The Handbook of Global Security Policy

Handbook of Global Policy Series

Series Editor
David Held
Master of University College and Professor of Politics and International Relations at Durham University

The *Handbook of Global Policy* series presents a comprehensive collection of the most recent scholarship and knowledge about global policy and governance. Each Handbook draws together newly commissioned essays by leading scholars and is presented in a style which is sophisticated but accessible to undergraduate and advanced students, as well as scholars, practitioners, and others interested in global policy. Available in print and online, these volumes expertly assess the issues, concepts, theories, methodologies, and emerging policy proposals in the field.

Published

The Handbook of Global Climate and Environment Policy
Robert Falkner

The Handbook of Global Energy Policy
Andreas Goldthau

The Handbook of Global Companies
John Mikler

The Handbook of Global Security Policy
Mary Kaldor and Iavor Rangelov

The Handbook of Global Health Policy
Garrett Brown, Gavin Yamey, and Sarah Wamala

The Handbook of Global Security Policy

Edited by

Mary Kaldor and Iavor Rangelov

WILEY Blackwell

This edition first published 2014
© 2014 John Wiley & Sons Ltd

Registered Office
John Wiley & Sons Ltd, The Atrium, Southern Gate, Chichester, West Sussex, PO19 8SQ, UK

Editorial Offices
350 Main Street, Malden, MA 02148-5020, USA
9600 Garsington Road, Oxford, OX4 2DQ, UK
The Atrium, Southern Gate, Chichester, West Sussex, PO19 8SQ, UK

For details of our global editorial offices, for customer services, and for information about how to apply
for permission to reuse the copyright material in this book please see our website at
www.wiley.com/wiley-blackwell.

The right of Mary Kaldor and Iavor Rangelov to be identified as the authors of the editorial material in
this work has been asserted in accordance with the UK Copyright, Designs and Patents Act 1988.

Library of Congress Cataloging-in-Publication Data

The handbook of global security policy / edited by Mary Kaldor and Iavor Rangelov. – Global security
and international law.
    pages cm
  Includes bibliographical references and index.
  ISBN 978-0-470-67322-5 (cloth)
  1. Security, International. 2. Security, International–Forecasting. I. Kaldor, Mary, author, editor of
compilation. II. Rangelov, Iavor, 1977–, author, editor of compilation.
  JZ5588.H358 2014
  355′.0335–dc23

                                                                              2013049094

A catalogue record for this book is available from the British Library.

Cover image: A model of a drone is lofted over protesters during a rally held to end the wars at home
and abroad in New York April 9, 2011. Photo © Jessica Rinaldi / Reuters.
Cover design by Design Deluxe.

Set in 10/12pt Sabon by Aptara Inc., New Delhi, India
Printed in Malaysia by Ho Printing (M) Sdn Bhd

1 2014

Contents

Notes on Contributors   ix

Introduction: Global Security Policy in the Twenty-First Century   1
Mary Kaldor and Iavor Rangelov

Part I   Key Concepts   **9**

1   Global Security   11
Ken Booth

2   Security and Social Critique   31
David Mutimer

3   Gender and Security   51
Natasha Marhia

4   Security Policy and (Global) Risk(s)   68
Sabine Selchow

5   Human Security   85
Mary Kaldor

Part II   Policy Arenas   **103**

6   Nuclear Disarmament and Nonproliferation   105
Maria Rost Rublee

7   Terrorism and Antiterrorism   126
Ekaterina Stepanova

8   Genocide and Large-Scale Human Rights Violations   145
    Martin Shaw

9   Transnational Crime   160
    John P. Sullivan

10 Natural Resources and Insecurity   175
    Anouk S. Rigterink

11 The Web of Water Security   190
    Mark Zeitoun

Part III   Policy Tools   **209**

12 Civilian Protection   211
    Sarah Sewall

13 Humanitarian Assistance   232
    Henry Radice

14 The Evolution of International Peacekeeping   247
    Renata Dwan

15 State-Building, Nation-Building, and Reconstruction   265
    Vesna Bojicic-Dzelilovic, Denisa Kostovicova,
    and David Rampton

16 Strengthening Democratic Governance in the Security Sector:
    The Unfulfilled Promise of Security Sector Reform   282
    Nicole Ball

17 Diplomacy and Mediation   300
    Àlvaro de Soto

18 Global Security and International Law   320
    Richard Falk

19 Transitional Justice   338
    Iavor Rangelov and Ruti Teitel

Part IV   Global Security Actors   **353**

20 Reframing the Use of Force: The European Union as a
    Security Actor   355
    Mary Martin

21 China   371
    May-Britt U. Stumbaum and Sun Xuefeng

22 India as a Global Security Actor   388
    Jivanta Schöttli and Markus Pauli

23 Security Agenda in Russia: Academic Concepts, Political
    Discourses, and Institutional Practices   408
    Andrey Makarychev

24 Contextualizing Global Security: The Case of Turkey   426
    Aslı Çalkıvik

25 The United States   446
    Adam Quinn

26 Civil Society in Fragile Contexts   463
    Willemijn Verkoren and Mathijs van Leeuwen

27 Protest and Politics: How Peace Movements Shape History   482
    David Cortright

28 Corporate Actors   505
    Shantanu Chakrabarti

Index   525

Notes on Contributors

Ken Booth is Senior Research Associate, Department of International Politics, Aberystwyth University, where he was formerly E.H. Carr Professor and Head of Department. He is a Fellow of the British Academy (FBA) and a former Chair of the British International Studies Association. In 2004, he was recipient of the ISA's Susan Strange Award in recognition of his contribution to International Studies.

David Mutimer is Director of the York Centre for International and Security Studies and Associate Professor of Political Science at York University. His research considers issues of contemporary international security through lenses provided by critical social theory, as well as inquiring into the reproduction of security in and through popular culture. Much of that work has focused on weapons proliferation as a reconfigured security concern in the post-Cold War era, and has tried to open possibilities for alternative means of thinking about the security problems related to arms more generally. In the past few years, this program of research has concentrated on small arms and light weapons. More recently, he has turned his attention to the politics of the global War on Terror, and of the regional wars around the world presently being fought by Canada and its allies.

Natasha Marhia has recently completed a PhD in Gender Studies at the London School of Economics and Political Science (LSE) Gender Institute. Her research, funded by the Economic and Social Research Council, explores gendered everyday (in)security through an analysis of police discourses and practices surrounding violence against women in Delhi. Her research interests include gender, violence, militarism, (human) security, masculinities, and the state. Her recent work also engages with broad theoretical questions of power, performativity and the imbrication of the material and the discursive, particularly in relation to gender, violence, and security. She has previously conducted research on sexual and gender-based violence for women's organizations in both London and Delhi, and taught on gender theory and on conflict and globalization at LSE.

Sabine Selchow is Fellow in the Civil Society and Human Security Research Unit, Department of International Development at the London School of Economics and Political Science (LSE). At LSE, she directs the "Culture/s'-research component in the 5-year-project "Security in Transition", funded by the European Research Council. Sabine is involved in various initiatives and international working groups, such as the working group "Cosmopolitan Communities of Risk", established by Professor Ulrich Beck at the Center of Advanced Studies in Munich, Germany. She holds a PhD in Government from LSE.

Mary Kaldor is Professor of Global Governance and Director of the Civil Society and Human Security Research Unit at the London School of Economics. She is the author of many books, including *The Ultimate Weapon is No Weapon: Human Security and the Changing Rules of War and Peace*; *New and Old Wars: Organised Violence in a Global Era*; and *Global Civil Society: An Answer to War*. Professor Kaldor was a founding member of European Nuclear Disarmament and of the Helsinki Citizen's Assembly. She was also convener of the Human Security Study Group, which reported to Javier Solana.

Maria Rost Rublee is a senior lecturer at the Australian National University in Canberra, Australia. Her book, *Nonproliferation Norms: Why States Choose Nuclear Restraint*, received the Alexander George Book Award for best book in political psychology, awarded by the International Society for Political Psychology. *Nonproliferation Norms* has also been positively reviewed in 14 journals, including *Foreign Affairs* and *Political Psychology*. Rublee has received major grants from the United States Institute of Peace, the Norwegian Ministry of Foreign Affairs, and the Japan Foundation. Her work uses social constructivism and social psychology to understand how material and normative factors interact to shape elite and civil society conceptions of "security". She has published articles in numerous international journals, including *International Studies Review*, *Comparative Political Studies*, and the *Nonproliferation Review*. She serves as editor for the journal *International Studies Perspectives* and is a member of the international Fissile Materials Working Group. Rublee earned her PhD in political science from the George Washington University in 2004.

Ekaterina Stepanova is a lead researcher and Head of the Peace and Conflict Studies Unit at the Institute of the World Economy and International Relations (IMEMO), Moscow. In 2007–2009, she was on leave from IMEMO to direct the Armed Conflicts and Conflict Management Program at Stockholm International Peace Institute (SIPRI). She is the author of six books, including *Terrorism in Asymmetrical Conflict: Ideological and Structural Aspects*. She serves on editorial boards of the journals *Global Governance, Terrorism and Political Violence, International Journal of Conflict and Violence*; on the expert panel of Global Peace Index; and Advisory board of the "Security in Transition" program, London School of Economics. She is also a member of the US–Russia Expert group on Afghan narcotrafficking. She lectures in English at the European University in St Petersburg. For more details, see http://www.estepanova.net

Martin Shaw is a sociologist of global politics, war, and genocide and author of numerous books including *What is Genocide?* and *Genocide and International Relations: Changing Patterns in the Upheavals of the Late Modern World*. He is Research Professor at the Institut Barcelona d'Estudis Internacionals (IBEI), Professorial Fellow in International Relations and Human Rights at the University of Roehampton, London, and Emeritus Professor of International Relations at the University of Sussex. His website is http://www.martinshaw.org

John P. Sullivan is a Senior Fellow at the Stephenson Disaster Management Institute at Louisiana State University. He also serves as a lieutenant with the Los Angeles Sheriff's Department. Sullivan holds a Bachelor of Arts in Government from the College of William and Mary, a Master of Arts in Urban Affairs and Policy Analysis from the New School for Social Research, and a PhD in Information and Knowledge Society from the Open University of Catalonia. He is a Member of the Advisory Board for Southern Pulse/Networked Intelligence, and an adjunct researcher on society and global crime at the VORTEX Research Group, Bogotá, Colombia. His current research focus is terrorism, transnational gangs and organized crime, conflict disaster, intelligence studies, post-conflict policing, sovereignty, and urban operations.

Anouk S. Rigterink is a PhD Candidate at the London School of Economics and Political Science, Department of International Development. She is associated with the ERC-funded Security in Transition Programme headed by Professor Mary Kaldor and the Department for International Development-funded Justice and Security Research Programme, headed by Professors Tim Allen and Alex de Waal.

Mark Zeitoun is Director of the Water Security Research Centre, School of International Development, University of East Anglia, UK. He has worked as a water resources engineer in conflict and post-conflict zones throughout Africa and the Middle East, and regularly advises bilateral and multilateral donor and implementing organizations on water policy, emergency preparedness, and water conflict negotiations.

Sarah Sewall teaches international affairs at the Harvard Kennedy School. A pioneer in the field of civilian protection, she helped revise US counterinsurgency doctrine, created new joint US military doctrine to stop genocide, and led the first comprehensive US field study on reducing civilian casualties in war. Previously, Dr Sewall served as the inaugural Deputy Assistant Secretary of Defense for Peacekeeping, as Director of Harvard's Carr Center for Human Rights Policy, and as Foreign Policy adviser to Senate Majority Leader George Mitchell.

Henry Radice is Research Fellow and Research Manager of the Justice and Security Research Programme at the London School of Economics and Political Science. His work focuses on the politics of humanity, that is, on how our understandings of common humanity and concepts of solidarity are shaped by our responses to moments of crisis, practices of inhumanity, and other humanitarian challenges such as climate change.

Renata Dwan is an official of the United Nations who has served in the Democratic Republic of the Congo, Haiti, Afghanistan, and Syria. She received her doctorate from the University of Oxford where she was Hedley Bull Junior Research Fellow in

International Relations. Previous positions include Head of Stockholm International Peace Research Institute (SIPRI)'s project on armed conflict and conflict management and Special Advisor to EU civilian crisis management operations. The views expressed in this chapter are personal and do not represent the official position of the United Nations.

Vesna Bojicic-Dzelilovic is Senior Research Fellow at the Department of International Development at the London School of Economics and Political Science. Her main area of research is political economy of transition, conflict and post-conflict reconstruction, political economy of policy making and decentralization, and regional development. She has published academic and policy papers on these topics with a focus on South East Europe. Her published work includes co-edited a volume on *Persistent State Weakness in the Global Age*.

Denisa Kostovicova is Associate Professor in Global Politics at the Government Department, London School of Economics and Political Science. She is the author of *Kosovo: The Politics of Identity and Space*, and co-editor of several volumes including *Bottom–up Politics: An Agency-Centred Approach to Globalization* and *Civil Society and Transitions in the Western Balkans*. Her research interests concern challenges of post-conflict recovery in the global context from a bottom–up perspective. She has studied state-building, human security, transitional justice, and Europeanization in the Western Balkan, which is her area of expertise.

David Rampton is a Fellow in Global Politics in the Government and International Relations Departments of the London School of Economics. He completed his PhD, which focused on hegemony, identity, and Sinhala nationalism, at the School of Oriental and African Studies. His current research focuses on the biopolitics of nationalism and the governmental interface between nationalist and international state-building projects. He has recently published articles in *Commonwealth and Comparative Politics* and in edited volumes.

Nicole Ball is Senior Fellow at the Center for International Policy, Washington, DC; Senior Visiting Fellow at the Conflict Research Unit, Clingendael Institute, The Hague; and Enough Fellow at the Center for American Progress, Washington, DC. For much of her career, she has worked on issues relating to security-sector governance in non-OECD countries. Since 1998, she has consulted for the governments of the United Kingdom, The Netherlands, Germany and the United States; United Nations Development Programme; the Organisation for Economic Co-operation and Development Development Assistance Committee; and the World Bank on issues relating to security sector governance, conflict-affected states and multilateral financing arrangements. Recent publications include three reports for the INCAF Peacebuilding, Statebuilding and Security Task Team: "The Challenges of Undertaking Effective Security and Justice Work" (with Luc van de Goor, 2011); "From Quick Wins to Long-Term Profits? Developing better approaches to support security and justice engagements in fragile states: Burundi case study" (with Jean-Marie Gasana and Willy Nindorera, 2012); and "From Quick Wins to Long-Term Profits? Developing better approaches to support security and justice engagements in fragile states: Report of the Netherlands MFA headquarters visit" (2012). In 2013, she was participating in an evaluation of the EU's African Peace Facility.

Àlvaro de Soto held senior positions at the United Nations for 25 years, and during this time led the 1990–1991 negotiations that ended the war in El Salvador and the 1999–2004 negotiations on Cyprus. He was Special Envoy for Myanmar (1995–1999) and Special Representative for Western Sahara (2003–2005). He was the chief envoy for the Arab–Israeli conflict (2005–2007). He now teaches conflict resolution at Sciences Po, in Paris. He is a member of the Global Leadership Foundation and a Fellow at the Ralph Bunche Institute in New York.

Richard Falk is Albert G. Milbank Professor of International Law Emeritus at Princeton University where he was a member of the faculty for forty years (1961–2001). Between 2002 and 2013, he has been associated with Global & International Studies at the Santa Barbara campus of the University of California. He currently conducts a research project on "Climate Change, Human Security, and Democracy" under the auspices of the Orfalea Center. Professor Falk is currently the Special Rapporteur on Occupied Palestine for the United Nations Human Rights Council. He served as Chair of the Board, Nuclear Age Peace Foundation, 2004–2012, and now is Senior Vice President. Over the years, Falk has published more than 50 books, including *Legal Order in a Violent World* (1968); *This Endangered Planet: Prospects and Proposals for Human Survival* (1971); *A Study of Future Worlds* (1975); *Predatory Globalization: A Critique* (1999); *Religion and Humane Global Governance* (2001). His most recent books *Achieving Human Rights* (2009); a co-edited volume entitled *Legality and Legitimacy in Global Affairs* (2012); *Global Parliament* (with Andrew Strauss) (2011); *Path to Zero: Dialogues on Nuclear Dangers* (with David Krieger) (2012). Forthcoming is *(Re)Imagining Humane Global Governance* (2013).

Iavor Rangelov is Global Security Research Fellow at the Civil Society and Human Security Research Unit, London School of Economics and Political Science, and Co-Chair of the London Transitional Justice Network. He is fellow of the research and training programme European Foreign & Security Policy Studies (EFSPS), which supported his post-doctoral research and visiting fellowships at the European Policy Centre, Brussels; EU Institute for Security Studies, Paris; Institut Barcelona d'Estudis Internacionals, Barcelona; and T.M.C. Asser Instituut, The Hague. He is the author of *Nationalism and the Rule of Law: Lessons from the Balkans and Beyond* (2014).

Ruti Teitel is a Fellow at New York University Law School's Straus Institute for the Advanced Study of Law and Justice (2012–2013); the Ernst C. Stiefel Professor of Comparative Law, New York Law School; Fellow, London School of Economics; and Affiliated Visiting Professor, Hebrew University of Jerusalem. She is the author of *Transitional Justice* (2000) and many articles and book chapters on international and comparative law, often focusing on political transitions. Her latest work is *Humanity's Law* (2011). She is founding Co-Chair of the American Society of International Law Interest Group on Transitional Justice and Rule of Law, a life member of the Council on Foreign Relations, and a member of the ILA International Human Rights Law Committee.

Mary Martin is Associate Research Fellow at the Civil Society and Human Security Research Unit, and a Visiting Fellow at the Government Department of the London School of Economics. She was previously coordinator of the Human Security Study

Group, which reports to the High Representative of the European Union. She is the editor of several books on human security. Her research interests also include the privatization of security, the role of corporate actors in conflict and peacebuilding, and European Union security policies.

May-Britt U. Stumbaum heads the NFG Research Group "Asian Perceptions of the European Union" at the Freie Unviersität, Berlin. She has worked both in policy research and academia, and has held positions at Harvard, SIPRI, DGAP, as well as other institutions in Europe, China, and the United States. May-Britt U. Stumbaum has published widely on security policy and EU–Asia/EU–China relations.

Sun Xuefeng is Associate Professor at the Department of International Relations at Tsinghua University and Executive Editor of the Chinese Journal of International Politics. Dr Sun Xuefeng is also a resident scholar at the Carnegie–Tsinghua Center for Global Policy. His research focuses on the rise of great powers, China's foreign policy, and international relations in East Asia.

Jivanta Schöttli is Lecturer in Comparative and International Politics at the Department of Political Science, South Asia Institute, Heidelberg University. Along with a Masters in Economic History and Bachelors in International Relations from the London School of Economics and Political Science, she holds a PhD, *summa cum laude* in political science from Heidelberg University. Her thesis was on the subject of policy-making and institution-building during the crucial transition period following independence under Prime Minister Jawaharlal Nehru. It has been published with Routledge, London in 2012 as *Vision and Strategy in Indian Politics*. She is co-author of *A Political and Economic Dictionary of South Asia*, has written articles on Indian foreign policy, and edited various publications. Jivanta was a research fellow at the Institute for Defence Studies and Analyses, New Delhi and at the India Study Centre, Beijing University. She is a member of the Heidelberg University, Cluster of Excellence, *Asia and Europe in a Global Context* and Deputy Editor of *Heidelberg Papers in South Asian and Comparative Politics* (HPSACP). Her research interests include India's international politics and the interplay between domestic and systemic dynamics of change and continuity in policy-making.

Markus Pauli studied Political Science at the Freie Unviersität in Berlin (FU) and the London School of Economics and Political Science. His research interests include political economy and international relations. Previously, he worked as project coordinator for InWEnt – Capacity Building International, a nonprofit organization dedicated to human resource development commissioned by the German Federal Government. His doctoral thesis at Heidelberg University explores the impact of microfinance in South India through an operationalization of the capability approach.

Andrey Makarychev is Professor at Institute of Government and Politics, University of Tartu, Estonia. His previous international employers were the Danish Institute for International Studies and the Center for Security Studies and Peace Research (ETH, Zurich). Andrey Makarychev lectured in the University of Tartu (Estonia), Diplomatic Academy of Azerbaijan, and National Mechnikov University (Odessa, Ukraine), and published in "*Cooperation and Conflict*", "*International Spectator*", "*Journal of International Relations and Development*" and other journals.

Aslı Çalkıvik is a Faculty Member at the Department of Humanities and Social Sciences at Istanbul Technical University. She received her PhD at the University of Minnesota in 2010 with her dissertation thesis, *Dismantling Security*. Her major research interests include global politics of security, international political theory, and critical security studies.

Adam Quinn is Lecturer in International Studies at the University of Birmingham. He is presently leading an ESRC Seminar Series on The Future of American Power and was convener of the US Foreign Policy Group of the British International Studies Association (BISA) 2008–2012. He is the author of *US Foreign Policy in Context: National Ideology from the Founders to the Bush Doctrine* (2010) and "The Art of Declining Politely: Obama's Prudent Presidency and the Waning of American Power", *International Affairs* (July, 2011).

Willemijn Verkoren is Associate Professor and Head of the Centre for International Conflict Analysis and Management (CICAM) at the Institute of Management Research (IMR) of Radboud University Nijmegen, the Netherlands.

Mathijs van Leeuwen is Assistant Professor with the CICAM/IMR, and researcher at the African Studies Centre at Leiden University, the Netherlands.

David Cortright is the Director of Policy Studies at the Kroc Institute for International Peace Studies at the University of Notre Dame. He is the author or editor of 17 books and has written widely on nonviolent social change, nuclear disarmament, and the use of multilateral sanctions and incentives as tools of international peacemaking. Cortright has a long history of public advocacy for disarmament and the prevention of war. He opposed the Vietnam War as an active duty soldier (1968–1971); was the Executive Director of SANE, the Committee for a Sane Nuclear Policy (1978–1988); and was co-founder and co-chairs Win Without War, a coalition of national organizations opposed to US policies of war and military occupation in Iraq and Afghanistan.

Shantanu Chakrabarti is currently an Associate Professor in the Department of History, University of Calcutta. He also holds the honorary position of the Convener, Academic Committee, Institute of Foreign Policy Studies, and University of Calcutta. He was formerly a Research Fellow at the Institute for Defence Studies and Analyses (IDSA), New Delhi. His current research interests include peace studies and conflict resolution; South Asian regional trends; Indian foreign policy making; privatization of security, and comprehensive security agenda in Asia.

Introduction: Global Security Policy in the Twenty-First Century

Mary Kaldor and Iavor Rangelov*

We live in insecure times. We trust our institutions because we believe they keep us safe; yet the present moment is characterized by a pervasive worldwide sense of insecurity. In places like Syria, Iraq, Afghanistan, Democratic Republic of the Congo, Somalia, and Mali, people live under the daily threat of being killed, expelled from their homes, or being robbed, raped, tortured or kidnapped. In places like Bangladesh, Oklahoma, Japan, and Australia, people are increasingly vulnerable to flooding, earthquakes, tsunamis, or fires. In much of the world, access to water, food, or shelter is scarce. And in the richer parts of the world, growing fears about welfare and pensions, or terrorism and criminality, are probably the basis of a growing mistrust of political institutions and the political class.

Security policy is supposed to address insecurity. During the Cold War, the institutions that were responsible for security policy were largely provided by nation-states and political blocs. Even though the United Nations (UN) had security functions, these were constrained by the continuing East–West conflict. Traditionally, security policies consist of military forces that are designed to repel an attack by a foreign state and police forces who are supposed to uphold the rule of law and deal with criminality. What Ulrich Beck (1992) calls the "master narrative" of the modern state was constructed around its role in protecting people against risk: the dangers posed by nature, personal risks of ill health and unemployment, as well as threats posed by foreign enemies. Indeed the idea of defense against a foreign enemy became

*We are grateful to five anonymous reviewers; the general editor of the series, David Held; the entire team at Wiley Blackwell that worked with us on the book; and the European Research Council. We are hugely indebted to Pippa Bore for her hard work and remarkable attention to detail in providing assistance.

a metaphoric umbrella term for security in general. Yet in a world where inter-state war is declining, the metaphor is much less reassuring than in the past. It is this mismatch between security policies as traditionally conceived and people's everyday experience in which the pervasive sense of insecurity resides.

This book is about global security policy. By global, we do not mean universal; rather we refer to the changes in security policy "in these global times". In part, global security policy is about the interconnectedness of contemporary sources of insecurity. Conflict, terrorism, criminality, climate change, or economic crisis can no longer be addressed only or even primarily at the level of the nation-state; hence the term global implies beyond the nation-state and often refers to a multiscalar system that is local, regional, and national, as well as global. But we mean more than that. Global security policy is not just about a change of level; it is about a change in kind. It is about how we understand and conceptualize security and how our understandings are implemented. It is about concepts and tools and not just actors. It entails a contradictory process of overlapping arenas that are public and private, and local and transnational, as well as national.

Much of the contemporary literature on security deals with the new range of world risks in place of the threat of attack by foreign military forces. Some of these risks, like cyber warfare or climate change, are clearly new; some, like terrorism or the spread of weapons of mass destruction or sectarian conflict, appear in a new guise. Some have new features that are the consequence of, for example, growing interconnectedness; new forms of communication that speed up mobilization and facilitate long-distance violence; or weak states that are the legacy of the collapse of dictatorships, the drying up of superpower aid to clients, and the pursuit of neoliberal economic strategies. Our point, however, is that many of these risks are risks that we used to think about in domestic terms – they only became visible as global risks after the end of the Cold War. During the Cold War, bipolar security was a mechanism for world order. Because an East–West conflict seemed like the worst possible eventuality, other sources of insecurity were accorded a low priority. Growing risk and complexity reflects not so much a change in how the world works, although it changes all the time, but rather the absence of a simple narrative to understand the world.

This book uses the term security to address primarily issues relating to violence. Nowadays, security discussions, including climate change, energy security, food security, and so on, tend to take a wider approach. This has the advantage of stressing the urgency of these issues. But it also allows for "securitization" – that is to say, co-option by those institutions traditionally responsible for security, such as the military and intelligence agencies (Buzan et al., 1998). It also carries the implication that if we solve these other problems, peace will follow. Of course, the sources of insecurity are much wider than this and, moreover, different sources of insecurity are interrelated; indeed, we touch upon this relationship in several of the chapters in this volume. There are, for example, complex linkages between high levels of military spending and global imbalances, strategies of structural adjustment and weak rule of law, sporadic violence, and poor economic performance. But a book that covered all sources of insecurity would be a book about global problems in general; thus we have chosen a perhaps arbitrary limitation on our subject matter although we do acknowledge that issues of war and crime need to be addressed on their own terms as well as in relation to wider global problems.

In identifying the sources of insecurity covered in this book, we have decided against any attempt to categorize or code different gradations of what are considered global risks; rather, we have adopted an empirical approach of identifying those sources of insecurity with which existing policy is actually concerned. We describe them as policy arenas rather than risks or sources of insecurity and they are addressed in Part II of the book.

Much has been written about conceptual and theoretical issues raised by global security (Booth, 2007; Buzan and Hansen, 2009) but much less about global security as policy. While there is growing literature on aspects of global security – terrorism, state-building, peace-keeping, and so on – we are not aware of any work that pulls all this together. Our interest is less in abstract theorizing about the possible directions and meanings of global security, although that is important, but more in the way that global security policy is actually practiced: how is it conceptualized and implemented, who is responsible, and what tools do they use? The book does not assume that a global security policy is being developed that offers a more effective answer to contemporary sources of insecurity. On the contrary, the global security landscape is characterized by multiple and often contradictory tendencies. The legacies of the Cold War period still shape the geo-political preoccupations of what could be described as the national players on the global stage; in fact, a very large proportion of world security expenditure is devoted to these preoccupations. The War on Terror launched in response to the events of 9/11 seems to have mutated into a global binary dynamic involving, on the one hand, long-distance air power, especially drones, carried out by new combinations of private security contractors, local non-state actors, and intelligence agencies, as well as traditional security actors and, on the other hand, networks of extremists and criminal groups tied together through an increasingly operational narrative of resistance. In international institutions like the UN, the European Union (EU), or the African Union, security policies are evolving largely around what Duffield (2001) describes as the "liberal peace": the combination of formulations, strategies, tools, and preoccupations conjured up in terms like stabilization, crisis management, human security, post-conflict reconstruction, etc. Many of the chapters in this book primarily address the concerns of the liberal peace, although they are less about setting up norms and more about understanding actual practice, achievements and inadequacies. However, the authors do take into account alternative tendencies and consider how they shape the evolution of different aspects of global security policy.

Structure and Organization of the Book

The Handbook has four parts: key concepts; security risks, which we describe as policy arenas; policy tools or instruments; and global security actors. Collectively, they provide an original account of global security policy in the twenty-first century and a comprehensive introduction to the main subjects and ideas that animate scholarly and policy discussions in this field.

Part I comprises five contributions, which elaborate some of the key concepts that constitute global security policy as a distinctive field of practice and scholarship. In Chapter 1, Ken Booth argues that arriving at a consensual understanding of "global security" is critical for promoting the well-being of humanity and nature in general.

He elaborates the concept of global security in relation to existential and emancipatory global threats and places them in their contemporary historical context. The chapter examines the emergence of a new global "securityscape" at the current juncture, shaped by the tension between the urgency of developing what Booth calls "global domestic security politics" on one side and the continuing power of statist rationality on the other.

The next two chapters examine the contribution of Critical Security Studies, focusing on a series of unsettling questions that scholars in this field have raised about security policy. David Mutimer (Chapter 2) introduces three stands of critical security scholarship: Feminism; post-Marxist Critical Theory; and post-structuralism. He demonstrates how despite their differences, all these approaches share a commitment to interrogating troubling simplicities and certainties in the name of those who are marginalized, oppressed, or made insecure by security policy. The aspiration of the work surveyed in the chapter, Mutimer argues, is not to promote better security policy, even though it may help contribute to it; instead, critical security scholars seek freer people engaged in more productive politics. Natasha Marhia (Chapter 3) deepens the analysis of the relationship between gender and security. In particular, she examines with a critical eye the securitization of sexual and gender-based violence under the Women, Peace and Security Agenda of the UN and the mobilization of gender narratives in the War on Terror.

Next, Sabine Selchow (Chapter 4) highlights the growing significance of the logic of "risk" for security policy, especially in the West, and examines some if its far-reaching implications. She introduces two different approaches to risk in this context. The first approach reflects the increased reliance on the concept of risk in security practices, setting in motion important dynamics that have implications extending well beyond the security field itself. These developments require sustained public discussion because what is at stake here, Selchow argues, is nothing short of the future of affected societies. The second approach emerges from Ulrich Beck's work on "global risk" and "risk society", and here the main implication is the need to rethink modern (security) institutions.

The final contribution to this part of the book is Mary Kaldor's discussion of human security (Chapter 5). The concept of human security came to the fore in the 1990s and since then it has attracted multiple critiques articulated from diverse positions and perspectives. Kaldor traces the evolution of the concept and takes issue with its radical critics, arguing that these critiques could be seen as representing the discursive achievement of the War on Terror. She suggests that the critical debates about what it is to be human, the meaning of security, and the use of the idea of biopower, add value and could help substantiate the concept of human security. The problem is their normative standpoint. By taking human security as their target, Kaldor argues, the radical critics have fallen into the trap set by the War on Terror and contributed to the narrowing of emancipatory space. The challenge is to reconstitute the idea of human security by harnessing some of the insights introduced by its critics.

Part II shifts the focus from concepts to risks that constitute key policy arenas in the evolving landscape of global security. Maria Rost Rublee (Chapter 6) discusses the related fields of nuclear disarmament and nonproliferation, starting with a critical examination of the meaning of these two terms. She considers traditional and more recent approaches in these arenas and addresses a series of questions about the frontiers of research on disarmament and nonproliferation, as well as their potential contribution to broader debates over global security. Next, Ekaterina Stepanova (Chapter 7) draws attention to important trends, dynamics, and explanatory frameworks of terrorism and their implications for the pursuit of antiterrorism policies in the early twenty-first century. Her account highlights key insights from recent statistical data, in particular the significance of terrorist activity by insurgencies against foreign forces and their local allies in Iraq and Afghanistan/Pakistan as a share of terrorism in the 2000s. In thinking about long-term strategies to prevent terrorism, these insights call for developing solutions at the level of global governance to the underlying problem of internationalization of conflict in weak or dysfunctional states. Martin Shaw's contribution to the volume (Chapter 8) evaluates the global policy challenges arising from genocidal violence. The chapter introduces the conceptual, theoretical and political background that shapes this policy arena and examines the character and extent of genocidal violence in a global era. Shaw takes a closer look at global policy-making aimed at preventing and punishing acts of genocide and offers reflections on the appropriate global institutions and policy frameworks for genocide prevention.

John Sullivan (Chapter 9) introduces an issue that is attracting growing attention from scholars and policymakers: transnational crime. He conveys the diversity of organized criminal groups that operate across borders in terms of their activities but also their relationship to global flows and state power. Sullivan considers how such groups increasingly operate as transnational networks and examines the role of actors such as transnational gangs, cartels, mafias, and pirates. The chapter reviews recent developments in key global regions and explores the potential of transnational networks to challenge states through criminal insurgencies. Next, Anouk Rigterink (Chapter 10) investigates the relationship between natural resources and insecurity. She argues that the evidence for the proposition that natural resources cause civil war is not as robust as popularly believed and points out that, from a policy perspective, it is equally important to understand the mechanisms that connect resources and violent conflict in order to develop effective policy interventions. In the final contribution to this part of the book, Mark Zeitoun (Chapter 11) explores the reasons why efforts to promote water security, whether by states or the international water policy community, often fall short of their goals. He proposes a new conceptual tool – the "web of water security" – as a partial remedy, combining consideration for the social and physical processes that either enable or prevent water security. Zeitoun argues that in the long term, sustainable water security depends on the balance between related security areas and equitable distribution of resources among the actors involved.

Part III comprises a set of chapters that focus on some of the "tools" available to policymakers: key instruments of global security policy. Sarah Sewall (Chapter 12) opens this part of the book with a discussion of civilian protection. She examines three approaches that have emerged in recent decades: international humanitarian law; the Protection of Civilians initiated by the United Nations in peacekeeping operations; and the Responsibility to Protect (R2P) norm, which at the sharp end may include humanitarian intervention. While each of these frameworks is a work in progress and may engender tensions, Sewall argues that they create new opportunities for protecting human rights. Henry Radice (Chapter 13) engages some of these issues from another perspective in his analysis of a related policy instrument: humanitarian assistance. He points out that the definition of humanitarianism in conflict-affected environments has been broadened to encompass not only alleviation of insecurity but also provision of security though concepts such as humanitarian intervention and R2P, prompting concerns that it risks becoming a driver of insecurity in its own right. Radice also introduces the debate over humanitarian space, suggesting that what is often left out of these discussions is the sense that such spaces are sites of governance, which bear out the consequences of humanitarianism for the in/security of the intended beneficiaries of assistance. Renata Dwan (Chapter 14) traces the evolution of international peacekeeping since 1948 – from limited monitoring of ceasefires between states to a comprehensive exercise in enforcing and building peace within states. The chapter shows how the scope and effectiveness of peacekeeping reflects the consensus of the authorizing states and explores the extent to which changes in global governance may be even more important than operational challenges in shaping the future direction of international peacekeeping.

In a co-authored contribution, Vesna Bojicic-Dzelilovic, Denisa Kostovicova and David Rampton (Chapter 15) consider the meanings and implications of a range of international instruments employed in state-building, nation-building, and reconstruction efforts in the aftermath of conflict. The chapter highlights the tensions and contradictions inherent in externally driven, liberal peace-based interventions by focusing on accountability, legitimacy, ownership, and sovereignty, but also considers the turn to hybridity as an alternative framework and draws out some of the implications for policy-making. Next, Nicole Ball (Chapter 16) turns to security sector reform (SSR), introducing the concept with a discussion of its definition, evolution, and application. She explores four main challenges for effective implementation of the SSR agenda: the international political and security landscape; the extent to which reforming countries own SSR efforts; the ability of international actors to navigate the local politics; and the effectiveness of donor approaches to SSR. Àlvaro de Soto (Chapter 17) discusses diplomacy and mediation, drawing attention to some of the new challenges and issues that have come to the fore since the end of the Cold War and highlighting the evolving roles of key players, old and new, active in this field. He argues that the War on Terror has narrowed mediation space while, paradoxically, the proliferation of conflict-resolution actors has ended up complicating the search for peace.

The last two chapters in this part of the book focus on the role of law and legal institutions in global security policy. Richard Falk (Chapter 18) interrogates the complicated relationship between international law and global security policy. He examines issues such as nuclear weapons, the threat and use of force, and climate change, arguing that in these domains international law has failed to protect the human interest in the face of structural constraints and pressures associated with world order, such as geopolitical control and the national interest of leading states. On this account, the link between global security policy and international law is complex and contradictory: part adherence, part interpretive manipulation, and part expedient violation. Iavor Rangelov and Ruti Teitel (Chapter 19) examine a range of novel legal instruments for addressing mass atrocity and human rights abuse, usually discussed under the rubric of transitional justice. The authors discuss the evolution of transitional justice in recent decades and introduce the "justice dilemma" – a set of perceived tensions and trade-offs between normative concerns and strategic considerations, which often underpins debates over justice and security – and the critiques it has elicited. The chapter identifies the state-centricity of transitional justice as the main challenge for scholars and policy makers and argues for engaging alternative normative frameworks, actors and geographies beyond the state in rethinking the relationship between justice and security.

Part IV of the book comprises nine chapters that explore the role of key actors in global security policy. Mary Martin (Chapter 20) traces the evolution of the EU as a security actor on the world stage, focusing on its contribution in terms of ideas, policies, and resources. The outcome of these efforts, Martin argues, is a distinctive but ambiguous concept of security, the effectiveness of which is yet to be proven in practice. Next, May-Britt Stumbaum and Sun Xuefeng (Chapter 21) examine China as a global security actor. The chapter discusses a range of traditional and non-traditional security challenges that China is facing and the capabilities that are used to meet them. It also introduces the debates over China's role in global security that are currently taking place internationally and within China itself, conveying the perspective of outsiders but also those internal dynamics that are rarely visible in Western-dominated discussions. The contribution by Jivanta Schöttli and Markus Pauli (Chapter 22) emphasizes the growing demands on India to play a greater role in global security affairs. The authors locate India's current aspirations in their historical context, which is inextricably tied to the idea and practice of non-alignment. They assess the relevance of India in the global security landscape by focusing on specific zones of (in)security and conclude by examining some of the constraints and challenges that are shaping India's contribution to global security.

Turning to Russia, Andrey Makarychev (Chapter 23) shows how the Russian security agenda is formulated and how security messages are communicated to the outside world. In doing so, he employs the lens of "securitization" and interrogates security discourses, the interplay of academic concepts and political narratives, as well as their institutional effects. Next, Aslı Çalkıvik (Chapter 24) discusses the transformation of Turkey's security policies in recent decades and their relationship to the broader agenda of global security. The chapter places these developments in the changing policy-making context of the post-Cold War era, emphasizing the ways in which Turkey sees itself as contributing to global security but also the emergence of security itself as a site of major contestation domestically. Adam Quinn (Chapter 25) examines the changing role of the United States in global security policy at a time when its power is seen as declining while, at the same time, many security threats arise from sources beyond the command and control of nation-states. Some of the key challenges facing the United States, such as rising powers, "rogue" states, jihadist terrorism, weapons proliferation, and economic instability, present serious questions about its ability to manage the new security landscape with existing capabilities and policy frameworks, without producing unintended consequences that may be aggravating these very problems or creating new ones.

The last three chapters of the volume shift the focus to non-state or private actors who have become more prominent in the formulation and implementation of global security policy in the early twenty-first century. Willemijn Verkoren and Mathijs van Leeuwen (Chapter 26) interrogate the role of civil society in fragile contexts. The chapter directs attention to the problem of distinguishing between state and society, and between "civil" and "uncivil" in such environments, and explores the tensions between local and international legitimacy. These problems, the authors argue, complicate the work of those who seek to strengthen civil society as part of broader efforts towards building peace. David Cortright (Chapter 27) distills key lessons from some of the largest civil society mobilizations in recent decades, including the Vietnam antiwar movement, the nuclear disarmament campaign of the 1980s, and the opposition to the US-led invasion of Iraq. While many dismiss the effectiveness of peace movements, Cortright offers a nuanced assessment of their role in constructing norms and values, constraining decision-making options with tangible impact on policies, and influencing electoral, legislative, and policy outcomes. Finally, Shantanu Chakrabarti (Chapter 28) explores the proliferation of corporate actors in global security provision. The chapter relates the growth of the private security industry to broader changes in the nature of the state and governance in the context of globalization. Corporate actors are seen as key players in the global security marketplace but they also raise unsettling questions about legality and legitimacy that need to be tackled head-on.

References

Beck, Ulrich. 1992. *Risk Society: Towards a New Modernity*. London: Sage Publications.
Booth, Ken. 2007. *Theory of World Security*. Cambridge and New York, NY: Cambridge University Press.
Buzan, Barry, and Lene Hansen. 2009. *The Evolution of International Security Studies*. Cambridge: Cambridge University Press.
Buzan, Barry, Ole Wæver, and Jaap de Wilde. 1998. *Security: A New Framework for Analysis*. Boulder, CO and London: Lynne Rienner Publishers.
Duffield, Mark. 2001. *Global Governance and the New Wars: The Merging of Security and Development*. London: Zed Books.

Part I   Key Concepts

Chapter 1

Global Security

Ken Booth[1]

"Global security" is a powerful idea, yet a settled understanding of the term remains elusive. This is not surprising because it couples together two concepts that are themselves individually contested. It will be argued that developing a common understanding of "global security" is a fundamental building-block in the construction of a better world – a world that works for all its human inhabitants and the natural world on which we depend.

What is a Global Security Issue? *Existential* and *Emancipatory* Threats

Every hour, for a growing proportion of people on earth, we are reminded of the shrinking of time and space and the reality of living in a truly global age. It is imperative therefore to situate the theory and practice of "security" in the context of the global, while incorporating the changing realities of the "global" in understandings and agendas of security. If a globalized *we* cannot define *global security* and develop a shared understanding of the term, how can we hope ever to achieve it? Concern with semantics is not always academic indulgence; here, this concern is fundamental in establishing what will later be called a *global domestic security politics*.

"Security"

Security is a fundamental human value. It is the condition of feeling or being safe from threats. Radical *insecurity* on the other hand is virtually synonymous with a person's struggle for survival as a biological organism, whether the source of that insecurity is fear of hunger or the threat of imminent injury and death in a violent conflict. Security, therefore, is what Philippa Foot (2001) might have called a "fact of human existence", namely a value that is rational for humans to pursue because we

The Handbook of Global Security Policy, First Edition. Edited by Mary Kaldor and Iavor Rangelov.
© 2014 John Wiley & Sons, Ltd. Published 2014 by John Wiley & Sons, Ltd.

cannot sustain social life in its absence, whether this involves attending to the needs of babies, developing communities, or exploring what it might mean to be "human".

"Security" performs its central political role as a "speech act" (Buzan, Wæver, and de Wilde 1998, p. 26) and once an issue is labeled "security", things happen. Significant features of world affairs over recent centuries can be explained by the power of the label "national security". This chapter will explore the meaning and significance of the label "global security" to see whether it should or could have similar future leverage.

"Security" in the context of politics comprises three key elements: a referent (some person, group, or entity that is threatened); an actual or impending danger to that referent (a threat to which a probability of risk can be assigned); and the desire of the referent to be free from the dangers identified (resulting in strategies to mitigate or escape from them). How individuals and groups think about these elements in particular situations involves choices deriving from their most basic ideas about politics. One's underlying political theory (even if not explicitly articulated) shapes security choices regarding the referent to privilege (particular collectivities or individuals?), the threats and risks to be prioritized (which danger is most pressing and/or most consequential?), and the strategies to be pursued (by confrontation or cooperation?).

Mainstream opinion in academic International Relations (IR) generally defends a narrow concept of security, focusing on the so-called nation-state as the privileged referent, war as the ultimate danger, and successful military strategy as the basic mode of survival. The concept has been broadened since the end of the Cold War to include other referents, dangers, and strategies. The way for this significant move in thinking about international relations was lit earlier by – among others – Johan Galtung (1971) with his idea of "structural violence" and Richard Falk (1975) with his framework of "world order" values. This rethinking of the security of real people in real places, as opposed exclusively to "national security", helped encourage the reconceptualizing of security beyond (but also including) the Westphalian international framework.

These deeper conceptions of what is at stake when we talk about security have been built upon in contemporary IR theory, for example, Andrew Linklater's (2011) theorizing of "harm", and the "security-as-emancipation" theme in Critical Security Studies (Booth, 2007). As a result of the prizing open of the "iron cage" of statist[2] security thought, paths have been opened to explore poverty, patriarchy, tyranny, environmental destruction, cultural imperialism, and so on as legitimate concerns for Security Studies in addition to interstate war and other aspects of the traditional agenda.

"Global"

The term "global" is hardly more settled than "security" itself. In academic and political discourse "global" is generally used lazily. It is assumed that we know what is "global" when we see it, or that we will accept its promiscuous usage in publications uncritically. The following discussion emphasizes analytical clarity and offers a particular conceptualization, while accepting that the term will remain somewhat contested, characteristic of art not science.

Central to the term "global" must be a notion of "reach". *Reach* is a necessary element and can refer to the actual physical range of something (e.g. global telecommunications) or an activity achieving coverage across the earth (e.g. global capitalism) or a project seeking to expand a particular aim everywhere (e.g. global democracy). As will become obvious, however, "reach" is not entirely straightforward.

The term "global" is obviously associated with the cognate terms "universal" and "world", but they are not synonymous. *Universal* refers to "all people or things" (as in "universal human rights"), whereas *world* is less demanding, pertaining to something involving the whole of the earth in some sense, but in general rather than particular (as in "world history"). In other words, human rights pertain to every individual, anywhere, but an account of world history would be an exercise in what to omit rather than attempting to include everything. If universal therefore means *all in particular*, while world means *all in general*, "global" inserts itself fuzzily in between.

These distinctions involve judgment not exactitude. It might be argued for example that poverty is a world issue because it is widespread, but not a universal issue because many people are not poor; nonetheless, poverty is certainly a global issue because all parts of the globe are implicated in, and affected by its existence. In the different case of the conflict between 1939–1945, we can say that it was clearly worldwide in its scope, though it impinged only peripherally on some regions. It was therefore appropriately labeled a "World" and not a "Global" war. The latter term would have been applicable if the superpowers during the Cold War had unleashed what Herman Kahn called a nuclear "wargasm" involving upwards of 50,000 nuclear weapons. Nuclear destruction on this scale would have resulted in the collapse of the infrastructure of modern life globally, and in some predictions might have brought about a "nuclear winter" threatening the existence of all human life.

This semantic discussion is critical in relation to the referent for global security. Because no existing political or social grouping embraces the entirety of humankind, it follows logically that the human referent for global security must be the universal collectivity of individual persons. This *global-we* is an *actual* "community of fate" because of accelerating and densifying human interconnectedness, and a *potential* global identity group associated with ideas of "global citizenship". In this global quasi-community, individuals and their groupings live in a natural (or "post-natural") environment whose own flourishing is fundamental to human existence; the environment must therefore constitute a basic referent for global security. This chapter focuses on the human dimension, but the non-human must never be ignored.

"Global Security Threats"

A concept of global security requires a framework for understanding the dangers threatening the referent (the *global-we*). What follows is based on a schema of Arnold Wolfers (1962, pp. 73–77), who distinguished the foreign policy objectives of states in relation to their "possession" or "milieu" goals. The former pertains to "national possessions" (the "things to which it attaches value", such as territory) while the latter pertains to "the shape of the environment in which the nation operates" (meaning the external conditions in which a people's values might flourish). The privileged referent for "global security" differs radically from Wolfers's state-centrism, but his distinction is nonetheless instructive.

First: global existential threats. These threats involve a danger of global reach, which poses a potential or actual risk to the continued being of individuals or groups. Such threats include nuclear weapons, "climate chaos" (the coinage of the World Wide Fund for Nature) threatening food and water security, and pandemics. The risks from climate change and disease underline that global existential threats do not necessarily have to be intentional or politically targeted. Global existential threats involve the survival of people and groups from physical dangers of global reach, whether or not a specific referent is designated as the target.

Second: global emancipatory threats. Emancipation involves freedom from oppression: the latter might be material threats such as hunger and poverty, social threats such as religious and cultural dogmatism, and political threats such as conquest, tyranny, and institutionalized racism (Booth 2007, pp. 95–116). Emancipatory goals are the equivalent for individuals and groups of the "milieu" goals that Wolfers identified for nation-states, namely those conditions that enhance or diminish the prospect of experiencing flourishing lives. By this conception, the abuse of human rights anywhere is a threat to human rights everywhere. Global emancipatory threats are local challenges to global human flourishing, whereby the political, social, and economic ideas and structures that promise to lift humans out of oppression are seriously challenged.

Existential and emancipatory securities are related in logic and in politics. Clearly, security-as-survival is logically prior to security-as-emancipation: existential security is the necessary condition for human flourishing. Politically, security-as-emancipation changes the conditions of possibility in relation to meeting existential threats. Above all, the wider and deeper the political identification with the referent of a global community embedded in shared values, the greater the likelihood of rational decisions being made in the global existential interest. Put simply, existence is the condition of possibility for emancipation, while furthering global emancipatory goals improves the conditions of possibility for global existential security.

The themes of human survival (in relation to threats of global reach) and emancipation (in relation to flourishing under conditions of global interconnectedness) will run through the rest of the discussion. "Global security", for the moment, can therefore be defined as *a condition in which humankind has a stable pattern of structures and processes, with associated institutions, attitudes, and behavior, that work towards the reduction and elimination of existential and emancipatory threats of global reach. The higher the level of global security experienced, the greater the conditions of possibility for people everywhere to explore the potentialities of being "human", beyond the merely animal.*

Global security threats, like those at any level, may be objective (existing but not necessarily perceived) or subjective (believed to exist, but doing so only in the perceiver's mind). Whether threats are objective or only felt subjectively, security is always relative: a condition of *absolute* security is unimaginable in any recognizable world. Because security is in the mind, as well as external to it, the reality of global security is importantly a construction of ideas. As such, history is partly an account of the way new ideas and patterns of thought emerge, resulting in things never quite being the same again. We need think only of how human society changed with the birth of monotheistic proselytizing religions, or with the spread of ideas such as democracy, nationalism, capitalism, and state sovereignty. History periodically gets written by ideas that were previously unthought.

In the twentieth century, the symbol of "national security" in the context of Westphalian international politics came to have phenomenal leverage on human behavior: on inventions, on industry, on culture, on social mobilization, and on the human capacity to contemplate mutual destruction. Might the symbol of "global security" come to have similar leverage, but towards cooperation rather than conflict? It is argued in the following section that a continuation of established practices, ideas, symbols, and global business-as-usual threaten an era of disaster. In these circumstances, re-imagining how to live globally is a rational priority, with the symbol of "global security" having reality-changing potential. Progressive change can never be guaranteed however. Before developing these arguments, it is necessary to look at the developing global context.

Where Are We In History? The Paradoxes of Proximity

The global age has been immanent in human biological exuberance. It became commonplace in the 1960s, following Marshall McLuhan (1962, p. 31), to hear reference to the "global village". By the 1990s, we were given the image of the "global neighborhood", the coinage of the Commission on Global Governance (1995). Both villages and neighborhoods are idealized as sites of community, but they are also known to be places of potential tension. When the space shared is the whole planet, "moving to get away from bad neighbours is not an option" (Commission on Global Governance, 1995, p. 44).

Specialists on globalization have endlessly debated the moment when the global age *really* began. Few would question the general observation of Peter Worsley, expressed in the mid-1980s, that "until our day, human society has never existed" (Mennell, 1990, p. 359). His point was that the human species could finally be conceived as one entity. Stephen Mennell nonetheless qualified this view by arguing that it was valid "only in the sense that never before have all the possible actors been on stage at once". Mennell emphasized that "some of the processes" that have made the human world one "have been at work in human societies as long as the species *Homo sapiens* has existed".

If the arrival of the global age was a process rather than an event, can the same be said about global security? I think so. With reference to global emancipatory threats, one noteworthy milestone was Immanuel Kant's recognition in *Perpetual Peace* (1795) that "the peoples of the earth have reached a stage of (narrower and broader) community where a violation of rights in one place is felt in all places" (Kant, 1988, p. 445). For Kant, justice was a "milieu" issue, arguing that the idea of a "*cosmopolitan* right" was not an empty phrase but a requirement in an interconnected world. Without justice and law, there would be chaos and disorder. From his home in Königsberg, Kant understood the dynamics of human global proximity, the interconnectedness of the emancipatory milieu, and the imperative of global reform.

Global existential security threats were earlier identified as being either targeted or untargeted. A symbolic marker of the latter was the "Spanish" flu pandemic of 1918–1919, when an estimated one-third of the world's population was infected and between 50–100 million people died. The fearful symbol of targeted global existential threats was the arrival in the 1950s of "nuclear overkill" and intercontinental delivery systems. This led some analysts to see the territorial "nation-state" as obsolete as a security provider (Herz, 1959). As nuclear plenty escalated to bizarre levels of "overkill", the prospect was raised of "nuclear winter" and the disappearance of all human life. "Mutual Assured Destruction" was embedded in the logic of national security. But history need not have gone this way.

Mike Featherstone (1990, p. 6) has argued that global historical sociology could have developed through various trajectories "through the imperial hegemony of a single nation or power bloc, or the triumph of a trading bloc, the universal proletariat, a form of religion or the world-federalist movement." Just as the past was open, so is the future, though it is wise to remember Karl Marx's warning: "Men make their own history, but they do not make it just as they please; they do not make it under circumstances chosen by themselves" (1992, p. 92).

When contemplating where we are in the developing human story, it is helpful to contemplate the immense historical panorama against which it is always enacted. For Norbert Elias, we still live in "humankind's prehistory" (Linklater, 2011, p. 22). Similarly, Michael Geyer and Charles Bright (2005, p. 29) remind us that "World history has only just begun". But we are as we are, and in that regard Anthony Giddens (Hutton and Giddens, 2001, p. 1) noted at the high-point of globalization in the 1990s: "Something very new is happening in the world". And it is not necessarily benign. While hyper-globalizers enthused about the "borderless world", others saw difficulties in the transformations taking place: the something new appeared to be a "runaway world" (Giddens, 1998, p. 309), a site of "turbulence" (Rosenau, 1990), a place of "new wars" (Kaldor, 1999), a "Risk Society" (Beck, 1992), and a world "on the edge" (Hutton and Giddens, 2001). Other writers, focusing on the international dimension of globalization, expressed concerns about "the ambiguity of interconnectedness" (Linklater, 2011, pp. 10, 16, 26, 112, 151, 253), "violence interdependence" (Deudney, 2007), and the "fragmentation" that accompanies globalization (Clark, 1997). Some were sure globalization would make us happy; Zygmunt Bauman thought it imperative to warn that it is "the cause of unhappiness in others" (1998, p. 1). These are all the paradoxes of proximity.

These paradoxes will intensify as human society globally is confronted by a historic "Great Reckoning" (Booth, 2007, pp. 395–470). A *reckoning* occurs when an individual or group has to come to terms with entrenched (even valued) ways of thinking and behaving that are dysfunctional. Faced by such a challenge, individuals or groups have to change how they have become accustomed to thinking and behaving, or pay the future price of business-as-usual. The Great Reckoning confronting human society in this period of history is the result of the "ideas that made us" – that constructed today's global living – being now out of time (Booth, 2007, pp. 21–27).

The dominant ideologies that have interacted to construct the dynamics of living globally have been patriarchy (the idea that men know best and should dominate society); proselytizing religions (the belief that "our" faith – whatever it is – represents the only true way and so deserves to be universalized); capitalism (a fantastically successful means of production, but one that requires losers as well as winners – with nature being amongst the most prominent losers); statism/nationalism (the game of sovereignty allied with national narcissism, producing the conflictual logic of international politics); racism (the idea of superior and inferior human beings, based on minor biological differences); and consumer democracy (which led to what J.K. Galbraith called a "culture of contentment" on the part of the winners within and between societies).

The interaction through history of this combination of ideas and their related institutions has delivered structures and processes that do not work for countless millions of people, do not work for nature, and do not promise a harmonious global future. These ideologies do not offer the positive, humane, long-term, and inclusive policies and institutions that that make it probable that the global-we will emerge from the Great Reckoning in good shape. The "ideas that made us" once seemed to make sense; they do so no longer except for the current winners on the world stage. They remain powerful and humans are their products, but we are not their prisoners, for "biology … makes us free" (Rose, 1997, p. 309). This includes the freedom to become differently global – but what sort of globalized animal might we become?

Where Are We Going? The Evolving Global Securityscape and the Inconvenient Truth of the International

The developing shape and character of the Great Reckoning can be conceived as a global "securityscape", that is, a terrain of insecurities characterized by the flux, flows, and persistent interaction of global dangers. The image of a securityscape is extrapolated from an idea of Arjun Appadurai (1990) regarding complex global cultural flows under globalization. These flows, he said, follow non-isomorphic paths, with various agents (states, multinational companies, interest groups, and so on) attempting to manipulate or channel or resist them with varying degrees of success, depending on their power.

The developing securityscape of the Great Reckoning is being shaped by the flux, flows, and persistent interaction of existential and emancipatory insecurities of actual or potential global reach. Our quasi-global community has varying capacities to manipulate or channel or resist these insecurities, be they international (multilateral organizations, states, or international nongovernmental organizations), small group, or individual. The following projections are offered in full recognition that those who predicted the twentieth century from its foothills got things badly wrong, and there is no reason to believe that human foresight has improved in this century.

Space forbids a detailed discussion of particular threats and risks within the developing securityscape. The aim here is simply to establish a framework for thinking about types of dangers in order to contemplate appropriate policy counters:

Global Existential Threats

Nuclear Weapons   Nuclear weapons allied to long-range delivery systems remain the most obvious destructive force with global reach and implications. While the fear of a nuclear war resulting in a global catastrophe has diminished, nuclear weapons continue to exist in large numbers and nuclear proliferation remains a pressing issue in several regions. If – probably when – the number of nuclear weapons states increases, so will the danger of any war between them producing a contagion of nuclear destruction. In this regard, all eyes are focused on the Middle East, and the behavior of Iran and Israel in particular. In the longer term, nuclear confrontations cannot be ruled out between the world's major military powers. A cottage industry thrives on speculation regarding a nuclearized Cold War resulting from (exaggerated) images of "the rise of China" and "the decline of the United States". Risks of nuclear war will exist as long as there are nuclear weapons, "worst-case forecasting", and security dilemma dynamics (Booth and Wheeler, 2008, pp. 265–272).

While there is widespread agreement about the declining utility of war between major powers (Lebow, 2010), history warns against complacency. Recall that observers of the international scene in 1913 looked back on a "long peace" and forward to its indefinite continuation. Today there are several geopolitically sensitive spots, where conventional war is not "unthinkable". Where potential parties are also nuclear armed, the risk of escalation is a rational calculation, and preparing for such an eventuality is part of the routine of some militaries. This being so, the "Sarajevo syndrome", symbolizing a local quarrel escalating through interlocking structures into a general war, remains a stark warning against complacency.

Conventional War   Conventional wars can have global reach. In the period since 1945, there have been two distinct models.

First, the global struggle for power between the superpowers in the Cold War resulted in several highly destructive "proxy wars". These took place far from the central front of the confrontation but were justified in relation to it. What is more, the threat and outbreak of violence in the name of this ideological/geopolitical struggle was not confined to the international level; violence was also globalized and legitimized at the human level in the form of vicious internal repression by allies on both sides.

The second model of globalized violence was the Global War on Terror declared by the Bush Administration in the aftermath of 9/11. The United States was attacked by al-Qaeda, a non-state terrorist organization that had declared a cosmic war against its "Far Enemy". When a superpower (which by definition has global reach) is challenged, what follows can become global. Other states may be drawn in directly as targets or allies, while general insecurity is spread through the excuse that a supposedly "global struggle" gives to all governments (including liberal democracies) to increase internal repression. This second model of globalized violence might be the result of traditional (conventional) military aggression or various non-traditional forms of attack, such as a terrorist "spectacular" or a cyber-attack aiming to cripple a rival's economic system.

These models of globalized conventional violence go against the optimistic image of a future peopled by *Better Angels* (Pinker, 2011), but sober contemplation of the developing securityscape offers abundant reasons for concern – what Gramsci would have called "morbid symptoms". These include the dangers that might arise from growing insecurity over access to future energy, water, and food; the risks of violence spreading through the combination of good intentions and military means flagged as "humanitarian intervention"; the militarization of space; and the unintended consequences of new sovereignty-threatening technology such as drones. Sparks anywhere have the potential of setting light to combustible material in the "global neighborhood". This happened a century ago, in the European neighborhood.

Environmental Degradation   It will be recalled that a global existential threat does not require explicit targeting by a political actor. People do not, for example, buy gas-guzzling cars to create fragile societies elsewhere, but there are regions where the prospect of famine, land loss, and migration as a result of human-made climate change might spark wars over territory (Booth and Wheeler, 2008, pp. 267–268). In these scenarios, the term "collateral damage" can be applied to the civilian casualties of global climate change; they are untargeted but real victims.

The existential threat of "climate chaos" is not driven by traditional state-to-state strategies, but the risks do have state-to-state implications as a result of the risks arising from such issues as food scarcity, water shortages, boundary disagreements, mass migration, and the loss of territory through sea-level rises. "Climate chaos" confronts human society with one of its biggest "known unknowns" over the coming century, and will be an important contributory factor to the sense of insecurity pervading the securityscape. When the corridors of power, and of powerlessness, are pervaded by uncertainty, fear, and mistrust, they are not places where rational policymaking can be guaranteed. That said, it is to the credit of far-sighted individuals – originally from within global civil society rather than governments – that they lobbied governments to take climate change seriously, long before the worst imagined consequences occur.

Biothreats   Biothreats include both strategic and natural dangers; the former have political intentionality and involve the specific targeting of people, while the latter are unintended and untargeted. What is common is infectious disease and its potential for global reach. *Strategic dangers* result from the threat of biological attacks by governments or "bioterrorists"; *natural dangers* are the result of threats to health on a global scale arising out of complex and widespread human interaction these days. It is the natural rather than strategic threats that seem to pose the far greater risk of harm.

The danger of the deliberate spread of biological agents (pathogens) for strategic purposes is an old one in war. In recent years, especially following the 9/11 "spectacular", the fear of bioterrorism has caused periodic scares, especially in the West. This concern has not been confined to the media or the popular imagination. One distinguished scientist, Martin Rees (2003, pp. 47–60) has argued that "the potential hazards stemming from microbiology and genetics" will be more "disquieting" than nuclear dangers in the years ahead. Significant obstacles face the weaponization of biological agents, especially when it comes to the dispersal of the agents, but work on biological warfare continues, for defensive as well as offensive purposes. Whether exaggerated or not, there is a conceivable threat: this work is not easily detected, advances in understandings of the human immune system raise the danger of advances in engineered viruses, and there are risks from "laboratory errors" (the escape of pathogens) as well as planned attacks.

Natural health threats (the risks of the spread of infectious disease) belong on the agenda of global security as one of the perils of proximity. Pandemics have periodically swept the world, as was mentioned earlier. The most recent ("swine flu" in 2009) quickly infected people in over one-third of the countries in the world, although death rates were relatively low. While the media are sometimes guilty of exaggerating the risks – playing on what Rees (2003, p. 49) calls the "dread factor" – the existential threat from a variety of diseases (AIDS, smallpox, and malaria can all kill in the millions) is potentially enormous. And new diseases, such as SARS, stoke new fears. Deadly diseases can threaten the stability of states and impact negatively on global emancipatory potentialities. Health is a fundamental dimension of human capability (Nussbaum, 2011).

Global Emancipatory Threats

Human Security   Global existential threats were previously classified according to the sources of danger. Global emancipatory threats can be better classified according to the level at which the insecurity operates.

The concept of "human security" was developed by the United Nations Development Programme (UNDP) (1994) at the end of the Cold War. Its relevant *Human Development Report* identified the need to shift from a superpower "cataclysmic world event" with its focus on weapons to "a concern with human life and dignity". The report emphasized that human security is a matter of universal concern, that its issues are interdependent and better dealt with earlier rather than later, and that it is people-centered. The issues listed were economic, food, health, environment, personal, community, and political. The threats identified were population growth, economic disparities, migration pressures, environmental degradation, drug trafficking, and international terrorism (UNDP, 1994, pp. 22–24). While one might quibble with the UNDP's detailed characterization of the issues and threats, what matters for present purposes is the international recognition of this level of security/insecurity, and the emphasis that was placed on interdependence and universality.

The notion of human security has attracted controversy – its meaning has been challenged for being too expansive, while governments have been criticized for shortcomings in their policies. Nonetheless, in historical terms the report represents another milestone in the international politics of emancipation. At the report's heart was the following: "In the final analysis, human security is a child who did not die, a disease that did not spread, a job that was not cut, an ethnic tension that did not explode into violence, a dissident who was not silenced" (UNDP, 1994, p. 23). The report was a milestone, but the journey remains a long one because human security in international practice attends mostly to symptoms rather than causes – an unemployed person might, at root, be a casualty of the workings of capitalism, for example, but the UNDP's role is not to overthrow the prevailing global economic system.

One criticism of the concept of human security has been that it merely reformulates "human rights". The view has some merit, but this merely underlines the legitimacy of the idea of individuals as the ultimate referent for security in international relations. While honoring the individual, human security implicitly and explicitly recognizes that individuals exist in groups. Likewise, a discussion of global emancipatory threats must also consider the risks facing groups. The personal is the social.

Societal Security   The idea of societal security, developed originally by Barry Buzan (1991), focuses on the sustainability and evolution of traditional patterns of language, culture, and religious and other identities and customs. Societal security is implicated in the conceptions and practices of both state and human security.

Societal security can be hostile to both human security and emancipation. The greater the security of some cherished identities and customs in some societies (manifest in practices of ethnic purity and patriarchy, for example), the greater the insecurity of other people and groups in those societies. In this regard, emancipation – like security – must be a universal project: neither emancipation nor security can be at the expense of others.

Globalization has had both positive and negative impacts on societal security. Positively, it has accelerated the growth of global consciousness and the densification of networks of "global civil society" – this is evident in the promotion of transworld solidarities on issues such as peace, human rights, and the environment. Negatively, globalization has threatened traditional identities through the cultural reach of "McWorld". Rampant consumerism and marketization have been powerful alienating forces on some local communities and personal fulfillment.

The risks to the emancipatory aspects of societal security are magnified by the "morbid symptoms" that characterize the developing securityscape. The situation is fragile in many places, and a longer-term danger of a downward spiral exists, analogous to other periods of decline in social and international order. In an interconnected world, local crises cannot be easily contained – this was demonstrated by the financial crisis of 2008. Violence can also be contagious. This was argued by Mary Kaldor (1999) in her exploration of the "new wars" associated with globalization. Here, distinctions become blurred between soldiers and civilians, between legitimate force and terrorism, between the inside and outside of states, and between politics and criminality. These "new wars" across central Africa, central Asia, and parts of the Middle East tear whatever fabric of order exists, together with whatever prospects there are for peaceful emancipatory politics. They constitute local global threats.

Tears in the fabric of global emancipatory possibilities begin with regressive ideas. Stereotypes ("men know best"), any relativization of the idea of human rights ("Asian values"), and the trumpeting of traditionalist common sense ("the poor will always be with us") help sustain anti-emancipatory behavior. It may be difficult to think of the slogans just mentioned as *global* threats, but they represent the mentality Kant thought essential to resist over 200 years ago. When enlightenment is torn anywhere, the fabric is weakened everywhere. The behavior of the Bush administration towards human rights and the rule of law, which legitimized similar or worse on the part of other governments, is a powerful reminder of the fragility of human rights in anxious times (Cole and Lobel, 2007).

The flows, flux, and persistent interactions of insecurity in the developing securityscape will appear in different (non-isomorphic) forms, and will affect specific referents to a greater or lesser extent. The latter will be evident in the subsequent chapters of this volume, in the discussions of key actors (states, international organizations, nongovernmental organizations, global civil society, corporations, etc.), different arenas (international, local, legal, and military), and with reference to specific tools (such as peacekeeping and statebuilding). It may well be that most risks to the security of most people in coming decades will not come from direct military threats – the traditional focus of national security – but from damage to the fabric of existing emancipatory structures. The distinction between the two types of global threat must not be overdrawn because, as was argued earlier, existential and emancipatory security are logically and politically mutually implicated. The collapse of emancipatory values is likely to have existential consequences, while existential security is the necessary condition for emancipation. Prejudice against migrants, for example, legitimizes more general attitudes of racism in a society, which in turn can feed the ethnic hatred that leads to violence.

This brief overview of the developing securityscape offers a picture of flux, flows, and the interaction of insecurities. It is taking place in a landscape dominated by familiar structures, and notably those operating at the international level of world politics. This level has particular "causal weight" and a distinctive "texture" (Waltz, 1959, 1979). In other words, the international level of world politics causes "big and important things" to happen, while its characteristic features show impressive continuity across the centuries (balance of power politics, war and rumors of war, security dilemmas, power differentials, the domination of selfish national interest, and so on). This picture has been challenged by those who argued that globalization in the latter part of the twentieth century was causing a radical change in how the world works. We were said to be in a "post-international" world in which nations and states were being increasingly by-passed (Rosenau, 1990). While such analyses were correct in declaring the arrival of a global age, it was too soon to describe it as "post-international". This is evident in the daily news from around the world highlighting the continuing "causal weight" of nation-state structures and norms.

These arguments should not be read to imply that international politics is as unchanging as "doctrinal realists" maintain, however. Progressive change is possible: universal human rights have been collectively legitimized; legal and moral inhibitions on war have grown; and interdependence has become increasingly institutionalized through a profusion of international governmental and non-governmental bodies. Progress is possible, but the statist structure of international politics remains an "inconvenient truth" for idealists (Booth, 2011, pp. 325–342).

The Challenge: Can we Escape the "Madness of Sanity"?

We are seven billion people and still counting. We reach across habitable and barely habitable landscapes, and our attitudes and behavior remain structured by ideas and institutions that prioritize micro- rather than macro-perspectives and interests. Above all, the security of the potential community of humankind is constantly confronted by the historic dynamics of statism, nationalism, and the hyper-productive and exploitative economic juggernaut of capitalism. The emerging global securityscape therefore consists of a Great Reckoning characterized by an "iron cage" of old ways of thinking about living globally on the one hand, and the rational demands of security for the *global-we* on the other.

The transformation in global life towards which this chapter points can be conceived as a shift – in outlook and in practice – from a *national security* mindset to a mindset tuned into what might be called a *global domestic security policy*. This formulation is derived from Jürgen Habermas's conception of "global domestic policy" (2006, pp. 135–139). Space forbids much discussion of Habermas's conception, save to say that I think it overemphasizes the need for the continuing centrality of the nation-state in global matters, overworks the difference between what he calls the "supranational" and "transnational" levels of politics, and underemphasizes the need for *government* as opposed to *governance* at the global level (similar criticisms are made by Scheuerman, 2007, 2011, pp. 113–121).

A global domestic security policy, while focused on the referent of humankind as a whole, must of course begin where we are now – this includes accepting the centrality of sovereign states and nations. The aim, therefore, must be to change the centrality and meanings of those institutions, working towards a global polity characterized by states beyond statism and nations beyond nationalism.

Progress along the lines suggested cannot be guaranteed, but there are rational reasons for hope. Taking the concept of global security seriously is not utopian in the negative sense of that term because the standpoint of this essay has been the perspective that critical theorists call "immanent critique". This is the very opposite of thinking in a vacuum. It involves identifying the features that "already exist" within concrete situations that can be built upon to construct a different and better "reality" (Horkheimer, 1972, p. 227). This better reality must focus in the first place on our survival as *biological* beings (facing existential global threats), and then on securing the conditions of possibility when it comes to exploring *human* beings (facing global emancipatory threats). The referent discussed throughout the essay has been a *global-we*, which is a quasi-community of fate (whether subjectively felt or not), and potentially a cosmopolitan identity community (an "imagined [global] community", to extrapolate Benedict Anderson's (1991, pp. 5–7) famous definition of a nation). In the necessarily brief sketches that follow, I will identify four strands, each based on potentials that "already exist", whose strengthening would add momentum towards a working global domestic security policy, and which are particularly relevant to readers of a book on global security.

Global Consciousness

The growth of a distinct global consciousness – the progressive engagement of the human mind with the idea of the global – is the necessary strand in developing a global domestic security policy. The phrase "global consciousness" (applicable to individuals and collectivities) refers to a positive mental awareness of human and non-human life on a global scale.

Ideas are fundamental to global security realities, and in this regard a major challenge is to reject the fatalism associated with regressive ideas such as "human nature" (Allott, 1998). Human nature is a powerful idea, not destiny, and history on the biggest screen offers a picture of radical change in human society through time. Today, planning global political life beyond statism, nationalism, and capitalism, in the spirit of cosmopolitanism and equality, will appear fanciful to majority opinion, but so would have been the idea of democracy and republicanism in the era of the Divine Right of Kings.

Powerful immanent transnational solidarities "already exist" in the idea of cosmopolitanism, notions of "global citizenship", commitments to universal human rights, and a growing sense of humankind as a community of fate. The latter is evident, for example, in attempts to organize a collective response to the risks of climate change, and in on-going efforts to control the global spread of nuclear weapons. However disappointing the results of these initiatives – the traditional "texture" of national security and national economic power still hold sway – the very fact of some cooperation on these matters offers a glimpse of a developing global domestic security policy agenda.

The term "global consciousness" is closely associated with the ancient idea of "cosmopolitanism". The latter is the belief in a common humanity; in the idea that the "equal worth of all human beings" should be a "regulative constraint" on political actions and aspirations; in the view that differences between people will be "nonhierarchically understood" and "morally irrelevant"; and in the conviction that "right" comes before country, and "universal reason" before nationalism (Nussbaum, 1996, pp. 3–17, 131–144). Cosmopolitan thought, historically, has had "three major moments" according to Richard Beardsworth (2011, pp. 17–21): the Stoics in ancient Greece, the theorists of natural law, and the European Enlightenment. As is evident, these "moments" actually add up to centuries of cosmopolitan sentiment on which global citizens can build.

In the construction of global security consciousness, there is a potentially significant role for opinion-formers of all sorts, including intellectuals working on international and global matters. While one should never exaggerate the impact of the academic profession, our work spreads into society through teaching and wider public dissemination, and so plays a part in shaping what Gramsci called the "common sense" of society. This is important work because if global civil society cannot define "global security", show how the strands of a global domestic security policy are based in reality, and suggest feasible strategic options, then we can never hope to overcome developing global insecurities.

The greater the transformed consciousness about living globally, the greater the influence of specifically global interests when decisions are being made about key issues in world affairs. Earlier, it was suggested that in the nineteenth and twentieth centuries the symbol of "national security" gave a particular dynamic to international life; the same will be the case if the symbol of "global security" comes to be coupled with *the global-we* (and is expressed through feelings, politics, institutions, and resources). Big things happen when security is coupled with identity, and if the goal of global security were to be shared by an embryonic global identity community, the world would never be the same again.

Individual Engagement

Confronted by the challenges of our time, it is tempting to give way to a sense of hopelessness: but there are grounds for hope. Encouragement can be taken, for example, from the many who already attempt to live as "global citizens" (Campbell, MacKinnon and Stevens, 2010, pp. 22–30, 370–372). Today, self-defined global citizens conceive their "citizenship" in relation to a virtual *cosmopolis* in a manner comparable to the original sense of citizenship in relation to the *cité* – there is a sense of entitlement (universal human rights for the global citizen) and commensurate responsibility (for the global citizen to live a global life locally, working as far as possible to encourage the flourishing of people and the preservation of the natural environment).

Deciding to live as a "global citizen", to the extent that is possible in one's individual circumstances, adds another layer to one's existing identities. And becoming global can counter hopelessness by giving meaning to individual lives. Peter Singer (1997, pp. 279–280) is but one who has written persuasively about the way that giving something of oneself to the world also helps a sense of personal fulfillment. Individual answers to the question "What is to be done?" can take various forms.

At the most personal level, it can be done by attempting to change people's minds about patriarchy, racism, rampant consumerism, and so on. In this way, one can contribute, however little, to constructing a common sense on which a more inclusive global domestic security policy can build. In such (even small) ways, we can all act as (global) "organic intellectuals". In Gramsci's formulation, we are all intellectuals in some sense, with organic intellectuals being those who clarify, theorize, and articulate the ideas and values of a particular class or group (Gramsci, 1971, pp. 3–24, 323–377).

From the argument earlier, it should be apparent that specialists in IR have a particular role because of the "inconvenient truth" and "causal weight" of the international level of world politics. The academic project of IR is not merely about telling the score in the game of nations, it is an aspect of the social development of humans, a part of the growth of human consciousness about the biggest political questions. This is not to suggest that every IR specialist focuses exclusively on the global, but it is a call to make sure one brings the global dimension into whatever one does. In this way, one can also contribute to changing traditionalist horizons about living globally. One can contribute to constructing a different global consciousness, essay by essay, seminar by seminar, book by book.

Global Identity Formation

Individual global engagement is a first step; the next is using the agency released in an explicitly political way. It has been argued that there exists a global community of fate, but not a cosmopolitan identity community. In other words, we live in the global age empirically, but it is still a minority of people across the planet who act politically according to cosmopolitan ideas. It cannot be assumed that such an identity community will ever come to guide global affairs: global solidarities do not simply exist – they have to be constructed.

"Global civil society" already exists to a degree, though it is largely separated into different issue-areas and is somewhat controversial. In general, it refers to those transnational organizations that operate below the level of governments with the aim of using and expanding the global public sphere in the interests of promoting both existential and emancipatory aims such as peace, democracy, environmental sustainability, and economic justice (Kaldor, 2003, pp. 1–14 discusses five different usages of the term).

To act in this way is to construct an emancipatory human community challenging fatalism. The more that the idea of common humanity becomes a global reality, the greater the potential to build global institutions that are able to promote common law and act politically in the common (global) rather than the particular (national) interest. For this to develop, identity must be reimagined forwards, beyond our traditionalist "us and them" forms of socialization. In this way, what has invariably been seen as the "utopia of world society" may become "a little more real or at least more urgent" (Beck, 1992, pp. 47, 137). This is not fanciful. Forms of human identification have expanded geographically over time. In recent centuries, "the nation" has generally been supreme. But nations are relatively recent constructions. They are "imagined communities", and enormous pressure – some soft, some hard – has to be exerted to manufacture the completed nationalized person.

"Imagined communities" have come in multiple forms throughout history, and there is no limit to the human potential for expanding identity, as is evident from the growing identification of people with the welfare of the Earth's other animals. Politically, universal cosmopolitan moments have been evident in the identification of people across the world, with the breaking down of the Berlin Wall and the peaceful overthrow of apartheid in South Africa. Global identifications are wider than many think, even if they are not (yet?) deep politically.

Global Institutional Reform

There is no escape from the global age, short of some almost unimaginable catastrophe. Space and time will continue to shrink, and increasing numbers of people across the world will live out-of-geography existences that would have been unthinkable even a few generations ago. If globalization in this sense is inevitable, what matters is its quality and character.

A world that works better for humans as a whole, and for the rest of nature, requires much more than a changed collective consciousness about living globally and bottom–up initiatives. To begin with, a "cosmopolitics" requires change at the level of existing institutions operating at the highest level. The United Nations, World Trade Organization, and the European Union, for example, are in need of reform with a view to embedding a more global mindset in their cultures and processes. In this regard, there is a pressing need for the discussion and development of ideas pointing to the building-blocks of a new global common sense, such as "cosmopolitan democracy" (Archibugi, 2003), amalgamated and pluralistic "security communities" (Booth and Wheeler, 2008, pp. 182–190, 252–253), the idea of the "cosmopolitan state" (Beck, 2000), and the much-neglected notion of "world government" (Weiss, 2009).

Significant global reform requires movement beyond the discussion of global "governance" to the construction of global "government". Those of us who think that such radical global reform is necessary must be mindful of the criticism of intellectual escapism directed against Marx by Raymond Aron (2002, p. 468): Aron complained that Marx sketched merely an idyllic portrait of his long-term vision, and "never actually described it". Global security policies require political blueprints, even if they are lightly sketched and subject to change.

When it comes to global reform among those who operate in society as intellectuals, there is a fascinating immanent potential involving some of the key figures in realist IR who worked in the middle of the last century, together with today's critical theorists. William Scheuerman (2011) calls the former group "Progressive Realists" and has shown how they took morality seriously, recognized the growing dysfunctionality of the sovereign state, and understood the perils of nationalism. At the same time, their thinking was embedded in a thorough grounding of international realities. Likewise, today's critical IR theorists recognize that the historic challenge is not that of fine-tuning the problems *in* the international *status quo*, but rather of changing *the very status quo* itself (Booth, 2007).

Scheuerman's account shows that it is not just those usually marginalized as "idealists" who think the unthinkable about global reform. Leading realist thinkers were in the vanguard of those arguing for radical global reform decades before the term "globalization" became common. Growing intellectual solidarity around global reform is an objective necessity. In face of the Great Reckoning, what today might seem to be a huge leap could soon appear as common sense.

Radical movement in the directions indicated may seem unlikely at the moment, but the objective conditions are changing to such a degree that old thinking will increasingly be tested to the limit, if not beyond. Answers will soon be required to questions that, in recent times, have been considered politically irrelevant. As the rapid and unpredicted end of the Cold War reminded us, we cannot always assume that tomorrow will be like today.

The phrase "madness of sanity" used in the title of this concluding section was a coinage of Jean-Jacques Rousseau, one of the Enlightenment's most influential thinkers. His concern was with structural power in the age of kings, and specifically how the anarchical system of sovereign states demanded self-help as the behavioral logic of the game of nations. There might be stability in such a system, according to realist thinkers about international relations (through balances of power for example), but there can be no automatic harmony (Waltz, 1959, p. 182). This being so, Rousseau argued that being "public spirited" would be futile on the part of kings and their officials. Sanity – being "public spirited" – would be "downright dangerous". Indeed, he said, "to be sane in a world of madmen is itself a kind of madness" (quoted by Waltz, 1959, p. 181).

Such views still resonate in the corridors of power in the knee-jerk obsession with the "the national interest" defined traditionally. The nation-state behavioral imperative is to compete because "everyone's strategy depends upon everyone else's" (Waltz, 1959, p. 238). This insight is familiar to all involved in conflictual situations. Acting strategically in this way is seen by realists as neither moral nor immoral, but simply "a reasoned response to the world about us". From such a perspective – invariably understood as the responsibility of statecraft – the international level of world politics will (indeed must) remain dominated by the mistrust and conflict of statist sanity.

Against this view, the earlier discussion has offered some signposts towards an escape from the ideas that made the global age what it is today. As the immanent critique of what exists and what is possible brought out, it is rational to think that it will be possible to escape the "madness of sanity" and begin to construct a different politics. Security, as has been argued, is a condition that allows individuals and groups, locally and globally, to explore human being/human becoming when emancipated from the biological search for survival, which is an instinct we share with other animals. Global existential security and global emancipatory security are opposite sides of the same coin. That coin is a humane global domestic security policy.

Radical progressive change in human affairs typically occurs in the shadow of recent or predictable disaster: Europe needed two world wars to learn the wisdom of trying to build a post-statist community; "We the Peoples", to use the language of the UN Charter, needed the Holocaust to bring about the Universal Declaration of Human Rights and the Genocide Convention; and states needed the threat of the "climate chaos" to begin to engage the global politics of environmental justice. Our generation's challenge is to achieve progress without disaster, when once again disaster looms. The ideologies, institutions, and dynamics of nationalism, state sovereignty, and supercharged capitalism are being tested to – and beyond – their limits in an age of ever-growing global interconnectedness. The emerging securityscape offers various pathways, some more hopeful than others. The choice of political compass is ours.

Notes

1. I want to thank Kamila Stullerova and Nicholas Wheeler for comments on an earlier draft.
2. "Statism" in this chapter is taken to mean the belief (i) in the primacy of the nation-state as the referent for security; (ii) in the nation-state as the ultimate level of decision-making in politics; and (iii) in the nation-state as the most important focus of political loyalty for people.

References

Allott, Philip. 1998. "The future of the human past." In *Statecraft and Security: the Cold War and Beyond*, edited by Ken Booth, 323–337. Cambridge: Cambridge University Press.

Anderson, Benedict. 1991. *Imagined Communities: Reflections on the Origins and Spread of Nationalism*. London: Verso.

Appadurai, Arjun. 1990. "Disjuncture and difference in the global cultural economy." In *Global Culture: Nationalism, Globalization and Modernity*, edited by Mike Featherstone, 295–310. London: Sage Publications.

Archibugi, Daniele, ed. 2003. *Debating Cosmopolitics*. London: Verso.

Aron, Raymond. 2002. *The Dawn of Universal History*. New York, NY: Basic Books.

Bauman, Zygmunt. 1998. *Globalization: the Human Consequences*. New York, NY: Columbia University Press.

Beardsworth, Richard. 2011. *Cosmopolitanism and International Relations Theory*. Cambridge: Polity Press.

Beck, Ulrich. 1992. *The Risk Society: Towards a New Modernity*. London: Sage Publications.

Beck, Ulrich. 2000. *What is Globalization?* Cambridge: Polity Press.

Booth, Ken. 2007. *Theory of World Security*. Cambridge: Cambridge University Press.

Booth, Ken, 2011. "International Politics: the Inconvenient Truth." In *Realism and World Politics*, edited by Ken Booth, 325–342. Abingdon: Routledge.

Booth, Ken, and Nicholas J. Wheeler. 2008. *The Security Dilemma: Fear, Cooperation and Trust in World Politics*. Houndmills: Palgrave Macmillan.

Buzan, Barry. 1991. *People, States and Fear: an Agenda for International Security Studies in the Post-Cold War Era*. 2nd ed. London: Harvester Wheatsheaf.

Buzan, Barry, Ole Wæver, and Jaap de Wilde. 1998. *Security: a New Framework for Analysis*. Boulder, CO: Lynne Rienner.

Campbell, Patricia J., Aran MacKinnon, and Christy R. Stevens. 2010. *An Introduction to Global Studies*. Oxford: Wiley Blackwell.

Clark, Ian. 1997. *Globalization and Fragmentation: International Relations in the Twentieth Century*. Oxford: Oxford University Press.

Cole, David, and Jules Lobel. 2007. *Less Safe, Less Free: How America is Losing the War on Terror*. New York, NY: The New Press.

Commission on Global Governance (Report). 1995. *Our Global Neighbourhood*. Oxford: Oxford University Press.

Deudney, Daniel H. 2007. *Bounding Power: Republican Security Theory from the Polis to the Global Village*. Princeton, NJ: Princeton University Press.

Falk, Richard. 1975. *A Study of Future Worlds*. New York, NY: Free Press.

Featherstone, Mike, 1990. "Global Culture: an Introduction." In *Global Culture: Nationalism, Globalization and Modernity*, edited by Mike Featherstone, 1–14. London: Sage Publications.

Foot, Philippa. 2001. *Natural Goodness*. Oxford: Oxford University Press.

Galtung, Johan. 1971. "A Structural Theory of Imperialism." *Journal of Peace Research*, 8(1): 81–117.

Geyer, Michael, and Charles Bright, 2005. "World History in a Global Age." In *The Global History Reader*, edited by Bruce Mazlish and Akira Iriye, 20–29. New York: Routledge.

Giddens, Anthony. 1998. "Affluence, Poverty and the Idea of a Post-Scarcity Society." In *Statecraft and Security: the Cold War and Beyond*, edited by Ken Booth, 308–322. Cambridge: Cambridge University Press.

Gramsci, Antonio. 1971. *Selections from the Prison Notebooks*. London: Lawrence and Wishart.

Habermas, Jürgen. 2006. *The Divided West*. Cambridge: Polity Press.

Herz, John, 1959. *International Politics in the Atomic Age*. New York, NY: Columbia University Press.

Horkheimer, Max. 1972. *Critical Theory. Selected Essays*. New York, NY: Continuum Publishing Company.

Hutton, Will, and Anthony Giddens. 2001. *On the Edge: Living with Global Capitalism*. London: Vintage.

Kaldor, Mary. 1999. *New and Old Wars: Organised Violence in a Global Era*. Cambridge: Polity Press.

Kaldor, Mary. 2003. *Global Civil Society: an Answer to War*. Cambridge: Polity Press.

Kant, Immanuel. 1988. *Perpetual Peace in Kant Selections*, edited by L.W. Beck, 429–457. New York, NY: Macmillan.

Lebow, Richard Ned. 2010. *Why Nations Fight? Past and Future Motives for War*. Cambridge: Cambridge University Press.

Linklater, Andrew. 2011. *The Problem of Harm in World Politics: Theoretical Investigations*. Cambridge: Cambridge University Press.

Marx, Karl. 1992. "The Eighteenth Brumaire of Louis Bonaparte." In Karl Marx and Frederick Engels, *Selected Works*. London: Lawrence and Wishart.

McLuhan, Marshall. 1962. *The Gutenberg Galaxy*. Toronto, ON: University of Toronto Press.

Mennell, Stephen. 1990. "The Globalization of Human Society as a Very Long-term Social Process: Elias's Theory." In *Global Culture: Nationalism, Globalization and Modernity*, edited by Mike Featherstone, 359–71. London: Sage Publications.

Nussbaum, Martha. 1996. *For Love of Country. Debating the Limits of Patriotism*. Boston, MA: Beacon Press.

Nussbaum, Martha. 2011. *Creating Capabilities: the Human Development Approach*. Cambridge, MA: Harvard University Press.

Pinker, Steven. 2011. *The Better Angels of our Nature*. New York, NY: Viking.

Rees, Martin. 2003. *Our Final Century: Will Civilisation Survive the Twenty-First Century?* London: Arrow Books.

Rose, Steven. 1997. *Lifelines: Biology, Freedom, Determinism*. London: Allen Lane.

Rosenau, James. 1990. *Turbulence in World Politics: a Theory of Change and Continuity*. Princeton, NJ: Princeton University Press.

Scheuerman, William E. 2007. "Global governance without global government." *Political Theory*, 36: 133–151.

Scheuerman, William E. 2011. *The Realist Case for Global Reform*. Cambridge: Polity Press.

Singer, Peter. 1997. *How Are We to Live? Ethics in an Age of Self-Interest*. Oxford: Oxford University Press.

UNDP. 1994. *Human Development Report 1994*. New York, NY: Oxford University Press.
Waltz, Kenneth N. 1959. *Man, the State, and War*. New York, NY: Columbia University Press.
Waltz, Kenneth N. 1979. *Theory of International Politics*. New York, NY: Random House.
Weiss, Thomas G. 2009. "What happened to the idea of world government." *International Studies Quarterly*, 53: 253–271.
Wolfers, Arnold. 1962. *Discord and Collaboration. Essays on International Politics*. Baltimore, MD: The John Hopkins Press.

Chapter 2

Security and Social Critique

David Mutimer

In 1990, John Mearsheimer wrote an article for *The Atlantic Monthly* provocatively titled "Why we will soon miss the Cold War". Mearsheimer meant his "we" to be quite expansive and inclusive. It certainly meant the United States, but more broadly the people of Western Europe and the West more generally, and perhaps even everyone everywhere (Mearsheimer, 1990). Revealingly, however, it is not possible to know from reading Mearsheimer's article because he simply speaks of "we" without revealing who that "we" might be. His argument, in essence, is that the Cold War kept the peace in the latter half of the twentieth century, and so without it, peace becomes much less certain (and "we" all benefit from peace). Of course, this argument depends on seeing the latter half of the twentieth century as "peaceful", which is an odd judgment for one of the most violent global periods and one which was marked by the constant threat of instant nuclear annihilation.

There are those who might have missed the Cold War in 1990, however, and there are those for whom the Cold War provided some certainty of action, a stable framework in which to go on, and the opportunity for some sizeable profits. In other words, those for whom the Cold War provided security. This "we" is a much narrower, but rather more easily identified group. It is the state managers, particularly in the United States and Western Europe, who were able to conduct 'security" policy within a relatively well understood frame of reference. This "we" also includes those selling endless supplies of increasingly expensive military equipment to states who considered themselves to be trapped in an "arms race", the distinguishing feature of which was not numbers but rather levels of (vastly expensive) technological sophistication. The "we" would also comprise the scholars of international security for whom the strictures of the Cold War provided a simple schema within which to analyze, pronounce, and proscribe. One of the leading such scholars in 1990 was John Mearsheimer.

The Handbook of Global Security Policy, First Edition. Edited by Mary Kaldor and Iavor Rangelov.
© 2014 John Wiley & Sons, Ltd. Published 2014 by John Wiley & Sons, Ltd.

So there were those who might miss the Cold War, but what of the others? What indeed of those who were not made secure by living in a world under constant threat of a devastating nuclear war? What if, more than that, there were those who had been rendered *insecure* by the very Cold War practices that purported to guarantee "our" security? It was in posing and starting to answer these very questions that a group of scholars developed a set of alternative approaches to the questions of security, approaches that are now broadly called "Critical Security Studies". In this chapter, I will introduce three of the leading approaches to security that have developed into, in, and around Critical Security Studies. First of all, I will briefly set them into the context of the debate about security and security studies, which was sparked by the demise of the Cold War that Mearsheimer laments.

Security Studies Meets Social Critique

The end of the Cold War was almost immediately missed by scholars working in the mainstream of International Security Studies. Not only had the Cold War provided the assumptions on which that study proceeded, but the majority of the practicing scholars confidently asserted that these assumptions were a permanent feature of international life. The Cold War, in other words, could not end.[1] But of course, the Cold War did end, and its ending opened what Jim George has called a "thinking space", an opportunity to question the previously unquestionable assumptions about what security was and how it might work (George, 1994, pp. 32–34). The debate of the early post-Cold War period around security that filled this space has been reasonably characterized as taking place between a group of scholars counseling a "broadening" of security and another seeking a "deepening" of security. Both positions recognized the challenge posed to the study and practice of security by the end of the Cold War, but differed on what was needed to respond to this challenge.

The "broadening" argument was articulated early and forcefully by Jessica Tuchman Mathews in an article in *Foreign Affairs*, the journal of record for the US foreign policy establishment:

> The 1990s will demand a redefinition of what constitutes national security. In the 1970s the concept was expanded to include international economics as it became clear that the U.S. economy was no longer the independent force it had once been, but was powerfully affected by economic policies in dozens of other countries. Global developments now suggest the need for another analogous, broadening definition of national security to include resource, environmental and demographic issues. (Mathews, 1989, p. 162)

This call was answered with a burst of literature in the early 1990 in the areas that Mathews identified: economic security, environmental security (both of which centered on resource security), and what came to be called societal security. What this literature demonstrated was that the near-exclusive focus on the military as both the source of threat and of security was untenable in the post-Cold War world.

Those seeking to "deepen" security did not object to the suggestion that security was both threatened and found in places other than the military, but rather they took issue with the very first line of Tuchman's argument: that what was at stake was a redefinition of *national* security. The military focus of the traditional understanding of security was certainly a problem, but so too was its *statism*, the assumption that security was a matter of protecting the territory and interests of the (national) state. The second key position in the debate sought "to deepen the agenda of security studies by moving either down to the level of individual or human security or up to the level of international or global security, with regional and societal security as possible intermediate points" (Krause and Williams, 1996, p. 230).

The move to deepen security through considering the security of individuals, non-state collectives, regions, or even humanity as a whole, posed a significant challenge to the conventional ways of thinking about (national) security. The assumption of national security studies (and policy) is that the security of the individual is guaranteed by the security of the state, that the former can be simply subsumed by the latter, and that all "we" need to worry about is national security. Once that easy connection is refused and the security of individuals, for example, is examined directly, it quickly becomes clear that the security of the state does not necessarily provide for the security of the people living within it – not even necessarily of those who are also "citizens". Indeed, what becomes clear quickly is that the state, often through the very policies and practices designed to provide security, renders its own people insecure. More generally, what becomes apparent is that the provision of security is differential, and that while some are secured through conventional security policy, others are excluded or are actively made insecure. In other words, security is like all other realms of social structure, and is, therefore, ripe for critique.

Social critique is understood in a number of ways, but all would share the claim that it involves revealing the ways in which social organization is, in some fundamental manner, inequitable. Beyond this analytic project, however, social critique also has explicit politics: that the revelation of structures of inequality is to serve a social mobilization designed to change the fundamentals revealed in the interest of those oppressed by the system as it is presently found. With the recognition that the structure of national security was inequitable in such a fundamental fashion, the way was opened for critical social theory to engage with security policy and practice. Perhaps, unsurprisingly, what security studies found when it began to enter into that engagement was that there were others already there.

Feminism and the Critique of Violence

On 10 July 2012, Thomas Lubanga was sentenced to 14 years in prison. By itself this would seem unremarkable, but Lubanga was convicted of conscripting, enlisting, and using children as soldiers while the leader of rebel forces in the long-running war in the Democratic Republic of Congo. Lubanga was, in fact, the first person to be tried by the International Criminal Court (ICC), a court that had been created almost exactly ten years before the sentence was handed down. The prosecution in the case also argued that sexual violence should be considered an aggravating factor in sentencing, but the court ruled that they had failed to demonstrate that these crimes were directly attributable to Lubanga (ICC, 2012, p. 28). However, the Court also said that people could be charged before the court with sexual violence, and that it could be taken into account in sentencing, even without charge (ICC, 2012, p. 26). This prosecution, and the further recognition by the ICC that sexual violence is both a crime and an aggravating factor in the commission of other crimes, points to the success of some of the earliest critical engagement with security practices. Feminist scholars, even before the rethinking of security in the early 1990s, had been arguing that war was a "gendered" social practice – that it had fundamentally differential effects on men and women and on adults and children (see Chapter 3 of this volume, by Natasha Marhia).

The early 1980s was marked by a return of intense East–West competition and a global sense of insecurity, now known as the Second Cold War (Halliday, 1983). Unlike the initial Cold War, however, the 1980s was also marked by a mature feminism as both a political movement and an academic practice. State policy in the Second Cold War articulated a conventional understanding of security and how it was to be achieved. "Western" security was threatened by an aggressive Soviet Union (it had invaded Afghanistan), and such a threat was to be met by a robust military response. In particular, the nuclear deterrent, which was the foundation of post-World War II security policy in the West, needed to be bolstered. The United States announced plans to build a new range of inter-continental ballistic missiles (the MX, nicknamed with some black humor "the Peacemaker"), and put pressure on its European allies to accept basing new shorter-range American nuclear missiles on their territory. These new shorter-range missiles would include updated intermediate-range ballistic missiles (the Pershing II), a missile that greatly reduced the warning time the Soviet Union would have on launch and so would increase the pressure on nuclear hair-triggers. They would also include a newly developed category of missile, ground-launched cruise missiles. Cruise missiles are now commonplace, but in the late 1970s they were a technological marvel; a marvel, however, that could entirely eliminate the warning a target population would have of their impending destruction.

With greater and lesser enthusiasm, the Europeans agreed to host the new P-II and Cruise in a special meeting of NATO in December 1979. The greatest enthusiasm was shown by the UK's new Prime Minister, Margaret Thatcher. Thatcher agreed to stationing cruise missiles in the United Kingdom, missiles which would be based on Greenham Common. Christine Sylvester recounts what happened next:

> On August 27, 1981, thirty-six "women" and a few "men" and "children" left their homes in and around Cardiff, Wales for the 120 mile walk to Greenham Common in Berkshire, where ninety-six US nuclear cruise missiles were to be deployed. The walkers, evoking standard images of "women" as "nurturers" called themselves "Women for Life on Earth". Their message, however, was political: they wanted to bring pressure to bear on the Thatcher government for a parliamentary debate about the deployment of these missiles on British soil. They arrived at the base ten days later and, when the press and the British government effectively ignored them – perhaps because "women" are invisible in the politics of international relations – some walkers decided to remain and others joined them. In fits and starts they learned to be in-your-face in unexpected and still largely unheralded ways. (Sylvester, 1994, p. 184)

The fits and starts produced an ever-changing peace camp around the Greenham Common site that lasted, in one form or another, until 2000, even though the missiles based there were removed by 1991 as part of an arms control agreement.[2] The unexpected and largely unheralded practices of the campers included employing an anarchic, empathetic "decision-making" system that did not even aim to generate consensus; the production of human chains of up to 70,000 people; adorning the fences with the symbols of domestic life; and even collapsing large stretches of the fences that provided "security" to the base. In the process, the "women"[3] of Greenham Common subverted the very understanding of "security", which produced the missiles as its agents in the first place:

> The Camp failed in its main mission, one supposes, and succeeded in unexpected realms. It subverted the security-based strategic vision of international relations by showing that acts of everyday insecurity, borne of a collective endeavour to write insecurity differently, to homestead it with knowledges gained from leaving "secure" homes for "women", could unravel the security studies texts with incisive clarity. (Sylvester, 1994, p. 193)

The Greenham Peace Camp, however, was not an exercise in academic feminism but rather an expression of enraged activism, which can be understood through the tools that feminism provides. At the same time, the renaissance of nuclear strategy was attracting the attention of feminist scholars, most notably an American sociologist, Carol Cohn. In 1984, Cohn attended a summer school on nuclear deterrence and arms control:

> For two weeks, I listened to men engage in dispassionate discussion of nuclear war. I found myself aghast, but morbidly fascinated – not by nuclear weaponry, or by images of nuclear destruction, but by the extraordinary abstraction and removal from what I knew as reality that characterized the professional discourse. I became obsessed by the question, How can they think this way. (Cohn, 1987, p. 688)

The phrasing of Cohn's question is important. Conventional security studies, along with most conventional social science, is interested in why something happened; studies informed by critical social theory, by contrast, tend to be interested not so much in "why" questions, but rather in the (logically) prior question of how something is possible. For feminist scholars, the conditions of possibility that they want to reveal concern gender, that is the social constitution of "masculinity" and "femininity", together with the social structure that ties those constructions to particular social locations, roles, and resources. (For an extended discussion of gender analysis and its relationship to feminism, see Chapter 3 in this volume).

Cohn remained at the research center in which she took the initial summer course for a year, engaging in participant observation in an attempt to answer her question:

> Throughout my time in the world of strategic analysis, it was hard not to notice the ubiquitous weight of gender, both in social relations and in the language itself; it is an almost entirely male world (with the exception of the secretaries), and the language contains many rather arresting metaphors. (Cohn, 1987, p. 688)

In her report on this research Cohn explores a number of these metaphors, and the one that attracted much of the attention was "patting the missile". Her analysis of this seemingly innocuous, if rather strange, metaphor is indicative of the kind of results feminist security analysis can provide, and so is worth quoting at some length:

> What is all this "patting"? What are men doing when they "pat" these high-tech phalluses? Patting is an assertion of intimacy, sexual possession, affectionate domination. The thrill and pleasure of "patting the missile" is the proximity of all that phallic power, the possibility of vicariously appropriating it as one's own.

But if the predilection for patting phallic objects indicates something of the homo-erotic excitement suggested by the language, it also has another side. For patting is not only an act of sexual intimacy. It is also what one does to babies, small children, the pet dog. One pats that which is small cute, and harmless—not terrifyingly destructive. Pat it, and its lethality disappears.

Much of the sexual imagery I heard was rife with the sort of ambiguity suggested by "patting the missiles." The imagery can be construed as a deadly serious display of the connections between masculine sexuality and the arms race. At the same time, it can also be heard as a way of minimizing the seriousness of militarist endeavors, of denying their deadly consequences. A former Pentagon target analyst, in telling me why he thought plans for "limited nuclear war" were ridiculous, said, "Look, you gotta understand that it's a pissing contest – you gotta expect them to use every-thing they've got." What does this image say? Most obviously, that this is all about competition for manhood, and thus there is tremendous danger. But at the same time, the image diminishes the contest and its outcomes, by representing it as an act of boyish mischief. (Cohn, 1987, pp. 695–696)

The "weight of gender", therefore, men speaking to men in highly gendered language, provides some of the condition of possibility for which Cohn sought. They can think this way because their particularly masculine power enables a combination of mastery and denial that allows the deaths of millions to be "rationally" discussed, debated, threatened, and even planned for without the intervention of potentially debilitating guilt or horror – indeed, without emotion at all.

The intersection of masculinity and military power that Cohn identifies has been a consistent theme through the subsequent development of feminist work on security. As Sandra Whitworth notes,

Feminists have long argued … that militaries require a particular "ideology of manliness" in order to function properly. … [T]he ideology of manliness required by militaries is one premised on violence and aggression, individual conformity to military discipline, and "aggressive heterosexism and homophobia," as well as misogyny and racism. (Whitworth 2004, p. 16)

Whitworth then explores the effects of this "militarized masculinity" in the practice of United Nations Peacekeeping, where soldiers might not be characterized as much by violence, homophobia, misogyny, and racism. However, Whitworth found that the militarization of peacekeepers' masculinity contributed to outcomes that were not in keeping with the epithet "peace": "militarized peacekeeping results in greater insecurity for far too many people, women and men, who through the exclusionary practices of militarism and armed intervention become targets of sexual abuse and racist violence" (Whitworth, 2004, p. 186). Whitworth's conclusions were powerfully supported by Sherene Razack in *Dark Threats & White Knights* published at the same time as Whitworth's book. Razack was interested in the conditions of possibility for the horrifying "Somalia Affair", in which Canadian soldiers stationed to Somlia as part of a peacekeeping mission tortured a Somali teenager, Shidane Arone, to death. What she argues is that the comfortable official account of "a few bad apples" hides the systemic conditions that enabled the individuals in question, and that those structural conditions are the same that Whitworth identifies: an ideology of (militarized) masculinity and racism (Razack, 2004, pp. 151–152).

While much feminist work on security began with an exploration of the place of men and women (and masculinity and femininity) in the military (see Enloe, 1983, 2000), the notion of "militarized masculinity" led to a much more widespread and richer gendered critique of security and security policy. While the military required a virulent "ideology of manliness", this militarized masculinity was not restricted to the military, but was rather intimately linked to the hegemonic masculinity in broader society. So, for example, when feminist analysis turned to the place that rape and other forms of sexual violence play in militaries in general and war in particular, it became clear that this could not be disconnected from sexual violence in the broader society. Both of these findings undermined the conventional conception of security. The military was supposed to be that institution that *provided* security, but instances such as Tailhook in the United States[4] and the sexual violence associated with peacekeepers around the world, revealed its militarized masculinity to threaten the security, even of some of its own members (Whitworth, 2004). Sexual violence in war revealed that the monadic "nation" that was supposed to be the referent object of security was, in fact, differentiated on gender (and other) lines. Women were targeted as women of "the enemy" by sexual violence, but importantly they were targeted *as women*. But more broadly the very notion of security being the preserve of states was undone by the recognition of widespread sexual violence in our purportedly secure societies, and the intimate connection between that violence and the hegemonic/militarized masculinities that produced it.

United Nations Security Council Resolution 1325

On October 31, 2000, the United Nations Security Council unanimously adopted Resolution 1325, which sought to promote a gender perspective in responding to conflict, particularly in UN peace and reconstruction operations (for further discussion of UN Security Council Resolution (UNSCR) 1325 and the UN's Women, Peace and Security Agenda, see Chapter 3 within this volume). The resolution was introduced by the Minister of Women's Affairs in Namibia while her country was the President of Council. Its adoption can be seen as a consequence of the significant work that feminist scholars on security had produced in the preceding 20 years because the Preamble 1325 articulates a key finding of this scholarship:

> *Expressing* concern that civilians, particularly women and children, account for the vast majority of those adversely affected by armed conflict, including as refugees and internally displaced persons, and increasingly are targeted by combatants and armed elements, and recognizing the consequent impact this has on durable peace and reconciliation. (United Nations Security Council, 2000)

In terms of the substantive articles of the Resolution, most concern the practices of the United Nations or the place of women in post-conflict reconciliation and reconstruction efforts. However, Paragraphs 10 and 11 reflect feminist findings on the nature of violence and the conduct of armed conflict:

> 10. *Calls* on all parties to armed conflict to take special measures to protect women and girls from gender-based violence, particularly rape and other forms of sexual abuse, and all other forms of violence in situations of armed conflict;

11. *Emphasizes* the responsibility of all States to put an end to impunity and to prosecute those responsible for genocide, crimes against humanity, and war crimes including those relating to sexual and other violence against women and girls, and in this
regard *stresses* the need to exclude these crimes, where feasible from amnesty provisions. (United Nations Security Council, 1325)

Article 10 marks international recognition at the highest level of the gendered nature
of armed conflict, which feminist approaches to security had demonstrated throughout the 1980s and 1990s. Furthermore, Article 11 puts the weight of the Security
Council behind the prosecution of gender-based violence in international law – leading, among other things, to the conviction of Thomas Lubanga in 2012.

After Frankfurt: Security as Emancipation

Ten months or so before Thomas Lubanga was convicted, a group of Americans
gathered in a small park near the famed financial district in New York City. They
gathered to protest against the management of an American and global economy that
over the previous 30 years had seen more and more wealth concentrated in the hands
of fewer and fewer people.[5] They termed the protest "Occupy Wall Street", and
attempted in the first instance to occupy the small park in which they had gathered,
Zuccotti Park. They were able to remain in the park, with more than a hundred
people sleeping in the park each night, from the beginning of the protest on September
17, 2011 until November 15, 2011 when the security services, in particular the New
York Police, evicted them. By the time the protesters were removed, Occupy Wall
Street had sparked a global protest against the excesses of contemporary capitalism
under the slogan "We are the 99%". The Occupy Movement, as it has come to be
called, boasts movements in more than 1500 cities around the world.[6]

Conventionally, security studies would be blind to the Occupy protests. Political
protest against banks, even in the world's leading financial center, would not be considered a question of "security". As the broadening and deepening I discussed earlier
developed, however, some students of security began to think in ways that would
lead the protests in Zuccotti Park at least to register. The Occupy protests could be
seen as a threat to the financial stability of the United States, which, given its place
in the global financial system, might even be a threat to the global economic system
as a whole. It might not be a military threat, but it is certainly a threat of some kind
to the "security" of the state, understood a little more broadly than the conventional
understanding allowed. Seen in this way, the response by the state of using one of its
security arms seems quite understandable.

However, seen from the side of the protesters, security of a rather different sort can
come into view. The protest against the global economic system, and its inequitable
outcomes, put the Occupy Movement fully on the terrain of critical theory. Much
social critique has its origin, or at least one of its major influences, in the work of Karl
Marx and his later followers and interpreters. Indeed, Critical Theory, with the words
in capitals, generally refers to an important strand of this post-Marxist work. For
Marx and his descendants, of course, social critique is fundamentally about revealing
the workings of the modes of production and distribution of social wealth, showing how the system necessarily produces unequal outcomes, and indeed oppresses

(most of) those living and working within it. Furthermore, critique of this kind cannot simply stop with these revelations, as powerful as they may be, but must continue to work for the transformation of the system in the name of those oppressed. It must work, in other words, for emancipation.

In 1990, as the West was trying to come to terms with the passing of the Cold War, John Mearsheimer, a leading British security scholar, addressed the problem of security in the keynote address to a conference of International Relations. In the published version of that address, Ken Booth set out what was to become the touchstone of a second influential approach to rethinking the study and practice of security. He wrote:

> "security" means the absence of threats. Emancipation is the freeing of people (as individuals and groups) from those physical and human constraints which stop them carrying out what they would freely choose to do. War and the threat of war is one of those constraints, together with poverty, poor education, political oppression and so on. Security and emancipation are two sides of the same coin. Emancipation, not power or order, produces true security. *Emancipation, theoretically, is security.* (Booth, 1991, p. 319, emphasis added.)

While Booth's initial formulation of emancipation could be criticized as too liberal a representation of a fundamentally Marxist concept, the equation of security and emancipation proved very powerful. In order to develop what was initially, after all, an after dinner speech into a considered approach to the study and practice of security, Booth turned to the leading thinkers about emancipation. In particular, he turned to those who came from the Frankfurt School of social critique, the School that had given rise to the term "Critical Theory".[7]

Booth, together with a number of collaborators mainly from Aberystwyth University, set about to build what he calls a "critical theory of security". Booth is quite clear that what he means by this is a general singular theory of security, in the tradition of the Frankfurt School. Security's engagement with social critique, which animates this chapter, can lead, and has led, in a wide range of rich theoretical directions because social critique comprises a wide range of theoretical positions (beyond even the three broad theoretical domains of this chapter). Booth is not interested in that theoretical pluralism, but rather in building what he terms, in its most complete expression, a *Theory of World Security*, which seeks to "explain and advance a case for a particular theoretical framework with which to explore and engage with the security of real people in real places" (Booth, 2007, p. xii). This theory is not simply derivative of the Frankfurt School's Critical Theory, but rather takes that understanding of Critical Theory as its starting point to construct uniquely critical theory *of* security.

Booth's critical security theory derives four key themes from Critical Theory of a largely Frankfurt School variety:

- The first is that knowledge is produced through social and political processes, and so there are "interests of knowledge". In saying this, Booth echoes perhaps the most famous post-Marxist intervention into the study of world politics – Robert Cox's recognition that "theory is always *for* someone and *for* some purpose" (Cox, 1981, p. 128).

- The second theme follows from this first – that traditional theory (Horkeimer's term) does not recognize its social and political origins, and so is naturalist (taking the social world as "natural") and reductionist (open to mechanical explanation).
- The third theme characterizes Critical Theory in opposition to this traditional theory, suggesting critical theory provides the basis for political and social progress. Put another way, critical theory involves praxis.[8]
- Finally, returning to his own original point about security, Booth draws from the tradition of Critical Theory that the test of theory is emancipation (Booth, 2005, p. 268).

From these foundations, Booth seeks to build his critical theory of security. What distinguishes this approach from others discussed in this chapter, and more broadly all those which engage with critical social theory, is this final commitment to "emancipation" (Peoples and Vaughan-Williams, 2010, pp. 23–24). It is not that other approaches do not seek to engage in a practice of security aimed at overcoming structures of domination (as the feminist approach does in relation to gender), but rather that the Welsh School retains a commitment to an understanding of emancipation drawn from an explicitly post-Marxist tradition (despite Booth's commitment to theoretical eclecticism), which anchors all forms of domination in the capitalist system, in the last instance.

Zuccotti Park as Security "Policy"

If we look, therefore, through the lens of this form of Critical Theory of Security at the Occupy Movement, a rather different notion of security comes into view than that of the Occupiers as threats to global stability. If security, theoretically, is emancipation, and if emancipation, in turn, involves freeing people from the oppression of the structures in which they find themselves, in the final instance the economic system, then the Occupy Movement is a significant instance of security praxis. It is a practice aimed at the fundamental reform, if not replacement, of the global economic system, and as such does pose a threat to the stability of the global political economy in general, and the US political economy in particular. The point is that such a threat can be seen as a move toward security, rather than insecurity.

It is only by considering the Occupy Movement through the statist assumptions of the conventional understanding of security that the possibility of destabilizing the national, or even global, political economy is necessarily read as a threat to security. Recognizing the importance of the particular security theory is a consequence of accepting the first two of Booth's themes: the social production of knowledge and tendency to naturalism. Once it is recognized that even something so seemingly basic as 'security" or "the state" is a social product and not natural, it is possible to see security in places other than the defense of the state. Booth and those that follow him are committed to the security of "individuals and groups", or as Columba Peoples and Nick Vaughan-Williams have put it, "security should ultimately be concerned with real world security of human beings" (Peoples and Vaughan-Williams, 2010, p. 24). The central claim of the Occupy Movement is that the system of global capitalism that has been created, at least in its present form, since the early 1980s poses a threat to the security of the 99%.

There seems a natural fit, therefore, between the politics of the Welsh School of security studies and the Occupy Movement. In one of the earliest elaborations of this approach to security, Richard Wyn Jones stressed the importance of "praxis", that is of political engagement that proceeds from the academic practice of critique:

> [P]roponents of critical security studies should aim to provide support for those social movements that promote emancipatory social change. By providing a critique of the prevailing social order and legitimating alternative views, critical theorists can perform a valuable role in supporting the struggles of social movements. (Wyn Jones, 1999, p. 161)

The Occupy Movement would seem to represent just such a social movement, international in scope, which is promoting emancipatory change through the struggle against the very pinnacle of global capital.

The Radical Promise of Poststructuralism

Looking a little further back in time, almost exactly a decade before Wall Street was Occupied, it had served as the backdrop to a dramatic transformation of the global security terrain. On September 20, 2001, US President George W. Bush addressed a joint session of the US Congress with these, now famous, words: "Our war on terror begins with al Qaeda, but it does not end there. It will not end until every terrorist group of global reach has been found, stopped and defeated" (Bush, 2001b). While the speech launching the "War on Terror" was delivered in the Capital in Washington, its subject was the events a few days earlier in New York's financial district when hijacked commercial airliners had destroyed the World Trade Centre. Indeed, it has become commonplace to say that "the world changed" on September 11, 2001, but I am saying something slightly different. Following from the final approach to security to be examined in this chapter, I suggest that that the moment of transformation was not the sunny morning in Manhattan but the evening in Washington when the President of the United States declared war.

As with feminism, to suggest that "poststructuralism" is singular is to perform a violence on the multiplicity that the term comprises. The authors, whose work would generally be considered to take a poststructural approach to questions of security, draw eclectically on a range of continental social theory.[9] Nevertheless, the work in and on security that is generally identified as poststructural does share a number of important characteristics. Of these characteristics, none is perhaps more commonly accepted by the scholars in question, nor as misunderstood by those outside, than the commitment to "discourse". This central claim, from which much of the rest of the work follows, is captured most succinctly by Jacques Derrida's felicitous phrase: "*Il rein d'hors texte*", best translated into English as: "there is nothing outside discourse". In other words, while there is clearly a world "out there", our only access to it is mediated through the concepts, words, ideas, and practices that give it meaning. This collection of, predominantly though not exclusively, linguistic tools can be thought of collectively as "discourse".[10]

Following from this insight, poststructural approaches to security explore the discursive production of 'security", and ask questions about how they came to be as we find them, and what the consequences are of their particular production. For example, David Campbell begins his noted text, *Writing Security*, with the observation that Iraq became a danger to the United States on August 2, 1990 when it invaded Kuwait. However, he continues, that while this might seem to be stating the obvious, it is not:

> After all, an event of this kind (particularly one so distant from America) does not in and of itself constitute a danger, risk, or threat. ... Indeed, there have been any number of examples in which similar "facts" were met with a very different American reaction: only a decade earlier, the Iraqi invasion of Iran (an oil producing state like Kuwait) brought no apocalyptic denunciations or calls to action, let alone a military response, from the United States. (Campbell, 1998, p. 1)

So while Iraqi tanks did indeed enter Kuwait and attempt to engineer its annexation (or, if you take the Iraqi perspective, reattach stolen land to Iraq), it is not these "facts" that rendered Iraq dangerous to the United States. Rather, it was a particular (discursive) production of these facts in and around the United States that made Iraq dangerous, that created Iraqi actions as a matter of "security" for the United States.[11]

A similar logic obtains in the case of "9/11". "Terror group[s] of global reach" became a danger – indeed became the primary danger – to the United States in September 2001 partly, though not necessarily, as a result of the attacks on the World Trade Center and Pentagon. Even this kind of event, while in no way distant from the United States, is not in and of itself a "danger, risk, or threat", and certainly not a danger of a particular kind. The efforts of a group closely connected to the 9/11 attacks had tried to bring down the World Trade Center in 1993, and yet this "fact" did not produce a Global War on Terror. Rather, the 1993 attack was treated as a crime and so, by 1997, six people had been captured, tried, and convicted (Parachini, 2000). The events of September 11, therefore, were not acts of war and did not mean that the United States was at war. Indeed, in his address to the nation on the day of the attacks, President Bush said: "These *acts of mass murder* were intended to frighten our nation into chaos and retreat. But they have failed; our country is strong" (Bush, 2001a, emphasis added). Murder, even mass murder, is not an event of war, but rather a criminal act. Indeed, one of the points about "war" is that it legitimizes killing, removing it from the criminal category of "murder". In this initial address, Bush went further in framing the events of the day as a matter of law rather than of war: "The search is underway for those who are behind these evil acts. I've directed the full resources of our intelligence and law enforcement communities to find those responsible and to bring them to justice" (Bush, 2001a). The defining feature of our present global security order, the War on Terror, comes about from the interpretation of the events of 9/11 as an act of war rather than an act of mass murder. While that interpretation developed between September 11 and the President's speech on September 20, it was in the speech that the discourse of "War on Terror" was established as the dominant frame for the response to attacks.

The War on Terror discourse did more than produce the attacks as "acts of war" and the appropriate American response as "war". The articulation of a security problem, particularly in the case of a security problem as significant as "war", entails the identification of an enemy. Acts of war are carried out by groups of people, and so the identification of a war necessarily involves the identification of a group of people against whom you are going to war. In launching the War on Terror, the US President identified just such an enemy, but did so in a way that should appear rather surprising:

> I also want to speak tonight directly to Muslims throughout the world. We respect your faith. It's practiced freely by many millions of Americans, and by millions more in countries that America counts as friends. Its teachings are good and peaceful, and those who commit evil in the name of Allah blaspheme the name of Allah. The terrorists are traitors to their own faith, trying, in effect, to hijack Islam itself. The enemy of America is not our many Muslim friends; it is not our many Arab friends. Our enemy is a radical network of terrorists, and every government that supports them. (Bush, 2001b)

In identifying a series of small terrorist groups with "global reach" as the new enemy of the United States, the President felt it necessary to say that Muslims were not that enemy; that the War on Terror was not a war on Islam. The actual production of an enemy, however, involves more than simply a speech, even a Presidential speech; it is rather the product of the full range of utterances and practices that compose a "discourse". The War on Terror discourse, understood in this way, has tended to produce Muslims as the enemy, as the "other", in much the same way the war discourse of World War II tended to produce Japanese and Germans as enemies of the Allies, even if they were loyal, multigenerational citizens of those very Allied countries.

Every "security" discourse produces, among other things, an "other" who threatens. At the same time, indeed in the very act of doing so, it produces the self who is threatened. Security discourse is inescapably a discourse of identity. This insight drove much of the poststructural literature on security in the 1990s. Campbell's book *Writing Security*, to which I referred earlier, was published in 1992 with the subtitle: *United States Foreign Policy and the Politics of Identity*. Published in the same year, RBJ Walker's seminal text *Inside/Outside: International Relations as Political Theory* provided a broad context within which to fit the understanding of security as an identity discourse. Walker's work showed how the very foundation of international politics, the sovereign state, was a discursive product that, most importantly, marked an "inside" (self) from an "outside" (other).

> Simply put, then, the principle of state sovereignty expresses an historically specific articulation of the relationship between universality and particularity in space and time. As such, it both affirms a specific resolution of philosophical and political options that must be acknowledged everywhere and sets clear limits to our capacity to envisage any other possibility. ... As a practice of states, it is easily mistaken for their essence. (Walker, 1992, p. 176)

The tradition of security studies, of course, made precisely this mistake, reifying sovereignty and reducing security to its expression. The (sovereign) state provided security to those within its borders (citizens) against threats that were external in origin, other (sovereign) states. Once sovereignty is recognized as a practice, or more precisely a collection of interconnected and overlapping practices, it is no longer possible to see 'security" as a necessary effect of sovereignty, but rather sovereignty, and other identities, come into focus as contingent effects of security practices.

Much of the early poststructural scholarship on security, therefore, pursued these observations to explore the forms of identity produced by security discourses as "threatened", "threatening", and particularly those that were simply ignored. Some scholars explored the dominant discourses of security. Campbell's *Writing Security* was particularly significant, as was Simon Dalby's *Creating the Second Cold War: The Discourse of Politics* (1990) and Bradley Klein's *Strategic Studies and World Order: The Global Politics of Deterrence* (1994). These three books took on the central features of the conventional security studies agenda: the foreign and security policy of the United States, the US–Soviet Cold War, the nuclear confrontation, and the strategic studies that represented the scholarly response to the others. The works revealed not only the way in which all these features were produced, but also the ways in which they rendered some (notably in the "West") secure by rendering others (mainly in the global "South") insecure. Others turned their attention further afield from the traditional security terrain to inquire into the production of "security" and the identities of the secure and insecure at sites most commonly ignored by the tradition. Some of these were feminist scholars, who were also poststructural in their theoretical commitments – for example, Christine Sylvester's "Feminist Home-steadings" of security in her 1994 *Feminist Theory and International Relations in a Postmodern Era*. Others turned to questions of environmental security, for example, or the way in which narcotics have been treated through a "security" discourse (Dalby, 2002; Grayson, 2008).

With the declaration of the "War on Terror", much of the attention of poststructural security scholars turned to the nature and consequences of this new global security discourse. Poststructural, and the other critical approaches to security discussed in this chapter, emerged in the post-Cold War era when the certainties of security had been removed but not replaced. The most common refrain of the period was the lack of a defined era to follow the "Cold War". The "War on Terror" seemed (and still seems) a likely new era in security terms. Much of the work focused on the interplay of security and liberty that was difficult to avoid in an environment in which "security" became both pervasive and visible,[12] whether it was the reorganization of government around "homeland security", the proliferation of video surveillance, attempts to recreate cultures of informing on neighbors, the transformation of air travel, or the pervasive "racial profiling" that produced those who looked vaguely "Muslim" as potential enemy others (Bell, 2006; Bell, 2011; Dauphinee and Masters, 2007; Dillon and Lobo-Guerrero, 2008; Lyon, 2007; Muller, 2008; Salter, 2004, 2008).

The Biometric Border

One of the most visible sites of the new security practice was the international border. Now that security threats were refigured as individuals rather than (sovereign) states, the border took on an added significance. Borders had always been important to security, for they are, in Walker's terms, the point at which inside and outside meet, and so crossing the border is the moment at which the insecure becomes secure. The personalization of security, however, has meant that the way in which people are treated at the border has become significantly different under the "War on Terror", and that has drawn considerable attention from the community of poststructural security scholars. Many of these, in turn, have drawn on the later work of the French thinker Michel Foucault, and in particular his twin notions of biopolitics and governmentality to explore the functioning of the new border.

In his later work, Michel Foucault turned his attention to broad questions of government and politics, and although the work was left unfinished, it did introduce a number of important ideas to the contemporary study of government. Foucault argued that in the nineteenth century, the European state developed a new mode of power, organizing its citizenry into "populations" on the basis of the newly emerging techniques for the acquisition and analysis of statistical data. Where the traditional, modern state exercised power through its sovereign ability to kill or send to be killed, the statistical understanding of populations allowed the state to foster healthy (and importantly) productive people – to make live rather than kill. Furthermore, he argued that in a state that founds its legitimacy on this biopolitical "making live", it is increasingly difficult to order society through fiat and fear. Rather, the state engages in reshaping the subjectivity of the citizen to recruit them into governing themselves, developing within them a "government-mentality" or governmentality (Foucault, 1990, 2003, 2007, 2008).

Armed with these, and a number of other related ideas, a number of poststructural thinkers turned their attention to the reshaping of borders in the post-9/11 world. In the drive to make the border "secure" while impeding flow as little as possible, the United States led the way in creating what can be termed the "biometric border" (Amoore, 2006). Biometrics enables the rapid, technologically mediated identification of individuals, and if this is in turn married to a detailed database of information provided by travelers in advance of their journeys, the traveler can pass quickly across the border while the state can know who it is allowing in. While such convenience might seem initially appealing to the traveler, the system only works by giving up significant personal information to the state: retinal and fingerprint patterns, as well as far more extensive and intrusive information than has ever previously been collected for the purposes of issuing a passport. Poststructural security scholars have asked how this became possible, and with what effects?

Mark Salter and Geneviève Piché, for example, have shown how the Canada–US border was transformed from a site regulating economic activity to a site of security in the aftermath of the 9/11 attacks. As they put it, the world's longest undefended border "has fundamentally changed from undefended border to a smart border – and from a focus on facilitation to one of defense in depth" (Salter and Piché, 2011, p. 929). This transformation, with the "smart" border instantiated in biometric technology, has important consequences that Salter and others have been exploring. Louise Amoore introduced the term "biometric border" to think about this technology and, in an analysis of the US VISIT programme, considered the effects of smarter borders in terms of biopolitics and governmentality:

> [T]he governing of mobility through US VISIT's biometric borders is categorically not about new border threats in a post-9/11 world, but rather a means of identifying and designating the safe from the dangerous at multiple borders of daily life. US VISIT, then, is but one element of a liberal mode of governmentality that sees risk profiling in the war on terror pervade and claim every aspect of species life itself, or something akin to a shift from geopolitics to biopolitics. (Amoore, 2006, p. 338)

By investigating the particular "security" practices of the border, Amoore and others have revealed the way in which the biometric border is part of a much more extensive set of security practices, reshaping the very possibilities of political subjectivity in the contemporary West. What is more, the work also shows that while these practices are both intrusive and increasingly extensive, they are not necessarily effective, at least in the stated goal of increasing "security".

> The irony here, of course, is that not only do such schemes fail to guarantee that a citizen will be regarded as safe by the state; they also ignore the fact that citizens might well be compromising their safety by enabling the state to transform them into a digital identity. (Muller, 2010, p. 85).

Conclusion

On December 14, 2012, the United States experienced another in a depressingly long series of school shootings. At Sandy Hook Elementary School in Newtown, Connecticut, a gunman killed 26 students and teachers, most of them between six and seven years old. Among the many reactions worldwide to this horror was the announcement by the Premier of the Canadian province of Ontario that an additional $10 million would be provided to schools to ensure all primary schools had video surveillance cameras, and also that schools would institute a "locked door" policy by September 2013. While Premier McGuinty argued that this was a "reasonable" response to the shooting in Connecticut, not everyone agreed. A leading Canadian columnist put it like this: "To instate a locked-door policy at 4,000 schools in reaction to a threat in a different country with much different gun laws is to surrender to fear. It is the job of governments to weigh risks, not safeguard us against every eventuality" (Gee, 2012).

McGuinty's reaction – to an event in another country with both different laws and a different culture around gun violence – is a clear indication of the pervasive logic of post-9/11 security to which Amoore, Muller, and others have directed our attention, in which the state takes upon itself to safeguard against "every eventuality". Locking doors and installing surveillance video in response to a horrifying but extremely unlikely event echoes precisely the hardening of borders and the resort to intrusive surveillance in response to the horrifying but extremely unlikely terrorist attacks of 2001. Indeed, it raises the question of whether "security" itself is fatally flawed, that just as "smart" borders do not necessarily make safer citizens, is it possible that security can any longer secure, if it ever could? Mark Neocleous has recently taken up this question, drawing on a number of the forms of critical social theory discussed in this chapter, to argue persuasively that the answer is yes.

Neocleous has provided what he terms a *Critique of Security*. Developed particularly out of the post-Marxist tradition of critical social theory, though with support from Foucault's arguments as well, Neocleous's critique echoes that of some post-structural thinkers in showing how security is a technology of government that is involved in reshaping our political subjectivity. Ultimately, however, he argues that contemporary security policy is simply a more transparent version of the same security logic that has shaped our politics throughout the twentieth century, to increasingly devastating consequences. Rather than seeking to enhance our security or to make "better" security policy, therefore, Neocleous ultimately concludes that we should "return the gift" of security entirely (Neocleous, 2008, pp. 185–186).

I began this chapter by citing John Mearsheimer's claim that we might miss the Cold War, that we might miss what his mentor, Kenneth Waltz, termed "its stark simplicities and comforting symmetry" (Waltz, 1993, p. 44). The end of those simplicities opened up a space in which various forms of critical social theory could be brought to bear on the apparent complexities of security, and more importantly in which the scholarship that resulted could be taken seriously. The result is the growth of a rich collection of literatures engaging questions of security from feminist perspectives, that of Critical Theory, and varied poststructural perspectives, among others. For all their differences, they share a commitment to troubling "simplicities" and "comforts",in the name of those who are marginalized, rendered insecure, and oppressed by security policy. The work I have surveyed, therefore, does not seek a better security policy, though it may help contribute to it; rather it seeks freer people engaged in more productive politics, even if that means forgoing the comfort of "security" altogether.

Notes

1. The most startling example of this assertion is found in Kenneth Waltz 1993 article, "The Emerging Structure of International Politics", in which he argues that the events of 1989 did not fundamentally alter the bipolarity that is characteristic of the Cold War world: "How does the weakened condition of Russia affect the structure of inter-national politics? The answer is that bipolarity endures, but in an altered state" (Waltz, 1993, p. 52).
2. The agreement was the Intermediate Range Nuclear Forces (INF) agreement (1987), which is credited as the first nuclear arms control agreement to eliminate an entire class of weapons.
3. The Greenham Common Peace Camp was largely produced by women, but not exclusively. In addition, Sylvester uses scare-quotes around "women" in her discussions of the camp to draw attention to the socially produced nature of gender, as she put it: the "politicization of slightly different anatomies in ways that support grand divisions of labor, traits, places, and power" (Sylvester, 1994, p. 4).
4. "Tailhook" refers to an incident in 1991 when a large number of US Navy and Marine personnel were accused of, and many disciplined for, sexual assault and other inappropriate behaviors at a symposium hosted by the Tailhook Association (McMichael, 1997).
5. The Organisation for Economic Cooperation and Development (OECD) reported in 2011 that income inequality grew in 17 of its members between the mid-1980s and the late 2000s, remained largely static in three, and was reduced in this period in only two of its members: Turkey and Greece (OECD, 2011, p. 6).
6. The figure is from the occupywallst.org/about (accessed December 17, 2012), which is one of the central web hubs of the Occupy Movement.
7. The term "critical theory" is generally credited to one of the original members of the Frankfurt School, Max Horkheimer, from his 1937 essay, "Traditional and Critical Theory". The essay can be found reprinted in Horkheimer (1975).
8. On the centrality of praxis to Critical Theory in the context of the study of security, see Wyn Jones (1999, pp. 145–163).

9. The term "continental" betrays the Eurocentrism and more particularly Anglocentrism of the discourse on philosophy. "Continental" philosophy generally refers to twentieth century social theory from either Germany or France, with the former broadly considered "post-Marxist" and the latter "poststructural".

10. There is a growing movement among security scholars to think about security through the so-called new materialism, which takes the material seriously as discourse, rather than simply as seen through (linguistic) discourse. See, for example, the 2012 Millennium Conference, "Materialism and World Politics" that featured a number of security-related panels engaging with the new materialism. (http://millenniumjournal.org/annual-conference/, accessed December 19, 2012).

11. While Campbell discusses the production of Iraq as a danger in *Writing Security*, the focus of this book is elsewhere. He returned to the question of Iraq, however, in his subsequent book: *Politics without Principle* (Campbell, 1993).

12. One of the most notable was the CHALLENGE Project (The Changing Landscape of European Liberty and Security) funded by the European Union and headed by RBJ Walker and Didier Bigo (See Bigo, Carrera, Guild, and Walker, 2010).

References

Amoore, Louise. 2006. "Biometric borders: Governing mobilities in the war on terror." *Political Geography*, 25(3): 336–351.

Bell, Colleen. 2006. "Surveillance Strategies and Populations at Risk: Biopolitical Governance in Canada's National Security Policy." *Security Dialogue*, 37(2): 147–165.

Bell, Colleen. 2011. *The Freedom of Security: Governing Canada in the Age of Counter-Terrorism*. Vancouver, BC: UBC Press.

Bigo, Didier, Sergio Carrera, Elspeth Guild, and RBJ Walker, eds. 2010. *Europe's 21st Century Challenge: Delivering Liberty*. London: Ashgate.

Booth, Ken. 1991. "Security and Emancipation." *Review of International Studies*, 17(4): 313–326.

Booth, Ken. 2005. *Critical Security Studies and World Politics*. Boulder, CO: Lynne Rienner.

Booth, Ken. 2007. *Theory of World Security*. Cambridge: Cambridge University Press.

Bush, George W. 2001a. "Statement by the President in His Address to the Nation." Accessed December 19, 2012 from http://georgewbush-whitehouse.archives.gov/news/releases/2001/09/20010911-16.html

Bush, George W. 2001b. "Address to a Joint Session of Congress and the American People." Washington, DC. Accessed December 18, 2012 from http://georgewbush-whitehouse.archives.gov/news/releases/2001/09/20010920-8.html

Campbell, David. 1993. *Politics without Principle: Sovereignty, Ethics, and the Narratives of the Gulf War*. Boulder, CO: Lynne Rienner.

Campbell, David. 1998 [1992]. *Writing Security: United States Foreign Policy and the Politics of Identity*. Revised Edition. Minneapolis, MN: University of Minnesota Press.

Cohn, Carol. 1987. "Sex and Death in the Rational World of Defence Intellectuals." *Signs*, 12(4): 687–718.

Cox, Robert. 1981. "Social Forces, States, and World Orders: Beyond International Relations Theory." *Millennium: Journal of International Studies*, 10(2): 126–155.

Dalby, Simon. 1990. *Creating the Second Cold War: The Discourse of Politics*. New York, NY: Guilford Press.

Dalby, Simon. 2002. *Environmental Security*. Minneapolis, MN: University of Minnesota Press.

Dauphinee, Elizabeth, and Cristina Masters. 2007. *The Logics of Biopower and the War on Terror: Living, Dying, Surviving*. New York, NY: Palgrave Macmillan.

Dillon, Michael, and Luis Lobo-Guerrero. 2008. "Biopolitics of Security in the 21st Century: An Introduction." *Review of International Studies*, 34(2): 265.

Enloe, Cynthia. 1983. *Does Khaki Become You? The Militarization of Women's Lives*. Boston, MA: South End Press.

Enloe, Cynthia. 2000. *Maneuvers: The International Politics of Militarizing Women's Lives*. Berkeley, CA: University of California Press.

Foucault, Michel. 1990. *The History of Sexuality: An Introduction*. New York, NY: Vintage Books.

Foucault, Michel. 2003. *Society Must be Defended: Lectures at the College de France 1975–1976*. London: Penguin/Allen Lane.

Foucault, Michel. 2007. *Security, Territory, Population: Lectures at the College de France 1977–1978*. London: Palgrave Macmillan.

Foucault, Michel. 2008. *The Birth of Biopolitics: Lectures at the College de France 1978–1979*. London: Palgrave Macmillan.

Gee, Marcus. 2012. "McGuinty's locked-door policy acquiesces to unfounded fears." *Globe and Mail*, December 26. Accessed January 2, 2013 from http://www.theglobeandmail.com/news/national/mcguintys-locked-door-policy-acquiesces-to-unfounded-fears/article6734304/

George, Jim. 1994. *Discourses on Global Politics: A Critical (Re)Introduction to International Relations*. Boulder, CO: Lynne Rienner.

Grayson, Kyle. 2008. *Chasing Dragons: Security, Identity, and Illicit Drugs in Canada*. Toronto, ON: University of Toronto Press.

Halliday, Fred. 1983. *The Making of the Second Cold War*. London: Verso.

Horkheimer, Max. 1975. *Critical Theory: Selected Essays*. New York, NY: Continuum International

International Criminal Court. 2012. "Situation in the Democratic Republic of The Congo in the Case of The Prosecutor v. Thomas Lubanga Dyilo: Decision on Sentence pursuant to Article 76 of the Statute." (ICC-01/04-01/06) July 10. Accessed July 19, 2012 from http://www.icc-cpi.int/iccdocs/doc/doc1438370.pdf

Klein, Bradley. 1994. *Strategic Studies and World Order: The Global Politics of Deterrence*. Cambridge: Cambridge University Press.

Krause, Keith, and Michael C. Williams. 1996. "Broadening the Agenda of Security Studies: Politics and Methods." *Mershon International Studies Review*, 40(2): 229–254.

Lyon, David. 2007. "Surveillance, Security and Social Sorting." *International Criminal Justice Review*, 17(3): 161–170.

Mathews, Jessica Tuchman. 1989. "Redefining Security." *Foreign Affairs*, 68(2): 162–177.

McMichael, William H. 1997. *The Mother of all Hooks: The Story of the US Navy's Tailhook Scandal*. Piscataway, NJ: Transaction Publishers.

Mearsheimer, John. 1990. "Why We Will Soon Miss The Cold War." *The Atlantic Monthly*, 266(2): 35–50.

Muller, Benjamin. 2008. "Securing the Political Imagination: Popular Culture, the Security Dispositif and the Biometric State." *Security Dialogue*, 39(2–3): 199–220.

Muller, Benjamin J. 2010. "Unsafe at any speed? Borders, mobility and 'safe citizenship'." *Citizenship Studies*, 14(1): 75–88.

Neocleous, Mark. 2008. *Critique of Security*. Montreal, QC: McGill-Queen's University Press.

Organisation for Economic Cooperation and Development (OECD). 2011. "Growing Income Inequality In OECD Countries: What Drives It And How Can Policy Tackle It?" OECD Forum on Tackling Inequality, Paris, May 2, 2011. Accessed from http://www.oecd.org/social/socialpoliciesanddata/47723414.pdf

Parachini, John V. 2000. "The World Trade Center Bombers (1993)." In *Toxic Terror: Assessing Terrorist Use of Chemical and Biological Weapons*, edited by Jonathan B. Tucker, 185–206. Cambridge, MA: MIT Press.

Peoples, Columba, and Nick Vaughan-Williams. 2010. *Critical Security Studies: An Introduction*. London: Routledge.

Razack, Sherene. 2004. *Dark Threats & White Knights: The Somalia Affair, Peacekeeping, and the New Imperialism*. Toronto, ON: University of Toronto Press.

Salter, Mark. 2004. "Passports, Mobility, and Security: How Smart can the Border be?" *International Studies Perspectives*, 5(1): 71–91.

Salter, Mark. 2008. *Politics at the Airport*. Minneapolis, MN: University of Minnesota Press.

Salter, Mark, and Geneviève Piché. 2011. "The Securitization of the US–Canada Border in American Political Discourse." *Canadian Journal of Political Science / Revue canadienne de science politique*, 44(4): 929–951.

Sylvester, Christine. 1994. *Feminist Theory and International Relations in a Postmodern Era*. Cambridge: Cambridge University Press.

United Nations Security Council. 2000. UN Security Council Resolution 1325 on Women, Peace and Security (S/RES/1325(2000). Adopted by the Security Council at its 4213th Meeting on October 31, 2000.

Walker, RBJ. 1992. *Inside/Outside: International Relations as Political Theory*. Cambridge: Cambridge University Press.

Waltz, Kenneth. 1993. "The Emerging Structure of International Politics." *International Security*, 18(2): 44–79.

Whitworth, Sandra. 2004. *Men, Militarism, and UN Peacekeeping: a gendered analysis*. Boulder, CO: Lynne Reinner.

Wyn Jones, Richard. 1999. *Security, Strategy, and Critical Theory*. Boulder, CO: Lynne Reinner.

Chapter 3

Gender and Security

Natasha Marhia

A useful way to understand "gender" is as a lens or perspective that casts a different light on social phenomena. In this view, gender is not limited to socially constructed sex, but encapsulates the way in which social life is implicitly and explicitly patterned by meanings, knowledges, and power relations inflected by constructions of masculinities and femininities, sex/gender, and categories such as "men" and "women". Such an understanding of gender has political implications: for many scholars of Gender Studies, the project of studying and researching gender is informed by the conviction that gender relations can and should be changed.[1] Gender is not a peripheral or niche issue so much a holistic view that illuminates the whole landscape of security studies and policy. Gender can also be conceived as intersectional and mutually constitutive of other axes of power and difference, such that adopting a gender perspective need not necessarily mean treating gender as primary over other differences or identifications. Sexuality, race, class, nation/nationality, age/generation, and (dis)ability are among the multiple and various vectors of power, which, at times, become salient in Gender Studies.

This chapter provides an overview of how feminist and gender research has impinged on and intervened in security studies debates, and its relevance and implications for thinking about global security policy. While there is a substantial overlap between what I call "feminist" and "gender" scholarship, there is also a subtle difference that should be noted. Many scholars resist abstracting gender from the "decades of feminist scholarship that worked to explore, expand on and elucidate what gender might mean" (Shepherd, 2009, p. 217), which is informed by the insight that all social life is gendered and gender is multidimensional and not reducible to a variable. There is also a body of work which does not share such an explicit feminist orientation but treats gender as a variable: for instance, investigating sex-specific behaviors in conflict and post-conflict situations (Shepherd, 2009, p. 218). This chapter will

The Handbook of Global Security Policy, First Edition. Edited by Mary Kaldor and Iavor Rangelov.
© 2014 John Wiley & Sons, Ltd. Published 2014 by John Wiley & Sons, Ltd.

focus primarily on feminist gender scholarship, but refers to both feminist and other gender research at times.

I start by elaborating feminist critiques of the state-centric conceptions of security that have dominated traditional Security Studies and how these intersect with feminist and gender perspectives on war, militarism, and militarization and the study of gendered violences across and in between "war" and "peace'. The following section considers how gendered violences – most notably, systematic sexual violence as a weapon of war – have been securitized and how gender has been cast as significant to international security issues, through United Nations Security Council Resolutions (UNSCR) and other international policy instruments and channels. The third section investigates the gendered dimensions of human security as an alternative paradigm to state-based conceptions of security, and the final section discusses the mobilization of gender narratives as part of the "War on Terror" as a particular kind of security project in the post-9/11 era.

State-Centric Security and Gendered Violences

A key contribution that feminist and gender research has made to perspectives on security is a body of incisive critique of state-based approaches to security stemming from the realist and neorealist paradigms (see for instance Morgenthau, 1960; Waltz, 1979) that gained significant policy relevancy in the Cold War era, especially in the United States (Nuruzzaman, 2006, 288; Tickner, 2005; Shepherd, 2009), and of the associated security institutions, discourses, and practices. There is an overlap with other postpositivist critiques of (neo)realism (Tickner, 2005), including critical security scholarship (see Krause and Williams, 1997; Booth, 2005; Peoples and Vaughan-Williams, 2010; Nuruzzaman, 2006), but feminist and gender research is distinctive in demonstrating the indispensability of *gender* as an analytical category informing such critiques. Gender perspectives are not simply about adding "women" in to discussions of security, but generating different ways of understanding, conceptualizing, and explaining social phenomena (Shepherd, 2009, p. 216) – significantly, in this case, violence in its relationship to security. Much of this work problematizes "security" as a discursive field and practice of (gendered and gendering) *power*. It makes visible the often *pernicious effects* of security discourses/practices, and their implication in the *reproduction of* a range of (gendered, gendering, and gender-based) *violences*. In doing so, these literatures emphasize different and more holistic ways of conceptualizing violence in relation to security, which have considerable (although contested) policy implications.

Peterson and True (1998, p. 19) and Tickner (1992, pp. 9, 16–19) argue that the International Relations theory, which produces "security" as a field of power/ knowledge, is structured by a system of gendered hierarchical dualisms or binaries that derive from a (masculinist) tradition of Western political thought (Blanchard, 2003, p. 1293), such as order/anarchy, domestic/foreign, protector/protected. The values that are privileged, argues Tickner, are "related to concepts of masculinity" (1992, p. 17), thus the idea of security is constructed as the rational use of power to control and domesticate man's primitive "state of nature" in the domestic realm and anarchic threats in the ungoverned world of states. Autonomy and separateness are valued over interdependence, attachment, and community; zero-sum forms of coercive power are valued over positive-sum, mutual enablement (Tickner, 1992, pp. 131–133; Peterson and True, 1998, p. 20).

Feminists challenge the reification of the sovereign state as the proper referent object of security, contending that the abstraction of the state effaces the flesh and blood human bodies that are endangered by security discourses/practices (Elshtain, 1987, p. 91; Hartsock, 1982). State-centric security discourse is founded on the assumption that order within the domestic body politic is tantamount to "security" – the "domestic" realm is naturalized as already secure – while (largely military) power secures its borders against the anarchic threats lurking "outside". In contrast, feminist scholarship throws into relief how everyday, gendered insecurities traverse the domestic/foreign, internal/external divides (Peterson, 1992; Tickner, 1992), and the state's complicity in such insecurities is effaced by the mystification of state violence as "protection" (Peterson, 1992). This reification of the state is wedded to profoundly gendered discourses/practices of militarism which (re)produce forms of hegemonic masculinity[2] (Connell, 1987, 1995) that valorize and glorify violence (Enloe, 1983, 1993, 2000; Price, 2001; Jones, 2006; Cockburn, 2004b; Cockburn and Hubic, 2002).

Feminist research has highlighted the prevalence of sexual violence in armed conflict as a systematic weapon of war and a means of accomplishing or performing militarized masculinities (Seifert, 1996; Price, 2001). Sexual violence in war has often been normalized by security discourses, which have dismissed these practices as either incidental, exceptional or inevitable (Brownmiller, 1977; Hansen, 2000, Seifert, 1996). Research on the wars in the former Yugoslavia has been particularly significant in demonstrating the systematic complicity of security forces in the propagation of sexual and gender-based violences (Nikolić-Ristanović, 1996, 1998; Korac, 1998; Kesić, 1999; Zarkov, 2001). Sexual and gender-based violence is not only a weapon of war but tends to increase in interpersonal relations during and after conflict and in militarized contexts (Kelly, 2000). Enloe (2000) has shown how militaries often organize sexual access to women's bodies for their soldiers to cultivate the "right" kind of masculinity for soldiering. This association between masculinity and violence is mediated by the eroticization and masculinization of violence, and the feminization of subjugation (Chapkis, 1988). Cohn (1986, 1993), for example, has shown how the "technostrategic" discourse of the America's nuclear defense intellectuals in the 1980s masculinized and eroticized weapons of mass destruction. Contemporary "international" practices of securitization, such as peacekeeping, are not exempt from these critiques – for instance, Cockburn and Hubic (2002) highlight the participation of peacekeeping forces in post-war Bosnia in the sexual exploitation of women.

It is important to note that these gendered violences are not targeted exclusively at women. Some gender researchers have shown how (militarized) masculinities associated with discourses/practices of security can endanger people indiscriminately (Cohn, 1993), while still others have focused on gendered violence affecting (particular groups of) men and boys. Gender-based violence in the Balkan conflicts included the systematic massacre of men and boys belonging to certain ethnic groups by security forces (Jones, 1994). Indeed, Jones (2006) highlights the vulnerability of "battle-age" males to violence in armed conflict, which he posits as a function of hegemonic (militarized) masculinities that in turn depend on culturally hegemonic heterosexuality. This vulnerability includes susceptibility to sexual violence. Critical discussion of sexual violence against men in armed conflict is limited, but DelZotto and Jones (2002) and Sivakumaran (2007) unearth evidence of its pervasiveness despite under-reporting. Existing analyses observe that sexual violence against men is more likely to take the form of genital damage/mutilation and/or castration than rape, and men in detention are especially at risk (Sivakumaran, 2007; DelZotto and Jones, 2002; Jones, 2006). A significant thread in this literature is the focus on the gendered meanings that sexual violence against men may be understood to carry and the connections between these and the logic of sexual violence against women. Emasculation (of the individual "enemy", the ethnic group, the nation) is an eminent theme. Theorizing sexual violence against men in the Balkan wars as part of a performance of racialized masculinity, Zarkov (2001, p. 78) writes: "emasculation annihilates the power of the ethnic Other by annihilating the power of its men's masculinity".

DelZotto and Jones (2002) take issue with the exclusion of male victims from the hegemonic, feminist framing of sexual violence as a security problem (I will return to this concern in the next section). However, a nuanced and sophisticated gender analysis is illuminating, indeed necessary, to understand and address sexual violence against men, and the complicity of security discourses/practices in its (re)production.

In underscoring the porous boundaries between violences, some theorists posit violence as a "continuum" (Cockburn, 2004a; Moser and Mcilwaine, 2001; see also Pearce, 2007). They argue that the continuities between organized, politicized, and/or securitized violences, and those that are everyday, routine, and privatized become visible from a gender perspective. In this view, military invasions, bombing campaigns, rape, and domestic violence are linked by the more diffuse violence of structural gender inequalities and the norms of hegemonic masculinities. Hence, Shepherd (2009, p. 212) points out that feminist and gender perspectives on security have been significant in troubling the "war/peace" dichotomy and investigating the in-between, everyday, and structural violences it eclipses. Attention to interconnections between different forms of violence highlights how feminist and gender perspectives on security draw on related and overlapping areas of feminist and gender research, such as scholarship on violence against women and its normalization and social reproduction (Kelly, 1988; Hester, Kelly and Radford, 1996; Dobash and Dobash, 1998; Kelly and Humphreys, 2000; Kannabiran, 2005), and the long-standing feminist critique of the public/private divide in liberal political theory (Pateman, 1989). Overall, feminist and gender perspectives make a compelling case for the importance of gender as a category of analysis – albeit always inflected by, and intersecting, other vectors of power and difference – in theorizing both security, and violence and its (re)production in many contexts.

The Securitization of Sexual and Gender-Based Violence

Advocates of women's rights have had some success in gaining recognition of how gender impinges on security. Since 2000, the United Nations Security Council has passed five resolutions under its "Women, Peace and Security" Agenda, beginning with the passage of UNSCR 1325 on Women, Peace and Security in 2000. UNSCR 1325 calls for increased participation and better representation of women at all levels of decision-making in conflict resolution and peace processes, and attention to the gender-specific protection needs of women and girls in armed conflict. It calls for gender perspectives to be integrated into UN programming and reporting, Security Council missions, post-conflict processes, and the training of staff for UN peace support operations. The resolution was strengthened on its ninth anniversary by the passage of UNSCR 1889, which introduced further institutional monitoring and reporting mechanisms relating to these commitments. UNSCR 1820, adopted in 2008, was the first resolution to confront and condemn systematic sexual violence in conflict while framing it as an international security issue. It was followed up with calls on member states to take measures to prevent sexual violence in war and end impunity under UNSCR 1888 in 2009, and new institutional tools were created under resolution 1960 in 2010.

These provisions have been significant in positioning a gender perspective as a key dimension of the UN's international security agenda. Contestation over, and changes, in dominant discourses of security since the end of the Cold War period have helped to produce institutional and discursive conditions conducive to the creation of such policy instruments – even if translating them into meaningful violence reduction and other material outcomes remains an enormous challenge. These conditions include the increasing prominence of women's rights discourses in the international institutional arena (exemplified by CEDAW,[3] DEVAW,[4] and the Beijing Declaration and Platform for Action,[5] for instance), alongside the increasing focus on the individual and a rights-based approach under the rubric of human security. Feminist and gender research has clearly contributed to such debates. I will discuss these changes in more detail in the next section.

Against this background, in 2001, a landmark UN Hague war crimes court set a precedent in recognizing systematic rape in war as a crime against humanity, finding three Bosnian Serb soldiers guilty of the offence. The prosecution had to show that rape was conducted on a widespread, systematic basis as part of a campaign of "ethnic cleansing" intended to attack, terrorize and/or drive away members of a particular ethnic group. They had to demonstrate that the rapes were implicated in a chain of command, and the complicity of those in authority (Hagan, 2003). It is notable, however, that insofar as gender-based violence has been recognized as a security issue, it is cast as exceptional. It must be perpetrated under conditions of armed conflict, verifiably pervasive and systematic. Feminist concerns about interconnections between more visible, organized, highly politicized forms of violence and the routine gendered and gendering violences of daily life are therefore not fully addressed. Feminist and gender scholars offer a variety of responses to these developments. Bergoffen's (2003) analysis, for instance, celebrates the 2001 Hague court ruling for its (in her view) inauguration of new possibilities for rethinking security through, "the politics of the vulnerable body" in ways that challenge its traditional construction as masculinist authority and protection. She argues that the ruling found the soldiers guilty, not of failing as the women's (the women who were raped) "protectors", so much as "violating the laws of heteronomy and trust", and failing to "respect the women's heterogeneous sexual identity" (Bergoffen, 2003, p. 133).

In contrast, other gender theorists assess the securitization of sexual and gender-based violences more ambivalently. I focus here on two pieces of research. Firstly, Hansen (2000) analyses three of the dominant representations around which the debate about the mass rapes in the war in Bosnia in the early 1990s crystallized. This debate played a particularly salient role in the coming to prominence of systematic sexual violence in armed conflict as an issue for international security discourse and policy (Hansen, 2000, p. 55). Hansen argues that the "rape as normal/Balkan warfare" argument, which she associates with realist, state-based constructions of security, failed to securitize the rapes at all, but rather reproduced the normalization and privatization of sexual violence. In contrast, the "rape as exceptional/Serbian warfare" discourse constructed the rapes as a collective security problem through a nationalist lens, understanding wartime rapes as distinct from "spontaneous" rapes in that they "serve as a means for destruction of a nation" (Hansen, 2000, p. 60, citing Nikolić-Ristanović, 1996, p. 202). This discourse failed to securitize rapes not committed by those security forces constructed as the aggressors. There are some notable similarities between this construction and the securitization of rape by The Hague ruling and the United Nations Security Council Resolutions, discussed earlier, which also distinguish (at least implicitly) between "spontaneous" and systematic sexual attacks. Maintaining this distinction means that many forms of sexual and other gender-based violence, and their connections with more organized and systematic forms of violence, remain obscured. A further representation, which Hansen calls the "Balkan patriarchy" discourse, securitized the rapes by pitting "women" as the victims against the nationalist regimes carrying out warfare. This does challenge the distinction between collective and individual rape; however, Hansen argues that both discourses through which rape was securitized carried ambivalent effects and implications. The former, for instance, is implicated in the (re)production of exclusivist national(ist) identities, while the latter reifies the categories "women" and "men", and obscures women's complicity in fostering nationalisms.

Hansen highlights the "productive power of rape" to "inscribe" the very nation(s) it seeks to attack and "reinforce national and gendered identity" (2000, p. 60). Her argument shows how the way in which rape is constructed as a security issue can add to, moderate, and/or amplify this productive power, and indeed, carries its own discursive/productive force. The effects of securitizing rape can be complex and myriad; they extend beyond and are not limited to securing those people who are threatened or harmed by the rapes. In the Balkan case, for instance, these effects included the (re)production of nationalist identity projects that were implicated in generating the violence.

Second, DelZotto and Jones (2002) also problematize the framing of sexual violence as a security issue. Their contention is that the experiences of sexually victimized men are rendered invisible in ways that reinforce the patriarchal/paternalist constructions of masculinity and femininity underscoring these and other gendered violences, including sexual violence against women. Feminist lobbying on sexual violence in conflict pre-dates the Balkan conflict and the ensuing explosion of interest in this problem. DelZotto and Jones argue that sexual violence as a human rights issue was strategically taken up by Western states as they reconstructed their identities after the demise of the Cold War. This involved a re-investment in paternalist constructions of sexual violence, which posit women as victims and as property to be protected (often from barbaric, hyper-masculinized ethnic "Others'). They contend that certain feminist discourses that began to command international attention following the Balkan wars, in their efforts to theorize women's gender-specific experiences of conflict and insecurity, ironically contributed to re-entrenching static constructions of masculinity and femininity that posit men as aggressors exerting power *over* women as victims. Sexual violence as a security problem thus became defined in exclusively heteronormative, male-on-female terms. Hence, prevalent forms of sexual violence against men were classed by the International Criminal Tribunal for the former Yugoslavia (ICTY) as torture or "inhuman treatment" rather than recognized as sexual offences – when they were acknowledged at all.

DelZotto and Jones show how dominant modes of securitizing sexual violence continue to efface sexual violence against men in a way that does not allow for a fully nuanced appreciation of the gender dynamics of violent conflict or its consequences. Adding "women" into the picture is not synonymous with gender analysis. They argue that this exclusion of male experiences of sexual victimization actually furthers the interests of elite men, and that those feminist discourses that collude in it are counterproductive. Indeed, in the final section, I will consider how reifying women as victims enabled the cooptation of certain feminist discourses into conservative, paternalist security projects in the era of the "War on Terror'. Again, it matters *how* gendered violence is securitized, and how gender is analytically deployed in the process.

Efforts to securitize gendered violences can produce unpredictable and ambivalent effects, and do not necessarily or seamlessly reduce or eradicate such violences, make the women, men, or children threatened by them more secure, or transform the way in which "security" is constructed and/or practiced. Importantly, it is not just a question of policy being poorly implemented, or barriers in translating it into practice. These effects, critically, flow from how key categories – gender, security, violence – are constructed. This underscores not only the significance of gender as an indispensable analytical category for conceptualizing security and analyzing the implications of security policies, but also Shepherd's (2008a, 2008b, 2009) contention that security should be understood "as a set of discourses", which feeds back into the (re)production of both gender and violence, rather than simply as a public good. Shepherd is therefore critical not only of state-centric conceptualizations of security, but of emancipatory security paradigms that have sought to displace the former. Her concerns suggest that gender scholarship must retain its critical edge. The next section considers a model of security as emancipatory that has been particularly salient in the international policy arena – human security – and how it has been both illuminated and troubled by gender perspectives.

Humanizing Security, Gendering Security?

Challenges to (neo)realist and state-centric formulations of security have proliferated since the end of the Cold War, a notable marker of which has been the rise of human security. Human security can be understood as the coalescence and repackaging of disparate, marginal strands of critical intervention questioning state-centric approaches to security (MacFarlane and Foong Khong, 2006; Christie, 2010, p. 171), which came to a head in the 1990s. It emerged, in part, from discontent with the (neo)realist security orthodoxy (Steans, 2006) and its tendencies towards militarism and war-making (UNDP, 1994). This reconfiguration of security thinking captured by human security discourse has evolved in tandem, if not always explicit dialogue, with increasing attention to women's rights discourses and recognition of sexual violence in armed conflict as a human rights and international security concern.

The uneven mainstreaming of human security in supranational policy arenas has prompted claims of a "paradigm shift" (Tadjbakhsh and Chenoy, 2007, pp. 19–21). It speaks to feminist concerns and critiques of the (neo)realist security orthodoxy in particular ways. For instance, the shift of the referent object of security from the state to the individual evokes feminist criticisms of dominant constructions of security shaped by "sovereign state systems that themselves constitute profound and pervasive insecurities" (Peterson, 1992, p. 49). For some feminist theorists, the inscription of the individual human being as the referent object of security is critically important in guarding against the subordination of the security and well-being of particular individuals to the (imagined) "security" of the collective or community. Nussbaum argues that women's lack of opportunities to realize the capabilities necessary for a "fully human life" stems in part from the instrumentalization of women's bodies and reproductive labor as *means* to the well-being of others, rather than as ends in themselves (2000, 2002). In contrast, human security (like Nussbaum's "capabilities" approach) posits each and every human being as having intrinsic value, "as ends in themselvs", regardless of nationality or sex, or any other marker of identity or difference. This is indispensable for a politics that positively demands that women's bodily integrity, dignity, and entitlement to a life free from violence are recognized as irreducible values in and of themselves, which governments and international organizations have a duty to secure (Marhia, 2013).

Second, human security's analytical emphasis on interconnections between multiple insecurities and the integrative character of threats (Gasper, 2005) resonates with feminist approaches to security, which emphasize the interrelationships between multiple violences (Tickner, 1992, p. 133), both direct and structural, including violences that traverse national borders. Human security thus resonates with feminist theories that posit violence as a continuum (Cockburn, 2004a; Moser and Mcilwaine, 2001). It appears to generate possibilities to transcend the restrictive (gendered) boundary distinctions characterizing (neo)realist conceptions of security, which feminist scholarship has problematized (Tickner, 1992, p. 23): public/private, domestic/foreign, national/international, order/anarchy, war/peace, self/other, us/them. In doing so, it ostensibly offers possibilities to foreground continuities between everyday violences located at the less visible end of the continuum, and the over-securitized violent threats (armed conflict, terrorism) at the other end. It suggests the potential to conceptualize insecurities as systemic, rather than as isolated "events", and therefore to develop frameworks for addressing structural violence. It revalues security as a "positive public good" (Hoogensen and Rottem, 2004, p. 157), rather than a negative response to the failures of politics (see Buzan, Wæver, and de Wilde, 1998).

Feminist and gender scholars have argued for orienting security towards people's everyday lives (Seckinelgin, Bigirumwami, and Morris, 2010, p. 525; Colak and Pearce, 2009, p. 17; Wibben, 2011, p. 87; Shepherd, 2009), and human security purports to concern itself with the latter in a way that national security frameworks do not. However, its construction of the "everyday" in relation to (in)security can undermine this stated aim. For instance, Seckinelgin, Bigirumwami, and Morris (2010) question some processes of securitization stemming from human security's "widening" rubric – processes that effectively *abstract* "threats" from their everyday contexts. They examine the securitization of HIV/AIDS under the rubric of human security in international policy discourse and show how it "is framed in static terms of state security" and "national and international security interests", projecting ordinary people/women potentially affected by HIV/AIDS (especially in African conflict zones) as a security threat, while reproducing the effacement of the (gendered) "structural vulnerabilities" that shape the course of the pandemic and how these condition people's everyday lives.

Such analyses indicate that in spite of its ostensible departure from (neo)realist, state-centric conceptions of security, human security can reproduce some of the latter's key assumptions. Some renditions of the concept do not claim to displace "national security", but to "complement" it (Commission on Human Security, 2003, pp. 2, 4), to add an extra layer of security, to cast a wider, deeper safety net in an increasingly globalized and interconnected world (Commission on Human Security, 2003; UNDP, 1994). This claim works on the assumption that securing *people* is harmonious with securing *the state* and that there is no conflict between the two. Human security is temporally positioned as additive to, but not supplanting, hegemonic models of national security in the face of a "new" and "changing" global situation: insecurities can "no longer" be contained within state boundaries, states alone can "no longer" respond effectively to the range of "new" and "emerging" threats (Commission on Human Security, 2003; UNDP, 1994) – as if, at some earlier, simpler time, a state-centric security approach could have fulfilled all our security needs. The fetishization of the sovereign state as the provider and arbiter of security, and the sole source of legitimate political authority (Shepherd, 2008a), which feminist and gender research has problematized, is left intact. A gender perspective that interrogates how the category of the "everyday" is constructed in and through human security discourse/practice, which pays particular attention to structural violences and their reproduction, and which questions the masculinism and presumed benign character of the sovereign state, is thus indispensable to thinking critically about human security and how it translates into security policy and practice.

Human security has attracted a still evolving body of gender scholarship (see Truong, Wieringa, and Chhachhi, 2006; contributions to *Peace Review* 16(1), 2004; Karamé with Bertinussen, 2001; Fox, 2004; Hoogensen and Rottem, 2004; McKay, 2004; Chenoy, 2005; Hudson, 2005; Hoogensen and Stuvøy, 2006; Denov, 2006; Robinson, 2008, 2011). This work encapsulates a range of perspectives, but despite the *prima facie* receptivity of human security discourse to feminist concerns, it is ambivalent in its slippage between celebration and critique. Some commentators see human security as potentially offering a framework through which to address women and girls' gender-specific experiences of insecurity (Denov, 2006; Fox, 2004), while others critique it as inadequate to this task (Bunch, 2004; McKay, 2004). Gender is also advocated as an analytic frame for (re)conceptualizing human security (Hoogensen and Rottem, 2004; Truong, Wieringa, and Chhachhi, 2006; Hudson, 2005, p. 157).

The usefulness of a gender lens for theorizing violences, both bodily and structurally, as discussed in the earlier section, implies that gender impinges significantly on human security as an alternative, emancipatory security paradigm, although this has not always been widely recognized. Denov's (2006) research on post-conflict interventions in Sierra Leone provides a poignantly illustrative example of how a lack of contextually grounded gender analysis can undermine the effective implementation of human security policies. Denov describes how the process of "disarmament, demobilization, and reintegration" (DDR) in Sierra Leone between 1998 and 2003, identified by the United Nations as an important aspect of the human security agenda, systematically discriminated against women and girls who had been involved in wartime violence. "Informed by conventional views of gender roles," the DDR process considered the conflict to have been fought between young men and rendered the girls' experiences invisible (Denov, 2006, p. 330). Women and girls were only visible as "wives" or "camp followers", not as combatants; therefore, they were not considered appropriate recipients of DDR benefits and were excluded outright from the "cash for weapons" program. Their weapons were appropriated by the men, who reaped the benefits, while many girls were left without the support networks they had come to depend upon during the conflict, and with nothing with which to replace them. The DDR process failed to address the after-effects of sexual violence against girls, but put them at further risk in the "perilous and insecure", "overcrowded" DDR camps (Denov, 2006, p. 335). Girls in Sierra Leone, argues Denov, experienced the DDR process not as "protective" or "empowering" (the human security buzzwords), but as "a struggle to fend for themselves and their children" (Denov, 2006, p. 331). The process, she concludes, had the effect of *reproducing* the very gender-based power differentials and insecurities that had characterized the conflict.

Denov accounts for these unintended consequences of a human security intervention, partly as a failure of policy *implementation*; however, there are potentially wider implications of her analysis. It indicates how human security discourse and associated policy measures, though not simply excluding considerations of gender, have tended to treat gender in a reductive way as an a priori or fixed variable, rather than appreciating its analytical potential. This can lead to its reduction to "women (and girls)" as a group subject to specific vulnerabilities (Hudson, 2005, p. 158). This approach may bring largely gender-based violations into discussions of security from which they were formerly excluded – but Robinson (2008, p. 175) problematizes the reinscription of precisely the "dichotomous ontologies that many feminists seek to overcome". Reifying the categories of "men" and "women" risks reproducing gender inequalities, gendered violences, and elite male privilege – as shown in the research of Hansen, DelZotto and Jones, and Denov.

In contrast, Robinson (2008, 2011) proposes a critical feminist ethics of care as an ontological and normative basis for rethinking human security. She draws on feminist theories of relational autonomy (Mackenzie and Stoljar, 2000) and feminist research on the ethics and politics of care, which overlaps with critiques of exclusively rights-based approaches. Robinson argues that the constellations of care that underlie the livelihoods, security, and well-being of the autonomous individual posited as the referent object of human security, are obscured by the lens of political and ethical liberalism that constructs human security's normative framework primarily in terms of rights (Robinson, 2011, pp. 161, 163). Relations of care, dependence, and interdependence, contends Robinson, form the basis of social life, and are deeply entangled with the (re)production of (in)security – that is, the risks associated with a multitude of security threats are minimized in contexts in which care is adequately, reciprocally, and non-exploitatively provided (Robinson, 2011, p. 163). However, care and care work are chronically undervalued in the current, neoliberal, global political economy, and the liberalism in which dominant conceptualizations of human security partake contributes to this devaluation of practices of care. Furthermore, she adds, the (variable, context-specific) construction of hegemonic masculinities is crucial not only to feminist critiques of the militarism that attends state-based security discourses, but also to the devaluation of care and its implications for realizing human security's substantive goals (Robinson, 2011, p. 165). However, Robinson resists idealizing practices of care, which would risk reproducing existing patterns of dominance and dependency, but favors a critical interrogation of contemporary care arrangements and their gendered, raced, and classed dimensions, while situating these against historical and contemporary relations of colonialism, race, and geopolitics (Robinson, 2011).

Extending beyond calls for the recognition of gender-based specificities and vulnerabilities to violence and insecurities, Robinson's framework again underscores the significance of gender as an analytical and, crucially, also an intersectional lens through which people's experiences of (in)security across the spectrum from the everyday to the exceptional can be conceptualized. Robinson rejects the rights-oriented individualism that she associates with emancipatory approaches to security and seeks to offer instead methods of analyzing how relations of power, which are typically hidden from view, are related to people's security (Robinson, 2011, p. 8). However, when she argues that "the struggle to ensure greater security for people must begin with attention to the state of care in their lives" (Robinson, 2011, p. 163) and for "a global commitment to care that complicates our understandings of the protectors and the protected, the strong and the vulnerable" (Robinson, 2011, p. 165), Robinson appears to be interested in security not exclusively as a set of discourses, but also as a public good. Her feminist critical ethics of care foregrounds both the discursive construction of security, and people's material experiences of (in)security, as well as the links between the two. In the next and final section, I consider how gendered constructions of security were both reproduced and reconfigured as part of the so-called "War on Terror" in the post-9/11 era.

Gender Narratives and the "War on Terror"

Some advocates of human security were concerned that the shifts in security discourses globally in the wake of 9/11 enabled a regrouping of hegemonic, state-based security paradigms and closed the window of opportunity for human security to take root as an alternative and emancipatory security paradigm (Duffield, 2006, p. 29). Subsequent analyses, however, have explored the problematic appropriation and instrumentalization of human security discourse and the liberal cosmopolitanist, rights-based framework in which it partakes into/by the "War on Terror" as a particular kind of security project (Marhia and Davies, 2013; Marhia 2013; see also Duffield, 2006; Christie, 2010, p. 174). A notable feature of this project, which feminist and gender researchers have problematized, was the co-option of the language of women's rights and freedoms in such a way as to discursively legitimate a range of forms of institutionalized and organized violence. This indicates again the impingement of gender on security, but in new ways that call attention to the importance of an intersectional, critical, and reflexive gender perspective in illuminating the implications of security policies for the (re)production of a range of violences.

Shepherd (2006) analyzes the rhetoric of "protecting Afghan women" mobilized by the Bush administration in justifying the post-9/11 invasion of Afghanistan as part of the fight against terrorism. She demonstrates how, "framing this fight through a gender lens enabled a stronger claim to moral righteousness" (2006, p. 34). On the one hand, this indicates the salience of women's rights and ostensibly feminist rhetoric at the level of national and international security discourse and policy, which accompanied the rise of human security as an alternative security paradigm competing with state-based approaches to security. However, feminist and gender researchers such as Shepherd (2006) and Young (2003, 2009), for instance, show how feminist rhetoric is deployed in ways that insidiously – or sometimes quite transparently – reinvigorate "existing cultural narratives of gender" (Shepherd, 2006, p. 34), which masculinize protectors and feminize victims. Young (2003, 2009) argues that the post-9/11 security regime in the United States has been characterized by the "logic of masculinist protection" in which the state functions as a protection racket, feminizing and infantilizing the citizenry.

Feminist and postcolonialist critics highlight, furthermore, the imperialist policy implications of the strategic mobilization of the language of women's rights by the orchestrators of the "War on Terror" security project. The association of "gender" and of women's rights and freedoms with development, democratization, modernity, and progress is, in part, what lends the gender narrative the "moral righteousness" it brings to the "War on Terror" project. However, such rhetoric was mobilized explicitly or implicitly to legitimate imperialist and neocolonialist forms of violence carried out in the name of "security" (Shepherd, 2006; Butler, 2008; Abu-Lughod, 2002; Ayotte and Husain, 2005), such as the invasions of Afghanistan and Iraq, and the torture and abuse of detainees at Abu Ghraib and Guantanamo Bay, to cite only the most obvious examples. The violent practices of securitization that emerged under the rubric of the "War on Terror" project were certainly gendered (and gendering), and often highly sexualized, although not always gender-based in a stable and predictable way: such violences are not reducible to a narrative of male perpetrators and female victims. A gender perspective enables a richer, critical analysis of the way in which gender narratives were mobilized and the kinds of violence they worked to legitimate, but such an analysis also requires sustained attention to the intersection of gender with, and its mutual constitution of, sexuality, nation, race, religion, culture, and coloniality.

Conclusion

In all its contextually specific complexity, gender inescapably impinges on security and on the (re)production and prevention of violence, with significant implications for policy. Gender and feminist research and analysis are a source of productive critical insight into the effects of security thinking and policy, and the power relations and violences that these are, at times, complicit in reproducing. Feminist scholars have thus argued that gender perspectives deserve a less peripheral position within the broader field of Security Studies and policy. Some have welcomed the rise of human security as an emancipatory alternative to state-based ("national") security paradigms and the attendant (gendered and gendering) militarism as potentially creating an opening for gender analysis to make a more widely recognized contribution to security thinking, policy, and practice. The liberal rights-based framework in which human security partakes, combined with feminist research and activism drawing attention to sex/gender-specific violations in armed conflict, for instance, have helped to carve out a space for bringing gender perspectives to bear on security policy within international institutional arenas such as the United Nations Security Council. However, the reconceptualization and "humanization" of security, as well as the securitization of systematic sexual violence, address some feminist concerns while raising new problems and dilemmas. The task of casting critical scrutiny on how gender is constructed, understood, and mobilized in and through security discourses and policies, and with what effects, remains ongoing.

Notes

1. I am indebted to Professor Clare Hemmings for sharing this formulation informally at an LSE Gender Institute seminar on Agency, May 2010.
2. Connell's (1987) theory of hegemonic masculinity has been extremely influential in Gender Studies, including in relation to militarism, violence, and security. According to Connell's original argument, hegemonic masculinity is a historically specific and constructed cultural ideal of masculinity, which achieves its hegemony or ascendency through cultural *consent*, persuasion, and institutionalization rather than violence – although it may also be backed up or enacted by/through force. Hegemonic masculinities are sustained by "configurations of practice", which relate to and valorize such ideals even if they are infrequently embodied. There is therefore a hierarchy of masculinities including those that are hegemonic, complicit, marginalized, and subordinated. Hegemonic masculinity is relational and defined against and in relation to both non-hegemonic masculinities and femininities. Although historically and culturally variable and subject to change, Connell argued that hegemonic patterns of practice generally enable (the continuation of) men's dominance over women, and contribute to ideologically legitimating it.
3. Convention for the Elimination of All Forms of Discrimination Against Women, adopted by the UN General Assembly in 1979.
4. Declaration for the Elimination of Violence Against Women, adopted by the UN General Assembly in 1993.
5. The official document prepared by delegates at the UN Fourth World Conference on Women: Action for Equality, Development and Peace, convened in Beijing, China, in September 1995. The Beijing Declaration and Platform for Action attempts to set out a global "agenda for women's empowerment" (UN Fourth World Conference on Women, 1995).

References

Abu-Lughod, Lila. 2002. "Do Muslim Women Really Need Saving? Anthropological Reflections on Cultural Relativism and Its Others." *American Anthropologist*, 104(3): 783–790.

Ayotte, Kevin J., and Mary E. Husain. 2005. "Securing Afghan Women: Neocolonialism, Epistemic Violence, and the Rhetoric of the Veil." *NWSA Journal*, 17(3): 112–133.

Bergoffen, Debra. 2003. "February 22, 2001: Toward a Politics of the Vulnerable Body." *Hypatia*, 18(1): 116–134.

Blanchard, Eric M. 2003. "Gender, International Relations and the Development of Feminist Security Theory." *Signs: Journal of Women in Culture and Society*, 28(4): 1289–1312.

Booth, Ken, ed. 2005. *Critical Security Studies and World Politics*. Boulder, CO: Lynne Rienner.

Brownmiller, Susan. 1977. *Against Our Will: Men, Women and Rape*. Harmondsworth: Penguin.

Bunch, Charlotte. 2004. "A Feminist Human Rights Lens." *Peace Review: A Journal of Social Justice*, 16(1): 29–35.

Butler, Judith. 2008. "Sexual politics, torture and secular time." *British Journal of Sociology*, 59(1): 1–23.

Buzan, Barry, Ole Wæver, and Jaap de Wilde. 1998. *Security: A New Framework for Analysis*. London: Lynne Rienner.

Chapkis, Wendy. 1988. "Sexuality and Militarism." In *Women and the Military System*, edited by Eva Isaksson. New York, NY: Harvester Wheatsheaf.

Chenoy, Anuradha M. 2005. "A Plea for Engendering Human Security." *International Studies*, 42(2): 167–179.

Christie, Ryerson. 2010. "Critical Voices and Human Security: To Endure, To Engage or To Critique?" *Security Dialogue*, 41(2): 169–190.

Cockburn, Cynthia. 2004a. "The Continuum of Violence: A Gender Perspective on War and Peace." In *Sites of Violence: Gender and Conflict Zones*, edited by Giles and Hyndman. Berkeley, CA: University of California Press.

Cockburn, Cynthia. 2004b. "Militarism, male power and the persistence of war." Seminar presentation *Militarism and Male Violence*, at the European Social Forum, London. Accessed October 18, 2012 from http://www.cynthiacockburn.org/Blogmilitmasc.pdf

Cockburn, Cynthia, and Meliha Hubic. 2002. "Gender and the peacekeeping military: a view from Bosnian women's organizations." In *The Postwar Moment: Militaries, Masculinities and International Peacekeeping, Bosnia and the Netherlands*, edited by Cynthia Cockburn and Dubravka Zarkov. London: Lawrence and Wishart.

Cohn, Carol. 1986. "Sex and death in the rational world of defense intellectuals." In *Feminist Theory in Practice and Process*, edited by Micheline. R. Malson. Chicago, IL: University of Chicago Press.

Cohn, Carol. 1993. "Wars, Wimps and Women: Talking Gender and Thinking War." In *Gendering War Talk*, edited by Miriam Cooke and Angela Woollacott. Princeton, NJ: Princeton University Press.

Colak, Alexandra Abello, and Jenny Pearce. 2009. "'Security from Below' in Contexts of Chronic Violence." *IDS Bulletin*, 40(2): 11–19.

Commission on Human Security. 2003. *Human Security Now*. New York.

Connell, Robert. 1987. *Gender and Power: Society, the Person and Sexual Politics*. Cambridge: Polity Press.

Connell, Robert. 1995. *Masculinities*. Cambridge: Polity Press.

DelZotto, Augusta, and Adam Jones. 2002. "'Male-on-Male Sexual Violence in Wartime: Human Rights' last taboo?" Paper presented to the Annual Convention of the International Studies Association (ISA), New Orleans, LA, March 23–27. Accessed April 29, 2013 from http://adamjones.freeservers.com/malerape.htm#N_11_

Denov, Myriam S. 2006. "Wartime Sexual Violence: Assessing a Human Security Response to War-Affected Girls in Sierra Leone." *Security Dialogue*, 37(3): 319–342.

Dobash, Rebecca Emerson, and Russell P. Dobash. 1998. "Violent Men and Violent Contexts." In *Rethinking Violence Against Women*, edited by Rebecca Emerson Dobash and Russell P. Dobash. London: Sage Publications.

Duffield, Mark. 2006. "Human security: linking development and security in an age of terror." In *New interfaces between security and development: Changing concepts and approaches*, edited by Stephan Klingebiel. Bonn: Dt. Inst. für Entwicklungspolitik.

Elshtain, Jean Bethke. 1987. *Women and War*. Brighton: Harvester Press.

Enloe, Cynthia. 1983. *Does Khaki Become You? The Militarization of Women's Lives.* London: Pluto Press.

Enloe, Cynthia. 1993. *The Morning After: Sexual Politics at the End of the Cold War.* Berkeley, CA: University of California Press.

Enloe, Cynthia. 2000. *Maneuvers: The International politics of Militarizing Women's Lives.* Berkeley, CA: University of California Press.

Fox, Mary-Jane. 2004. "Girl Soldiers: Human Security and Gendered Insecurity." *Security Dialogue*, 35(4): 465–479.

Gasper, Des. 2005. "Securing Humanity: Situating "Human Security" as Concept and Discourse." *Journal of Human Development*, 6(2): 221–245.

Hagan, John. 2003. *Justice in the Balkans: Prosecuting War Crimes in the Hague Tribunal.* Chicago, IL: University of Chicago Press.

Hansen, Lene. 2000. "Gender, Nation, Rape: Bosnia and the construction of security." *International Feminist Journal of Politics*, 3(1): 55–75.

Hartsock, Nancy. 1982. "Prologue to a feminist critique of war and politics." In *Women's views of the political world of men*, edited by Judith Stiehm. New York, NY: Transnational Publishers.

Hester, Marianne, Liz Kelly, and Jill Radford, eds. 1996. *Women, Violence and Male Power: feminist activism, research and practice.* Buckingham: Open University Press.

Hoogensen, Gunhild, and Svein Vigeland Rottem. 2004. "Gender Identity and the Subject of Security." *Security Dialogue*, 35(2): 155–171.

Hoogensen, Gunhild., and Kirsti Stuvøy. 2006. "Gender, Resistance and Human Security." *Security Dialogue*, 37(2): 207–228.

Hudson, Heidi. 2005. "'Doing' Security As Though Humans Matter: A Feminist Perspective on Gender and the Politics of Human Security." *Security Dialogue*, 36(2): 155–174.

Jones, Adam. 1994. "Gender and Ethnic Conflict in ex-Yugoslavia." *Ethnic and Racial Studies*, 17(1): 115–134.

Jones, Adam. 2006. "Straight as a Rule: Heteronormativity, Gendercide and the Non-Combatant Male." *Men and Masculinities*, 8(4): 451–469.

Kannabiran, Kalpana, ed. 2005. *The Violence of Normal Times: Essays on Women's Lived Realities.* New Delhi: Women Unlimited/Kali for Women.

Karamé, Kari, with Gudrun Bertinussen. 2001. *Gendering Human Security: From Marginalisation to the Integration of Women in Peace-building.* Norwegian Institute of International Affairs.

Kelly, Liz. 1988. *Surviving Sexual Violence.* Cambridge: Polity Press.

Kelly, Liz. 2000. "Wars Against Women: Sexual Violence, Sexual Politics and the Militarised State." In *States of Conflict: Gender, Violence and Resistance*, edited by Susie Jacobs, Ruth Jacobson, and Jennifer Marchbank. London: Zed Books.

Kelly, Liz, and Catherine Humphreys. 2000. "Stalking and Paedophilia: Ironies and Contradictions in the Politics of Naming and Legal Reform." In *Women, Violence and Strategies for Action: Feminist research, policy and practice*, edited by Jill Radford, Melissa Friedberg, and Lynne Harne. Buckingham: Open University Press.

Kesić, Obrad. 1999. "Women and Gender Imagery in Bosnia: Amazons, Sluts, Victims, Witches, and Wombs." In *Gender Politics in the Western Balkans: Women and Society in Yugoslavia and the Successor States*, edited by Sabrina P. Ramet. University Park, PA: Pennsylvania State University Press.

Korac, Maja. 1998. "Ethnic-Nationalism, Wars and the Patterns of Social, Political and Sexual Violence Against Women: The Case of the Post-Yugoslav Countries." *Identities*, 5(2): 153–181.

Krause, Keith, and Michael C. Williams, eds. 1997. *Critical Security Studies: Concepts and Cases.* Minneapolis, MN: University of Minnesota Press.

MacFarlane, S. Neil, and Yuen Foong Khong. 2006. *Human Security and the UN: A Critical History*. Bloomington, IN: Indiana University Press.

Mackenzie, Catriona, and Natalie Stoljar. 2000. "Introduction: Autonomy Refigured." In *Relational Autonomy: Feminist Perspectives on Autonomy, Agency and the Social Self*, edited by Mackenzie and Stoljar. New York, NY: Oxford University Press.

Marhia, Natasha. 2013. "Some Humans Are More *Human* than Others: Troubling the 'Human' in Human Security from a Critical Feminist Perspective." *Security Dialogue*, 44(1): 19–35.

Marhia, Natasha, and Chloe Davies. 2013. "A 'Force for Good'? British national security and human security in an age of counter-terrorism." In *National, European and Human Security: From co-existence to convergence*, edited by Mary Martin, Mary Kaldor and Narcís Serra. London: Routledge.

McKay, Susan. 2004. "Women, Human Security and Peace-building: A Feminist Analysis." In *Conflict and Human Security: A Search for New Approaches of Peace-building*, edited by Hideaki Shinoda and Ho-Won Jeong. IPSHU English Research Report Series, No. 19.

Morgenthau, Hans. 1960. *Politics Among Nations: The Struggle for Power*. New York, NY: Knopf.

Moser, Caroline, and Cathy Mcilwaine. 2001. "Gender and Social Capital in Contexts of Political Violence: Community Perceptions from Colombia and Guatemala." In *Victims, Perpetrators or Actors? Gender, Armed Conflict and Political Violence*, edited by Caroline Moser and Fiona Clark. London: Zed Books.

Nikolić-Ristanović, Vesna. 1996. "War and Violence against Women." In *The Gendered New World Order: Militarism, Development and the Environment*, edited by Jennifer E. Turpin and Lois Ann Lorentzen. London: Routledge.

Nikolić-Ristanović, Vesna. 1998. "War, Nationalism, and Mothers in the Former Yugoslavia." In *The Women and War Reader*, edited by Lois Ann Lorentzen and Jennifer E. Turpin. New York, NY: New York University Press.

Nuruzzaman, Mohammed. 2006. "Paradigms in Conflict: The Contested Claims of Human Security, Critical Theory and Feminism." *Cooperation and Conflict*, 41(3): 285–303.

Nussbaum, Martha C. 2000. *Women and Human Development: The Capabilities Approach*. Cambridge: Cambridge University Press.

Nussbaum, Martha C. 2002. "Women's Capabilities and Social Justice." In *Gender Justice, Development and Rights*, edited by Molyneux and Razavi. New York, NY: Oxford University Press.

Pateman, Carol. 1989. *The Disorder of Women: Democracy, Feminism and Political Theory*. Cambridge: Polity Press.

Pearce, Jenny. 2007. "Bringing Violence 'Back Home': Gender Socialisation and the Transmission of Violence Through Time and Space." In *Global Civil Society 2006/7*, edited by Helmut Anheier, Mary Kaldor, and Marlies Glasius. London: Sage Publications.

Peoples, Columba, and Nick Vaughan-Williams. 2010. *Critical Security Studies: An Introduction*. New York, NY: Taylor & Francis.

Peterson, V. Spike. 1992. "Security and Sovereign States: What Is at Stake in Taking Feminism Seriously?" In *Gendered States: Feminist (Re)Visions of International Relations Theory*, edited by Peterson. Boulder, CO: Lynne Rienner.

Peterson, V. Spike, and Jacqui True. 1998. "'New Times' and New Conversations." In *The 'Man' Question in International Relations*, edited by Marusia Zalewski, and Jane L. Parpart. Boulder, CO: Westview Press.

Price, Lisa S. 2001. "Finding the man in the soldier-rapist: some reflections on comprehension and accountability." *Women's Studies International Forum*, 21(2): 211–227.

Robinson, Fiona. 2008. "The importance of care in the theory and practice of human security." *Journal of International Political Theory*, 4(2): 167–188.

Robinson, Fiona. 2011. *The Ethics of Care: A Feminist Approach to Human Security.* Philadelphia, PA: Temple University Press.

Seckinelgin, Hakan, Joseph Bigirumwami, and Jill Morris. 2010. "Securitization of HIV/AIDS in Context: Gendered Vulnerability in Burundi." *Security Dialogue*, 41: 515–535.

Seifert, Ruth. 1996. "The Second Front: the logic of sexual violence in wars." *Women's Studies International Forum*, 19(1/2): 35–43.

Shepherd, Laura J. 2006. "Veiled References: Constructions of Gender in the Bush Administration Discourse on the Attacks on Afghanistan." *International Feminist Journal of Politics*, 8(1): 19–41.

Shepherd, Laura J. 2008a. *Gender, violence and security: Discourse as practice.* London: Zed Books.

Shepherd, Laura J. 2008b. "Power and Authority in the Production of United Nations Security Council Resolution 1325." *International Studies Quarterly*, 52: 383–404.

Shepherd, Laura J. 2009. "Gender, Violence and Global Politics: Contemporary Debates in Feminist Security Studies." *Political Studies Review*, 7: 208–219.

Sivakumaran, Sandesh. 2007. "Sexual Violence Against Men in Armed Conflict." *The European Journal of International Law*, 18(2): 253–276.

Steans, Jill. 2006. *Gender and International Relations: Issues, Debates and Future Directions.* Cambridge: Polity Press.

Tadjbakhsh, Shahrbanou, and Anuradha Chenoy. 2007. *Human Security: Concepts and Implications.* London: Routledge.

Tickner, J. Ann. 1992. *Gender in International Relations: Feminist Perspectives on Achieving Global Security.* New York, NY: Columbia University Press.

Tickner, J. Ann. 2005. "Gendering a Discipline: Some Feminist Methodological Contributions to International Relations." *Signs: Journal of Women, Culture and Society*, 30(4): 2173–2188.

Truong, Thanh-Dam, Saskia Wieringa, and Amrita Chhachhi. 2006. "Introduction: gender questions in the human security framework." In *Engendering human security: feminist perspectives*, edited by Thanh-Dam Truong, Saskia Wieringa and Amrita Chhachhi. London: Zed Books.

United Nations Development Programme (UNDP). 1994. *Human Development Report.* New York, NY: Oxford University Press.

United Nations Fourth World Conference on Women. 1995. *Beijing Declaration and Platform for Action.* Beijing: United Nations. Accessed December 9, 2003 from http://www.un.org/womenwatch/daw/beijing/platform/

Waltz, Kenneth N. 1979. *Theory of International Politics.* London: Addison-Wesley.

Wibben, Annick T. R. 2011. *Feminist Security Studies: A narrative approach.* London: Routledge.

Young, Iris Marion. 2003. "The Logic of Masculinist Protection: Reflections on the Current Security State." *Signs: Journal of Women, Culture and Society*, 29(2): 1–25.

Young, Iris Marion. 2009. "Feminist Reactions to the Contemporary Security Regime." *Hypatia*, 18(1): 223–231.

Zarkov, Dubravka. 2001. "The Body of the Other Man: Sexual violence and the Construction of Masculinity, Sexuality and Ethnicity in Croatian Media." In *Victims, Perpetrators or Actors? Gender, Armed Conflict and Political Violence*, edited by Caroline O. N. Moser and Fiona Clark. London: Zed Books.

Chapter 4

Security Policy and (Global) Risk(s)

Sabine Selchow

Introduction

Over the past decades there has been an explosion of scholarly engagements with "risk". While the issue of "risk" used to be one of particular interest to scholars in management and economics, it has come to be of concern to an increasing number of scholars from across the social and political sciences, such as sociologists and criminologists, and most recently also those interested in the study of security as it is understood in this *Handbook*. This rise in scholarly interest in "risk" is, of course, not detached from developments in socio-political reality, where the issue of "risk" has come to be important in various policy fields, among them security practices. As David Garland (2003, p. 49) observes, risk "has, out of nowhere, come to stand center stage in contemporary politics and social theory".

While it is apparent that "risk" matters these days more than ever, it is less obvious what is actually meant by "risk" in the various scholarly instances in which the term is used. Like a chameleon, the term "risk" changes color from context to context and from use to use. "Risk" is taken as a commodity, a capital, a technique of government, as something objective and scientifically knowable, as subjective and socially constructed, as a problem, a threat, a source of insecurity, as a pleasure, a thrill, a source of profit and freedom, a means whereby we colonize and control the future (Garland, 2003). Needless to say, each of these understandings draws on and implies complex and diverse world-views, and diverse conceptual assumptions, as well as different epistemological and ontological bases. So, talking about security policy and "risk" is not a straightforward endeavor. Putting it differently, it is an endeavor that could be embarked on from a variety of different angles, focusing on a variety of different socio-political phenomena.

The aim of this chapter is to introduce two different approaches to "risk". The chapter starts by introducing the concept of "risk" as a modern invention to "tame"

The Handbook of Global Security Policy, First Edition. Edited by Mary Kaldor and Iavor Rangelov.

the uncertainties of the future in order to enable action in the present. Based on this foundation, the chapter then proceeds in two different directions. First, the chapter takes up the post-Cold War phenomenon of an increasing reliance on the concept of "risk" in security practices and highlights four dynamics that are set in motion through its application in policy-making. This part of the chapter suggests that these dynamics need to be both recognized and critically considered in the context of Security Studies because they turn security practices into a complex social practice, which has profound implications reaching far beyond the narrow realm of "security". As such, the increasing significance of the logic of "risk" in security policy-making must become subject to a broader public discussion about nothing short of the future (of the constitution) of affected societies. Second, given the relatively high number of references to it in the social and political sciences in general and recently in Security Studies in particular, the chapter provides an account of Ulrich Beck's notion of "global risk" and its implied imperative to rethink (the way we currently think about) modern (security) institutions.

The Modern Invention Called "Risk"

"Risk" is a child of Modernity. It is a modern invention, a central tool in the modern endeavor of "colonising the future" (Giddens, 1991, p. 111), that is, of actively dealing with the uncertainties of the future. In the context of "risk", these uncertainties of the future are, however, not traditional uncertainties, such as (potential) natural disasters, but human-made uncertainties, which occur because of some form of human action (or inaction). So, the possibility of an earthquake is not a "risk" per se but might become a "risk", for instance, within the context of the development of a housing complex in an area in which an earthquake could happen. In other words, an earthquake can only become a "risk" within the context of human agency and decisions made by actors and responsibilities that could be identified in the case of unwanted consequences of these decisions. As such, "risk" is about decisions and responsibilities. It only exists and makes sense within a cultural context, in which the idea of human agency and the idea of the future as something that is "open" in the sense of something that could be shaped by human action in the present, exist. As Anthony Giddens (2002, p. 24) puts it, "risk" is "the mobilising dynamic of a society bent on change, that wants to determine its own future rather than leaving it to religion, tradition, or the vagaries of nature." This does not mean, however, that the future could ever *actually* be determined through the logic of "risk". The future remains as "unknown" as it has always been, no matter if it is approached through the logic of "risk" or not. What is determined through the logic of "risk" is an *imagination* of the future. As Gerda Reith (2004, p. 396, emphasis in original) puts it, "risk" "cannot make the future predictable or the world certain, [but] it can create the means for *acting as though it were*." As such, "risks" need to be understood as "non-existent, constructed and fictitious" (Beck, 2009, p. 214); they "exist [...] as a feature of *knowing*, not as an aspect of *being*" (Reith, 2004, p. 387, emphasis added). As Niklas Luhmann stresses, "[t]he outside world itself knows no risks, for it knows neither distinctions, nor expectations, nor evaluations, nor probabilities" (quoted in Reith, 2004, pp. 385–386). So, through "risk", the future is brought into the present. More precisely, the imagined "future" *becomes* the present. And it is this present of the *imagined* future that then constitutes the basis for action and decisions. Putting all this the other way around, "risk" can be understood as the *imagination* of potential future consequences of a decision and action in the present.

This means that "risk" is something like a double social product. On the one hand, as a logic, "risk" is a social product in that it is built on the premises of modernity and its idea of human agency. On the other hand, whatever is actually assessed and treated as "risk" in a society is socially, culturally, and historically contingent. As Ulrich Beck (2009, p. 13) emphasizes, "[t]he risks which we believe we recognize and which fill us with fear are mirror images of our selves, of our cultural perceptions." Thus, "risk" is "an artificial entity of calculation" (Krasmann, 2007, p. 306) that is not objective or value-free; it is politically loaded.

Security Policies and the Logic of "Risk'

Security policies are always guided by conceptions of "what"/"who" is to be secured "against what". In modern politics, the "what"/"who" that is to be secured has been the nation – more precisely, the nation-state. Needless to say, the conceptions of what is to be secured in general and the (naturalized) focus on the nation-state in particular, are historical. This is apparent in the face of the recent shift from a strict focus on the nation-state as the unit to be "secured" towards the individual, the "human" that Mary Kaldor observes in Chapter 5 on "Human Security". Just as the conception of the subject of security policies is historical, so are the notions of the "against what" it is to be "secured". As the authors of the Introduction and a number of chapters in this volume demonstrate (see also Bonss, 2011; Daase, 2010), over the past decades there has been a general widening of the concept of "security" and this has implied a widening of what constitutes the security threat. While the threat used to be a relatively narrow and clear idea of a "national Other" outside one's own national boundaries, a look into recent national security strategies shows that the "against what" has broadened these days to an almost infinite extent. As the 2010 UK National Security Strategy explains:

> Our predecessors grappled with the brutal certainties of the Cold War – with an existential danger that was clear and present, with Soviet armies arrayed across half of Europe and the constant threat of nuclear confrontation between the superpowers. Today, Britain faces a different and more complex range of threats from a myriad of sources. Terrorism, cyber-attacks, unconventional attacks using chemical, nuclear or biological weapons, as well as large scale accidents or natural hazards – anyone could do grave damage to our country. These new threats can emanate from states, but also from non state actors: terrorists, home-grown or overseas; insurgents; or criminals. The security of our energy supplies increasingly depends on fossil fuels located in some of the most unstable parts of the planet. Nuclear proliferation is a growing danger. Our security is vulnerable to the effects of climate change and its impact on food and water supply. So the concept of national security in 2010 is very different to what it was ten or twenty, let alone fifty or a hundred years ago. (National Security Strategy (UK), 2010, p. 3)

This widening of what is perceived and treated as a security threat is intriguing in various respects (e.g. see Booth, Chapter 1, in this volume). What is particularly remarkable, however, is, that it came along with a deep conceptual shift that has come to shape the practice of contemporary security policy-making, especially in the West.

This conceptual shift is the increasing reliance on the logic of "risk". As Michael Williams (2008, p. 57) observes, "[s]ince the end of the Cold War, Western security institutions have become increasingly obsessed with the management of global security risks, rather than the deterrence of a monolithic threat from another state." Williams substantiates his observation of what he describes as an "increasingly evident conceptual shift" (Williams, 2008, p. 58) by referring to security policy documents of NATO, the European Union (EU), and the United States. Particularly obvious here is this shift in the aftermath of the terrorist attack in New York City and Washington, DC on September 11, 2001, i.e. within the context of the "War on Terror". As Louise Amoore and Marieke de Goede (2008, p. 9) suggest, "risk" has elevated to be "the dominant technology of the war on terror", in which, as President George W. Bush (2002; emphasis added) made clear, the "defense of the homeland" "not only means dealing with real, immediate threats; it also means *anticipating* threats before they occur, before things happen." A look at the current US Homeland Security strategy makes the striking and explicit reference to the logic of "risk" apparent. In her 2013 Annual Address on the State of Homeland Security, US Secretary of Homeland Security Janet Napolitano (2013) highlights the reliance on "risk" as a key strategy of her department's "completely different" approach to security, which she describes as "more efficient, risk-based, and designed to detect, prevent, and respond to a range of threats – from terrorist attacks to natural disasters." As she explains,

> [t]his approach is built upon the notion that in a world of evolving threats, we can no longer simply be reactive or isolated. We have to leverage information to identify threats sooner, target our security measures to areas where they will have the greatest impact in decreasing risk, allocate our resources according to risk-based priorities, and engage a full range of partners in our work. (Napolitano, 2013)

Providing an outlook into the future of US Homeland Security, Napolitano stresses, "[w]e must continue to embed our risk-based approach within everything we do." In sum, what is particularly remarkable is that in contemporary security discourses, there are not simply only new issues perceived to threaten (national) security but, importantly, that these issues have come to be approached through the logic of "risk".

In order to understand the significance and profound implications of this conceptual development, we need to be aware of four dynamics that are set in motion once the logic of "risk" is applied. Two of these apply to policy-making in general: (1) the dynamic of the decoupling of political acts from the grounds of actuality; and (2) the dynamic of a "depolitization" of policy issues. The other two dynamics are specific to *security* policy-making in particular: (3) the dynamic of an "internalization" of (global) security issues, which is linked to a process of responsibilization; and (4) the dynamic of an expanding process of "securitization". In the following, each of these dynamics are considered in turn.

The Dynamic of the Decoupling of Political Acts from the Grounds of Actuality

The first dynamic that is set in motion through the application of the logic of "risk" in security practices relates to the decoupling of political decisions and political action from the grounds of actuality. This dynamic arises from the specific temporal conception that is characteristic of "risk". As we have seen in the previous section, "risk" is the *imagination* of an unwanted side effect of a decision in the present and the probability that this unwanted side effect might occur in the future. This means that political decisions and actions that are based on "risk" cannot be assessed against an *actual* happening. They are by nature decoupled from the grounds of actuality in that they are about prevention and preemption, as opposed to reaction. As an Organisation for Economic Co-operation and Development (OECD) report on risk-based security policy regarding terrorism and international transport acknowledges, "[s]ecurity is characterised by uncertainty, meaning that no objective probabilities can be determined for the occurrence of attacks" (OECD, 2009, p. 20). This means that risk-based actions can only be assessed against the "actuality" of the *claim* that something, which could (have) happen(ed), was avoided thanks to, but not against the *knowledge* that something actually happened, or would have *actually* happened without the relevant "risk"-based measure. In other words, it is not possible to determine "with any degree of finality" (Rasmussen, 2006, p. 4) if an undesired event would have *actually* happened because it is the very idea of "risk"-based approaches to act preventively *before* something happens (i.e. before one *knows*) that "risk"-based action always remains in the realm of the unknown. This means that the increasing popularity of "risk" as a guiding conception within security policy-making involves a decoupling of security policy-making from the grounds of actuality.

The Dynamic of a Depolitization of (Security) Policymaking

The second dynamic that is set in motion through the application of the logic of "risk" in security practices is the dynamic of a depolitization of security policy-making. Three interlinked aspects constitute this dynamic.

The first aspect that amounts to the depolitization of security policy-making is the pretense of "objectivity" that is implied in the concept of "risk" and in "risk"-based action. We have seen earlier that "risk" is about determining the likelihood that an action in the present leads to an undesired event in future. This determination is made by bringing a complex (imagined) setting into a calculable form. Hence, despite the fact that, by nature, "risk" is a double *social* product, this translation of an imagination of an undesired future event into a calculable form "implies precision of calculation, which suggests objectivity and control" (Joffe, 1999, p. 4). As Helene Joffe (1999, p. 4) suggests, it is this powerful sense of "objectivity" that means that "[t]he concept of risk not only conceals the emotional facet of danger, but also obscures the value-laden nature of choices made in societies concerning risks". It also obscures the essentially political nature of the categories that constitute the ground for "risk" assessments. For instance, Louise Amoore and Marieke de Goede (2008, p. 8) attest for US security screening practices at airports, in particular through the Automated Targeting System (ATS) introduced in 2006 (see Department of Homeland Security, 2006), that the datasets which are used to establish "risk" "are always already made on grounds that are absolutely racialized and prejudicial". In fact, it is this supposed "objectivity" that public and private security actors use in legitimizing "risk"-based measures; the US government, for instance, explicitly "sells" their ATS and its "risk-based screening [...] to civil liberties groups as being more objective, neutral and expert led than the potentially discriminating and prejudicial decisions taken by airport security personnel and border guards", Amoore and de Goede (2008, p. 8) state. "ATS provides equitable treatment for all individuals in developing any individual's risk assessment score, because ATS uses the same risk assessment process for any individual using a defined targeting methodology for a given time period at any specific port of entry", claims the Department of Homeland Security (2006, p. 2) on its website.

The second, closely related aspect that constitutes the dynamic of the depolitization of "security" through the application of the logic of "risk" is that, in "risk"-based categories, *individual cases* are translated into *types*. As Robert Castels (1991, p. 281, emphasis in the original) explains in the context of mental health and social work, "risk"-based strategies "dissolve the notion of the *subject* or a concrete individual, and put into its place a combinatory of *factors* of risk." This means that, by nature, "risk"-based security measures are not about engagements with human individuals (and their personal histories) but about engagements with types, categories, and factors. As Susanne Krasmann (2007) argues, it is in the logic of "risk"-based assessments that it is not necessary anymore to actual *see* the person one "engages" with and judges. Related to the translation of individual cases into types is the *production* of "new" identities through "risk"-based measures. These "new" identities not only coexist with the respective person's "real" identity, but also replace it within the field of security and for the purposes of security "risk"-assessments. Someone "who attempts to cross a national border may find that she is already welcome or already excluded on the basis of an identity that is established by the codes", observes David Lyon (quoted in Amoore and de Goede, 2005, p. 162). What we see is that the extensive and expanding surveillance system, which serves as the data provider for the "risk"-assessment exercises that constitute contemporary security measures (see Lyon, 2003), "operates by abstracting human bodies from their territorial settings, and separating them into a series of discrete flows. These flows are then reassembled in different locations as discrete and virtual 'data doubles'" (Haggerty and Ericson, 2003, p. 605).

The third aspect that amounts to the dynamic of the depolitization of "security" through the application of the logic of "risk" relates to the fact that, as Henning Schmidt-Semisch (2004) points out, the logic of "risk" is not about the normative categories of "right" or "wrong". The application of "risk" means a lifting of policy-making into a realm outside the collectively negotiated and socially ratified normative horizon of a society. Instead, as Schmidt-Semisch (2004) explains, decisions that are taken based on "risk" assessments are about how *adequate* they are in following the imperatives of their respective socio-political ("risk") context. As such, the logic of "risk" provides the basis for *responsible* behavior and decisions – as opposed to explicitly "right" or "wrong" decisions. As Niklas Luhmann (quoted in Reith, 2004, p. 399) explains, this means that the technology of "risk" can easily lead to paradoxical situations in which a "wrong decision is right", namely "right" in accordance with risk assessment rules and procedures. Thus, "[i]f the impossible happens, one can defend oneself with the argument that one decided correctly, namely in risk-rational manner" (Reith, 2004, p. 396). In other words, through the application of the logic of "risk", discussions are (naturally) lifted outside the realm of critical discourse and are placed within discussions of adequacy, which, in turn, is closely linked to conceptions of effectiveness and efficiency. Overall, therefore, the shift towards "risk"-based security policies means a shift towards a managerial rationale.

It is the interplay of these three aspects that together comprise the multifaceted and profound dynamic of the depolitization of security policy-making as a result of the reliance on the logic of "risk". These two dynamics that are set in motion through the application of the logic of "risk" in security practices are of general nature. By contrast, the following two dynamics are specific to contemporary *security* policy-making.

The Dynamic of an "Internalization" of (Global) Security Issues and the Process of Responsibilization

The third dynamic that is set in motion through the application of the logic of "risk" in security practices – practices that we are currently experiencing – relates to the "responsibilization" of society and of the individual to secure security. Linked to this is an "internalization" of global security issues.

The previous section sketched out the way that decisions, which are made based on the logic of "risk", are not subject to normative assessments of "right" and "wrong". This, however, does not mean that they are not subject to a *moralistic* discourse. The notion of "morality" is key to the logic of "risk" because, as we have seen earlier, "risk" establishes a direct link between human action (i.e. a particular decision) and its (undesired) consequences in the future. As we have also seen earlier, recent security discourses are shaped by a widening of the notion of security and by a conceptual shift from being guided by the idea of a monolithic threat towards perceptions of a variety of security "risks". It is thanks to this shift, i.e. thanks to the logic of "risk", that we have seen an expansion of the idea of who is to serve as security actors, from distinct state actors to (potentially) each individual. This is apparent in the following account of contemporary US understanding of security by US Secretary of Homeland Security Janet Napolitano:

> Today, a decade after the creation of a Cabinet-level agency bearing that name, home-land security has come to mean much more [...] it means the coordinated work of hundreds of thousands of dedicated and skilled professionals, and more than ever, of the American public, of our businesses and families, communities and faith-based groups. (Napolitano, 2013)

Looking into the future of the US Department of Homeland Security, she states, "I think we must do even more to inform and *engage the public* in this *shared responsibility* for our safety and security" (2013, emphasis added). So, the shift towards the logic of "risk" enabled and produced a security environment that responsibilitized the individual for the securing of security. Putting it differently, it produced an environment in which it has come to be the US citizens' responsibility to spot and report "behavior reasonably indicative of criminal activity related to terrorism"

(Department of Homeland Security, n.d.), and the Londoners' responsibility "to be vigilant, trust [their] instincts and tell [the police] about anyone or anything [they] see which is out of place in [their] normal day to day lives" (Metropolitan Police Service, n.d.). "Everyone who works, lives and visits the capital has a role to play in helping to counter the terrorist threat which remains real and serious", explains the Metropolitan Police Service (Metropolitan Police Service, n.d.) in London.

The responsibilization of society, and the individual to secure security, goes hand-in-hand with another remarkable dynamic – the "internalization" of global security issues. Given that security issues, such as global terrorism, have come to be subject to the responsibility of the individual underground traveler in London or citizen in New York City, it has come to be strangely internalized in the respective societies. Through the application of the logic of "risk", global security threats are not (only or simply) external issues anymore, to be dealt with by public security measures but which become subject to everybody's responsibility; they become part of lived everyday experience. This dynamic of the "internalization" of global security issues is remarkable because it fundamentally undermines the concepts of "internal" and "external" that has shaped security policy-making for the past decades and is at the heart of the notion of "international relations.

The Dynamic of an Expanding Process of "Securitization'

The fourth dynamic that is set in motion through the application of the logic of "risk" in security discourses is closely related to those discussed earlier and could be called an expanding "securitization". There are two aspects to this dynamic.

First, it refers to the necessity to act that the logic of "risk" implies. Given that the concept of "risk" is inevitably linked to responsibility, it implies the inescapable imperative to act; one cannot *not* act. The imperative to act fuels the process of securitization.

Second, it relates to the fact that, by nature, the logic of "risk" is productive. It is productive in two senses. On the one side, it produces the necessity of "risk"-based action *ad infinitum*. This is due to the fact that "risk" is about the *imagination* of an undesired future event. As discussed previously, action that is guided by the logic of "risk" is not "tamed" by a distinct, tangible actuality that occurs in a specific moment in time. This means that there is something "unlimited" about "risk"-based action. "Risk"-based action initiates a process of unlimited "risk"-based action. It expands over time, so to say, because it requires a subsequent active "taming" of further "risk". As Mikkel Vedby Rasmussen (2006, p. 4) puts it, "risks are infinite because they multiply over time since one can always do more to prevent them from becoming real." It is in this sense that the logic of "risk" is "productive". It produces (further) uncertainties, or, better, the *sense* of (further) uncertainties that need to be "tamed" – again through measures based on the logic of "risk". As Richard Ericson and Kevin Haggerty (1997, p. 85) observe,

> [t]he yearning for security drives the insatiable quest for more and better knowledge of risk. However, in the search for inexhaustibly detailed and continuous risk management knowledge, each new form of knowledge and the measure of protection it makes visible gives rise to new knowledge about insecurity.

On the other side, the logic of "risk" is productive in terms of the "security" subjects and normalized ways of conduct it produces – through the measures of reward, punishment, encouragement, surveillance etc. that are implied in the moralistic "risk"-discourse. This means that the logic of "risk" *expands* itself over time and spreads into, and shapes, society deeply and fundamentally.

It is the interplay of these two aspects that account for the dynamic that means a "securitization" of society.

Summary

This section has highlighted four dynamics that are set in motion when the logic of "risk" is applied in policy-making. These are the dynamic of the decoupling of political acts from the grounds of actuality; the dynamic of a "depolitization" of policy issues; the dynamic of an "internalization" of (global) security issues, which is linked to a process of responsibilization; and the dynamic of an expanding process of "securitization". Each of these dynamics, which have only been outlined here, open a variety of interesting questions and fields of critical empirical engagement. Taken together, they reveal that the recent popularity of "risk" within security policy-making is about more than simply a replacement of the idea of a "monolithic threat" with an array of global "risks", such as climate change and terrorism. It constitutes a profound shift in the *logic* that shapes security policy-making. For instance, as we have seen previously, it lifts security policy-making out of the realm of the normative and into the realm of the adequate. As we have also seen, it leads to a situation in which security measures cannot be assessed against an actuality anymore; it further depoliticizes the security discourse; and it actually *produces* specific subjects and conduct.

This is remarkable and, indeed, explosive because through "risk", a logic is brought into the security discourse that is by nature expansive, i.e. constitutes a process that is hard to stop. As we have heard previously, "risk" is expansive because it inevitably produces more "risk", which produces more "risk", which produces more "risk" *ad infinitum*. But it is also inherently expansive in the sense that, as Ulrich Broeckling (2004) ellaborates, it implies the infinite need for ever more knowledge and data. In order to be able to assess "risk", relevant "factors" need to be identified and grasped, knowledge about the environment needs to be gathered that brings out relevant "factors", and, not least, knowledge about the relationship between relevant "factors" that might lead to the occurrence of the undesired event has to be gained. In this sense, recent practices, such as the extensive collection of personal data, notably biometric data, need to be understood as nothing less than the *natural* outcome of the logic of "risk". Yet, given that the assessment of "risk", i.e. the probability of an undesired event, inevitably builds on past experiences and is gathered against the background of the *imagination* of the future, preventive knowledge is essentially "incomplete": it is always partial and *naturally* implies the need to gain further knowledge (Broeckling, 2004, p. 211). As Broeckling (2004, p. 211) puts it, "those who aim to prevent, never know enough", in other words, the hunger for preventive knowledge is insatiable. On the one hand, one could argue that this is problematic because it produces new potential security risks. Given that the name of one of the alleged offenders of the 2013 bombing in Boston was actually already listed in the US master database "Terrorist Identities Datamart Environment" (TIDE), critics suggest that the data that has been continuously collected to serve as the basis for "risk"-based security measures has reached a volume that is counterproductive, in the sense that it is increasingly hard to handle in an effective way (see Karen Greenberg quoted in Hosenball, 2013).[1] On the other hand, it is also problematic beyond a narrow security-focus because through the increasing reliance on the logic of "risk" in security policy-making, an inherently expansive process is set in train, one that, recalling the earlier dynamics, has a profound impact on nothing short of the constitution of affected societies.

Consequently, it is crucial to understand and be aware of the earlier-outlined dynamics that are set in motion when the logic of "risk" is applied in security policy-making. This is because they show that risk-based security practices do more than securing security. They need to be understood as a complex social practice that has a profound and comprehensive social impact. Hence, as Loughnan and Selchow (2013) argue in their engagement with one particular "risk"-based measure, the practice of "preventive detention", risk-based security policy-making needs to be subject to public debates that go beyond a narrow "security"-focus. They require a debate about nothing less than how the respective public imagines the (future) constitution of its society.

"Global Risks" and the Imperative to Rethink Modern (Security) Institutions

The preceding part of this chapter discussed the dynamics that are set in motion when the logic of "risk" enters security policy-making. In this section, the chapter moves to a different direction. Given the relatively high number of references to it in the social and political sciences in general and recently in Security Studies in particular (see e.g. Heng, 2006; Rasmussen, 2006; Spence, 2005; various contributions in Amoore and de Goede, 2008; Coker, 2009), the chapter provides an account of Ulrich Beck's concept of "global risk" and the implied imperative to rethink (the way we think about) modern (security) institutions.

"Global Risks"

In the short introduction of the concept of "risk" at the beginning of this chapter, we have seen that "risk" is about an *imagined* future – it is about the anticipation of a possibility. We have further seen that "risk" implies the idea of agency. The notion of "risk" presupposes an understanding of the future as something that is open to being shaped by human agents. Hence, "risk" is about the *imagination* of *potential* outcomes of a *decision*. Where there is no "decision", there is no "risk"; and where there is a "decision", there is "responsibility". Hence, "risk" is inevitably and closely linked to the notion of "responsibility". As such, "risk" is a child of modernity. For "risk" to exist, it depends on, or more accurately it pre-requires, a modern outlook at the world. But this is not all there is to the relationship between "risk" and Modernity because "risk" is also *constitutive* of Modernity – more precisely of the process of modernization and industrial development. This is not only because "risk" enables action in the face of an "uncertain", though "open" future to begin with, but because it enables a societal context built on the premise and promise of (institutionalized) compensation for (potential) unwanted side-effects, i.e. the "bads" of the process of modernization and industrial development (that is, a society built on what Beck (2009, p. 7) calls the "risk contract"). We will return to this point in due course because it is a key aspect of Beck's argumentation; however, before doing so, it is useful to clarify what Beck actually means by "global risk".

With "global risk", Beck refers specifically to a certain kind of uncertainty, namely to the potential consequences of "industrial, that is, techno-economic decisions and considerations of utility" (Beck, 1992b, p. 98). "Industrial, techno-economic decisions and considerations of utility" are, as he explains, those decisions and considerations that have "their 'peaceful origin' in the centres of rationality and prosperity with the blessings of the guarantors of law and order" (Beck, 1992b, p. 98). There are two distinct aspects to these potential consequences of "industrial, techno-economic decisions and considerations of utility", i.e. "global risks". Each of these is considered in turn.

First, the potential consequences of "industrial, techno-economic decisions and considerations of utility", i.e. "global risks", constitute a specific kind of uncertainty that can no longer be simply "tamed" through a "traditional" modern imagination, i.e. through the logic of "risk" as we know it. "Global risks" constitute a "new dimension of risk", as Beck (2009, p. 6) puts it; they are "different in kind" in a three-fold sense.

1. "Global risks" are "different in kind" because they cannot be readily and "naturally" understood as something "unknown", in the sense of "not yet known". Rather, "industrial, techno-economic decisions and considerations of utility" need to be understood as producing non-knowledge (*Nichtwissen*; see especially Beck, 2009; also in depth Wehling, 2006). Non-knowledge is not to be misconceptualized as knowledge that is (still) *absent*, something we do not know *yet*, in that it is not yet there. Rather, it needs to be understood as an unknown unknown, i.e. it captures the fact that there are things we do not know that we do not know. For instance, the reduction of the ozone layer through chlorofluorocarbon (CFC) can be seen as a consequence of a "techno-economic decision and considerations of utility", namely the decision to use CFC in refrigerators, blowing agents, etc. Yet, when refrigerators and blowing agents were produced with CFC, the reduction of the ozone layer was not a (modern) "risk", i.e. it was not imagined as a potential consequence of the decisions in the then-present imagined future. It was not a "risk" because it was not simply a "not-yet-known". Rather, it was an unknown unknown, which did not enter relevant "industrial, techno-economic decisions and considerations" because there is no space for the unknown unknown (*Nichtwissen*) in the modern logic of "risk".

2. Further, the potential consequences of "industrial, techno-economic decisions and considerations of utility", i.e. "global risks", constitute a "different in kind" uncertainty that can no longer be simply "tamed" through a "traditional" modern imagination, i.e. through the logic of "risk" as we know it, because we *know* that there are potential consequences that produce instances that stand and remain *beyond* knowledge. For instance, it needs to be taken as known that it is impossible to provide a comprehensive and reliable picture of all long-term consequences of the explosion of reactor four of the nuclear power plant

in Chernobyl in 1986 and the subsequent release of radioactivity. So, in addition to imagining them as non-knowledge (*Nichtwissen*), potential consequences of "techno-economic decisions and considerations", i.e. "global risks", also need to be imagined as instances that are and indeed might *remain beyond* knowledge.

3. Last but not least, the potential consequences of "industrial, techno-economic decisions and considerations of utility", i.e. "global risks", are "different in kind" because they need to be imagined as "socially delimited in space and time" (Beck and Grande, 2010, p. 418). For instance, the potential consequences of the decision, i.e. the "global risks", of planting maize that is genetically modified for glyphosate tolerance in one place needs to be imagined as affecting and playing out beyond its (social) locality as well as in future generations.

Overall, as Beck (2009, p. 5, emphasis added) suggests, potential consequences of "techno-economic decisions and considerations of utility", i.e. "global risks'", cannot be taken in a modern sense, namely as if they could be "tamed" by "more knowledge but [are] instead a *result* of more knowledge."

This last point leads us directly to the second aspect that makes the potential consequences of "industrial, techno-economic decisions and considerations of utility", i.e. "global risks", distinct.

The second key characteristic of what Beck conceptualizes as "global risk" is that the potential consequences of "industrial, techno-economic decisions and considerations of utility", i.e. "global risks", need to be seen as the "*fruits*" of the process of modernization. "Global risks" are not the dark side effect but the result of the *success* of modernization. As suggested in Beck's own words, extracted earlier, they are "the result of *more* knowledge", that is, for instance, they are the outcome of our advanced understanding of the low toxicity, low reactivity, and low flammability of CFCs that made these gases attractive to be used in refrigerators, or our ability to genetically modify organisms, to enrich uranium, and to be mobile and travel the globe by plane. "Climate change, for example, is a product of *successful* industrialization which systematically disregards its consequences for nature and humanity", argues Beck (2009, p. 8, emphasis added). The potential consequences of "industrial, techno-economic decisions and considerations of utility", i.e. "global risks", therefore, are not to be seen as the (not yet "tamed') shortcomings of the process of modernization and industrialization but as its realization, indeed, its triumph.

The significance of understanding this specific, "different in kind"-nature of "global risk" is that it accounts for their transformative impact on modern societies. "Global risks" play a key role in a *structural* transformation of modern societies that Beck observes and is at the center of his scholarly interest.

"Risk Society" and "Reflexive Modernity"

At the heart of Beck's scholarship is his argument that modern societies have been subject to a profound structural transformation. This profound transformation is, however, not the product of contradictions, class struggles, or violent confrontations *within* societies. Rather, Beck argues, it is the product of the process of modernization itself. "[I]t is the process of modernization itself that calls the institutional order of first modernity into question, steals its clarity, he argues (Beck and Lau,

2005, p. 528). What he observes is that modern industrial societies are subject to the modernization of Modernity, which transforms them by catapulting them into a "radicalized Modernity" (Beck, 2008, p. 1), into "reflexive Modernity" (especially Beck, 1994). The attribute "reflexive" captures Beck's understanding of the way that the process of modernization "backfires"; it confronts modern industrial societies with their modern self (Beck, 2009, p. 6).

Throughout his scholarship, Beck conceptualizes and discusses three interlinked dynamics that contribute to this process of the modernization of Modernity: two of these dynamics are "individualization" (especially Beck, 1992b, pp. 91–155) and "cosmopolitization" (especially Beck, 2006), and the third is the process that he captures in his concept of "risk society" (especially Beck, 1992a), and later "world risk society" (especially Beck, 2009). This is "the process of problematizing the assumption that it is possible to control and compensate for industrially generated insecurities and dangers" (Beck, 2009, p. 7). In this sense, the concept of "risk society" captures "a constellation in which the idea of the controllability of decision-based side effects and dangers which is guiding for modernity has become questionable" (Beck, 2009, 15). This is because of the "different in kind"-nature of "global risks" as outlined earlier. Given that potential consequences of "industrial, techno-economic decisions and considerations of utility", i.e. "global risks", can no longer be imagined simply as "not yet known" unknowns, the basis for decisions needs to be built on a different (reflexive modern) idea of "control". What we are experiencing is a "return of uncertainty" (Beck, 1994, p. 8) in the process of modernization – yet, of a kind of uncertainty that can no longer be grasped and "transformed" through the modern logic of "risk" as we know it.

The significance of this insight is that it poses a fundamental question about the idea of a specific controllability and, to return to the beginning of this section, the premise and promise of the (institutionalized) insurance (of the possibility) for compensation for potential unwanted consequences of techno-economic decisions (e.g. pollution, accidents, etc.) – what Beck calls "risk contract" – which provide nothing less of the very basis for the process of modernization itself. It is this breakdown of the "risk contract" that motivates Beck to conceptualize contemporary societies as "*risk* societies", i.e. as societies that are shaped by a "reflexivity of uncertainty" (specifically Beck, 2009). He uses the term "*risk* society" in order to express his point that "the indeterminability of risk in the present is for the first time becoming fundamental for society as a whole" (Beck, 2009, p. 15).

This does not mean, however, that Beck detects an *awareness* of, in other words, a reflexion on the reflexivity of modernity. In fact, looking at the increasing reliance on the modern logic of "risk" outlined in the previous section of this chapter, it seems that social and political actors do not share Beck's understanding of the new constitution of contemporary societies (but see Selchow, 2013). Rather, Beck speaks of a *structural* change of modern societies. He argues that "global risks" produce new realities, whether or not there is an *awareness* of this fact in societies. One of the new structural features is, for instance, that "the 'global other' is in our midst" creating "new cosmopolitan responsibilities, cosmopolitan imperatives, which no one can escape" (Beck and Grande, 2010, p. 417). "Cosmopolitan" is, however, not to be misunderstood as an adjective that captures the assumptions underlying the normative project of cosmopolitanism (which may be familiar to some readers of this

Handbook), but as an adjective that captures the product of the *social force* that Beck grasps with his *analytical concept* "cosmopolitanization" (especially Beck and Grande, 2010; see also Beck, 2011). As such, "global risks" pave the ground for the "universal possibility" of new kinds of communities, "which spring up, establish themselves and become aware of their cosmopolitan composition" (Beck and Grande, 2010, p. 417) – though, again, as Beck emphasizes, this does not necessarily mean a move towards a "normative cosmopolitanism of a world without borders" (Beck and Grande, 2010).

Summary

From time to time, scholars take Beck's writing on "risk society" as suggesting that we are living in an increasingly dangerous time, that contemporary societies face an increasing number of "risks". Not often is his "risk society"-thesis read as support for claims that contemporary societies are shaped by cultures of fear (e.g. Kahmann, 2011, p. 358). Although his, at times alarming, rhetoric (and maybe because it is hard to avoid intuitively associating the term "risk society" with an idea of a society shaped by "risks") might support this misinterpretation, a closer look at his writing (the outcome of such a look has been condensed earlier) shows that this is not the most adequate interpretation of Beck's work. The brief summary of his "risk society"-thesis earlier makes it obvious that Beck's sometimes alarming rhetoric is less triggered by a discovery of an increased dangerousness of the world, let alone by a claim that there are more "risks" in contemporary "risk societies", than by a concern about the inadequacy of existing (modern national) institutions, which have been designed to respond to and handle "the adventure involved in opening up and conquering new markets and in developing and implementing new technologies" (Beck, 2009, p. 7), i.e. the products of the process of modernization and the very process that reflexively "backfires" in the form of "global risks". This leads to Beck's main argument and concern, which is the imperative to rethink modern national institutions or, more precisely, to rethink the way we *think about* modern national institutions. As Beck (e.g. 2003) suggests, given that our conceptual tools are products of and shaped by the modern national outlook, the main and first task is to develop a new conceptual language that enables us to imagine reflexive modern institutions to begin with.

For scholars in Security Studies, Beck's concepts of "global risk" and "risk society" are of interest in three respects, two being of general nature and one being particular for Security Studies. First, Beck's theory provides a theoretical and conceptual basis and inspiration for thinking about a "reinvention of politics" (Beck, 1994). In keeping with Beck's take on the world, a "reinvention of politics" needs to take into account that "we live in a world that has to make decisions concerning its future under the conditions of manufactured, self-inflicted insecurity" (Beck, 2009, p. 8). More precisely, that decisions concerning the future take place under the condition of uncertainties that are self-inflicted and are part of the realm of the unknown. Second, Beck's take on the world provides a theoretical and conceptual basis and inspiration for imagining political practices beyond (the logic of) "risk" because, as Beck (Beck, 2009, p. 5) suggests, it is "[t]hrough risk [that] the arrogant assumption of controllability [...] can increase in influence" and "tame" societies in their modern selves. Third, and specific for Security Studies, Beck's concept of "global risk" and his theory

of "risk society" provide a theoretical and conceptual basis and inspiration for reconceptualizing recent security practices and technologies, such as armed and unarmed
drones, in order to understand and uncover the concrete shortcomings of existing
(modern) institutions in dealing with them and the consequences of their existence.
That this is a fruitful task is apparent, for instance, in light of UK Surveillance Commissioner Andrew Rennison's acknowledgement that the current use of surveillance
technology has escaped existing regulatory institutions (Hastings, 2013).

Conclusion

Current and future scholarly engagements with security practices and policies will
not be able to avoid engagement with the concept of "risk". This is because of the
apparent increasing reliance on the logic of "risk" in security practices, especially in
the West.

There are a growing number of scholarly engagements with "risk" in the context of security that apply a variety of different conceptions of "risk". The aim of
this chapter was to introduce two different approaches to "risk". The chapter started
with a general introduction of the concept of "risk" as a modern invention to "tame"
the uncertainties of the future in order to enable action in the present. Based on this
foundation, it then proceeded into two different directions. First, the post-Cold War
phenomenon of an increasing reliance on the concept of "risk" in security practices
was discussed and four dynamics that are set in motion through its application in
policy-making were highlighted. It was suggested that these dynamics need to be
both recognized and critically considered in the context of Security Studies because
they turn security practices into a complex social practice, which has profound implications reaching far beyond the narrow realm of "security". As such, the increasing
significance of the logic of "risk" in security policy-making must become subject to
a broader public discussion about nothing short of the future (of the constitution)
of affected societies. Second, an account of Ulrich Beck's concepts of "global risk"
and "risk society" and its implied imperative to rethink (the way we currently think
about) modern (security) institutions was provided.

Note

1. Between 2008 and 2013 the number of entries in TIDE increased from 540,000 to 875,000
   (Hosenball, 2013).

References

Amoore, Louise, and Marieke de Goede. 2005. "Governance, risk and dataveillance in the
    war on terror." *Crime, Law & Social Change*, 43: 149–173.
Amoore, Louise, and Mareike de Goede, eds. 2008. *Risk and the War on Terror*. London:
    Routledge.
Beck, Ulrich. 1992a. *Risk Society*. Cambridge: Polity Press.

Beck, Ulrich. 1992b. "From Industrial Society to Risk Society: Questions of Survival, Social Structure and Ecological Enlightenment." *Theory, Culture & Society*, 9: 97–123.

Beck, Ulrich. 1994. "The Reinvention of Politics: Towards a Theory of Reflexive Modernization." In *Reflexive Modernization*, edited by Ulrich Beck, Anthony Giddens, and Scott Lash, 1–55. Cambridge: Polity Press.

Beck, Ulrich. 2003. "The Analysis of Global Inequality: From National to Cosmopolitan Perspective." In *Global Civil Society 2003*, edited by Mary Kaldor, Helmut Anheier, and Marlies Glasius, 45–55. Oxford: Oxford University Press.

Beck, Ulrich. 2006. *The Cosmopolitan Vision*. Cambridge: Polity Press.

Beck, Ulrich. 2008. "World at Risk: The New Task of Critical Theory." *Development and Society*, 37(1): 1–21.

Beck, Ulrich. 2009. *World Risk Society*. Cambridge: Polity Press.

Beck, Ulrich. 2011. "Cosmopolitanism as Imagined Communities of Global Risk." *American Behavioral Scientist*, 55(10): 1346–1361.

Beck, Ulrich, and Edgar Grande. 2010. "The Cosmopolitan Turn in Social Theory and Research." *The British Journal of Sociology*, 61(3): 409–437.

Beck, Ulrich, and Christoph Lau. 2005. "Second modernity as a research agenda: theoretical and empirical explorations in the "meta-change" of modern society." *The British Journal of Sociology*, 56(4): 525–557.

Bonss, Wolfgang. 2011. "(Un)Sicherheit in der Moderne." In *Zivile Sicherheit: Gesellschaftliche Dimensionen gegenwaertiger Sicherheitspolitiken*, edited by Peter Zocher, Stefan Kaufmann and Rita Haverkamp, 43–69. Bielefeld: Transcript.

Broeckling, Ulrich. 2004. "Praevention." In *Glossar der Gegenwart*, edited by Ulrich Broeckling, Susanne Krasmann and Thomas Lemke, 210–215. Frankfurt: Suhrkamp.

Bush, George W. 2002. "Remarks to the Community in Trenton, New Jersey." September 23, 2002.

Castels, Robert. 1991. "From dangerousness to risk." In *The Foucault Effect: Studies in Governmentality*, edited by Graham Burchell, Colin Gordon and Peter Miller, 281–298. Chicago, IL: University of Chicago Press.

Coker, Christopher. 2009. *War in an Age of Risk*. Cambridge: Polity Press.

Daase, Christoph. 2010. "Der erweiterte Sicherheitsbegriff." Sicherheitskultur im Wandel, Working Paper 1. Accessed February 13, 2012 from http://www.sicherheitskultur.org/fileadmin/files/WorkingPapers/01-Daase.pdf

Department of Homeland Security. 2006. "Privacy Impact Assessment for the Automated Targeting System" 22 November. Accessed January 17, 2013 from http://www.dhs.gov/xlibrary/assets/privacy/privacy_pia_cbp_ats.pdf

Department of Homeland Security. n.d. "If You See Something, Say Something." Accessed January 17, 2013 from http://www.dhs.gov/if-you-see-something-say-something

Ericson, Richard V., and Kevin D Haggerty. 1997. *Policing the Risk Society*. Toronto, ON: University of Toronto Press.

Garland, David. 2003. "The Rise of Risk." In *Risk and Morality*, edited by Richard V. Ericson, and Aaron Doyle, 48–86. Toronto, ON: University of Toronto Press.

Giddens, Anthony. 1991. *Modernity and Self-Identity: Self and Society in the Late Modern Age*. Stanford, CA: Stanford University Press.

Giddens, Anthony. 2002. *Runaway World: How Globalization is Shaping Our Lives*. London: Profile Books.

Haggerty, Kevin D., and Richard V. Ericson. 2003. "The Surveillant Assemblage." *The British Journal of Sociology*, 51(4): 605–622.

Hastings, Rob. 2013. "From Grainy CCTV to a Positive ID: Recognising the Benefits of Surveillance." *The Independent*, January 1.

Heng, Yee-Kuang. 2006. "The 'Transformation of War' Debate: Through the Looking Glass of Ulrich Beck's World Risk Society." *International Relations*, 20(1): 69–91.

Hosenball, Mark. 2013. "Number of Names on US Counter-Terrorism Database Jumps." *Reuters* U.S. Edition, May 2. Accessed May 3, 2013 from http://www.reuters.com/article/2013/05/03/us-usa-security-database-idUSBRE94200720130503

Joffe, Helene. 1999. *Risk and "the Other'*. Cambridge: Cambridge University Press.

Kahmann, Elke. 2011. "Beck and Beyond: Selling Security in the World Risk Society." *Review of International Studies*, 37(1): 349–372.

Krasmann, Susanne. 2007. "The Enemy on the Border: Critique of a Programme in Favour of a Preventive State." *Punishment & Society*, 9(3): 301–318.

Loughnan, Arlie, and Sabine Selchow. 2013. "Preventive Detention Beyond the Law: The Need to Ask Socio-Political Questions." In *Preventive Detention: Asking the Fundamental Questions*, edited by Patrick Keyzer. Portland, OR: Intersentia.

Lyon, David. 2003. *Surveillance after September 11*. Cambridge: Polity Press.

Metropolitan Police Service. n.d. "It's probably nothing, but…" Accessed January 17, 2013 from http://content.met.police.uk/Campaign/couldbenothingbut

Napolitano, Janet. 2013. "The Evolution and Future of Homeland Security. Secretary of Homeland Security Janet Napolitano's Third Annual Address on the State of Homeland Security." February 26. The Brookings Institution, Washington, DC.

National Security Strategy (UK). 2010. "A strong Britain in an Age of Uncertainty: The National Security Strategy." Accessed May 16, 2013 from https://www.gov.uk/government/publications/the-national-security-strategy-a-strong-britain-in-an-age-of-uncertainty

Organisation for Economic Co-operation and Development (OECD). 2009. "Terrorism and International Transport: Towards a Risk-Based Policy." OECD/ITF Roundtable 144.

Rasmussen, Mikkel Vedby. 2006. *The Risk Society at War: Terror, Technology and Stratgey in the Twenty-First Century*. Cambridge: Cambridge University Press.

Reith, Gerda. 2004. "Uncertain Times: The Notion of 'Risk' and the Development of Modernity." *Time & Society*, 13(2–3): 383–402.

Schmidt-Semisch, Henning. 2004. "Risiko." In *Glossar der Gegenwart*, edited by Ulrich Broeckling, Susanne Krasmann and Thomas Lemke, 222–227. Frankfurt: Suhrkamp.

Selchow, Sabine. 2013. "An Interplay of Traditions: The 'Return of Uncertainty' and its Taming in Post-9/11 US Security Thinking." In *Interpreting Global Security*, edited by Mark Bevir, Oliver Daddow, and Ian Hall. London: Routledge.

Spence, Keith. 2005. "World Risk Society and War Against Terror." *Political Studies*, 53(2): 284–302.

Williams, Michael J. 2008. "(In)Security Studies, Reflexive Modernization and the Risk Society." *Cooperation and Conflict: Journal of the Nordic International Studies Association*, 43(1): 57–79.

Wehling, Peter. 2006. *Im Schatten des Wissens? Perspektiven der Soziologie des Nichtwissens*. Konstanz: UVK.

Chapter 5

Human Security

Mary Kaldor

According to David Chandler, the heyday of human security was during the decade of the 1990s. In the early 2000s, the human security discourse was integrated into international institutional apparatuses and "the radicals appeared to be on the other side, critiquing human security as the ideological tool of biopolitical, neoliberal global governance" (Chandler, 2011, p. 117).

In this chapter, I argue that the burgeoning of radical critiques of human security during the last decade can be construed as representing the discursive achievement of the War on Terror. Both because of the way in which the language and even some of the practices of human security and humanitarianism appeared to be appropriated in the pursuit of the War on Terror and because of the way counterterror practices have influenced development and civil society policies – the space for emancipatory intervention has been narrowed. By focusing their critiques on human security, the radical critics have fallen into the trap set by the War on Terror and have, as it were, contributed to that narrowing of emancipatory space.

This is not to say that the critiques do not add value to the concept. On the contrary, the debates about what it is to be human, the meaning of security, or the use of the idea of biopower all have potential to substantiate our understanding of human security. The problem is not the critiques; rather it is their normative standpoint.

The narrowing of the space for emancipatory intervention is starkly illustrated by what is happening in Syria. There is a general consensus against any form of intervention. Despite the reams that have been written about the protection of civilians or support for civil society, the only international agenda is top–down political negotiations. It is taken for granted that the only alternative to political negotiations is military intervention, to which the West are reluctant and the other powers opposed. Radical critiques of military intervention based on the assumption that Iraq and Afghanistan are the only models, close down the sort of debates that were current in the 1990s about the indivisibility of security and human rights, how to promote

The Handbook of Global Security Policy, First Edition. Edited by Mary Kaldor and Iavor Rangelov.
© 2014 John Wiley & Sons, Ltd. Published 2014 by John Wiley & Sons, Ltd.

human rights while opposing war, how to construct security in the sense of safety. In a word, a discussion about what might constitute a human security approach to Syria is non-existent.

In elaborating this argument, I start by tracing the evolution of the concept of human security and the ways in which it has been mainstreamed into international conduct. I then analyze the radical critiques of human security. And in the last section, I discuss how we might reconstitute the idea of human security, building on some of the insights that the critiques have introduced.

The Evolution of the Concept of Human Security

Origins

The story of human security usually starts with the United Nations Development Programme (UNDP) Human Development Report of 1994 (UNDP, 1994); yet, the ideas and practices that came together under the umbrella of the term "human security" had a much longer trajectory.[1] In particular, the concept can be said to have emerged from two strands of thinking that became increasingly salient in the last decades of the Cold War.

One strand of thinking had to do with disarmament and development; concern with the burden of the East/West arms race and the idea that those resources devoted to the arms race could be better directed towards solving the problems of poverty and disease. This preoccupation was the subject of a series of a reports undertaken by the United Nations, as well as a number of independent commissions (Brandt, Brundtland, Palme, Nyere) that all tried to broaden the concept of security. Actually, the term "human security" was used in the press release for the 1993 Human Development Report (a year before the 1994 Report), which drew attention to

> new concepts of human security that stress security of the people not just nations and territory. This means accelerated disarmament using defence cuts to boost development. It also means a new role for the United Nations, increasingly intervening to provide human security in areas such as the former Yugoslavia and in Somalia, where people are fighting within countries rather than between countries. (Quoted in Bosold, 2011, p. 32)

For the UNDP, the emphasis was on material security, even though it insisted on the link between freedom from fear and freedom from want. The 1994 Report lists seven types of security (economic, food, health, environmental, personal, community, and political), of which only one "personal security" referred to safety from violence. There was an underlying assumption that deprivation is the main cause of war and, through development, the problem of war and violence could be solved. This understanding of human security is evident in the writing of Mahboob ul Haq, the person in charge of the UNDP Report and credited with the concept of human security:

> Two major issues dominated the creative period of international rethinking during and just after the Second World War. One was to avoid a catastrophic war. The other was to avoid another economic depression and to ensure universal economic and social well-being. The first preoccupation was with military security, the second with human

security – and the link between the two was never forgotten. Unfortunately, with the start of the Cold War between the superpowers, the first component often dominated the second. (Quoted in Bosold 2011, p. 34)

This version of human security has been followed through by UNDP with a series of human security reports in different regions and countries and is also widely used within the broader UN system. A Human Security Unit has been established to administer the Japanese-funded United Nations Trust Fund for Human Security. The fund has undertaken a series of human security projects that largely, but not exclusively, focus on material insecurity. A human security advisor to the Secretary-General has been appointed and he is responsible for regular reporting on the implementation of human security.

A second strand of thinking drew on the growing influence of human rights and the link that came to be made between security and human rights. The Human Rights Conventions, which came into effect in the years following the Second World War, stimulated the emergence of a human rights movement, particularly in places like Eastern Europe and Latin America. A key moment was the Helsinki Agreement of 1975, which ushered in a period of East–West détente. The three baskets of Helsinki (security, economic and social cooperation, and human rights) essentially constituted a human security concept even though the term was not used at the time. This human rights focus was very influential in both Canada and Australia where innovative foreign ministers (Lloyd Axworthy and Gareth Evans) pioneered the idea of human security. Writing in 1994, Gareth Evans argued:

> Two approaches seem particularly worthy of further exploration. The first is to develop the notion that 'security' as it appeared in the Charter is as much about the protection of individuals as it is about the defense of the territorial integrity of states. ... A second approach, which could either stand alone, or be seen as reinforcing the 'human security' reading just described, would pursue to its logical limits the international community's obligations under the UN Charter, to protect basic human rights bearing in mind that the most basic human rights of all, that of life, is violated on a very large scale in intra-state conflicts. (Quoted in Bosold, 2011, p. 36)

The high point of the human rights approach is often considered the International Commission on Intervention and State Sovereignty (ICISS), established by the Canadian government and chaired by Gareth Evans and Mahmoud Sahnoun. This was the report that developed the concept of Responsibility to Protect (RTP) – the idea that the international community has a responsibility to intervene, even to the extent of using military force, in cases of genocide, ethnic cleansing, and massive violations of human rights, where states fail to act (ICISS, 2001).

The concept of RTP was adopted in the report by the UN Secretary-General's High Level Panel on Threats, Challenges and Change, "A more secure world: our shared responsibility" (United Nations, 2004), which was supposed to consider how the United Nations could be reformed, and it was approved by the General Assembly in the World Summit Outcome document of 2005. Since his appointment as Secretary General in January 2007, Ban Ki Moon has said that "he will spare no effort to operationalise Responsibility to Protect" (quoted in Orford, 2011, p. 17). He has appointed special advisors on genocide prevention and RTP. He has established a $2 million Responsibility to Protect Fund supported by Sweden, the United Kingdom, and Australia and produced a series of reports on the implementation of RTP.

The idea that human security is linked to RTP and is primarily about the right to life is also reflected in the Human Security Reports and Briefs produced at Simon Fraser University in Canada, which reports on trends in armed conflict. The Human Security Report Project (2010) defines human security as "the combination of threats associated with war, genocide, and the displacement of populations. At a minimum, human security means freedom from violence and from the fear of violence."

These two strands of thinking produced a debate about the narrow versus the broad version of human security. Those who favored the broad version argued that the narrow version was too focused on military intervention, while those who favored the narrow version argued that the broad version was indistinguishable from development and covered too much to be analytically useful; moreover, it was argued the broad version risked "securitizing" development. The debate about the broad versus narrow version was, to some extent, reconciled by the report of the Commission of Human Security "Human Security Now" chaired by Sadako Ogata and Amartya Sen (Ogata and Sen, 2003). The report developed what has become known as the threshold approach to human security (Owen, 2004). The definition of human security contained in the report was:

> to protect the vital core of all human lives in ways that enhance human freedoms and human fulfillment. Human security means protecting fundamental freedoms— freedoms that are the essence of life. It means protecting people from critical (severe) and pervasive (widespread) threats and situations. It means using processes that build on people's strengths and aspirations. It means creating political, social, environmental, economic, military and cultural systems that together give people the building blocks of survival, livelihood and dignity. (Ogata and Sen, 2003)

This notion of the "vital core of all human lives" implied that human security comprises both human rights and human development but is concerned with what Amartya Sen called the "downside risks".

Worth noting is the emphasis put by Sadako Ogata in the Japanese version of human security on empowerment. Ogata emphasized the bottom–up character of human security. According to the Japanese Ministry of Foreign Affairs:

> In addition to protection by the state and the international community, it is necessary for the international community to put the focus on individuals and endeavour to empower people and societies through co-operation by countries, international organisations, non-governmental organisations (NGOs) and civil society so that people can live self-sufficient lives. This is the thinking behind "human security". (Quoted in Bosold, 2011, p. 37)

The Context

These ideas were being developed against the backdrop of a spike in wars in places like the Balkans and Africa and a dramatic growth in UN interventionism. At the start of the 1990s, there were only eight United Nations peacekeeping operations, involving some 10,000 troops. As of the end of 2000, there were some 15 United Nations operations, involving some 38,000 military troops. And a number of regional organizations were also involved in various missions concerned with conflict prevention or management, including NATO, the Commonwealth of Independent States, the European Union (EU), the Organization for Security and Co-operation in Europe (OSCE), the Economic Community of West African States (ECOWAS), and the then Organization for African Unity (OAU). Many proposals of the 1990s associated with ideas about human security came out of the experience both of international agencies operating in difficult situations and from locally based peace and human rights groups with links to the broader peace and human rights community. In particular, the war in Bosnia became the focus of an often-agonized public debate about how international intervention could protect people from ethnic cleansing and massive violations of human rights (Kaldor, 2001).

New proposals emanating from the insecurity actually experienced in different parts of the world included:

- Safe havens, no-fly zones or humanitarian corridors aimed at the direct protection of civilians
- New justice mechanisms in relation to war crimes and crimes against humanity
- Ways to control forms of finance for war through transparency and accountability especially for valuable resources like diamonds or oil
- The transformation of peacekeeping from separating sides to protecting civilians

Proposals of this kind potentially constituted a radical change in the nature of international intervention in war situations, which can be sharply distinguished from classic military intervention, even though such interventions involved military personnel. The tasks of those personnel are primarily civilian protection, dampening down violence, and the arrest of war criminals rather than defeating enemies and winning. Of course, for the most part, interventions of this kind have not been sufficiently robust but this does not necessarily mean such interventions are not possible. There were examples, such as the British experience in Northern Ireland, the safe haven in Northern Iraq in 1991, or the British intervention in Sierra Leone in 2001 that represent relatively successful examples of this type of intervention.

Alongside these proposals, much economic assistance was increasingly directed towards what became known as state-building and nation-building, involving public sector reform, election monitoring, security sector reform and DDR (disarmament, demobilization, and reintegration), or support for civil society, in addition to the more classic socio-economic tasks of development assistance.

The growth of multilateral interventionism and the mainstreaming of terms like RTP and human security gathered pace in the early 2000s. The Stockholm International Peace Research Institute's database of multilateral peace operations includes nearly 600 multilateral missions between 2000 and 2009.[2] And the number of UN troops deployed worldwide had increased by the end of the first decade of the twenty-first century to more than 100,000. It is now standard for United Nations Security Council (UNSC) Resolutions to refer to the protection of civilians, although the Libya resolution in 2011 (S/RES/1973) was the first to name the protection of civilians as the main goal, and almost all current UN peacekeepers are now mandated to protect civilians.

In the European Union, the new European Security and Defence Policy (ESDP) was developed following the Anglo–French summit in St Malo during the Kosovo war. ESDP has been designed for the so-called St Petersburg tasks, that is to say, multilateral interventions in crisis situations, rather than classic defense of borders. The European Union has incorporated the concept of human security, understood as upholding human rights, and has been developing combined military/civilian capabilities. Indeed, it is the first institution to have a combined military/civilian planning cell and it has pioneered civilian crisis management, largely consisting of missions aimed at restoring or establishing a rule of law and system of justice. It has undertaken some 23 missions, including EU Navfor (the current mission to counter piracy in Somalia) and the missions to the Democratic Republic of the Congo (DRC), which were considered successful in using a robust approach to preventing massacres and maintaining order, if too short (see Martin, 2010).

And in Africa, the African Union, which succeeded the Organization of African Unity (OAU), has institutionalized a "right of humanitarian intervention" in "grave circumstances", namely war crimes, genocide, and crimes against humanity, in Article 4h of the Constitutive Act. It has established a Peace and Security Council and an African Standby Force. This represents a considerable change from the earlier insistence on noninterference. Several African countries including Botswana, Ghana, Lesotho, Nigeria, Rwanda, and Tanzania have formally endorsed the RTP.

A particularly significant development in the twenty-first century has been the establishment of the International Criminal Court (ICC), even though there are widely differing opinions about its utility. The Rome Statute, the legal basis for the court, was adopted by 120 states on July 17, 1998 and entered into force on July 1, 2002. The establishment of the ICC was part of the general pressure for humanitarian norms as a result of the war in Bosnia and the Rwandan genocide (Glasius, 2006). The new emphasis on crimes against humanity has generated a whole new machinery of transitional justice (Rangelov and Teitel, 2011). So far, three state parties have referred situations in their territories to the ICC – Uganda, DRC, and the Central African Republic. In addition, the Security Council has referred the situations in Darfur and Libya to the court and the Prosecutor has opened an investigation into Kenya. Some 23 people have been indicted. In addition to the court, the Yugoslav and Rwandan tribunals established in the 1990s continued their work; the highly public arrests of Vojislav Seselj, the leader of the Serbian radical party; Radovan Karadzic, the former leader of Republika Serbska; and Ratko Mladic, the General responsible for the Srebrenica massacre, could be said to represent a further achievement in institutionalizing humanitarian norms.

Alongside these multilateral initiatives, many countries have begun to reconceptualize security as something broader than national defense. There has been much discussion about new or non-traditional threats or risks and the appropriate capabilities needed to complement military force; even countries like Russia and China refer to non-traditional threats. And even the United States has partly begun to move away from classic defense thinking. Members of the Bush Administration argued when they first came to power that it was not the job of the military to undertake constabulary duties or nation-building (see Rice, 2000). However the experience of Iraq and

Afghanistan led to profound rethinking in the Pentagon. General Petreaus produced a new counterinsurgency manual in 2006 that emphasized the protection of civilians, the need for a rule of law and the integration of military and civilian capabilities (Department of the Army and United States Marine Corps, 2006). Former Secretary of Defense Robert Gates made the case for "rebalancing" the defense budget so as to give greater priority to these new roles. And the State Department under Hillary Clinton introduced a Quadrennial Diplomacy and Development Review to complement the Quadrennial Defense Review and plan civilian capabilities for crisis management.

Of course, these developments do not constitute the adoption of a human security approach. Despite the emphasis on civilian protection, the lives of international personnel are still privileged over the lives of local people. An independent report on the protection of civilians in UN operations undertaken for the United Nations finds that there is still insufficient clarity of mandates, lack of planning, training and preparation, and lack of appropriate structures, resources and tools, despite the perseverance of "many dedicated and creative individuals" (Holt and Taylor, 2009, p. 8). Resources are still inadequate for the task of human security. Stories abound of overlap and duplication, of layers of agencies both official and non-governmental absorbing large chunks of aid budgets. Moreover, these new forms of intervention are often seen as secondary to the core task of defending nations from attack by a foreign enemy. It is argued that the "high end" of defense spending – advanced equipment and war fighting capabilities – can be applied at the "low end" but not the other way round. The financial crisis has meant a closing-in on core tasks, thereby weakening an already fragile capability for the new crisis tasks. Even though those directly engaged in international operations, especially the military, recognize the need for change, few political leaders are ready to embrace new approaches.

All the same, even if inadequate and ineffective, this new interventionism does represent a move towards recognizing the importance of contributing to the safety of people in far away places instead of focusing only on national concerns.

The Barcelona Version of Human Security

The European Union published its first security strategy in December 2003. Although it did not use the term human security, the basic themes could be said to broadly follow human security lines. The Study Group on European Security Capabilities (later renamed the Human Security Study Group) that reported to Javier Solana, then High Representative for Common Foreign and Security Policy, adopted the term "human security" to describe its distinctive approach. Its first report to Solana, presented in Barcelona in September 2004 was entitled "A Human Security Doctrine for Europe" (Human Security Study Group, 2004). The version of human security put forward by the study group had its roots in the experience of the Helsinki process in Europe but it could not be construed as the "narrow version" of human security. It was not the same as RTP; rather it added a third component to the definition of human security. As well as the usual elements of human security, the focus on the individual as opposed to the state and the link between "freedom from fear" and "freedom from want", it put particular emphasis on the link between human security and law and the blurring of the difference between internal and external security.

Human security, according to the Human Security Study Group, is about the kind of security that individuals expect in rights-based law-governed societies where law is based on an implicit social contract among individuals. Fundamental to law-governed societies is the assumption of equality before the law. This is different from the idea of a state-based international system in which, even if this system is law-governed, it is law, based on state rights rather than individual rights. In such a system, from an individual point of view, nationals are privileged over foreigners. In a law-governed national society, where law applies to individuals, it is assumed that the state will protect individuals from existential threats and emergency services – ambulances, firefighters, and police – are part of state provision. In most such societies, civil and political rights tend to receive more attention than social and economic rights in practice, even though all these rights are enshrined in law.

Human security is about extending individual rights beyond domestic borders and about developing a capacity at a global level to provide those kinds of emergency services to be deployed in situations where states either lack capacity or are themselves the violators of rights. What this means is that national security cannot be assured unilaterally, that the security of any part of the world depends on a global or human security system. Thus, instead of defending borders against external attack the security capabilities of states are designed to contribute to global emergency services.

The Barcelona Report and its follow-up, the Madrid Report, focused on the kind of capabilities required to operationalize this understanding of human security. It was proposed to establish human security forces composed of both military and civilian officers under civilian control. This coming together of military and civilians for human security is only possible if they conform to certain principles, which guide the way they are used. It is these principles that distinguish a human security intervention from a classic military intervention.

These principles are:

- *The primacy of human rights.* The primacy of human rights is what distinguishes the human security approach from traditional state-based approaches. What this principle means is that the primary goal is protecting civilians rather than defeating an adversary. Of course, sometimes it is necessary to try to capture or even defeat insurgents, but it has to be seen as a means to an end – civilian protection – rather than the other way round. Torturing suspects who have been arrested is also illegitimate and illegal. So-called collateral damage is unacceptable. At the same time, the application of this principle to saving life directly under threat from other parties may require a greater readiness to use force and to risk the lives of soldiers or aid workers – a shift in the balance between force protection and civilian protection.

  Human rights include economic and social rights, as well as political and civil rights. This means that human rights, such as the right to life, the right to housing, or the right to freedom of opinion, are to be respected and protected even in the midst of conflict.

- *Legitimate political authority.* Human security can only be guaranteed by a rule of law that depends on the existence of legitimate institutions that gains the trust of the population and have some enforcement capacity. This applies both to physical security, where the rule of law and a well-functioning system of justice are essential, and to material security, where increasing legitimate employment or providing infrastructure and public services require state policies. Legitimate political authority does not necessarily need to mean a state, it could consist of local government, a city for example, or regional or international political arrangements like protectorates or transitional administrations. Since state failure is often the primary cause of conflict, the reasons for state failure have to be taken into account in reconstructing legitimate political authority. Measures like justice and security sector reform, DDR, extension of authority, and public service reform are critical for the establishment of legitimate political authority (see Wulf, 2005), as is the involvement of civil society in political debate.

This principle explicitly recognizes the limitations on the use of military force. The aim of a human security operation is to stabilize the situation so that a space can be created for a peaceful political process rather than to win through military means alone. It is the political process that is critical.

- *Effective multilateralism.* This is related to legitimacy and distinguishes a human security approach from neocolonialism. Human security means a commitment to work with others, with international institutions, creating or complying with existing common rules and norms and solving problems through rules and cooperation, as well as with individual states, regional actors, and NGOs. It also means a better division of tasks and agreeing the appropriate means to resolve conflict and build peace. It is also closely related to international law and the need to operate within an international legal framework. In the current "strategic complexes", with layers of contracting and numerous agencies and an internal logic of competition, this may turn out to be one of the biggest obstacles to the implementation of human security.

- *The bottom–up approach.* Notions of "partnership", "local ownership", and "participation" are already key concepts in development policy, and soldiers often refer to the "ground truth" or to knowledge of the "human terrain". Decisions about the kind of security and development policies to be adopted, whether or not to intervene with military forces or through various forms of conditionality, and how, will only work if they take account of the most basic needs identified by the people who are affected by violence and insecurity. This is not just a moral issue; it is also a matter of effectiveness. People who live in zones of insecurity are the only ones able to sustain long-term security. There is a tendency among outsiders to focus on those who carry guns. Yet those who carry guns may often be those with a long-term interest in insecurity. Thus communication, consultation, and dialogue are essential tools for human security not simply to win hearts and minds nor even to gain knowledge and understanding but to empower those who will have to be responsible for security in the long run. The participation of teachers, doctors, tribal leaders, religious leaders, and young people are all critical for both understanding and operationalizing human security. Particularly important, in this context, is the role of women. The importance of gender equality for development, especially the education of girls, has long been recognized. The same may be true when managing violence. Women play a critical role both in dealing with the everyday consequences of the violence and overcoming divisions in society. Involvement and partnership with women's groups could be a key component of a human security approach.

- *Regional focus.* The tendency to focus attention on areas that are defined in terms of statehood has often meant that relatively simple ways of preventing the spread of violence are neglected. Time and again, foreign policy analysts have been taken by surprise when, after considerable attention had been given to one conflict, another conflict would seemingly spring up out of the blue in a neighboring state. The war in Sierra Leone could not be solved without addressing the cause of conflict in Liberia, for example. Today's war in Afghanistan can only be contained if the neighboring states, especially Pakistan, are involved.
- *Clear Civilian Command.* In human-security operations, civilians are in command. This means that the military must operate in support of law and order and under rules of engagement that are more similar to those of police work than to the rules of armed combat. Everyone needs to know who is in charge and leaders must be able to communicate politically with local people as well as people in the sending countries.

Fundamental to all these principles is a change of mindset. It is about the equality of human beings. This sounds obvious, but in war zones, local civilians are not treated as though they were equal in importance to civilians back home or indeed to the forces themselves.

The Impact of the War on Terror

David Chandler is probably right to argue that the 1990s represented the high point for human security. Despite the continued mainstreaming of human security concepts by international institutions in the early 2000s, the War on Terror, starting with the terrible events of September 11, 2001 has blunted and sidelined the distinctiveness of a human security approach and muffled those voices advocating such an approach.

First, the reaction to the attacks on the World Trade towers and the Pentagon was a national security reaction. They were treated as an attack by a foreign power on the United States and compared to the Japanese attacks on Pearl Harbor in 1940. A human security approach would have treated what happened as a humanitarian catastrophe and focused on the needs of the victims, methods of preventing any repetition, and efforts to arrest those responsible. As it turned out, the national security response led to the wars in Iraq and Afghanistan, which are classic military interventions.

There are several explanations for the way in which these wars undermined the distinctiveness of a human security approach. Neither of the interventions was formally justified in terms of humanitarianism or human security. The intervention in Afghanistan in October 2001 was justified in terms of self-defense. On October 7, 2001, the United States informed the United Nations Security Council that it was launching air strikes against al-Qaeda as a unilateral action in self-defense. In the case of Iraq, the formal justification was preemptive self-defense in order to remove the weapons of mass destruction that were supposed to have been possessed by Iraq. Nevertheless, many of those who supported those wars used humanitarian justifications. Liberal internationalists, like Michael Ignatieff or Christopher Hitchens, favored the war because of the abhorrent nature of both regimes, the Taliban and

Saddam Hussein. Yet in neither case was there an imminent humanitarian disaster. As Human Rights Watch (2004) argued at the time:

> In considering the criteria that would justify humanitarian intervention, the most important, as noted, is the level of killing: was genocide or comparable mass slaughter underway or imminent? Brutal as Saddam Hussein's reign had been, the scope of the Iraqi government's killing in March 2003 was not of the exceptional and dire magnitude that would justify humanitarian intervention. We have no illusions about Saddam Hussein's vicious inhumanity. Having devoted extensive time and effort to documenting his atrocities, we estimate that in the last twenty-five years of Ba'th Party rule the Iraqi government murdered or "disappeared" some quarter of a million Iraqis, if not more. In addition, one must consider such abuses as Iraq's use of chemical weapons against Iranian soldiers. However, by the time of the March 2003 invasion, Saddam Hussein's killing had ebbed.
>
> There were times in the past when the killing was so intense that humanitarian intervention would have been justified ... But on the eve of the latest Iraq war, no one contends that the Iraqi government was engaged in killing of anywhere near this magnitude, or had been for some time. "Better late than never" is not a justification for humanitarian intervention, which should be countenanced only to stop mass murder, not to punish its perpetrators, desirable as punishment is in such circumstances.[3] (Human Rights Watch, 2004)

Indeed, the interventions precipitated humanitarian crises in both countries as a result of lack of access to remote areas (Afghanistan) and the unfolding conflicts in both countries.

Once the wars were underway, new ideas that had many parallels with the human security discourse developed with the United States and other militaries. These included an emphasis on "population security" in the new counterinsurgency manual put together by General Petreaus, as well as on the rule of law and the establishment of legitimate political authority and the integration of military and civilian capabilities (Department of the Army and United States Marine Corps, 2006). In Afghanistan, the McCrystal plan (NATO, 2009) for stabilization even used the term "human security". Despite the brief success of this approach during the surge in Baghdad, these ideas have been discredited by the failures in Afghanistan. However, it should be stressed that counterinsurgency is different from human security in that it is based on a military rather than a civilian logic. McCrystal's idea was essentially defeated by the preoccupation with killing the Taliban (using kill or capture metrics much like in Vietnam) and by the pervasiveness of military culture.[4]

Second, humanitarian agencies came under attack because they depended on military protection, thus calling into question the demand for integrated military and civilian capabilities. The attack on the UN headquarters in Baghdad in August 2003, which killed the greatly respected UN Special Representative Sergio de Mello, caused a profound rethinking in the humanitarian community. For many, this was a signal to return to the classic precepts of humanitarianism, developed originally by the International Committee of the Red Cross, with an emphasis on principles such as neutrality and impartiality and the preservation of humanitarian space. What this line of argument fails to appreciate is that the main task of human security interventions is the creation of humanitarian space. Of course, when humanitarian agencies are identified with one side in a war, they become a target. But in a human security operation, the aim is civilian protection and empowerment not the winning or defeating enemies, and in areas where civilians are the main targets, it is not always possible to establish humanitarian space with some sort of military support.

Third, the counterterror measures introduced worldwide, led to new forms of regulation, surveillance, and control over a range of development actors (Howell and Lind, 2009). In places like the Horn of Africa, the demands of counterterror overwhelmed earlier human security approaches. It led to the "securitization" of aid in the sense that development functions increasingly came under the purview of security agencies (the Pentagon, the intelligence agencies, Africom, etc.) (Duffield and Waddell, 2006).

Fourth, and perhaps most importantly, the War on Terror polarized the public debate between those in favor of classic military intervention and those against all forms of intervention. In particular, it pulled apart the humanitarian community. Some – the liberal interventionists – joined the warrior camp. Others, like the veteran war correspondent David Rieff, have become disillusioned and cynical about humanitarian intervention and have joined the anti-interventionist camp. Those who remain, largely in the human rights movement, argue that humanitarian intervention is different from war and has to be conducted appropriately. Yet their position has little public resonance nowadays except perhaps among civil society groups inside war zones, such as in Afghanistan or Syria.

So, although the momentum of the 1990s carried the idea of human security through the international institutions during the early 2000s, by the end of the decade, vocal public support for human security seems to have virtually disappeared. The absence of a human security discourse is echoed in the academy where scholarship has focused on critiquing rather than remolding the concept of human security.

The Critiques of Human Security

The radical critiques of human security are drawn from feminist and post-colonial scholarship, as well as making use of the theories of Michel Foucault, Giorgio Agamben, and Carl Schmitt. As Suvi Alt (2011) points out, these various sources of criticism are often lumped together in confusing and misleading ways. In what follows, I attempt to outline different lines of argument taken from different sets of critiques.

What it is to be Human

The first set of arguments has to do with what it is to be human. Feminist scholars point out, not necessarily critically, that humans cannot be conceived as autonomous individuals. They are social beings intimately connected through networks of social relationships. Fiona Robinson's fine book draws attention to the importance of incorporating the ethics of care into concepts of human security and to situate such approaches in real lived experience. Human security has to encompass attentiveness, responsibility, and responsiveness to the needs of others, and a rethinking of the relation between private and public spheres. She notes the tendency of human security to focus on state discourses, "international law and the macropicture of global governance" (Robinson, 2011, p. 50). And she points out that "feminist ontology reveals the extent to which the continuity of life and a sense of security in people's day-to-day lives are impossible without relations of care and responsibility" (Robinson, 2011, p. 44).

The argument about autonomous individuals is also taken up by those who put forward the proposition, drawing on Agamben, that human security reduces human beings to "bare life". Similar to the feminist point, the argument is that human security neglects "the cultural context within which the individual realises his/her self-consciousness" and produces a "de-historicized and deracinated individual" (Shani, 2011, p. 57). For Agamben, bare "life" refers to the simple fact of living taken from the Greek term Zoë. "Bare life" is contrasted with social cultural human being. According to Agamben, "bare life" reached its apogee in the concentration camps. Human security, it is argued, fails to recognize the culturally contested and embedded nature of individual identities. Humanitarian emergencies, it is argued, "strips people of their history, culture and identity" (Alt, 2011, p. 146). The implication is that human security entrenches systems of power and depletes the possibility of human agency.

Interestingly, Chandler criticizes this argument on the grounds that human rights are indeed embedded in political struggles but, for him, these struggles emerge out of national political communities and his critique of human security follows from his skepticism about the possibility of a global political community. But the absence of a global political community is equally unrealistic. Human rights did indeed emerge from national struggles but often in conjunction with international groups and agencies. In the post-war period, it was the alliance of human rights groups with international NGOs and agencies and even governments that strengthened international human rights instruments.

While the importance of the everyday and of the cultural context cannot be over emphasized, it is also important not to romanticize the local. As feminists are only too aware, the family is often a site of insecurity and so is the local community. Moreover, what is regarded as "local" is often globally connected. Warlords, jihadists, and drug and diamond smugglers are often integrated into global networks. The "bottom–up" principle of human security involves alliances of care among local citizens seeking outside help to escape the nexus of violence in which they are caught. In other words, the blurring of public and private also involves a blurring of local and global.

The Meaning of Security

A second set of arguments has to do with the meaning of securitization. The idea of "securitization" developed by the Copenhagen School is that by calling something a security issue, it does something. What it does, however, depends on how the term security is understood.

One meaning of security is safety or, as Fiona Robinson (2011) points, free of care. This is the sense in which it was used by those who formulated the original version of human security. For them, calling something a security issue meant that it was important. And so by calling development a security issue, they wanted to draw attention to its importance. Understood in this way, the significance of securitization is rather trivial and the charge that the broad vision of security "securitizes" development is not serious; indeed it may have positive consequences, as the originators of human security believed, to securitize in this sense.

The second meaning of security is the identification with security services (the police, the military, intelligence services, etc.). In this sense, securitization refers to the way in which security services expand their remit to cover fields formerly addressed by social services or development agencies. This sense of securitization is evidently very relevant and worrying in understanding the effect of extensive counterterror measures.

But it is the third meaning of security that preoccupies the critics of human security. This is the understanding of security as having to do with a supreme emergency, which is intrinsically linked to sovereign power. In this sense, securitization is defined as the "speech act of labelling an issue a 'security Issue' [which] removes it from the realm of normal day-to-day politics casting it as an 'existential threat' and justifying extreme measures"(Robinson, 2011, p. 42). Sovereignty, from a Schmittian perspective, is all about the ability to decide what is an "existential threat". Carl Schmitt is famous for the dictum: "Sovereign is he who decides on the exception" (Schmitt, 1985, p. 1). What he means by this is that the ability to act is revealed at moments of crisis or emergency when normal laws can be suspended. Thus the USA PATRIOT Act of October 26, 2001 and the subsequent "Military Order" issued by President Bush on November 13, 2001 gave the President far-reaching powers to suspend the rule of law and, in particular, permitted the indefinite detention and trial of non-citizens suspected of involvement in terrorism. Effectively, it established a "state of exception"; indeed, Agamben argues that a state of exception has become normality for contemporary states.

Critics of human security suggest that if sovereignty is constructed through the exception, then human security represents a way of establishing global sovereign power. The ICISS argued that the RTP applies in "cases of violence which so genuinely 'shock the conscience of mankind' or which present such a clear and present danger to international security, that they require coercive intervention" (quoted in Doucet and de Larrinaga, 2011, p. 139). According to Doucet and de Larrinaga,

> In this the concept of human security plays a central role in identifying and defining those extreme and exceptional circumstances that not only set the conditions for the suspension of the law but also for its refounding in the language of new international norms on intervention. (2011, 139)

A very similar argument is put forward by Anne Orford (2011) in relation to RTP. She suggests that RTP is the way in which the United Nations acquires executive power.

Even if it were the case that international institutions had the capacity to act decisively in emergencies and were not constrained both by their member states and by lack of resources, this reading of sovereignty is at variance with the idea of conditional sovereignty that underpins a human security approach. What conditional sovereignty means is that the sovereignty of states (and international institutions) depends on respect for the framework of international rules, including human rights. Sovereignty, on this reading, is constructed through a social contract negotiated at national levels but supplemented by negotiations in the international arena on which the international rules are based. Any human security intervention has to operate within the framework of rules just as would be the case for emergency services in domestic settings. This is what makes a human security intervention different from a military intervention. The rules of war do represent a suspension of "normal" laws. This cannot be the case for human security.

The sovereignty argument is linked to the idea that human security reduces human beings to 'bare life'. It is also linked to Schmitt's critique of wars for humanity. Writing during World War II, on the German side, Schmitt argued that wars for humanity reduce the enemy to non-human and justifies extreme and brutal methods. But a human security intervention is not a war; in a war, the enemy is collective. If human security is viewed as human rights-based international law enforcement, rather than war, then there are no collective enemies, but there may be individual criminals whose lives also have to be respected.

Biopower

The third set of arguments have to do with the Foucauldian idea that human security and the strategic complexes it has spawned constitutes a form of biopower. In some critiques, the term biopower is confused with the concept of "bare life". Alt (2011) points out that this is a misreading of Foucault. Biopower refers to the form of power that focuses on the population rather than territory. It has to do with technologies of health and welfare rather than with disciplinary technologies; it is about the "power to make live" rather than the "right to kill". Mark Duffield (2001), who pioneered this approach, suggested that biopower can be regarded as a social mechanism used to maintain stability in what he describes as the uninsured part of the world – a way to maintain the quarantine of rich countries and salve their consciences. The strategic complexes of human security constitute a new paraphernalia of international intervention – a technology of power that preserves the submission of conflict ridden parts of the world to an unequal world order.

But actually to describe human security as a global extension of biopower is not necessarily a critique of human security. As Alt points out, whereas the concept of "bare life" offers a bleak prospect of human agency, for Foucault, the possibility of resistance is always present. Not only do people govern themselves through various techniques of the self, but also life is not "inescapably integrated into techniques of governance; it escapes constantly" (Alt, 2011, p. 152) "Whereas a Foucauldian perspective would see human security as a perspective that is constantly being reshaped, an Agambenite perspective would claim that it cannot be reshaped" (Alt, 2011, p. 153).

Of course human security is about power. Power is intrinsically linked to notions of security; the question concerns which notions of security. The normative question is not about power but about the specific practices and ideas that comprise the dominant paradigm (what Foucault would call *dipositif*) within which power is exercised. In other words, to suggest that human security is a form of biopower is a research strategy rather than a normative standpoint. What is then required is an empirical dissection of the way that power functions.

The Duffield argument that human security is a way of protecting the quarantining of the insured world is relevant, of course, whether or not the term biopower is applied. Similar arguments relate to the way in which human security "pathologizes" what are known as weak states (McCormack, 2011) and entrenches existing power inequalities by focusing on the individual rather than on structural inequalities (Newman, 2004). These are arguments that are always raised in relation to the partial adoption of progressive strategies. Does the welfare state, for example, help the poorest people or maintain capitalism? Undoubtedly ideas of human security have coincided with the dominance of neoliberal ideas and it can be argued that human security offers the sort of minimum safety net that neoliberalism requires. The question is whether such approaches actually make life form obstacles to structural change or whether, by offering an alternative set of norms, they contribute to further pressure for change. Whether people are being helped whatever the consequences, whether such help sustains existing inequalities of wealth and power, or whether it represents a challenge to such structural inequalities has to be determined through empirical research.

Reconstructing Human Security

The critiques of human security offer a bleak future. They offer no alternative for protecting and empowering people in faraway places. The implication of the critiques is that all forms of state-based international intervention are harmful. Yet in our globalized world, the local is imbued with the global – surely the refusal of all types of intervention amounts to the application of laisser-faire in the political arena alongside dominant laisser-faire economics?

Human security needs to be reconstructed as a strategy of resistance – an alternative to the War on Terror, not an adjunct. In contrast to the top–down character of RTP (which is about the right of outside powers to intervene), human security needs to be understood as the right to be protected. The value of some of the critiques is that they do offer some pointers to how this might be accomplished. First, human security has to understand the human as gendered, contextual, and social. It has to be a strategy that emanates from the context rather than imposed from above. Second, human security does have to be about the extension of rights-based international law, but that process is also contextual. Law can be used as an instrument of resistance by local groups trying to reduce violence and enhance the safety of their communities, and it is only through such pressure that international tendencies to override law can be constrained. Third, we need a micro empirical picture of the variety of international intervention in practice, what Duffield calls the strategic complexes of global governance to identify nodal points of resistance.

The drawing down of the wars in Iraq and Afghanistan has not left people in those regions any safer. On the contrary, the continuing violence in Iraq and Afghanistan, the wars in Syria and Palestine, the spread of both the drone campaign and jihadism, combined with growing economic crisis, suggest that the world is entering a dangerous phase. Can the concept of human security help us to ponder ways of navigating the new dangers?

Notes

1. Indeed David Bosold (2011, p. 30) suggests that the first person to use the term was Nils Bohr in 1945 when he said that "active atomic materials" represent a "perpetual menace to human security".

2. The database can be found on SIPRI's website http://www.sipri.org/research/conflict/pko/multilateral

3. See especially Chapter 1 – "War in Iraq: Not a Humanitarian Intervention" for Human Rights Watch's argument against war in Iraq.

4. For a more extensive treatment of this failure, see the chapter on Iraq and Afghanistan in the third edition of Kaldor (2012).

References

Alt, Suvi. 2011. "Problematizing Life Under Biopower: A Foucauldian Versus an Agambenite Critique of Human Security." In *Critical Perspectives on Human Security: Rethinking Emancipation and Power in International Relations*, edited by David Chandler and Nik Hynek, 144–156. Abingdon: Routledge.

Bosold, David. 2011. "Development of the Human Security Field: A Critical Examination." In *Critical Perspectives on Human Security: Rethinking Emancipation and Power in International Relations*, edited by David Chandler and Nik Hynek, 28–42. Abingdon: Routledge.

Chandler, David. 2011. "Rethinking Global Discourses of Security." In *Critical Perspectives on Human Security: Rethinking Emancipation and Power in International Relations*, edited by David Chandler and Nik Hynek, 114–128. Abingdon: Routledge.

Department of the Army and United States Marine Corps. 2006. "Counterinsurgency Field Manual No 3–24." *Marine Corps Warfighting Publications*, No 3–33.5, Washington DC, December 2006.

Doucet, Marc, and Miguel de Larrinaga. 2011. "Human Security and the Securing of Human Life: Tracing Global Sovereign and Biopolitical Rule." In *Critical Perspectives on Human Security: Rethinking Emancipation and Power in International Relations*, edited by David Chandler and Nik Hynek, 129–143. Abingdon: Routledge.

Duffield, Mark. 2001. *Global Governance and the New Wars: The Merging of Development and Security.* New York, NY: Zed Books.

Duffield, Mark, and Nicholas Waddell. 2006. "Securing Humans in a Dangerous World." *International Politics*, 43(1): 1–23.

Glasius, Marlies. 2006. *The International Criminal Court: A Global Civil Society Achievement.* London: Routledge.

Holt, Victoria, and Glyn Taylor. 2009. *Protecting Civilians in the Context of UN Peacekeeping Operations: An Independent Study Commissioned by the UN Office for the Coordination of Humanitarian Affairs (OCHA) and the UN Department of Peacekeeping Operations (DPKO).* New York: United Nations. Accessed December 19, 2013 from http://www.peacekeepingbestpractices.unlb.org/PBPS/Pages/Public/viewdocument.aspx?id=2&docid=1014

Howell, Jude, and Jeremy Lind, eds. 2009. "Civil society under strain: counter-terrorism policy, civil society and aid post-9/11." Connecticut, CT: Kumarian Press.

Human Rights Watch. 2004. *Human Rights and Armed Conflict.* Accessed December 19, 2013 from http://usiraq.procon.org/sourcefiles/hrw2004.pdf

Ogata, Sadako, and Amartya Sen (Co-Chairs). 2003. *Human Security Now: Report of the Commission on Human Security.* United Nations.

Human Security Report Project. 2010. "Human Security Backgrounder." Accessed April 2012 from http://www.hsrgroup.org/press-room/human-security-backgrounder.aspx

Human Security Study Group. 2004. "A Human Security Doctrine for Europe: The Barcelona Report of the Study Group on Europe's Security Capabilities." Barcelona, Spain.

ICISS. 2001. *The Responsibility to Protect (Report of the International Commission on Intervention and State Sovereignty)*. Ottawa, ON: International Development Research Centre. Accessed December 19, 2013 from http://responsibilitytoprotect.org/ICISS%20Report.pdf

Kaldor, Mary. 2001. "A Decade of Humanitarian Intervention: The Role of Global Civil Society." In *Global Civil society 2001*, edited by Helmut Anheier, Marlies Glasius, and Mary Kaldor. Oxford: Oxford University Press.

Kaldor, Mary. 2012. *New and Old Wars*. 3rd ed. Cambridge: Polity Press.

Martin, Mary. 2010. "The European Union in the Democratic Republic of Congo – a force for good?" In *The European Union and Human Security: external interventions and missions*, edited by Mary Martin and Mary Kaldor, 55–75. London: Routledge.

McCormack, Tara. 2011. "The Limits to Emancipation in the Human Security Framework." In *Critical Perspectives on Human Security: Rethinking Emancipation and Power in International Relations*, edited by David Chandler and Nik Hynek, 99–113. Abingdon: Routledge.

NATO. 2009. *Commander's Initial Assessment*, 30 August 2009. NATO International Security Assistance Force, Afghanistan, Afghan US Forces [on file with author].

Newman, Edward. 2004. "The 'New Wars' Debate: A Historical Perspective Is Needed." *Security Dialogue*, 35(2): 173–189.

Orford, Anne. 2011. *International Authority and the Responsibility to Protect*. Cambridge: Cambridge University Press.

Owen, Taylor. 2004. "Human Security – Conflict, Critique and Consensus: Colloquium Remarks and a Proposal for a Threshold-Based Definition." *Security dialogue*, 35(3): 373–387.

Rangelov, Iavor, and Ruti Teitel. 2011. "Global Civil Society and Transitional Justice" In *Global Civil Society 2011: Globality and the Absence of Justice*, edited by Martin Albrow and Hakan Seckinelgin. Basingstoke: Palgrave Macmillan.

Robinson, Fiona. 2011. *The Ethics of Care: A Feminist Approach to Human Security*. Philadelphia, PA: Temple University Press.

Rice, Condoleeza. 2000. "Campaign 2000: Promoting the National Interest." *Foreign Affairs*, Jan/Feb.

Schmitt, Carl. 1985. *Political Theology (translated by George Schwab)*. Chicago, IL: Chicago University Press.

Shani, Giorgio. 2011. "Securitizing 'Bare Life': Critical Perspectives on Human Security Discourse." In *Critical Perspectives on Human Security: Rethinking Emancipation and Power in International Relations*, edited by David Chandler and Nik Hynek, 56–68. Abingdon: Routledge.

IPRI. 2013. "SIPRI Multilateral Peace Operations Database." Accessed March 1, 2013 from http://www.sipri.org/research/conflict/pko/multilateral

United Nations. 2004. *A more secure world: Our shared responsibility*. Accessed December 19, 2013 from http://www.unrol.org/doc.aspx?n=gaA.59.565_En.pdf

United Nations Development Programme (UNDP). 1994. *Human Development Report*. New York: UNDP and Oxford University Press.

Wulf, Herbert. 2005. "The Challenges of Re-Establishing a Public Monopoly of Violence." In *A Human Security Doctrine for Europe: Project, Principles and Practicalities*, edited by Marlies Glasius and Mary Kaldor. Oxford: Routledge.

Part II Policy Arenas

Chapter 6

Nuclear Disarmament and Nonproliferation

Maria Rost Rublee

Conventional wisdom about nuclear weapons decision-making argues that nuclear policy is based on material cost-benefit calculations, with systemic forces propelling states into a narrow range of choices. Nuclear proliferation is unsurprising, given the anarchical state system; nonproliferation will succeed only if the great powers can enforce it through a system of benefits and sanctions; disarmament is both unlikely and undesirable. This chapter examines conventional wisdom on all counts and finds it wanting. Nuclear weapons decision-making is more than a simple response to material conditions; ideational influences, including norms, psychology, language and beliefs, shape global nuclear futures in incontrovertible ways. As a result, nuclear proliferation is rare, nonproliferation is more often embraced than forced, and the issue of disarmament has become more, not less, potent.

This chapter specifically focuses on the latter two topics, nonproliferation and disarmament, both neglected by conventional scholarship. First, these ambiguous and sometimes overlapping terms will be examined: what exactly is meant by disarmament and nonproliferation? Next, the chapter will explore each topic in-depth before moving into an exploration of the future frontiers in research on the topic. What can new perspectives on disarmament and nonproliferation add to global security policy debates? The chapter ends with comparative conclusions, examining how trends from related disarmament treaties may shape global nuclear futures.

Deconstructing Nonproliferation and Disarmament

The distinction between nuclear nonproliferation and disarmament seems clear-cut: nonproliferation refers to prevention of state acquisition of nuclear weapons, whereas disarmament refers to a state's relinquishment of actual nuclear weapons

The Handbook of Global Security Policy, First Edition. Edited by Mary Kaldor and Iavor Rangelov.
© 2014 John Wiley & Sons, Ltd. Published 2014 by John Wiley & Sons, Ltd.

and the accompanying military nuclear program. However, in both the academic and policy literature, the distinctions are often blurred, as Burford notes:

> Theorists have often been vague about whether they are addressing nuclear nonproliferation or nuclear disarmament in their accounts of nuclear decision making. This is exemplified by the insouciance with which scholars interchangeably use terms such as restraint, forbearance, rollback, denuclearisation, nonproliferation, disarmament, and more recently, deproliferation. These terms have been used in cases which variously involve the conscious restraint from a decision to acquire nuclear weapons; a decision to renounce an established nuclear weapons programme not yet come to fruition; the reduction or complete dismantlement of existing arsenals; or surrender of nuclear weapons inherited from other countries. (Burford, 2013, p. 4)

There are only four cases of nuclear disarmament: South Africa and the three former Soviet republics (Ukraine, Kazakhstan, and Belarus), which inherited Soviet nuclear weapons after the collapse of the regime. Nevertheless, these cases tend to be lumped together with cases of nuclear rollback by scholars without any distinction between the different processes of nonproliferation and disarmament. In addition, the messiness of reality blurs the categories because whether the Ukraine, Kazakhstan, and Belarus can be truly considered disarmament is a matter for debate, given that the countries' leaders never made a decision to acquire nuclear weapons and did not have access codes to use the weapons once inherited.

Distinguishing between nuclear nonproliferation and disarmament is important for both theoretical and policy reasons.[1] One cannot assume that motivations for nonproliferation will also explain motivations for disarmament. Acquiring nuclear weapons irreversibly changes a state, from the public prestige (or scorn) that accrues to the domestic bureaucracy that forms to manage and maintain the weapons program. Reversing that type of decision will involve a different set of processes than the processes involved in nuclear restraint. The policy importance of separating nonproliferation from disarmament flows from this analysis: policymakers and activists who want to encourage disarmament will need to go beyond the policies that have successfully promoted nonproliferation.

Nevertheless, the distinctions between the concepts of nonproliferation and disarmament do not negate the deep and complex relationship between them. Serious discussion and action in nuclear nonproliferation and disarmament concentrated heavily on the nonproliferation side of the bargain, but the end of the Cold War brought optimism for more equal progress. Multiple challenges, however, overwhelmed the push for global nuclear disarmament, from concern over nuclear weapons programs by state members of the Nuclear Non-Proliferation Treaty (NPT, North Korea and Iraq) to nuclear weapons tests by two NPT holdout states (India and Pakistan). In particular, the administration of George W. Bush focused heavily on nonproliferation, to the exclusion of global disarmament negotiations. For example, at the 2004 NPT PrepCom, US Under-Secretary of State John Bolton argued that states were focusing on Article VI violations "that did not exist" (Wurst, 2004). It is not hard to understand the frustration of non-nuclear weapons states that wanted balance between the obligation of nonproliferation and the obligation of disarmament.

However, just as it was mistaken to focus exclusively on nonproliferation, it would also be incorrect to focus entirely on disarmament to the exclusion of nonproliferation. Indeed, global nuclear disarmament is impossible without success in nuclear nonproliferation. Should Iran acquire and operationalize nuclear weapons, the likelihood of Israel disarming falls to almost zero – and several other states in the Middle East may rush to join Iran as nuclear powers (Kaye and Wehrey, 2007). The task of disarmament grows more difficult with each additional state that joins the nuclear club. Surprise and stringent inspections of civilian nuclear facilities ensures countries do not cheat and create a nuclear "break-out" capability; just as important, the inspections create confidence in the global community that nuclear power is not being used for nuclear weapons. This creates a positive environment for disarmament because nuclear weapons states are unlikely to disarm if they fear others are engaging in nuclear hedging. Inspections also foster greater global confidence in the International Atomic Energy Agency (IAEA), the likely candidate to verify disarmament measures such as the Fissile Material Cut-Off Treaty (FMCT). Certainly, the bargain swings the other way as well: non-nuclear weapons states are less likely to adhere to strict rules and inspections if the nuclear weapons states do not show progress on their obligations. Nuclear disarmament and nonproliferation require each other.

Nuclear Nonproliferation

History of the Nuclear Nonproliferation Regime

Less than a year after the United States conducted its first nuclear test, Washington presented the first plan for nuclear nonproliferation to the United Nations. In June 1946, the United States proposed the Baruch Plan, which argued for international oversight of all civilian nuclear programs and international control of any nuclear facilities that could be used to create nuclear weapons. One of the primary purposes of the plan was to prevent any other states from acquiring nuclear weapons. In addition, the United States pledged to disarm after international control was established. The Soviet Union rejected the plan, in part due to its skepticism that the United States would actually disarm.

Later negotiations for agreements related to nuclear weapons were significantly more modest than the Baruch Plan. After the United States and the Soviet Union began testing hydrogen bombs (1952 and 1953, respectively), the concern over radioactive fallout led to negotiations for a nuclear test ban treaty. By August 1955, the world's first conference protesting nuclear weapons was held in Hiroshima. The next year, the US Democratic presidential candidate, Adalai Stevenson, proposed an end to above-ground nuclear tests (Bunn, 1992). While Eisenhower dismissed the proposal when he was reelected, "considerable pressure by powerful popular movements" prodded him to begin expert talks with the Soviets on the possibility of an enforceable test ban (Müller, Fischer, and Kötter, 1994, p. 18). These grassroots movements – composed of diverse elements such as intellectuals, scientists, students, religious organizations, pacifists, and housewives – led Eisenhower to remark in August 1958, "The new thermonuclear weapons are tremendously powerful; however, they are not … as powerful as is world opinion today in obliging the United States to follow certain lines of policy" (Tannenwald, 2001, p. 65).

By 1962, the negotiations were formalized in the United Nations' Eighteen-Nation Disarmament Committee (ENDC). Within a year, the Partial Test Ban Treaty had been concluded. In July 1968, the NPT was opened for signature and entered into force in 1970. The treaty's nonproliferation provisions have been quite successful. Since 1970, only four states have developed nuclear weapons (India, Pakistan, North Korea, and Israel), although some argue that Israel had obtained the bomb as early as 1967. However, the nuclear weapons states' promise to engage in good faith nego- tiations for nuclear disarmament has been more disappointing, as will be discussed later in the chapter.

The Causes of Nuclear Restraint

For decades the literature on nuclear policy was dominated by discussions of nuclear proliferation: strategy and deterrence, nuclear rivalries, and the causes of nuclear acquisition. Only recently has the academic community begun to seriously examine the causes of nuclear restraint. As I argue elsewhere,

> Why have so many states abstained from nuclear weapons, why do a few continue to pursue them against all odds? Of all the states in the today's world, the fact that only four have "gone nuclear" since the introduction of the NPT is a fact pregnant with potential for both theoretical and policy insights. If we can understand what influenced these states – those with the motive, means and opportunity to develop nuclear weapons but that instead abstained – we will be much better prepared to handle today's potential proliferators. (Rublee, 2009, pp. 1–2)

Researchers have focused both on different substantive reasons and different levels of analysis to understand state decisions to remain non-nuclear. In terms of substantive content, arguments have been made about the importance of traditional security con- cerns (such as great power pressure and security alliances), economic orientations, and ideational factors (including the impact of norms and elite psychology).

Realist explanations about nuclear restraint revolve around explaining why the proliferation predicted by the theory has failed to materialize. The basic tenets of realism – anarchy and self-help – combine to create powerful incentives for states to achieve the maximum military capability possible. If the international system makes cooperation unlikely and self-reliance imperative, then acquiring nuclear weapons is the most reasonable response by a rational state. However, the power- ful structural arguments of realism do not match up to the empirical record, as T.V. Paul notes:

> To begin with, hard realists, based on their assumption of anarchy, argue that cooper- ation is difficult if not impossible in the security area. The empirical evidence – i.e., the cooperation thus far developed in non-proliferation – challenges this basic argument. Many states, both capable and not so capable of producing nuclear weapons, have adhered to the regime, which takes away part of their sovereignty in this matter. It seems that the number of countries that acquired nuclear weapons from the original five is so small that these cases seem more like an anomaly than the norm. (Paul, 2000, p. 8)

Realists respond to the surprising lack of proliferation through a variety of theoretical explanations. Benjamin Frankel argues that the Cold War bipolarity artificially reduced proliferation, but after the collapse of the Soviet Union, proliferation would increase because multipolarity increases uncertainty, making states less likely to depend on alliances and security guarantees (Frankel, 1993, p. 38). In fact, Mearsheimer predicted just such a spread of nuclear weapons in Europe after the end of the Cold War because of "substantial incentives" that non-nuclear states will have in order to acquire a nuclear deterrent. Not only will small states seek nuclear weapons to avoid blackmail by Russia, Mearsheimer predicted, but Germany would also feel insecure without its own nuclear force (Mearsheimer, 1990, p. 37). However, again realist predictions failed to materialize. Since the end of the Cold War, only three states have joined the nuclear club (India, Pakistan, and North Korea), whereas seven states gave up nuclear weapons or serious nuclear weapons programs (South Africa, Ukraine, Belarus, Kazakhstan, Argentina, Brazil, and Libya).

Another popular realist argument explaining the lack of proliferation is security guarantees. While strong states balance against threats by developing indigenous nuclear capability, weaker states are more likely to balance by aligning with a powerful, nuclear-armed ally. Clearly, credible security guarantees have been an important component of nuclear decision-making in states such as Japan and Germany. However, security guarantees alone cannot explain nonproliferation. At what point did Japan and Germany move from "weak" to "strong," and why didn't their nuclear decision-making change at that point? Why have some weak states managed, against all odds, to create their own nuclear deterrent? More to the heart of realist assumptions, however, is the question to what extent can a security guarantee truly be credible to a survival-conscious state? As Jacques Hymans argues,

> It is hard to see why, from a realist perspective, anything less than an indigenous nuclear arsenal would be sufficient to deter outside threats. Realists spent the entire Cold War bemoaning the lack of credibility of extended deterrence: Could anyone really expect us to trade New York for Berlin? (Hymans, 2006a, p. 456)

The lack of credibility springs from the realist focus on self-help. Mearsheimer argues that while self-help does not rule out alliances, "alliances are only temporary marriages of convenience, where today's alliance partner might be tomorrow's enemy, and today's enemy might be tomorrow's alliance partner" (Mearsheimer, 1994/1995, p. 11). Thus, if today's friend could be tomorrow's enemy, why would you trust anyone for a nuclear guarantee? Ultimately, realism offers powerful structural explanations for proliferation, but its attempts to deal with nonproliferation do not match the empirical record or fundamental realist assumptions.

Another important explanation for nuclear nonproliferation can be found in the work of Etel Solingen, whose economic arguments posed the first major challenge to realist orthodoxy. Solingen argues that economic orientations of domestic coalitions shape state nuclear decision-making:

> Leaders or ruling coalitions advocating economic growth through integration in the global economy have incentives to avoid the costs of nuclearization, which impair domestic reforms favoring internationalization. By contrast, nuclearization implies

fewer costs for inward-looking leaders and for constituencies less dependent on inter-national markets, investment, technology, and institutions, who can rely on nuclear weapons programs to reinforce nationalist platforms of political survival. (Solingen, 2007, p. 17)

Thus, strategies of domestic survival led to the practice of nonproliferation in East Asia, while proliferation became the dominant norm in the Middle East. Solingen positions her arguments within the "world time" after 1968, when the NPT opened for ratification. In doing so, she elevates the importance of the NPT, but in her anal-ysis, leaves the impact of the NPT unexamined. As Scott Sagan notes, her

> "focus on the post-1968 NPT world time, however, makes it more puzzling that Solin-gen denigrates the role of the treaty and does not examine whether the NPT was nec-essary for "liberalizing" governments to be concerned that movement toward a nuclear weapons program would lead to international sanctions or other restrictions on the potential benefits from integrating into the global economy" (Sagan, 2011, p. 236).

Another problem with a narrow focus on economic incentives is that Solingen misses the identity and normative-based drivers that shape domestic coalitions' decisions about nuclear weapons. These coalitions are not acting on solely rational economic concerns, but rather a broader set of ideas about either being part of the international community or autarkic rejection of Western philosophies of progress and modern-ization (Rublee, 2009, pp. 11–13).

The newest research about nuclear forbearance looks to ideational causes, whether beliefs, culture, or norms. The two main authors who focus on ideational reasons for nuclear nonproliferation are Jacques Hymans and Maria Rost Rublee. Both authors blend constructivism and social psychology, and both argue for the importance of understanding individual beliefs. There, however, the similarities end. Hymans contends that we shouldn't question why so few states have nuclear weapons, but rather why any states at all have nuclear weapons. Acquiring nuclear weapons is a "leap in the dark", and few elites are willing to risk such a revolutionary choice. What drives those who do make the leap is a psychological identity profile of oppositional nationalist:

> Oppositional nationalists see their nation as both naturally at odds with an external enemy, and as naturally its equal if not its superior. Such a conception tends to gen-erate the emotions of fear and pride – an explosive psychological cocktail. Driven by fear and pride, oppositional nationalists develop a desire for nuclear weapons that goes beyond calculation, to self-expression. Thus, in spite of the tremendous complexity of the nuclear choice, leaders who decide for the bomb tend not to back into it. For them, unlike the bulk of their peers, the choice for nuclear weapons is neither a close call nor a possible last resort but an absolute necessity (Hyman, 2006b, p. 2).

Hymans's in-depth research into four country's nuclear choices (France, India, Aus-tralia, and Argentina) makes a powerful case for the importance of the oppositional nationalist leader in driving proliferation. But his conclusions are less than satisfying when it comes to understanding nonproliferation. When elites who are not oppo-sitional nationalists express interest in nuclear weapons programs, Hymans would argue that they are not seriously interested and would not commit to a full-fledged program. But serious progress on nuclear weapons can be made in such instances, and given that experts have identified up to 14 cases of nuclear rollback, it would be unwise to dismiss the proliferation implications of such work. In addition, the policy recommendations from Hymans' work are disconcerting. If proliferation is limited because of elite psychology, rather than the nonproliferation regime, can we ignore the many hard questions involved in strengthening the regime, such as whether to universalize the Additional Protocol, which allows for unannounced and intrusive inspections of state nuclear facilities? As Jeffrey Lantis notes, "Hymans' singular focus on the revolutionary decision means that 'ancillary questions' are moved to the margins of the study. Yet, decisions regarding these questions seem every bit as relevant as the ultimate order to build nuclear weapons" (Lantis, 2007, p. 651).

Although I also focus on ideational causes for nuclear nonproliferation, my work emphasizes the importance of systemic factors, in particular, the international social environment created by the nuclear nonproliferation regime. The nonproliferation norm, embedded in the NPT, has changed not only state cost-benefit equations when considering nuclear weapons, but also has transformed the way some state elites conceptualize the value of nuclear weapons (Rublee, 2009). Thus, nonproliferation policies cannot be taken for granted; if the NPT and associated norm is weakened, state thinking on military nuclear capability is likely to shift in response. My work also draws from the social psychology literature to create a framework through which analysts can measure whether norms are actually influencing elite decisions (Rublee, 2008). Particularly in democracies, antinuclear peace groups, using the international norm to gain credibility, were critical in raising the political costs for conservative elites to go nuclear. Indeed, Malet contends that this line of argument points to a need for a deeper focus on the norm entrepreneurs responsible for shifting debate: "If states are to use social psychology to prevent proliferation – whether through persuasion, the pressure of social conformity, or in fostering new identifications as responsible international actors – it will be necessary to identify the best messengers or interlocutors" (Malet, 2010, p. 70).

Restraint, Hedging, or Ambiguity?

Nonetheless, some analysts raise questions about whether "restraint" is the best characterization for the lack of proliferation today. In particular, two authors have offered innovative interpretations for limited nuclear proliferation: Ariel Levite and Itty Abraham. Levite argues that nuclear restraint may better be understood as nuclear hedging, "a national strategy of maintaining, or at least appearing to maintain, a viable option for the relatively rapid acquisition of nuclear weapons, based on an indigenous technical capacity to produce them within a relatively short time frame ranging from several weeks to a few years" (Levite, 2003, p. 69). Article VI of the NPT allows non-nuclear weapons states to acquire nuclear technology for civilian purposes, including uranium enrichment and plutonium reprocessing facilities. This same technology can be used to create nuclear weapons, and a state with very advanced civilian nuclear facilities could potentially withdraw from the NPT and create nuclear weapons within months. Being able to deliver those nuclear weapons through reliable means is another matter, but more than one country has come under suspicion because of its advanced civilian nuclear complex, including Japan and Brazil (Rublee, 2010). Nevertheless, ascribing motives of nuclear hedging to a country because of civilian nuclear programs is problematic. While it is true that politicians in both Japan and Brazil have made comments about nuclear acquisition, these are individuals who, by themselves, have no real influence over the scientific, energy, diplomatic, and military bureaucracies that would need to be marshaled to create serious nuclear weapons programs (Hughes, 2007). In addition, societal barriers in countries must be acknowledged; for example, talking in a pro-nuclear fashion in Japan still can wreak havoc on a politician's career, at least in the short term (Rublee, 2009). An advanced nuclear industry may provide psychological comfort for conservative elites who wish for an indigenous nuclear capacity, but by itself, it is only one of the necessary building blocks of a military nuclear capacity.

Indeed, innovative analysis by Itty Abraham points to the fact that concern over "hedging" and "restraint" may actually push countries toward proliferation. Abraham argues that what is typically termed restraint or hedging may actually be ambiguity: elites may be undecided or have not committed to any particular nuclear choice. The nature of nuclear technology is such that "both war and peace are always present in the meanings attributed to nuclear programs" (Abraham, 2006, p. 56). Ambivalence, then, is central to "nuclear", rather than a half-completed state or a failure to know enough about intentions. But because of the academic and policy focus on proliferation, "the multiple meanings of nuclear power are shrunk into one register – the desire to produce weapons" (Abraham, 2009, p. 117). The resulting distorted analysis turns every nuclear program into a possible weapons program, leading to increased restrictions and surveillance – and resentment. In addition, "[T]his reinforces the particular aura of nuclear weapons to be coveted and desired, the very opposite effect sought by policy makers concerned with nuclear proliferation" (Abraham, 2009, p. 117). According to this logic, nonproliferation policies may be responsible for actual proliferation.

Nuclear Disarmament

History of Negotiations for Nuclear Disarmament

While the history of nuclear nonproliferation is largely a success story, the history of nuclear disarmament is often painted as a failure. More than 40 years after the NPT entered into force, the numbers are not encouraging: none of the five original nuclear weapons states have disarmed; an additional four states currently have nuclear weapons; as of 2102, approximately 19,000 nuclear weapons remain (Ploughshares Foundation, 2012). After the failure of the Baruch Plan in 1946, the Cold War stifled serious discussion of nuclear disarmament for the major powers. After the end of the Cold War, movement on disarmament has been slow and halting, and even recently, despite the full support of US President Barak Obama, gains have been few and disappointing.

While factual, such a broad-brush portrayal of the record on disarmament misses numerous important achievements. For example, nuclear-weapon-free zones (NWFZ) have carved out regional disarmament zones since the late 1960s. The first NWFZ, the Treaty of Tlatelolco, entered into force in 1969, covering Latin America and the Caribbean (BASIC and Oxford Research Group, 2005). Since then, four other NWFZs have been negotiated and entered into force: the Treaty of Rarotonga (1986, covering South Pacific, Australia, and New Zealand), the Treaty of Bangkok (1997, Southeast Asia), the Treaty of Pelindaba (2009, Africa), and the Treaty on a Nuclear-Weapon-Free Zone in Central Asia (2009). In addition, Mongolia declared itself a single-state NWFZ in 1992, and uninhabited areas (including Antarctica, the sea bed, the moon, and outer space) are also de facto NWFZs. NWFZ treaties prohibit the development, acquisition, and possession of nuclear weapons, as well as assistance with research for any of these tasks (Magnarella, 2008, p. 511). As a result, their spread creates "geographical areas that are completely free of nuclear weapons and thereby constitute steps towards a nuclear-weapon-free world" (Center for Nonproliferation Studies, 2010). Today, this disarmament zone extends over 116 countries and the entire Southern hemisphere. Until and unless a nuclear weapons convention is negotiated (discussed next), NWFZ may be the best tool for the promotion of nuclear disarmament.

Another significant disarmament achievement was brought about during the height of the Cold War by unparalleled public protests. In the 1980s, mass public demonstrations against nuclear weapons in both Europe and the United States led to significant policy changes and new disarmament initiatives. Within America, the nuclear freeze movement began as a grassroots movement focused on the local level, but quickly became the largest citizen's movement in the United States up to that time. In response, US President Ronald Reagan was compelled into dropping his opposition to nuclear arms control (Wittner, 2010). European leaders faced perhaps even greater pressure from the antinuclear mass movement. The 1979 NATO decision to pursue the development of intermediate-range nuclear forces (INF) led to the largest demonstrations in history for multiple European countries, including Britain, Belgium, and Germany. Both besieged and traumatized by the unprecedented protests, European leaders pressured Washington into making concessions in negotiations for an INF treaty. By 1987, the Soviets and the Americans signed the INF treaty, the first treaty to completely ban an entire class of nuclear weapons. As Wittner notes,

> Boxed in by the movement and Gorbachev, Reagan and his successor, George H.W. Bush, were drawn into the most substantial burst of nuclear arms control and disarmament ventures in history. By the early 1990s, the United States and the Soviet Union had ceased the testing, development, and deployment of nuclear weapons and had reduced their nuclear arsenals. (Wittner, 2010)

The indefinite extension of NPT in 1995, and resulting commitments for disarmament in 2000, can also be counted as disarmament achievements. Originally negotiated for a period of 25 years, in 1994 the NPT faced either another extension of a specific period or indefinite extension. Many non-nuclear weapons states felt agreeing to indefinite extension would give up their only leverage for disarmament. As Squassoni notes,

> When states met in 1995 to decide whether or not to extend the NPT indefinitely, it was important to obtain a serious commitment to disarmament steps by the nuclear-weapon states. In fact, it is doubtful that the NPT would have been extended indefinitely in 1995 without such a commitment. (Squassoni, 2009, p. 2)

At the Review Conference, states agreed on several steps toward disarmament, including early conclusion of the Comprehensive Test Ban Treaty, and the treaty was indefinitely extended. Just three years after the Review Conference, a cross-cutting group of states formed the New Agenda Coalition (NAC) with the goal of pressing the nuclear weapons states for concrete movement on disarmament. Composed of Brazil, Egypt, Ireland, Mexico, New Zealand, Africa, and Sweden, the NAC included US friends and allies and thus could not be easily dismissed as a grouping of states composed only of member of the nonaligned movement. At the next NPT Review Conference in 2000, the NAC was able to pressure the nuclear weapons states into a commitment of thirteen practical steps for nuclear disarmament, including "unequivocal undertaking by the nuclear-weapon States to accomplish the total elimination of their nuclear arsenals leading to nuclear disarmament to which all States parties are committed under Article VI" (United Nations, 2000, p. 14).

While disarmament took a back seat during the administration of US President George W. Bush, the election of Barak Obama propelled global zero back to the top of the agenda. With the election of US President Barak Obama, however, the tone underwent another dramatic shift. Just months after his inauguration, Obama declared that the United States was committed to a world without nuclear weapons. In his famous Prague speech in April 2009, he said, "as nuclear power – as a nuclear power, as the only nuclear power to have used a nuclear weapon, the United States has a moral responsibility to act. We cannot succeed in this endeavor alone, but we can lead it, we can start it" (The White House, 2009). Despite a hostile reception from many Republicans, Obama's work was supported by earlier calls for disarmament from unlikely allies: the four horsemen (Henry Kissinger, George Shultz, William Perry, and Sam Nunn), who jointly published an opinion piece in the *Wall Street Journal* entitled "A World Free of Nuclear Weapons" in 2007 and then a follow-up piece in 2008. The foreign policy giants argued that unless the United States seriously pursued disarmament, we would end up with a much more proliferated world.

While the change in discourse in Washington was enabling, similar changes occurred around the world. Australia announced the International Commission on Nuclear Non-Proliferation and Disarmament, co-chaired by former Australian and Japanese foreign ministers Gareth Evans and Yoriko Kawaguchi. The Commission was especially focused on empirical opportunities and roadblocks to disarmament (Hanson, 2012). A number of NATO members were able to force the security organization to confront questions about the necessity of tactical nuclear weapons in Europe. Within Britain, debate over renewal of the Trident submarines – the United Kingdom's only delivery vehicle for nuclear weapons – led to serious discussion about possible unilateral disarmament.

Perhaps the most remarkable disarmament achievement is the serious discussion of a Nuclear Weapons Convention (NWC), which would ban the development or possession of nuclear weapons. Taking their cue from the success of the land mine ban treaty and the cluster munitions treaty, a group of like-minded states and activists argued that the NPT lacks the force to compel the nuclear weapons states to give up their military nuclear capability, and the best option open to the international community is to pursue a NWC. At the 2010 RevCon, outspoken states such as Austria and Switzerland raised the NWC forcefully; for the first time, the final document referenced a possible NWC. While endorsement of a NWC was not possible due to opposition from some nuclear weapons states, the final language on disarmament commitments was not unsubstantial:

> The Conference affirms that the final phase of the nuclear disarmament process and other related measures should be pursued within an agreed legal framework, which a majority of States parties believe should include specified timelines. (NPT/CONF.2010/ 50 Vol. I: 13)

With nuclear disarmament seriously on the table for the first time, both friends and critics began to analyze obstacles to getting to zero. In the space of a few years, the academic literature on the topic blossomed (see, for example, Perkovich and Action, 2009; Sagan *et al.*, 2010, O'Hanlon, 2010; Blechman and Bollfrass, 2010; Kelleher and Reppy, 2011; Burford, 2012; Ogivile-White and Santoro, 2012). The academic literature on disarmament has focused on two key questions: is disarmament desirable, and is it achievable?

Is Disarmament Desirable?

The first debate raised by the serious consideration of nuclear disarmament is whether it is even desirable. In his Prague speech, Obama committed the United States to "seek the peace and security of a world without nuclear weapons," but critics say that a world without nuclear weapons will have neither peace nor security. In fact, as realist Ken Waltz says, "Those who like peace should love nuclear weapons" (Sagan and Waltz, 2010, p. 93). Disarmament critics offer two main arguments for why global zero is undesirable. First is the argument pioneered by Waltz, that nuclear weapons reduce the possibility of war. Countries with nuclear weapons will not use them against other nuclear-armed states because of fear over mutually assured destruction. Moreover, states are very unlikely to start conventional wars with nuclear weapons states: non-nuclear states do not want to pick fights with a nuclear-armed opponent, and a country with military nuclear capability would hesitate to attack another nuclear state for fear the conflict could lead to a nuclear exchange.

Many experts disagree with Waltz's assessment of the value of nuclear weapons. Chief among his critics is Scott Sagan, who argues that Waltz misreads history. Nuclear-armed countries have fought each other: the 1999 Kargil conflict between India and Pakistan led to more than one thousand military deaths. As Sagan notes, "The Kargil war occurred not *despite* Pakistan developing nuclear weapons but rather *because* Pakistan got the bomb. Pakistani generals thought that their new nuclear arsenal was a shield behind which they could safely sneak Pakistani soldiers into Indian-controlled Kashmir without triggering a war" (Sagan and Waltz, 2010, p. 94, emphasis in original). In addition, proponents of nuclear weapons ignore the organizational and human facets of command and control (Sagan and Waltz, 2003); weapons are managed and guarded by human beings, who make mistakes and could be tempted by money or ideology to transfer sensitive nuclear materials. Nuclear disarmament is the only way to ensure this does not happen.

The second key critique is that global zero may actually cause nuclear proliferation. As Evangelista notes, some argue that nuclear weapons have not spread because of the stability brought about by extended nuclear deterrence, in particular the US nuclear umbrella (Evangelista, 2011). If the United States makes deep cuts to its nuclear forces as it moves toward disarmament, this could generate concern among allies over America's ability to protect them – and thus could stimulate nuclear proliferation as allies seek their own indigenous nuclear deterrent (Kyl and Perle, 2009). While the argument has been applied to a number of allies, including Australia and Turkey, the main focus of concern is Japan, which relies on US extended deterrence and faces nuclear threats from North Korea and China. However, this argument does not hold up to scrutiny. It assumes that nuclear choices are determined by systemic strategic forces; a nuclear withdrawal by the United States would mean a necessary nuclear step forward by the countries involved. However, as the literature on nuclear restraint demonstrates, systemic security concerns are filtered and given meaning through regional, domestic, and even individual conditions, both material and normative. As Llewelyn Hughes argues about the "hard" case of Japan, "a hollowing out of the U.S. deterrent is unlikely to automatically translate into the inclusion of a nuclear deterrent within Japan's force structure" (Hughes, 2007, p. 96).

Is Disarmament Achievable?

Another key debate about nuclear disarmament is whether it is actually technically feasible. As Catherine Kelleher notes, the question that critics often ask, "Can we really restore the genie to its bottle, given the global spread of civil nuclear technologies, the near instantaneous distribution of technical literature, and a global commerce system poised to deliver any and all necessary components through a myriad of legal and illegal channels?" (Kelleher, 2011, p. 3). The technical difficulties are numerous, but can be collapsed into two main problems: reaching and then maintaining global zero. First, how do we ensure all current nuclear weapons are destroyed? How can it be confirmed that all nuclear weapons states actually dismantle all of their weapons and dispose of their weapons-grade fissile material? Second, once global zero is achieved, how do we ensure that no new nuclear weapons are built? The most difficult step in building a military nuclear capacity is the creation of fissile material: either uranium-235 or plutonium-239. While most technologies available today to create weapons-grade fissile material are detectable, some are easier to hide than others. For example, South Africa used jet nozzle technology to secretly create enough enriched uranium for a handful of atomic bombs. Waltz comments that even if the international community were able to verify nuclear disarmament, "one state or another might eventually come to believe that it faced a threat to its very existence. A mad scramble to rearm with nuclear weapons would then take place" (Sagan and Waltz, 2010, p. 93).

Analysts who support movement toward disarmament do not underestimate the challenges that verification will pose. As Trevor Findlay argues,

> The verification and compliance regime for a nuclear weapon-free world will need to be more effective than any disarmament arrangement hitherto envisaged. One hundred per cent verification of compliance with any international arms agreement is highly improbable. In the case of nuclear disarmament, however, the security stakes will be so high that states will not agree to disarm and to disavow future acquisition of nuclear weapons unless verification reduces to a minimum the risk of non-compliance. (Findlay, 2003, p. 2)

Nevertheless, the sense of realism about the magnitude of the obstacles does not dampen enthusiasm that the technical verification challenges can be overcome. First, some question whether perfect verification will be necessary. As Perkovich and Acton muse, "If, as zero is approached, robust verification finds no unresolvable indications of possible cheating and states become convinced that each truly intends to fulfill the agreement, they might no longer require such stringent verification" (Perkovich and Acton, 2009, p. 52). Next, scholars and scientists have just begun to apply considerable talent and energy to disarmament obstacles, and they have already begun to make inroads. Developing nuclear weapons requires creating fissile material, either highly enriched uranium or plutonium – a process that is detectable. For example, recent advances in mass spectrometry have enabled the IAEA to detect fissile material at levels ten times lower than previously possible, and thus increasing the agency's ability to detect cheating (IAEA, 2012). Another example can be found in the work of the United Kingdom, Norway, and the nongovernmental organization VERTIC on verification of nuclear warhead dismantlement, illustrating how fruitful cooperation can be in solving seemingly intractable technical and political problems associated with disarmament (Ritchie, 2010). Finally, Donald MacKenzie and Graham Spinardi argue that nuclear weapons may not be easily redeveloped once successfully banned because of the importance of tacit knowledge ("embodied in people rather than words, equations, or diagrams") to nuclear weapons development. They contend, "If design ceases, and if there is no new generation of designers to whom that tacit knowledge can be passed, then in an important (though qualified) sense nuclear weapons will have been uninvented" (MacKenzie and Spinardi, 1995, p. 44).

New Frontiers in Policy and Research

Nuclear politics will dominate headlines for years to come, and the academic literature will continue to proliferate as scholars attempt to understand and solve key global nuclear issues. Several new openings in research deserve special attention for their policy relevance and/or theoretical innovations.

Questioning Deterrence

Nuclear deterrence lies at the heart of realist thinking on the atomic bomb; without it, the logic may collapse like a house of cards. But is nuclear deterrence "real", or is it a social construct that has become embedded in policy without justification? These questions are not new. More than 20 years ago, Mary Kaldor argued that deterrence served an ideational function, allowing political and military elites to create an imaginary war through which they could exert control. "[D]eterrence, instead of preventing war, actually turns out to be a way of keeping the idea of war and the idea of a conflict alive, either to legitimize the growth of military forces or for domestic or intra-bloc purposes" (Kaldor, 1990, p. 194). Today's scholars have developed numerous other creative analyses to disturb the idea of "deterrence". Ward Wilson has provocatively argued that the fundamental assumptions behind deterrence are unsound:

> [T]hree practical arguments put the efficacy of nuclear deterrence into doubt: 1) the characteristic attack threatened in most nuclear deterrence scenarios – city attack – is not militarily effective or likely to be decisive; 2) the psychology of terror that is supposed

to work in nuclear deterrence's favor actually creates the circumstances for unremitting resistance; and 3) even though the field is mostly conjectural, what little unambiguous evidence does exist contradicts the claim that nuclear deterrence works. (Wilson, 2008, p. 421)

If the logic behind deterrence is unpersuasive, why has it carried so much weight, for so long? Applying Karl Marx's discussion of commodity fetishism, Anne Harrington de Santana argues deterrence has remained unquestioned because nuclear weapons have become fetish objects.

> [N]uclear weapons are the embodiment of power. Just as access to wealth in the form of money determines an individual's opportunities and place in a social hierarchy, access to power in the form of nuclear weapons determines a state's opportunities and place in the international order. In both cases, the physical form of the fetish object is valuable because it serves as a carrier of social value. In other words, the power of nuclear weapons is not reducible to their explosive capability. Nuclear weapons are powerful because we treat them as powerful. (Harrington de Santana, 2009, p. 327).

In challenging the conventional wisdom of nuclear deterrence, these and other authors have questioned unexamined assumptions and in doing so, forced significant rethinking of the value of nuclear weapons.[2]

Norm Entrepreneurs: Promoting Both Disarmament and Proliferation?

Martha Finnemore and Kathryn Sikkink's seminal article (1998) on the norm life cycle spurred enormous interest in applying the concept to international relations, particularly the concept of norm entrepreneurs. While some scholars have analyzed nuclear politics through the framework of norms (Tannenwald, 2007; Rublee, 2009; Lantis, 2011), surprisingly little work has been done on the drivers of change in nuclear norms. A strong literature on civil society and nuclear protest does exist, for example, Lawrence Wittner's three-volume set, *The Struggle Against the Bomb* (1993, 1997, 2003) and Jeffrey Knopf's *Domestic Society and International Cooperation* (1998). But in terms of analyzing normative change through the framework of norm entrepreneurs, less work has been done. Rublee examines how antinuclear norm entrepreneurs might interact with international organizations to advance their goals (2011); Carmen Wunderlich explores Iran as an advocate of nuclear norms (2011); Malfrid Braut-Hegghammer focuses on how nuclear entrepreneurs can drive proliferation (2009); and Karl-Erik Passonen (2007) documents the successful tactics that activists used against uranium mining in the Northern Territory of Australia. Nonetheless, more research is needed to explore the questions, how and through what methods can individuals outside of the state apparatus dramatically shape the meaning of "nuclear weapons" through normative argumentation?

The Individual: Future Plains of Research

The bulk of scholarly work on nuclear proliferation uses realism, which seeks to understand nuclear politics through systemic security drivers. This trend has slowly turned toward a greater theoretical focus on other variables, including economic conditions, domestic coalitions, normative concerns, institutional constraints, and even supply and demand. Few theoretically informed works, however, have specifically spotlighted the role of individuals in nuclear decision-making; some notable exceptions include Matthew Evangelista's analysis of the importance of scientists in US–Soviet arms control discussions (1999), Peter Lavoy's exploration of nuclear "mythmakers," individuals who have the access and ability to promote the mythical qualities of nuclear weapons to decision makers (2006), and Hymans's focus on psychological characteristics of decision-makers (2006b). The lack of attention to individuals may be in part due to the dominance of realism, but also due to the more general neglect of the first image in international relations.

However, in nuclear politics, it is time for a renaissance for the individual level of analysis – to bring the individual back in. The field needs to curtail its unending gaze on the state, and researchers need to deconstruct some of the basic ways of thinking about nuclear politics. Rather than seeing it as an inevitable march towards a state's security interests – complete with all the post-hoc justifications – people have an unrelenting and undeniable influence on what we call "nuclear politics". The extension of work on norm entrepreneurs is an excellent start, but this type of project requires more than just inserting a few footnotes about individuals in the state-centered study of nuclear politics.

Hymans contributes to such a project in his latest work *Achieving Nuclear Ambitions: Scientists, Politicians and Proliferation* (2012). He argues that management style may have as much to do with nuclear weapons success as any other variable. Sara Kutchesfahani (2010) focuses on the importance of epistemic communities in persuading elites to pursue nonproliferation policies. Jan Ruzicka and Nicholas Wheeler (2010) present intriguing hypotheses on the importance of trust in the nuclear nonproliferation regime; this work would be applicable in looking at relationships between key individuals (diplomats, scientists, decision makers) in nuclear negotiations. My recent work (Rublee, 2012) takes a broad look at antinuclear advocacy – focusing on individuals – to understand the tactics, strategies, and effectiveness of multiple antinuclear norm entrepreneurs in both developed and developing countries. But the field is open for others to investigate the importance of individuals in nuclear politics – leading to a crumbling of what we "know" and uncovering the chaotic and contingent sources of nuclear-related activities.

Comparative Conclusions: Beyond Nuclear Politics

Comparing nuclear nonproliferation and disarmament, the literature offers a much deeper and broader understanding of nonproliferation. In terms of methodology, the number of cases of nonproliferation far outnumbers the cases of disarmament, making the topic easier to study. Just as important, the policy biases of Western states likely help to focus academics on nonproliferation – most of the researchers hail from nuclear weapons states and thus are more likely to be naturally interested in nonproliferation as opposed to disarmament. Finally, the lack of serious consideration of disarmament has likely contributed to the dearth of interest in it as a subject of academic study, and given its renewed place on policy agendas around the world, both theoretical and empirical studies of disarmament are likely to increase.

Comparing the NPT with other disarmament treaties leads to the obvious insight of the relative failure of the NPT in achieving its disarmament goals. The Chemical Weapons Convention (CWC) has a time-bound disarmament framework with verification measures, and although not all deadlines have been met, chemical weapons stocks have been reduced dramatically and the treaty is seen as a relative success. The Biological Weapons Convention (BWC) lacks verification measures, but the norm against the acquisition and use of biological and toxic weapons is strong: "Biological weapons remain, essentially, outside the arsenals and war plans of most states and violent non-state actors" (Littlewood, 2010, p. 16). While neither the Mine Ban Treaty (MBT) nor Cluster Munitions Convention (CMC) has near universal adherence, these two disarmament treaties were negotiated outside of normal channels and without the blessing of major powers. That they even exist shows the success of the initiating movements; the fact that both treaties have shaped security policy in non-signatories is even more of an achievement.

However, comparing the NPT with other disarmament treaties can make the treaty seem less successful that it actually is. The NPT was designed with three pillars: nuclear nonproliferation, nuclear energy, and nuclear disarmament. While the first two are meant to be supportive of the ultimate aims of the latter, at times the embedded norms (nonproliferation, right to civilian nuclear technology, and disarmament) are in conflict with one another. Because the CWC, BWC, MBT, and CMC are all strictly disarmament treaties, their implementation is more straightforward. Other key comparative issues that disadvantage the NPT include whether disarmament is time bound (in the NPT, it is not), whether all parties openly accept the need for disarmament (in the NPT, they do not), and whether decisions must be negotiated by consensus versus majority vote (in NPT Review Conferences, the final document is adopted by consensus).

Nevertheless, scholars and policymakers concerned with nuclear disarmament can learn from the other disarmament treaties. The first lesson is that disarmament in the general sense is not impossible. As Burford notes, "These [disarmament treaties] all provide strong evidence of both the will and the capacity of states to collaborate on multilateral disarmament projects, when they perceive the mutual benefit in doing so" (Burford, 2013, p. 3). The key point here is "mutual benefit", and because of the embedded conflicts within nuclear politics, achieving consensus on mutual benefit may not be possible. For this reason, like-minded states and activists have been pushing for the movement of disarmament-related measures outside of the Conference on Disarmament (CD), which operates by consensus rules. Similar obstacles were faced by the supporters of the landmine ban treaty, who decided to negotiate a new regime outside of the regular fora, leading to the Ottawa Treaty banning antipersonnel landmines (Rutherford, 1999).

Like-minded states and NGOs have taken note of this success, and will likely attempt to replicate it with nuclear disarmament measures. One of the key treaties necessary for nuclear disarmament is a ban on the creation of new fissile material (uranium 235 or plutonium 239). However, negotiations for a Fissile Material Cutoff Treaty (FMCT) have been stalled in the CD because of opposition by Pakistan (which believes it will be hurt by such a ban because of India's advantage in fissile material). As a result, in 2011, Norway, Austria, and Belgium put forward a resolution to move the negotiations outside the CD – the UN Secretary-General suggested that negotiations might take place in the UN General Assembly. Indeed, the UN Secretary-General has made the FMCT a priority and it is likely that negotiations for it will follow the pattern established by the MBT and the CMC. If this process is successful, then pressure to move negotiations for a nuclear weapons convention outside the CD will almost certainly build as well.

The final lesson for nuclear disarmament from other treaties relates to whether it is worth pursuing a treaty that will not have universal adherence: is a weak or non-universal treaty better than no treaty at all? While no conclusive answer can be given, it is worth noting the experiences of the landmine ban treaty. Negotiated without the support of major powers, such as the United States, Russia, or China, the treaty today has been ratified by more than 75% of the countries in the world. More important, many states that are not party to the treaty still abide by its provisions. The case of the United States is illustrative: "The United States hasn't used land mines on the battlefield in more than two decades. It has poured nearly $2 billion into mine clearance, helping the injured and other assistance since 1993, making it a commanding force in the global battle against antipersonnel land mines" (Alpert, 2012). Despite its lack of universality, the normative power of the treaty has grown tremendously. As Richard Price argues, "As the number of crucial states supporting a ban reached critical mass, concerns of reputation and identity fostered emulation, which became an increasingly powerful mechanism through which the new norm was adopted" (Price, 1998, p. 640). In normative terms, the regulative norm took on a constitutive effect; the logic of appropriateness convinced even non-parties to conform to the treaty. Landmines are not nuclear weapons, but the normative power of the NPT has effectively promoted nonproliferation for six decades. To see similar success in the field of nuclear disarmament, a separate treaty banning nuclear weapons may be necessary to bring the full power of regulative, and over time, constitutive norms to bear.

Notes

1. For a thorough discussion of the differences between disarmament and arms control, see Neil Cooper. 2006. "Putting Disarmament Back in the Frame." *Review of International Studies,* 32: 353–376.
2. On questioning deterrence, see also Robert Green, *Security Without Nuclear Deterrence* (2010); Ward Wilson, *Five Myths about Nuclear Weapons* (2013); and Ken Berry, Patricia Lewis, Benoît Pélopidas, Nikolai Sokov and Ward Wilson, *Delegitimizing Nuclear Weapons: Examining the validity of nuclear deterrence* (2010). For an opposing view, see Elbridge Colby (2011) "Hiroshima, Nagasaki and the New Logic of Nuclear Deterrence," *The National Interest,* October 19, 2011. Accessed July 2, 2012 from http://national interest.org/commentary/hiroshima-nagasaki-the-new-logic-nuclear-deterrence-6032

References

Abraham, Itty. 2006. "The Ambivalence of Nuclear Histories." *OSIRIS,* 21: 49–65.
Abraham, Itty. 2009. "Contra-Proliferation: The Indian Bomb and Nuclear Developmentalism." In *Inside Nuclear South Asia,* edited by Scott Sagan, 106–136. Stanford, CA: Stanford University Press.

Alpert, Emily. 2012. "Why Hasn't the US Signed an International Ban on Land Mines?" *Los Angeles Times*, April 5, 2012. Accessed May 12, 2012 from http://latimesblogs.latimes.com/world_now/2012/04/mine-treaty-us-ottawa-convention.html

Berry, Ken, Patricia Lewis, Benoît Pélopidas, Nikolai Sokov, and Ward Wilson. 2010. *Delegitimizing Nuclear Weapons: Examining the Validity of Nuclear Deterrence*. Monterey, CA: Monterey Institute for International Studies.

Blechman, Barry M., and Alexander K. Bollfrass, eds. 2010. *Elements of a Nuclear Disarmament Treaty*. Washington, DC: Stimson Center.

Braut-Hegghammer, Malfrid. 2009. *Nuclear entrepreneurs: drivers of nuclear proliferation*. Unpublished PhD thesis. London School Economic and Political Science.

British American Security Information Council (BASIC) and Oxford Research Group. 2005. *Nuclear Weapons Free Zones: The Untold Success Story of Nuclear Disarmament and Nonproliferation*.

Bunn, George. 1992. *Arms Control by Committee: Managing Negotiations with the Russians*. Stanford, CA: Stanford University Press.

Burford, Lyndon. 2012. "No Such Thing as a Free Lunch: A Nuclear-User-Pays Model of International Security." *The Nonproliferation Review*, 19(2): 229–239.

Burford, Lyndon. 2013. "Nuclear Disarmament Advocacy by Non-Nuclear Armed States: Motivations, Policies and Outcomes." PhD diss. (unpublished), University of Auckland.

Center for Nonproliferation Studies. 2010. *Nuclear-Weapon-Free Zone Clearinghouse*. Monterey Institute for International Studies. Accessed June 4, 2012 from http://cns.miis.edu/nwfz_clearinghouse/

Colby, Elbridge. 2011. "Hiroshima, Nagasaki and the New Logic of Nuclear Deterrence." *The National Interest*, October 19, 2011. Accessed July 2, 2012 from http://nationalinterest.org/commentary/hiroshima-nagasaki-the-new-logic-nuclear-deterrence-6032

Cooper, Neil. 2006. "Putting Disarmament Back in the Frame." *Review of International Studies*, 32: 353–376. DOI: 10.1017/S0260210506007066

Evangelista, Matthew. 1999. *Unarmed Forces: The Transnational Movement to End the Cold War*. Ithaca, NY: Cornell University Press.

Evangelista, Matthew. 2011. "Nuclear Abolition or Nuclear Umbrella: Choices and Contradictions in US Proposals." In *Getting to Zero: The Path to Nuclear Disarmament*, edited by Catherine Kelleher and Judith Reppy. Stanford, CA: Stanford University Press.

Findlay, Trevor. 2003. *Verification of a nuclear weapon-free world*. London: VERTIC.

Finnemore, Martha, and Kathryn Sikkink. 1998. "International Norm Dynamics and Political Change." *International Organization*, 52: 887–917.

Frankel, Benjamin. 1993. "The Brooding Shadow: Systemic Incentives and Nuclear Weapons Proliferation." In *The Proliferation Puzzle: Why Nuclear Weapons Spread*, edited by Zachary Davis, and Benjamin Frankel. London: Frank Cass.

Green, Robert. 2010. *Security Without Nuclear Deterrence*. Christchurch, NZ: Astron Media and the Disarmament & Security Centre, 2010.

Hanson, Marianne. 2012. "Advocating the Elimination of Nuclear Weapons: The Role of Key Individual and Coalition States." In *Slaying the Nuclear Dragon: Disarmament Dynamics in the Twenty-First Century*, edited by Tanya Ogilvie-White and David Santoro, 56–84. Athens, GA: University of Georgia Press.

Harrington de Santana, Anne. 2009. "Nuclear Weapons as the Currency of Power: Deconstructing the Fetishism of Force." *Nonproliferation Review*, 16(3): 325–345.

Hughes, Llewelyn. 2007. "Why Japan Will Not Go Nuclear (Yet): International and Domestic Constraints on the Nuclearization of Japan." *International Security*, 31(4): 67–96.

Hymans, Jacques. 2006a. "Theories of Nuclear Proliferation: The State of the Field." *Nonproliferation Review*, 13(3): 455–465.

Hymans, Jacques. 2006b. *The Psychology of Nuclear Proliferation: Identity, Emotions and Foreign Policy*. Cambridge: Cambridge University Press.

Hymans, Jacques. 2012. *Achieving Nuclear Ambitions: Scientists, Politicians and Proliferation*. Cambridge: Cambridge University Press.

International Atomic Energy Agency (IAEA). 2012. "IAEA Nuclear Scientists Employ More Precise 'Fingerprinting'." May 7, 2012. Accessed June 17, 2012 from http://www.iaea.org/newscenter/news/2012/spectrometer.html

Kaldor, Mary. 1990. *The Imaginary War: Understanding the East–West Conflict*. Oxford: Blackwell.

Kaye, Dalia Dassa, and Frederic Wehrey. 2007. "A Nuclear Iran: The Reactions of Neighbors." *Survival*, 49(2): 111–128. DOI: 10.1080/00396330701437777

Kelleher, Catherine, and Judith Reppy, eds. 2011. *Getting to Zero: The Path to Nuclear Disarmament*. Stanford, CA: Stanford University Press.

Knopf, Jeffrey. 1998. *Domestic Society and International Cooperation: The Impact of Protest on US Arms Control Policy*. Cambridge: Cambridge University Press.

Kutchesfahani, Sara. 2010. "Who Shapes the Politics of the Bomb? The Role of Epistemic Communities in Creating Nuclear Nonproliferation Policies." Working Paper 03/2010, London School of Economics.

Kyl, Jon and Richard Perle. 2009. "Our Decaying Nuclear Deterrent." *Wall Street Journal*, June 30. Accessed July 13, 2012 from http://online.wsj.com/news/articles/SB124623202363966157

Lantis, Jeffrey. 2007. "Nuclear Hearts and Minds." *International Studies Review*, 8(4): 650–652.

Lantis, Jeffrey. 2011. "Irrational Exuberance? The 2010 NPT Review Conference, Nuclear Assistance, and Norm Change." *Nonproliferation Review*, 18(2): 389–409.

Lavoy, Peter R. 2006. "Nuclear Proliferation Over the Next Decade: Causes, Warning Signs, and Policy Responses." *Nonproliferation Review*, 13(3): 433–454.

Levite, Ariel. 2003. "Never Say Never Again: Nuclear Reversal Revisited." *International Security*, 27(3): 59–88.

Littlewood, Jez. 2010. "The Verification Debate in the Biological and Toxin Weapons Convention in 2011." *Disarmament Forum*, 3: 15–25.

MacKenzie, Donald and Graham Spinardi. 1995. "Tacit Knowledge, Weapons Design, and the Uninvention of Nuclear Weapons." *The American Journal of Sociology*, 101(1): 44–99.

Magnarella, Paul J. 2008. "Attempts to Reduce and Eliminate Nuclear Weapons Through the Nuclear Nonproliferation Treaty and the Creation of Nuclear-Weapon-Free Zones." *Peace & Change*, 33(4): 507–521.

Malet, David. 2010. "Book Review." Review of *Nonproliferation Norms: Why States Choose Nuclear Restraint* by Maria Rost Rublee. *Journal of Human Security*, 6(3): 69–70.

Mearsheimer, John. 1990. "Back to the Future: Instability in Europe after the Cold War." *International Security*, 15(1): 5–56.

Mearsheimer, John. 1994/1995. "The False Promise of International Institutions." *International Security*, 19(3): 5–49.

Müller, Harald, David Fischer, and Wolfgang Kötter. 1994. *Nuclear Non-Proliferation and Global Order*. Oxford: Oxford University Press.

O'Hanlon, Michael. 2010. *A Skeptic's Case for Nuclear Disarmament*. Washington, DC: Brookings Institution Press.

Ogilvie-White, Tanya, and David Santoro, eds. 2012. *Slaying the Nuclear Dragon: Disarmament Dynamics in the Twenty-First Century*. Athens, GA: University of Georgia Press.

Paasonen, Karl-Erik. 2007. "Between Movements of Crisis and Movements of Affluence: An analysis of the campaign against the Jabiluka uranium mine, 1997-2000." PhD diss. (unpublished). University of Queensland.

Paul, T.V. 2000. *Power versus Prudence: Why Nations Forgo Nuclear Weapons*. Quebec City, QC: McGill-Queen's University Press.

Perkovich, George, and James M. Acton, eds. 2009. *Abolishing Nuclear Weapons: a debate*. Washington, DC: Carnegie Endowment for International Peace.

Ploughshares Foundation. 2012. *World Nuclear Weapons Stockpiles*. Washington, DC: Ploughshares Foundation.

Price, Richard. 1998. "Reversing the Gun Sights: Transnational Civil Society Targets Land Mines." *International Organization*, 52(3): 613–644.

Ritchie, Nick. 2010. "Relinquishing Nuclear Weapons: Identities, Networks and the British Bomb." *International Affairs*, 86(2): 465–487.

Rublee, Maria Rost. 2008. "Taking Stock of the Nuclear Nonproliferation Regime: Using Social Psychology to Understand Regime Effectiveness." *International Studies Review*, 10: 420–450.

Rublee, Maria Rost. 2009. *Nonproliferation Norms: Why States Choose Nuclear Restraint*. Athens, GA: University of Georgia Press.

Rublee, Maria Rost. 2010. "The Nuclear Threshold States: Challenges and Opportunities Posed by Brazil and Japan." *Nonproliferation Review*, 17(1): 49–70.

Rublee, Maria Rost. 2011. "Norms, Norm Entrepreneurs, and International Organizations." Paper presented at the 2011 International Studies Association Annual Conference, Montreal, Canada.

Rublee, Maria Rost. 2012. "Norms, Volition and Nuclear Futures." Paper presented at the Oceanic Conference on International Studies, University of Sydney, July 2012.

Rutherford, Ken. 1999. "The Hague and Ottawa Conventions: A Model for Future Weapon Ban Regimes?" *Nonproliferation Review*, Spring/Summer: 36–50.

Ruzicka, Jan, and Nicholas J. Wheeler. 2010. "The Puzzle of Trusting Relationships in the Nuclear Non-Proliferation Treaty." *International Affairs*, 86(1): 69–85.

Sagan, Scott. 2011. "The Causes of Nuclear Weapons Proliferation." *Annual Review of Political Science*, 14: 225–244.

Sagan, Scott, and Kenneth Waltz. 2003. *The Spread of Nuclear Weapons*. New York, NY: W.W. Norton & Company.

Sagan, Scott, and Kenneth Waltz. 2010. "Is Nuclear Zero the Best Option?" *The National Interest*, Sep/Oct: 88–96.

Sagan, Scott, James M. Acton, Jayantha Dhanapala, Mustafa Kibaroglu, Harald Müller, Yukio Satoh, Mohamed I. Shaker, and Achilles Zaluar. 2010. *Shared Responsibilities for Nuclear Disarmament: A Global Debate*. Washington, DC: American Academy of Arts and Sciences.

Squassoni, Sharon. 2009. *Grading Progress on 13 Steps Toward Disarmament*. Washington, DC: Carnegie Endowment for International Peace.

Solingen, Etel. 2007. *Nuclear Logics: Contrasting Paths in East Asia and the Middle East*. Princeton, NJ: Princeton University Press.

Tannenwald, Nina. 2001. "U.S. Arms Control Policy in a Time Warp." *Ethics and International Affairs*, 15(1): 51–70. DOI: 10.1111/j.1747-7093.2001.tb00343.x

Tannenwald, Nina. 2007. *The Nuclear Taboo: the United States and the Non-Use of Nuclear Weapons*. Cambridge: Cambridge University Press.

The White House. 2009. "Remarks by President Barak Obama." Office of the Press Secretary, The White House, April 5, 2009. Accessed June 27, 2012 from http://www.whitehouse.gov/the_press_office/Remarks-By-President-Barack-Obama-In-Prague-As-Delivered/

United Nations, 2000. *Final Document 2000. Review Conference of the Parties to the Treaty on the Non-Proliferation of Nuclear Weapons*. New York, NY: United Nations.

Wilson, Ward. 2008. "The Myth of Nuclear Deterrence." *Nonproliferation Review*, 15(3): 421–439.

Wilson, Ward. 2013. *Five Myths about Nuclear Weapons*. New York, NY: Houghton Mifflin Harcourt.

Wittner, Lawrence. 1993. *The Struggle Against the Bomb. Volume One, One World or None: A History of the World Nuclear Disarmament Movement Through 1953*. Stanford, CA: Stanford University Press.

Wittner, Lawrence. 1997. *The Struggle Against the Bomb. Volume Two, Resisting the Bomb: A History of the World Nuclear Disarmament Movement*. Stanford, CA: Stanford University Press.

Wittner, Lawrence. 2003. *The Struggle Against the Bomb. Volume Three, Toward Nuclear Abolition: A History of the World Nuclear Disarmament Movement, 1971–Present*. Stanford, CA: Stanford University Press.

Wittner, Lawrence. 2010. "The Nuclear Freeze and Its Impact." *Arms Control Today*, 40(10): 53–56.

Wunderlich, Carmen. 2011. "Black Sheep or Sheep in Wolf's Clothing: Rogue States as Norm Entrepreneurs?" Paper presented at International Studies Association Annual Conference, Montreal, Canada.

Wurst, Jim. 2004. "NPT Parties Criticized on Nonproliferation, Disarmament Compliance." *Global Security Newswire*, April 26.

Chapter 7

Terrorism and Antiterrorism

Ekaterina Stepanova

Terrorism is violence specifically tailored to affect politics through blackmailing the state and intimidating the society. Of all violent tactics, it arguably has the highest potential to do so. In the information and communications age, it is the broader destabilizing effect of violence on society and the state and its ability to affect politics that quickly acquires central importance. As demonstrated by high profile, mass-casualty terrorist attacks of the early twenty-first century, especially the September 11, 2001 attacks – unprecedented in scale, lethality, and impact – it no longer takes a major conventional war with hundreds of thousands of deaths to dramatically affect and even distort the global security agenda.

Terrorism is a threat at the interface of national/state and human security. It involves the direct use or threat to use violence against civilians (or is intentionally indiscriminate), but always goes beyond its immediate targets to serve as an asymmetrical tactic employed by a weaker non-state actor against a stronger protagonist of higher status, i.e. against a state, or a group of states, or an international organization, or the international community as a whole. The highly asymmetrical nature and disproportionately destabilizing manipulative effect of terrorism on politics explains why it will continue to pose a threat to many states and societies and to international security.

Progress in Defining Terrorism

Academic research on terrorism has largely evolved since the 1970s (Schmid, 2011). However, due to the high level of politicization of all matters related to terrorism, the definitional aspects had for decades remained the most contentious issues. Discussions on definition and typology of terrorism gained new momentum in the aftermath of the 9/11 attacks, as the heavily militarized "war on terrorism" introduced new confusion and revived old controversies, especially regarding the interface of

The Handbook of Global Security Policy, First Edition. Edited by Mary Kaldor and Iavor Rangelov.
© 2014 John Wiley & Sons, Ltd. Published 2014 by John Wiley & Sons, Ltd.

"terrorism" and "war", "terrorism" and "insurgency", and non-state terrorism and "state terror".

Despite hundreds of existing definitions, the single largest advance in recent terrorism research has been the formation of a degree of academic consensus on definitional issues. While the emerging consensus definition (Schmid, 2011, pp. 86–87) has not yet made it into an international political agreement (e.g. a UN convention), it gains ground in research and expert circles, is used in strategic documents of some international organizations such as the European Union, and dominates in the methodology of the world's largest database on terrorism – the Global Terrorism Database (START).

Mainstream terrorism research strongly emphasizes the political nature of terrorism as a tactic to achieve political goals (Hoffman, 1998; Laqueur, 2001; Crenshaw, 1995). Central to the consensus definition are also the asymmetrical nature and "communication" function of terrorism, which uses "soft" (civilian/non-combatant or indiscriminate) targets as victims to generate a broader political message. By targeting these victims in a specific political context, terrorists seek to intimidate and create "virtual" pressure on the state and society. For successful terrorist acts, this resulting political pressure is disproportionately high compared to perpetrators' real political and military capacity.

While a degree of consensus on the main definitional criteria of terrorism is emerging in academia, most experts also acknowledge the highly context-specific nature of concrete forms and manifestations of terrorism.

The Rise of Terrorism in the Early Twenty-First Century

Terrorism's main hallmark – its destabilizing political effect that exceeds its actual damage – is hard to measure quantitatively. Numbers of incidents, casualties, terrorist groups per country, and other measurable parameters cannot fully reflect the final impact and political significance of terrorist attacks in a specific political context; however, in the early twenty-first century, terrorism has been on the rise, even in terms of sheer numbers.

The Global Terrorism Index (GTI) that integrates several parameters (incidents, fatalities, injuries, level of material damage) shows a 234% overall increase in terrorist activity over the 2002–2011 period (IEP, 2012, p. 23). Terrorism peaked in 2007 and then leveled off at a high level through 2011. This major increase in terrorist activity in the 2000s amounts to a new – historically, third – wave of terrorism, following the first historical peak of the late nineteenth to early twentieth century and the second peak of the late 1970s and 1980s.

According to the Global Terrorism Database (GTD), the decade following 2001 was marked by approximately 31,000 terrorist incidents and 64,000 fatalities. The number of incidents increased sharply (see Figure 7.1) – by 464% in 2011, compared to 2002 (they started to rise in 2005, jumped in 2007–2008 and crossed the highest peak of 5000 attacks/year in 2011) (START, 2013). Fatalities from terrorism, overwhelmingly civilian, increased by 195% since 2002 and reached a peak of 10,000 in 2007 (an equivalent of battle-related deaths from several major armed conflicts). Terrorism-related injuries increased by 224% over the same period and peaked in 2009 at 19,000 (IEP, 2012, pp. 6, 25). More countries (72) displayed a rise in

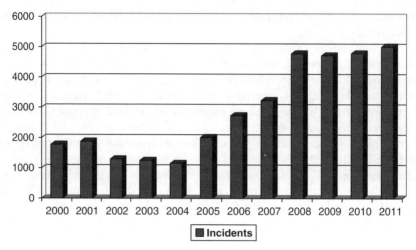

Figure 7.1 Terrorist incidents worldwide, 2000–2011.
Source: Data from Global Terrorism Database (START, 2013).

terrorist activity after 2001 than those (63) that showed decline in terrorism (IEP, 2012, pp. 6, 12).

While the 9/11 attacks had a demonstrative effect on many militant actors in the more localized contexts, terrorism rose most sharply in the few years after 2001 – since the mid-2000s. Remarkably, terrorism increased the most in those countries that had become central targets for the US-led "war on terrorism" *after* they had become such targets: Iraq since 2004, Afghanistan in the second half of the 2000s, and Pakistan in the late 2000s to early 2010s. According to GTD, these three countries alone accounted for 57% of all terrorist incidents in 2002–2011 (see Figure 7.2). Iraq alone accounted for more than one-third of all terrorism-related fatalities worldwide. The GTI ranks Iraq, Pakistan, and Afghanistan as the top three countries affected by terrorism after 2001 (IEP, 2012, p. 4; see Figure 7.3).

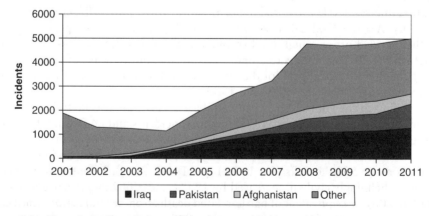

Figure 7.2 Terrorist incidents in Iraq, Afghanistan, and Pakistan, 2001–2011.
Source: Data from Global Terrorism Database (START, 2013).

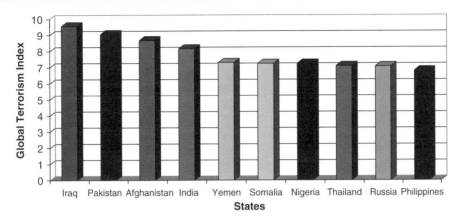

Figure 7.3 Top 10 countries most affected by terrorism.
Source: Data from Global Terrorism Index 2011 (IEP, 2012).

Few countries are free from terrorism: of the 158 countries ranked by GTI, only 20 did not experience any terrorist attacks in 2002–2011. While high-impact terrorist attacks may take place even in peaceful states (e.g. the August 2011 attacks in Norway by a racist extremist), much of the terrorist activity today either takes place in areas of armed conflict or is linked to the political agenda of a particular conflict. Terrorism correlates strongly with intense organized conflict, as measured by the Uppsala Conflict Data Program (UCDP) or Global Peace Index.

From this it could be suggested that global dynamics of terrorism should mirror global trends in armed conflicts. However, the relationship is more complex and context-specific. While the 40% decline in annual totals of armed conflicts between the early 1990s and early 2000s (UCDP, 2012a) appeared to be paralleled by falling or stabilizing terrorism indicators, the sharp rise of terrorism since the mid-2000s does not correspond to overall stabilization or minor increases in conflict numbers. One explanation of this discrepancy is the high concentration of global terrorist activity in the early twenty-first century in just ten conflict-affected countries, which accounted for 87% of all terrorist incidents in 2011 (IEP, 2012, p. 12).

Global terrorism statistics from the 2000s were heavily dominated by the two largest armed conflicts – the wars in Iraq and Afghanistan. By the 2010s, they were joined by Pakistan, where cross-border terrorism linked to the conflict in Afghanistan and the pressures of the US-led "war on terrorism" merged with effects from multiple other terrorist threats. Remarkably, Iraq and Afghanistan – the two most heavily internationalized wars of the early twenty-first century, both involving armed insurgencies in Muslim countries primarily against Western troops backing very weak local proxy governments – have had stronger effects on global terrorism dynamics than all conflicts in the rest of top 20 terrorism-affected states combined. The latter range from conflicts in weak states (either fully internationalized, such as Somalia, or not formally internationalized, such as Yemen) but with no direct Western intervention, to dozens of non-internationalized conflicts of ethnoseparatist/religious or socio-political types in peripheral areas of relatively functional states (such as in India, Thailand, Nigeria, Russia, the Philippines, or Turkey).

The disproportionate role of the few most heavily internationalized and intense conflicts in generating terrorism prevents close parallels between global trends in terrorism and armed conflicts. However, terrorism dynamics do reflect some broader trends in organized collective violence.

Some generally positive developments, such as a decline in conflict numbers, major conventional wars, inter-state conflicts and battle-related deaths (UCDP, 2012a; Human Security Report Project, 2011), have been effectively counterbalanced by the rise in other forms of armed violence and violent actors. One of the counterbalancing trends is the growing role of non-state actors (from locally based groups to transnational networks) in world politics and in armed violence, from combat to one-sided (direct and premeditated) violence against civilians. Since 1989, non-state actors made up over 70% of all perpetrators of one-sided violence, and since 2001, non-state actors unprecedentedly killed more unarmed civilians in one-sided violence than governments (UCDP, 2012b). This shift is partly explained by the growing number of militant groups resorting to terrorist methods and is manifested in increasing number of terrorism-related deaths compared to fatalities from other forms of one-sided violence (such as massacres or communal violence).

Overall, the rise of terrorism in the early twenty-first century forms an integral part of two broader global trends in organized violence:

- the lack of positive dynamics in all forms of one-sided violence against civilians; and
- the growing role of non-state actors in organized armed violence.

Transnationalization of Terrorism

It has become commonplace in policy, media, and expert circles to recognize the high degree of transnationalization of terrorism. What is often ignored is that transnationalization primarily manifests itself in qualitative rather than quantitative terms. If quantitative parameters are still measured in line with the old-fashioned "technical" definition of any terrorist activity conducted on the territory of more than one state and involving citizens of more than one state as "international", then incidents of "domestic terrorism" still outnumber acts of "international terrorism" by a large margin (MIPT, 2008). Of over 2000 terrorist groups recorded by the GTD, only a few attacked civilians in another country (START, 2013).

Instead, the very line between domestic and international terrorism becomes increasingly blurred. Terrorist groups with a localized political agenda may be partly based in and operate from abroad and may also tend to increasingly transnationalize some or most of their logistics, fund-raising, propaganda, and even planning activities, often extending them to regions far beyond their main areas of operation. For many groups, particularly those driven by ideologies with religious imperative, the high degree of transnationalization of their activities is also a progression of their universalist ideologies. For instance, a violent Islamist cell in Europe, comprised of Muslims that may be citizens of European states, may have limited or no direct operational guidance, financial, or logistical support from other violent Islamist groups, but engage in terrorist activity guided by a universalist ideology and carried out in the name of the "Islamic world" (*umma*). This is transnational terrorism, even if it results in casualties primarily among the perpetrators' fellow citizens.

In a globalized world, all terrorism is transnationalized to some degree, which makes it critically important to distinguish between different levels, stages and qualities of transnationalization (Saikia and Stepanova, 2009). Minimal transnationalization of a terrorist group's activities may be confined to conducting terrorist acts abroad or extending logistics and fund-raising activities to foreign countries. A more advanced form of transnationalization implies interaction between separate, independent groups in different countries or amounts to the formation of fully fledged inter-organizational networks. At the most advanced stage, transnational terrorist networks emerge.

Of decisive importance today are no longer questions of how many countries a group raises funds in, whether or not its members attended a training camp abroad, or citizens of how many states were hit by its terrorist activity, especially in major urban centers. As terrorism may be transnationalized even at the localized levels, the mechanical distinction between purely "domestic" and "international" terrorism makes little sense. The main criterion to establish the qualitative type of transnationalization is the level of a group's ultimate goals and agenda – local, regional, or global.

"Global Terrorism" After 9/11: Transformation and/or Decline?

Terrorism has long been employed as a standard tactic in armed conflicts and as extreme violence by marginal left-wing, right-wing, and other radical groups in peacetime. However, at the turn of the century, a qualitatively new phenomenon of "global terrorism" appears to have emerged. This new type/level of terrorism has been primarily associated with al-Qaeda and, later, the al-Qaeda-style cells and networks.

In contrast to the more traditional conflict-related and peacetime terrorism, "global terrorism" is practiced by actors with an explicitly universalist agenda and ultimately pursues existential, non-negotiable, global and unlimited goals (e.g. challenging the world order). Such terrorism is exterritorial because it is not tied to any single political context or even several local contexts. It is also global in its impact, if not necessarily in its physical reach.

Although "global terrorism" has gained a high profile in international politics and security after 9/11, it has not become the dominant type of terrorism. The bulk of global terrorist activity is accounted for by militant actors that pursue more limited goals in more localized contexts and combine terrorism with other violent tactics in local/regional armed conflicts. Why then has al-Qaeda-style "global terrorism" gained such disproportionately high attention and created an impression that it dominates the present discourse on terrorism?

First, the effect of terrorism is judged not only on the basis of its physical and measurable parameters, but, more importantly, by the scale of its political impact. Despite the minimal number of incidents after 2001 (in 2011, al-Qaeda was responsible for just one kidnapping out of 5000 terrorist incidents worldwide (IEP, 2012, p. 6)), and relatively few operatives and ideologues, al-Qaeda-style "global terrorism" has been unprecedentedly effective from the political point of view. In contrast to the more familiar types of terrorism, ideologues and practitioners of "global terrorism" managed to cause truly global political impact and address the world as a whole through limited means (i.e. by carefully timed, spectacular mass-casualty attacks on high-profile Western-affiliated targets, usually in homeland/peacetime settings, which magnified the effect, in the name of explicitly transnational goals). These are characteristics of the 9/11 attacks, but also of subsequent bombings in Bali, Istanbul, Madrid, and London. Also, disproportionate strategic importance assigned to "global jihad" terrorism in the West may be partly explained by the fact that most of its high-profile targets have been either located in, or associated with, the developed Western world (whereas conflict-related terrorism in the name of more localized goals primarily affects regions such as the Middle East or South Asia and has only limited manifestations in Western Europe).

Second, the "global jihad" movement poses a major ideological challenge. In fact, "global jihad" is now the only set of doctrines and beliefs that effectively plays the role of global antisystem protest ideology, and is able to come up with a coherent, even if totally utopian, alternative concept of a global order based on God's direct rule and to inspire enough adepts ready to promote it with violent means. This ideology is not merely *inter*nationalist or *trans*national, but *supra*national, rejecting the very notion of a "nation state" and pretending to exist in another dimension, with no states or borders, where people are characterized not by their ethnicity or citizenship, but solely by whether or not they share the faith in one God. This ideology is not simply "reactionary" – its main strength lies in offering a very radical response to challenges of a globalizing world.

Third, another of al-Qaeda's strengths has been its organizational and operational flexibility, ability to adapt, appeal to more localized groups with a limited agenda, and ability to inspire autonomous cells. Analytical approaches to the evolution of the "global jihadi" terrorism can be grouped into three categories, depending on how they assess the speed, scale, and substance of al-Qaeda's transformation: "al-Qaedaization", "regionalization", and the "post-Qaeda" approach.

The "al-Qaedaization" approach maybe on the wane, but it prevailed in the immediate aftermath of 9/11. It manifested itself in a flawed tendency to link all militant/terrorist actors, at least of Islamist bent, to al-Qaeda in one way or another and to grossly overestimate the vertical command and control role for Bin Laden's "al-Qaeda Central" (Gunaratna, 2002). While inaccurate, this approach was used to inform and justify the policies of the world's lead powers, with dramatic effects on international politics and security, particularly in view of the US-led interventions in Iraq and Afghanistan.

Ambiguous and even counterproductive effects of the George W. Bush-style "war on terrorism", reinforced by new international developments such as a wave of mass protests and revolutions across the Middle East, pushed the Barack Obama administration to revise US counterterrorism strategy. Academics and policy experts started to talk about *"regionalization"* as the main direction of al-Qaeda's evolution, arguing that the main level of al-Qaeda-style terrorism had shifted towards its "regional affiliates" in Muslim regions – al-Qaeda in the Arabian Peninsula, al-Qaeda in Iraq, al-Qaeda in the Lands of the Islamic Maghreb, or al-Qaeda in East Africa (Rollins, 2011). By the 2010s, the regionalization approach prevailed in mainstream expertise and policy-making in the West and has been gaining prominence in international organizations such as the United Nations.

While more adequate, a focus on "regionalization" has its own problems. It appears to not only shape, but also reflect certain policy priorities, particularly on the part of the United States. For instance, an emphasis on the degradation of "al-Qaeda Central", attempts to dissociate it from Afghanistan by shifting the focus to the "al-Qaeda core in Pakistan", and the belated assassination of Bin Laden in May 2012 (apparently timed for the US election cycle) provided the badly needed public cover-up for the decision to withdraw the bulk of US forces from Afghanistan, despite the lack of counterinsurgency successes, functional governance, or progress towards political settlement.

Also, in contrast to alleged al-Qaeda "regional affiliates" in Muslim countries, small self-generating cells and "lone-wolf" individuals – "ideological adherents" of "global jihad" – have been largely interpreted as a sign of al-Qaeda's weakness and organizational degradation (White House, 2011; Rollins, 2011). Underestimation of the significance of this micro-level of small "jihadi" terrorist cells may partly reflect the reluctance to recognize – and the political embarrassment about – the fact that the overwhelming majority of such micro-cells emerge and function not in far-away conflict zones deep inside the Muslim world, but in the Western states themselves.

In contrast, the more strongly revisionist *"post-al-Qaeda" approach* sees the multilevel, extraterritorial network of autonomous, self-generating cells in different parts of the world – particularly in the West itself – as the main center of gravity of the dynamic "global jihad" movement (Sageman, 2007; Stepanova, 2008). These cells' activities are not directed from any center; rather, in planning and carrying out terrorist activity, they follow general ideological/strategic guidelines formulated by dispersed leaders and ideologues in line with the explicitly universalist ideology of "global jihad". This approach questions the role of most radical jihadist groups in Muslim regions as "al-Qaeda regional affiliates". It points instead to their largely authentic origin and emergence in parallel to, rather than as branches of, al-Qaeda, their deep integration into respective local/regional contexts, and the lack of credible evidence to prove their operational links to "al-Qaeda Central". Furthermore, the post-al-Qaeda vision implies that "al-Qaeda Central" in Afghanistan/Pakistan has lost any practical/operational meaning beyond residual symbolic significance. This understanding contradicts attempts to blame the US/NATO counterinsurgency failures in Afghanistan primarily on the interference of "al-Qaeda-linked terrorist elements" from Pakistan.

Causes and Explanations of Terrorism

While the terrorism literature initially paid much attention to studying the manifestations of terrorism, in the twenty-first century scholars have increasingly addressed its causes and explanations. In particular, a rather simplistic "root causes" approach came under scrutiny – a general agreement has emerged in the field that it may be more accurate to refer to different types, levels, and combinations of causes, contributing factors, and other explanations of terrorism (Bjorgo, 2005; Lia and Skjolberg, 2005; Crenshaw, 2010).

One way (Bjorgo, 2005) is to differentiate between *structural, or macro-level, causes* (demographic imbalances, globalization, rapid modernization, transitional societies, "relative deprivation", social alienation, marginalization of segments of the population), *facilitating factors* (symbiotic relationship between terrorism and mass media, advances in weapons technology, weak state control of territory, interconnections with crime), and the more direct and context-specific *motivational causes* (discrimination and other grievances among a subgroup, elite dissatisfaction, lack of opportunity for political participation or civil rights).

Another way is to look for explanations *at different levels of social structure* – i.e. the individual level dominated by the psycho-sociological school (Horgan, 2005), the social group, societal/national and systemic/international levels – and analyze them in combination, where appropriate. For instance, the failure of much of Western literature to adequately explain the phenomenon of suicide terrorism may be partly explained by its over-reliance on psycho-sociological explanations at the individual level and also at the expense of attention to social-group and societal levels of analysis.

Structural Causes

Some of the most contentious issues in terrorism research concern the alleged relationship between poverty or underdevelopment and terrorism on the one hand, and between modernization and terrorism on the other.

Most scholars agree that terrorism is not a product of underdeveloped (traditional) society. The general impact of modernization on socio-political violence has long been the subject of debate between radical, or dependency, theorists (the followers of Emile Durkheim who argue that political violence is a by-product of modernization, e.g. Karl Deutsch, Ernst Gellner, and Samuel Huntington, amongst others) and Erich Weede, Nils P. Gleditsch and other proponents of the liberal theory who insist that development brings prosperity and social and political peace (Lia and Skjolberg, 2005). If the central focus is on the *process* of modernization, rather than on its perceived *end-products*, then the chances for resorting to terrorist methods increase in areas affected by particularly rapid and painful ("traumatic") modernization, socio-cultural marginalization, and frustration that is associated with the socio-psychological gap between the rising expectations and reality (*relative deprivation*).

Current research also supports this view by questioning direct or decisive causal effect of poverty (underdevelopment) on terrorism (Krueger, 2008). It is not the low-income countries that are most vulnerable to terrorism: over a decade after 2001, 65% of all terrorist incidents, 69% of fatalities, and 73% of injuries were recorded in lower-middle countries (IEP, 2012, p. 12).

Cutting-edge research emphasizes political conditions, long-standing feeling of indignity and frustration, and lack of political and civil rights as the indicators far more directly associated with terrorism than poverty, underdevelopment, or lack of education. The factors that show strongest positive correlation to terrorism (measured by the UN Terrorism Prevention Branch's Terrorism Index and the recent GTI, or integrated into broader indicators such as Political Terror Scale) include acute group grievances, low respect for human rights, low levels of political stability, and weak intergroup cohesion and rule of law.

This, however, does not automatically imply that "more democracy" means "less terrorism". Current research stresses a complex and ambiguous *relationship between terrorism and the type of political regime*. The latter is just one of several factors affecting the state's vulnerability to terrorism (along with general functionality of the state or ethno-confessional diversity and other identity/cultural factors). Terrorism is more likely to manifest itself in states with hybrid regimes, or "anocracies" (that combine democratic and authoritarian features) than in either consolidated democracies or rigid autocracies. Hybrid regimes accounted for 46% of all terrorism incidents, 54% of fatalities and 60% of injuries between 2002–2011 (IEP, 2012, p. 12). They are followed by "flawed"/weak democracies such as India, Thailand, or Pakistan where terrorist incidents have doubled since 2002.

Although developed democracies ensure higher levels of civil and political rights and give fewer pretexts for domestic socio-political violence, of all forms of such violence, terrorism is the one they are most vulnerable to. Specific vulnerability of democracies to terrorism lies in the higher value they attach to the lives of civilians, which may make these governments easier for terrorists to pressure and blackmail. This vulnerability is a side-product of the essential characteristics of democracy and cannot be "removed". Also, although developed democratic states are less affected by domestic socio-political violence, they sometimes get involved in asymmetrical armed conflicts, military interventions, and controversial state-building experiments in other parts of the world that provokes violent resistance, including terrorism directed at "soft" targets associated with the West.

Ideological and Organizational Asymmetry

Terrorism research has moved beyond identifying the more static "causes" to the more dynamic and actor-oriented approaches exploring how contextual socio-political and psycho-sociological factors merge with ideologies and organizational patterns to explain mechanisms of radicalization of individuals and groups into terrorism.

Terrorist groups were traditionally categorized by dominant ideology as either *socio-political/secular ideological* (of a revolutionary leftist, anarchist, right-wing, or other bent), *nationalist* (ranging from national liberation movements to ethno-separatist organizations), or *religious* (ranging from totalitarian sects and cults to broader movements whose ideology is dominated by religious imperative). In practice, there are few groups with a pure motivation formulated in accordance with a single ideology. Many militant-terrorist groups are driven by more than one motivation and ideology, and it may not always be clear which motivation is the dominant one – one motivation may replace another with time or they can gradually merge.

After the end of the Cold War and the global decline of radical socialism and communism, the role of secular socio-political ideologies of leftist bent, as a basis for groups engaged in terrorism, decreased relative to the rise of nationalist and religious terrorism. However, "political terrorism" driven by ideologies other than religious or nationalist extremism should not be neglected – in absolute terms, left-wing terrorism has even somewhat increased in the early twenty-first century (MIPT, 2008). By 2011, five out of the top ten most active terrorist groups were "political organizations" other than religious and nationalist groups (IEP, 2012, p. 32).

While recent research on ideologies of terrorism has been dominated by studies of religious, particularly Islamist, extremism (Esposito, 2002; Juergensmeyer, 2000; Kepel, 2004), claims about the absolute dominance of religious terrorism in the early twenty-first century are inaccurate. Nationalist terrorism continues to account for most terrorist incidents not only at the domestic level, but also for the bulk of all terrorist incidents worldwide. Religious terrorism has been the most, and increasingly, lethal and shows a clear rise in incidents (MIPT, 2008; START, 2013; IEP, 2012, p. 32). If a typical ideological set for a standard terrorist group of the second half of the twentieth century was a mix of left-wing radicalism and secular nationalism, the dominant combination of the early twenty-first century is a mix of religious extremism and radical nationalism (either of the more inclusive "national liberation" type or of the more exclusive ethno-separatist bent).

In terms of terrorist groups' structures, the general spread of networks is qualified by the prevalence of hybrid types, with most real-life groups displaying vertical and horizontal, and formal and informal links. The increasingly sophisticated information and communication capacities of terrorists allow them to expand their audiences and amplify the demonstrative effect of attacks. Organizational and information/communication upgrades affect terrorists' training and recruitment patterns, which evolve from the more structured and centralized recruitment involving combat training and/or experience, to the speedier, often voluntary process, frequently via online radicalization of individuals or cells who join the broader network as self-generating actors through informal links and sometimes even through "direct action". Analysis of novel organizational forms of terrorism is no longer confined to the study of networks, in line with either organizational network theory (Arquilla and Ronfeldt, 2001) or social networks theory (Sageman, 2004, 2007), but also involves research on "post-network" organizational features of terrorist groups that are not typical for either networks or hierarchies (Mayntz, 2004; Stepanova, 2008, pp. 140–149).

Facilitating Factors

Even major terrorist acts have been relatively inexpensive and most attacks involve standard and relatively easily accessible means and weapons (up to 80% rely on dynamite, grenades, and firearms (IEP, 2012, p. 41)). Although money and weapons may not be terrorists' main strategic assets, their role in facilitating terrorism cannot be neglected, particularly in view of growing financial and economic independence of terrorist actors. This includes their increasingly active and diversified involvement in criminal activities (Shelley and Picarelli, 2002), stimulated by decline in state support of terrorism since the end of the Cold War. However, terrorists' links to organized crime should not be overstated because it risks reducing terrorism to another form of "serious crime", de-emphasizing its political nature, and neglecting terrorism financing from non-criminal sources (such as religious donations), especially in the case of Islamist militant groups.

The rise of "global terrorism" with universalist goals, increased attention to the possibility of the use of weapons of mass destruction (WMD) by terrorists (Ranstorp and Normark, 2009). Although the specific challenges posed by what should be more accurately referred to as "unconventional" or "CBRN (chemical, biological, radiological, nuclear) terrorism" should by no means be ignored, the level of attention to the potential use of WMD by terrorists appears to greatly outmatch the real scale of the threat (Pikayev and Stepanova, 2008). The main feature of terrorism as a form of political violence is that it seeks to create asymmetrical, *disproportionately large* political effect through the use of *limited* means. Consequently, weapons, explosives, means of delivery employed even in high-profile attacks as in New York and Washington (2001), Madrid (2004), or London (2005) tend to be relatively available, inexpensive and not particularly sophisticated. When it comes to inflicting mass casualties and/or mass destruction, the main terrorist method remains conventional bombings. Less frequently, "unconventional" use of conventional means is involved (e.g. flying the hijacked civil aviation airliners into the World Trade Center and Pentagon buildings on September 11, 2001). Of only three mass-casualty terrorist attacks involving unconventional weapons since the 1970s, only one – the Aum Shinrikyo attack on the Tokyo subway in 1995 – actually aimed at mass casualties, but even that attack by a religious cult, whose unique fascination with unconventional weapons is very atypical for terrorist groups, resulted in less damage and disruption than most high-profile conventional terrorist attacks (Parachini, 2001). In sum, massive conventional attacks are incomparably more widespread, consistently more deadly and have caused more damage than unconventional attacks. In the future, terrorists may be more likely to experiment with targets (e.g. by increasingly targeting critical infrastructure such as transport, energy, water systems, information and communication networks) than with weapons and materials, including unconventional means.

Finally, a recent tendency to primarily confine sources of terrorism to the so-called failed states is inaccurate. The absence of a minimally functional state does not leave much space for asymmetrical violence, including terrorism, in the local/national context; rather, such ungoverned areas can provide "facilitating environments" for terrorism. First, terrorist methods can be used by domestic militant actors against neighboring states, especially if the latter are perceived as meddlers or occupying powers. Also, in the case of foreign or international security presence, terrorist methods can be locally applied against domestic or foreign targets associated with foreign presence. Second, dysfunctional or weak states offer external or transnational terrorist network opportunities for relocation, sanctuary, and transshipment of arms and people. In both cases, the impact of terrorism is not confined within a "failed state", but has wider regional and international implications. It is also difficult to apply antiterrorist measures in such states because they lack effective national capacity to fight terrorism.

Specifics of Antiterrorism

Not only is terrorism a highly contextual phenomenon (with its asymmetrical communicative and intimidation effect largely depending on how well it is timed with and tailored to specific political context), and not only does it display a variety of forms and manifestations, but it also affects most countries in the world (138 out of 158 indexed by GTI). The highly diversified and widespread nature of terrorism implies that, all international discourse on "the fight against terrorism" notwithstanding, any discussion of antiterrorism in a global context allows for very broad generalizations only.

Terrorism strikes at the intersection of "national security" (security of the state) and "human security" centered on civilian populations and society. This dual nature of terrorism is well reflected in terminology denoting activity to confront terrorism.

While the narrow notion of "counterterrorism" refers primarily to a range of specialized functions undertaken by the state security sector, "antiterrorism" is both an
umbrella term to encompass all activity to prevent and manage terrorism, and a term
for political, legal, civil society and other measures against terrorism that go beyond
"security functions". The growing importance of antiterrorism is well reflected by
the shift in research from the dominant criminological paradigm (Crelinsten, 2009)
to the growing attention to broader political, social, and other aspects of antiterrorism, and on de-radicalization and preventing radicalization (English, 2010; Ashour,
2009; Bjorgo and Horgan, 2005). Still, some general reservations should be kept
in mind.

First, the highly asymmetrical nature of terrorism transforms into a "reverse
asymmetry" in antiterrorism. Terrorism as a tool of the weaker side by default
is much cheaper and requires more limited means, resources and manpower than
anti/counterterrorism. Counterterrorism is a much more expensive, sophisticated,
time- and resource-consuming activity requiring a wide range of different skills,
resources, and capacity to be conducted on a permanent basis. Antiterrorism in general and prophylactic measures in particular tend to be very personnel-intensive.

Second, different types of terrorism – by dominant motivation (ideological mix),
degree of transnationalization or relation to broader armed conflict – may require
significantly nuanced anti/counterterrorism strategies. In particular, a range of
resources, actors, and strategies to address terrorist threats linked to the agenda and
context of an ongoing or concluding armed conflict will vary significantly, depending
on which of the following two broad categories a case in point falls under:

- Security ("stabilization", counterinsurgency) operations carried out by functional
  states (India, Nigeria, Pakistan, the Philippines, Russia, Thailand, the United
  Kingdom, in Northern Ireland etc.) in the peripheral parts of their own territory,
  with or without a formal peace process;
- International security/peacebuilding operations in failed, weak, seriously fractured, or emerging states (Afghanistan, Iraq, Somalia, Libya, or Mali).

Third, effective antiterrorism always requires a combination of measures undertaken
by different actors, at different levels, and within different time-frames, ranging from
reactive to preventive, from short-term to long-term, from security (intelligence, law,
and order) to political, legal, public information, and other measures. Short-term
preemption and response would hardly have a tangible effect if they were not part
of a comprehensive antiterrorism strategy that included mid-term and long-term
strategies. While in the early twenty-first century, security strategies to address direct
manifestations of terrorism and attention to the long-term underlying "causes" of
terrorism have been upgraded from local to global levels, the critical "meso-level"
of antiterrorism – the need to undermine terrorists' ideologies and organizational
structures – remains inadequately addressed (Stepanova, 2008).

Confronting Manifestations of Terrorism

Paradoxically, even as terrorism itself is increasingly transnationalized, the center of
gravity of antiterrorist activity firmly remains at the national level. This is partly

due to the specifics of counterterrorism, especially its heavy reliance on intelligence and (counter)intelligence capacity and the extremely contextualized character of the threat.

A major problem intrinsic both to the international "war on terrorism" and to national counterterrorist strategies is the failure to understand and accommodate the highly specific nature of counterterrorism as a security activity distinct from traditional military or policing tasks. In contrast to police or military operations, counterterrorism is a security function whose primary goals *are not post hoc* coercion, enforcement, or retaliation. The central tasks of counterterrorism are prevention, preemption, and preemptive disruption of terrorist activity. Ninety percent of this work should be conducted before, not after, a terrorist attack occurs. At the core of counterterrorism are highly specialized, carefully targeted "special operations" conducted by (counter)intelligence services and aimed at prevention, preemption and preemptive disruption of terrorist acts and networks. These operations are completely dependent on timely, comparative analysis of solid and accurate intelligence of strategic, psychological, and tactical type (the latter is the hardest to achieve because it concerns terrorists' specific plans of action). This intelligence has to be collected and analyzed on a permanent basis, with an emphasis on combining technical, human/undercover, and open-source intelligence, but it will only be effective if it is coupled with resolute government decision-making capacity to act upon timely analysis of such intelligence.

This underscores the need to find (depending on a national context or any specific international security institution) an optimal balance in counterterrorism between (in declining order of importance):

- More specific tasks performed by specialized segments of the professional (counter)intelligence community on a permanent, not *ad hoc*, basis (ranging from intelligence collection, detective, investigative and other analytical work to demining and hostage rescue operations conducted by special counterterrorism units with support from law enforcement and the military);
- More general law enforcement tasks centered on broad prophylactic and preventive measures, such as physical protection of the population and critical infrastructure (to be mainly performed by police forces);
- The support role that the military can play in counterterrorism (including in crisis management operations);
- *Post hoc* consequence management, with an emphasis on civil protection.

Legal and judicial measures are also essential, above all, to balance between *functionality* and *legitimacy* in antiterrorism. Only a balance between the two can ensure that counterterrorism does not produce more terrorism than it seeks to counter. These measures range from antiterrorism legislation to the use of (preferably civil) criminal justice processes to prosecute terrorists. The role of the judiciary tends to be most effective when it establishes some form of mutually dependent working cooperation with the (counter)intelligence community and – with no significant derogation from the due process of law – adapts specific procedures to increase the level of professionalism on antiterrorism, make the system more adaptive to antiterrorism needs, and allow "preliminary" inquiries predating the occurrence of a terrorist act, rather than just *post hoc* investigations. Some form of codification of the "terrorism conspiracy" norm is also needed to target terrorists' logistics/financial networks and to open investigations *before* a terrorist act occurs. A combination of some specialization of judicial process (preferably, within the overall framework of normal legal procedure) and complementarity of intelligence and judicial capabilities (e.g. in France) is one institutional way to balance functionality and legality in antiterrorism. Although a broader strategy, in theory, should ensure full legal protection of human rights in terrorism-related cases, in practice such protection depends on a specific national context and is unlikely to materialize in states with a low level of respect for human rights (who are also more likely to create pretexts and preconditions for terrorism in the first place).

Transnationalization of terrorism and erosion of the distinction between "internal" and "international" terrorism reinforce the interrelation between domestic and foreign counterterrorist strategies, with some measures and policies relevant for preventing and combating terrorism both at home and abroad. Although international cooperation on counterterrorism, especially operational cooperation, still remains most effective at the bilateral level, it has also significantly increased at the macroregional and broader international levels and is now firmly on the agenda of most international security institutions.

Intelligence cooperation is the most important form of international counterterrorism cooperation, but is still mainly confined to intelligence sharing. Joint counterterrorism operations such as the French–Spanish efforts to confront "Euskadi ta Askatasuna" (ETA) are much less frequent. Legal, judicial, and police cooperation (including adoption and review of the implementation of international/UN legal instruments against terrorism, the growing role for Interpol and regional institutional mechanisms) is equally important. It centers on ensuring physical protection of citizens, property and businesses abroad, and international transport and communications security, and prosecuting suspected terrorists and accomplices (including joint antiterrorism investigations) and countering terrorists' logistics and financial networks. The potential for international military cooperation on counterterrorism (rather than on tasks that may be undertaken in the name of counterterrorism, but are not specific or tailored to counterterrorism needs) is inherently limited. However, even military-to-military cooperation and regional military blocs have a unique role to play, e.g. in critical infrastructure protection, terrorism consequences management, and CBRN security and safety measures, in cooperation with other security/civil defense structures.

Political coordination is easier to declare than to exercise at the international level due to ubiquitous double standards, conflicts of interest or simply different scales and types of terrorist threats to one state over another. Cooperation in this field mostly bears fruit if it takes place between close bilateral partner states or within regional security blocs. It often takes the form of providing counterterrorism (security, technical, legal, immigration) assistance to countries less experienced in these matters, but increasingly affected by terrorist threats. However, broader international cooperation on a few select issues, such as depriving individual high-profile terrorists (especially the ones on respective UN or Interpol lists) of safe havens and political legitimacy, has greatly improved in recent years.

Undermining Terrorists' Ideologies and Structures

No antiterrorism strategy is effective unless it addresses two key asymmetrical advantages of terrorist actors, i.e. unless it challenges ideological extremism and effectively neutralizes terrorists' organizational advantages.

However, when it comes to the dominant ideology of "global terrorism" – the "global jihad" ideology – the reality is that its violent adepts may not in principle be amenable to alternative ideological influence, persuasion, moderation, or pressure because they are fighting for a new global social order and mode of existence and not for any tangible benefits, such as political power in existing states or control of territory. This shifts the central focus of any "de-radicalization" efforts from committed jihadists to potential recruits who have not yet been radicalized into this type of terrorist. Still, in the more localized (regional, national, local) contexts, a variety of methods could be employed to reduce the degree of ideological extremism of militant actors employing terrorist means, both at the individual and at the social group level. This includes ideological methods, such as widespread policies encouraging moderate Islamic clergy, madrasa, and charities in their debates with Islamic radicals on concepts of martyrdom and jihad and efforts to promote traditional religious/legal bans on targeting the enemy's women and children. More unorthodox solutions include attempts to refocus religious extremism to develop a pragmatic stake in a concrete political process and context, including by tolerating an (ethno)nationalist agenda as a hedge against and a more manageable alternative to transnational and supra-national violent Islamism (ranging from a "chechenization" policy in the North Caucasus to "palestinization" of Hamas or "lebanonization" of Hizbullah).

Ways to neutralize and normalize structural capabilities of militant/terrorist actors, especially of the larger mass-based movements that cannot be neutralized by special or military means, may range from introducing elements of network organizational design into the state's own security structures to overt and covert efforts to formalize the informal links within militant/terrorist organizations and to turn relatively decentralized hybrid networks into more formal and streamlined hierarchies, making them easier to deal with.

In confronting terrorism at the local/national/regional level, especially in conflict and post-conflict contexts, an integrated strategy aimed at undermining ideological and organizational pillars of terrorism hinges on progress towards general demilitarization of politics. A majority of today's conflicts are not ended by decisive military victory, but either involve a peace process resulting in a political settlement or fade away (often to recur later) with a lack of either a military or political solution. This underscores the critical importance of stimulating – or at least not hindering – political transformation of armed movements who have included or may include terrorism in their tactical arsenal, but are major "veto players" (politically and militarily viable and organizationally cohesive groups that enjoy a degree of local support (such as the Taliban in Afghanistan) or are even mass-based grassroots movements (Palestinian Hamas, the Sadrist movement in Iraq, Lebanese Hizbullah, or Maoist Naxalite movement in India). Depending on the context, different strategies, pressures, and concessions may be applied to get this type of actor to become increasingly politicized, form distinct fully-fledged political wings (rather than mere "front organizations" for fund-raising and propaganda), develop a stake in greater formal legitimization, and eventually incorporate their mainstream core into the political process. In parallel, this requires efforts to do everything at the national or international level to encourage and ensure marginalization, isolation, relocation, or eventual liquidation of the more radical, hardline, often splinter factions.

The evolution of a major militant non-state group enjoying a degree of grass-root support into a legal political actor could be extremely painful, may be preceded by or lead to violent splits and intensification of internal/sectarian violence and even drive more radical factions to more actively resort to terrorist means in an increasingly irrational manner. However, promoting this evolution is essential to widen the gap between more moderate elements that could be demilitarized and included in the political process and the more radical underground hardline, often splinter, factions whose violent activity is likely to be dominated by terrorist means. This would make the latter easier for either a national government or, in the absence of functional governance, for external/international forces, to isolate, marginalize, delegitimize and, ultimately, force them to "freeze" or relocate to places where they will be removed from their social base, and facilitate their dissolution or destruction by targeted counterterrorist operations.

Conclusion

In addition to confronting manifestations of terrorism in a variety of contexts and undermining terrorists' ideologies and organizational patterns, efforts to prevent, and mitigate the effects of terrorism in the long run requires addressing the underlying causes of terrorism. This includes socio-economic measures aimed at moderating some of the most painful effects of "traumatic" modernization. In the case of conflict-related terrorism, the basic incompatibilities over which the conflict has been fought need to be addressed (whether as part of the formal peace process or de facto, even in the absence of such). Any more general efforts aimed at increasing both the basic functionality and political legitimacy of the state (first and foremost, for its own population) and at fostering socio-political integration and preventing marginalization of significant segments of society in and of themselves have a long-term antiterrorism effect.

Still, if the dominant patterns of terrorism in the early twenty-first century have anything to teach us, they show that it is not domestic terrorism in functional states, employed by peripheral militant actors of the mixed (ethno)nationalist/religious or, less frequently, secular socio-political orientation, that accounts for the largest share of terrorist activity worldwide. Nor, for that matter, is it the transnationalized "global terrorism" driven by markedly universalist, existential, and utopian agendas. Instead, the main challenge for antiterrorism on a global scale involves a different kind of paradox.

On the one hand, weak states and ungoverned areas may be used by locally based militants and/or transnational terrorist networks to pose terrorist threats to neighboring states or other international actors. In the absence of functional national antiterrorist capacity or where it is very weak, foreign and international actors, particularly if they feel affected by terrorist threats emanating from these areas, may take up certain antiterrorist tasks that are normally associated with a functional state. This also underscores the dependence of effective antiterrorism in these areas on progress in peacebuilding and, more narrowly, state-building.

On the other hand, a disproportionately large share of global terrorist activity – and the fastest rise in terrorism over the past decade – has been accounted for by two highly intensive armed conflicts (in Iraq and in the Afghanistan/Pakistan context) that escalated *following* direct Western-led multilateral military interventions initially linked to the "war on terrorism" as a result of armed resistance to these interventions. Against this background, building more adequate global governance mechanisms to ensure that strategies undertaken by a handful of the world's lead states to manage major "threats to international peace and security", such as terrorism, do not actually contribute to the escalation, and further internationalization of the threat itself may need to be prioritized as a long-term terrorism prevention strategy on a global scale.

References

Arquilla, John, and Daniel Ronfeldt. 2001. *Networks and Netwars: The Future of Terror, Crime, and Militancy*. Santa Monica, CA: RAND.

Ashour, Omar. 2009. *The De-Radicalization of Jihadis: Transforming Armed Islamist Movements*. Abingdon: Routledge.

Bjorgo, Tore, ed. 2005. *Root Causes of Terrorism: Myths, Reality and Ways Forward*. Abingdon: Routledge.

Bjorgo, Tore, and John Horgan, eds. 2008. *Leaving Terrorism Behind: Individual and Collective Disengagement*. Abingdon: Routledge.

Crelinsten, Robert. 2009. *Counterterrorism*. Cambridge: Polity Press.

Crenshaw, Martha. 1995. *Terrorism in Context*. University Park, PA: Pennsylvania State University Press.

Crenshaw, Martha. 2010. *Explaining Terrorism: Causes, Processes and Consequences*. London: Routledge.

English, Richard. 2010. *Terrorism: How to Respond*. Oxford: Oxford University Press.

Gunaratna, Rohan. 2002. *Inside Al Qaeda: Global Network of Terror*. New York, NY: Columbia University Press.

Esposito, John L. 2002. *Unholy War: Terror in the Name of Islam*. Oxford: Oxford University Press.

Hoffman, Bruce. 1998. *Inside Terrorism*. New York, NY: Columbia University Press.

Horgan, John. 2005. *The Psychology of Terrorism*. London: Routledge.

Human Security Report Project, Simon Fraser University. 2011. *Human Security Report 2009/2010: The Causes of Peace and the Shrinking Costs of War*. New York, NY: Oxford University Press.

IEP (Institute of Economics and Peace). 2012. *Global Terrorism Index: Capturing the Impact of Terrorism in 2002–2011*. Sydney: Institute for Economics and Peace.

Juergensmeyer, Mark. 2000. *Terror in the Mind of God: The Global Rise of Religious Violence*. Berkeley, CA: University of California Press.

Kepel, Gilles. 2004. *Jihad: The Trail of Political Islam*. London: IB Tauris.

Krueger, Alan B. 2008. *What Makes a Terrorist: Economics and the Roots of Terrorism*. Princeton: Princeton University Press.

Laqueur, Walter. 2001. *A History of Terrorism*. New Brunswick, NJ: Transaction.

Lia, Brynjar, and Katja Skjolberg. 2005. *Causes of Terrorism: An Expanded and Updated Review of Literature*. Kjeller: Norwegian Defence Research Establishment (FFI).

Mayntz, Renate. 2004. *Organizational Forms of Terrorism: Hierarchy, Network or a Type Sui Generis?* Cologne: Max Planck Institute for the Study of Societies.

MIPT (Memorial Institute for Prevention of Terrorism). 2008. Terrorism Knowledge Database. Okhlahoma City, OK: MIPT. Accessed April 1, 2008 from http://www.mipt.org

Parachini, John V. 2001. "Comparing motives and outcomes of mass casualty terrorism involving conventional and unconventional weapons." *Studies in Conflict and Terrorism*, 24(5): 389–406.

Pikayev, Aleksandr, and Ekaterina Stepanova. 2008. "Non-proliferation and nuclear terrorism." In *Nuclear Weapons After the Cold War*, edited by Alexei Arbatov and Valery Dvorkin, 271–306. Moscow: Elinin Publ.

Ranstorp, Magnus, and Magnus Normark. 2009. *Unconventional Weapons and International Terrorism: Challenges and New Approaches*. London: Routledge.

Rollins, John. 2011. *Al Qaeda and Affiliates: Historical Perspective, Global Presence, and Implications for US Policy*. Congressional Research Service (CRS) Report for Congress no. R41070. Washington, DC: CRS.

Sageman, Mark. 2004. *Understanding Terror Networks*. Philadelphia, PA: University of Pennsylvania Press.

Sageman, Mark. 2007. *Leaderless Jihad: Terror Networks in the Twenty-First Century*. Philadelphia, PA: University of Pennsylvania Press.

Saikia, Jaideep, and Ekaterina Stepanova, eds. 2009. *Terrorism: Patterns of Internationalization*. London: Sage Publications.

Schmid, Alex P., ed. 2011. *The Routledge Handbook of Terrorism Research*. London: Routledge.

Shelley, Louise, and John T. Picarelli. 2002. "Methods Not Motives: Implications Of The Convergence Of International Organized Crime and Terrorism." *Police Practice and Research*, 3(4): 305–318.

START (National Consortium for the Study of Terrorism and Responses to Terrorism), University of Maryland. 2013. "Global Terrorism Database." Accessed January 20, 2013 from http://www.start.umd.edu/data/gtd/

Stepanova, Ekaterina. 2008. *Terrorism in Asymmetrical Conflict: Ideological and Structural Aspects*. Oxford: Oxford University Press.

UCDP (Uppsala Conflict Data Program) and PRIO (Peace Research Institute, Oslo). 2012a. "UCDP/PRIO Armed Conflict Dataset v.4-2012, 1946–2011." Accessed January 20, 2013 from http://www.pcr.uu.se/research/ucdp/datasets/ucdp_prio_armed_conflict_dataset/

UCDP. 2012b. "*One-sided Violence Dataset v 1.4-2012, 1989–2011*." Accessed January 20, 2013 from http://www.pcr.uu.se/research/ucdp/datasets/ucdp_one-sided_violence_dataset/

The White House. 2011. *National Strategy for Counterterrorism*. Washington, DC: The White House.

Chapter 8

Genocide and Large-Scale Human Rights Violations

Martin Shaw

In the post-Cold War era, the idea of global policy to prevent and punish genocide and crimes against humanity has finally begun to be realized, involving a multiplicity of agencies and initiatives. However, genocidal violence and other rights violations remain recurring problems in the twenty-first century world, and existing policy frameworks are by no means adequate to the challenge that they pose. In this chapter, I shall discuss the scope of these problems in the current period and of the various forms of global policy to address them, but first I shall define the conceptual and historical parameters of the problem.

The idea of global policy to prevent genocide dates to December 1946, when the United Nations (UN) General Assembly passed Resolution 96(1) defining genocide as a crime and initiating a process of drafting a convention to ban it. Two years later, in December 1948, the United Nations adopted the Convention on the Prevention and Punishment of the Crime of Genocide, at the same time as it adopted the Universal Declaration of Human Rights. Although the lawyer, Raphael Lemkin, who had developed the idea of genocide only four years earlier (Lemkin, 1944), claimed that the Convention was superior to the Declaration because it had the force of law, for more than four decades it seemed that the former's capacity for enforcement was no greater than the latter's, and that the Convention's main significance was also declaratory. The United Nations failed to establish the international criminal court envisaged as necessary for enforcement, and during the Cold War the Convention seemed a dead letter. Both the United States and the Soviet Union were responsible for large-scale human rights violations and willing to condone those of their allies. Even the Cambodian genocide of 1975–1979, whose leaders were allied to China rather than one of the superpowers, passed without serious attempts at international action.

Although human rights became more important in international politics in the 1980s, it was only after the end of the Cold War that practical efforts were made to prevent and punish genocide and other large-scale rights violations on a global

The Handbook of Global Security Policy, First Edition. Edited by Mary Kaldor and Iavor Rangelov.
© 2014 John Wiley & Sons, Ltd. Published 2014 by John Wiley & Sons, Ltd.

scale. New initiatives were taken, both in "humanitarian intervention" to prevent
or halt violence against civilians, and in the prosecution of perpetrators. Although
the United Nations failed to prevent either the large-scale violations in the Yugoslav
wars of the 1990s or the highly murderous Rwandan genocide of 1994, it established international criminal tribunals (the first since those at Nuremberg and Tokyo
in 1945–1946) to deal with perpetrators in each case. Partly because of the achievements of these tribunals, in 2002, an International Criminal Court (ICC) was finally
established. In 2004, the UN Secretary-General appointed a Special Advisor on the
Prevention of Genocide, and by the late 2000s, the United Nations supported the idea
of a Responsibility to Protect (R2P) for civilian victims of mass violence. In the United
States, genocide became, for the first time, a mass campaigning political issue during
the violence in Darfur, Sudan, which peaked in 2002–2003. A Genocide Prevention
Task Force, chaired by two former secretaries of state, produced a report in 2008
and the Obama administration established an Atrocities Prevention Board in 2011.

Conceptual and Legal Parameters

This chapter will discuss how extensive genocide and other violations are in the current period, and evaluate proposals for dealing with them. But in order to open up
these issues, we need to establish some parameters. This field is notorious for its
conceptual and terminological issues, which have been not only of academic importance, but also highly significant for policy-making. The 1948 Convention remains
the main benchmark for global policy, to which legal and political actors necessarily refer because of its established character and international legitimacy (140 out of
194 states have ratified it). However, lawyers also use the categories of crimes against
humanity and war crimes to encompass large-scale rights violations, and political
actors often invoke ideas like "ethnic cleansing" and "humanitarian crisis" as alternative labels. This labeling has been an important question in the policy debates of
the United Nations, governmental and nongovernmental actors because "genocide"
carries with it the legal obligations of the Convention, which other categories do not.
More than this, of course, the idea of genocide has acquired some of the "sacred-
evil" quality associated first of all with the Holocaust, which is regarded in Western
culture as the supreme evil of modern times (Alexander, 2002). Representatives of
victim-groups invariably seek to apply "genocide" rather than alternative labels to
their experiences, although both perpetrators and actors, who might be called on to
intervene, typically resist this label. (Perpetrators, however, also often invoke real or
imagined "genocide" against "their" people as an excuse for their atrocities.)

The matter is complicated further because the Genocide Convention – although
embedding a broad definition of genocide as various acts "committed with intent
to destroy, in whole or in part, a national, ethnical, racial or religious group, as
such" – represented a political compromise between the victorious great powers who
founded the United Nations. These powers were themselves responsible, directly and
indirectly, for huge atrocities against civilian populations during and immediately
after the Second World War. By protecting only certain types of "groups" ("national,
racial, ethnical, and religious"), the Convention excluded other types, such as political groups and social classes, which had also been subjected to destructive violence. It
also created an apparent requirement to determine in each case whether the attacked

population counted as one of the named types. Likewise, although the Convention embodied the multifaceted approach to the definition of the acts that constituted genocide, which had been proposed by the idea's originator, Raphael Lemkin (1944, pp. 79–80), it left some ambiguity as to the scope of these acts. In particular, as the legal scholar William Schabas comments,

> There is no doubt that the drafters of the Convention quite deliberately resisted attempts to encompass the phenomenon of ethnic cleansing within the punishable acts. According to the comments accompanying the Secretariat draft, the proposed definition excluded "certain acts which may result in the total or partial destruction of a group of human beings … namely … mass displacements of population." (Schabas, 2000, p. 196, quotation abbreviated in original)

Yet such forced removals of population – encouraged or tolerated by the great powers even as the Convention was adopted – were (as they remain) the most common method through which armed power destroyed civilian population groups.

These deficiencies have resulted in considerable legal confusion. Since courts have begun to apply the Convention, they have had to adjudicate its meaning and have expanded its definitions. The Rwanda tribunal, for example, declared Tutsis to be a protected group, even though it did not agree that they could be classified as an ethnic (or any of the other named types of) group. The Yugoslav tribunal used the Convention's specification of "physical and mental harm" as one of the means of genocide in order to argue that forced population removal, which causes great mental harm, constitutes genocide. Similarly, rape, although not named in the Convention as one of the means of group destruction, has been recognized in the courts as a method of genocide. However, courts have adopted a variety of positions on the applicability of genocide law. They have often charged perpetrators with crimes against humanity or war crimes because these charges are considered easier to prove, even though the acts in question might be regarded as genocide. In particular, they have often embraced the idea that "ethnic cleansing" is different from genocide. At times, it has also been difficult to avoid the conclusion that their judgments have involved, at least in part, rationalizations of political imperatives to avoid the determination of genocide. Therefore, we cannot take their judgments as definitive for global policy purposes.

In this chapter, therefore, I assume that although global policy must undoubtedly refer to the Genocide Convention, it is unacceptable to regard it as a sufficient basis for defining genocide. Global policy needs to be developed on the basis of a coherent, intellectually defensible understanding, even if that means pushing beyond the Convention. In the following discussion, I assume that genocidal action is "action in which armed power organizations treat civilian social groups as enemies and aim to destroy their real or putative social power, by means of killing, violence and coercion against individuals whom they regard as members of the groups" (Shaw, 2007, p. 154). I see this action as setting up genocide as "a form of violent social conflict or war, between armed power organizations that aim to destroy civilian social groups and those groups and other actors who resist this destruction" (Shaw, 2007, p. 154).

I thus return to Lemkin's original idea of genocide as a general class of actions directed towards group destruction. Genocide includes many different crimes against

humanity, and encompasses all sustained destructive violence in which civilian populations are attacked as enemies in themselves, rather than purely as a means of attacking an armed enemy. Genocide is closely related to war, but distinguished from it by
the fact that the enemy to be destroyed is a civilian population or group. It is therefore a practice that usually develops out of conventional political conflict or war,
whenever armed actors (states, armies, movements, militias, etc.) regard population
groups, as well as other armed actors, as distinct enemies.

The History of Genocide in Academic Perspectives

In this chapter, I deal with genocide in the period since the end of the Cold War,
because this is the period in which global policy-making on these questions has
become a serious area of policy. Indeed I call this the global era, not only because
the world is increasingly understood as a single social space but also because in this
context, the idea of shared global values has begun to have practical meaning (Shaw,
2000). Yet to grasp the problem of genocide in the current period, we need a larger
historical perspective, not least because policy responses are constantly informed by
references to events of the recent past. The phenomenon was first defined in the
context of what Lemkin (1944) called "the Nazi genocide", by which he meant the
regime's widely destructive policies towards *all* the peoples under German occupation. However, this seminal case often came to be understood in the late twentieth
century exclusively or mainly in terms of the mass murder of the Jews, now called
the Holocaust or Shoah, despite the fact that there were many other victims.

This historical re-interpretation was accompanied in turn by a growing tendency
to narrow the definition of genocide itself to "mass murder" (e.g. by Chalk and Jon-
ahsson, 1991, p. 23; Charny, 1994). In this perspective, the only cases that can be
unequivocally accepted as genocide are "mega-genocides" like the Armenian and
Rwandan genocides which, in terms of scale, organization, speed and above all mur-
derousness, most closely resemble the Holocaust. This in turn has led a number of
scholars to agree, as Scott Straus (2007, p. 497) concludes from a survey of recent
work, that genocide is a "rare" event. In line with these assumptions, the academic
field, understood as "comparative genocide studies", is conceived primarily as the
comparison on a transhistorical basis of these few historically exceptional events.

The problem with this paradigm is that it excludes most of the violence against
civilian populations which, on either Lemkin's or the Convention's definition, could
be regarded as genocide. Both define genocide as a type of destructive action (and
crime) against groups, which is neither limited to the particular method of mass
murder, nor confined to events of a certain scale. Leo Kuper (1981) pointed out that
genocide may take the form of relatively discrete, localized, small-scale "genocidal
massacres" as well as of large-scale centralized campaigns. The latter may be (almost
by definition) exceptional, but to confine the scope of genocide to these conceals from
view a great range of violence that is of the same type. It is as though we were to
confine the study of war to the world wars, and then argue that war is a rare event,
ignoring all the local and regional wars, civil as well as international, that occur.

Recent historiography has challenged this view of genocide from three directions.
First, several accounts (e.g. Moses, 2000, 2008; Levene, 2005; Kiernan, 2007) have
shown that genocide was extensively practiced in colonial contexts. During several

centuries of European colonization in the Americas, Australasia, Asia, and Africa, there were many violent episodes, recurring intermittently but often in linked series of events, each of which involved scores, hundreds, thousands, or tens of thousands of victims. These constitute a formidable history of genocidal violence, even if there are few if any Nazi-like centralized campaigns.

Second, new accounts of Europe in the first half of the twentieth century have emphasized that the Nazi genocide itself was an evolving, multitargeted process, in the context of a genocidal violence committed by many actors in the Second World War (Bloxham, 2009). Moreover, it was the culmination of three-quarters of a century of genocide in the eastern half of the continent. Thus it can be traced back to many smaller-scale, less murderous events of mass expulsion in a number of places and by numerous authors, during what Donald Bloxham (2007) calls the "great game of genocide" in south-eastern Europe from the 1870s to the early 1920s.

Third, accounts of genocide have increasingly stressed the limits of idea that it is normally highly centralized and state-centric. Settlers, not imperial authorities, were most often the direct perpetrators of colonial genocide, and even the Holocaust has been shown to have involved complex interactions between various Nazi agencies, allied actors, and population elements. Michael Mann (2005) proposes that "ethnic cleansing" and genocide typically involve a trinity of actors: radical regimes, paramilitaries, and popular constituencies (there are echoes here of Carl von Clausewitz's famous trinity of government, generals, and people in war). Christian Gerlach (2010) goes further, suggesting that variable coalitions of state and non-state actors are typically responsible for mass violence, in what he calls "extremely violent societies".

Historical Parameters of Global-Era Genocide

Although there has been, as we shall see, much attention to individual episodes of genocide in recent years, few attempts have been made to consider the general scope of genocide in the global era. Instead, two partly contradictory assumptions frame discourse about the current period. On the one hand, the occurrence of large-scale episodes like those in Rwanda and Darfur feeds arguments that the dangers of genocide are essentially unchanged compared to the Nazi era. On the other hand, it is widely assumed that because genocide has now been criminalized, worldwide enforcement of genocide law is now possible through the ICC, and because the United Nations and United States have taken initiatives, genocide prevention can easily be achieved today in a way that it could not be in the past. Taken together, these assumptions often feed a simplistic campaigning politics of genocide prevention. Yet a careful historical evaluation will lead us to question both these assumptions, indicating a more complex context for global policy development.

Just as the high genocidal period in Europe (roughly 1875–1949) involved a shift in the locus of genocide from the colonies to the European imperial heartlands, so the period since 1949 has seen a shift back to some of the (now post-colonial) regions of the global South. After three-quarters of a century in which Europe was the world epicenter of genocide, the phenomenon disappeared from the continent during the Cold War. Mann (2005) argues that there was a decline in the global North, largely as a result of the success of earlier waves in creating mono-ethnic states. (In the remaining Northern multiethnic states, he argues, politics is largely defined by class, region, and gender, while continuing ethnic politics, both historic and new, is largely nonviolent.) Although this is true, the reason that mono-ethnic states were consolidated in the late 1940s was because the result of the Second World War caused the success of the Soviet programme for ethno-national reorganization (accepted by the West) in which borders and populations were homogenized in line with Stalin's political and security objectives. Even as the Genocide Convention was being drafted, the forced removal of Germans and others completed this programme. The definitive nature of this settlement was reinforced by the discipline of the Cold War, which threatened that any attempt to further revise borders or move populations would ignite a nuclear confrontation.

In the global South, however, it was a different matter. First, the global Cold War (Westad, 2005) was far more murderous than the European. The outcome of the Second World War was a definitive defeat of the German and Japanese empires, but whereas territories liberated from Germany were divided up by agreement, those liberated from Japan were the subject of titanic struggles for power. A destructive civil war in China led to the establishment of Mao's Communist regime, whose instability produced in the following two decades both the genocidal famine of the Great Leap Forward (1958–1961) in which at least 15 million people died, and the violent attacks on urban society of the Cultural Revolution (1966–1969). Civil wars in Korea, Vietnam, and Cambodia were internationalized in wars between nationalist forces (mostly Communist-led) and the United States. All of these involved huge violence against civilians, both strategic and genocidal, culminating in the Cambodian genocide of 1975–1979. In Indonesia, military leaders and paramilitaries carried out large-scale mass killings of Communists in 1965. Likewise, if on a smaller scale, in Latin America, anti-Communist Cold War dictatorships continued to "disappear" and kill leftists, often stealing their children, into the 1980s and even afterwards.

Second, even where the Cold War was not pivotal, the terminal crises of the European empires produced huge power struggles. In some places, for example in Algeria and Kenya, these arose because the empires and their colonists were not willing to cede power. Wars of "national liberation" were often characterized by genocidal violence as insurgents targeted colonial defenders, including ethnic groups allied to colonial power, and counterinsurgents evicted and massacred populations believed to support insurgents. In other cases, for example India and Rwanda, where empires negotiated their withdrawals, the struggle for the succession of power between rival nationalist elites produced massive forced removals of population, massacres, and rape. Furthermore, when post-colonial states became established, new "national" elites were often drawn from particular ethnic groups and ruled over diverse populations in a quasi-imperial, authoritarian fashion, leading to wars of secession from states like Indonesia (after its conquest of East Timor), Nigeria, Pakistan, Sri Lanka, Sudan, Ethiopia, and Iraq, all of which involved partly genocidal insurgencies and/or counterinsurgencies.

All of these conflicts were affected by the Cold War, chiefly because competing states and insurgent groups were sponsored by the superpowers and their European allies, but none of them were rooted primarily in the East–West conflict. This meant that the end of the Cold War, the decline of Communism, and the weakening of international sponsorship by no means resulted in an end to genocidal conflict worldwide.

On the contrary, instabilities of state structures and rivalries between armed movements based on different sections of society remained, even appeared, in new regions and were often internationalized within regions after 1989.

The post-Cold War specter of genocide was first raised on the fringes of Europe. The opening up and collapse of the Soviet empire in the 1980s led to partial democratization, but this opened the door to ethnic nationalism that often took more or less exclusive forms. In Azerbaijan, conflict over the partly Armenian-populated Ngorno–Karabakh region led to genocidal massacres and expulsions and countermassacres and counterexpulsions by Azeri and Armenian nationalists. Similar conflicts developed in Georgia, and later in Chechnya (part of the Russian Federation) and Kyrgyzstan. None of these conflicts, however, became of great global significance, mainly because they occurred within the Russian sphere of influence, and Russia (like China and other great quasi-imperial states) was less affected by Western-centered global policy-making than were many smaller or weaker states.

However, the question of genocide became of huge significance in post-Cold War international politics because of the break-up of Communist Yugoslavia, an independent federation on the borders of the European Community. In the wars of succession, both Serbian and Croatian nationalists sought to create ethnically homogenized territories through "cleansing" their territories of other ethnic groups. The Bosnian war, with its forced removals of populations, concentration camps, systematic rape, and the siege of the multiethnic capital, Sarajevo, culminating in the massacre of 7000–8000 Bosnian men and boys at Srebrenica, was a prime catalyst for Western and UN responses to genocide in the post-Cold War period. The European Union, United States and NATO as well as the United Nations were involved in repeated efforts to influence the course of events, through diplomatic initiatives, humanitarian aid, and military intervention. The conflict introduced the term "ethnic cleansing" into global discourse, and raised the idea of "humanitarian intervention" to a major question of Western and global policy-making. In the Yugoslav context, these issues reverberated throughout the 1990s, at least until the final major war of the series in Kosovo in 1998–1999. Here the Serbian regime responded to NATO intervention by escalating mass expulsions, but NATO's own escalation in response ultimately brought about the return of most Albanians.

The genocidal wars in Yugoslavia were notorious for UN and Western policy failures that allowed local nationalist elites to perpetrate extensive violence and to block international attempts to promote multiethnic states (Rieff, 1996; Simms, 2001). However, in a global perspective, it could be argued that this new genocidal violence in the North was relatively well internationally managed compared to that in other world regions. Indeed, the European genocide of the 1990s appears to have subsided in the twenty-first century. Although genocidal nationalism has had some successes (for example, the Bosnian–Serbian statelet, Republika Srpska, remains largely autonomous and in control of the region "cleansed" in 1992–1995), new genocide has been prevented since around 2000. After a further decade, the principal perpetrators indicted by the International Criminal Tribunal for former Yugoslavia have finally been arrested. The states of the Western Balkans are being brought within the orbit of the European Union and NATO, constraining rivalries between states and nationalist movements from becoming extensively violent once more. It is now plausible to interpret genocide in Yugoslavia, and to a lesser extent in the former

Soviet region, as a phenomenon of transition, linked to the crises of quasi-imperial and multinational Communist states during the ending of the Cold War system.

In many regions of the South, in contrast, recent genocidal violence has been more long-lasting, often rooted in Cold War-era conflicts, even if these have changed their forms, and given less global attention and resources than the Yugoslav wars. Mann (2005) argues that in the South, the diffusion of the "ideal of the nation-state" and the confusion of demos and ethnos are creating new threats of "cleansing", rein-forced by the decline of class politics, the weakening of liberalism and socialism, and the rise of fundamentalism (including "theo-democracy", which he suggests could represent a third variant of his perversion of democracy thesis, alongside ethnic and class versions). Settler "cleansing" continues against indigenous peoples, especially in Latin America and "middlemen ethnicities", like the Chinese in Southeast Asia, remain threatened.

Nevertheless, Mann (2005, p. 517) argues that "cleansing" is less likely than in the past to lead to large-scale, national, exterminatory "genocide". According to him, there are few cases in which rival bi-ethnic claims are capable of fuelling the most murderous developments that occurred in Rwanda and Burundi: "I can think of no other closely analogous case to Rwanda/Burundi elsewhere in the world. Per-haps this was the last of the world's [large-scale] genocides" (Mann, 2005, p. 517). This speculation is difficult to test. Exceptional events are, by definition, unusual and unpredictable: no one foresaw the extent of the Rwandan genocide even shortly beforehand. And the crises in the Congo in the late 1990s and in Darfur, Sudan, in the early 2000s were certainly on a large scale, even if genocidal killing was less concerted and more episodic than in Rwanda.

Mann (2005, p. 518) also argues that genocidal violence might be less globally important: "Most [ethnopolitical] conflicts occur in some of the poorest, most iso-lated parts of the world, and so they become only local black holes." This suggests a more fruitful line of analysis. In Europe in the first half and in East Asia in the third quarter of the twentieth century, genocidal violence was, to a considerable extent, produced in and driven by central geopolitical conflicts of the interstate system. Today, it is concentrated in less strategically central regions, especially sub-Saharan Africa, and in more localized conflicts. Moreover, if there is a lower likelihood of "mega-genocides", this could be related to the reduction in the number of interstate wars. Genocidal violence, while implicated in transnational and global relations, is not linked to large-scale conventional armed conflicts, but to civil wars or "new wars" (Kaldor, 1999).

Reasons Not To Be Cheerful

Yet five factors should lead us to reject an optimistic reading of these trends. First, even limited interstate wars can have genocidal consequences. For example, the US invasion of Iraq in 2003 initially appeared to have succeeded as a quick-fix operation, but led to years of war in which civilian populations were widely targeted by rival militias. Within six weeks, President George W. Bush was boasting of the cessation of "major combat", and civilian casualties during this phase of the operation were unintended consequences of military operations, estimated in the low thousands. However, the invasion led to resistance by militia based in the Sunni population, reinforced by non-Iraqi fighters, some of which turned their violence against the softer targets of the Shia and Kurdish populations who were perceived to have benefited from the US-installed regime. In the subsequent low-grade civil war between Sunni- and Shia-based militia that peaked in 2005–2007, each sought to drive the "other" population from local areas they controlled, resulting in hundreds of thousands of forced removals and tens of thousands of deaths. Iraq, a decade after the US invasion, is a country with much more complete local segregation and millions of internally displaced people, as well as a country from which large numbers of refugees have fled to neighboring states.

Second, even localized civil conflicts can be extremely destructive. The Rwandan genocide occurred, after all, in a tiny state with a small population and no global strategic significance; the genocidal civil war in Darfur occurred in an isolated region, the strategic significance of which was limited even in regional terms. Yet both of these cases saw hundreds of thousands of deaths and even more displacements.

Third, local conflicts are typically connected in regional patterns of international relations. The Rwandan genocide was the culmination not only of a genocidal history in post-colonial Rwanda that could be traced back over thirty years, but of genocidal violence in neighboring Burundi and Uganda. The genocide led, in turn, to new civil and international wars in neighboring Zaire (subsequently renamed the Democratic Republic of the Congo), in which further genocidal violence was committed. René Lemarchand identifies recurring regional cycles of cross-border refugee flows and violence:

> the central pattern which recurs time and time again is one in which ethnic polarization paves the way for political exclusion, exclusion eventually leading to insurrection, insurrection to repression, and repression to massive flows of refugees and internally displaced persons, which in turn become the vectors of further instability. (Lemarchand, 2009, p. 31)

Fourth, local and regional patterns of conflict may be worsened as well alleviated by well-meaning global interventions. The Rwandan genocide followed the attempt of the United States and other powers, backed up by the United Nations, to resolve the armed conflict between the Hutu-nationalist Rwandan government and the Rwandan Patriotic Front (RPF), formed by Uganda-based Rwandan Tutsi exiles, and to promote democracy by involving internal opponents of the regime as well. Global intervention led to a power-sharing and democratization agreement, adopted at Arusha (Tanzania) in 1993, but this satisfied neither the government nor the RPF, and set up commitments on each side that the other did not trust it to carry out. This led fairly directly to the final stage of the civil war, in which a new invasion by the RPF was followed by the coordinated genocidal campaign carried out by elements of the Rwandan regime.

Finally, even some apparently positive current global trends and policies are clearly associated with new patterns of genocidal violence. The democratization of the post-Cold War era, actively encouraged by Western democracy-promotion, has seen many more states hold free or semi-free elections. However, there is evidence that democratization is often associated with war and violent conflict. Indeed, elections are often focal points for violence because elites often use manipulation and intimidation to rig their results, provoking conflict, or mobilize group identities to create violence against the presumed supporters of political opponents. Even in India, a well-established democracy, antipopulation violence is a regular (if usually contained) accompaniment of elections (Wilkinson, 2006). In many democratizing countries, especially where leaders seek to steal elections or mobilize against electoral theft (for example, Zimbabwe in 2008, Kenya in 2009, and Ivory Coast in 2011), more serious violence often accompanies elections. Mann (2005), who argues that stable democracies do not see "ethnic cleansing" or genocide, argues that democratizing states are actually more at risk than stable authoritarian regimes.

Policies and Politics of Genocide Prevention

"Prevention" has been at the heart of the law, politics, and scholarship of genocide since Lemkin invented the term and the Convention committed the United Nations as well as the signatory states to "punish and prevent" it. However, its emergence as a serious strand of global policy-making is not just a post-Cold War development, as I noted earlier, but can be dated even later, to the late 1990s and 2000s, as a reaction against the continuing *failure* to prevent genocide in former Yugoslavia and Rwanda in the early 1990s.

Over Yugoslavia, the widespread failure to recognize genocide, reflected in the global adoption of the perpetrator euphemism "ethnic cleansing" to describe the antipopulation violence, largely continued after the conflict. However, while international discourse generally failed to recognize the genocidal character of Serbian (and some Croatian) policies, courts and international institutions did subsequently recognize the 1995 Srebrenica massacre as an instance of genocide. This recognition highlighted failures of global policy-making, moreover because it was the Dutch battalion of the UN forces who had handed over Muslim men and boys to Serbian forces before they were slaughtered, and UN commanders in Sarajevo and policymakers in New York who had failed to back up the Dutch forces and resist the Serbian conquest of the Srebrenica enclave.

Over Rwanda, the initial UN and Western resistance to recognizing genocide, reflected in its ignoring the reports and warnings of the local UN commander, Canadian General Roméo Dallaire, and the preference for regarding the violence as the "excesses" of civil war, had given way within a few weeks to the adoption of genocide language. But by then, most of the estimated 800,000 victims had died, and even after recognizing genocide, the United Nations failed to intervene to prevent its continuation (the only effective intervention being the belated introduction of French forces that protected perpetrators as much as victims). These failures, the product of a lethal combination of great-power indifference and the UN's bureaucratic culture, led in 1998 to fulsome apologies in the Rwandan capital, Kigali, by US President Bill Clinton and UN Secretary-General Kofi Annan. The US failure was influentially generalized in a prize-winning book by Samantha Power (2002), while the UN's failure was cogently analyzed by Michael Barnett (2002), who had been a UN insider during the genocide.

Although the United Nations had failed to prevent most of the atrocities in former Yugoslavia and Rwanda, it had established international criminal tribunals for both in quick succession (in 1993 and 1994), which made important contributions to developing a legal framework for responding to international atrocities. The post-Second World War international tribunals at Nuremburg and Tokyo had represented victors' justice: all defendants were German and Japanese leaders and commanders, and there was no question of Allied leaders facing charges for any crimes for which they were responsible. The International Criminal Tribunal for former Yugoslav (ICTY), in contrast, arraigned figures from all sides of the conflict. Although Serbians and to a lesser extent Croatians predominated, reflecting the balance of responsibility for atrocities, Bosnian government and Kosovo Liberation Army figures were also charged. The ICTY also upheld the principle that Western states, too, should be accountable for their actions, in establishing a committee that examined the conduct of NATO's campaign over Kosovo (although it concluded that no charges should be brought). The ICTY often shared the official Western ambivalence about "ethnic cleansing" as genocide, laying charges mainly for war crimes and crimes against humanity, but laid genocide charges against the main Serbian leaders. The International Criminal Tribunal for Rwanda, in contrast, was overwhelmingly concerned with genocide, and achieved the first international convictions for the crime; however, it avoided indicting the RPF for the atrocities for which it was responsible, reflecting the international guilt for the inaction during the 1994 genocide. Despite the mixed records of the tribunals, they proved crucial precedents, leading to the establishment of the permanent International Criminal Court (ICC) in 2002.

Also responding to the global failures over Rwanda, the Canadian government established an International Commission on Intervention and State Sovereignty whose report (Evans and Sahnoun, 2001) urged the global adoption of the principle of a "responsibility to protect" threatened civilian populations. This idea enshrined both the idea of states' responsibilities to protect their own populations and the principle of international intervention when states failed to do so. As noted earlier, in 2004, the United Nations appointed a Special Advisor on the Prevention of Genocide, and in 2005, the Responsibility to Protect (R2P) was adopted by a UN world summit and incorporated in a Security Council resolution in 2006. In 2009, the Secretary-General proposed a report on implementing the principle that was adopted by a resolution of the General Assembly. The R2P agenda could be seen as more closely specifying the principle of genocide prevention, although R2P debates were not always framed in terms of genocide. This reflected both the continuing international ambiguity about the term and the desire of those who pushed for adoption of R2P to overcome terminological barriers to action.

The global commitment to stopping genocide had meanwhile been tested in the crisis over Darfur, which erupted in 2003. In response to rebel movements, the Sudanese government – in alliance with the Janjaweed militia drawn from the Arab population – attacked various "African" populations perceived as linked to the insurgents. Within two years the civilian death toll, direct and indirect, was in the hundreds of thousands. Although both populations were Muslim, the Sudanese regime was already an issue for the Christian Right in the United States because of the earlier conflicts involving southern Sudan, and this combined with a liberal genocide-prevention lobby to pressurize the Bush administration. The US Secretary of State, Colin Powell, first declined to acknowledge genocide, but in 2004 changed his stance, the first time the United States had charged another state with ongoing genocide. A UN-backed force from the African Union was sent to Darfur and the United Nations established an international commission on the crisis. The latter's report (International Commission on Darfur, 2006) studiously avoided the conclusion that the Sudanese government was responsible for genocide, in a move widely seen as reflecting political pressures to avoid recognizing genocide. However, after the United Nations referred the report to the ICC, in 2008 its prosecutor charged the Sudanese president, Omar al-Bashir, and others with genocide.

By the late 2000s, moreover, genocide-prevention politics had moved further in the United States. In 2007, the US Holocaust Memorial Museum, the US Institute of Peace, and the American Academy of Diplomacy set up a Genocide Prevention Task Force (GPTF), convened by two former secretaries of state, which reported the following year (Albright and Cohen, 2008). It urged that prevention should be a "presidential priority" and made detailed recommendations for harnessing the US governmental apparatus to this cause. In 2011, President Barack Obama established an Atrocities Prevention Board, which Samantha Power would chair, and in 2012 laid out the responsibilities of the various branches of government following the GPTF's model. In principle, the world's greatest political and military power was now fully committed to the cause of genocide prevention.

Limitations of Global Genocide Policy

The rapid development of global policy-making on genocide and mass atrocities since the late 1990s has been impressive, given the overwhelming failure to advance this process in the half-century after the adoption of the Genocide Convention in 1948. Clearly genocide prevention is now increasingly embedded in the normative and institutional frameworks of the United Nations and, perhaps even more important, of the greatest military power, the United States. Moreover, the conclusion of the work of the ICTY, including the trials of Radovan Karadzic and Ratko Mladic (under way at the time of writing), together with the beginnings of the work of the ICC, dealing so far with a range of African cases, promise a consolidation of the international commitment to punish genocide and crimes against humanity.

However, there are several reasons for caution about these developments. To be effective, the commitment of the United Nations to protecting civilians and preventing genocide requires the active support of the Security Council and therefore of its permanent members. Two of these, China and the Russian Federation, remain authoritarian or semi-authoritarian states and are consistently unsupportive of international action that might infringe the sovereignty of states, even where these are perpetrating genocide and atrocities. Although they sometimes tolerate Western initiatives, such as the 2011 Libya intervention, they often block all but the most minimal action, as is happening (as I write) during debates about action against the Syrian regime over its serial massacres of civilians in 2012. Moreover, the Libya intervention also posed very clearly one of the major dilemmas of "humanitarian intervention", whether under the R2P or not: atrocities result from political and armed conflict, and action to protect civilians is also an intervention in conflict. While NATO's intervention, under UN auspices, undoubtedly protected some civilians from the Ghadaffi regime's violence, it also stimulated the civil war that caused more civilian deaths, and its latent goal was to support the insurgents' overthrow of Ghadaffi. This experience was, of course, one of the reasons for Russian and Chinese opposition to action over Syria.

Effective global policy concerning genocide and atrocities thus depends heavily on support from Western states, and especially the three permanent members of the Security Council, the United States, Britain, and France. Certainly the European Union, other Western states, nongovernmental organizations, social movements, and global media (including Internet activists) also impact on the commitment of the United Nations to pursue antigenocidal policies; however, ultimately the decisive factor is the attitude of the permanent members and above all the United States. The latter's crucial role is reinforced by the fact that global genocide awareness, discourse, campaigning, education, and scholarship are all heavily centered in the United States. This centering is itself the outcome of the US's global military, political, economic and cultural preeminence, as well as the recognition of its past failures. However, it also reflects the distinctive role of the Holocaust as a reference point in US culture and politics to a much greater extent than in other Western countries, let alone non-Western regions.

This dependence of global genocide policy on the United States may often be a strength. By definition, the world's strongest and most sophisticated state has a lot to offer to all dimensions of efforts to prevent, halt, and mitigate the effects of atrocities. However, it is also problematic because it means that genocide-prevention will depend on the United State's perceptions of its national interests and priorities, and will inevitably be tied to its wider international policies and alliances, and indeed to the domestic politics of the United States. The perceptions of global genocide policy by other actors, both state and non-state, will be skewed by their relationships to the United States, and the limitations of US policy will impact strongly on global policy.

There are many clear signs of the problems this causes. First, the idea of "humanitarian intervention" was heavily tarnished by its linkage to the US invasion of Iraq. Although the intervention did not have humanitarian ends, the Saddam Hussein regime had previously committed genocide against the Kurds and others, and this record was used to support the intervention. Second, the United State's own record includes atrocities, and its military methods produce new atrocities. The United States was primarily responsible for maintaining UN sanctions against Iraq in the 1990s, even at the cost of high levels of civilian suffering, which raised questions of genocide (Gordon, 2010). The US reliance on high-level bombing and drone attacks predictably produces regular massacres of civilians: in Afghanistan there has even been a pattern in which wedding parties have repeatedly been massacred (Rockel, 2012). Third, US military action may indirectly provoke genocidal violence by others, as we saw in Iraq.

Furthermore, the close US alliance with Israel, coupled with the centrality of the Holocaust to US genocide politics, creates a danger that genocide-prevention will be harnessed to Israel's military goals. Israel is the world's most militarily active small state, founded on the destruction of Palestinian Arab society through the expulsions of 1948 (these can be seen in a genocide frame: Shaw, 2010), which continue to be consolidated by Israeli policies today. Israel's attacks on Gaza in 2008–2009 included targeted killings of Hamas members and their families, and also of police personnel, as well as a "collective punishment" of the civilian population for voting for Hamas. Since the Iranian president Mahmoud Ahmadinejad's outrageous Holocaust denial and call for the destruction of the Israeli regime in 2005, Israeli politicians have identified a genocidal threat to Israeli Jews from the Iranian nuclear programme (even though Israel itself has nuclear weapons and Iran is believed to be engaged in "nuclear hedging" rather than active acquisition of weapons). This cause has been reinforced by the campaigning of an organization called Genocide Prevention Now, led by the veteran genocide scholar Israel Charny, and even secured the backing in 2006 of the International Association of Genocide Scholars. In 2012, Israeli Prime Minister Benyamin Netanyahu directly invoked the Holocaust in his attempt to pressure the United States to endorse an attack on Iran.

Clearly the US Atrocities Prevention Board is unlikely to act to stop the United State's own atrocities or to counter the Holocaust militarism of its close ally. Nor will the United States be a consistent advocate of international justice: the Bush administration refused to ratify the Rome treaty establishing the International Criminal Court, and went to extraordinary lengths to ensure that other states would never submit US citizens to prosecution in front of it. Although the United States pragmatically supported the Security Council's reference of Darfur to the ICC, its cooperation with the court, even under Obama, is restricted and could easily be reversed by a future Republican administration. The ICC's inability, to date, to pursue cases outside the African continent reflects the fact that international justice applies only to lesser states and non-state actors under certain conditions. The fact that the United States gives only very limited support to the ICC, while China, the emerging superpower, does not support it at all and other major powers are also reluctant, indicates the probability that international law will continue to see very limited enforcement in the future.

We can conclude from this survey that global policy on genocide is a heavily contested field, closely entwined with the divisions between major states. The two decades since the Rwandan genocide have certainly placed the issue of genocide and atrocity prevention much higher on the agenda of world politics, and have led to important initiatives. But the difficulties of genocide protection, civilian protection against atrocities, and punishment of perpetrators are unlikely to be consistently overcome in the near, or probably even the medium, future. Only deeper civil-society involvement and a broadening of its international base are likely to give permanent strength to the new impetus to consistent global policy to prevent genocide.

References

Albright, Madeleine, and William Cohen. 2008. *Preventing Genocide: A Blueprint for US Policymakers (Report of the Genocide Prevention Task Force)*. United States Institute of Peace/United States Holocaust Memorial Museum.

Alexander, Jeffrey C. 2002. "On the Social Construction of Moral Universals: The "Holocaust" from War Crime to Trauma Drama." *European Journal of Social Theory*, 5(1): 5–85.

Barnett, Michael. 2002. *Eye-Witness to a Genocide*. Ithaca, NY: Cornell University Press.

Bloxham, Donald. 2007. *The Great Game of Genocide*. Oxford: Oxford University Press.

Bloxham, Donald. 2009. *The Final Solution: A Genocide*. Oxford: Oxford University Press.

Chalk, Frank, and Kurt Jonassohn. 1990. *The History and Sociology of Genocide: Analyses and Case Studies*. New Haven, CT: Yale University Press.

International Commission of Inquiry on Darfur. 2005. "Report of the International Commission of Inquiry on Darfur." Accessed December 4, 2013 from http://www.un.org/News/dh/sudan/com_inq_darfur.pdf

Charny, Israel W. 1994. "Toward a Generic Definition of Genocide." In *Genocide: Conceptual and Historical Dimensions*, edited by George Andreopoulous, 64–94. Philadelphia, PA: University of Pennsylvania Press.

Evans, Gareth, and Mohamed Sahnoun, 2001. *The Responsibility to Protect: Report of the International Commission on Intervention and State Sovereignty*. Ottawa, ON: International Development Research Centre, Minister of Foreign Affairs.

Gerlach, Christian. 2010. *Extremely Violent Societies: Mass Violence in the Twentieth Century World*. Cambridge: Cambridge University Press.

Gordon, Jay. 2010. *Invisible War: The United States and the Iraq Sanctions*. Cambridge, MA: Harvard University Press.

Kaldor, Mary. 1999. *New and Old Wars*. Cambridge: Polity Press.

Kiernan, Ben. 2007. *Blood and Soil: A World History of Genocide and Extermination from Sparta to Darfur*. New Haven, CT: Yale University Press.

Kuper, Leo. 1981. *Genocide*. Harmondsworth: Penguin.

Lemarchand, René. 2009. *The Dynamics of Violence in Central Africa*. Philadelphia, PA: University of Pennsylvania Press.

Lemkin, Raphael. 1944. *Axis Rule in Occupied Europe*. New York, NY: Carnegie.

Levene, Mark. 2005. *Genocide in the Age of the Nation State* (2 volumes). London: IB Tauris.

Mann, Michael. 2005. *The Dark Side of Democracy*. Cambridge: Cambridge University Press.

Moses, A. Dirk. 2000. "An Antipodean Genocide? The Origins of the Genocidal Moment in the Colonization of Australia." *Journal of Genocide Research*, 2(1): 89–107.

Moses, A. Dirk, ed. 2008. *Empire, Colony, Genocide*. New York: Berghahn Books.

Power, Samantha. 2002. *A Problem from Hell: America and the Age of Genocide*. New York, NY: Basic Books.

Rieff, David. 1996. *Slaughterhouse: Bosnia and the Failure of the West*. New York, NY: Simon & Schuster.

Rockel, Stephen. 2012. "Wedding Massacres and the War in Afghanistan." In *Theatres of Violence: Massacre, Mass Killing and Atrocity throughout History*, edited by Philip G. Dwyer and Lynndal Ryan, 271–284. Oxford: Berghahn Books.

Schabas, William A. 2000. *Genocide in International Law*. Cambridge: Cambridge University Press.

Shaw, Martin. 2000. *Theory of the Global State: Globality as Unfinished Revolution*. Cambridge: Cambridge University Press.

Shaw, Martin. 2007. *What is Genocide?* Cambridge: Polity Press.

Shaw, Martin. 2010. "Palestine in an International Historical Perspective on Genocide." *Holy Land Studies*, 9(1): 1–24.

Simms, Brendan. 2001. *Unfinest Hour: Britain and the Destruction of Bosnia*. London: Allen Lane.

Straus, Scott. 2007. "Second-Generation Comparative Research on Genocide." *World Politics*, 59: 476–501.

Westad, Arne. 2005. *The Global Civil War: Third World Intervention and the Making of Our Times*. Cambridge: Cambridge University Press.

Wilkinson, Stephen I. 2006. *Votes and Violence: Electoral Competition and Ethnic Riots in India*. Cambridge: Cambridge University Press.

Chapter 9

Transnational Crime

John P. Sullivan

Broadly speaking, transnational crime involves criminal enterprises that cross national boundaries. For our purposes, we are looking at transnational criminal organizations (TCOs) that engage in transnational organized crime (TOC). Phil Williams (1994) suggested that transnational organizations, including TCOs, conduct centrally directed operations in the territory of two or more nation-states, mobilize operations and optimize strategies across national boundaries. For Williams, these enterprises were functionally specific and sought to penetrate, not acquire new territories. That is changing. That loose definition is only a starting point for understanding the dynamics and logic structure of what is perhaps best understood as "global crime".

The United Nations Convention against Transnational Organized Crime, known as the *Palermo Convention*, defines an organized criminal group as:

> a structured group of three or more persons, existing for a period of time and acting in concert with the aim of committing one or more serious crimes or offences established in accordance with this Convention, in order to obtain, directly or indirectly, a financial or other material benefit ... (United Nations, 2000, Article 2(a), p. 2)

Essentially, transnational or global crime exploits global economic flows to garner profit and power. In the traditional view, TOC and TCOs are concerned only with profit; that is, exploiting the black market to concentrate wealth. As Phil Williams (1994) noted:

> Most transnational criminal organizations are concerned about profit rather than politics, and are unlikely to want to undermine a system that they are able to exploit and abuse for their own purposes. A few other groups, especially those linked to "pariah states" may have more disruptive goals. Treating these very different organizations as part of a single global challenge is not only misleading conceptually, but could encourage a policy response that is as ineffective as it is undifferentiated. (Williams, 1995, p. 58)

The Handbook of Global Security Policy, First Edition. Edited by Mary Kaldor and Iavor Rangelov.
© 2014 John Wiley & Sons, Ltd. Published 2014 by John Wiley & Sons, Ltd.

Profits attributed to TOC are vast. According to the United Nations Office on Drugs and Crime (UNODC, 2011, p. 7), TCOs generated an estimated $870 billion or about 1.5% of the global gross domestic product (GDP) in 2009. According to Havocscope, the global black market is valued at $1.82 trillion, with organized crime valued at $322 billion, money laundering valued at $2.5 trillion, and corruption and bribery valued at $1.6 trillion (Havocscope, 2013). Almost certainly these values, which are interrelated, are understated due to the occult nature of organized crime and black markets. In addition, a large gray market certainly raises the profits of TCOs. Many TCOs are primarily concerned with profit, and most seek to sustain equilibrium (Bailey and Taylor, 2009) with the state or states they operate in. Others, as in the case of some Mexican cartels, seek much more.

Transnational Groups and Enterprises

The participants in the global criminal arena include a range of actors. These include traditional mafias (like the Sicilian mafia or Cosa Nostra, Camorra, 'Ndrangheta in Italy, which are estimated to earn €100 billion – about 7% of Italy's GDP annually with a corresponding €65 billion in annual liquidity (Squires, 2012)), the American mafia (like New York's traditional "Five families"), the Russian *mafiya*, outlaw motorcycle gangs (like the Hells Angels), drug cartels (like the Mexican and Columbian cartels), Chinese Tongs and Triads, transnational gangs or *maras*, pirates, and hybrid entities (like Colombia's FARC and Taliban insurgents) that merge crime, terrorism, and insurgency (Sullivan, 2002).

TCOs are involved in a range of enterprises – both illicit and licit. The largest profit center is illicit *pharma* or drugs, including heroin (opium), cocaine, cannabis, synthetic drugs (like methamphetamine and ecstasy), and the illicit use of prescription drugs. The international narcotic trade generates vast sums of money. While the true value is hard to accurately define, it is estimated that the global illicit *pharma* market is worth at least $411.44 billion, with marijuana topping the list valued at $141.80 billion, followed by cocaine at $85 billion, prescription drugs at $68 billion, heroin at $68 billion, methamphetamine at $28.25 billion, and ecstasy at $16.07 billion (Havocscope, 2013).

For the United States, illicit drugs are a $60 billion per year industry patronized by at least 16 million (Caulkins, Reuter, Iguchi, and Chiesa, 2005). Havocscope (2013) places the values higher, estimating the drug market value in the United States at $215 billion. Spain follows closely with its market valued at $95 billion, Italy at $83 billion, Canada at $44.5 billion, Mexico at $40 billion, and the United Kingdom at $28 billion. This global drug trade has significant destabilizing effects on society, nations, communities, crime, and policy. Attempts to address this illicit business have been fraught with frustration, political and policy stalemates, and growing violence and instability (Sullivan, 2010).

In the Americas, the narcotics trade has had a discernible impact on other forms of crime – violent crime in particular. In extreme cases, it can even fuel insurgency, as seen in Colombia. Drug violence leads to extreme rates of violent crime, interacts with the small arms trade that leads to enhanced gang violence, and stimulates money laundering and corruption that collectively undermine the economy and governance

(UNODC, 2008). According to the International Crisis Group (ICG), the situation in the Americas can be characterized as follows:

> Well-armed, well-financed transnational trafficking and criminal networks are flourishing on both sides of the Atlantic and extending their tentacles into West Africa, now an important way station on the cocaine route to Europe. They undermine state institutions, threaten democratic processes, fuel armed and social conflicts in the countryside and foment insecurity and violence in the large cities across the Americas and Europe. In Colombia, armed groups derive large incomes from drug trafficking, enabling them to keep up the decades-long civil conflict. Across South and Central America, Mexico and the Caribbean, traffickers partner with political instability. (ICG, 2008, p. 3)

Drugs are only one component of the global illicit economy. Other enterprises or profit centers that comprise what some analysts term "deviant globalization" include human trafficking (including the global sex trade and trafficking migrants); arms smuggling; trade in wildlife; resource extraction (illegal mining, petroleum theft, illegal logging); exploitation of intellectual property – software, CDs, movies, video; contraband smuggling including tobacco; gambling; loan sharking; money laundering; and toxic waste trafficking and dumping (Gilman, Goldhammer, and Weber, 2011). Emerging profit centers for TOC include cybercrime, identity-related crime, trafficking in cultural property, environmental crime, piracy, and organ trafficking (UNODC, 2013). TCOs also operate legitimate businesses, including shops and restaurants (Squires, 2012), both as profit centers and as a venue for laundering illicit funds.

Networks of Gangs and Cartels

Transnational crime is moving in some cases from hierarchical, command-and-control organizations to a constellation of interactive and adaptive networks. Here we see the impact of "netwar", a hybrid form of conflict waged by irregular adversaries including drug traffickers (*narcos*), gangsters, and terrorists (Arquilla and Ronfeldt, 2001). Collectively, these articulations of gangs and cartels could be viewed as a strain of violent non-state-actors (VNSAs) or irregular armed forces. Sullivan (2002) categorized these actors into five basic types: (1) terrorists; (2) criminals (organized crime); (3) insurgents (rebels); (4) warlords (including pirates); and (5) private military companies (PMCs). All of these types are abstractions and the groups interact through strategic alliances (Williams, 1994) and hybrid combinations facilitated by Internet communication technology (ICT) stimulated by globalization (deviant or otherwise).

Gangs are the simplest instantiation of organized crime (transnational or local). As Sullivan (1997, 2000, 2008) has observed, gangs can fit into one of three generations: turf, market, and mercenary/political.

- **First Generation Gangs** are traditional street (or prison) gangs with a turf orientation. Operating at the lower end of extreme societal violence, they have loose leadership and focus their attention on turf protection and gang loyalty within their immediate environs (often a few blocks or a neighborhood). When they engage in criminal enterprise, it is largely opportunistic and local in scope. These turf gangs are limited in political scope and sophistication.

- **Second Generation Gangs** have a business focus. They are entrepreneurial and drug-centered. They protect their markets and use violence to control their competition. They have a broader, market-focused, sometimes overtly political agenda and operate in a broader spatial or geographic area. Their operations sometimes involve multi-state and even international areas. Their tendency for centralized leadership and sophisticated operations for market protection places them in the center of the range of politicization, internationalization, and sophistication.
- **Third Generation Gangs** have evolved political aims. These are the most complex gangs and they operate – or aspire to operate – at the global end of the spectrum, using their sophistication to garner power, aid financial acquisition, and engage in mercenary-type activities. To date, most 3 GEN Gangs have been primarily mercenary in orientation; in some instances they have sought to further their own political and social objectives (e.g. Mara Salvatrucha 13 (MS-13) in Central America).

Three factors influence gang evolution: politicization, internationalization, and sophistication. Transnational gangs fit into the second and third generations. Notable transnational gangs include MS-13 and 18th Street that operate throughout the United States and in Central America, and Barrio Azteca/Los Aztecas that operates along the United States–Mexico border near Texas and Chihuahua. Barrio Azteca was a key player in the intense bloodbath during the battle for the plaza (or drug distribution zone) in Ciudad Juárez. The Barrio Azteca formed part of the enforcement arm of the Juárez Cartel known as La Línea.

La Línea is exemplary in depicting the networked actors emerging among contemporary transnational gangsters:

> Comprised of drug dealers, *sicarios* (hit men), and corrupt police officials, it protects the cartel's business interests and trafficking operations. It may merely be wording designed to convey control or garner loyalty – a case of sophisticated branding. Alternatively, it might be a unifying concept to consolidate efforts to protect the market. Practically, it is both of these – a salient example of the adaptive organizational forms evolving within the narco-conflict.
>
> Essentially, La Línea is a networked gang, a specialized node in a transnational criminal enterprise. It appears to be operating as more than a turf-oriented street gang (a first-generation gang) or even a narco-trafficking gang (a second-generation gang). It appears to act as a specialized variant of a third-generation gang essentially serving as mercenaries. It has transnational reach through its allies and inter-networked cross-border gangs and cartel partners. It demonstrates a higher degree of sophistication than many gangs, and it even fulfills para-political functions for its cartel employer. Its network configuration enables morphing form to exploit custom network links to carry out specific, specialized missions. (Sullivan and Logan, 2011, p. 48)

Gangs often inter-operate with cartels and other organized crime groups. They act as enforcers – foot soldiers and hit men (*sicarios*). They also frequently occupy the retail rung of TCO drug distribution structures. Sometimes they forge alliances as in the case of MS-13 and Los Zetas (Sullivan and Elkus, 2012a). Occasionally, they morph into powerful transnational actors in their own right (as in the case of MS-13). These *maras* are no longer just street gangs. They have morphed across three generations through interactions with other gangs and transnational organized crime organizations (e.g. narcotics cartels/drug trafficking organizations) into complex networked threats and have evolved into a transnational security concern. As a result of globalization, the influence of information and communications technology, and travel/migration patterns, gangs that were formerly confined to local neighborhoods have spread their reach across neighborhoods, cities, and countries. This reach is increasingly cross-border and transnational (Sullivan, 2012a).

While TCOs are traditionally viewed as static, hierarchical, profit seeking entities, drug cartels seem to present a case for adaptation and a preference for seeking power. Drug cartels are also evolving as we see in the case of Mexico's *narcotraficantes*. Three stages of cartel evolution have been identified (Bunker and Sullivan, 1998, p. 59):

1st Phase Cartel (Aggressive Competitor)
The first phase cartel form originated in Colombia during the 1980s and arose as an outcome of increasing US cocaine demand. This type of cartel, characterized by the Medellín model, realized economies of scale not known to the individual cocaine entrepreneurs of the mid-1970s. This early cartel was an aggressive competitor to the Westphalian state because of its propensity for extreme violence and willingness to directly challenge the authority of the state.

2nd Phase Cartel (Subtle Co-Opter)
The second phase cartel form also originally developed in Colombia, but in this instance, is centered in the city of Cali. Unlike their Medellín counterparts, the Cali cartel was a shadowy organization devoid of an actual kingpin. Its organization is more distributed and network-like, rather than hierarchical. Many of its characteristics and activities were stealth-masked and dispersed, which yielded many operational capabilities not possessed by the first phase cartel form. Specifically, it possessed leadership clusters that are more difficult to identify and target with a decapitation attack. The Cali cartel was also more sophisticated in its criminal pursuits and far more likely to rely upon corruption, rather than violence or overt political gambits, to achieve its organizational ends. This cartel form has also spread to Mexico and the dynamic is still evolving.

3rd Phase Cartel (Criminal State Successor)
Third phase cartels have the potential to pose a significant challenge to the modern nation-state and its institutions. A third phase cartel is a consequence of unremitting corruption and co-option of state institutions. While this "criminal state successor" has yet to emerge, warning signs of its eventual arrival are present in many states worldwide. Of current importance in the United States are the conditions favoring narco- or criminal-state evolution in Mexico. Indeed, the criminal insurgency in Mexico could prove to be the genesis of a true third phase cartel, as Mexican cartels battle among themselves and the state for dominance. Essentially, third phase cartels rule "criminal enclaves," acting much like warlords.

Gangs and cartels have the ability to act like warlords in "failed communities" and weak states, potentially generating the development of "other governed spaces"

(Sullivan, 2002). Here we see TCOs acting as new warmaking (and potentially statemaking) entities. This blurs the distinctions between crime and war and the distinctions among criminals, terrorists, and insurgents. Pirates are a special case in this new war-making paradigm. Pirates are non-state actors that challenge not only state integrity, but also specifically the ability of all states to protect the flows of commerce on the open seas. Typically viewed as a sea-borne threat, they need a secure base of operations on the land. They frequently find this operating haven in failed or weak states and within criminal enclaves. Pirates elude the rule of law, especially customary international law. Piracy is a crime of opportunity. In the case of the Somali pirates:

> Piracy is an economic activity: well-organized criminals exploiting the horrible deterioration of present-day Somalia. These criminals have made a rational assessment of risk. The political dimension is important not because this piracy is politically motivated but because internal political protection – and the lack of external political response – lessens the risks that pirates face. That is how politics has generally aided piracy throughout history. If the situation is to change, pirates must perceive that their jeopardy has increased. (Murphy, 2010)

Piracy is essentially a local or regional problem with global ramifications. It also has the potential to interact with TOC and extreme stateless political Islam (as seen in Somalia). Pirates are specialized littoral variant of warlords:

> Pirates are a sea-borne analog to the land-based warlord. Pirates seek to dominate a spatially defined area – usually sea lanes, shipping lanes, straits and similar segments of littoral regions. Piracy is on the rise in many contested regions of the globe ... Profit, plunder (greed), war, revolutionary motives and lawlessness are fueling this maritime variation of the land-locked warlord. (Sullivan, 2002, p. 246)

A Global TCO Sampler: AfPak, Mexico, Central America, and West Africa

Chronicling the entire breath of TOC goes beyond the scope of this chapter and would likely fill many volumes. That said, pertinent examples of contemporary TOC activity provide depth to the discussion and outline key elements of the evolution of this global threat. Three specific regions are highlighted to demonstrate emerging potentials. These are Afghanistan/Pakistan (AfPak), Mexico and Central America, and West Africa.

Afghanistan/Pakistan (AfPak)

TCOs in the AfPak region are intricately tied to Islamist militancy. Indeed, the narcoeconomy of the region empowers a mix of both state and non-state actors. This mix has been called "Narco-Jihad" (Ahrari, 2009). Narcotics are the chief economic driver in the AfPak conflict zone. The Taliban funds its military operations with the proceeds from the lucrative drug trade. As Vanda Felbab-Brown (2009, p. 2) observes, "a multitude of actors are involved in Afghanistan's opium poppy production, including the Taliban, all levels of the Afghan government, law enforcement, unofficial powerbrokers, and tribal elites." Opium drives the informal economy in Afghanistan. The actors in the trade range from village elites to official and unofficial Taliban power brokers in Afghanistan and Pakistan to international smuggling networks. Afghanistan produces 90% of the global opium supply and is the second largest cannabis resin producer in the world. Other illicit enterprises in the AfPak border regions include illicit timer trade, antiquities, and cigarette smuggling. These goods transit Pakistan to the south and Iran to the west. Central Asian states to the north provide connectivity to Russia. The drug trade and other illicit flows weaken state control and cement linkages among the Taliban, insurgents, and criminal enterprises (Shelley and Hussain, 2009).

According to Ahrari (2009) a "narco-jihad" is being funded by the opium trade in the AfPak region. The conflict is intense in Afghanistan and growing in Pakistan's North-West Frontier Province and the Federally Administered Tribal Areas, as well as Baluchistan. The Taliban derives a 20% tax (*zakat*) from the trade. Ahrari states that an "iron triangle" of warlords, corrupt government officials, and Taliban–al-Qaeda enable the narco-trade and fuel the Islamist insurgency. In addition, the

> Narco-trade in both Afghanistan and Pakistan interfaces with actors in Iran, Turkey, and Central Asia, which serve as transit routes to the global market. Terrorist groups and transnational drug and crime syndicates are involved in protection, price control, and distribution of opium to regional and global markets. (Ahrari, 2009, p. 44)

Mexico and Central America

Mexico is ground zero for one of the most intense criminal wars in contemporary times. Since 2006, Mexico's drug cartels and associated gangs have been waging a brutal war against their criminal rivals and the state. The war has been punctuated by hyper-violence and barbarism. Beheadings, assassinations of journalists, mayors, and police punctuate the battle for spoils and power. Car bombings, the use of infantry tactics and information operations sustain the cartels' grip on power (Sullivan, 2012b, 2012c; Sullivan and Bunker, 2012; Sullivan and Elkus, 2012b). Somewhere over 100,000 people have been killed in the conflict; another 24,000 are missing or disappeared. At least 230,000 refugees or internally displaced persons have fled the violence and between 45 and 67 journalists have been killed. Accurate numbers are hard to find (Sullivan, 2012b).

Instrumental and symbolic violence are the tools of the cartels as they battle for control of the *plazas (*drug transshipment points, cities, and routes). Typically, organized crime seeks to elude the state, if not able to do so it seeks to co-opt state actors through bribes and corruption. When those fail, the gangsters have only one option left: confronting the state (Bailey and Taylor, 2009). In Mexico, the cartels are currently confronting the state. Entire regions or "zones of impunity" are under cartel control. Assassinations and atrocity are common:

> Individuals and teams of *sicarios* wage brutal war against their adversaries. The result: assassinations, kidnappings, torture, dismemberment, beheading, persons hung from bridges, rivals boiled in pots to become what is euphemistically called *posole* (or soup), and at least one recent crucifixion. Notable attacks have included grenades launched against Mexican Independence day celebrations in Morelia, killing 8 and wounding over 100 in 2008; the brutal murder of 13 high school students at a party in Ciudad Juárez in 2010; the ambush of Rodolfo Torre, candidate for Governor in Tamaulipas along with 4 others; and an armed assault on a birthday party in Torreón that killed

17 and wounded 18 others. Mass graves (*narcofosas*) are a recurring gruesome reality. Notable *narcofosas* include 51 corpses found near Monterrey in July 2011 and 450 mass internees in mass graves in Durango and Tamaulipas in April 2011. The August 2011 arson attack on a Monterrey gambling house – the Casino Royale – left 52 dead in under 3 minutes. Numerous mass killings accompany this small sample. (Sullivan, 2012b)

The cartels involved include the Sinaloa cartel, Los Zetas, La Familia Michoacana, Los Cabelleros Templarios (Knights Templar), the Cartel del Golfo, the Juárez cartel and others. The cartels are frequently shifting alliances, adapting and morphing to sustain operations, secure power, and garner profit. The cartels are linked to a range of actors including transnational gangs, local turf gangs, and international mafias. While drugs are their mainstay, many cartels have branched out into other profit centers, including petroleum theft, mining, timber theft/illegal logging, kidnapping, human trafficking, arms trafficking, software and intellectual property piracy, and protections (street taxes/extortion).

The cartels run their own communications networks (radio towers), suborn police forces, and provide local security (and insecurity). They mark their vehicles with distinct markings and sometimes wear uniforms. They also force mayors to pay taxes for protection (Agence France-Presse, 2013). Cartel information operations (including *narcomensajes* [narcomessages] in the form of *narcomantas* [narcobanners], *narcopintas* [narcograffiti], *narcobloqueos* [narcoblockades], "corpse-messaging" – or leaving a message on a mutilated corpse – are used to shape the operational space. The cartels want their unique message out. Kidnappings (*levantóns*), mass graves (*narcofosas*) and social cleansing (mass targeted murders within cartel zones of influence) reinforce their message. The cartels also provide utilitarian social goods to secure community support. Some cartels, like La Familia Michoacan and Los Cabelleros Templarios cast themselves as "social bandits" (Hobsbawm, 2000/1969) to enhance their legitimacy and secure support.

Narcocultura, including *narcocorridos* (folk songs) and alternative belief systems, complement the cartels' activities. Narcos venerate folk saints, including Jesús Malverde, Santa Muerte, and San Nazario (deceased leader of La Familia). *Narcocultura* is a powerful way of forging alternative primary loyalties (Sullivan, 2012c).

Organized crime's assault on the Mexican state results in "criminal insurgency". Criminal insurgency differs from conventional insurgency because the gangsters don't wish to overtly takeover the mechanisms of the state; rather they seek freedom of action – autonomy and economic control of territory and economic flows. The narcos seek to dominate the market free from state interference. As a result, they "hollow" out the state. Criminal insurgency can exist at several levels (Sullivan, 2012a; Sullivan and Bunker 2012):

- *Local Insurgencies* (gangs dominate local turf and political, economic, and social life in criminal enclaves or other governed zones);
- *Battle for the Parallel State* (battles for control of the "parallel state". These occur within the parallel state's governance space, but also spill over to affect the public at large and the police and military forces that seek to contain the violence and curb the erosion of governmental legitimacy and solvency);

- *Combating the State* (criminal enterprise directly engages the state itself to secure or sustain its independent range of action; cartels are active belligerents against the state);
- *The State Implodes* (high intensity criminal violence spirals out of control; the cumulative effect of sustained, unchecked criminal violence and criminal subversion of state legitimacy through endemic corruption and co-option. Here the state simply loses the capacity to respond).

The end result is the development of "criminal enclaves" where gangsters rule in a "parallel state" under conditions of "dual sovereignty". Neighborhoods (*colonias*), towns, and prisons come under control of cartels and gangs in this situation. For example, six out of ten prisons in Mexico are subject to gangster self-rule (*The Scotsman*, 2012). This situation exists in Mexico and in parts of Central America (e.g. El Salvador, Honduras) where both Los Zetas and the *maras* (MS-13 and 18th Street) are the *de facto* rulers of cities, towns, and exurban regions. Gangsters orchestrate all meaningful subnational political life. Governments seek to regain control, but the diffuse gang structures are hard to contain and operate a shadow web of control.

Mexican cartels are also expanding their reach. They operate in the United States, in Europe, throughout Latin America, and in West Africa. They are also spreading their tentacles to the Pacific with operations in Australia. Essentially they go where the money is. Los Zetas are reported to have links with the 'Nhdrangheta, and the Sinaloa cartels reportedly operate in Africa, Asia, Australia, and Europe. Basically, all Mexican cartels have operations and alliances with local and transnational gangs in the United States. The Sinaloa cartel and Los Zetas are bitter rivals and, through a series of alliances, battle each other for control of turf and transport routes. MS-13 engages in opportunistic alliances with drug cartels.

West Africa

Transnational crime in West Africa includes: "drug trafficking, advanced fee and Internet fraud, human trafficking, diamond smuggling, forgery, cigarette smuggling, illegal manufacture of firearms, trafficking in firearms, armed robbery and the theft and smuggling of oil" (UNODC, 2005, p. iii). As in other regions of the world, crime and corruption are mutually supportive. In many aspects, West African organized crime relies on opportunist networks as opposed to hierarchical mafias. In addition, several West African countries serve as operational bases for transshipment of drugs from Latin America or Asia to Europe. Cross-border crimes in West Africa also include the recruitment of child soldiers and mercenaries (de Andrés, 2008). Social condition and weak states make the impact of transnational crime a pervasive threat to stability and the rule of law. Post-conflict scenarios, weak state structures and corruption favor exploitation by TCOs. As de Andrés observed:

> The very structure of West African economies, based on exploitation of natural resources (mining or single crop export oriented agriculture), coupled with a patrimonial conception of the State, contribute too in creating an enabling environment within which disrespecting existing laws and using institutional prerogatives for private goals are not

only justified, but considered as an indicator of power. All such factors also attract unscrupulous economic operators, facilitate the establishing and development of local and transnational criminal networks, and promote the rooting of a cultural model under which money can buy everything including impunity, political power, social considera- tion and respectability. (de Andrés, 2008, p. 204)

Organized criminal networks in sub-Saharan Africa are entrepreneurial. In many senses, they are defined by the activities and contacts of key actors with personal ties and shifting alliances framing networks that coalesce around a portfolio of crimi- nal projects (de Andrés, 2008, p. 219). Links between organized crime and terrorist organizations are also believed to be a threat in the region. Both Hezbollah (which retains a significant criminal funding arm) and al-Qaeda affiliates are believed to be active in the region.

Guinea-Bissau has a vibrant drug trade and Nigeria has an active petro-insurgency (criminal insurgency variant). The MEND (Movement for the Emancipation of the Niger Delta) and affiliated and competing gangs and militias are engaged in a bat- tle with state forces, oil companies, and each other. A state of lawlessness prevails with organized robberies, kidnappings, car bombings, armed attacks, and oil theft (bunkering) joining with corruption to fuel the power base of rival warlords (Watts, 2008). Criminal enterprises fuel the conflict. Terrorist-criminal overlap is also a con- cern. As Felbab-Brown and Forest (2012) note, interaction between these two types of group center on resources and mutual benefit. Both terrorists and organized crime seek control over resources and the population. As Sullivan noted:

Organized crime and terrorism are related in complex and diverse ways. Crime of many varieties is frequently used to fund terrorist activity. This may include smuggling, iden- tity theft, sales of counterfeit goods (cigarettes, clothing, videos, etc.), illicit technology transfer, gems smuggling, piracy, high-tech crime and many varieties of fraud. Money laundering is at the core of global organized criminal enterprise. It is in this fiscal trans- action or enterprise where terrorists, gangsters and other illicit actors are most likely to cooperate. These links sometimes mature into alliances of convenience. (Sullivan, 2002, p. 241)

According to Cockayne and Williams (2009), West Africa is being buffeted by an invisible tide of transnational organized crime. This tide forms a "narco- intervention" that impacts urban slums, coastlines, and banking systems that are subject to weak state control. Foreign trafficking organizations have found West Africa's permissive environment to be a benefit for their operations. Easily corrupted law enforcement agencies with weak territorial reach favor TCOs. While Nigerian gangsters pioneered the local drug trade, global actors are moving into the lucra- tive space. Essentially West Africa forms a pivot in a tri-continental South America– Africa–Europe space of illicit flows.

Cockayne and Williams (2009) foresee a period of "coming drug wars" as the tide of cash fuels political instability and violence among local and foreign factions. They point out that West African politics are predatory and often produce "vampire" or "mafia" states driven by resource extraction. As a consequence some areas of the state are contested. Contested zones favor transnational drug trafficking organiza- tions either because the state acquiesces to their presence or because they are "no-go zones" for the police and state security forces. Cockayne and Williams (2009) suggest that "criminal enclaves" may result from this situation. This parallels the suggestion by Sullivan (2012a) that criminal enclaves could and do emerge in areas dominated by cartels and gangs. These criminal enclaves challenge state and state institutions and could range in geospatial scope from "failed communities" (or neighborhoods) to "failed" or "feral" cities (Norton, 2003; Bunker and Sullivan, 2011).

Violent Non-State Actors, Statemaking, and State Reconfiguration

Some cartels have formulated part of their operations as private armies; hence, they are effectively irregular armed actors or violent non-state actors (VNSAs). These groups challenge the solvency (legitimacy plus capacity) of states and contribute to insecurity when they erode the state monopoly on violence. Using both instrumental and symbolic violence, the criminal soldiers/VNSAs intimidate government officials, attack journalists, and gain concessions from legitimate political mechanisms. By usurping state authority they create new "primary loyalties" and networks of obligation and reciprocity (Davis, 2010). For Davis, this can lead to "fragmented sovereignty", which is essentially a neomedieval stratified sovereignty where gangsters rule some spheres and the state and its institutions rule over others. Corruption is the glue that binds the two alternative power structures. For Williams (2008), this neofeudal arrangement is a feature of potential "new middle ages" where competing structures, fragmented authority, and "no-go zones" challenge the Westphalian state, and possibly the rise of a new dark age. As such, it is possible to view TOC as a driver on new statemaking potentials (Tilly, 1985).

State change and formation is likely to involve state reconfiguration. Gangs and cartels (TCOs) can have profound impacts on sovereignty. These illicit networks have the potential to reconfigure states. Such reconfiguration could include erosion of state capacity (or the exploitation of a state capacity gap), corrupting and co-opting state organs (government, the police, the judiciary) in all or part of the state – through the development of criminal enclaves – or at the extreme edge, state failure. State reconfiguration is potentially a more common outcome than abject state capture or state failure (Garay-Salamanca, Jorge, Salcedo-Albarán, and De Leoán-Beltrán, 2009, 2010).

Conclusion: Illicit Networks of Crime and Disorder

US policy scholars call the hybrid threat convergence of crime, terrorism, and insurgency the triple threat (Center for Strategic Leadership-Homeland Security Policy Institute, 2011). TOC ranges from urban gangs, through transnational gangs to drug trafficking organizations, mafias, and poly-crime cartels. Mexico's cartels are exemplary for both their brutal violence and confrontation with the state. They are also pioneers in moving from drug trafficking to multiple criminal enterprises (the Colombian cartels remained largely focused of the drug trade). Not all TCOs directly confront the state. Most prefer the traditional organized crime *modus operandi* of evading or eluding the state and using corruption and bribes to co-opt the state. Nevertheless, some TCOs (notably Mexico's cartels) have engaged the state in direct battle. While this challenges the conventional wisdom, the cartels are still able to make vast sums of money to fuel their quest for power and plunder.

TOC is present in all regions of the world. In the contemporary threat spectrum, both traditional mafias and criminal VNSAs form the constellation of transnational crime. Transnational gangs and enterprises are increasingly networked (some internally, some are hierarchical internally and networked externally). Their activities range from local to global, and all (even local actors) are linked to global illicit flows. Activities embraced by transnational crime include trafficking in persons (both the sex trade and migrant smuggling), drug trafficking, arms trafficking, counterfeit products, environmental extraction and trafficking of wildlife, maritime piracy, and increasingly cybercrime (UNODC, 2010). In contested zones, TOC threatens governance and stability and potentially changes the nature of sovereignty. In areas where organized crime avoids direct state confrontation, it still threatens the state and rule of law through the corroding influence of corruption. In all cases, TOC threatens democratic consolidation.

Increasingly, TOC utilizes network configurations to pursue its goals. This could include linking with other transnational gangs of mafias to conduct joint operations or alliances of convenience. It also includes links with corrupt arms of the state in collusive exploitative relationships. Insurgents and terrorists also combine with TCOs to forge alternative funding mechanisms and create enclaves free from state interference to pursue their individual and collective goals. The cumulative result is a kind of "recombinant *delectiva*" (crime) where adaptive multipurpose illicit networks reconfigure their structure, alliances, and enterprises to ensure survival and maximum profit. Gangsters embrace limited terrorism and terrorism embraces limited criminal enterprises to pursue their goals of political change. Insurgencies are criminalized and criminals wage insurgencies (criminal insurgency).

This insurgent consequence of "deviant globalization", which fuels "new wars" that mix war, organized crime, and massive humanitarian atrocities, demands new security structures (Kaldor, 2007). New security structures that feature attributes of policing, intelligence, and stability operations are needed to ensure global stability. Essentially this results in the "gendarmification of war". New multilateral efforts, including global gendarmerie forces that are able to link local policing and security with expeditionary stability policing, investigations, and prosecutions, are needed to negotiate this new security environment.

References

Agence France-Presse (AFP). 2013. "Mexican mayors admit paying cartels to stay alive." *France 24*, February 8. Accessed February 11, 2013 from http://www.globalpost.com/dispatch/news/afp/130208/mexican-mayors-admit-paying-cartels-stay-alive

Ahari, Ehsan. 2009. "The Dynamics of "Narco-Jihad" in the Afghanistan-Pakistan Region." In *NBR Report #20, Dec 2009: Narco-Jihad: Drug Trafficking and Security in Afghanistan and Pakistan*, by Ehsan Ahari, Peter Mandaville, Vanda Felbab-Brown, Louise I. Shelly, and Nazia Hussain, 43–57. The National Bureau of Asian Research.

de Andrés, Amado Philip. 2008. "West Africa Under Attack: Drugs, Organized Crime and Terrorism as the New Threats to Global Security." *UNISCI Discussion Papers No. 16*, January. Accessed February 11, 2013 from http://www.defensesociale.org/xvicongreso/usb%20congreso/2ª%20Jornada/01.%20Panel%206/07.%20UNISCI%20DP%2016%20-%20Andres.pdf

Arquilla, John, and David Ronfeldt, eds. 2001. *Networks and Netwars: The Future of Terror, Crime, and Militancy*. Santa Monica, CA: RAND.

Bailey, John, and Matthew M. Taylor. 2009. "Evade, Corrupt, or Confront? Organized Crime and the State in Brazil and Mexico." *Journal of Politics in Latin America*, 1(2): 3–29.

Bunker, Robert J., and John P. Sullivan. 1998. "Cartel Evolution: Potentials and Consequences." *Transnational Organized Crime*, 4(2): 55–74.

Bunker, Robert J., and John P. Sullivan. 2011. "Integrating Feral Cities and Third Phase Cartels/Third Generation Gangs Research: The Rise of Criminal (Narco) City Networks and BlackFor." *Small Wars & Insurgencies*, 22(5): 764–786.

Caulkins, Jonathan P., Peter Reuter, Martin Y. Iguchi, and James Chiesa. 2005. *How Goes the 'War on Drugs'? An Assessment of US Drug Problems and Policy*. Santa Monica, CA: RAND, Drug Policy Research Center.

Center for Strategic Leadership-Homeland Security Policy Institute (CSL-HSPI). 2011. "The Hybrid Threat: Crime, Terrorism and Insurgency in Mexico." Proceedings for the Joint Policy and Research Forum, US Army War College, October 20.

Cockayne, James, and Phil Williams. 2009. "The Invisible Tide: Towards an International Strategy to Deal with Drug Trafficking Through West Africa." New York, NY: International Peace Institute, October. Accessed February 11, 2013 from http://www.ipinst.org/media/pdf/publications/west_africa_drug_trafficking_epub.pdf

Davis, Diane E. 2010. "Irregular Armed Forces, Shifting Patterns of Commitment, and Fragmented Sovereignty in the Developing World." *Theory and Society*, 39: 397–413.

Felbab-Brown, Vanda. 2009. "The Drug Economy in Afghanistan and Pakistan, and Military Conflict in the Region." In *NBR Report #20, Dec 2009: Narco-Jihad: Drug Trafficking and Security in Afghanistan and Pakistan*, by Ehsan Ahari, Peter Mandaville, Vanda Felbab-Brown, Louise I. Shelly, and Nazia Hussain, 1–22. The National Bureau of Asian Research.

Felbab-Brown, Vanda, and James J.F. Forest. 2012. "Political Violence and the Illicit Economies of West Africa." *Terrorism and Political Violence*, 24(5): 787–806.

Garay-Salamanca, Luis Jorge, Eduardo Salcedo-Albarán, and Issac De Leoán-Beltrán. 2009. "From State Capture towards the Co-opted State Reconfiguration: An Analytical Synthesis." *Working Paper No. 61*, June. Bogotá: METODO.

Garay-Salamanca, Luis Jorge, Eduardo Salcedo-Albarán, and Issac De Leoán-Beltrán. 2010. *Illicit Networks Reconfiguring States: Social Network Analysis of Colombian and Mexican Cases*. Bogotá: METODO.

Gilman, Nils, Jesse Goldhammer, and Steven Weber. 2011. *Deviant Globalization: Black Market Economy in the 21st Century*. New York, NY: Continuum.

Havocscope. 2013. "Havocscope Black Market Information." Accessed February 10, 2013 from http://www.havocscope.com/black-market-value/

Hobsbawm, Eric. 2000/1969. *Bandits*. New York, NY: The New Press.

International Crisis Group (ICG). 2008. "Latin American Drugs I: Losing the Fight." *Latin America Report No. 25, March 14*. Accessed February 10, 2013 from http://www.crisisgroup.org/~/media/Files/latin-america/25_latin_american_drugs_i_losing_the_fight_final.pdf

Kaldor, Mary. 2007. *New & Old Wars* (2nd ed). Stanford, CA: Stanford University Press.

Murphy, Martin N. 2010. "Dire Straights: Taking on Somali Pirates." *World Affairs*, July/Aug. Accessed February 10, 2013 http://www.worldaffairsjournal.org/article/dire-straits-taking-somali-pirates.

Norton, Richard J. 2003. "Feral Cities." *Naval War College Review*, 65(4): 97–106.

The Scotsman. 2012. "Report claims gangs and drug cartels run most of Mexico's jails." September 28. Accessed February 11, 2013 from http://www.scotsman.com/news/international/report-claims-gangs-and-drug-cartels-run-most-of-mexico-s-jails-1-2546721

Shelley, Louise I., and Nazia Hussain, "Narco-Trafficking in Pakistan- Afghanistan Border Areas and Implications for Security." In *NBR Report #20, Dec 2009: Narco-Jihad: Drug Trafficking and Security in Afghanistan and Pakistan,* by Ehsan Ahari, Peter Mandaville, Vanda Felbab-Brown, Louise I. Shelly, and Nazia Hussain, 23–27. The National Bureau of Asian Research.

Squires, Nick. 2012. "Mafia is Italy's biggest business." *The Telegraph,* January 10. Accessed February 10, 2013 from http://www.telegraph.co.uk/finance/financialcrisis/9006027/Mafia-is-Italys-biggest-business.html

Sullivan, John P. 1997. "Third Generation Street Gangs: Turf, Cartels and Netwarriors." *Transnational Organized Crime,* 3(3): 95–108.

Sullivan, John P. 2000. "Urban Gangs Evolving as Criminal Netwar Actors." *Small Wars and Insurgencies,* 11(1): 82–96.

Sullivan, John P. 2002. "Terrorism, Crime and Private Armies." *Low Intensity Conflict & Law Enforcement,* 11(2/3): 239–253.

Sullivan, John P. 2008. "Transnational Gangs: The Impact of Third Generation Gangs in Central America." *Air & Space power journal-Spanish edition, Second Trimester.* Accessed February 10, 2013 from http://www.airpower.maxwell.af.mil/apjinternational/apj-s/2008/2tri08/sullivaneng.htm

Sullivan, John P. 2010. "Counter-supply and counter-violence approaches to narcotics trafficking," *Small Wars & Insurgencies,* 21(1): 179–195.

Sullivan, John P. 2012a. "From Drug Wars to Criminal Insurgency: Mexican Cartels, Criminal Enclaves and Criminal Insurgency in Mexico and Central America. Implications for Global Security." *Working Paper No. 9, FMSH-WP-2012-09,* April. Paris: Fondation Maison des sciences de l'homme.

Sullivan, John P. 2012b. "Barbarization in Mexico Punctuated by Hyper Violence." *IVN,* September 25. Accessed February 11, 2013 from http://ivn.us/2012/09/25/barbarization-in-mexico-drug-war/

Sullivan, John P. 2012c. "Criminal Insurgency: Narcocultura, Social Banditry, and Information Operations." *Small Wars Journal,* December 3. Accessed February 11, 2013 from http://smallwarsjournal.com/jrnl/art/criminal-insurgency-narcocultura-social-banditry-and-information-operations

Sullivan, John P., and Robert J. Bunker. 2012. *Mexico's Criminal Insurgency: A Small Wars Journal-El Centro Anthology.* Bloomington, IN: iUniverse.

Sullivan, John P., and Adam Elkus. 2012a. "Los Zetas and MS-13: Nontraditional Alliances." *CTC Sentinel, Combating Terrorism Center, United States Military Academy,* 5(6). Accessed February 10, 2013 from http://www.ctc.usma.edu/posts/los-zetas-and-ms-13-nontraditional-alliances

Sullivan, John P., and Adam Elkus. 2012b. "Tactics and Operations in the Mexican Drug War." Infantry, Sep-Oct: 20–23.

Sullivan, John P., and Samuel Logan. 2011. "La Línea: Network, gang, and mercenary army." *The Counter Terrorist,* 4(4) Aug/Sept. Accessed February 10, 2013 from http://www.homeland1.com/domestic-international-terrorism/articles/1098212-La-L-237-nea-Network-gang-and-mercenary-army/

Tilly, Charles. 1985. "War Making and State Making as Organized Crime." In *Bringing the State Back In,* edited by Peter Evans, Dietrich Rueschemeyer, and Theda Skocpol, 169–191. Cambridge: Cambridge University Press.

United Nations. 2000. "United Nations Convention against Transnational Organized Crime." General Assembly Resolution 55/25, November 15. Accessed February 10, 2013 from http://www.unodc.org/documents/treaties/UNTOC/Publications/TOC%20Convention/TOCebook-e.pdf

United Nations Office on Drugs and Crime (UNODC). 2005. "Transnational Organized Crime in the West African Region." Vienna. Accessed February 11, 2013 from http://www.unodc.org/pdf/transnational_crime_west-africa-05.pdf

United Nations Office on Drugs and Crime (UNODC). 2008. "The Threat of Narco-Trafficking in the Americas." Vienna, October. Accessed February 10, 2013 from http://www.unodc.org/documents/data-and-analysis/Studies/OAS_Study_2008.pdf

United Nations Office on Drugs and Crime (UNODC). 2011. "Estimating Illicit Financial Flows Resulting from Drug Trafficking and Other Transnational Organized Crimes: Research Report." Vienna, October. Accessed February 10, 2013 from http://www. unodc.org/documents/data-and-analysis/Studies/Illicit_financial_flows_2011_web.pdf

United Nations Office on Drugs and Crime (UNODC). 2010. "The Globalization of Crime: A Transnational Organized Crime Threat Assessment." Vienna. Accessed February 11, 2013 from http://www.unodc.org/documents/data-and-analysis/tocta/TOCTA_Report_2010_low_res.pdf

United Nations Office on Drugs and Crime (UNODC). 2013. "Emerging Crimes." Accessed February 10, 2013 from http://www.unodc.org/unodc/organized-crime/emerging-crimes.html

Watts, Michael. 2008. "Blood Oil: The Anatomy of a Petro-Insurgency in the Niger Delta, Nigeria." *Economies of Violence, Working Paper No. 22*. Berkeley, CA: University of California, Berkeley. Accessed February 11, 2013 from http://oldweb.geog.berkeley.edu/ProjectsResources/ND%20Website/NigerDelta/WP/22-BloodOil_Watts.pdf

Williams, Phil. 1995. "Transnational Criminal Organizations: Strategic Alliance," *The Washington Quarterly*, 181(1): 57–72.

Williams, Phil. 2008. *From the New Middle Ages to a New Dark Age: The Decline of the State and US Strategy*. Carlisle Barracks: Strategic Studies Institute, US Army War College, June.

Further Reading

Williams, Phil. 1994. "Transnational Criminal Organisations and International Security." *Survival*, 36(1): 96–113.

Chapter 10

Natural Resources and Insecurity

Anouk S. Rigterink

Introduction

Over the past twenty years, terms such as "natural resource curse", "natural resource trap" and "blood diamond" have been added to our vocabulary, all illustrating that natural resources adversely affect countries that possess such "riches" in large amounts. Natural resources are said to be associated with bad economic performance, undemocratic regime types, and civil conflict (Collier and Hoeffler, 2004; Sachs and Warner, 2001; Ross, 2001). This chapter will explore the last relationship by reviewing theoretical and empirical literature on whether natural resources cause insecurity.

As this literature is extensive, and the supposed negative effects of natural resources are many, setting some boundaries and definitions is in order. For the purpose of this chapter, insecurity is taken to mean insecurity stemming from *physical violence* by a *politically organized* actor. On a country level, this is commonly translated as the risk of civil war onset, although it is also interpreted as the intensity of (political) violence. This focus on the political excludes criminal violence, although it often proves difficult to distinguish the two, as the World Development Report 2011 (World Bank, 2011) highlights. Defining security as the absence of physical violence excludes other important dimensions of security. The Human Development Report 1994 (United Nations Development Programme (UNDP), 1994) distinguishes six such additional dimensions: economic, food, health, environmental, community, and political security. The absence of these dimensions of violence and insecurity in this chapter is by no means a denial of their importance or existence, but merely an acknowledgement that the factors driving them may be different.

Furthermore, the term "natural resources" refers to tradable primary commodities, including agricultural products, timber, narcotics, fossil fuels, metals and gemstones. Focusing on natural resources such as commodities, this chapter does not

The Handbook of Global Security Policy, First Edition. Edited by Mary Kaldor and Iavor Rangelov.
© 2014 John Wiley & Sons, Ltd. Published 2014 by John Wiley & Sons, Ltd.

engage with the effect of scarcity, degradation, or depletion of stocks of renewable resources (such as water, forests, fisheries, or land) on violent conflict. A flourishing literature surrounding this topic exists (a good starting point for the interested reader is the theme number of *Political Geography*, volume 26, issue 6). This literature seems, at least on the surface, at odds with research on primary commodities and conflict: the former argues that *scarcity* of resources leads to violence, the latter that an *abundance* of resources leads to violence.

Lastly, I will focus almost exclusively on quantitative literature. This is not to say that this is the only field in which interesting research on natural resources and violent conflict is being done. However, quantitative research on resources and war has been very prominent in influencing policy makers and popular perceptions: the most-cited article(Collier and Hoeffler, 2004) on this topic uses quantitative methods, an early version of which was published under auspices of the World Bank, whilst the popular translation, *The Bottom Billion* (Collier, 2008), made the bestseller lists in 2007. As the idea that natural resources and violence are connected has definitely conquered a place in the public consciousness, it is interesting to examine more closely how rigorous the quantitative analyses are that form the foundation of this belief.

This chapter will argue that the link between natural resources and civil war onset, as apparent from studies exploiting cross-country variation is not as strong as popularly believed. Furthermore, in recent years, evidence that these studies fail to identify a *causal* relationship between natural resources and violence is piling up. Another critique of these studies is that they lack a theoretical model detailing exactly how this relationship works: the mechanisms connecting natural resources and war. This question is important from a policy point of view because some policies that would seem effective if we have one mechanism in mind would not be ineffectual, or even have adverse effect, from the perspective of another. A number of mechanisms follow from various theoretical models, not all of which have been tested empirically till this date. Interestingly, the mechanism that has been investigated most empirically, hypothesizing that the price of natural resources influences wages or income and thereby the opportunity costs of conflict, has not been widely translated into policy.

The remainder of this chapter is organized as follows. The first section will review conclusions from studies using cross-country variation, consider a number of reasons for why these conclusions differ markedly between studies and relate some critiques of this research design. The second section will provide the intuition behind several theoretical models of the mechanisms connecting resources and conflict. The third section reviews studies using variation over time that attempt to empirically test these models. The fourth section draws out policy implications.

Cross-Country Empirical Studies: Are Resources and Civil War Related?

One way to try to establish whether natural resources and violent conflict are related is to investigate whether countries that have or produce more resources are more prone to civil war than countries with fewer resources. This set-up compares different countries to each other and therefore uses cross-country variation – as opposed to variation over time (does a particular country or area experience more violence at a time when it has or produces more resources?). This section will focus on studies that rely at least partially on cross-country variation, which I will refer to as "cross-country studies" for ease of reference. It should be noted that most studies discussed use panel data and base their conclusions on variation over time as well as comparisons between countries.

The basic set-up of cross-country studies is remarkably similar. They attempt to explain the onset of civil war, using a range of economic, social, political, and geographical factors as explanatory variables, of which the production, rents, exports, or stocks of natural resources is one. The period under study starts at either 1945 or 1960 and extends as far as data availability allows, and all the world's countries for which data is available are included in the sample. Civil war onset is measured as a "1" or a "0", where "1" means that a civil war started in a particular country in a particular year and "0" means no such war started. For violence to constitute a civil war, it has to have some political motivation, the government needs to be party to it and it has to have resulted in at least 1000 "battle-related deaths". In practice, the last criterion is usually the hardest to satisfy, so whether violence gets coded as a civil war depends heavily on the number of battle deaths recorded. In addition to natural resources, factors hypothesized to influence the chance of a civil war onset may include gross domestic product (GDP), the size of the population, level of ethno-linguistic or religious fractionalization/polarization, levels of democracy and inequality, years since the last civil war, an indicator for how mountainous a country is, and an indicator for non-contiguous territory.

Despite the similarities in set-up, conclusions from cross-country studies differ markedly, as Table 10.1 illustrates. The table shows how various studies measure natural resource abundance and whether the study finds a positive (+), negative (–), or no statistically significant relationship (0) between natural resources and civil war onset. From the top panel, we can see that there is no consensus on whether natural resources as a single category increase the chance of violent conflict, with roughly half of the studies finding a positive relationship between the two and the other half concluding no relationship exists. Most studies that do find that natural resources increase the risk of war use primary commodity exports as percentage of GDP as an independent variable, although Fearon and Laitin (2003) and Fearon (2005) do not support this conclusion, even though they use the same measure. Studies using stocks of natural resources generally fail to find a connection between resources and violent conflict onset.

A more clear-cut picture emerges from investigations into oil or fossil fuels specifically: all studies conclude that oil is associated with civil war onset and results are similar for virtually all measures of oil abundance. The only notable exception is oil reserves, again a measure of resource stocks (Humphreys, 2005).

Studies investigating the impact of diamonds on war risk in the bottom panel of Table 10.1 provide an inconclusive myriad of results. Many of these studies distinguish between primary diamonds (those that are mined in capital-intensive mines) and secondary diamonds (those that can be mined using artisanal techniques and are considered easily "lootable"). Humphreys (2005) concludes total diamond production is positively related to civil war onset, whilst Lujala, Gleditch, and Gilmore (2005) find that both primary and secondary diamond production are unrelated to war onset in general. The latter continue to conclude that primary diamonds are negatively, and secondary diamonds positively related to *ethnic* war onset, whilst Ross

Table 10.1   Summary of findings of various cross-country empirical studies.

Study resources – War	Measure natural resources	Relationship
	Aggregated natural resources	
Brunnschweiler and Bulte (2009)	Stock of all natural resources per capita	0
Collier and Hoeffler (1998)	Primary commodity exports as % of GDP	+
Collier and Hoeffler (2004)	Primary commodity exports as % of GDP	+
Collier, Hoeffler, and Rohner (2009)	Primary commodity exports as % of GDP	+
De Soysa (2002)[a]	Stock of all natural resources per capita	0
	Stock of mineral resources per capita	+
De Soysa and Neumayer (2007)	Mineral rents as % of GNI	0
Elbadawi and Sambanis (2002)	Primary commodity exports as % of GDP	+
Fearon and Laitin (2003)	Primary commodity exports as % of GDP	0
Fearon (2005)	Primary commodity exports as % of GDP	0
Rigterink (2010)	Stock of all natural resources per capita	0
	Stock of mineral resources per capita	0
	Oil	
De Soysa (2002)	Oil exporter dummy	+
De Soysa and Neumayer (2007)	Energy rents as % of GNI	+
Fearon and Laitin (2003)	Oil exporter dummy	+
Fearon (2005)	Fuel exports as % of GDP	+
Humphreys (2005)	Proven oil reserves per capita	0
	Quantity of oil produced per capita	+
Ross (2006)	Fuel rents per capita	+
	Diamonds	
Humphreys (2005)	Total quantity of diamonds produced per capita	+
Lujala, Gleditsch, and Gilmore (2005)	Dummy primary diamond production	0 (–)[b]
	Dummy secondary diamond production	0 (+)[b]
Ross (2006)	Value of primary diamonds produced per capita	+
	Value of secondary diamonds produced per capita	0

[a]De Soysa (2002) investigates a considerably shorter period (1989–1999) than the other studies in Table 10.1, and uses a 25 battle-related deaths threshold as opposed to 1000 battle-related deaths. Results for Stock of Mineral Resources are insignificant when adding a dummy for oil exports to the model.
[b]Lujala, Gleditsch, and Gilmore (2005) only find significant results when taking the onset/incidence of *ethnic* conflict as a dependent variable. Sign of these results are in parentheses.

(2006) finds the exact opposite, concluding that primary diamonds are positively, and secondary diamonds negatively related to both civil war onset in general and ethnic war onset.

What explains this surprising lack of agreement (with the exception of results on oil)? It is likely that many reasons exist, but a number have been systematically explored. Fearon (2005) investigates why Collier and Hoeffler (2004) and Fearon and Laitin (2003) do not come to the same conclusion, despite using the same measure of natural resource abundance. He concludes that Collier and Hoeffler's results are an artifact of how they split up the research period (in intervals of five, rather than one year); their decision to disregard observations for which no data is available, rather than to impute the missing data and keep them in the sample; and their specific set of control variables. When Fearon changes some combination of these relatively arbitrary decisions, he is no longer able to find a positive and significant relationship between natural resource exports as a percentage of GDP and civil war onset.

Another potential reason for the lack of consensus may be that various studies use different datasets on civil war onset (Sambanis, 2004). Although these datasets have very similar definitions of war as noted ealier, Sambanis shows that seemingly minor differences in coding rules can have substantial consequences for how many wars are included and in what year the war start is recorded. Some examples of these differences are: is the 1000 battle-deaths threshold cumulative over the entire duration of the conflict or per year? When is a conflict first recorded: in the year the first violence takes place or the first year the conflict crosses the death threshold? What to do with a conflict that slowly accumulates deaths over time until it exceeds the threshold, whilst we would intuitively not characterize it as a civil war? What to do when violence "dips" below the casualty threshold for one or more years – when would we code this as a continuation of an old conflict and when would we code a new war start? Sambanis shows that very few variables that supposedly explain civil war onset consistently do so across all war databases. Even the dummy for oil exporters, a measure that has given consistent results across all studies in Table 10.1, is sometimes positively related and sometimes unrelated to war, depending on the database chosen.

In another attempt to establish how sensitive conclusions are to reasonable changes in research set-up, Hegre and Sambanis (2006) investigate whether different combinations of explanatory variables consistently give the same results. They take 18 concepts that are supposedly related to civil conflict, of which natural resources is one, and identify 88 variables measuring these concepts. Then, they systematically try all possible combinations of these 88 variables and look at the distribution of the coefficients on each one. None of the five measures for natural resources, including two measuring oil exports, makes their cut-off for variables that are systematically related to civil war onset.[1]

Does it matter that results are not the same across studies? It matters if we think that all studies are equally credible, and had they all come up with the same conclusions, we would have believed that natural resources cause civil war. It matters less if we think that not all of these studies credibly identified a causal relationship to begin with, so we would not trust their conclusions even if they had all drawn the same one, or if we are more inclined to believe certain studies over others.

Do cross-country empirical studies succeed in showing that natural resources *cause* civil war? A major problem in identifying a causal relationship is that natural resource exports or production may be *endogenous* to the models estimated. In other words, certain countries may export or produce a large amount of natural resources for a reason, and that reason may not be independent of violence. Natural resource exports as a percentage of GDP is most suspicious in this regard. This indicator does not measure resource abundance, but rather resource dependence (Brunnschweiler, 2008). Countries that are resource dependent usually display a number of other characteristics, such as poverty, "bad" governance and "bad" institutions, any one of which can make a country more likely to experience a civil war. So if we observe a positive relationship between natural resource exports over GDP and civil war start, it is impossible to tell whether this means that natural resources cause war or that any of these other characteristics causes both natural resource dependence and war risk. Expressing natural resource exports as a percentage of GDP is a further source of endogeneity. It is plausible that productive activity, and with that GDP, will decline *in anticipation of* civil war. Furthermore, natural resources exports will likely not decline as steeply because these industries are location-specific and hence harder to move out of the country. Thus, the ratio of natural resource exports over GDP may increase in anticipation of civil war, rather than the civil war breaking out in response to natural resource exports (Ross, 2004).

It has been argued that the production, rents (the value of production net of extraction costs) or exports of natural resources *per capita* are free of these endogeneity problems (Ross, 2006). However, over the last years, numerous theoretical models have suggested that they are not. A first argument for this is that the pace at which a country extracts natural resources is a choice, usually made by its government. It stands to reason that a government that cares for the future more will both choose a slower pace of natural resource extraction and better overall policies, and will therefore be less at risk of civil war. Hence, slow natural resource extraction and low war risk may go together, even if one does not cause the other. Indeed, a theoretical model by Robinson, Torvik, and Verdier (2006) predicts that governments will over-extract resources compared to the efficient extraction path, especially when their political position is insecure. Furthermore, two of the theoretical models covered in the next section predict that countries in conflict export more natural resources if the property rights to that resource are insecure (Garfinkel, Skaperdas, and Syropoulos, 2008) and that the production of capital intensive natural resources increases with conflict (Dal Bó and Dal Bó, 2004). Thus, the models expect exports and production of resources to increase in response to conflict *as well as* the other way around, and this two-way causation poses a challenge for studies using export or production numbers.

From the measures of natural resource abundance in Table 10.1, I would argue that stocks of natural resources per capita are plausibly the least endogenous because the amount of resources a country possesses is a geological fact. It is not entirely free from suspicion though because the present stock of natural resources is a result of past extraction decisions and we may simply not have discovered natural resource deposits in the world's most unstable areas yet. However, it seems harder for a government to meaningfully influence future resource stocks than present resource extraction, and it seems doubtful that resources nobody knows about will affect politics at all. If we believe that resources stocks are more exogenous, we would put most faith in the conclusions of studies using stock measures. From Table 10.1, we can see that virtually all of these conclude that there is no causal relationship between natural resources and the onset of civil war.

Some studies explicitly attempt to find out to what extent conclusions are driven by endogeneity problems and to what extent they can be given a causal interpretation. Brunnschweiler and Bulte (2009), instrumenting for natural resource dependence using the stocks of natural resources, find that any positive relationship between natural resource dependence and civil conflict is due to endogeneity. I find that the relationship between natural resources and war, which is so prominent in Collier and Hoeffler (2004) and Collier, Hoeffler, and Rohner (2009), disappears when I replace natural resource exports over GDP in their model with a more exogenous measure of resource stocks (Rigterink, 2010). Lastly, Cotet and Tsui (2010) show that the relationship between oil production per capita and civil war onset does not survive either controlling for country-specific characteristics or instrumenting for oil production using proven oil reserves, again providing evidence that endogeneity drives the results of many cross-country studies.

In sum, cross-country studies do not provide a clear-cut result on the relationship between natural resources and civil war onset, with the exception of results on oil. This is partly due to relatively minor differences between studies that we would expect solid conclusions to be "resistant" to. Additionally, there is increasing evidence that positive associations between natural resources and civil war are a result of endogeneity, and cannot be interpreted causally. This has led Bruckner and Ciccone (2010) to sum up as follows: "According to the latest evidence, there does not appear to be a robust link between natural resource wealth and civil war".

Theoretical Models and Mechanisms: the "How" of this Relationship

The previous section dealt with *whether* there is a connection between natural resources and war. An equally interesting question is *how* this relationship exactly works because different *mechanisms* through which natural resources may lead to violence suggest different solutions to the problem. For example, if we believe that natural resources with poorly protected property rights incite more violence because they are easily "lootable", we may suggest giving the state more control over the resources. However, if we believe that the rents flowing from natural resources result in poor quality government, this may well be the last thing we want to do.

A (further) criticism directed at cross-country studies is that they lack a theoretical model (Besley and Persson, 2010), although they suggest numerous mechanisms connecting resources and war. Having a theoretical model is useful because some mechanisms that sound reasonable at first glance are actually incomplete, require unrealistic assumptions, or make unrealistic predictions. For example, the best known mechanisms supposedly connecting resources and war is "greed" (Collier and Hoeffler, 2004). A layman's interpretation of "greed" could be something similar to "if there is lootable wealth lying around in the form of resources, there will always be people willing to fight to obtain it". However, some lootable asset is likely present that at all times and all places (if not natural resources, then land, tools, cash, bicycles, or smartphones), so this way of thinking unrealistically predicts that people will always be fighting everywhere (if anything, more in rich countries because they have more assets). This "model" lacks some sense of the costs of conflict. Another example is that the existence of insurgent groups financed by the proceeds of natural resource sales is sometimes regarded as "smoking gun" evidence that natural resources cause conflict. However, how can we be sure that these insurgent groups would not have found some other source of funding in absence of natural resources? And how do we explain countries without insurgency, despite sufficient funding? This "model" requires information on why it was deemed advantageous to start an insurgency in the first place and on whether funding is a constraining factor.

In response to the call for more theoretical models, numerous ones have been developed in the past years. They hypothesize that one or more of the following four mechanisms connect natural resources and violence. It is possible that natural resources affect the *returns to conflict*. This comes in two variations: resources may either increase the returns to holding territory or the "prize" of obtaining government power. Second, resources may affect the *opportunity costs of conflict* through impacting the wage rate. A third possible mechanism suggests that natural resources impact the *quality of government*, meaning the government invests less in productive policies or strengthening of institutions, and more in clientelistic handouts and/or oppression of the opposition. Finally, proceeds of natural resources may finance conflict, and thereby *relieve a credit constraint*. This section will outline the intuition behind various theoretical models, deferring the question of whether they adequately describe reality to the next section.

Focusing on the returns to holding territory, Garfinkel, Skaperdas, and Syropoulos (2008) construct a model of a country in which two groups can decide to allocate labor to fighting over some contested amount of oil-producing land. If the price of oil increases, the contested land becomes more valuable (returns to conflict go up) and the groups allocate more labor to conflict in order to obtain it. Hence, the model predicts that an increase in the price of a resource with insecure property rights leads to an increase in violent conflict.

An alternative model by Dal Bó and Dal Bó (2004) also assumes that labor is the main input to conflict, yet focuses on the opportunity costs of violence. It features a country with two productive sectors (one capital-intensive and one labor-intensive) and one expropriation sector violently stealing a fraction of total production. Individuals face the decision whether to use their labor to produce or to expropriate; the opportunity cost of allocating labor to violent expropriation is the wage that this labor could have earned in the productive sectors. Wages, thereby the opportunity costs of violence, decrease as the price of a capital-intensive good increases, for the following reason. As the price of a capital-intensive good increases, the capital-intensive sector expands and the labor-intensive sector contracts. The contracting labor-intensive sector releases more labor onto the market than the capital-intensive sector can absorb at the going wage rate, hence wages decrease. In real world terms, the model predicts that an increase in the price of a natural resource with a capital-intensive production process depresses wages and encourages violence. Conversely, violence decreases with the price of a labor-intensive natural resource.

Janus (2012) combines both the opportunity cost and returns to conflict mechanisms in one model, and adds a third, natural resources as relieving a credit constraint. In contrast to other models, it allows for a resource stock that is exhaustible and for capital to be an input to violence, in addition to labor. In the model, two groups possess a fixed amount of labor that can be allocated to producing agricultural goods, to producing natural resources, or to fighting over the remaining stock of natural resources. Earnings from natural resources can be used to purchase a capital input to fighting (such as weapons). It is possible that natural resources earnings are not sufficient to buy as much "fighting capital" as a group would optimally want, in which case the group faces a binding credit constraint. Janus shows that whether his model supports the opportunity cost mechanism (a decrease in agricultural productivity leads to increased fighting) or the returns to conflict mechanism (an increase in the stock or price of natural resources leads to increased fighting) depends on whether this credit constraint is binding. In addition, he shows that an increase in the price of the capital input to conflict (the aim of an arms embargo) could have adverse effects if the credit constraint does not bind (Janus, 2012). Although pointing to important omissions of other models, these results may depend on a number of contestable assumptions for which Janus offers few justifications, such as the assumed production functions for the three sectors, the assumption that earnings from agriculture cannot be used to purchase "fighting capital" and the premise that the amount of natural resources extracted is large enough relative to the remaining stock to meaningfully influence the returns to fighting.

What is perhaps most notably absent from all these models is a policy-making government. Yet, numerous arguments have been made for proceeds from natural resources (mainly oil revenues) to impact the behavior of governments, creating so-called "petro-states" combining strong dependence on oil revenue, extensive rent-seeking, unsuccessful development policies, and political instability (Karl, 1997). Kaldor, Karl, and Said (2007) formulate this as an "oil rent-seeking cycle", in the later stages of which governments need to rely increasingly on rent-seeking and repression to remain in power, eroding state institutions, leading to "new oil wars" and eventual state failure. A variation on this argument is that natural resource wealth attracts corrupt politicians garnering support through identity politics, which makes war along real or imagined ethnic lines more likely (Kaldor, Karl, and Said 2007).

Besley and Persson (2010) construct a model explaining why extensive natural resource extraction, low income, low state capacity, and violent conflict so often go together. In the model, the government receives natural resources and tax revenue, which it can use to fund army wages, public goods, investments in state capacity and/or *de facto* transfers to its own group. An opposing group can raise an army to replace the government. If natural resource rents increase, the "prize" attached to obtaining government power increases because this means more revenue that the government can potentially redistribute to its own group. This gives both the opposition and the government a greater incentive to arm. Furthermore, when there is violent conflict, the government has a smaller interest in investing in state capacity because supporting economic development increases wages and thereby the government's costs of raising an army (Besley and Persson, 2010). Hence, natural resource rents raise the returns to conflict *and* decreases the opportunity costs of conflict through low quality government. Employing a similar reasoning, Caselli (2006) presents a model in which a government of a natural resource rich country faces a greater chance of being displaced and therefore invests less in long-term economic growth.

However, not all theoretical models predict that natural resources are an economic as well as a political curse. In a model by Tsui (2010), natural resource rents actually induce governments to choose more optimal economic policies. This follows from the assumption that taxing the natural resources sector is subject to lower dead-weight transaction costs than taxing other productive activity and that the incumbent can gain political support by increasing citizens' income. Tsui further expands on the possibility that increasing natural resource rents may not necessarily lead to outright civil war but to more government repression discouraging the opposition from engaging in violence (Tsui, 2010).

More Empirics: Which Mechanism(s) do the Data Support?

The previous section has identified four potential theoretical mechanisms through which natural resources can lead to violent conflict: returns to conflict (either the returns to holding territory or the "prize" of obtaining government); opportunity costs of conflict; quality of government; and relieving a credit constraint. However, the fact that a theory is coherently formulated and internally consistent does not necessarily make the theory "true" in the sense that it successfully describes reality. Therefore, this section returns to empirics, asking which of the four theoretical mechanisms are supported by real-world information. It reviews studies using variation over time, either single-country studies or cross-country studies using fixed effects to control for time-invariant country-specific factors to attempt to mitigate some of the endogeneity problems described earlier.

First, consider the opportunity costs of conflict mechanism. A number of studies take GDP as an indicator for income or wage, and investigate whether the price of natural resources affects GDP and thereby conflict risk (using the same definition of civil conflict as cross-country studies). Studies of this type essentially attempt to find evidence that as the price of a particular natural resource decreases, GDP decreases and conflict risk increases more in countries possessing this particular resource than in countries without this resource. Aggregating all types of resources, Bruckner and Ciccone (2010) conclude that this is the case, supporting the opportunity cost mechanism, while Bazzi and Blatmann (2011) find no evidence for this supposition. However, this seems like rather a rough test of the opportunity costs of conflict mechanism: GDP does not translate directly into individuals' incomes and depending on whether a resource is labor or capital intensive, shocks to its price may have opposite effects on wages (Dal Bó and Dal Bó, 2004). It seems useful therefore to distinguish different types of resources. When doing so, Bazzi and Blatmann (2011) find some evidence that an increase in the price of certain agricultural resources is associated with less conflict and conclude that the opportunity cost mechanism is the only mechanism supported by their data, although weakly.

Dube and Vargas (2009) and Rigterink (2011) provide a direct test of the theory put forward by Dal Bó and Dal Bó. Both studies compare the impact of changes in the price of a capital-intensive resource (oil and primary diamonds, respectively) to those of a labor-intensive resource (coffee and secondary diamonds). The Dal Bó and Dal Bó model would predict that an increase in the price of the capital-intensive resource would lead to an increase in violence in areas possessing this resource, whilst an increase in the price of a labor-intensive resource would lead to a *decrease* in violence. Both studies provide empirical support for this prediction, employing data on violent events in Colombian districts (Dube and Vargas, 2009) and African countries (Rigterink, 2011).

In contrast to these works, Angrist and Kugler (2008) fail to find any evidence supporting the opportunity cost mechanism in the case of coca. They investigate the impact of a military campaign cutting off the supply of raw coca to Colombia, dramatically increasing domestic production. This could potentially have a positive effect on livelihoods in coca-growing regions. However, the military campaign is concluded to be unrelated to local livelihoods and to have *increased* rather than decreased violent deaths in coca-growing regions (Angrist and Kugler, 2008).

Overall, there has been a reasonable amount of research on the opportunity cost mechanism, most of it providing support for it. However, the case of illegal drugs is an exception.

The critical reader may remark that a positive relationship between the price of a capital-intensive resource (like oil or primary diamonds) and violence could also be considered evidence in favor of the returns to conflict or quality of government mechanism. Proceeds from capital-intensive resources commonly accrue directly to the government, potentially contributing to the "prize" of capturing the government or providing incentives for unproductive policies.

One way to distinguish between the opportunity costs of conflict mechanism and the returns to conflict mechanism is to consider where the violence takes place: if wage rates were the true mechanism, we would expect violence to go up in the region the resource is produced, whilst the returns to conflict mechanisms would predict that violence would increase in the capital, where the government is located. Dube and Vargas (2009) and Rigterink (2011) find increasing violence in resource-producing regions, but not in the capital, failing to support the returns to conflict mechanism. Furthermore, the latter study finds that secondary diamonds, one of the archetypically "lootable" resources with poorly protected property rights, are unrelated or even negatively related to violence, providing an argument against the returns to conflict mechanism suggested by the Garfinkel, Skaperdas, and Syropoulos (2008). Other studies equally fail to find evidence in support of the returns to conflict mechanism. Bazzi and Blatmann (2011) conclude that an increase in the price of so-called "extractive" resources does not increase conflict risk. Cotet and Tsui (2010) find that the chance of experiencing a coup or irregular leader transition does not increase after an oil discovery. In sum, there has been very little empirical support for the returns to conflict mechanism.

The link between capital-intensive resources and violence may also indicate indirect support for the quality of government mechanism. More detailed evidence would then have to show both that government natural resource revenue is associated with unproductive government policies or identity politics, and that these policies lead to violence. With regards to the former, there is research suggesting that natural resources increase the level of repression or autocracy in non-democratic countries. For example, Caselli and Tesei (2011) find that an increase in the price of a countries' principal export commodity is associated with a decrease in polity score for non-democratic countries. Similarly, Cotet and Tsui (2010) conclude that military spending as a percentage of GDP increases in non-democratic countries following an oil discovery, suggesting that governments increase the level of repression; however, it seems difficult to connect these decreases in government quality to increased risk of civil war or other forms of violence. Caselli and Tesei do not attempt this, and Cotet and Tsui (2011) find no increase in the chances of civil war, coups, or irregular leader transitions after oil discoveries. In general, polity score does not consistently explain civil war (Sambanis, 2004).

This does not necessarily mean that the quality of government mechanism is not valid. Government quality is multifaceted and extremely difficult to measure and the process from resource discovery to government behavior to political violence may take a long time, making it difficult to identify such a relationship. Keeping this in mind, we have to conclude that there is some evidence to connect natural resources to government quality, but very little for a direct link to forms of political violence.

The final mechanism suggests that proceeds from natural resources relieve some credit constraint for individuals intending to fight. I am not aware of a study directly testing this mechanism. Possibly, this is because it is difficult to establish whether potentially violent groups are credit constraint. Angrist and Kugler (2008) do suggest that coca production provides funding for violent groups in Colombia as an explanation for their result that coca production and violence are linked; however, they do not provide information suggesting that funding was prohibitively scarce before coca production soared. More research and a credible way to determine credit constraints seem required.

In conclusion, the current state of research on what connects natural resources and violence provides most evidence in favor of the opportunity cost of conflict mechanism and most evidence contrary to the returns to conflict mechanism. There is little indication either way for the quality of government and credit constraint mechanisms.

Conclusion and Policy Implications

What bearing does this have on policy? Although evidence from cross-country studies that natural resources starts civil war is weak, studies using variation over time give us reason to believe that the value of natural resources does have some impact on violence. Various mechanisms explaining this link have been proposed, not all of which are equally well supported by empirical studies. Mechanisms are important because, as mentioned earlier, which mechanism we think connects natural resources and violent conflict determines, to a large extent, which policy we deem effective.

Consider two well-known policies intending to break the link between natural resources and conflict: a ban on the export of natural resources from conflict zones and initiatives to improve the transparency of revenue flows associated with resources. Interestingly, if we look at these policies from the perspective of the opportunity cost mechanism (the one most strongly supported by empirical work), we may expect them to be ineffective or even to have adverse effects. The following will illustrate this.

Trade bans can take the form of a blanket ban on the export of a particular natural resource (commonly oil) or a selective ban on the trade in illegally obtained resources that may finance conflict. An example of the latter is the Kimberley Process Certification Scheme (KPCS), which forbids signatory countries to import or export diamonds that do not carry a certificate stating they were legally mined. Campaigns that incite consumers not to buy so-called "conflict resources" could be considered an informal selective trade ban.

Proponents of trade bans appear to have some variation of the returns to holding territory mechanism or credit constraint mechanism in mind. The reasoning seems to be that if we take trade in valuable resources away, this would decrease the incentive to fight over territory and/or insurgents would lack the capital to continue violence; however, these mechanisms have received little empirical support. Trade bans do not necessarily decrease the incentive for violence if we think obtaining government is the "prize" of conflict: selective trade bans usually consider all government-traded resources legal (in fact, in case of the KPCS, it is the government that issues the certificates of "clean health" for diamonds) and blanket bans are often lifted after one party has obtained some decisive victory and forms a recognized government, so this may still be a high-return goal to strive for. Executed in this manner, trade bans equally do not seem particularly effective from the perspective of the quality of government mechanism.

Whether the opportunity cost mechanism predicts a trade ban to be effective depends on whether the ban hits a capital- or a labor-intensive resource. In the former case, it gives cause for high hopes, but in the latter, the opportunity cost mechanism would suggest that a trade ban can have the adverse effect of decreasing wages and thereby *increasing* violence. The KPCS, which almost exclusively hits "lootable", labor-intensive secondary diamonds, is a potential example of this. Lastly, the opportunity cost mechanism predicts that any capital-intensive resource may be related to violence via the wage rate, regardless of whether the proceeds are spent on weapons or used for perfectly legal ends. From this perspective, campaigns that expose dealings of resource extraction companies with armed groups, though laudable for informing consumers, are not the most effective way to curb violence.

A second policy attempts to improve the transparency of revenue flows, with the intention of inciting governments to use proceeds from natural resources for socially beneficial goals, such as education. An example of this is the Extractive Industries Transparency Initiative (EITI). This policy appears to be inspired by the quality of government and/or the government as "prize" mechanism, attempting to either directly improve governance or to prevent natural resource proceeds to be distributed as rents. However, there is no strong empirical evidence in favor of either mechanism. As this policy restricts governments and the dealings of companies with governments, there is little reason to expect it to be effective from the perspective of the returns to territory mechanism or the credit constraint mechanism. Equally, the opportunity cost mechanism only predicts success for transparency initiatives if and when better governance leads to meaningful increases in the wage rate. This is possible, though likely to be a time-consuming process. Hence, although transparency initiatives may provide a possible long-term solution, we would not expect them to decrease violence in the short term, taking the view of the opportunity cost mechanism.

In sum, we have policies tailored to all but one mechanism, potentially connecting resources and violent conflict. Interestingly, the exception is the opportunity cost mechanism, the mechanism garnering most empirical support. What policies would flow from this? One suggestion that comes to mind is to directly support the wage rate, by labor-intensive (reconstruction) spending. In theory, this could decrease the chances of conflict and thereby benefit society as a whole, even if the labor hired through such a scheme is completely unproductive (Dal Bó and Dal Bó, 2004). In practice, labor-intensive reconstruction spending by the US military has proven to be successful in decreasing violence in Iraq (Iyengar, Monten, and Hanson 2009), suggesting it may be an effective short-term policy. Despite initial success, the execution of such a policy seems key: if these schemes become another source of rents to be distributed by the government, they could even have adverse effects.

Note

1. Although it should be noted that when using the lower death threshold of 25 battle-related deaths, oil exports as a percentage of GDP does make the list of variables that are robustly related to violence.

References

Angrist, Joshua D., and Adriana D. Kugler. 2008. "Rural Windfall or a New Resource Curse? Coca, Income and Civil Conflict in Colombia." *The Review of Economics and Statistics*, 90(2): 191–215.

Bazzi, Samuel, and Christopher Blattman. 2011. "Economic Shocks and Conflict: The (Absence of?) Evidence from Commodity Prices." *Working Paper 274*. USCD and Yale University.

Besley, Timothy, and Torsten Persson. 2010. "State Capacity, Conflict, and Development." *Econometrica*, 78(1): 1–34.

Bruckner, Markus, and Antonio Ciccone. 2010. "International commodity prices, growth and the outbreak of civil war in Sub-Saharan Africa." *The Economic Journal*, 120: 519–534.

Brunnschweiler, Christa. 2008. "Cursing the blessings? Natural resource abundance, institutions and economic growth." *World Development*, 36(3): 399–419.

Brunnschweiler, Christa, and Eric H. Bulte. 2009. "Natural resources and violent conflict. Resource abundance, dependence and the onset of civil wars." *Oxford Economic Papers*, 61: 651–674.

Caselli, Francesco. 2006. "Power struggels and the natural resouce curse." Unpublished Working Paper.

Caselli, Francesco, and Andrea Tesei. 2011. "Resource windfalls, political regimes, and political stability." *NBER Working Paper Series*. Cambridge MA: National Bureau of Economic Research.

Collier, Paul. 2008. *The Bottom Billion*. Oxford: Oxford University Press.

Collier, Paul, and Anke Hoeffler. 1998. "On economic causes of civil war." *Oxford Economic Papers*, 50: 563–573.

Collier, Paul, and Anke Hoeffler. 2004. "Greed and grievance in civil war." *Oxford Economic Papers*, 56: 563–595.

Collier, Paul, Anke Hoeffler, and Dominic Rohner. 2009. "Beyond greed and grievance: Feasibility and civil war." *Oxford Economic Papers*, 61: 1–27.

Cotet, Anca M., and Kevin K. Tsui. 2010. Oil and Conflict. What Does the Cross-Country Evidence Really Show? *American Economic Journal: Macroeconomics*, 5(1): pp. 49–80.

Dal Bó, Ernesto, and Pedro Dal Bó. 2011. Workers, warriors and criminals. Social conflict in general equilibrium. *Journal of the European Economic Association*, 6(4): pp. 646–677.

De Soysa, Indra. 2002. "Paradise is a bazaar? Greed, creed and governance in civil war, 1989–1999." *Journal of Peace Research*, 39(4): 395–416.

De Soysa, Indra, and Eric Neumayer. 2007. "Recourse wealth and civil war onset. Results from a new dataset of natural resource rents 1970–1999." *Conflict Management and Peace Science*, 24: 201–218.

Dube, Oeindrilla, and Juan Vargas. 2009. "Commodity price shocks and civil conflict. Evidence from Colombia." Unpublished Working Paper.

Elbadawi, Ibrahim, and Nicholas Sambanis. 2002. "How much war will we see? Explaining the prevalence of civil war." *Journal of Conflict Resolution*, 46(3): 307–334.

Fearon, James. 2005. "Primary commodities exports and civil war." *Journal of Conflict Resolution*, 49(4): 483–507.

Fearon, James, and David Laitin. 2003. "Ethnicity, insurgency and civil war." *American Political Science Review*, 97(1): 75–90.

Garfinkel, Michelle, Stergios Skaperdas, and Constantinos Syropoulos. 2008. "Globalization and domestic conflict." *Journal of International Economics*, 76: 269–308.

Iyengar, Radha, Jonathan Monten, and Matthew Hanson. 2011. Building Peace: The impact of aid on the labor market for insurgents. *NBER Working Paper Series*, #17297. Available at http://www.nber.org/papers/w17297

Hegre, Håvard, and Nicholas Sambanis. 2006. "Sensitivity analysis of emperical results on civil war onset." *Journal of Conflict Resolution*, 50(4): 508–535.

Humphreys, Macartan. 2005. "Natural resources, conflict and conflict reslution. Uncovering the mechanisms." *Journal of Conflict Resolution*, 49(4): 508–537.

Janus, Thorsten. 2012. "Natural resource extraction and civil conflict." *Journal of Development Economics*, 97: 24–31.

Kaldor, Mary, Terry Lynn Karl, and Yahia Said, eds. 2007. *Oil Wars*. London: Pluto Press.

Karl, Terry Lynn. 1997. *The Paradox of Plenty. Oil Booms and Petro-States*. Berkeley, CA: University of California Press.

Lujala, Päivi, Nils Petter Gleditsch, and Elizabeth Gilmore. 2005. "A diamond curse? Civil war and a lootable resource." *Journal of Conflict Resolution*, 49(4): 538–562.

Rigterink, Anouk S. 2010. *The wrong suspect. An enquire into the endogeneity of natural resources to civil war*. London: London School of Economics and Political Science.

Rigterink, Anouk S. 2011. *Diamonds and Violence in Africa. Uncovering Relationships and Mechanisms*. London: London School of Economics and Political Science.

Robinson, James A., Ragnar Torvik, and Thierry Verdier. 2006. "Political foundations of the resource curse." *Journal of Development Economics*, 79(2): 447–468.

Ross, Michael. 2001. "Does Oil Hinder Democracy?" *World Politic,s* 53: 325–361.

Ross, Michael. 2004. "What do we know about natural resources and civil war." *Journal of Peace Research*, 41(3): 337–356.

Ross, Michael. 2006. "A closer look at oil, diamond and civil war." *Annual Review of Political Science*, 9: 265–300.

Sachs, Jeffrey, and Andrew Warner. 2001. "The curse of natural resources." *European Economic Review*, 45: 827–838.

Sambanis, Nicholas. 2004. "What is civil war? Conceptual and empirical complexities of an operational definition." *Journal of Conflict Resolution*, 48(6): 814–858.

Tsui, Kevin K. 2010. "Resource Curse, Political Entry and Deadweight Costs." *Economics & Politics*, 22(3): 471–497.

United Nations Development Programme (UNDP). 1994. *Human Development Report*. New York, NY: Oxford University Press.

World Bank. 2011. *World Development Report. Conflict, Security and Development*. Washington, DC: The International Bank for Reconstruction and Development.

Chapter 11

The Web of Water Security

Mark Zeitoun

Not Water Secure

This chapter addresses shortcomings of analysis and policy related to water security. It notes how such policy can lead to insecurity of related natural resources and to short-term water security for some, at the cost of water insecurity for others. A conceptual tool that may help guide both research and policy towards longer-term and more sustainable national water security is proposed – the "web" of water security. The chapter does not offer a fully grounded analytical framework or prescription for the analytical pitfalls and incoherent policy identified. The approach taken to broaden and deepen the concept of water security does serve, however, as a basis to understand and tackle the complex and interconnected water security challenges we all face.

The approach to national water security taken here stresses that social and physical processes occur simultaneously across the many "security areas" so intimately related to water. The breadth, complexity, and immediacy of the Nile River conflict and UK consumption of Peruvian asparagus serve briefly to demonstrate.

For the want of a clause, the end of centuries of conflict over the Nile River was lost. The wording of Article 14b – titled *Water Security*, and hidden in the annex of the May 2010 Nile Cooperative Framework Agreement – has been interpreted by some to open up the possibility of discussion of reallocation of Nile flows. The opportunity was immediately endorsed by Ethiopia and other upstream governments,[1] and fiercely resisted by the downstream governments of Sudan and Egypt. These latter two had grown accustomed over half a century to use of the entire flow of the river, having "secured" the distribution according to the 1959 bilateral agreement (with about one-quarter for Sudan and three-quarters plus excess flows for Egypt, not including water lost to evaporation). Through its negotiations within the World Bank-facilitated Nile Basin Initiative (NBI) and the Cooperative Framework

The Handbook of Global Security Policy, First Edition. Edited by Mary Kaldor and Iavor Rangelov.
© 2014 John Wiley & Sons, Ltd. Published 2014 by John Wiley & Sons, Ltd.

Agreement, the Egyptian government was eventually confronted with two options to maintain the water "security" it had already achieved. It could either accommodate the expressed interests of the upstream states, which might lead to more equitable allocation of the flows, or it could maintain its lion's share of water use through other means, as it had done in earlier decades[2] (Brunnée and Toope, 2002; Mekonnen, 2010). It chose the latter, and inter-state tensions on the Nile are rising again.

The same sort of decisions may have to be made by governments of wetter climes, such as the United Kingdom. Nearly two-thirds of the water used in the United Kingdom comes through food imported from abroad (WWF, 2008, p. 13). Some of this "virtual water" (Allan, 1997) comes from environmental conflict zones, that is, in the form of oranges from Egypt (Nile Delta), potatoes from Israel (Jordan River), and asparagus from the desertic Ica Valley in Peru. Much of the water used to irrigate the Peruvian asparagus is abstracted at rates far beyond the sustainable capacity of the aquifers, and applied to green the desert on either side of the valley floor (Hepworth, Postigo, and Delgado, 2010). With financial support from the World Bank, the agro-food industry employs thousands of local residents. It also perpetuates local inequities, particularly with established Ica Valley alpaca herders – who find themselves at once in competition for the water and in tension with the farm hands. The "Carhuancho water conflict" (Hepworth, Postigo, and Delgado, 2010, p. 56) has developed through a proposal to divert water away from communities living in the neighboring Carhuancho basin. Both aggrieved groups (the Ica Valley herders and the Carhuancho communities) have turned to the Latin American Water Tribunal for justice, which has led to increased strain between locals and the national political and business elites. In many ways similar to the hidden costs of mining in Peru (Budds and Hinojosa, 2012; Sosa and Zwarteveen, 2012), British demand for asparagus thus fuels the conflict – and its people are not fully independent of the unsustainable exploitation of the Peruvian people or the groundwater. Evidently not as pressed as the Egyptian government about its food and water policies, the UK government will be obliged at some point to question just how "secure" these are – at least for its own citizens.

With such tensions rising from riverbeds all over the globe, it is at first reassuring to see the extensive policy and research effort devoted to "water security". Indeed, the hydrological cycle seems to be gaining part of the global attention devoted to the carbon cycle (Stern, 2009). But as the Nile and Ica Valley cases demonstrate, the largely uncoordinated approach taken to regional and global water security issues lags far behind the emerging global policy regime for climate change, and attempts to achieve water security fall well short of their mark.

Where it is developed, water security policy is at best incoherent; at worst, it creates situations of *in*security for other natural resources that people and states have come to depend upon, or for the communities and nations themselves.

The first step this chapter takes is to review critically the water security literature in academic and policy circles. The prevailing approaches to water security are found to (a) overemphasize and place too much confidence in the physical aspects of water security; and (b) be environmentally determinist and narrow, as if environmental policy was driving politics, and water security was independent of the many other related security areas. The case of British consumption of Peruvian asparagus demonstrates that water security is actually coupled with food security (for the United Kingdom), human or community security (of the alpaca farmers) and state security (of Peru). Water security is also interdependent with energy and climate security, through the competition for water by crops driven by the need to fill stomachs or petrol tanks, or the fossil fuel burned to get the vegetables from the desert floor on to a dinner plate in rural England.

The processes that drive such transactions are considered to be fundamentally socioeconomic and political, much as water *scarcity* in many cases is primarily "social". The complex networks of interrelated actors and resources involved in any case of water security drives the development of the water security "web", which is the second step of this chapter.

The "web" approach to water security reframes the term, recognizing it as (very) broad, interdisciplinary in analysis, and cross-sectoral in application. The suggested conceptual tool emphasizes the inseparability of social and biophysical processes related to water, and an understanding of how these mediate and are mediated by the socioeconomic and political context within which they occur. Security is then discussed in relation to stability and the interdependencies of associated security areas, where two guiding principles are proposed: (1) seeking a balance between water security and related natural "security resources"; and (2) equitability in distribution of benefits and effects of any policy. The chapter concludes with a brief discussion of the implications the web has for policy and analysis.

Why Narrow and Deterministic is not Good Enough

This section critically reviews the academic and policy literature related to water security. Shortcomings of prevailing conceptions of water security are found to stem from an overreliance on the physical aspects of water, and on narrow and determinist analysis.

Water Resources Security, Water Links, Water Nexus

The world's rivers, lakes, and aquifers are under constantly increasing strain to meet the human demands for water from agriculture, industry, and for domestic supply. The environmental impact is evident in over-abstraction (Pittock and Lankford, 2010), pollution (United Nations Environmental Programme (UNEP), 2012, p. 19), and ecosystem collapse (Vörösmarty et al., 2010). Meanwhile, a rapid rise in "thirsty" middle-class lifestyles around the globe is coinciding with altered physical water scarcity due to changes in climate (Milly, Dunne, and Vecchia, 2005). The only constant in this fluid picture is the inequitable distribution of the clean water that remains – towards money (Reisner, 1986) and the powerful.

Global water policymakers have anticipated and followed the evolving pressures, developing a number of paradigms such as Integrated Water Resources Management (IWRM), Dublin Principles (1992), and International Water Law (United Nations International Law Commission (UN ILC), 1997). "Water Security" seems to be the latest idea, and has evidently extended its grip beyond the international water "development" community to also reach national security communities as well.

Possible back-steps to earlier simplifications about international "development" and water wars are thus possible. As Zeitoun and Mirumachi (2008) discuss, the compelling notion of water wars is undermined by the stress-reducing role of (water-consuming) food imports, the low economic value of water, and power asymmetries between states. A variety of geographers (particularly Wolf, 2007) and constructivist International Relations thinkers (e.g. Warner, 2008; Julien 2012) have further helped situate water within the broadened scope of security analysis that Buzan, Waever, and de Wilde (1998) have developed. These thinkers clearly understand the causes of tensions driven by and over water – and solutions to them – in the complex local and global governance that define local and international political economies. One would thus hope the emerging interest in "water security" would build on such social scientific contributions to knowledge.

Yet, the researchers and policy makers who make up the international water community make liberal use of the term "water security". Cook and Bakker (2012) review a wide variety of definitions to demonstrate how early definitions that were purely anthropocentric[3] have broadened to consider water quality and related environmental issues. Some of these less narrow definitions, the authors note, have been used in state-building and "international development" efforts (e.g. Global Water Partnership (GWP), 2000), and have drawn a fair share of criticism.

The association between water security, dams, and national economic growth is a case in point. A select group of wealthy states and continents are found to have a high water storage capacity (dams and associated impoundments, chiefly), and a causal link between storage, flood protection, and poverty is asserted (Brown and Lall, 2006; Grey and Sadoff 2007, Figure 3; Briscoe, 2009, Figure 5). Working backwards, the variability in river flow that storage eliminates is cast as water security[4], and the construction of dams is recommended along with the development of related water institutions. The evidence base for such policy recommendations is shaky, however. The selection of presented cases is not justified, the reams of socio-economic analysis carried out on the multiple factors that contribute to national economic growth are ignored, and the quality of the relation between national water security and economic growth links remain untested. Indeed, direct causality between the two is cautioned against, at least in the case of Ethiopia (Grey and Sadoff, 2007, p. 22), while further analysis of the reliability of the method and data series employed (Conway and Schipper, 2011, p. 231) cast further doubt on the robustness of the evidence base. Despite these shortcomings, the "increased storage = increased wealth" assertion is gaining currency in policy circles – in the name of water security (see, e.g. UNEP, 2006; Department for International Development (DFID), 2009; GWP, 2009, p. 9; World Bank, 2009).

Such less narrow definitions of water security, furthermore, cannot consider the interdependency of water and water use with related natural "security resources", such as food, climate, and energy. For their limited breadth and water resource-centric perspective, this body of work may be more accurately referred to as relating to "water *resources* security".[5]

Research conducted on the links between water security and a single other natural "security resource" was perhaps the first step beyond simple water resources security. With agriculture accounting for over 80% of global water use (Rogers, 2008), the water security–food security link has been explored at length, as in the *Ministerial Declaration on Water Security* at the 2000 World Economic Forum. The resulting virtual water and "water footprint" work (e.g. Aldaya, Hoekstra, and Allan, 2008) is increasingly taken up by water research institutes, think tanks, and implementing agencies (e.g. International Water Management Institute (IWMI), 2007; Stockholm International Water Institute (SIWI), 2005).

The link between water and *energy* security is relatively less developed. The competition between food and biofuels for water ("water for energy") is directly related to the demand (and cost) of fossil fuels (Berndes, 2002; Lundqvist *et al.*, 2007, p. 56). The water footprint of biomass is 70 to 400 times larger than that of conventional fuels (Gerbens-Leenes, Hoekstra, and van der Meer, 2008, p. 5), raising concerns about competition for water, particularly in India and China. Concerns about energy used for the treatment, production, and delivery of water ("energy for water") is also receiving attention (e.g. King, Holman, and Webber, 2008).

Water and *human* (or *community*) security is most frequently discussed in relation to water and sanitation concerns, or individual access to water (Barlow, 2007). Vörösmarty *et al.* (2010) also reconcile a particular understanding of "human water security" with the biophysical aspects of river flows. The "bottom–up" approach has been explored in relation to armed conflict through water and climate issues (Smith and Vivekananda, 2007) while the emerging concept of *climate* security has developed in relation to national security (CNA, 2007; WBGU, 2008), as well as to human security (Adger, Paavola, Huq, and Mace, 2006). Fertilization of the concept with water security remains relatively undeveloped however.

Examination of the intersection of two water-related security areas has eventually given way to studies of water "nexus", that is, the intersection of water processes with three or more related resources. Climate–water–national security links have been discussed in relation to the Middle East (Brown and Crawford, 2009), and more tangentially by water and agriculture think tanks concerned about impacts of climate change on food production (IWMI, 2009). Houdret, Kramer, and Carius (2010) connect water–human–state security while Magsig (2010, p. 62) refers to the "security triad" of environment, energy, and food. The water–food–climate nexus has also been explored in the Middle East and North Africa (Food and Agriculture Organization (FAO), 2008; Zeitoun, Cascão, England, and Hodbod, 2012).

Even more-encompassing water security work explores the links between water and human security, food security, economic security, and health security (e.g. FAO, 2000; Grobicki, 2009, p. 14; Hellegers Zilberman, Steduto, and McCornick, 2008; McCornick, Awulachew, and Abebe, 2008). The international water legal academic community is leading development of the legal perspective on multidimensional water security, which may form the platform from which a deeper understanding of the challenges involved may embark (Tarlock and Wouters, 2010). This chapter's approach of the "web" of water security complements this latter body of work, but with a much less deterministic view of the links between water and national security, and a more critical interpretation both of politics and of natural resource science.

Overconfidence in the Physical, and Ignoring the Social

Political ecological readings of science studies demonstrate how uncritical application of the scientific method can lead to the development of very deeply held and unquestioned explanations of environmental phenomena (e.g. Demeritt, 2006). Forsyth (2003, p. 38) documents a number of these "environmental orthodoxies", including conventional wisdom on the positive relation between forests and river flow quantity and quality. The orthodox thinking determines policy, he demonstrates, despite physical scientific evidence of flaws associated with it.

The perpetuation of environmental orthodoxies in the face of evidence questioning them suggests blinkered science, or underlying agendas. Some of the views of water security appear to suffer from such constricted thinking, particularly in relation to water *scarcity*.[6] One is struck when reviewing the mounting literature on water security just how much the *physical* component of water scarcity alone has been used as a basis for policy. If physical scarcity were calculated with a reasonable degree of certainty, this would only be half as bad.

Despite roughly a century of effort devoted to the study of the hydrological cycle, there is no agreement on methods to calculate the basic quantities of water (in all of its forms) flowing in and out of a river basin. The established hydrological watershed models are just beginning to incorporate *ground*water into their water balance models. As Taylor (2009) points out, however, modelers do not yet incorporate the *soil water* that sits above the groundwater and sustains all non-irrigated plant matter, including the bulk of global food production. In the case of the Nile River, this means that half or more of the water in the basin is not even counted, much less deliberated over, in negotiations at the NBI.

Flawed understandings of water scarcity are perpetuated by simplistic but very popular classifications, such as the national "water stress" thresholds. The classification asserts that countries with less than 1000 m^3 of water available annually per person are "chronically stressed" and those with less than 500 m^3/year are "beyond the water barrier" (Perveen and James, 2010). The originator of the idea has proposed a more sophisticated approach to scarcity (Falkenmark *et al.*, 2007), and has acknowledged that the original thresholds can mischaracterize national water issues for a number of reasons, including lack of consideration of soil water within a country and the pressure-reducing feature of food ("virtual water") imports. Despite their very significant conceptual shortcomings, the water stress thresholds are taken up or used as departure points by the Intergovernmental Panel on Climate Change (see, e.g. Bates, Kundzewicz, Wu, and Palutikof, 2008, p. 7) and many other high-profile water or climate change studies (e.g. Vörösmarty *et al.*, 2010; Walker and King, 2008).

Such solely biophysical studies of water scarcity and security are limited most of all, perhaps, by their failure to consider how water is *distributed* within a country. Recognition that water scarcity for the masses does not necessarily mean water scarcity for the economic elite led to the development of the concept of "social" (or "economic") water scarcity (Ohlsson, 1999). The social side of scarcity considers politics, ethics, justice, economics, and human water and food consumption in examination of distributional issues. As the concept is very well established (see, e.g. Mollinga, 2008; United Nations Development Programme (UNDP), 2006), avoidance of its use by the high-profile studies is disconcerting. Privileging research of the relatively neat biophysical aspects of water security over its messy social realities cannot be expected to form a cohesive policy basis.

Narrow and Determinist Views

The second shortcoming of the prevailing interpretations of water security that constrains policy options is the narrow and determinist approach relied upon. "Environmental determinism" authors have struggled in interpreting complex sociopolitical phenomena such as water and security. Competition over scarce (or overabundant) natural resources will lead to peace, it is suggested, or to violent conflict – what Bakker (1999, p. 221) refers to as a "seductive but problematic" neoMalthusian message. The killing in Darfur has attracted media headlines as the world's first climate conflict (Borger, 2007), for example, with somewhat less deterministic reports drawing similar conclusions (e.g. Bromwich *et al.*, 2008; Burke *et al.*, 2009; UNEP, 2007). "Dig more water wells" is the typical policy recommendation, as water and human security are conflated.

The intended audience of this book may have scant respect for advice arising from analysis that sees mono-causes of war (Cramer, 2006), and may consider that tensions between the Fur and the Zaghawa (or Khartoum and the Sudan Liberation Army) have more to do with the violence in Darfur than does the rainfall variability to which the residents have long adapted (see, e.g. Kevane and Gray, 2008). But the determinist and narrow "resource scarcity leads to war (or peace)" message is heard and repeated in academic and policy circles around the world (e.g. CNA, 2007; Ki-Moon, 2007) to the point that it too may be considered an "environmental orthodoxy". Meanwhile, the very important roles that food trade, energy security, and human agency can play as opportunities for resolution of the conflict or community water security are passed up.

Water security policy based on a narrow and deterministic view of the issues involved can lead, furthermore, to water *in*security, as the UK Royal Association of Engineers (RAE) has noted (RAE, 2010, p. 5). When selective water security policy is developed through power asymmetries, the effects can be far-reaching. Physically water-scarce Saudi Arabia, as just one example, has (sensibly) gone from being the world's sixth largest exporter of cereal to a net importer. The shift in water security policy from unbridled farming of the desert has not, however, led to resolution of the conflict over the Disi Aquifer with Jordan (Ferragina and Greco, 2008), or to concern for more equitable internal distribution of water and food within the country. The concern did lead – in the wake of the 2008 cereal price spike – to agricultural "land grabs", for example in Sudan (Cotula, Vermeulen, Leonard, and Keeley, 2009). The same price spike called community and national security into question through the riots it led to in Egypt – the direct result of an (unacknowledged) dependence on cereal imports,[7] and an incoherent (what Allan and Mirumachi (2010) call "apparent") water security policy.

The tensions in the Ica Valley so distant from Lima may not be of the same geopolitical dimension, but are of the same character and importance locally. Policymakers would do well to consider the effects of the fact that water security for the powerful does not mean water security for the rest, and question how tenable and "secure" their policies are in the long term.

The "Web" of Water Security

This section proposes a "web" as metaphor for a conceptual tool that can help guide water security research and policy formation through the shortcomings identified. It then discusses the important interdependencies between water and other security areas, seeing these as developing from within a context that can usefully be interpreted through political ecology and other disciplines.

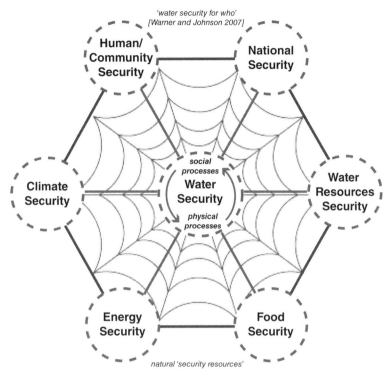

Figure 11.1 The global "web" of national water security.

A conceptual tool is preferred over the published definitions of water security because these are either insufficiently narrow or all-encompassing to the point that they are not operationable (e.g. GWP, 2009, p. 6). The "web" in Figure 11.1 centers on the interdependencies and a combined reading of how social and physical processes combine to create or deny water security.[8] Sustainable water security is interpreted as a function of the degree of equitability and balance between interdependencies of the related security areas, played out within a web of socioeconomic and political forces at multiple spatial levels. *Analytical* application of the web is necessarily interdisciplinary; the development and implementation of *policy* deriving from the web is necessarily cross-sectoral.

The "web" of water security identifies the "security areas" related to national water security. These include the intimately associated natural "security resources" (water resources, energy, climate, food), as well as the social groups concerned (individual, community, nation). The "web" recognizes the interaction occurring at all spatial scales, from the individual through to river basin and global levels. In this sense, an individual's water security may coexist with national water *in*security, as in the case of wealthy farmer-sheikhs with the deepest wells (who may be temporarily water secure) in the dry highlands of Yemen (which is not, on the whole, water secure) (Lichtenthaler, 2002).

While Figure 11.1 is symmetrical and clear, we can be certain that the shape, character, and extent of each filament and the web in its entirety are anything but.

The conceptual tool suggests consideration of the complex "simultaneously political, economic, and ecological processes" (Bakker 2003, p. 36), as indicated by the cyclical arrows at the center of the figure. It follows on from political ecology work on environmental vulnerability and risk (Wisner, Blaikie, Cannon, and Davis, 2004), international political economy research on water (e.g. Allan, 2001) and the growing interest in socioecological systems (Agrawal and Chhatre, 2011). Like that work, the "web" of water security eschews direct bivalent causal relationships of water and socioeconomic and political processes for an understanding of the multivalent underlying causes of water insecurity. This means, for example, less effort spent on prediction of the outbreak of a water war in the Ica Valley, and more spent on the (perhaps seemingly more bland) study of the effect of British vegetable consumption on the water resources and human and community security there. Similarly, the implications for UK national security of water leaving the Nile in the form of fruit destined for European supermarkets would be understood in the context of mounting tensions (and regional security) on the Nile, and would question if, how, and for whom the NBI is generating national, food, or water resources security.

At the risk of overextending a metaphor, analysis of the web in its entirety is not generally feasible because tugging like a fly on the filaments will inevitably break some, or tie one up methodologically. The approach suggests that if an analytical focus on any part of the web is necessary, the scope taken should be analytically nested within the web in its entirety. Interpretation of the physical and social components of interdependencies between two or more security areas may be assisted by the work that has been done by disciplines specialized in those areas. National security research concerned about climate security could apply the nondeterministic work done on the environment and security field (Hartmann, 2002; Mobjörk, Eriksson, and Carlsen 2010), for instance.

Interdependency and Sustainable Water Security

As national water security is a function of the interdependencies between the related security areas at multiple levels, it is important to understand both the way and the context within which security and interdependencies relate to each other. In their discussion of "water security for who", Warner and Johnson (2007, p. 71) point out that "interdependence ... means opportunity for some, but dependence and vulnerability for others. Virtual water trade delivers water-poor states from one type of dependency (on limited resources), but can usher in dependency of another type: on the unequal terms of world trade". The remarks demonstrate that the trade-offs that occur in the pursuit of water security are made as much between groups as they are between natural "security resources".

It follows that the study of interdependencies should occur in two ways. One is to pursue the extent to which different natural security resources are interdependent. To what degree does the production of biofuels generate national energy security at the expense of national water resources insecurity (and hence national water security), for example? Here, "balance" is the suggested operating principle, if a semblance of sustainability is sought.

The second research pursuit is to understand how the water security of different actors in the web is affected by interdependence. "Equitability" is suggested as the operating principle towards sustainable water security here, with an understanding that instability and uncertainty are reduced by greater codependence (in ecosystems, as in the European Union) rather than independence (for discussion see, e.g. Buzan, Waever, and de Wilde, 1998; Kaldor, 2007). Sustainable long-term water security may thus be assisted by thinking and action on human security in ways that are being tentatively explored (see, e.g. Pachova, Nakayama, and Jansky, 2008). The power asymmetries that enable short-term and "selective" water security suggest that greater examination should be conducted of the mediating potential of international water law (McCaffrey, 2007; WWF–DFID, 2010), or injustices meted out through international food trade (e.g. Via Campesina, 2006).

The relationship between interdependencies and various relevant security areas requires considerable testing and theorization, as brief testing of the upper and right side of Figure 11.1 shows. The interdependency created by transboundary waters flowing through or under state borders challenges the traditional view of national security assured through sovereignty and independence. Attempts to exert full sovereign territorial control over a "fugitive resource" such as water (Frederick, 1996) clash with thinking on, and implementation of, natural resource management. These have evolved from seeing nature as static (which leads to attempts to "conserve" it) to an appreciation of global biophysical processes being resilient and in "non-equilibrium". *Adaptive* natural resources and water management (see, e.g. Ostrom, 1990) developed as a result of the recognition that a sense of security is possible without stability and full control. Infrastructure, built on the logic that variability in rainfall, river flow, or aquifer recharge is a source only of *in*security, goes against the grain of the adaptive approach, and precludes alternative methods of dealing with the variability (e.g. Lankford, 2004).

Yet the sociopolitical and economic context in which transboundary water dynamics occur is just as fluid as the resource itself, and a firm understanding of the interdependencies for any country is difficult to pin down for long. A "web" of water security reading of Egyptian water security would factor in the shifting political context between Nile Basin states, including the strengthening alliance between Ethiopia and the United States, the 2011 secession of South Sudan, Sudan's newfound financial independence from the exploitation of oil and Chinese investment (including for new dams on the Nile River), and soil water, which makes up so much of the Nile Basin water balance. Seen in this light, the decision by Cairo (along with Khartoum) not to sign the Cooperative Framework Agreement in May 2010 selects security through independence over security through (more or less equitable) interdependence. The water security achieved through the position is tenable as long as the power asymmetry that sustains it is maintained.

The current political deadlock blocking any progress on cooperation along the Nile may also be seen in light of criticism that the World Bank has drawn from NBI member states for driving its own agenda (see, e.g. Cascão, 2009, p. 59), or for taking a stand during the negotiations in support of the Egyptian position (Doya, 2009). The efforts to create a Nile Basin Commission were not perceived by all as an equitable process, and did not explicitly confront the inequitable allocation of Nile flows cemented in the 1959 Agreement. In that sense, the divisive impact of the *Water Security* Article 14b was entirely predictable (and was in fact predicted) (Cascão, 2008). Any water security ensured by Egypt through preservation of the inequitable and contentious *status quo* is, on this reading, expected to survive only in the short term.

With the outcome of the latest round of the Nile conflict yet undecided, it is difficult to judge whether the NBI on its own has resulted in greater or less water security for all the Nile states, or for individuals and communities living within the basin. The attention drawn indirectly by the NBI to the core water-sharing issue and the extensive interaction between state representatives and epistemic communities may yet prove to generate a constructive distribution of resources and security. The notion that cooperation over transboundary rivers will lead eventually to stability between states (and eventually regional economic integration) marches on elsewhere, in any case. Experience from the Mekong and Nile Basins initiatives is drawn upon for a similar World Bank-led initiative with Nepal, India, and Bangladesh on the Ganges River (Rahaman, 2009). The same policy based on similar determinist analysis is thus applied to a completely different political, social, and economic context. If the lessons learned on the other basins lead to a broader and less deterministic conception of water security, the expected selective and short-term water security may be avoided.

Analytical and Policy Implications of the "Web" of Water Security

The water security "web" reading of transboundary waters and national security has highlighted the previously discussed shortcoming of water security policy. The narrow and deterministic approach blames water insecurity chiefly on physical phenomena, and reacts through infrastructure, institutions, or treaties. When a relationship between a country's GDP (as seen in Ethiopia) is found to correspond with river flow variability, dams are proposed. When an opportunity to convert fossil water into cash is spotted (as in Peru), asparagus spears are cultivated. When tensions are sensed between riparian states, a basin initiative that sets about to share collection of data (but not the water itself, as with the NBI) is deployed, under the assumption that environmental issues shape the broader political context, and not vice versa.

Such prescriptions are likely to lead to water security for some in the short term. They are unlikely, however, to lead to long-term national water security, for the reasons discussed. Yet the development of practical long-term national water security policy is no mean feat. A tentative first step outside the water box is helpful. Koch, for example, has identified the need to shift from IWRM to Integrated Water Energy and Food Management (Tickner and May, 2011).

A second useful step is to reconsider policy based on environmentally determinist analysis. This should be recognized as potentially interesting and subjective, and as excluding solutions that may arise from the agency of local population to adapt and develop appropriate solutions. Between the "pro-storage" and "anti-dam" ideologues, for instance, there is space for "good dams" (Gyawali, 2001; Skinner, Niasse, and Haas, 2009). It follows that researchers would do well to investigate the interests and agendas behind all recommendations put forward as attempts to achieve "water security".

The "web" of water security further opens analytical eyes up to the political constraints on and less conventional opportunities for progress. The recognition of the influence of soil water on the water balance of the Nile Basin, for example, could lead to examination of the benefits to be gained from increased food trade within the basin (see, e.g. Phillips and Woodhouse, 2010). The impact of food exports or innovative water resource management policies (e.g. water demand management) would be factored into externally imposed basin initiatives. Interpretation of the formation of international regimes dealing with the water, global food trade, and energy nexus would consider the opportunities and constraints engendered from alliances developed in a world shifting in order to have regional multilateralism.

If analytical application of the "web" is forcibly interdisciplinary, policy deriving from it is necessarily cross-sectoral. Making water security a core component of national security and putting water security at the center of "international development", as the RAE (2010) suggests, means harmonization of policy across sectors and with foreign policy. Coherent national-level policy addressing water resources security, energy security, food security, or national security will oblige transcending departmental borders. This would imply the training of experts in cross-sectoral policy, as well as increase cross-departmental policy committees, and the dispatch to rivers of lawyers and environmental diplomats along with hydrologists. These would interact with the relevant ministers and ministries of agriculture, trade, and finance, and seek equitability of resource distribution between the actors involved as a matter of course, not exception.

Conclusions

This chapter has offered a critical review of academic and policy work on water security, arguing that prevailing conceptions both overemphasize the physical aspects of water, and are narrow and determinist. High-profile work on water security has been found to have built-in judgments and assumptions about watershed balances and scarcity thresholds that render them less solid than they first appear. Any hydrological, engineering, or diplomatic initiative for water security should recognize the vast quantities of *soil* water therein, for instance. Just as importantly, it has been noted that the links between water and other related natural "security resources" – food, energy, climate – are not routinely addressed or fully understood. Uncoordinated policy aimed at security in one area may result in less security in another: less water security as the cost of greater energy security through biofuel production, for example.

The formulation of direct causal relationships between society and the environment (i.e. dams lead to water security, and this leads to state wealth) was found to yield correspondingly simple policy recommendations. The possibility that insufficiently broad working definitions of water security become unquestioned "environmental orthodoxies" was identified, such that poor policy is expected to be perpetuated.

Policy downplaying the social aspects of water scarcity and security has been noted as leaving out half or more of any issue or options for policy. Ignoring inequitable distribution of water flows or associated resources will compromise the viability of efforts and lead to selective short-term, rather than sustainable, water security. The massive oversight comes at a cost – first, to those who suffer from the selective water "security" policy, and second, to the budget lines of their financial backers.

A "web" of water security has been offered as a conceptual tool to guide research and policy. "Sustainable" water security is interpreted as a function of the degree of equitability and balance between interdependencies of the related security areas, played out within a web of socioeconomic and political forces at multiple spatial levels. Its understanding of combined social and physical processes leads to a number of implications for analysis and policy. The social, economic, and political context that mediates the relationships between the related security areas must be considered, for instance. As that context is replete with trade-offs and asymmetries, equitability and balance are suggested as principles to counter the potential development of selective and short-term water security.

A significant amount of research and testing of the various filaments of the web is required, before the suggested approach can adequately support national water security policy. The nexus research already under way (e.g. water–food–climate) would thrive by considering the other interdependent water security-related security areas (e.g. "water security for whom"), the governing principles of water allocation (Lankford, 2013) and ties with national economic security. Perhaps the most fertile gap to fill is the insight that may be garnered through incorporation of epistemological views on "risk", as well as the philosophical foundations of uncertainty and "security" itself. In the absence of this exploration, our collective ability to develop and implement long-term water security will remain compromised.

Acknowledgements

The author would like to thank T. Allan, D. Conway, T. Forsyth, E. Kistin, B. Lankford, N. Mirumachi, D. Phillips, J. Warner, colleagues at the UEA Water Security Research Centre, and three anonymous reviewers for the comments they have provided on the original version of this chapter.

Notes

1. These include Tanzania, Kenya, Uganda, Rwanda, Burundi, and Democratic Republic of Congo. Eritrea was not part of the negotiations.
2. As predicted, the national water security achieved was tenable only as long as the power asymmetry that sustains it was maintained (Nicol and Cascão, 2011).
3. Cook and Bakker (2012) cite Clarke (1993), for example: water security means "the ability to provide adequate and reliable water supplies for populations living in the world's drier areas so as to meet agricultural production needs"
4. "Africa is deeply water insecure" (Grey, 2006, p. 2).
5. Water resources security may be understood to comprise the same principles and ideas about environmental "quality" as "environmental security" (e.g. Dalby, 2006), and may be informed by the lessons drawn from the considerable effort spent globally on Integrated Water Resources Management (Molle, 2008).
6. Although the discussion focuses on water *scarcity*, an overabundance of water is equally relevant to water security, for instance in the Peruvian town of Ica (Warner and Oré, 2006).
7. Between 1998 and 2003, for instance, Egypt annually imported approximately 32 billion cubic metres of virtual water (mostly in the form of beef) from outside the Nile Basin – the equivalent of about one-third of the flow of the river itself (Zeitoun, Allan, and Mohieldeen, 2010).

8. The "web" metaphor comes from a draft World Economic Forum (WEF) report by the Global Agenda Council on Water Security: "Water security is the gossamer that links together the web of food, energy, climate, economic growth and human security challenges that the world economy faces over the next two decades", (WEF, 2009, p. 5).

References

Adger, W. N., J. Paavola, S. Huq, and M. J. Mace, eds. 2006. *Fairness in Adaptation to Climate Change*. Cambridge, MA: MIT Press.

Agrawal, A., and A. Chhatre. 2011. "Against Mono-consequentialism: Multiple Outcomes and Their Drivers in Social-Ecological Systems." *Global Environmental Change*, 21: 1–3.

Aldaya, M. M., A. Y. Hoekstra, and J. A. Allan. 2008. *Strategic Importance of Green Water in International Crop Trade*. Value of Water Research Report Series No. 25. Delft: UNESCO-IHE Institute for Water Education.

Allan, J. A. 1997. "Virtual Water: A Long Term Solution for Water Short Middle Eastern Economies?" SOAS Water Issues Study Group, School of Oriental and African Studies/King's College London, Occasional Paper 3.

Allan, J. A. 2001. *The Middle East Water Question: Hydropolitics and the Global Economy*. London: I.B. Tauris.

Allan, J. A., and N. Mirumachi. 2010. "Why Negotiate? Asymmetric Endowments, Asymmetric Power and the Invisible Nexus of Water, Trade and Power that Brings Apparent Water Security." In *Transboundary Water Management: Principles and Practice*, edited by A. Earle, A. Jägerskog, and J. Öjendal. London: Earthscan.

Bakker, K. 1999. "The Politics of Hydropower: Developing the Mekong." *Political Geography*, 18(2): 209–232.

Bakker, K. J. 2003. "A Political Ecology of Water Privatization." *Studies in Political Economy*, 70: 35–58.

Barlow, M. 2007. *Blue Covenant: The Global Water Crisis and the Coming Battle for the Right to Water*. Toronto, ON: McClelland & Stewart Ltd.

Bates, B. C., Z. W. Kundzewicz, S. Wu, and J. P. Palutikof, eds. 2008. *Climate Change and Water: Technical Paper of the Intergovernmental Panel on Climate Change*. Geneva: IPCC Secretariat.

Berndes, G. 2002. "Bioenergy and Water: The Implications of Large-Scale Bioenergy Production for Water Use and Supply." *Global Environmental Change*, 12: 253–271.

Borger, Julian. 2007. "Darfur conflict heralds era of wars triggered by climate change, UN Report warns." *The Guardian*, June 23.

Briscoe, J. 2009. "Water Security: Why It Matters and What to Do about It." *Innovations*, 4(3): 3–28.

Bromwich, B., A. A. Adam, A. A. Fadul, *et al.* 2008. *Darfur: Relief in a Vulnerable Environment*. Teddington, UK: Tearfund.

Brown, O., and A. Crawford. 2009. *Rising Temperatures, Rising Tensions: Climate Change and the Risk of Violent Conflict in the Middle East*. Winnipeg, MB: International Institute for Sustainable Development.

Brown, C., and U. Lall. 2006. "Water and economic development: The role of variability and a framework for resilience." *Natural Resources Forum*, 30: 306–317.

Brunnée, J., and S. J. Toope. 2002. "The Changing Nile Basin Regime: Does Law Matter?" *Harvard International Law Journal*, 43(1): 105–159.

Budds, J., and L. Hinojosa. 2012. "Restructuring and Rescaling Water Governance in Mining Contexts: The Co-Production of Waterscapes in Peru." *Water Alternatives*, 5(1): 119–137.

Burke, M. B., E. Miguel, S. Satyanath, et al. 2009. "Warming Increases the Risk of Civil War in Africa." *Proceedings of the National Academy of Sciences of the United States of America*, 106(49): 20670–20674.

Buzan, B., O. Waever, and J. de Wilde. 1998. *Security: A New Framework for Analysis*. London: Lynne Rienner.

Cascão, A. E. 2008. "Counter-Hegemony in the Nile River Basin." *Water Policy*, 10(S2): 13–28.

Cascão, A. E. 2009. *Institutional Analysis of the Nile Basin Intitative: What Worked, What did Not Work and What are the Emerging Options?* Report prepared for International Water Management Institute, the International Livestock Research Institute, the Nile Basin Initiative and the Eastern Nile Technical Organization.

CNA. 2007. "National Security and the Threat of Climate Change." Alexandria, VA: CNA Corporation.

Conway, D., and E.L.F. Schipper. 2011. "Adaptation to climate change in Africa: Challenges and opportunities identified from Ethiopia." *Global Environmental Change*, 21: 227–237.

Cook, Catherine, and Karen Bakker. 2012. "Water Security: Debating an emerging paradigm." *Global Environmental Change*, 22(1): 94–102.

Cotula, L., S. Vermeulen, R. Leonard, and J. Keeley. 2009. *Land Grab or Development Opportunity? Agricultural Investment and International Land Deals in Africa*. London/Rome: IIED/FAO/IFAD.

Cramer, C. 2006. *Civil War is Not a Stupid Thing*. London: Hurst & Co.

Dalby, S. 2006. "Security and Environment Linkages Revisited." In *Globalization and Environmental Challenges: Reconceptualizing Security in the 21st Century*, edited by H. Gunter Brauch, U. Oswald Spring, C. Mesjasz, et al., 165–172. Heidelberg: Springer.

Demeritt, D. 2006. "Science Studies, Climate Change and the Prospects for Constructivist Critique." *Economy and Society*, 35(3): 453–479.

Department of International Development (DFID). 2009. "Water Storage and Hydropower: Supporting Growth, Resilience and Low Carbon Development: A DFID Evidence-into-Action Paper." *Policy Booklet*. London: Department for International Development.

Doya, M. 2009. "Donors Back Egypt, Sudan on Nile Water Pact." *The East African*, Nairobi, August 10.

Dublin Principles. 1992. *The Dublin Statement on Water and Sustainable Development*, International Conference on Water and the Environment.

Falkenmark, M., A. Berntell, A. Jägerskog, et al. 2007. *On the Verge of a New Water Scarcity: A Call for Good Governance and Human Ingenuity*. Brief, S. P. Stockholm: Stockholm International Water Institute.

Ferragina, E., and F. Greco. 2008. "The Disi Project: An Internal/External Analysis." *Water International*, 33(4): 451–463.

Food and Agriculture Organization (FAO). 2000. *New Dimension in Water Security: Water, Society and Ecosystem Services in the 21st Century*. AGL/MISC/25/2000. Rome: Food and Agriculture Organization of the United Nations, Land and Water Division.

Food and Agriculture Organization (FAO). 2008. *Climate Change, Water and Food Security*. Technical Background Document from the Expert Consultation, 26–28 February. Rome: Food and Agriculture Organization of the United Nations.

Forsyth, T. 2003. *Critical Political Ecology: The Politics of Environmental Science*. London: Routledge.

Frederick, K. D. 1996. "Water as a Source of International Conflict." *Resources*, 123: 9–12.

Gerbens-Leenes, P. W., A. Y. Hoekstra, and T. H. van der Meer. 2008. "Water Footprint of Bio-energy and Other Primary Energy Carriers." *Value of Water Research Report Series No. 29*. Delft, UNESCO-IHE Institute for Water Education.

Global Water Partnership (GWP). 2000. *Towards Water Security: A Framework for Action*. Stockholm: Global Water Partnership.

Global Water Partnership (GWP). 2009. *GWP Strategy 2009–2013*. Stockholm: Global Water Partnership.

Grey, D. 2006. "Water, Poverty and Growth in Africa." Paper presented at Department for International Development's Africa Growth Conference, London, July 6, World Bank.

Grey, D., and C. W. Sadoff. 2007. "Sink or Swim? Water Security for Growth and Development." *Water Policy*, 9: 545–571.

Grobicki, A. 2009. "Water Security: Time to Talk across Sectors." *SIWI Water Front*, 14–15.

Gyawali, D. 2001. *Rivers, Technology and Society: Learning the Lessons of Water Management in Nepal*. London: Zed Books.

Hartmann, E. 2002. "Strategic Scarcity: The Origins and Impact of Environmental Conflict Ideas". Unpublished PhD diss., Development Studies Institute, London School of Economics and Political Science.

Hellegers, P., D. Zilberman, P. Steduto, and P. McCornick. 2008. "Interactions between Water, Energy, Food and Environment: Evolving Perspectives and Policy Issues." *Water Policy*, 10(S1): 1–10.

Hepworth, N., J. C. Postigo, and B. G. Delgado. 2010. *Drop by Drop: A Case Study of Peruvian Asparagus and the Impacts of the UK's Water Footprint*. Progressio, in association with Centro Peruano De Estudios Sociales, and Water Witness International.

Houdret, A., A. Kramer, and A. Carius. 2010. "The Water Security Nexus: Challenges and Opportunities for Development Cooperation." GTZ International Water Policy and Infrastructure Concept Paper. GTZ/Adelphi, Eschborn, Germany.

International Water Management Institute (IWMI). 2007. *Water for Food, Water for Life: A Comprehensive Assessment of Water Management in Agriculture*. International Water Management Institute. London: Earthscan.

International Water Management Institute (IWMI). 2009. *Flexible Water Storage Options and Adaptation to Climate Change*. Water Policy Brief Issue 31. Colombo: International Water Management Institute.

Julien, F. 2012. "Hydropolitics is what societies make of it (or why we need a constructivist approach to the geopolitics of water." *International Journal of Sustainable Society*, 4(1/2): 45–71.

Kaldor, M. 2007. *New and Old Wars: Organized Violence in a Global Era*. 2nd ed. London: Polity Press.

Kevane, M., and L. Gray. 2008. "Darfur: Rainfall and Conflict." *Environmental Research Letters*, 3. DOI:10.1088/1748-9326/3/3/034006.

Ki-Moon, B. 2007. "What I Saw in Darfur." *Washington Post*, September 14.

King, C. W., A. S. Holman, and M. E. Webber. 2008. "Thirst for Energy." *Nature Geoscience*, 1(55): 283–286.

Lankford, B. 2004. "Resource-Centred Thinking in River Basins: Should we Revoke the Crop Water Requirement Approach to Irrigation Planning?" *Agricultural Water Management*, 68: 33–46.

Lankford, B. 2013. *Resource Efficiency Complexity and the Commons: The Paracommons and Paradoxes of Natural Resource Losses, Wastes and Wastages*. London: Routledge.

Lichtenthaler, G. 2002. *Political Ecology and the Role of Water: Environment, Society and Economy in Northern Yemen*. Aldershot: Ashgate.

Lundqvist, J., J. Barron, G. Berndes, *et al.* 2007. *Water Pressure and Increases in Food & Bioenergy Demand: Implications of Economic Growth and Options for Decoupling*. Swedish Environmental Advisory Council Memorandum 2007:1, Chapter 3, Stockholm.

Magsig, B.-O. 2010. "Introducing an Analytical Framework for Water Security: A Platform for the Refinement of International Water Law." *The Journal of Water Law*, 20(2–3): 61–69.

McCaffrey, S. 2007. *The Law of International Watercourses*. Oxford: Oxford University Press.

McCornick, P. G., S. B. Awulachew, and M. Abebe. 2008. "Water–Food–Energy–Environment Synergies and Tradeoffs: Major Issues and Case Studies." *Water Policy*, 10(S1): 23–36.

Mekonnen, D.Z. 2010. "The Nile Basin Cooperative Framework Agreement Negotiations and the Adoption of a "Water Security" Paradigm: Flight into Obscurity or a Logical Cul-de-sac?" *European Journal of International Law*, 21: 421–440.

Milly, P.C.D., K. A. Dunne, and A. V. Vecchia. 2005. "Global pattern of trends on streamflow and water availability in a changing climate." *Nature*, 438(17): 347–350.

Mobjörk, M., M. Eriksson, and H. Carlsen. 2010. *On Connecting Climate Change with Security and Armed Conflict: Investigating Knowledge from the Scientific Community*. Stockholm: Swedish Defence Research Agency Defence Analysis.

Molle, F. 2008. "Nirvana Concepts, Narratives and Policy Models: Insights from the Water Sector." *Water Alternatives*, 1(1): 131–156.

Mollinga, P. P. 2008. "Water, Politics and Development: Framing a Political Sociology of Water Resources Management." *Water Alternatives*, 1(1): 7–23.

Nicol, A., and A. E. Cascão. 2011. "Against the Flow - New Power Dynamics and Upstream Mobliisation in the Nile Basin." *Review of African Political Economy*, 38(128): 317–325.

Ohlsson, L. 1999. "Water Conflicts and Social Resource Scarcity." *Physics and Chemistry of the Earth, Part B: Hydrology, Oceans and Atmostphere*, 25(3): 213–220.

Ostrom, E. 1990. *Governing the Commons: The Evolution of Institutions for Collective Action*. Cambridge: Cambridge University Press.

Pachova, N. I., M. Nakayama, and L. Jansky. 2008. "National Sovereignty and Human Security: Changing Realities and Concepts in International Water Management." In *International Water Security: Domestic Threats and Opportunities*, edited by N. I. Pachova, M. Nakayama, and L. Jansky, 289–295. Tokyo: United Nations Press.

Perveen, S. and L. A. James. 2010. "Scale Invariance of Water Stress and Scarcity Indicators: Facilitating Cross-Scale Comparisons of Water Resources Vulnerability." *Applied Geography*. DOI: 10.1016/j.apgeog.2010.07.003.

Phillips, D., and Woodhouse, M. 2010. *Benefit Sharing in the Nile River Basin: Emerging Strategies for Fresh Water Use at the Country and Selected Sub-basin Levels, as Revealed by the Trans-boundary Waters Opportunity Analysis*. Windhoek, Nile Basin Initiative, Socioeconomic Development and Benefit Sharing component.

Pittock, Jamie, and Bruce Lankford. 2010. "Environmental Water Requirements: Demand Management in an Era of Water Scarcity." *Journal of Integrative Environmental Sciences*, 7(1): 75–93.

Royal Academy of Engineering (RAE). 2010. *Global Water Security: An Engineering Perspective*. London: The Royal Academy of Engineering.

Rahaman, M. M. 2009. "Integrated Ganges Basin Management: Conflict and Hope for Regional Development." *Water Policy*, 11(2): 168–190.

Reisner, Marc. 1986. *Cadillac Desert – The American West and its Disappearing Water*. New York, NY: Penguin Books.

Rogers, P. 2008. "Facing the Freshwater Crisis." *Scientific American*, July.

Skinner, J., M. Niasse, and L. Haas, eds. 2009. *Sharing the Benefits of Large Dams in West Africa*. London: International Institute for Environment and Development.

Smith, D. and J. Vivekananda. 2007. *A Climate of Conflict: The Links between Climate Change, Peace and War*. London: International Alert.

Sosa, M., and M. Zwarteveen. 2012. "Exploring the Politics of Water Grabbing: The Case of Large Mining Operations in the Peruvian Andes." *Water Alternatives*, 5(2): 360–375.

Stern, N. 2009. *A Blueprint for a Safer Planet: How to Manage Climate Change and Create a New Era of Progress and Prosperity*. London: Random House.

Stockholm International Water Institute (SIWI). 2005. *Let it Reign: The New Water Paradigm for Global Food Security*. Final Report to CSD-13. Stockholm: Stockholm International Water Institute, with IFRPI, IUCN and IWMI.

Tarlock, D., and Wouters, P. 2010. "Reframing the Water Security Dialogue." *The Journal of Water Law*, 20(2): 53–60.

Taylor, R. 2009. "Rethinking Water Scarcity: The Role of Storage." *Transactions of the American Geophysical Union*, 90(28): 237–238.

Tickner, D., and R. May. 2011. "Thirsty Crops: social and environmental outcomes from a partnership approach to agriculture in Pakistan and India." Presentation given on behalf of the Worldwide Fund for Nature to the UEA Water Security Research Centre. University of East Anglia, Norwich, March 13.

United Nations Development Programme (UNDP). 2006. *Beyond Scarcity: Power, Poverty and the Global Water Crisis*. Human Development Report 2006. New York: United Nations Development Programme.

United Nations Environment Programme (UNEP). 2006. "Rainfall variability and economic growth in Zimbabwe." United Nations Environment Programme. Accessed November 20, 2010 from http://maps.grida.no/go/graphic/rainfall-variability-and-economic-growth-in-zimbabwe

United Nations Environment Programme (UNEP). 2007. *Sudan: Post-conflict Environmental Assessment*. Nairobi: United Nations Environment Programme.

United Nations Environment Programme (UNEP). 2012. *Global Environment Outlook – 5: Environment for the future we want*. Valletta, United Nations Environment Programme.

United Nations International Law Commission (UN ILC). 1997. *Convention on the Law of the Non-navigational Uses of International Watercourses*, United Nations International Law Commission.

Via Campesina. 2006. *Rice and Food Sovereignty in Asia Pacific*. Jakarta: La Via Campensina.

Vörösmarty, C. J., P. B. McIntyre, M. O. Gessmer, *et al.* 2010. "Global Threats to Human Water Security and River Biodiversity." *Nature*, 467: 555–561.

Walker, G., and D. King. 2008. *The Hot Topic: How to Tackle Global Warming and Still Keep the Lights On*. London: Bloomsbury.

Warner, J. 2008. "The Politics of Flood Insecurity: Framing Contested River Management Projects." PhD thesis, Wageningen University, Netherlands.

Warner, J., and C. L. Johnson. 2007. ""Virtual Water" – Real People: Useful Concept or Prescriptive Tool?" *Water International*, 32(1): 63–77.

Warner, J. and M. T. Oré. 2006. "El Niño Platforms: Participatory Disaster Response in Peru." *Disasters*, 20(1): 102–117.

WBGU. 2008. *Climate Change as a Security Risk*. German Advisory Council on Global Change. London: Earthscan.

World Economic Forum (WEF). 2009. *The Bubble is Close to Bursting: A Forecast of the Main Economic and Geopolitical Water Issues Likely to Arise in the World during the Next Two Decades (Draft for Discussion at the World Economic Forum Annual Meeting 2009)*. World Economic Forum Initiative: Managing Our Future Water Needs for Agriculture, Industry, Human Health and the Environment.

Wisner, B., P. M. Blaikie, T. Cannon, and I. Davis. 2004. *At Risk: Natural Hazards, People's Vulnerability and Disasters*, second edition. London: Routledge.

World Bank. 2009. *Directions in Hydropower*. Washington: Energy, Transport, Water – The World Bank Group.

WWF. 2008. *UK Water Footprint: The Impact of the UK's Food and Fibre Consumption on Global Water Resources*. London: Worldwide Fund for Nature.

WWF–DFID. 2010. *International Architecture for Transboundary Water Resources Management: Policy Analysis and Recommendations*. London: Worldwide Fund for Nature and the

UK Department for International Development, with Pegasys Strategy and Development, and the UNESCO Centre for Water Law, Policy and Science.

Wolf, A. T. 2007. "Shared Waters: Conflict and Cooperation." *Annual Review of Environmental Resources*, (32): 241–269.

Zeitoun, M., and N. Mirumachi. 2008. "Transboundary water interaction I: Reconsidering conflict and cooperation." *International Environmental Agreements*, 8: 297–316.

Zeitoun, M., J. A. Allan, and Y. Mohieldeen. 2010. "Virtual Water "Flows" of the Nile Basin, 1998–2004: A First Approximation and Implications for Water Security." *Global Environmental Change*, 20: 229–242.

Zeitoun, M., A. Cascão, M. England, and J. Hodbod. 2012. *Water Demand Management and the Water–Food–Climate Nexus in the MENA Region*. Ottawa, ON: International Development Research Council.

Further Reading

Global Water Partnership (GWP). 2010. *Water Security for Development: Insights from African Partnerships in Action*. Stockholm: Global Water Partnership.

Lankford, B.A. 2011. "Responding to water scarcity – beyond the volumetric." In *The Limits to Scarcity: Contesting the Politics of Allocation*, edited by L. Mehta. London: Earthscan.

Part III   Policy Tools

Chapter 12

Civilian Protection

Sarah Sewall

Introduction

Our expectations of why and how global citizens should be protected from violence has evolved dramatically in recent decades, challenging existing conceptual, legal, and normative frameworks and pitting important international principles against one another. This chapter is concerned with the evolution and varied manifestations of the concept of protecting civilians primarily during armed conflict and from physical threats. It traces the character of civilian protection as a *military* responsibility, explaining how it has expanded to incorporate broader humanitarian imperatives. The essay discusses three different genres of civilian protection: avoiding civilian casualties in armed conflict, protecting civilians at the tactical level during military operations, and conducting military interventions for the primary purpose of protecting civilians. This chapter does not explore issues of humanitarian action (see Chapter 13: Humanitarian Assistance).

Since the end of the Cold War, and with hastening momentum, the idea of civilian protection has assumed entirely new dimensions. At the conceptual level, the international human rights movement has driven this change and the related evolution of cultural norms. At a practical level, the concept takes shape through the actions of national governments and international political bodies, particularly the United Nations. Civilian protection began as a highly limited concept that roughly equated to avoiding intentionally targeting civilians in war. Ever since, the idea of civilian protection has been continuously recast, expanding who is to be protected, by whom, and from what. This transition is hopeful for expanding protections to victims of organized violence, but it is also fraught with contradictions and complications.

First, we must address language and definitions. Clarity about who is a civilian and what civilian protection encompasses is vital to understanding both the operational and political challenges associated with this emerging global norm. In this

The Handbook of Global Security Policy, First Edition. Edited by Mary Kaldor and Iavor Rangelov.

essay, the term "civilian protection" is an umbrella term to describe three different types of efforts by *military forces* to shield civilians from physical violence. The initial building block is the requirement to *avoid causing civilian casualties* in the course of armed conflict (an obligation embodied in Geneva Conventions). Civilian protection further includes *affirmative military tasks* undertaken during military operations – including UN peacekeeping operations – where the tasks specifically aim to protect civilians from violence (such actions will be referred to here as tactical civilian protection). The third genre of civilian protection is strategic civilian protection – a *military intervention* that aims primarily to prevent or halt violence against civilians. The United Nations Security Council mandate for intervention in Libya in 2011 provides such an example.[1]

It is worth noting here that the international discourse highlights non-military aspects of protecting civilians. For example, the United Nations uses a term called "Protection of Civilians" or POC to refer to a wide range of activities to protect civilians from physical violence. Similarly, proponents of the emerging norm of the "Responsibility to Protect" (R2P) emphasize prevention and non-military tools rather than the use of military force. The military challenges of civilian protection are unique but they remain underappreciated, in part because the international community prefers to emphasize the non-military options for enhancing civilian security.

A further complexity is the meaning of "civilians", or the persons deserving protection. Historically, civilians are defined by what they are *not*. Combatants are persons who are members of any armed forces (national militaries or paramilitaries with continuous combat functions), or are part of a *levee en masse* (spontaneously arming themselves without sufficient time to become "organized", while still openly carrying weapons and respecting the law of war). All other persons are civilians. Civilians may nonetheless lose their protected status under international human rights law (IHL) by participating directly in military hostilities.[2]

The International Committee of the Red Cross (ICRC) notes trends in modern warfare have made classifying a civilian more complex.[3] This is not simply the result of combatants increasingly violating IHL by locating their forces amidst civilians or by refusing to identify themselves with uniforms. Conflicts frequently take place in civilian population centers where civilians become involved in activities closely related to military operations. Also, the outsourcing of military activities to government civilians and private contractors has further increased the involvement of non-uniformed personnel in warfare. Finally, the complexity of military operations may involve geographically dispersed civilians and combatants in the same military activity (such as conducting drone strikes). For our purposes, we should assume that while the definition of a civilian may remain contested, "civilian protection" would not logically extend to civilians who had lost their protected status by taking a direct part in hostilities.

Normative Principles: Origins and Tensions

The concept of civilian protection has two competing points of origin. The first is in ancient notions of the morality of war, which states codified into the law of war at the turn of the twentieth century. The second source is the modern human rights movement, which, since the 1970s, has become increasingly robust thanks to the efforts of a burgeoning civil society. The older, state-centric understanding that armed conflict might affect non-combatants (even if its violence should be limited) contrasts markedly with the newer human rights ideal of inviolable individual rights. These two independent strands of civilian protection have begun to intersect, creating new notions of how to protect civilians in war.

Yet, important tensions persist partly because humanitarian principles and military power coexist uneasily. Humanitarians are suspicious of military power; they seek to impartially alleviate human suffering, not to impose violence for political ends. Competing values and institutional tensions prevent humanitarianism from fully adopting a political lens of analysis or accepting the role of military force. This stance can undermine humanitarian objectives when an at-risk population's fundamental need is physical protection rather than the provision of material, services, or rights advocacy of humanitarian response.

Civilian protection also challenges traditional distinctions within the ethics of war. The Just War tradition separates the morality of when and how war should be waged (*jus ad bellum* and *jus in bello*, respectively). Civilian protection figured centrally in the conduct of war, but it was not considered a distinct aspect of *jus ad bellum* decision-making. Today, international debate about the purpose and morality of using force is becoming intermingled with debate about how force is used, complicating our analytic framework for thinking about the moral use of force.

Three Genres of Civilian Protection

Despite the very real tensions between upholding human rights and using military force, humanitarian impulses continue to expand and redefine the idea of civilian protection. Today, there are at least three discernable genres of expectations and efforts to protect civilians from certain types of organized violence. The first is the longstanding expectation that the violence of armed conflict should be inflicted upon combatants, and that armed actors should seek to avoid harming civilians. This is a "negative protection" in that it aims to exempt civilians from the otherwise legitimate use of organized violence. But it is not the only form of protection. Combatants' failure to respect this negative protection, along with states' failure to respect or ensure citizens' security, have given rise to two new "affirmative" genres of protection.

The second genre may be called tactical protection. International and regional organizations conducting peace operations increasingly integrate tasks to physically protect non-combatants. The third genre of civilian protection is a military intervention conducted primarily to protect civilians in another nation. This can be described as the strategic protection of civilians. These three genres of protection are discussed in great detail next.

Civilian Protection as Acts of Omission: Avoiding Civilian Harm in Armed Conflict

International law to protect civilians during war differs from international or national laws that apply in times of peace. During armed conflict, military necessity is enshrined as a paramount principle because the pursuit of victory is the legally sanctioned purpose of war. The legal responsibility to avoid killing civilians during armed conflict initially belonged to state combatants at war with one another, but by the mid-1970s, the obligation was formally extended to non-state actors involved in internal armed conflicts. Civilian protection during armed conflict is largely negative in character, focusing more on acts of omission. Specifically, the law obliges combatants to avoid harming civilians in the course of their operations rather than requiring that they organize and conduct their military operations to protect civilians from the enemy's violence. Such "negative protection" is further limited in its scope because avoiding harm hinges largely upon the combatant's intent, not upon the results of his actions.

However circumscribed, this requirement to avoid civilian harm remains the foundation of civilian protection.[4] IHL has helped to shape military forces' actions in circumstances where armed forces seek to uphold norms and laws. By design, IHL countenances actions during internal or international armed conflict that cause unintended "collateral damage" as long as those actions comply with other IHL rules, such as proportionality. Such lawful civilian harm remains a source of suffering worldwide. A more fundamental problem is the blatant disregard for IHL by many global armed actors.

Although the ratio of civilian to combatant deaths in recent armed conflicts is disputed,[5] the vulnerability of civilians has become a growing international concern (Mack, 2007, p. 42). In the post-Cold War era, prolonged internal conflicts, such as those in the Democratic Republic of Congo (DRC) and Sudan have led to millions of civilian deaths. Dramatic incidents prompt international outrage, as in the cases of the US air bombing of the Amiriyah shelter during Operation Desert Storm in 1991, Russia's missile attacks against citizens of Grozny in 1999, and Sri Lanka's artillery shelling of a civilian population toward the end of its conflict with Tamil insurgents in 1999. Furthermore, when military force is used in part to halt the killing of civilians (e.g. NATO interventions in Kosovo in 1999 and Libya in 2011), unintentional civilian harm undermines the intervention's strategic rationale. For instance, the United Nations Security Council expressed particular concerns about the African Union Mission in Somalia (AMISOM) forces inflicting civilian casualties in Somalia.[6]

Contemporary debate about civilian protection sometimes neglects to emphasize the longstanding responsibilities codified in IHL. Perhaps because these obligations have long been part of the normative landscape, they can appear to be taken for granted. IHL obligations also may be overlooked because they are a largely negative form of protection – involving acts of omission, rather than affirmative, positive acts implied by the verb "protect". The gap also might reflect the fact that civil society groups often focus their institutional efforts upon advocacy for expanded types of civilian protection rather than ensuring enforcement by state and non-state actors. Indeed, the lack of enforcement mechanisms for IHL, short of the International Criminal Court (ICC), remains a weakness of the regime.

Concept

Ethical Traditions   The requirement to avoid imposing harm upon civilians during armed conflict has deep roots in a variety of religious and ethical traditions (Turner Johnson, 1981; Best, 1983). A common theme has been the importance of killing only the "enemy" – although the enemy has been defined in various ways. In the

Judeo–Christian ethical tradition, individuals are either combatants or fall into various categories of "non-combatants". In this tradition, the only legitimate targets are individuals who are both combatants *and* capable of inflicting harm. In other words, civilians who are not participating in the fighting and combatants who could or would not fight are not to be killed. Importantly, however, the Just War Ethic distinguished between intent and results. Its "principle of double effect" essentially held that unintended harm was acceptable as long as other criteria were met. Thus, it was not immoral for civilians to die in war, nor was it unethical to kill them as long as the combatants did not purposefully aim to kill them. After all, these were the ethics of war, not of peace.

The Just War Ethic also distinguished between the justice of how one fights in war (*jus in bello*) and the justice of fighting a war at all (*jus ad bellum*). Just War criteria for when to fight a war do not explicitly address the question of civilian harm, although several provide a logical basis for incorporating this concern (such as the criteria that belligerents have just cause and that the expected benefits of war exceed the anticipated costs). Instead, the concrete focus on civilian protection lay in the rules governing the conduct of war, including limits on the types of weapons and the principle of distinction between combatants and non-combatants.

International Law   Many of the earliest ethical principles about the conduct of war gradually became the customary practice of states and were formally codified in the Law of Armed Conflict (LOAC), which is also referred to as IHL. The law's main texts are the Hague Convention of 1907 and the four Geneva Conventions of 1949 and their 1977 Additional Protocols International Committee of the Red Cross 2010. These instruments establish rules regarding types of weapons and their use, protection of non-combatants, and other aspects of warfare. Core principles of the law include "military necessity", (the use of force must be related to military requirements), "distinction" (the requirement to only target combatants), and "proportionality" (the need to appropriately balance non-combatant harm with the military benefits of force) (Roberts and Guelff, 1982, pp. 9–10).

The law's principles make sense intuitively, but they largely defy precise definition. Moreover, the need to protect non-combatants, protect forces, and accomplish the mission may often be in tension. The legal obligation to avoid inflicting civilian harm is ultimately qualified because it must coexist with the successful conduct of war.

Implementation

Several factors impede the realization of IHL's promise of civilian protection. Some are technical and institutional, while others are political or normative. Armed forces can advance civilian protection in two primary ways. The first is by making, monitoring, and adjusting efforts to reduce civilian casualties during their actual conduct of operations. The second, deeper type of commitment is institutionally integrating the principles and best practices of civilian protection into the preparation and equipment of their forces. The latter activities, though, are generally undertaken only by national armed forces rather than by irregular forces. The advanced military powers that have the improved technological capacity and political will to avoid civilian casualties during operations have managed, in relative terms, to vastly reduce the scale of civilian harm even though their commitments to institutional change varies.[7] A greater problem, though, exists with regard to armed groups that do not have a moral and legal commitment to avoiding non-combatant casualties.

In armed conflict, the goal and nature of military operations, the technological capabilities involved, the actions of the enemy, and the combatants' intentions all shape outcomes for civilians. In particular, technological improvements have allowed advanced military powers to apply force with far greater precision and discrimination than was possible during the Second World War or the armed conflicts in Korea and Vietnam. As advanced powers have extended this technological advantage, weaker actors have chosen "asymmetric" strategies that not only reject, but also, in some cases, purposefully exploit the protections accorded to civilians under the law. Such behavior has vastly complicated and increased the costs of upholding IHL by parties seeking to do so. Retired Air Force MG Charles Dunlap uses the word "lawfare" to describe the use of IHL as a weapon by non-compliant parties (Dunlap, 2001, 2007). By hiding among civilian populations and refusing to wear uniforms, national militaries and informal armed groups increase the likelihood that their opponents will cause unintended civilian harm, which the non-compliant parties then use to discredit those opponents and gain recruits. These developments have led some observers to argue that IHL is becoming a liability because it is no longer a reciprocal legal regime among combatants.

When Western powers faced criticism for civilian deaths, they sometimes adjusted their tactics during war. In the case of Operation Allied Force in 1999, NATO responded to such criticism by changing its rules of engagement (ROE), and some members even stopped using cluster munitions. Some NATO states with advanced air forces began developing computer models to predict civilian harm from air strikes and devising tactics and munitions to reduce it in future conflicts. By 2006, the US-led coalition's ground forces in Iraq began refocusing their tactics to reduce civilian casualties. By 2009, tactical directives to minimize civilian harm were a central focus of International Security Assistance Forces (ISAF) in Afghanistan. These operational changes in turn created demands for changes in pre-deployment training and command and control of military assets in the field.

A deeper level of change is institutional, pertaining to how armed forces plan, organize, equip, and train to avoid causing civilian harm in future operations. Here, even the most advanced military powers still have enormous room for improvement. Many militaries still approach civilian protection as simply not intending to cause civilian deaths during war, rather than proactively preparing to fight wars with reduced civilian deaths. Reflecting this attitude, some militaries address the avoidance of civilian harm only in doctrine related to peace operations or counterinsurgency operations, rather than as an integral aspect of waging war. While such militaries may imperfectly realize the requirement to avoid civilian harm in combat operations, they at least remain committed to the principle.

The greater challenge is the plethora of armed forces and groups that fight without any meaningful commitment to the principle of avoiding civilian harm or awareness of the LOAC. While some armed groups fail to acknowledge the requirement to distinguish between civilians and combatants in applying violence, many armed groups specifically target civilians as a matter of course. The ability to influence these criminal behaviors through education and advocacy appears limited at best.[8] The ICC aims, in part, to promote adherence to the international law by holding individuals accountable for the most egregious violations; however, the ICC's investigative and prosecutorial capabilities remain limited in scope.

While the aforementioned type of civilian protection entails avoiding the infliction of harm upon civilians, armed forces (and other actors) may also act affirmatively to protect civilians from physical harm imposed by others. Such affirmative acts may be discrete and limited tasks (tactical actions), or they may be the strategic goal of a military operation. Two primary variations of affirmative civilian protection have emerged in international practice over the past few decades. They are differentiated by the extent of protection they intend to provide and by the nominal degree of consent they enjoy from the state within which they are conducted. Specifically, the United Nations has developed a theory and practice of "the protection of civilians" that enjoys (and only tactically confronts) the consent of the state. The United Nations and a collection of predominantly Western states have also pioneered the theory and nascent practice of an international responsibility to protect civilians that exists where the state will not or cannot provide such protections to its citizens. In other words, the two genres of protection considered next exist in different political contexts.

Peacekeeping and the Protection of Civilians

Concept

The United Nations has developed an integrated civil–military approach to advancing many aspects of civilian well-being, a concept it refers to as the "Protection of Civilians" (POC). The UN's concept encompasses a full range of human rights (not just physical security) and envisions the use of force only where necessary to prevent imminent physical harm. The United Nations regards the military's role as a subset of the UN's POC work. This section focuses on this military component within the UN's civilian protection framework, and it also references relevant military protection tactics in other regional security organizations and national military forces.

The United Nations is the international body responsible for promoting global peace and security, including the authorization of force for purposes other than self-defense. It is not a military organization *per se*, but instead relies upon member states for any military action. The United Nations is also concerned with promoting human rights and the well-being of persons, articulating those rights, and developing civilian capacities to promote them through broad-based social development, and emergency relief programs. Thus, while the organization's objectives propel it toward civilian protection, its dependence on consensus among sovereign states limits the scope and capabilities with which it might realize that goal.

UN peacekeeping missions, for example, often provide the security needed in post-conflict areas to achieve political goals. Yet, UN missions are generally restricted in their ability to use force in support of them. Furthermore, UN efforts in a country generally address critical humanitarian needs involving a range of Agencies, Funds, and Programs, each shaped by competing institutional approaches to civilian protection.

For instance, humanitarian organizations within the United Nations have long seen their work meeting civilian needs and promoting human rights in conflict and post-conflict areas as civilian protection (Interagency Standing Committee, 2011).[9] Their collective tools ranged from legal advocacy, to humanitarian assistance, to security sector reform. They consider the humanitarian assistance to be a form of short-term protection while development and the promotion of human rights constitute a longer-term protection effort. Thus, even within the UN's humanitarian community, agencies have different mandates, authorities, and character.[10]

Humanitarians differentiate their work from military action and its presumed "political", need-based objectives. Indeed, the humanitarian community remains ambivalent about the relationship of military force to humanitarian action. While some humanitarian actors promoted the idea of UN peacekeeping forces providing "protection by presence," many humanitarian groups remain concerned that the concept of protection itself has become militarized. Additionally, humanitarian actors fear that the UN emphasis on integrated field missions could undercut the independence of humanitarians (see Glad, 2012).

Therefore, when the United Nations began to address civilian protection as a *military* issue, it pushed peacekeeping forces into a field that had been defined in civilian and humanitarian terms, and whose practitioners were generally skeptical towards military power.

This began in 1999, when the UN Secretary-General started to provide regular reports to the United Nations Security Council on the protection of civilians. The United Nations Security Council also began directing peacekeeping forces to protect civilians from the imminent threat of violence and adopted broader resolutions on civilian protection (e.g. United Nations Security Council Resolutions 1265, 1296, and 1674) and specific resolutions on the protection of women, children, and humanitarian workers.

Yet the understandings and priorities of civilian protection remain contested within the United Nations, both because of humanitarian–military tensions and also organizational differences within the multiagency UN system (Holt, 2006). The Department of Peacekeeping Operations (DPKO), for example, is one of many UN agencies defining the organization's identity and carrying out its work. DPKO directs the military, civilian, and police components of peacekeeping missions, combining military expertise with specialists in areas like protection of civilians, child protection, rule of law, and security sector reform, along with civil and political affairs. Other UN humanitarian agencies, including the Office for the Coordination of Humanitarian Affairs (OCHA), United Nations High Commissioner for Refugees (UNHCR), United Nations Children's Fund (UNICEF), Office of the High Commissioner for Human Rights (OHCHR), and World Food Programme (WFP) have different forms of "civilian protection" mandates that draw upon human rights and refugee law, and often include monitoring the conduct of war by military forces.

Under the UN's POC concept, halting imminent threats of violence against civilians with military force has emerged as a routine function of UN peacekeeping forces. This practice faces many challenges, however.

The United Nations has become a central global forum for envisioning how to protect civilians using military force. With the rise of UN peacekeeping, the conception of civilian protection has shifted from the responsibility of states in conflict (to avoid harming non-combatants and protecting their citizens) to the responsibility of the international community as a whole. As such, the United Nations has come to regard the protection of civilians in armed conflict as a key institutional rationale and identity.[11]

Implementation

UN peacekeepers (as well as the military forces serving regional organizations) were pushed into the military tactics of civilian protection by widespread concerns about ongoing violence against civilians, and by a desire among Member States that the United Nations should remain relevant in times of conflict. These pressures sometimes overrode the concerns of troop-contributing nations about the risks of action. The United Nations Security Council began directing that peacekeepers protect civilians under imminent threat of physical violence. The mandate language, however, was not coupled with guidance on what was expected of forces, nor did the United Nations initially have doctrine from which to draw.

Since 2000, twelve UN peacekeeping operations have been given POC-mandates: UNAMSIL (Sierra Leone); MONUC, now MONUSCO, (DRC); UNMIL (Liberia); ONUB (Burundi); MINUSTAH (Haiti); UNOCI (Cote d'Ivoire); UNMIS (Sudan); UNIFIL (Lebanon); UNAMID (Darfur); MINURCAT (Central African Republic); UNMISS (South Sudan); and UNISFA (Abyei).[12] While the mandates have varied, most have authorized the use of all necessary means to protect civilians under imminent threat of physical violence.

Over the past decade, DPKO has led the UN bureaucracy in fleshing out the specific military demands of civilian protection in peace operations. But military tasks are just one tactical aspect of POC within an overarching political–military protection strategy developed for individual operations. DPKO has sought to accommodate demands for military action while remaining sensitive to the primacy of political and humanitarian efforts in integrated peace operations. Reflecting this, its 2010 Operational Concept delineates force as but one tool among many for use across the three "tiers" of engagement. These tiers are differentiated by their goals: (I) Protection through political process, (II) Protection from physical violence, and (III) Establishment of a protective environment (DPKO/DFS, 2010).

The military tasks in Tier II include: forward field deployments; day and night patrols in vulnerable communities and in targeted locations (such as markets, schools, refugee sites), [and] responding to violent attacks with all necessary means, including, if necessary, the use of force, to protect civilians and stabilize the situation. These are the tasks that have been incorporated into draft protection strategies, identified as training requirements for troop-contributing nations, and envisioned in resource and capabilities discussions about implementation (Kjeksrud et al., 2011).

Some national armed forces consider what the United Nations deems "civilian protection" tasks as part of an existing repertoire of activities within the spectrum of operations from war to peace. Where these tactics, techniques, or procedures are considered routine components of military operations, they are only deemed "civilian protection" tasks when conducted *for that purpose*. The United Nations requests that troop-contributing militaries should be prepared to conduct civilian protection tasks may eventually prompt associated changes in national lexicons and doctrine.

NATO's views of civilian protection are more tightly coupled to high-intensity military operations. Unlike the United Nations, NATO is a military alliance conceived and prepared to conduct major combat operations. NATO concepts therefore do not reflect a humanitarian legacy, a tradition of monitoring rather than using force, or a political requirement for state consent. Further, NATO does not envision a new requirement for tactical protection tasks because it would simply apply traditional military tasks for the different purpose of civilian protection.

NATO does not use the UN's POC language, but NATO doctrine acknowledges the utility of traditional military activities for that purpose, principally in peacekeeping. These include no-fly zones, the forcible separation of belligerent parties, the establishment of protected areas, and the creation of "safe corridors" for civilians and aid delivery (Holt, 2006). Such protection activities are distinct from the general requirement to secure the civilian protection described in NATO's counterinsurgency doctrine.[13]

NATO's *Peace Support Operations (AJP 3.4.1)* anticipates the requirement for combat in peacekeeping operations. These operations:

> are increasingly conducted in situations in which there are widespread and ongoing abuses to basic human rights, ethnic cleansing and genocide ... Only a PSF [peace support force] prepared for combat can operate in such an environment, curtail human rights abuses, and create a secure environment in which civilian agencies can redress the underlying causes of the conflict and address the requirements of peace building. (Holt, 2006, p. 57)

The European Union also regards civilian protection as potentially requiring the use of force. Indeed, the European Union has employed force for protection purposes, as in Operation Artemis in the DRC in 2003, and in Cote d'Ivoire in 2011.[14] The African Union on the other hand has draft guidelines for the protection of civilians that mirror the UN's broad definition, but the African Union has not yet fully integrated this approach in mission planning (African Union draft guidelines, cited in Williams, 2010, p. 17). Nonetheless, the African Union has carried out specific civilian protection activities. During the African Union Mission in Somalia, for example, the police had a role in civilian protection alongside military forces that guarded internally displaced person (IDP) camps, conducted firewood patrols, and protected market places and wells (Kjeksrud *et al.*, 2011).

Overall, at this stage the theory of civilian protection at the tactical level is more coherent than its practice. Given the conceptual ambiguities in the United Nations Security Council and among UN agencies, UN implementation of civilian protection should be expected to be uneven, even as it clearly progresses. Actors "often understand POC in ways that may contradict one another, causing friction, misunderstanding, and frustration in missions" (Kjeksrud *et al.*, 2011). Furthermore, while POC is seen as an effort demanding a comprehensive approach, the associated tasks are sometimes in tension or contradictory both for military actors and especially for military and civilian actors working in the same operation (Kjeksrud *et al.*, 2011). There is also a limit to the level of civil–military integration that is achievable and desirable (United Nations DPKO/DFS, 2009).

Tensions can arise from the UN's understanding of a POC mandate. The UN's Framework document seeks to square the circle between an operation based on state consent and the impartial use of force to protect civilians: "Bearing in mind that missions operate within the principles of peacekeeping and in accordance with the mandate, missions are authorized to use force against any party, including elements of government forces, where such elements are themselves engaged in physical violence against civilians" (United Nations, n.d., p. 3). There are obvious, though largely untested, limits to this nominal reconciliation of political consent and military clashes under the protection of civilians rubric. Yet, a

> dual role of supporting the local authorities and potentially acting directly – sometimes against local authorities that may themselves be engaged in violations against civilians – is very difficult to reconcile, and none of the strategies give enough attention to how these often conflicting roles should be managed. These missions have, at times, been required to balance the goal of maintaining consent of the state in which they operate, and the desire to act forcefully to protect civilians in specific cases. (Kjeksrud, *et al.*, 2011)

Other implementation challenges pertain to the level of protection the United Nations Security Council mandate implies, as well as the question of what participating national military forces are actually willing or able to do. First, there is significant scope for interpretation of which military actions are authorized by UN mandates. How much force can be used? Can it be used offensively or only defensively? What degree of protection is seemingly obligated, as opposed to being just theoretically allowed? Second, civilian protection outcomes often hinge upon the political will of the force commander and troop contributing nations. A commander can push against or hide behind a POC mandate. Moreover, even where a commander is forward-leaning, contributing nations may not allow their military or police forces to undertake specific actions (such as using force to halt attacks on civilians). National caveats on participating personnel can be a severe hurdle to the realization of protection.

Finally, UN forces will always struggle to fulfill others' expectations regarding civilian protection. The United Nations is aware of the need to address this challenge more directly as part of a POC strategy.

> [I]t is vital that the mission consider how it will clearly communicate to the local population, host authorities, and other key stakeholders, what it can and cannot do regarding the protection of civilians in the mission area, in addition to the fact that the ultimate responsibility for POC rests with the host government. (United Nations, n.d., p. 14)

Few national militaries have developed doctrine or training for civilian protection tasks, which in their requisite levels of initiative, risk, and intensity, would fall somewhere between major combat operations and traditional Chapter Six peacekeeping actions. Some nations like Canada and the United States have begun to use civilian protection terminology and are wrestling with the specific implications for their forces.[15] At the other end of the spectrum, however, national military forces may reject the idea that peacekeeping tasks could require significant use of force and give little thought to the relevant components of civilian protection.

Fortunately, the United Nations recently developed a resource and capability matrix for UN missions to use in drafting umbrella civilian protection strategies.

DPKO has also developed training modules, which set training standards for POC that include 12 scenario-based exercises that address the range of operational challenges involved in protecting civilians. The tools are now being shared globally by preparing trainers and integrating their work into senior military leadership at both national and regional training centers. The UN's efforts to clarify requirements and create standards for training and assessment of troop contributing forces offer hope for elevating civilian protection within UN operations.

As the United Nations increasingly pursues and realizes civilian protection within its consent-based peacekeeping operations, sensitive political questions will likely emerge about the relationship of such actions to the international responsibility to protect civilians, even when a state actively opposes international intervention.

Strategies of Civilian Protection and R2P

The third genre of civilian protection is intervening forcibly in another state for the purpose of protecting endangered citizens. This differs from the protection actions described earlier in two key respects. First, unlike in UN peacekeeping operations, there is no pretense of state consent to the protection function. Thus, despite the humanitarian impetus, the intervention is decidedly partial in that it sides with threatened civilians over the government and/or other actors threatening them.

Second, the strategic purpose and concept of the intervention is to halt threats to the physical well-being of civilians. The operational design itself can take many forms and adopt other objectives as means toward the end of protection. Importantly, the means may not necessarily be perceived as "civilian-friendly" military operations, either with regard to the first genre of civilian protection (the avoidance of civilian casualties) or the second genre of civilian protection (tactical actions directly linked to "imminent threats" to civilians).

Strategic interventions to protect civilians are controversial for numerous reasons, including the potential violation of sovereignty, the potential that humanitarian language may mask other motivations for intervention, and the inherent difficulties of ensuring consistency between operational means and strategic ends.

Military interventions to protect civilians can be considered part of the emerging norm of a "Responsibility to Protect" or R2P. Just as tactical military actions are one subset of the UN's broader POC concept, strategic *military* intervention to protect civilians is one aspect of the R2P concept that has emerged over the past decade. This is essentially the idea that sovereign states have responsibilities toward their citizens and that the international community is obliged to assume those responsibilities should states be unwilling or unable to protect their civilians from specific types of harm.

Concept of R2P

Historically, there has been little international consensus about when states might use force for humanitarian ends. Following the horrors of the Holocaust, the 1948 Convention on the Prevention and Punishment of the Crime of Genocide committed states to act in the event of a future genocide. The commitment's precise meaning remains disputed and, more significantly, the obligation has been honored largely in the breach. Retrospective analyses have characterized several military interventions in the 1970s as humanitarian interventions: India's war with Pakistan that led to the independence of Bangladesh; Vietnam's invasion of Khmer Rouge Cambodia; and Tanzania's invasion of Uganda under Idi Amin (see Walzer, 1977, Chapter 6). Yet, at the time, the invading states justified their actions in the name of self-defense and received varying degrees of international criticism.

Following the end of the Cold War, new possibilities emerged under the UN charter for parties to use force in support of humanitarian objectives. After the United Nations authorized a multilateral coalition to free Kuwait from Iraqi occupation, the United Nations provided Chapter Seven authority to continue implementing no-fly zones to prevent the Iraqi government from attacking threatened populations in its territory. The United Nations also directed or authorized a series of Chapter Seven peace operations in Somalia and the Balkans. During this period of high expectations, however, the United Nations had uneven success and several glaring failures. These include the 1995 murder of over 8000 Bosnian men in the UN-declared "safe haven" of Srebenica, and most notably, the slaughter of some 800,000 Rwandan citizens as the United Nations pared down its peacekeeping forces.

These travesties prompted a rethinking of how the norm of sovereignty – a Westphalian legacy aimed to promote peace through international order – should be balanced against expectations that states should protect individual human rights within their borders. The effort was galvanized by an influential 2001 report on what was called the "Responsibility to Protect" (R2P), which articulated a new concept to justify international action to prevent mass atrocities against civilians.

The R2P concept regards sovereignty as no longer absolute but as conditional under specific circumstances. A state's right to control activity within its borders was now paired with a responsibility to respect its citizens' most fundamental rights to physical integrity. R2P recognizes that governments retain primary responsibility for protecting their citizens, but stipulated that when rulers violate (or allow widespread and systematic violation of) their citizens' basic human rights, sovereignty can no longer bar other states from acting to protect them. In such a case, R2P doctrine holds that the international community has a responsibility to act to protect those citizens. But R2P proponents are quick to point out that the concept's intent is to encourage national governments to ensure civilian protection, not to encourage foreign intervention for that purpose.

The R2P concept also emphasizes the desirability of preventive measures like diplomacy and socioeconomic sanctions, and regards the use of force as a last resort to ensure civilian protection. The concept's emergence coincided with the creation in 2002 of an International Criminal Court (ICC) to prosecute individuals – including state leaders – suspected of responsibility for mass atrocity crimes.

R2P's adoption by key states such as Canada, along with influential civil society actors, helped to socialize this new norm throughout the UN system. By 2005, the United Nations General Assembly included R2P in its World Summit outcome document. The document anticipated the three major objections to R2P by (1) clarifying its scope (the international responsibility applies only to genocide, war crimes, ethnic cleansing, and crimes against humanity); (2) emphasizing sovereignty (the responsibility to protect populations resides primarily with states and only secondarily with the international community); and (3) stressing the importance of prevention and the use of peaceful rather than forcible measures. The following year, the United Nations Security Council formalized its support for R2P in Resolution 1674 (S/RES/1674) reaffirming the United Nations General Assembly provisions. Further, the 2009 UN Secretary-General report called *Implementing the Responsibility to Protect* prompted a General Assembly debate and the first R2P resolution (A/RES/63/308).

Implementation of Strategic Military Intervention   This section considers several challenges arising during military interventions to protect civilians: the diversity of operational choices regarding *how* to "protect"; the inherent contradiction of risking civilian lives as "collateral damage" as forces act to protect civilian life; the threshold of violence that can justify the use of force; and the viability of prevention versus responses to mass violence.

There is great variety in how military forces might go about "protecting civilians". Contrary to some perceptions, protection does not automatically entail regime change. For example, France's 1995 Operation Turquoise created a safe zone in southwestern Rwanda. While it was a technically successful combined arms operation, Turquoise was widely seen as supporting the very Hutu actors that were responsible for the wider genocide in that country. Nonetheless, the French operation did not transfer permanent political authority to a Hutu leadership operating in the safe zone – the region reverted to the control of the Rwandan Patriot Front and subsequent Rwandan government. NATO's Operation Allied Force aimed to stop Serb atrocities against Kosovars and coerce Serb authorities to agree to a political settlement of the conflict – but it did not specifically seek to overthrow the Milosevic regime.

The 2011 intervention in Libya was controversial in part because it was perceived to evolve to embrace the goal of regime change rather than remaining focused on civilian protection. NATO, the Arab League and the United Nations Security Council all supported military efforts to protect civilians. The United Nations Security Council Resolution authorized all necessary measures to protect Libyan civilians and civilian-populated areas under threat of attack, but did not require that such threats be "imminent" (the language commonly used in UN peacekeeping mandates).[16]

Resolution 1973 also authorized an arms embargo and a no-fly zone to protect civilians, but prohibited the stationing of a "foreign occupation force of any form on any part of Libyan territory".[17] NATO's sea and air power was initially focused on defending the city of Benghazi where Libyan rebels had taken refuge. Over time, the military target list expanded from the neutralizing of enemy air defenses and heavy weapons to the destruction of the Libyan military's command and control mechanisms, military supply depots, and training centers.

As the NATO-led mission evolved, some advocates of the intervention grew uncomfortable about the mission's military objectives and their apparent links to the rebel offensive and the goal of regime change.[18] NATO members maintained that any government policy seeking regime change reflected a political goal that was independent of NATO's Operation Unified Protector's (OUP) military objective to protect civilians. However, once NATO bombing had successfully thwarted the initial Libyan assault on Benghazi, the difference between military actions to protect civilians and military actions to topple the Libyan regime became difficult to discern.

Civilian casualties proved to be another controversial aspect of the Libya operation. Concerns about civilian deaths had provided the key impetus for political support of the military intervention. But OUP, like most bombing campaigns near population centers, caused civilian deaths. The apparent contradiction of killing civilians in order to save them continues to haunt OUP and the commanders who led it (MacFarquhar, 2012). Both targeting choices and their unintended consequences created controversy about which military tasks and operational objectives were intended or implicit in the operation's civilian protection mandate.

These controversies reflect a lack of understanding and consensus regarding what military forces can or should do in the name of civilian protection. Of course, ambiguity is often a product of diplomatic artifice and the need to gain political consensus for the UN mandate; indeed, such pressures will never disappear. The deeper problem, though, is the breadth of operational choices that accompany any operation to protect civilians. Based on historical experience, political leaders can closely envision what a naval blockade or a no-fly zone would entail, but face difficulty anticipating the implementation and implications of civilian protection efforts. The absence of military doctrine and analysis also precluded military leaders from articulating requirements and choices in advance.

Because the challenges related to strategic civilian protection are diverse and highly contingent upon the specifics of the case, it may be impossible to fully anticipate the related operational requirements and dilemmas for every civilian protection mission. But OUP shows that the international community has a great deal of work to do in thinking through these issues, particularly because civilian protection relates to regime change.

The future of strategic military intervention to protect civilians faces many questions. One concern is the acceptable *means* of "operationalizing" civilian protection, or put differently, whether civilian protection missions demand a different way of using force. Should it be comprised only of defensive actions (protecting from attack), or is broader offensive action in the name of protection acceptable? Many operational concepts exist for responding to mass atrocities. These include saturating the entire area of operations with ground forces to provide security, expanding secure areas over time with an "oil spot" approach, separating perpetrators and victims, creating safe areas, enabling partners to protect civilians, containing the areas in which violence occurs, and finally, directly attacking and defeating perpetrators of the violence (Sewall, Raymond, and Chin, 2010, pp. 70–86). In theory, and often in practice, attacking a limited number of perpetrators of violence may be more effective than seeking to defend every potential victim; yet, the offensive choices may seem at odds with a protective mission.

Another question the international community must address is the level of civilian harm that can be justified in the name of civilian protection. The humanitarian nature of the mission suggests that special care should be taken to ensure success with minimal civilian harm. If civilian harm is accepted as an inevitable result of military intervention, should the bar for initiating military intervention be set that much higher?

If civilian harm is considered antithetical to the purpose of the intervention, does this increase the demands and costs for intervening forces? Must the operation be fought with greater restraint or in different ways, or can it be, as with Operation

Allied Force, virtually indistinguishable from a traditional military campaign – simply fought with a different rationale? In either case, are ground forces to assist civilians required or can airpower alone provide an appropriate civilian protection capability? The more demanding the concept – and particularly if it requires a ground force and the associated risks for those forces – the less likely the international community may be to undertake the mission. At the same time, a less demanding intervention may be less effective or cause more harm to civilians than other options. The international community and its member states should begin an effort to articulate expectations or guidelines for operations fought to protect civilians – R2P or otherwise.

A third issue is the threshold of harm or potential harm that should justify intervention. There is an enormous tradeoff between waiting for the situation to develop and building political will for military action on the one hand and acting *before* the need for action becomes self-evident on the other. Many observers argue that if NATO had waited for Libyan troops to enter Benghazi, it would have proved impossible to use airpower to protect civilians. If acting late can be militarily daunting but more politically acceptable, acting early may be more militarily feasible but politically fraught. Such early action is also more likely to invite criticisms that intervening states have simply masked other national security rationales in humanitarian terms. Indeed, it is important to accept that intervening powers will almost always have mixed or ulterior motives in their desire to protect civilians.

Political suspicions of humanitarian intervention are exacerbated because mass atrocities arise from underlying conflicts. Their cessation is therefore often connected with other processes or outcomes. Protecting civilians with military force may entail enforcing a particular electoral outcome, protecting a perpetrator of mass violence from reprisal, or forcing regime change. In other words, it may not be a viable goal unto itself. Therefore, while "mission creep" to other objectives beyond civilian protection may not be inevitable or desirable, it is predictable given the underlying conditions that often give rise to mass atrocity. If the term "civilian protection" is to be more than a political marketing slogan, and to become a genuine strategic objective, the international community must unpack cause and effect and means and ends in each contingency.

The role of force in international politics is a fourth major issue concerning R2P, particularly when that force is sanctioned by the United Nations. Many states would prefer to see a UN emphasis on non-military measures to enhance security and protect rights. This is not only a matter of values, but also of power because advanced military means are the purview of just a handful of states. While the United Nations has inched toward tactical POC, civilian protection at the strategic level threatens to depart (at least temporarily) from the principles that have formerly characterized UN peacekeeping operations, such as consent of the parties, impartiality, and minimal use of force.

There is an enormous gap between the military actions required for strategic intervention and the integration of POC tasks into peace operation. Even as the United Nations and troop-contributing countries work to increase skills and training as part of ongoing POC reform efforts, the initial United Nations General Assembly World Summit statement reflected member states' concerns about a perceived overreliance on military means at the expense of other tools and the temptation to respond after the fact of crimes against civilians rather than to prevent them. The UN's R2P discussion is tempered by fears that its humanitarian principles and practices might be overwhelmed by a militarized implementation of the concept.

Such concerns have only grown in the aftermath of the Libyan operation. In particular, the perceived disconnect between the United Nations Security Council mandate for the Libyan air campaign and NATO's conduct of operations has raised questions about how the UN community should define and monitor civilian protection operations. In November 2011, Brazil articulated the concept of "Responsibility While Protecting" (RWP) in an effort to better define the threshold for using force to protect civilians and to engage UN Member States more fully in oversight of military operations. The topic is likely to become a focus of UN discussion regarding operational civilian protection.

Conclusion

In many respects, the future of civilian protection looks bright. More capable national military forces are able to conduct military operations with far greater precision and less harm to civilians than was possible even twenty years ago. International and regional organizations have begun implementing tactical protection elements within peacekeeping missions to save civilians from the imminent threat of physical harm. Importantly, the international community has taken a revolutionary step by endorsing the collective use of force as a last resort to protect civilians from specific types of physical threats – even at the cost of violating the core international principle of sovereignty.

Nonetheless, significant obstacles remain and some underlying trends bode poorly for civilian protection. Specifically, the eroding state monopoly of violence dilutes the impact of international humanitarian law. Armed groups operating as insurgents, criminal networks, and terrorist actors have little regard for longstanding rules to protect non-combatants and may even purposefully target civilians. The growing reach of these actors threatens the longstanding core of civilian protection.

This phenomenon also produces a second-order negative effect. When armed groups fail to respect non-combatant immunity in war, they further increase the costs for opponents that are committed to civilian protection. Reducing civilian harm frequently forces accommodations with other national objectives, such as protecting forces and accomplishing the mission (achieving victory). As other armed actors increase the costs of civilian protection by collocating with civilians, refusing to wear uniforms, etc., the price of norm compliance may become prohibitive even for the "good guys" in warfare.

In other words, while IHL's civilian protections are the oldest and most firmly codified, they cannot be taken for granted in the twenty-first century. After all, the affirmative approaches to civilian protection (peacekeeping tactics and R2P) have emerged in part to compensate for the violence inflicted by actors that lack respect for IHL.

Another key challenge to civilian protection is "operationalizing" its many concepts, especially newer ones. Many nations pay lip service to IHL but fail to invest in the technical capabilities and training that could better uphold those commitments. States routinely insert civilian protection tasks into peace operations mandates, but they have not fully accepted responsibility for the requirements associated with implementation. Some states lack capabilities, and others the willingness to carry out key tasks. R2P is so new and controversial that it even lacks operational concepts. While the Libyan operation has initiated an important dialogue about the associated demands of strategic civilian protection, the answers will face many practical and political obstacles.

Finally, the community of states needs to address the contradictions within, and the interrelationships among, the three genres of civilian protection. Wishful thinking or piecemeal approaches will underserve the vulnerable, at a minimum, and may discredit civilian protection as an objective. For example, the United Nations has not confronted the tensions between sustaining state consent for a peacekeeping operation and confronting government complicity in causing civilian harm. Civilian protection tasks can swiftly consume an operation as they draw on the usually limited mission resources. Without setting clear parameters about the expectations of tactical civilian protection, political authorities risk misleading citizens at risk, and military forces risk being drawn into a level of conflict they did not anticipate. At the same time, the tactics that peacekeeping forces use in consent-based operations should be adopted for use in strategic R2P intervention concepts (which have yet to be developed). And for both genres of military interventions, preparing forces to minimize civilian harm can better reconcile the means and ends of civilian protection.

Louise Arbour has argued that the international community faces a paradigm shift as it reorients its focus from how to avoid harming civilians during war to how to protect civilians by waging war (cited in Stanley Foundation, 2012). It would be a mistake, however, to see these as alternatives. International law and actors treat the three genres of civilian protection as distinct. Each has its own constituency and political context. Yet, the three genres of civilian protection are intertwined and overlapping. The international and academic communities would do well to consider them as a whole with discrete but interrelated parts.

Changing human rights norms and the continuation of egregious violence against civilians have expanded both the international understanding and practice of affirmative civilian protection. But it is premature to be triumphant because core IHL principles are under siege. And while the evolution of state practice to protect civilians is auspicious, it remains controversial, complicated, and underdeveloped. Civilian protection has emerged as a multifaceted and challenging issue on the international agenda, but its future is still under negotiation.

Acknowledgements

The author would like to thank Vivek Chilukuri, Sally Chin, and Bharathi Rhadakrishnan for their research or editing assistance and the United Nations and nongovernmental organization experts who kindly provided comments on this chapter.

Notes

1. This example is discussed later in this chapter.
2. The precise meaning of this principle has been a subject of fierce debate in recent decades and the ICRC sought to clarify the matter by issuing "interpretive guidance" in 2009.

The United States, among other nations, does not fully accept the ICRC guidance. For an extensive discussion of this subject, see http://www.icrc.org/eng/assets/files/other/irrc-872-reports-documents.pdf (accessed December 5, 2013).

3. See http://www.icrc.org/eng/assets/files/other/irrc-872-reports-documents.pdf (accessed December 5, 2013).

4. Terrorism and genocide are related causes of civilian harm that involve the purposeful targeting of civilians that can occur independently of internal or international armed conflicts.

5. It is frequently asserted that a majority of victims of modern war are civilians, but see analysis in Roberts (2010).

6. This led to AMISOM's creation of a civilian casualty tracking cell and new policies on indirect fire. See https://www.un.org./News/Press/docs/2011/sc10399.doc (accessed December 5, 2013).

7. In my view, the Sri Lankan and Russian actions in 1999 did not reflect a commitment to avoiding civilian casualties; NATO operations in Kosovo and Libya, while flawed, did reflect this commitment.

8. The ICRC and other nongovernmental organizations work to improve IHL compliance by non-state actors; perhaps the most notable example of success would be the Geneva Call effort to encourage non-state actors to abide by Landmine Ban Treaties. See http://www.genevacall.org/Themes/Landmines/landmines.htm (accessed August 15, 2012).

9. The ICRC brokered a common definition in 1996: "[Protection is] all activities aimed at obtaining full respect for the rights of the individual in accordance with the letter and spirit of the relevant bodies of law (i.e. human rights law, international humanitarian law and refugee law). Human rights and humanitarian organizations must conduct these activities in an impartial manner (not on the basis of race, national or ethnic origin, language or gender)." (ICRC, 1999, p. 21)

10. The central player within the UN system is the Office for the Coordination of Humanitarian Affairs (OCHA), which holds that "Protection involves creating an environment conducive to respect for human beings, preventing, and/or alleviating the immediate effects of a specific pattern of abuse, and restoring dignified conditions of life through reparation, restitution, and rehabilitation." (Lie and de Carvalho, 2008). United Nations High Commissioner for Refugees has a different understanding (see United Nations High Commissioner for Refugees, 2007). To the World Food Program, civilian protection means "safe and dignified programming": employing a protection-oriented analysis of hunger; seeking to ensure that programming does not incur new risks; and agreeing procedures for action when abuses are witnessed. See Sorcha O'Callaghan and Sara Pantuliano, 2007.

11. As the UN Secretary-General said in 1998: "The plight of civilians is no longer something which can be neglected, or made secondary because it complicates political negotiations or interests. It is fundamental to the central mandate of the Organization." 12 S/1999/957, para 68.

12. UNSCR 1270 for UNAMSIL, October 22, 1999; UNSCR 1279 for MONUC, November 30, 1999; UNSCR 1509 for UNMIL, September 19, 2003; UNSCR 1545 for ONUB, May 21, 2004; UNSCR 1542 for MINUSTAH, April 30, 2004; UNSCR 1528 for UNOCI, February 27, 2004; UNSCR 1590 for UNMIS, March 24, 2005; UNSCR 425 and 426 for UNIFIL, originally in March 1978 and expanded on August 11, 2006; UNSCR 1769 for UNAMID, July 31, 2007; UNSCR 1778 for MINURCAT, September 25, 2007; UNSCR 1996 for UNMISS, July 8, 2011 as of this writing.

13. However, US COIN doctrine fails to disaggregate and specify the general requirement to protect the population. This gap allows forces to default more readily to enemy-centric military activities.

14. See Chapter 8 of Holt and Berkman, 2006.
15. In its 2002 Joint Doctrine Manual, Canada describes civilian protection as a military task. Alternately, the United States is still wrestling with whether civilian protection should be considered an aspect of peace operations doctrine or is instead part of a broader protection mission that includes force protection. A handful of nations including Canada, the United Kingdom, and the United States acknowledge that significant force might be required in order to prevent genocide. See also Holt, 1988.
16. Some observers have argued that preamble language ("*Reiterating* the responsibility of the Libyan authorities to protect the Libyan Population. ...") is a nod to R2P, adding another dimension of complexity to the civilian protection language. See http://daccess-dds-ny.un.org/doc/UNDOC/GEN/N11/268/39/PDF/N1126839.pdf?OpenElement (accessed July 19, 2012).
17. The occupation force language was not determinate – it could have been interpreted loosely to allow for ground forces that were not to serve as a permanent occupation force.
18. See, for example, http://www.pbs.org/wnet/religionandethics/episodes/june-10-2011/reassessing-libya-intervention/8977/ (accessed December 5, 2013).

References

Best, Geoffrey. 1983. *Humanity in Warfare: The Modern History of the International Law of Armed Conflicts*. New York, NY: Routledge.

DPKO/DFS. 2010. "Operational Concept on the Protection of Civilians in United Nations Peacekeeping Operations." New York, NY: United Nations.

Dunlap, Charles J. Jr. 2001. "Law and Military Interventions: Preserving Humanitarian Values in 21st Century Conflicts." *Carr Center for Human Rights Policy's National Security and Human Rights Program Working Papers Series*, Vol 1.

Dunlap, Charles J. Jr. 2007. "Lawfare amid warfare." *Washington Times*, August 3.

Glad, Marit. 2012. "A partnership at risk? Norwegian Refugee Council Discussion Paper: 16.02.2012." Accessed July 13, 2012 from http://www.nrc.no/?did=9608295

Holt, Victoria. 1988. "Chapter 4: The Military and Civilian Protection: Developing Roles and Capacities." In *HPG Report 21: Resettling the Rules of Engagement*, March 2006, 60. UK Army, *Army Field Manual* Volume 5, Part I. London: HMSO.

Holt, Victoria. 2006. "The Military and Civilian Protection: Developing Roles and Capacities." In *HPG Report 21: Resettling the Rules of Engagement*, edited by Victoria Wheeler and Adele Harmer, 53–66. Overseas Development Institute.

Holt, Victoria K., and Tobias C. Berkman. 2006. *The Impossible Mandate?* Accessed 5 December, 2013 from http://www.stimson.org/books-reports/the-impossible-mandate/

Interagency Standing Committee. 2013. Human Rights Guidance Note For Humanitarian Coordinators, November 2005. Accessed December 5, 2013 from http://rconline.undg.org/wp-content/uploads/2010/12/IASC-Guidance-note-for-HCs-on-Human-Rights.pdf

International Committee of the Red Cross. 1999. "Third Workshop on Protection." *Background Paper.* 7 January 1999, p. 21.

Kjeksrud, Stian, Jacob Aasland Ravndal, Andreas Øien Stensland, *et al.* 1 November 2011. "Protection of Civilians in Armed Conflict – Comparing Organizational Approaches." *Norwegian Defense Research Establishment (FFI)*.

Lie, Jon Harald Sande, and Benjamin de Carvalho. 2008. "A Culture of Protection? Perceptions of the Protection of Civilians from Sudan." *NUPI Report: Security in Practice, 7.*

MacFarquhar, Neil. 2012. "UN Faults NATO and Libyan Authorities in Report." *New York Times,* 2 March.

Mack, Andrew (ed.). 2007. "Human Security Brief 2007." *Human Security Report Project.* Vancouver, BC: Simon Fraser University.

O'Callaghan, Sorcha, and Sara Pantuliano, 2007. "Protective Action: Incorporating Civilian Protection into Humanitarian Response." *Humanitarian Policy Group, Report 26,* December 2007, p. 20. Accessed December 5, 2013 from http://www.odi.org.uk/sites/odi.org.uk/files/odi-assets/publications-opinion-files/1640.pdf

Roberts, Adam. 2010. "Lives and Statistics: Are 90% of War Victims Civilians?" *Survival,* 52(3): 115–136.

Roberts, Adam, and Richard Guelff, eds. 1982. *Documents on the Laws of War.* New York, NY: Oxford University Press.

Sewall, Sarah, Dwight Raymond, and Sally Chin. 2010. *Mass atrocity response operations: a military planning handbook.* Cambridge, MA: Carr Center for Human Rights Policy, Harvard Kennedy School, and the US Army Peacekeeping and Stability Operations Institute. Accessed 5 December, 2013 from http://www.hks.harvard.edu/cchrp/maro

Stanley Foundation. 2012. "A Coming of Age for Human Protection." *Courier,* 7. Accessed 5 December, 2013 from http://stanley.dynamicwebware.com/courier/courier74/Courier74.pdf

Turner Johnson, James. 1981. *Just War Tradition and the Restraint of War: A Moral and Historical Inquiry.* Princeton, NJ: Princeton University Press.

Walzer, Michael. 1977. *Just and Unjust Wars: A Moral Argument with Historical Illustrations.* New York, NY: Basic Books.

Williams, Paul D. 2010. *Enhancing Civilian Protection in Peace Operations: Insights from Africa.* Washington, DC: National Defense University Press.

United Nations. n.d. *UN's Framework for Drafting Comprehensive Protection of Civilians (POC) Strategies in UN Peacekeeping Operations.* Accessed December 5, 2013 from http://www.refworld.org/pdfid/523998464.pdf

United Nations DPKO/DFS. 2009. "A New Partnership Agenda: Charting a New Horizon for UN Peacekeeping." New York, NY: United Nations.

United Nations High Commissioner for Refugees (UNHCR), 2007. "Handbook for the Protection of Internally Displaced Persons." p. 8. Accessed February 7, 2012 from http://www.unhcr.org/cgi-bin/texis/vtx/home/opendocPDFViewer.html?docid=4c2355229&query=civilian%20protection

Further Reading

International Committee of the Red Cross. 2010. "War and International Humanitarian Law." Accessed January 23, 2012 from http://www.icrc.org/eng/war-and-law/overview-war-and-law.htm

The Report of the International Commission on Intervention and State Sovereignty. 2001. "Responsibility to Protect." Ottawa ON, Canada: International Development Research Centre, Minister of Foreign Affairs.

United Nations. 2005. "World Summit Outcome." Accessed 5 December, 2013 from http://www.un.org/womenwatch/ods/A-RES-60-1-E.pdf

Chapter 13

Humanitarian Assistance

Henry Radice

Introduction

Humanitarian assistance takes place on the frontline of global security policy where, for many, insecurity often takes the form of violent death. According to conventional understandings of humanitarianism, the proper role of humanitarian assistance should be to deliver a partial alleviation of insecurity for those caught up in or fleeing conflict and disaster. One standard definition provided by the United Nations Office for the Coordination of Humanitarian Affairs (OCHA) refers to aid in the context of humanitarian assistance as seeking "to save lives and alleviate the suffering of a crisis-affected population. Humanitarian assistance must be provided in accordance with the basic humanitarian principles of humanity, impartiality and neutrality..." (OCHA, 2003, p. 13). A well-established body of international humanitarian law, built around the Geneva Conventions and Additional Protocols, enshrines many core humanitarian concerns, places key obligations on belligerents to mitigate the excesses of war, and provides legal space for humanitarians to act. In principle, therefore, the place of humanitarian assistance within global security policy should be relatively straightforward.

However, debates have arisen in recent years that cast professional humanitarians as both potential producers and consumers of security, and as both perpetrators and victims of insecurity. These four potential roles will be at the heart of this chapter, and will be examined in the context of ongoing debates about the definition and boundaries of humanitarian assistance itself, about the nature of the "humanitarian space" within which professional humanitarians try to operate, and about the extent to which humanitarians should embrace or reject the lure of politics and power. Behind all this lies a fundamental concern: that humanitarianism often radically affects the security of those it aspires to serve, the end-users of humanitarian assistance, and

The Handbook of Global Security Policy, First Edition. Edited by Mary Kaldor and Iavor Rangelov.
© 2014 John Wiley & Sons, Ltd. Published 2014 by John Wiley & Sons, Ltd.

that the ways in which this happens need to be examined if it is to be used wisely as a tool to alleviate the insecurity of the most vulnerable.

The first part of the chapter, on the scope of humanitarian practice, will discuss how the sense of humanitarianism as the provision of humanitarian assistance in response to insecurity has been broadened from the alleviation of the consequences of insecurity to include the provision of security and in so doing, risked, it is sometimes alleged, becoming a driver of insecurity in its own right.

The second part of the chapter will explore the contested notion of humanitarian space, arguing that debates about the proper extent and protection of humanitarian space have become the foci for key discussions about the security of professional humanitarians and those they aspire to serve. It will then argue that what is omitted from discussions of humanitarian space is often the sense of such spaces as sites of governance, in which humanitarianism's consequences for the security and insecurity of intended beneficiaries needs to be examined more closely.

Humanitarianism, Security, and Politics

This first section will discuss the different ways in which humanitarianism has been conceptualized as a response to insecurity. These different conceptualizations have been at the heart of a profound and prolonged crisis of identity among professional humanitarians over the last few decades (Barnett and Weiss, 2008; Rieff, 2002). Craig Calhoun notes that "humanitarians have long felt a need to police the boundary of their field" (Calhoun, 2010, p. 51). The spectrum of different types of humanitarian action is often defined in terms of the relationship between humanitarianism and politics (Weiss, 1999, p. 67). At the supposedly apolitical end of this spectrum sits the classical variant of humanitarianism, inspired by the core principles of the Red Cross movement and limited to the provision of basic relief in conflict and disaster contexts, according to the principles of humanity, neutrality, impartiality, and independence. At the other end of the spectrum are so-called military humanitarian interventions, in which lethal force is deployed in the service of putatively humanitarian ends through an uneasy alliance with unambiguously political actors such as states. This end of the spectrum has been further reinforced in recent years by the discourse of the Responsibility to Protect (R2P), in which humanitarianism and global security policy arguably become inextricably intertwined (ICISS, 2001).

There are several problems with this starting point though. First, the parameters of that spectrum are themselves contestable: it is not at all clear that the scope of humanitarian practice is exhausted by those activities explicitly labeled "humanitarian" and widely recognized as such. Many claim the label humanitarian for purposes that are anything but, while others engage in activities that bear all of the hallmarks of humanitarian action, but are labeled under a different rubric, such as international development. However, in the context of a discussion of global security policy, it makes sense to limit the focus to actions conventionally described as, at least potentially, part of the humanitarian toolkit, for these tend to be those most closely associated with visceral insecurity and violence.

Still, here we encounter a second problem, which is that defining the spectrum of types of humanitarian assistance in relation to politics does not really seem entirely satisfactory. To do so is to define politics in a very narrow way, limited to the actions of explicitly political actors. Increasingly, humanitarians concede this point, acknowledging that humanitarian action almost always has political consequences. But this does not go far enough. In fact, all kinds of humanitarian action represent forms of politics, visions of how best to mitigate inhumanity in a context in which others perpetuate or tolerate inhumanity. These may involve different kinds of relationships to a variety of different political actors, but do not represent positions on a political/apolitical spectrum. To do so is to mistake both the rhetoric of humanitarianism for its reality, and to misunderstand the relationship between ethics and politics (Collinson and Elhawary, 2012; Radice, 2010).

As such, a more convincing strategy in formulating a taxonomy of humanitarianism may therefore be to plot the varieties of humanitarian action according to the different forms of insecurity that either prompt calls for humanitarian action, or are themselves caused by the deployment of inappropriate models of humanitarian action. For the purposes of this discussion, it shall be limited to the various forms of insecurity linked to the direct presence or threat of violence, a significant restriction in light of the fact that much humanitarian action deals with insecurity arising from natural disasters, even if there is often little that is "natural" about the consequences of such events in terms of human suffering (Oxfam, 2008; Sen, 1983).

Classical Humanitarian Assistance

This, still dominant, model of humanitarian assistance was born on the battlefield of Solferino in 1859, where the Swiss businessman Henry Dunant's encounter with the extreme suffering caused by conflict led to the foundation of the International Committee of the Red Cross (ICRC) and the wider community of the Red Cross movement (Dunant, 1986; Moorehead, 1999). Classical humanitarian assistance of the Red Cross variety attempts to alleviate the suffering that arises from insecurity. Since we are concerned here with insecurity relating to violence, the humanitarian assistance under scrutiny is the provision of relief in conflict situations. Action is generally taken according to four core principles of international humanitarianism: humanity, neutrality, impartiality, and independence (the full list of seven fundamental principles set out by the Red Cross also includes voluntary service, unity, and universality) (ICRC, 1986; Pictet, 1979). By adhering to strict neutrality and treating cases of suffering with impartiality, while maintaining independence from belligerents of any sort, it is argued that access to the wounded and threatened can best be achieved, most lives can be saved, and, ultimately, the principle of humanity can best be honored. It is this last principle that sits at the apex of humanitarian concerns. For Tony Vaux, "the principle of 'humanity' represents the fundamental moral value of humanitarianism. It takes precedence over all others" (Vaux, 2001, p. 5).

There is little doubt that the Red Cross model of humanitarian assistance still represents the gold standard to which most professional humanitarians aspire, even if a high degree of negotiation needs to take place to put those principles into practice on the ground (Magone, Neuman, and Weissman, 2011). The Red Cross movement still carries a unique symbolic weight within the humanitarian sector, and the ICRC has a special status within international humanitarian law (ICRC, 1998). For many, it defines the very notion of humanitarian assistance, and other practices are simply using the label "humanitarian" in bad faith. Yet for others, it has shown itself lacking in several crucial respects with regard to the security of those it aims to help.

First, the provision of relief aspires to save lives and thus to reduce, in a fundamental sense, the insecurity of those at threat. But this ability depends very much on the nature of the threat. If a life is saved only to be attacked anew the next day, questions could well be asked as to the appropriateness of an approach that refuses to engage with the root causes of suffering (Anderson, 1998). The most famous, and still traumatic, example of this is the case of Red Cross engagement in the Nazi concentration camps during the Second World War (Favez, 1999). The organization's failure to speak out in the face of what would soon come to be legally defined as genocide arguably marked a nadir of the model of classical humanitarian assistance. The fundamental problem here was that the kind of relief the Red Cross was able to deliver was utterly unable to mitigate the primary danger to the lives of those in the camps – that of mass murder. Rony Brauman, one of Médecins Sans Frontières' (MSF) sharpest minds, notes that the Red Cross was above all "guilty of not having taken into account the fact that the very notion of humanity already had been abolished" (Brauman, 2004, pp. 403–404).

This much-discussed case posed, and continues to pose, a fundamental challenge to the classical model. It presupposes a certain degree of equality between belligerents, in which, when all is said and done (and what is said, and done, may still be very violent indeed, even within the confines of international humanitarian law), one's enemies are nevertheless recognized as human, and accorded some basic respect as a result. Where the aim is, as in genocide, precisely to expel a certain category of person outside of the category of human, classical humanitarian assistance would appear to reveal its limitations.

Moreover, where neutral, impartial aid has not paid sufficient attention to the underlying political dynamics of a situation, it has sometimes been manipulated by belligerents or inadvertently served to prolong conflict. David Keen's work has revealed the different functions of violence in "complex emergencies" in which the aim of war is not necessarily to win (Keen, 2008). Paradoxically, two landmark (in terms of their role in broader normative shifts) moments in the development of a global humanitarian consciousness, Biafra and the Ethiopian famine, are now seen as deeply flawed humanitarian operations, while a much longer list of humanitarian "failures" haunts the literature.

A camp, even a refugee camp, however well-run in terms of classic humanitarian provision, nevertheless runs the risk of merely rounding up future victims for the slaughter, if sufficient notice is not paid to the causes of insecurity beyond the lack of basic food, shelter, etc. Two traumatic cases put the issue in particularly sharp relief in the 1990s. In 1992, the dread phrase the "well-fed dead" reared its head with regard to the siege of Sarajevo (*New York Times*, 1992). It was later to haunt many defenders of a "neutral" humanitarian approach after the so-called "safe area" of Srebrenica became the site of a notorious massacre in July 1995. In the aftermath of the 1994 Rwandan genocide, a catastrophe that revealed the limitations of international humanitarians, many humanitarians became troubled by the fact that in many refugee camps they were sustaining not the victims of the genocide, but its perpetrators (Terry, 2002).

The question of how to resolve, from a humanitarian perspective, the many different manifestations of the particular form of insecurity, arguably the most extreme form of insecurity possible, of being cast outside of the protections afforded by the category of common humanity, continues to trouble and torment humanitarians. It remains so troubling because it frequently involves a discussion of whether force should be harnessed in the service of humanitarian ends. This in turn raises the risk, ever-present when lethal means are under discussion, of creating new forms of insecurity, violating the injunction to "do no harm" (Anderson, 1999). Also crucial are questions of responsibility, which we will revisit next in the context of the debates around the R2P: for many humanitarians, this simply goes beyond what it is reasonable to ask of them and of the practice they represent.

Military Humanitarian Intervention

The classical model of humanitarian assistance, which we might term "rescue by consent", mainly took place in a world in which state sovereignty was largely upheld at the level of official state discourse, if rather less upheld at the level of state practice (Krasner, 1999). The OCHA definition of humanitarian assistance offered in the introduction earlier goes on to state that "the UN seeks to provide humanitarian assistance with full respect for the sovereignty of States" (OCHA, 2003, p. 13). But over the past few decades, the notion that the norm of state sovereignty should trump human rights norms has become much more overtly contested (Brown, 2002; Wheeler, 2002). Some have begun to consider that a more robust humanitarianism might sometimes be called for, leading to the emergence of humanitarian intervention as a prominent element of the global security toolkit. A standard definition of humanitarian intervention is offered by Holzgrefe:

> the threat or use of force across state borders by a state (or group of states) aimed at preventing or ending widespread and grave violations of the fundamental human rights of individuals other than its own citizens, without the permission of the state within whose territory force is applied. (Holzgrefe, 2003, p. 19)

This definition appears promising in suggesting a practice that might address some of the limitations addressed earlier, but raises a number of obvious problems from the perspective of classical humanitarian action, which have so far been evident in a number of cases of putative (the label is almost always contested) humanitarian intervention.

First, in terms of the violation of state sovereignty at stake, this clearly goes against the tradition of acquiring the consent of all relevant parties before acting. But professional humanitarians and other civil society actors have played their part in this normative shift (Kaldor, 2007). Prominent among these was the group of doctors who broke with ICRC procedure over Biafra in a split that led to the formation of MSF. One of the leading figures here, Bernard Kouchner, has been influential in pushing the case for what in French has been called a *droit d'ingérence* (right of interference) through roles at the head of a succession of nongovernmental organizations

(NGOs) and, later, government ministries and intergovernmental missions (Allen and Styan, 2000).

Though Kouchner has been comfortable moving across the boundaries between non-state, state, and inter-state actors, many professional humanitarians are not, and raise a second objection to the very notion of humanitarian intervention, that the key actors at stake – states (and, crucially, their militaries) – would seem to violate the principle of independence. For many in the humanitarian sector, no state or political leader, however well-intentioned, can carry out humanitarian action. They can act more or less ethically within the realm of politics, but that is, it is claimed, ultimately a different realm. As we saw earlier, this distinction between politics and humanitarianism is at the very least contestable. It is certainly the case, however, that states do not have the kind of singular, focused mandate that humanitarian agencies have, and thus bring a great deal of baggage into the field.

Third, the use of violent means would simply seem to preclude any characterization of humanitarian intervention as humanitarian assistance in a "true" sense. The notion of "killing to save" would appear to be so oxymoronic as to defy humanitarian reason. Rather than increase the security of those on the ground, it runs the risk of fatally increasing the insecurity of the inevitable victims of "collateral damage", without necessarily increasing the security of those it aspires to save, due to the unpredictability of any war and its aftermath. But the question persists as to whether an effective military action to alleviate suffering should not, in some cases, fall under the umbrella of humanitarian action. There are powerful hypotheticals that resonate in the humanitarian folk imaginary, such as the persistent "what if" of a reinforcement and more forceful use of UN personnel in the run-up to and early stages of the Rwandan genocide. There are also the, at least arguably partial, successes of liberal interventionism of the turn of the century, such as Kosovo, Sierra Leone, and East Timor.

Fourth, if we return to Holzgrefe's definition of humanitarian intervention, it is important to note that he refers to human rights as the justification for humanitarian intervention. This distinction might appear small to some, but is of crucial importance to many humanitarians for whom their practice is strictly limited to the provision of life-saving relief, not the defense of rights. Classifying humanitarian intervention as a legitimate extension of humanitarian assistance therefore represents a category error. Indeed, David Rieff remarks that "human rights interventions" would be a less misleading term for what we commonly term "humanitarian interventions" (Rieff, 2006, p. xi) if we are to countenance at all the use of military means for such ends.

Rieff is an interesting figure in these debates. The cases of the early 1990s, especially Bosnia, made him something of an advocate for humanitarian intervention, but by the turn of the century, after years of close scrutiny of the full spectrum of humanitarian action, he was thoroughly disillusioned with the promises of the more expansive humanitarian agendas of the late 1990s, and argued that the provision of "a bed for the night" is perhaps all humanitarianism should aspire to. Rieff notes that, "[like] most humanitarians I have known, I am not a pacifist," going on to make the case for military intervention and protectorates in certain extreme cases (Rieff, 2002, p. 329). He maintains that "to argue for military intervention on political grounds ... is not the same thing as arguing for military intervention on humanitarian grounds. For me, that will always be a contradiction in terms. It is a perversion of humanitarianism, which is neutral or it is nothing." (Rieff, 2002, p. 330) A decade on, the sense of disillusion grows: "humanitarian space is a sentimental idea, neutrality a bogus one, and impartiality an abstraction, however necessary, and it is a lost cause to try to defend any of them. The sooner they are given a decent burial, the sooner we can all move on" (Rieff, 2011, pp. 253–254).

It is not clear though, that Rieff's warnings have been heeded and the deployment of the rhetoric of humanitarianism made more circumspect, for while the record of cases of humanitarian intervention is certainly a mixed one, the response has not necessarily been a retrenchment towards a limited understanding of how humanitarian concerns should inform the practice of protection, but rather a major expansion, in the form of the doctrine of R2P.

The Responsibility to Protect

The emergence of R2P as a discourse offered the potential to shift the discourse away from the assertion of a "right to intervene" to the need to assure the protection of the most vulnerable. It stemmed from the confluence of a number of policy debates, all of which had humanitarian concerns at their core, and took place alongside other attempts to institutionalize the normative developments of the 1990s, such as the International Criminal Court.

The Independent International Commission on Kosovo (IICK) famously described the NATO intervention as "illegal but legitimate" (IICK, 2000). This put the intervening states, and those who supported them, including many NGOs, in the position of acting both irresponsibly, and therefore unaccountably in legal terms, but responsibly in broader humanitarian terms. This cognitive dissonance was a key impetus behind the formulation of R2P.

The initial report was the product of a high-level commission featuring many of the key protagonists of the 1990s debates on humanitarian intervention. It linked them to ongoing debates on how to reconceptualize sovereignty to resolve the tension between sovereignty norms and human rights norms, through notions such as Francis Deng's "sovereignty as responsibility", which stemmed from his work on internally displaced persons (IDPs) in the mid-1990s (Evans, 2008; ICISS, 2001). It created a framework in which, for the worst "mass atrocity crimes", there would always be a responsible agent: in the first instance the host state, and, if unwilling or unable to fulfill its responsibilities, the wider community of states, under the auspices of the UN Security Council's ultimate arbitration. Responsibility here is conceived of across three parameters: preventing, reacting, and rebuilding. A watered-down version of R2P was endorsed by the 2005 UN World Summit.

Since then, there has been much debate on what R2P represents. In the absence of new international legal obligations, it is at best a doctrine. But a doctrine implies a consistent impact on the shape of international policymaking, which is as yet difficult consistently to detect, though the language of responsibility is increasingly informing international discussion of cases such as Libya. Of course, for much of the 2000s, the alternative security meta-narrative of the War on Terror was perhaps a more powerful influence in constraining humanitarians' room for maneuver and in determining the context for military–humanitarian relations in interventions such as Afghanistan and Iraq. Alex Bellamy, who has been providing almost real-time academic commentary on the evolution of R2P, concluded in one interim assessment that because

> indeterminacy makes it unlikely that RtoP will act in the near future as a catalyst for international action in response to genocide and mass atrocities, it seems reasonable to argue that the most prudent path is to view the principle as a policy agenda in need of implementation rather than as a "red flag" to galvanize the world into action. (Bellamy, 2010, p. 166)

That is, it provides no shortcut to professional humanitarians in search of reliable, consistent action, and a robust internationalized responsibility for mass atrocity crimes. R2P does not appear to offer a magic bullet for a situation like Syria. R2P offers a change, and perhaps a useful one, in vocabulary, but it does not alter the fundamental problem that faced those professional humanitarians who denounced the failure of the West to engage with the Rwandan genocide in 1994: how to generate the political will to intervene to protect the most insecure (and what exactly should that intervention look like)? Professional humanitarians cannot *a priori* detach themselves from involvement in this conversation (although some organizations may reasonably wish to for operational reasons). The risk that concerns many though, is that by identifying their practice with broader developments in global security policy, they risk restricting the scope of humanitarian space.

Securing Humanitarian Space

Humanitarian space is a highly contested concept, and a vital trope in recent humanitarian discourse. Each of the models of humanitarian action outlined has different implications for thinking about what humanitarian space might mean, both conceptually and in terms of consequences for security policy. Whether one considers humanitarian space to be shrinking or expanding depends to a large extent on what position one takes in relation to these models. Furthermore, it has different implications for the relationship between humanitarianism and security, and for the security of humanitarians themselves.

Types of Humanitarian Space

Humanitarian space serves to describe and ring-fence humanitarian action within an international context. For Stephen Hopgood, humanitarian identity is intimately intertwined with the concept, in the sense that "legitimacy comes from the idea of a humanitarian space bordered by neutrality, impartiality, and independence" (Hopgood, 2008, p. 119). It can evoke many different types of space: rhetorical, physical, legal, political, ethical, or functional. If we cannot define it outside of or against politics, we can still examine its distinctive elements within.

In one study of state fragility, the question was posed "of whether humanitarian space means primarily the space for humanitarian agencies to operate safely and effectively on the ground, or whether it relates to a wider social, political or geographical space within which human welfare is preserved and promoted" (Collinson, Elhawary, and Muggah 2010, p. 14). The ICRC's Johanna Grombach

Wagner attributes the phrase "humanitarian space" itself to Rony Brauman, who defined it as "a space of freedom in which we are free to evaluate needs, free to monitor the distribution and use of relief goods, and free to have a dialogue with the people" (Grombach Wagner, 2005). OCHA simply views it as a synonym of "humanitarian operating environment" (Grombach Wagner, 2005). Brauman's definition gives humanitarians a privileged status to define the terms of debate, access, and action. Indeed, Robert DeChaine sees the MSF understanding of humanitarian space as part of an attempt to forge a global "imagined community" (DeChaine, 2005, pp. 91–99). This resonates with some of the more ambitious uses of the term, which, in retrospect, appear as key rhetorical groundwork for concepts like R2P, taking the debate in a direction perhaps rather different from that intended by the likes of Brauman. For instance, in 1995, Thomas Weiss (later, crucially, to be research director of the 2001 International Commission on State Sovereignty that developed R2P) and Jarat Chopra posited that:

> the identity of populations is also expanding beyond nationality to be all-inclusive of the human species, irrespective of origin. This is the basis of a developing global humanitarian space, which is significantly eroding the distinction between concepts of "internal" and "external." Because humanitarian space is not linked to territory and transcends sovereign boundaries, it becomes increasingly difficult to speak of "*inter*vention" within it. Consequently, humanitarian assistance shifts from being a potential violation of sovereign rights to being a safeguard for fundamental human rights. (Weiss and Chopra, 1995, p. 88)

Amidst these various definitions, we can identify two tendencies. On the one hand, the view of professional humanitarians of a classicist bent for whom the notion of humanitarian space is primarily a question of securing autonomy for humanitarian actors within conflicted environments, though some recognize that in securing that autonomy it can become a "space for negotiation, power games and interest-seeking between aid actors and authorities" (Allié, 2011, pp. 2–3). On the other hand, broader perspectives that see humanitarian assistance and the defense of humanitarian space around it as a Trojan horse (in a positive sense) for normative developments such as R2P and the emergence of a more cosmopolitan global political order embodied by other new institutions such as the International Criminal Court. This is, of course, a putative order that many remain suspicious of, seeing R2P as a Trojan horse of more imperialistic tendencies and therefore potentially a threat to the security of many in the global South (Bellamy, 2005; Weiss, 2012, pp. 134–137).

Humanitarians in Peril

Prominent humanitarians, such as Fred Cuny, killed in Chechnya in 1995, and Sergio Vieira de Mello, victim of an attack on the UN headquarters in Iraq in 2003, number among the many fallen of recent conflicts. The security of humanitarians themselves within humanitarian space is an important part of the discussion of humanitarian assistance as part of the policy toolkit, not least because how humanitarians respond to real or perceived insecurity has consequences for the security of those around them, including local staff (who are often the softest targets within the aid community) and those they aspire to help. There has certainly been an increase in recent years in violent attacks on aid workers and kidnappings in absolute terms, although it is important to note that numbers of aid workers have also increased in absolute terms. Several arguments have been put forward for this and they all intersect with broader security debates. The security of humanitarians is now a major object of study in its own right and is yielding a rich sub-literature that is rapidly clarifying what has been a relatively uncertain picture (Bruderlein and Gassmann, 2006; Egeland, Harmer and Stoddard, 2011; Gassmann, 2005; Harmer, 2008; Stoddard, Harmer, and Haver, 2011; Stoddard, Harmer, and Hughes, 2012; Van Brabant, 2010).

The provision of humanitarian assistance has, of course, always been a risky business. But in recent years, discussions of humanitarian space have often revolved around the extent to which humanitarians are increasingly at risk of kidnap or killing, and whether this increase is a consequence of a humanitarianism that is insufficiently neutral, or at least not perceived as such. Many humanitarians feel that it is precisely the politicization, and sometimes militarization, of humanitarian assistance that has put them at risk. They worry that they have been imperiled by having their identify as neutral purveyors of help muddied by too close an involvement with military and political actors, or by surrounding themselves with hired protection, and are therefore just seen as another set of partial Western interventionists. This is a difficult concern to test because where conflicts involve parties with a sophisticated understanding of how to shape the media narrative, they may well be perfectly aware of the operational distinctions between actors, and yet desire to exploit their vulnerability to put across a particular message about the relations of power on the ground.

With respect to the despicable abduction and murder of Margaret Hassan, Iraq country director for CARE, in 2004, Thomas Weiss has written: "Living in the country for 30 years and being married to a Muslim Iraqi did not make her less vulnerable, but rather a perfect symbolic target to send a message about insecurity" (Weiss, 2012, p. 79). As Laura Hammond argues, such an act of violence is performative and can serve multiple purposes: to draw attention to the insecurity on the ground in Iraq; as a show of strength on the part of the insurgents and a demonstration of the weakness of the occupying forces; and of the vulnerability of all internationals without exception (Hammond, 2008, pp. 178–179).

Mark Duffield looks at how humanitarians have responded to this sense of insecurity and explores the "bunkerization" of the aid industry, and its resultant impact in terms of creating "an archipelago of international space", leading to further practices of inclusion and exclusion (Duffield, 2010, 2012a, 2012b). The physical geography of humanitarian assistance serves to remind us of the power that humanitarians have, and of the consequences that has for the security and insecurity of those surrounding them.

Humanitarians in Power

We now briefly turn to a particularly important dimension of contemporary humanitarianism, that of humanitarian assistance as a mechanism of governance. At times, of course, humanitarians have literally found themselves in government, with considerable power over the security outcomes of local populations. One example of this was Bernard Kouchner's spell as Special Representative and Head of the United

Nations Interim Administration in Kosovo (UNMIK) in the aftermath of the NATO intervention. But at every level of the humanitarian enterprise, humanitarians wield life and death power over the people they aspire to serve, and the critical literature of humanitarian failures that prompted the humanitarian identity crisis of recent years is, among other things, a shopping list of the ways in which humanitarians can increase the insecurity of those they aspire to serve. Alex de Waal, a key voice in these debates over several decades, recently described the humanitarians' tragedy, for all the improvements in effectiveness, as being caught between escapable and inescapable cruelties (de Waal, 1997, 2010). Troublingly, Tony Vaux writes that:

> The problem for humanitarians is that the motive of pity so easily interacts with the motive for cruelty, and the desire to help so easily becomes the desire for power. Outer values often mean that we overcome or hide such feelings, but this does not mean that they have no effect. (Vaux, 2001, p. 95)

Moreover, humanitarians have not only a practical, but also a discursive role in shaping perceptions. Craig Calhoun points out that the notion of emergency is entwined with that of the exception, reminding us of Carl Schmitt's understanding of sovereignty as the ability to define the exception (Calhoun, 2010, pp. 45–47). Humanitarians play a key role in describing crises and in mediating our awareness of distant suffering (Boltanski, 1999; Chouliaraki, 2006). As such they have a powerful role in influencing the political economy of humanitarian concern. Triage is of course a reality of humanitarian action (Orbinski, 2009; Reed, 2007). But there is then, arguably, a kind of triage – a global selection – of the suffering that deserves attention, which precedes the actual acts of medical triage that take place on the ground. In both cases, inevitably, some suffering is included, some excluded, by such appeals to technical knowledge. Jenny Edkins presents a strong critique of the risks inherent in such practices, concluding that: "The search for technical answers is itself political and supports the powerful, not the suffering. It is the buttress for forms of governance that reduce life to calculability" (Edkins, 2000, p. 159).

Indeed, Didier Fassin describes humanitarianism as "a mode of governing" (Fassin, 2012, p. x). He explores the role of "humanitarian reason" in the "politics of precarious lives" (Fassin, 2012, p. 5). He then maps the various forms of "humanitarian government" that pervade our contemporary political orders. What Fassin's work really brings home is that humanitarianism – in drawing on resources of authoritative technical knowledge and in structuring the way precarious lives are perceived, categorized, ranked, and engaged with – has a powerful role that necessarily shapes the security of the precarious in profound ways.

Moreover, there is increasing recognition that humanitarian assistance is often not a brief interlude in the lives of those living in fragile and conflict-affected situations, but can become a key ongoing intervention in situations of near-permanent emergency. With this comes a power that is not necessarily sought but needs to be acknowledged as humanitarians become embedded in formal, informal, or hybrid structures of public authority, whether this is at the level of donor influence on host governments or at ground level in terms of how programming decisions affect the provision of all kinds of basic goods and services. Furthermore, decisions made by humanitarians arguably run the risk of prejudging people's own understandings of their security needs. In the most fragile and difficult contexts, the evidence remains patchy on what these are (Luckham and Kirk, 2012).

Conclusion: Humanitarian (In)coherence, or Humanitarian Purity?

How humanitarian assistance should now be understood and located within the toolkit of global security policy remains essentially contested. For many, the best contribution humanitarianism can make to the security of the most vulnerable is to restrict itself rigorously to the core humanitarian principles of humanity, neutrality, impartiality, and independence. For others, that has always been an overly idealistic vision of humanitarian assistance, and while such efforts may remain valuable, they need to be seen as part of a broader humanitarian agenda within international policymaking that encompasses high-level normative developments such as R2P. Recently, there have been attempts to resolve some of the tensions set out in this chapter through a "coherence" agenda that aims to achieve greater coordination of humanitarian efforts. This has certainly had some success in improving the effectiveness of humanitarian assistance, but questions remain of whether coherence is compatible with independence and of whether humanitarian efforts, however well-coordinated, are sufficiently underpinned by evidence about the constantly changing everyday insecurities of those at the receiving end of their efforts.

References

Allen, Tim, and David Styan. 2000. "A right to interfere? Bernard Kouchner and the new humanitarianism." *Journal of International Development*, 12: 825–842.

Allié, Marie-Pierre. 2011. "Introduction: Acting at Any Price?" In *Humanitarian Negotiations Revealed: The MSF Experience*, edited by Claire Magone, Michaël Neuman, and Fabrice Weissman, 1–11. London: Hurst & Company.

Anderson, Mary B. 1998. "'You Save My Life Today, But For What Tomorrow?' Some Dilemmas of Humanitarian Aid." In *Hard Choices: Moral Dilemmas in Humanitarian Intervention*, edited by Jonathan Moore, 137–156. Oxford: Rowman & Littlefield.

Anderson, Mary B. 1999. *Do No Harm: How Aid Can Support Peace – Or War*. Boulder, CO: Lynne Rienner.

Barnett, Michael, and Thomas G. Weiss, eds. 2008. *Humanitarianism in Question: Politics, Power, Ethics*. Ithaca, NY: Cornell University Press.

Bellamy, Alex J. 2005. "Responsibility to Protect or Trojan Horse? The Crisis in Darfur and Humanitarian Intervention after Iraq." *Ethics & International Affairs*, 19: 31–54. DOI: 10.1111/j.1747-7093.2005.tb00499.x

Bellamy, Alex J. 2010. "The Responsibility to Protect – Five Years On." *Ethics & International Affairs*, 24: 143–169.

Boltanski, Luc. 1999. *Distant Suffering: Morality, Media and Politics*. Translated by Graham Burchell. Cambridge: Cambridge University Press.

Brauman, Rony. 2004. "From Philanthropy to Humanitarianism: Remarks and an Interview." *South Atlantic Quarterly*, 103: 397–417. DOI: 10.1215/00382876-103-2-3-397.

Brown, Chris. 2002. *Sovereignty, Rights and Justice: International Political Theory Today*. Cambridge: Polity Press.

Bruderlein, Claude, and Pierre Gassmann. 2006. "Managing Security Risks in Hazardous Missions: The Challenges of Securing United Nations Access to Vulnerable Groups." *Harvard Human Rights Journal*, 19: 63–93.

Calhoun, Craig. 2010. "The Idea of Emergency: Humanitarian Action and Global (Dis)Order." In *2010*, edited by Didier Fassin and Mariella Pandolfi, 29–58. New York, NY: Zone Books.

Chouliaraki, Lilie. 2006. *The Spectatorship of Suffering*. London: Sage Publications.

Collinson, Sarah, and Samir Elhawary. 2012. *Humanitarian Space: A Review of Trends and Issues*. London: Overseas Development Institute.

Collinson, Sarah, Samir Elhawary, and Robert Muggah. 2010. *States of Fragility: Stabilisation and its Implications for Humanitarian Action*. London: ODI.

de Waal, Alex. 1997. *Famine Crimes: Politics and the Disaster Relief Industry in Africa*. Oxford: J. Currey.

de Waal, Alex. 2010. "The humanitarians' tragedy: escapable and inescapable cruelties." *Disasters*, 34: 130–137.

DeChaine, D. Robert. 2005. *Global Humanitarianism: NGOs and the Crafting of Community*. Lanham, MD: Lexington Books.

Duffield, Mark. 2010. "Risk-Management and the Fortified Aid Compound: Everyday Life in Post-Interventionary Society." *Journal of Intervention and Statebuilding*, 4: 453–474. DOI: 10.1080/17502971003700993.

Duffield, Mark. 2012a. "Challenging Environments: Danger, Resilience and the Aid Industry." *Security Dialogue*, 43: 475–492. DOI: 10.1177/0967010612457975.

Duffield, Mark. 2012b. Risk Management and the Bunkering of the Aid Industry. *Development Dialogue*, April.

Dunant, Henry. 1986. *A Memory of Solferino*. Geneva: ICRC.

Edkins, Jenny. 2000. *Whose Hunger? Concepts Of Famine, Practices Of Aid*. Minneapolis, MN: University of Minnesota Press.

Egeland, Jan, Adele Harmer, and Abby Stoddard. 2011. *To Stay and Deliver: Good Practice for Humanitarians in Complex Security Environments*. OCHA.

Evans, Gareth. 2008. *The responsibility to protect: ending mass atrocity crimes once and for all*. Washington, DC: Brookings Institution Press.

Fassin, Didier. 2012. *Humanitarian Reason: A Moral History of the Present*. Berkeley and Los Angeles: University of California Press.

Favez, Jean-Claude. 1999. *The Red Cross and the Holocaust*. Cambridge: Cambridge University Press.

Gassmann, Pierre. 2005. "Rethinking humanitarian security." *Humanitarian Exchange Magazine*, June.

Grombach Wagner, Johanna. 2005. "An IHL/ICRC Perspective on 'Humanitarian Space'." *Humanitarian Exchange Magazine*, November.

Hammond, Laura. 2008. "The Power of Holding Humanitarianism Hostage and the Myth of Protective Principles." In *Humanitarianism In Question: Politics, Power, Ethics*, edited by Michael Barnett and Thomas G. Weiss, 172–195. London: Cornell University Press.

Harmer, Adele. 2008. "Integrated Missions: A Threat to Humanitarian Security?" *International Peacekeeping*, 15: 528–539.

Holzgrefe, J. L. 2003. "The humanitarian intervention debate." In *Humanitarian Intervention: Ethical, Legal and Political Dilemmas*, edited by J. L. Holzgrefe and Robert O. Keohane, 15–52. Cambridge: Cambridge University Press.

Hopgood, Stephen. 2008. "Saying 'No' to Wal-Mart? Money and Morality in Professional Humanitarianism." In *Humanitarianism in Question: Politics, Power, Ethics*, edited by Michael Barnett and Thomas G. Weiss, 98–123. London: Cornell University Press.

ICISS. 2001. *The Responsibility to Protect: Report of the International Commission on Intervention and State Sovereignty*. Ottawa, ON: International Development Research Centre.

ICRC. 1986. "The Fundamental Principles of the International Red Cross and Red Crescent Movement." Accessed May 7, 2013 from http://www.icrc.org/eng/resources/documents/red-cross-crescent-movement/fundamental-principles-movement-1986-10-31.htm

ICRC. 1998. "The International Committee of the Red Cross as Guardian of International Humanitarian Law." Accessed May 7, 2013 from http://www.icrc.org/eng/resources/documents/misc/about-the-icrc-311298.htm

IICK. 2000. *The Kosovo Report: Conflict, International Response, Lessons Learned*. Oxford: Oxford University Press.

Kaldor, Mary. 2007. *Human Security*. Cambridge: Polity Press.

Keen, David. 2008. *Complex Emergencies*. Cambridge: Polity Press.

Krasner, Stephen. 1999. *Sovereignty: Organized Hypocrisy*. Princeton, NJ: Princeton University Press.

Luckham, Robin, and Tom Kirk. 2012. *Security in Hybrid Political Contexts: an end-user approach*. London: Justice and Security Research Programme, LSE.

Magone, Claire, Michaël Neuman, and Fabrice Weissman, eds. 2011. *Humanitarian Negotiations Revealed: The MSF Experience*. London: Hurst & Company.

Moorehead, Caroline. 1999. *Dunant's Dream: War, Switzerland and the History of the Red Cross*. London: Harper Collins.

New York Times, The. 1992. "Editorial: The Well-Fed Dead in Bosnia." *The New York Times*, July 15.

OCHA. 2003. *Glossary of Humanitarian Terms: In Relation to the Protection of Civilians in Armed Conflict*. New York, NY: United Nations.

Orbinski, James. 2009. *An Imperfect Offering: Dispatches From The Medical Frontline*. London: Rider.

Oxfam. 2008. *Rethinking Disasters: Why Death and Destruction is not Nature's Fault but Human Failure*. New Delhi: Oxfam International.

Pictet, Jean. 1979. "The Fundamental Principles of the Red Cross: Commentary." Accessed May 7, 2013 from http://www.icrc.org/eng/resources/documents/misc/fundamental-principles-commentary-010179.htm

Radice, Henry. 2010. *The Politics of Humanity: Humanitarianism and International Political Theory*. PhD Thesis, Department of International Relations, London School of Economics and Political Science, London.

Reed, Patrick. 2007. *Triage: Dr. James Orbinski's Humanitarian Dilemma*. CanWest Global Television Network.

Rieff, David. 2002. *A Bed for the Night: Humanitarianism in Crisis*. London: Vintage.

Rieff, David. 2006. *At the Point of a Gun: Democratic Dreams and Armed Intervention*. New York, NY: Simon & Schuster.

Rieff, David. 2011. "Afterword." In *Humanitarian Negotiations Revealed: The MSF Experience*, edited by Claire Magone, Michaël Neuman, and Fabrice Weissman, 251–8. London: Hurst & Company.

Sen, Amartya. 1983. *Poverty and Famines: An Essay on Entitlement and Deprivation*. Oxford: Oxford University Press.

Stoddard, Abby, Adele Harmer, and Katherine Haver. 2011. *Aid Worker Security Report 2011: Spotlight on security for national aid workers: Issues and perspectives*. Humanitarian Outcomes.

Stoddard, Abby, Adele Harmer, and Morgan Hughes. 2012. *Aid Worker Security Report 2012: Host States and Their Impact on Security for Humanitarian Operations*. Humanitarian Outcomes.

Terry, Fiona. 2002. *Condemned to Repeat? The Paradox of Humanitarian Action*. London: Cornell University Press.

Van Brabant, Koenraad. 2010. *Managing Aid Agency Security in an Evolving World: The Larger Challenge*. London: European Interagency Security Forum.

Vaux, Tony. 2001. *The Selfish Altruist: Relief Work in Famine and War*. Sterling, VA: Earthscan.

Weiss, Thomas G. 1999. "Principles, Politics, and Humanitarian Action." *Ethics & International Affairs*, 13: 1–22. DOI: 10.1111/j.1747-7093.1999.tb00322.x

Weiss, Thomas G. 2012. *Humanitarian Intervention: Ideas in Action*. 2nd ed. Cambridge: Polity Press.

Weiss, Thomas G., and Jarat Chopra. 1995. "Sovereignty Under Siege: From Intervention to Humanitarian Space." In *Beyond Westphalia? State Sovereignty and International Intervention*, edited by Gene M. Lyons and Michael Mastanduno, 87–114. London: Johns Hopkins University Press.

Wheeler, Nicholas J. 2002. *Saving Strangers: Humanitarian Intervention in International Society*. Oxford: Oxford University Press.

Chapter 14

The Evolution of International Peacekeeping

Renata Dwan

Introduction

Peacekeeping refers to the authorized deployment of international personnel to maintain peace and security.[1] Traditionally the purview of the United Nations (UN), international peacekeeping is, today, a tool employed by regional and subregional organizations, as well as *ad hoc* coalitions of states, to enforce, maintain, and build peace between and within states. The breadth of the term, the range of actors involved, and the diverse contexts in which it is employed make international peacekeeping difficult – and often contentious – to define. Yet it is the lack of precise definition that has enabled peacekeeping to evolve and adapt to changing international politics and norms over seven decades. As international peacekeeping tackles more complex and protracted conflicts with increasingly ambitious mandates, imprecision is also a challenge for its effective use. Questions over the scope, authority, governance, impact, and sustainability of international peacekeeping reflect this tension.

This chapter is divided into three sections. The first describes the evolution of peacekeeping from a limited tool of the United Nations to maintain ceasefires between states to a multiactor enterprise focused primarily on establishing peace and supporting recovery after civil conflict. The second section explores key current debates, particularly relating to implementation of peacekeeping mandates. The concluding section identifies issues and trends that are likely to impact the way in which future international peacekeeping is conceived and conducted.

The Evolution of International Peacekeeping

International peacekeeping evolved in an *ad hoc* and generally reactive way. There is no reference to peacekeeping in the UN Charter,[2] and the first attempt to set out a coherent doctrine was the publication in 2008 by the UN Department of

The Handbook of Global Security Policy, First Edition. Edited by Mary Kaldor and Iavor Rangelov.
© 2014 John Wiley & Sons, Ltd. Published 2014 by John Wiley & Sons, Ltd.

Peacekeeping Operations of principles and guidelines for UN peacekeeping operations (United Nations, 2008).

"Traditional" Peacekeeping

UN peacekeeping began in 1948 with the decision of the Security Council to deploy unarmed military observers to monitor ceasefires agreed between the new state of Israel and its Arab neighbors. A similar small mission was established to monitor a ceasefire between India and Pakistan in the disputed region of Kashmir. Armed peacekeepers were deployed for the first time during the 1956 Suez Crisis to supervise the cessation of hostilities and the withdrawal of French, UK, and Israeli forces from Egyptian territory. These early experiences set the framework for what is often described as "traditional" peacekeeping. The context of UN peacekeeping was the Cold War and the recognition that rivalry between the United States, the Soviet Union and their allies had the potential to ignite limited conflicts into global conflagrations (Urquhart, 1972; Mazower, 2009). At the same time, Cold War tensions limited the scope of Security Council action and UN peacekeeping reflected the limited nature of its decision-making.

Early UN peacekeeping was directed at containing armed violence and maintaining established ceasefires in broadly two types of conflict: territorial disputes involving at least one newly established state (Israel, India, Pakistan, Yemen) and disputes relating to decolonialization, particularly with regard to the withdrawal of the former colonial power (Suez, Congo, West New Guinea). The 1960–1964 mission in the Congo to supervise the withdrawal of troops of the former colonial power, Belgium, and to provide technical assistance to the newly independent state, was also the first large-scale UN peacekeeping operation, involving at its height around 20,000 military, police, and civilian personnel.

UN peacekeeping missions were not deployed to parts of the world that came within the direct influence of the Soviet Union, the United States or China, or to conflicts in which they directly engaged such as the Korean War or the Sino–Indian War.

The scope and techniques of peacekeeping were similarly shaped by the geopolitical environment. Early UN peacekeeping was primarily a military tool deployed as an interim measure to stabilize a conflict situation and, by its presence, to deter parties from resorting to violence or to provide confidence to parties and local populations. The tasks of early peacekeepers were limited to observation, monitoring, and reporting of ceasefire and supporting agreed verification arrangements. In this context, the consent of the parties, the impartiality of international peacekeepers, and the non-use of force except in self-defense became the defining principles of early peacekeeping (United Nations, 2008).

As an accompaniment to a political process, the effectiveness of peacekeeping relied on the active cooperation of the parties and on the degree of political unity and engagement of the Member States. With the exception of the Congo operation, early UN peacekeeping missions were small in scale and ambition. They were put together on short order and for limited duration, composed of troops from countries willing to respond to the request of the Secretary-General, and managed in an informal and largely *ad hoc* way by a handful of UN bureaucrats. The most significant institutional development in the 1960s was the establishment of standardized procedures for the financing of peacekeeping operations according to an established scale of assessment, in which the rate paid annually by each Member States is determined by its national income (General Assembly Resolutions 1874 (S-IV) of 1963 & 2101 (XXVIII) of 1973). Although often contentious, this has provided significant stability for the financing of missions and remains one of the distinguishing features of UN peacekeeping.

Against the background of its origins, defining success was difficult. Speed of deployment, the safe conduct of mission tasks and the absence of renewed violence between the parties were the factors most frequently cited as indicators of success (see Fortna and Howard, 2008). Direct causal linkages between the presence of peacekeepers and incidences of violence were rarely demonstrated and long-term conflict settlement was not a criterion, as the continued existence of the UN's earliest peacekeeping operations testifies.

Multidimensional and Multi-Actor Peacekeeping

The end of the Cold War brought significant changes to international peacekeeping, expanding the objectives, scope, means, and actors involved. The end of superpower rivalry and their political, military, and financial support to previously perceived "client" states and the break-up of the Soviet Union, as well as the former Yugoslavia, saw a sharp increase in internal conflicts but, at the same time, greater international will for a collective response to address them. The United Nations was, initially, the main vehicle: between 1989 and 1994 the organization launched 20 new missions, with peacekeeping personnel increasing from 11,000 to 75,000. The scope of peacekeeping was equally expanded. In Angola, Namibia, El Salvador, Cambodia, Mozambique, and Tajikistan, operations were mandated to support the implementation of comprehensive peace agreements (see Stedman, Rothchild, and Cousens, 2002).

Reflecting this ambitious and fundamentally political objective, the tasks of peacekeeping grew exponentially over the 1990s. Security Council mandates increasingly included human rights monitoring; monitoring and supporting elections; disarmament, demobilization, and reintegration of former combatants; removal of mines and remnants of war; monitoring and training police forces; and support to judicial and correctional reforms – in addition to providing assistance to international humanitarian and development activities. The composition of UN peacekeeping operations also expanded with police officers, drawn from Member States, as well as civilians recruited by the UN Secretariat. Missions were increasingly headed by civilians, either UN senior officials or nominations from Member States.

"Multidimensional" peace operations, as the United Nations described these new operations, saw peacekeeping as a tool not only to prevent the recurrence of violence but as a mechanism to support the building of peace. This optimistic perception of the will of the international community and of the capacity of the United Nations to provide comprehensive and sustained assistance to peace processes was reflected in the UN's *Agenda for Peace* (United Nations, 1992). The perspective of peacekeeping as a permanent activity of the United Nations was reflected in the establishment of a dedicated department for peacekeeping operations.

The expansion of the objectives of peacekeeping was not matched, however, by a reassessment of its core principles. Consent, impartiality, and the non-use of force except in self-defense remained its avowed bedrock. Yet the conditions under which more and larger peacekeeping operations were deployed in the 1990s made these principles increasingly tenuous. In the former Yugoslavia, UN peacekeepers were deployed in the absence of a ceasefire or a peace agreement to protect civilian populations and to support the delivery of humanitarian assistance. In Rwanda, a UN assistance mission was deployed to support implementation of a comprehensive peace agreement in the face of stalled implementation by the parties and lack of political support by Member States. In Somalia, two successive UN missions (UNOSOM I and II) were deployed to establish a secure environment for humanitarian aid and to assist in the implementation of ceasefires that were never held by the parties.

In these contexts, UN peacekeepers did not have the force presence, capabilities, or authority required to enforce peace. Their deployment was not always accompanied by significant political initiatives to broker peace. The UN headquarters provided little strategic guidance on how mandates should be implemented or instructions on the use of force for the protection of civilians or the defense of the mission. The chain of command was incoherent, with troops responding to varying and contradictory orders from their national capitals, the mission leadership, and UN headquarters. The resulting abject failures of these missions to protect civilians, enforce peace, or defend themselves constituted the most serious crisis for UN peacekeeping in its history (Jett, 1999; Luttwak, 1999; Dallaire, 2003; Pugh, 2004). Two major self-critical reviews of the organization's failures in halting genocides in Rwanda, Srebrenica, and also Bosnia in 1999 (United Nations, 1999a, 1999b) reflected the UN's recognition that the ambitions of peacekeeping were out of step with the degree of political and operational support provided.

Peacekeeping initiatives by *ad hoc* multilateral and regional organizations launched in the 1990s faced similar difficulties in enforcing and maintaining peace. The 1993 US-led deployment to Somalia to support UN humanitarian objectives expanded to combat operations to capture the Somali warlord Mohammed Farrah Aidid, resulting in the death of 18 US soldiers and the withdrawal of US forces. The Economic Community of West African States Monitoring and Observation Group (ECOMOG) deployed to Liberia in 1990 and subsequently Sierra Leone used progressively more aggressive tactics to bring about an end to civil war before supporting the assumption of power in Liberia by Charles Taylor, the same actor whose ruthless exploitation of instability in Sierra Leone led to the resumption of civil war in both countries in less than five years (for ECOMOG, see Olonisakin, 2000). NATO launched its first out-of-area operation in 1993, enforcing a no-fly zone in Bosnia, which expanded in 1994 to limited air attacks on Serb targets at the request of the UN mission there. Sixty-thousand NATO peacekeepers were deployed to Bosnia in 1995 as part of the terms of the Dayton Peace Agreement, remaining in the divided country until 2004 when their functions were taken on by the European Union's (EU) first military crisis management operation (Tardy, 2009). In all of these cases, initially limited mandates were expanded – and extended – as peace processes stalled, generating tensions among the parties in the conflict as well as contributing countries about the objectives, the scope, and the means of peacekeeping operations.

The disconnect between politics and peacekeeping was at the heart of the 2000 Brahimi Report on UN Peace Operations (United Nations, 2000), which included a review of all aspects of peacekeeping planning and implementation by a panel of appointed experts. The report noted that peacekeeping was increasingly deployed with the objective to create, rather than to maintain, peace and called for Security Council mandates that were clear, credible, and achievable. It reasserted the principles of peacekeeping but underscored that impartiality did not mean equal treatment of all parties to a conflict. Peacekeepers deployed in volatile environments had to be robust enough to defend themselves, other mission components, and the mission's mandate (United Nations, 2000).

While asserting the primacy of politics in establishing a credible peace, the Brahimi Report acknowledged that more attention should be given to the challenges of building peace, including the role of peacekeeping in supporting rule of law and human rights, electoral processes, disarmament and demobilization, and reconciliation. The report therefore did not take issue with expanded use of peacekeeping; rather, it defined the minimum political conditions and support required for its effective use. It tentatively suggested a division of labor between international peacekeeping actors, with coalitions of the willing or militarily capable regional entities best suited to peace enforcement operations, and the United Nations best placed for multidimensional peace consolidation activities. And it set out a concrete agenda to strengthen UN support to comprehensive peace-building efforts.

New and Old Peacekeeping Models

The assertion of international peacekeeping as a tool for managing change within countries has shaped the operations of the past 15 years during which peacekeeping reached unprecedented levels of deployment and cost. Almost 100,000 military and police personnel were deployed to UN operations in 2010, with global figures (including NATO, African Union (AU), and EU deployments) reaching over 256,000 (for detailed figures of UN and non-UN peacekeeping personnel, budgets, and mandates, see Center on International Cooperation (CIC), 2012). The bulk of international peacekeepers continue to come from Africa and South Asia (Pakistan, Bangladesh, India, Nigeria), with negligible Western troop contributions. European military contributions are limited to the UN mission in Lebanon and EU operations in the Balkans, while the largest Latin American troop deployments center on the UN operation in Haiti.

Perhaps the most striking feature of modern peacekeeping is the diversification of activities. After the NATO intervention in Kosovo and an Australian-led military mission in East Timor in 1999, the United Nations established executive administrations to support the gradual transition of these countries to independence. Large numbers of UN police and civilian staff were deployed, and UN administrators established and enforced legislation covering all aspects of government (e.g. Dwan, 2003). These experiences of trusteeship demonstrated the gaps in international understanding, knowledge, capacity, and financing for consolidating peace and building new states (see Chapter 15 by Bojicic-Dzelilovic, Kostovicova, and Rampton). While there is little enthusiasm for taking on responsibility to deliver the state functions, multidimensional UN peacekeeping missions are now routinely mandated to support the authority and extension of the state in which they are deployed (CIC, 2012). This includes support to asserting monopoly on the use of force, reinforcing the state's legitimacy through constitutional and electoral processes, and building the capacity of state institutions, as currently in South Sudan.

This objective has led the United Nations to a more robust force posture that has extended in the Democratic Republic of Congo (DRC) and Côte d'Ivoire to combat operations in support of elected national authorities and to protect civilians from violence. African regional peacekeepers, including the AU force in Somalia and the recently established African-led International Support Mission in Mali, have been authorized to support government-led offensive operations against rebel groups (S/Res/2085 (2012)). In Afghanistan, the Security Council continues to endorse and extend the mandate of the International Security Assistance Force "to take all necessary measures" to fulfill its mandate (S/Res/2069 (2012)).

By contrast, UN peace operations in Afghanistan, Iraq, and Libya have been civilian missions directed at supporting political processes with a deliberate "light footprint". They are the largest of a growing body of UN special political missions intended to operate in parallel to an international military presence, to sustain attention and support to peacebuilding after the departure of peacekeepers (e.g. in Burundi, Sierra Leone) or to facilitate peace processes (e.g. in Nepal, Yemen). A variation of "light" non-military peacekeeping is the EU's crisis management operations, the majority of which are made up of small numbers of police and civilian personnel providing technical assistance to police and rule of law reform (Chivvis, 2010). The view that "traditional" peacekeeping was a feature of the past has also been challenged by events in the Middle East, particularly the bolstering of the longstanding UN observer mission in Lebanon following the Israeli–Lebanon war of 2006 and the short-lived deployment of a small UN military observer mission in Syria in 2012.

Parallel or, as in the case of the United Nations–African Union mission in Darfur, joint operations between United Nations and regional organizations are now a standard feature of the peacekeeping landscape. The concept of UN multidimensional peace operations deploying after regional or coalition-led military peace enforcement missions reflected the experiences of the late 1990s and, particularly in Africa, were seen as the way of the future, largely in terms of legitimacy, capacity for broad engagement, and sustainability. Yet in the Balkans, EU missions followed the departure of UN peacekeepers and, with the establishment of the African Union in 2001, the notion of regional peacekeepers being a more culturally attuned and popularly legitimate presence dominated discussions. That perspective has been challenged somewhat by the AU's experience in Somalia, where African peacekeepers met with the same levels of hostility as previous UN missions. In Somalia and now in Mali, the United Nations, as well as NATO and the European Union, have deployed logisticians and trainers in support of AU missions.

The diverse way in which international peacekeeping is currently employed is, perhaps, the strongest indication of its success. There is consensus among the international community that peacekeepers contribute to stabilizing conflicts, which has reinforced the legitimacy of the enterprise. The reassertion of the value of peacekeeping has been accompanied by efforts to improve its professionalism and capabilities and to design peacekeeping interventions that address the specific context and dimensions of individual conflicts. This notwithstanding, international peacekeeping remains a reflection of the state of the international community, its scope, form, and resources shaped as much by the views of major global and regional powers as by the degree of their coherence and commitment to cooperation. The more international peacekeeping seeks to become a policy tool to support comprehensive transformation in and between states, the more that international consensus is tested.

Current Implementation Challenges

Although the United Nations has advanced an agenda for the strengthening of UN peacekeeping – the 2009 "New Horizons" initiative (United Nations DPKO/DFS, 2009) – no major reassessment of international peacekeeping has taken place since the Brahimi Report. Tensions within the international community over the objectives and scope of peacekeeping have tended to be reflected in debates over means, particularly the operational and cost implications of comprehensive peacekeeping operations.

Consent

One of the implications of peacekeeping as a reflection of international will and consensus, particularly among the permanent five members of the Security Council, has been the relative lack of attention given to the views of the countries – and the people – in which international peacekeepers are deployed (Pouligny, 2006). This reflected both recognition of the reality of international power dynamics as well as the authority of the United Nations Security Council to direct parties to a conflict to accept the deployment and activities of a mandated operation. From the 1990s, however, the presumption of consent as well as the reach of the Security Council has been challenged. Ethiopia's demand that UN peacekeepers deployed along its disputed border with Eritrea in 2005 be drawn only from Africa was replicated in Darfur, where the Sudanese government repeatedly limited the nationalities, freedom of movement, and access of the UN peacekeeping operation. The government in the DRC responded to UN criticism of human rights abuses by Congolese military and police forces by calling for an accelerated downsizing of the UN peacekeeping force in that country. Syria, compelled to accept a UN military observation operation to observe a short-lived ceasefire during 2012, imposed restrictions on the communications equipment of unarmed observers and, as evidence of massacres were exposed, restricted the access of UN peacekeepers to many parts of the country, ostensibly on grounds of safety concerns.

Clearly, the acceptance by warring parties of a peacekeeping presence is often lukewarm, seen as distracting either party from pursuing victory, or giving perceived enemies cover to regroup and rearm. Mandates to transform the political and security institutions of the state – constitutional reviews, security sector reform, and overhauling of the justice system – are all processes that can profoundly alter the structure and distribution of power in a state. It is hardly surprising that parties to a conflict, including state authorities in the face of insurgent opposition, should perceive themselves threatened by such activities. The inherent assumption of peacekeeping has been that such opposition lacks the means or the legitimacy to oppose the will of the international community. Sudan, and more recently Syria, have provided stark demonstrations of the capacity of relatively capable states to resist the implementation of mandated tasks by international peacekeepers and to exploit limited international consensus to their own ends. As the representativeness and the authority of the Security Council are called into question, its ability to impose force – much less a proactive agenda for change on a country – is increasingly limited. In turn, the authority and ability of peacekeepers on the ground to deter, enforce, or implement is weakened. What begins as an externally driven process often becomes an internal exercise as peacekeepers, without sustained Security Council consensus or attention, try to coax and cajole consent on the ground.

Even where national authorities initially welcome the presence of peacekeepers, experiences in Kosovo, Haiti, the DRC, Liberia, or Sierra Leone point to the inherent time limitations of international interventions. The legitimacy of international peacekeepers, UN and regional, has been undermined by shameful actions such as sexual exploitation and abuse, illegal exploitation of natural resources, corruption and mistreatment of nationals, including, more recently in Haiti, the introduction of cholera by UN forces in that country. Ineptitude or failure to deliver on expectations further weakens popular support for the presence of peacekeepers. Development debates on whether international assistance supports or undermines national capacity have extended to peacekeeping, and with it an increasing emphasis on working in support of national priorities and capacity development, sometimes uneasily alongside human rights mandates, as in the DRC, or in the absence of political will among national elites for reform, for example in Haiti.

In recent years, more attention from the United Nations has been given to how to maintain support for peacekeepers within the countries in which they are deployed for the duration of the mission. "Heart and minds" funding (quick-impact projects) are now included in UN peacekeeping budgets, despite criticisms that such limited assistance is not sustainable or always well designed. Some efforts have been made to assess the views of the wider population, including through engagement with local, social, and religious authorities and through public outreach and polling (e.g. Krasno, 2005, 2006). These efforts remain limited, however, with little attention or resources devoted to looking at how international peacekeepers might use social media, mobile phone technology, or other tools to engage local communities in sustained and responsive dialogue.

Engaging beyond government elites is not without risk as national authorities draw on arguments of sovereignty to assert their claim to non-intrusion, supported in many cases, by members of the Security Council. Outreach also has to be balanced with consideration of the potential risks involved for citizens in engaging with peacekeepers in countries such as Syria and Sudan. Ironically, debates over the extent to which international peacekeepers can and should engage local populations have been somewhat muted recently because many of the states who are most assertive of their sovereign rights, including in the Arab world as well as China, have seen their own populations demand political, socio-economic, and human rights reforms.

Protection of Civilians

The reassertion of the importance of the state and the role of peacekeepers in supporting its authority and functioning is balanced, often awkwardly, with the parallel mandate to protect civilians in conflict (see Chapter 12 by Sewall). Once controversial, the protection of civilians as a norm of international, particularly UN, peacekeeping has become more widely accepted. Discussion increasingly centers on implementation, including the required guidance and training for civilian, military, and police peacekeepers to implement protection mandates; how peacekeepers work with humanitarian and development actors to deliver more comprehensive protection; and how peacekeepers can support host governments in strengthening national protection mechanisms.

Protection of civilians as a peacekeeping task is more controversial within the international humanitarian community. Many humanitarian agencies have well-founded concerns that the presence of armed peacekeepers may undermine the security of citizens either by their own behavior or by the potential of rebel groups using force against peacekeepers and thus contributing to an overall surge in violence. Somalia is frequently cited as a case in point. Others argue that the state-centric bias of peacekeeping mandates orients missions toward national authorities and to support those that may be responsible for some of the most serious threats to civilian security and safety. UN peacekeeping assistance to the armed forces of the DRC is the most infamous example of this. Engaging with political or military peace operations, for many humanitarians, risks the impartiality on which the delivery of life-saving humanitarian support depends. One consequence of this has been the increased reluctance of humanitarian agencies to work closely with UN or African peacekeeping operations, calling into question the feasibility of peacekeepers implementing a comprehensive protection agenda (see Chapter 12 by Sewall).

Perhaps the greatest challenge is the lack of uniform application of the principle of protection. That the Security Council authorized NATO air attacks on Libya in 2011 but remains paralyzed in the face of protracted civil war in Syria is the most powerful illustration of the tensions that can occur when human security-centered norms confront the realities of international politics and national interests. While Russian and Chinese veto of robust action has been seen as the main obstacle to a peace enforcement operation, Western countries have also been reluctant to countenance external intervention in light of regional complexities, as well as the cost of establishing and consolidating peace. The humanitarian corridors and "safe areas" that failed to protect civilians during the Balkan wars, and which hang over current debates on Syria, demonstrate the limitations of protection when it is not accompanied by significant political and military engagement.

Peacekeepers as Peacebuilders

The transformations underway in some African and Middle East countries have reinforced the focus on the role of peacekeeping in building national institutions and capacities, in support of national-led processes and as part of a long-term reform effort. Previously taboo areas, such as defense sector reform, women's empowerment, or decentralization processes, are now addressed by peacekeepers. Key developing nations that had once opposed such support on grounds of intrusiveness are now proponents for an activist peacekeeping agenda in those areas that they perceive to be critical for peace. Brazil and South Africa, for example, have called for peacekeepers to become more engaged in supporting economic recovery, including through job-creation initiatives. While opposing the perceived "Western" bias toward a human rights and rule of law agenda, countries such as India and Egypt routinely provide police and judicial personnel to UN peacekeeping. In some cases, it is Western nations, initially the drivers of a comprehensive peacebuilding agenda, that now oppose further expansion of the peacekeeping agenda on grounds of cost, as well as the technical capacity required to support large-scale transformation.

Certainly, the peacebuilding agenda has called into question the feasibility of peacekeeping operations assisting the design and reform of core state functions and capacity (Sambanis, 2008). Drawn from diverse states, peacekeepers have no common standards and limited technical knowledge of the issues, much less the politics and conditions of the country in which they are deployed. Peacekeeping budgets rarely include funding for capacity building programmes. What peacekeeping operations can do is to help create a secure and enabling environment for peacebuilding and to initiate some early steps that lay the ground for reform (United Nations DPKO/DFS, 2009). In this vision, international peacekeeping is a partner to sustained development assistance, but international aid operates under different governance and financial mechanisms, driven primarily by bilateral priorities and not beholden to Security Council directives. The gap between international peacekeeping and development interventions is most striking in the context of African regional peacekeeping where significant international aid rarely accompanies AU or ECOWAS military intervention. Even when enormous amounts of development assistance have been deployed to bolster peacebuilding processes, as in the Balkans, Iraq, or Afghanistan, the effectiveness of aid in supporting national institution reform and building has been questioned (see Chapter 15 by Bojicic-Dzelilovic, Kostovicova, and Rampton; Paris, 2004; Berdal and Suhrke, 2012).

Capabilities

If the scope of peacekeeping has become less controversial, the same cannot be said for the capabilities and resources required to implement wide-ranging mandates. The developing countries that contribute the bulk of international peacekeepers rarely come equipped with the material and resources to undertake expanded peacekeeping tasks in often difficult environments. Although a sustained effort has been made to improve peacekeeping training and standards within the United Nations and the African Union, enabling capabilities such as aircraft, armored vehicles, surveillance, and communications equipment remain in short supply (United Nations DPKO/DFS, 2009; United Nations, 2012). The United Nations has sought to facilitate partnerships between countries willing to assist troop contributors in building national capabilities, but this has been largely *ad hoc* and difficult to expand. Repeated calls by the United Nations for enabling capabilities, such as helicopters, have fallen short of demand and have been the source of some of the most significant tensions between those countries that authorize peacekeeping and those that implement it. In contexts where individual, coalition, or EU military action by Western countries has been employed under Security Council authorization, as in Libya, or at the request of a state, as currently in Mali, those military capabilities and assets have not been placed at the disposal of UN or AU command.

Significant capability gaps also exist for police and civilian peacekeepers where the United Nations, African Union, and the European Union all continue to encounter difficulty in recruiting specialized personnel. This is despite a decade of policy development in the wake of the Brahimi Report's call for a holistic approach to the rule of law and attempts by the European Union to develop civilian "packages" for crisis management operations. Countries such as the United States, United Kingdom, and Germany, whose own difficulties in deploying civilian expertise to Iraq and Afghanistan led to the creation of national rosters for civilian deployments, have been reluctant to make available these nascent capabilities to peacekeeping. Moreover, against the backdrop of planned withdrawal from Afghanistan, Western countries are cutting back on financing for internationally deployable civilian expertise. While many emerging countries have become more interested in providing civilian capacity and argue that their domestic experiences have more relevance for countries emerging from conflict, most of these potential providers lack the scale and financing to meet current demand.

Partnerships

There is no established division of labor between peacekeeping entities. The way in which UN, African, EU, and *ad hoc* coalitions peacekeeping interventions are designed and implemented varies in each context. To some extent, this is to be welcomed because it reflects the interests of states and the particular political context into which peacekeepers are deployed. NATO and EU operations dominate in the Balkans, AU missions focus on Africa, and coalitions of states maintain observation missions along Israel's borders. Nevertheless, this entails additional costs and duplications because no single intergovernmental organization prioritizes specific peacekeeping activities on which it can direct resources. Thus, NATO has developed a comprehensive approach to crisis management operations, including the development of civilian capabilities. The European Union has a similarly comprehensive approach, but has yet to deploy a multidimensional operation. The African Union and African sub-regional entities have modeled capability development on UN multidimensional peace operations, even as the United Nations struggles to find the resources required for such operations. The United Nations maintains – as the primary global actor and as the institution of last resort for international peacekeeping – that continued access to the full spectrum of peacekeeping resources and capabilities is essential. Regional organizations, while highlighting their comparative knowledge, have not sought to develop region-specific approaches to peacekeeping. For good or for bad, UN peacekeeping remains the knowledge leader in international peacekeeping and the basis on which regional initiatives build. To date, it is the only entity to integrate humanitarian, development, and human rights dimensions into peace operations.

The lack of standing arrangements complicates the implementation of parallel operations. Each experience of cooperation is *sui generis* for which case-specific coordination arrangements are constructed (Yamashita, 2012). The most intensive peacekeeping partnership, that between the United Nations and the African Union, has seen joint peacekeeping and mediation operations in Darfur, UN planning and logistical support for AU operations in Somalia and Mali, and collaboration in addressing cross-border threats posed by The Lord's Resistance Army. The United Nations is inextricably committed to the success of AU peacekeeping; yet the United Nations often fails to treat the African Union as an equal partner in all aspects of mission planning and implementation. For its part, the African Union claims its comparative advantage over continental peace and security, and mandates activities, sometimes on the basis of little feasibility assessment, for which it subsequently calls on UN support. This tension is particularly acute for the financing of peacekeeping operations, with the African Union calling on the United Nations to fund Security Council-mandated AU operations in Somalia and in Mali. From the perspective of some African countries, the Security Council appears a partial partner, demanding degrees of oversight and control over AU operations that it does not require of other entities over which it has little financial leverage (Williams, 2012). The more African peacekeeping is forced to seek alternative means of financing, the less likely African states will accept the authority and guidance of the body charged with the maintenance of international peace and security.

The multiplication of actors is potentially a significant advantage for the effective conduct of peacekeeping. It can enable context-relevant and case-specific interventions and, possibly, facilitate greater burden-sharing of peacekeeping risk and costs. For partnerships to be operationally effective, however, three changes are required. First, regional organizations must be willing to respect the authority of the Security Council and to uphold the principles of cooperation set out in the UN Charter, Chapter VIII (United Nations, 1945). Second, the Security Council must be willing to establish and consistently apply equitable cooperation arrangements with regional organizations. Third, Member States must be willing to address issues of task and cost-sharing between the United Nations and regional peacekeeping, including financing for those operations where wealthier countries are not willing to contribute personnel. Without these conditions, the potential for friction over limited peacekeeping resources is high.

Rethinking International Peacekeeping?

Questions about the scope, management, representativeness, and impact of international peacekeeping were more easily avoided when financial means for large-scale, multiple peace interventions existed. The current global recession may force fundamental re-evaluation of how peacekeeping is employed and for what ends. That may not be a bad thing insomuch as it may lead peacekeeping organizations to think more carefully about what peacekeeping can and cannot do, and to design mandates that are credible and achievable. It may encourage consideration of greater efficiencies, including how resources can be more effectively used, how states can collaborate on training and equipment, and how inter-mission and inter-organizational cooperation can be best pursued. It may encourage more sustained attention on peacekeeping operations to better track and assess progress and gaps. Fiscal constraints risk, however, exposing the ambiguities and the divisions between the international community in addressing difficult questions, such as the priority conflicts for peacekeeping attention, the scope of international resources to be directed at a conflict, and how UN, regional, and multilateral peacekeeping interventions are managed. Navigating these issues will require leadership and coherence for which the present divisions in the Security Council, and its perceived authority and representativeness, raise serious questions.

Smaller, Shorter, Sharper

The era when large multidimensional peacekeeping operations were the rule may be over. The fiscal crisis has already impacted UN peacekeeping with across-the-board budget costs for existing missions and for UN headquarters. Regional organizations face similar financial difficulties. While peacekeeping has not been hit as hard as voluntarily funded development and humanitarian activities, the anticipated decline in funding will have a major impact on what peacekeeping activities are undertaken and how. Current planning for a UN peace operation in Somalia is illustrative of the more limited scale of ambition. A UN mission in Somalia will deploy in parallel to the AU mission and will likely be civilian in nature, focused on supporting institution and capacity building in a limited set of areas. In Mali, despite recognition that weak institutions and poor governance have played a large role behind Tuareg rebels' calls for independence, the surge of Islamic extremists from Libya, Algeria, Nigeria and elsewhere into the north of the country, and the collapse of state institutions, there is little appetite within the international community to comprehensively tackle these issues (Gowan, 2013).

Limited military interventions, such as NATO air strikes in Libya or the French intervention in Mali, are likely to be the preferred response by countries with military capabilities to violently overthrow government or carry out large-scale attacks against civilians. Decisions to intervene will be taken on the grounds of national interest and will be partial and potentially contentious, as in the case of Libya. The threat on which there is likely to be most consensus and the dominant motivating factor behind Western military engagement today, is the threat of terrorism, primarily from Islamic extremist groups. This unity of view has enabled the international community to rally behind an undemocratic coup regime in Mali and to support discredited Malian forces. The focus of international peacekeeping in the next few years is likely to be on conflicts where such groups are parties to a conflict, namely the Sahel, Somalia, and potentially Syria. Whether international peacekeeping is suited to counterinsurgency warfare, or has the means and sustainment to defeat extremist groups bears careful consideration. The lessons from Afghanistan are not encouraging.

One consequence of the rise of extremist rebel actors has been greater attention to issues of justice and rule of law in conflict-affected states. Weak and partial rule of law is seen to be both a source of grievance as well as an opportunity for the rise of Islamic extremists to fund their activities, including through drug trafficking and co-opting corrupt officials (Cockayne, 2011). The trend toward the provision of specialist technical assistance in policing and justice reform is likely to continue and to address issues such as border security and organized crime, particularly in those countries that are transit routes for drugs. This could see "light" missions that resemble much more of a technical assistance programme than a peacekeeping operation, as is already the case with the European Union. To meet their stated objectives, however, these peacekeeping operations depend on the will of the host government for reform and a degree of stability to enable focus and capabilities to be devoted to reform. They depend on the ability of the international community to supply the expertise required – much of which is in high demand already at home – and for a sustained period. They depend on peacekeeping staff to have the experience and skill sets to design and manage technical assistance programmes and provide effective mentoring and institutional capacity building assistance. Above all, specialist peace-keeping interventions must be able to ground technical rule of law reforms in the political and economic context of the country concerned and to understand the task to be as political as it is technical. Evidence to date from UN and EU police and rule of law operations suggest these criteria are not easily met. For this reason, as current debates on Mali illustrate, the need for longer term, more comprehensive peacekeep-ing will remain, with the United Nations as the primary vehicle, for reasons of cost as much as political legitimacy.

Demonstrating Impact

Fiscal constraint is accelerating interest in measuring the impact of peacekeeping in meeting its mandated goals and tasks. There is a now significant body of databased research that points to the positive impact of the deployment of peacekeepers on maintaining fragile peace settlements and preventing relapse into conflict (Collier, 2007; Fortna, 2003). At the same time, this research has questioned the ability of peacekeeping interventions to implement peacebuilding mandates to support social and economic recovery or democratic transformation (Fortna, 2008; Sambanis, 2008). Although these findings echo the doctrinal position of the UN Secretariat, in times of recession these arguments have taken on greater resonance. While no effort is yet underway to review how mandates are established by the Security Council or regional organizations, or what "credible and achievable" might mean in practice, there is now far greater scrutiny of implementation of peacekeeping. In the United Nations, the Security Council has called for a mission to establish clear benchmarks to monitor and evaluate progress. The Secretariat, in its turn, has called on Member States to consider periodic strategic reviews to enable missions to respond to fast-changing conditions on the ground and to better sequence tasks and activities over the lifetime of the mission (United Nations, 2012). Increased scrutiny of peacekeep-ing budgets is likely to put further pressure on the need for better adaptive capacity.

In many ways, this is promising because it may lead to improved accountability of peacekeepers and to more sustained political engagement among Member States. Fiscal constraints and more stringent progress reviews may also facilitate a more pri-oritized and focused approach to tasks and more sustained engagement with host country actors as to what should be addressed and how. Yet there is a risk that the lessons of the 1990s on premature peacekeeping departures are forgotten. Balancing the need to address root causes of conflict, but at the same time narrowing focus and resources on key priorities, will require the strengthening of peacekeepers' assess-ment and planning capacities as much as their ability to deliver on the areas that are identified as critical for peace.

A second concern for cost-driven mandates and impact measurement is the issue of impact on who may be more narrowly defined. For the past two decades, peace-keeping has navigated the complex balance between security of the state and secu-rity of the individual. The human-centered approach behind the assertion of human rights and the protection of civilians' agendas have been reflected in peacekeeping activities, as well as in the perceptions of local populations. This evolution is still nascent and peacekeepers have yet to fully grapple with the tensions and trade-offs between state and individual-based peacekeeping (see Glasius and Kaldor, 2006). If peacekeeping was more narrowly circumscribed, the potential for it to be redirected toward a more classical conception of security, rooted in the state and those that represent it, is real. Indeed, this is what many fragile states are calling for, as evidenced in debates around the "New Deal"[3] between donors and recipients of international aid and the increased assertiveness of many host states with regard to the peacekeepers' access to local populations and engagement with nongovernmental organizations.

Authority and Leadership

Peacekeeping began as a reflection of the threats to international peace and security that a divided international community could coalesce around. It remains so. Peacekeeping does not deploy to conflicts in those parts of the world where the permanent members of the Security Council cannot reach agreement that the situation is sufficiently threatening to collective interests but not so threatening that it challenges their individual interests. It does not engage comprehensively unless Member States are agreed on the scope of the problem or unless those most committed are able to convince others and take on a disproportionate share of the cost. The fact that peacekeeping has grown in number, as well as function, reflects a consensus that the tool serves the purpose of preventing conflict escalation and that it is a useful mechanism for burden-sharing among states.

The consensus on what constitutes a threat to international peace and security has expanded. There is greater agreement that civil conflicts threaten regional and international security. There is greater acknowledgement that states without the will or the capacity to provide a minimum degree of security and welfare for their populations constitutes a collective problem. And there is acceptance of the rights of human beings to security and to equality of opportunity. The evolution of international peacekeeping since 1948 reflects these expanding norms.

Managing the uniform application of these norms through a consensus-led instrument is perhaps the greatest strategic challenge for international peacekeeping today. The emergence of powerful states challenges the authority of a body that may no longer reflect international power to determine and direct collective action. While states such as India, Brazil, or South Africa seek to play a greater role in global governance structures, their claim to greater decision-making in international peacekeeping is particularly powerful. They provide the majority of the military and police personnel, the operations that are deployed are often in or close to their countries or spheres of concern, and they believe, with some justification, that their transition and development experiences provide perspectives and skills relevant to countries emerging from conflict. How these states can be given a greater role in the management of international peacekeeping will be a critical issue for the future of the tool.

It is not only emergent global powers that seek a voice in the design and application of peacekeeping. Participation has been a means for many smaller and newly established states to assert their international or regional credentials and capabilities. It is a way of claiming a stake in international peace and security challenges and gaining some access into processes from which they may be otherwise excluded. For poorer countries, participation in UN peacekeeping even pays monetarily, as well as through the experience gained in service overseas.

The extent to which international peacekeeping can incorporate the aspirations, as well as the concerns of a wider number of states, will determine its future. This will not be easy because a wider set of stakeholders will make deciding the when, what, and how of each peacekeeping intervention even more challenging. There is no indication, so far, that the Security Council is prepared to seriously address this challenge. The complex conflicts that now confront it in Syria, Sahel, and elsewhere, and global fiscal constraints may make it increasingly more difficult to evade.

Notes

1. Authorized by the Security Council or, in cases of lack of Security Council unanimity, the UN General Assembly under Resolution 377 (1950) "Uniting for Peace". This definition excludes multilateral military interventions, such as the US-led operations in Afghanistan in 2001 and in Iraq in 2003, or non-authorized regional operations, such as the 1999 NATO air campaign on Kosovo, even though some of these operations were subsequently recognized by UN Resolutions. It also excludes fact-finding, good offices, and electoral assistance operations authorized by the Security Council, e.g. the UN Office in West Africa.
2. Chapter VI of the Charter refers to the specific settlement of disputes, while Chapter VII addresses actions with respect to threats to the peace, breaches of the peace, and acts of aggression, including the provision of Member States' armed forces and facilities, upon request of the Security Council, for the purpose of maintaining international peace and security.
3. For more on the New Deal, see http://www.newdeal4peace.org/about-the-new-deal/ (accessed January 29, 2013)

References

Berdal, M., and Suhrke, A., eds. 2012. *The Peace in-between: Post-War Violence and Peace-building*. London: Routledge.

Center on International Cooperation (CIC). 2012. *Annual Review of Global Peace Operations*. Boulder, CO: Lynne Rienner.

Chivvis, C. 2010. *EU Civilian Crisis Management: The Record So Far*. RAND.

Cockayne, J. 2011. *State Fragility, Organized Crime and Peacebuilding*. NOREF Working Paper. Oslo: NOREF.

Collier, P. 2007. *The Bottom Billion: Why the Poorest Countries are Failing and What Can Be Done About it*. Oxford: Oxford University Press.

Dallaire, R. 2003. *Shake Hands with the Devil: The Failure of Humanity in Rwanda*. New York, NY: Carroll & Graf.

Dwan, R., ed. 2003. *Executive Policing: Enforcing the Law in Peace Operations*. Oxford: Oxford University Press.

Fortna, V.P. 2003. "Inside and out: peacekeeping and the duration of peace after civil and interstate wars." *International Studies Review*, 5(4): 97–114.

Fortna, V.P. 2008. *Does Peacekeeping Work? Shaping Belligerents" Choices After Civil War*. Princeton NJ: Princeton University Press.

Fortna, V.P, and L.M. Howard. 2008. "Pitfalls and prospects in the peacekeeping literature." *Annual Review of Political Science*, 11: 283–301.

Glasius, M, and M. Kaldor, eds. 2006. *A Human Security Doctrine for Europe: Projects, Principles & Practicalities*. London: Routledge.

Gowan, R. 2013. "Diplomatic fallout: Is Mali Africa's war now?" *World Politics Review*, January 21, 2013. Accessed January 30, 2013 from http://www.worldpoliticsreview.com/articles/12640/diplomatic-fallout-is-mali-africa-s-war-now

Jett, D.C. 1999. *Why Peacekeeping Fails*. New York, NY: St Martin's.

Krasno, J. 2005. *Public Opinion Survey of UNAMSIL's Work in Sierra Leone. DPKO Peacekeeping Best Practices Section*. Accessed February 9, 2013 from http://pbpu.unlb.org/pbps/Library/UNAMSIL-Public%20Opinion%20Survey%20Full%20Report%20(19%20July%202005).pdf

Krasno, J. 2006. *Public Opinion Survey of UNMIL's Work in Liberia. DPKO Peacekeeping Best Practices Section*. Accessed February 9, 2013 from http://www.peacekeepingbestpractices.unlb.org/PBPS/Library/Liberia_POS_final_report_Mar_29.pdf

Luttwak, E.N. 1999. "Give war a chance." *Foreign Affairs*, 78(4): 36–44.

Mazower, M. 2009. *No Enchanted Palace: The End of Empire and the Ideological Origins of the United Nations*. Princeton, NJ: Princeton University Press.

Olonisakin, F. 2000. *Reinventing Peacekeeping in Africa: Conceptual and Legal Issues in ECOMOG Operations*. London: Brill.

Paris, R. 2004. *At War's End: Building Peace after Civil Conflict*. New York, NY: Cambridge University Press.

Pouligny, B. 2006. *Peace Operations Seen From Below: UN Missions and Local People*. Bloomfield, CT: Kumarian.

Pugh, M. 2004. "Peacekeeping and critical theory." *International Peacekeeping*, 11(1): 39–58.

Sambanis, N. 2008. "Short and long-term efforts of United Nations Peace Operations." *World Bank Econ Review*, 22(1): 9–32.

Stedman, S.J., D. Rothchild, E.M. Cousens, eds. 2002. *Ending Civil Wars: The Implementation of Peace Agreements*. Boulder, CO: Lynne Rienner.

Tardy, T., ed. 2009. *European Security in a Global Context: Internal and External Dynamics*. London: Routledge.

United Nations. 1945. *Charter of the United Nations*. Accessed January 21, 2013 from http://www.un.org/en/documents/charter/chapter8.shtml

United Nations. 1992. *An Agenda for peace. Preventive diplomacy, peacemaking and peacekeeping*. A/47/277-S/24111, 17 June 1992.

United Nations. 1999a. *Report of the Independent Inquiry on the Actions of the United Nations During the 1994 Genocide in Rwanda*. Accessed January 28, 2013 from http://www.un.org/News/dh/latest/rwanda.htm

United Nations. 1999b. *Report of the Secretary-General pursuant to General Assembly Resolution 53/35, The Fall of Srebrenica*. A/54/549, November 15, 1999.

United Nations. 2000. *Report of the Panel on United Nations Peace Operations*. A/55/305-S/2000/809, August 21, 2000.

United Nations. 2008. *United Nations Peacekeeping Operations: Principles and Guidelines*. Accessed February 8, 2013 from http://pbpu.unlb.org/pbps/Library/Capstone_Doctrine_ENG.pdf

United Nations. 2012. *Report of the Secretary-General on implementation of the recommendations of the Special Committee on Peacekeeping Operations*. A/67/632.

United Nations DPKO/DFS. 2009. *A New Partnership Agenda: Charting a New Horizon for UN Peacekeeping*. Accessed February 8, 2013 from http://www.un.org/en/peacekeeping/documents/newhorizon.pdf

Urquhart, B. 1972. *Hammarskjöld: A Life in Peace and War*. New York, NY: WW Norton & Co.

Williams, P. 2012. "Towards more effective partnership peacekeeping in Africa." *SSRC online forum*. Accessed February 10, 2013 from http://forums.ssrc.org/kujenga-amani/2012/11/19/towards-more-effective-partnership-peacekeeping-in-africa/

Yamashita, H. 2012. "Peacekeeping cooperation between the UN and regional organizations." *Cambridge Review of International Studies*, 38(1): 165–186.

Chapter 15

State-Building, Nation-Building, and Reconstruction

Vesna Bojicic-Dzelilovic, Denisa Kostovicova, and David Rampton

Introduction

The end of the Cold War has ushered in a new kind of engagement between external actors and volatile post-conflict states. Foreign states, multilateral institutions (such as the United Nations, European Union, NATO, and Organization for Security and Co-operation in Europe), and international nongovernmental organizations (such as Red Cross, Yellow Crescent, and Médicines Sans Frontièrs) have taken on the rebuilding of states, societies, and economies in the aftermath of war. The involvement of a multitude of external actors in comprehensive governance (Caplan, 2005a, pp. 16–44) in foreign states has evolved alongside a reconceptualization of post-Cold War threats whereby weak and failed states have emerged as a primary security concern. The understanding of state weakness and fragility as a security threat represents a shift away from great power security competition where threat was judged as commensurate with the strength of the state (cf. Fearon and Laitin, 2004; Rotberg, 2007). Within this post-Cold War framework, conflict-affected space, understood as a distant "zone of chaos", could no longer be isolated or ignored due to the intensification of globalization (Cooper, 2004). Increasingly, local governance failures have come to be perceived as sources of transnational insecurity, illustrated by criminal activity, terrorism, and mass refugee and migration flows. Tracing insecurity to the state function has, at the same time, shifted the political and policy spotlight on intensified intervention in the aftermath of conflict, justified explicitly by the conflict legacy. Wars fought in a global context have been characterized by the coalescence of a multitude of state and non-state actors, military as well as civilian, legal and criminal, in the war enterprise. Their legacy is the criminalization of both state and society, often combined with instrumental use of ethnic and sectarian identities to political ends (Kostovicova and Bojicic-Dzelilovic, 2009).

The Handbook of Global Security Policy, First Edition. Edited by Mary Kaldor and Iavor Rangelov.
© 2014 John Wiley & Sons, Ltd. Published 2014 by John Wiley & Sons, Ltd.

Nearly two decades of external involvement in rebuilding local political authority in foreign environments has kept the recurrence of violence at bay, as for example in Bosnia and Herzegovina. However, despite the changing scope and nature of external involvement, the goal of building sustainable and legitimate states remains largely elusive. Demonstrations of local resistance to external actors and their local projects, epitomized in the Taliban resurgence in Afghanistan, point to a crisis in both practice and theory. The international intervention in Libya suggests that a military intervention may not necessarily be followed by a comprehensive post-conflict engagement, as in Kosovo. And a critique of liberal peace – until recently a dominant framework for theorizing external intervention – has given rise to alternative understandings of the rationale for and the nature of international engagement.

This chapter, rather than focusing on the role of international actors in ending violence, concentrates instead on the challenges inherent in the post-conflict reconstruction of domestic political authority by external actors. It first defines three approaches that have guided the involvement of external actors: state-building, nation-building, and post-war reconstruction. The analysis then turns first to the liberal peace framework and second to the critique of the neocolonial dynamics implicit in state-building. The subsequent review of dilemmas and contradictions inherent in the external project of comprehensive reconstruction of post-conflict states and societies focuses on the norms of sovereignty, legitimacy, accountability, and ownership that are central to state formation and yet problematic within current mainstream frameworks of international state-building. This section is followed by a discussion of alternative theoretical perspectives. The chapter concludes with a reflection on policy implications.

Definitions

At the end of the 1990s and the beginning of the 2000s, state-building became the centerpiece of international peacebuilding guided by the liberal peace idea that predicates stable peace on the existence of functioning and effective political and economic institutions. Following the logic that the absence and/or weakness of liberal institutions is the main cause of underdevelopment and insecurity driving armed conflicts in the global era, mainstream scholarship has defined state-building as "the creation of new governmental institutions and the strengthening of existing ones" (Fukuyama, 2004, p. 17; Paris and Sisk, 2009, p. 8; Ottaway, 2002, p. 1004). In this narrow institutional understanding of state-building, the onus on external actors is to assist in putting in place institutional architecture across a broad spectrum encompassing representative democracy (e.g. elections, constitution, media, judiciary, rule of law), and a private market-based economy (e.g. private property, fiscal and monetary institutions, open competition rules). This task is primarily concerned with propping up institutional capacity in order to supply adequate human, material, and other resources to improve the functionality of key institutions, which are undermined by the combined legacies of conflict and *ancien régime* underdevelopment (Fukuyama, 2004, p. 30). Conceiving of institution building as a technical process of improvement in bureaucratic capacity, the relevant scholarly debates have emphasized a diverse set of priorities, including the scale of required resources and the sequencing and pace of reforms (Ball, 2001; Paris, 2004; Wolff, 2011). Paradoxically, the institutionalist state-building framework, which dominated the state-building scholarship for much of the 2000s, conceived of this process as an apolitical process of capacity building and evolved against the backdrop of the (European) nation state-building paradigm and its preeminent concern with forging political community. Nation building, according to Fritz and Menocal (2007, p. 15), is "a process of constructing shared sense of identity and common destiny, usually in order to overcome ethnic, sectarian or communal differences and to counter alternative sources of identity and loyalty." Thus, it is embedded in a much larger process of the "shaping of economy, polity and society into a condition of possible sovereignty" (Wesley, 2008, p. 373). This broad agenda addressing every aspect of societal function has been the subject of voluminous scholarship on post-war reconstruction. In its minimalist expression, and echoing the original meaning of the concept at its inception in the aftermath of the Second World War (Barakat and Zyck, 2009), post-war reconstruction has been conceived of as "the restoration of the conditions of the assets and infrastructure [...] to the same or similar state in which they were found before the outbreak of hostilities" (Etzioni, 2007, p. 27). The broader definition of post-war reconstruction that gained ground in response to the empirical evidence of the scale of the task at hand, effectively conflates reconstruction and development, and redefines the goals of reconstruction, necessary for the attainment of stable peace as "reconstituting legitimacy, re-establishing security and rebuilding effectiveness" (Brinkerhoff, 2005, p. 3). These goals have been pursued through a number of differentially prioritized, context-dependent processes, which include, *inter alia*, the rehabilitation of physical infrastructure, the design of new political institutions, security sector reform, macroeconomic stabilization, social sector reform, reconciliation, and the psychosocial healing of traumatized populations. Over time, discourses on both state-building and post-war reconstruction have moved in the same direction, recognizing the limitations of the rebuilding of state institutions as separate from the process of nation-building (Allen, 2010, p. 414), especially in the context of politicized identity characteristics of many contemporary conflicts. The next section takes a more detailed look at the framings that govern both mainstream and alternative models and the impact that they have on peacebuilding outcomes.

(Post-)Liberal and Critical Framings

State-building, nation-building, and reconstruction represent overlapping and connected modalities in the international toolkit for the transformation of post-conflict states and societies where a combination of issues including governance, statehood, and political community are seen to be reproductive of conflict. They thus continue to threaten regional and global order, extending insecurity that derives from violence within "emerging political complexes" (Duffield, 2001, p. 163). This contemporary and normatively dominant interventionist international framework has been variously described as the liberal and/or post-liberal peace model. Although, this model itself produces both a powerful seam of critique (e.g. Chandler, 2010; Cooper, 2007; Cooper, Turner, and Pugh, 2011) as well as qualified defenders (e.g. Paris, 2002, 2010), there is a general consensus differentiating contemporary international state-building as a conscious and intentional project from both historical and contemporary state-formation processes, through which Western states emerged and which

non-Western states experience but in a manner that is constrained by the very processes of state-building and development that continue to be enmeshed in Western-led
international structures of power (Bliesmann de Guevara, 2010, p. 113). As a result,
some critics have contrasted what they consider to be a "classical liberal" from "post-
liberal" framework of statehood, with the former referring to forms of autonomy and
self-determination that characterized the development of Western states and at least
initially the principles of post-Second World War sovereignty, sovereign equality, and
liberal democratic government, whilst the latter refers to the reproduction of shell-
like states that require permanent management of "governance" through external
diplomatic, developmental, and humanitarian engagement (Chandler, 2010).

This (post-)liberal peace framework operates through a particular understanding
of the correct relationship between state, society, and people and the kind of institutions that are conducive to peaceful and harmonious existence and therefore to development. Key to this framing is that a stable society cannot emerge without good governance, human rights, effective rule of law, a marketized economy, and democratic
institutions (Richmond, 2006). According to this logic, these institutions and apparatuses will in turn act as a check upon predatory and authoritarian rule, clientelism
and corruption, whilst also providing for social integration (at local, national, and
global levels) through the socio-economic interdependence created by markets. Key
to the liberal peace framework has been this core triangulation of markets, democracy, and governance as a way of developmentally resolving the dynamics of conflict
and the role of poverty and underdevelopment in the reproduction of cycles of war
and violence (Duffield, 2007).

Just as state-building is dependent on key institutions and concepts that constitute
the Western experience of liberal democracy, liberal frameworks of nation-building
ostensibly privilege the construction and consolidation of inclusive civic-secular and
cosmopolitan frameworks of identity that have been the outcome of the Western
liberal parceling out of politics, socio-economic and cultural activity, human life
and conduct into the spheres of the public and the private, and of civil society and
state. Indeed, civil society remains a key liberal concept and policy tool in both state-
building and nation-building practices precisely because it describes the way in which
society has become "civilized" through the carving out of a space for the independent
and autonomous association of interests that is potentially oppositional to both the
predatory and authoritarian tendencies of the state (Taylor, 1990), as well as the unre-
constructed forms of religious and/or ethnic identity that have impacted upon conflict
dynamics in both the West and non-West. Civil society, therefore, becomes a tool for
holding the state accountable through social contractual frameworks and, if necessary, for resisting forms of irresponsible state power and particularistic social forces.
These aforementioned aspects of civil society have led to its revival as a tool for
emancipation and social transformation at the end of the Cold War (Calhoun, 2007,
pp. 77–101). Nevertheless, this has led to a hierarchical tension within civil society,
as both concept and policy tool, between those civic-secular identities acceptable to
liberal order and "certain kinds of associational life", such as ethnic and religious
identity that must "be reworked or even eliminated" (Williams and Young, 2012,
p. 9; see also Kymlicka, 2005, pp. 22–55; Nadarajah and Rampton, 2012; Bojicic-
Dzelilovic, Kerr-Lindsay and Kostovicova, 2013). In this way, the nation-building
frameworks of liberal peace operate through a privileging of both civil society as a

check on state power and predation and a rationalized civic nationalism (or post-national belonging) as the correct and inclusive form of identification between state, people, and territory, which is, as far as possible, stripped of its affective, *gemein-schaftlich* or populist dimensions (e.g. see Habermas, 2001, pp. 74–76).

Although such frameworks form the core goals for liberal peace and this is borne out in the mainstream frameworks of liberal policies, it is in the shifting short-to-mid-term practices of post-conflict reconstruction that one is confronted by the compro-mises and negotiation that international liberal actors engage in as a way of navigat-ing the resistances to liberal peace frameworks they encounter in regional, national and local contexts. Such reconstruction processes have been widely criticized for a tendency to seek accelerated results in everything from the misuse of "post-conflict" as a descriptive category for contexts undergoing ongoing insecurity, to the coun-terproductive reinforcing of conflict and therefore state-unbuilding, which ensues from processes of accelerated democratization and marketization against the institu-tional backgrounds that are missing the key building blocks supportive of democratic peace (e.g. Paris, 2004; see also Mansfield and Snyder, 2007). Indeed, in many ways, the term "post-conflict" has itself become so normalized that it is rarely questioned today despite the tendency for the term to be utilized in such a way that it masks ongoing conflict dynamics with all the attendant risks that this implies for popu-lations, including returning refugees and internally displaced people, who become the object of post-conflict development (for critiques of the "post-conflict" term, see Crisp, 2001, p. 16; Moore, 2000). Likewise, the notion of reconstruction, mis-leadingly suggesting a return to what was there in the first place, obscures the fact that the institutional foundations of the stable democratic peace are yet to be "con-structed" (Kaldor, 2009). Other scholars have also censured reconstruction processes in Afghanistan, Iraq, and Bosnia for the tendency to dilute democracy (Chandler, 2010), to introduce forms of paternalist proxy governance, or to compromise the liberal civic-secular framework through the ethnicization of peace and thereby of state and social structures (Hughes, 2011).

A number of different critical approaches, including classical liberal, realist, political economy, poststructuralist, and postcolonial perspectives, share a core critique of the (post-)liberal peace framework. These perspectives state that the (post-)liberal peace is neocolonial in a number of overlapping ways. First, because it represents a novel form of the old *mission civilisatrice* diffused by colonial powers in their encounters with societies in the Global East and South (Paris, 2002). Second, because it continues to reproduce subjugation and disqualification of forms of local existence, self-government, and community in the Global South through the imposi-tion of a Eurocentric, top–down, rationalist, territorialized, Westphalian framework and model of statehood and state-society relations (Richmond, 2011, pp. 8–9). Third, because it represents the dominance of Western states and their perception of the emergence of autonomous sovereign states in the Global South as a threat to liberal order. According to this understanding, international state-building seeks the perpetual external regulation and proxy governance of states that are subject to constant monitoring and the potential threat of intervention through justificatory discourses and categories that judge such societies and states as dysfunctional or as "failed states" (Chandler, 2010, pp. 4–6, 45; Woodward, 2009). Finally, it effects, according to political economy and post-structuralist approaches, a form of "global riot control" in capitalism's encounter with the unstable and conflict-affected "borderlands" of the Global South as it seeks a containment of forms of social life perceived as threatening to liberal order and existence (e.g. Dillon and Reid, 2009; Duffield, 2007; Pugh, 2004). These critiques, with the exception of Paris (2010), argue that liberal peace and the conflict dynamics it encounters on its periphery are doomed to a process of recurrence in so far as the liberal peace framework in its current form cannot produce anything other than instability and further conflict due to the social disruption, unraveling, and state-unbuilding that these interventions effect. In this way, liberalism is reproductive of its own nemesis, a facet of international state- and nation-building that is manifest in many of the tensions, contradictions, and paradoxes that haunt its engagement with conflict-affected spaces and which are ultimately seen to produce recurrent failures in the construction of a viable social contract.

Dilemmas and Contradictions

The aim of international interventions in post-conflict areas has been the establishment of a legitimate political authority, understood as a democratic, accountable, and self-sustained state. It is premised on a belief that a state's capability in dispensing its functions equitably, impartially, and effectively is a guarantor of peace and a precondition for the exit of external actors. However, a checkered record of state-building projects, from Bosnia-Herzegovina to East Timor, points to contradictions and dilemmas that beset external post-conflict interventions (Paris and Sisk, 2009; Call, 2008). The analysis of interaction between global and local processes and actors reveals a tension in the reconstruction of political authority by international actors, itself reflective of the tensions associated with global governance arrangements, such as the "democratic deficit" between policy makers and policy beneficiaries. These tensions are particularly pronounced in comprehensive reconstruction efforts because external actors assume direct control over a range of policies in local states while retaining only an indirect link to local constituencies. They are understood through concepts that originate in the nation-state context, and are used to describe and qualify the relationship between the ruler and the ruled. As an example of global policy, post-conflict reconstruction efforts involve multiple stakeholders both at a global and local level. Furthermore, these stakeholders look to and are beheld by disparate sources of authority. Consequently, the challenges faced by the international community in reconstructing post-conflict states and societies need to be understood in relation to multiple actors and multiple sources of authority in terms of both interveners and policy beneficiaries. The following section looks at sovereignty, legitimacy, accountability, and ownership as norms used to understand the policy of reconstructing local political authority and its challenges.

Sovereignty

The concept of sovereignty is critical to understanding the justification for external actors' intrusive role in domestic affairs of post-conflict states after the end of the Cold War. In state-reconstruction operations, external actors exercise power, to various degrees, on behalf of the local population. Regardless of the degree to which external actors control executive authority, comprehensive interventions in the governance of local states embody a seemingly contradictory principle of "compromising sovereignty to create sovereignty" (Woodward, 2001). The rule of external actors runs against the idea of sovereignty understood to flow from the will of the people. Thus conceived, the international community's intervention in local affairs may be considered to be imposed from above and inherently illegitimate. However, post-Cold War interventionism in reconstruction efforts has been accompanied by reformulation of the bases of international and domestic authority in a rapidly changing and increasingly interconnected world.

The involvement of international actors in domestic affairs of post-conflict states goes hand-in-hand with the reconceptualization of the norm of sovereignty after the end of the Cold War; it is seen as the implementation of positive sovereignty. The invocation of positive sovereignty has shifted attention to the responsibilities of states to protect their populations and their rights, providing justification for international authority and denial of self-determination (Zaum, 2007, pp. 37, 323). The states' responsibility toward their constituencies has been directly related to their capacity and effectiveness, so that state sovereignty has become "contingent" (Duffield, 2007, p. 28). Chandler argues that sovereignty is understood:

> not as a ban on intervention but rather as necessitating intervention. The fact that states, which are held to lack capacity – or to potentially lack adequate capacity – are making sovereign decisions is held to be a major threat both to their own citizens and to the security of the international society itself. (Chandler, 2010, p. 3)

Echoing Jackson and Rosberg (1982), Ghani and Lockhart (2008, pp. 3–4) point to the "sovereignty gap" between *de jure* sovereignty, which dysfunctional states enjoy in the international system, and the *de facto* capabilities of these states in serving their populations and contributing to international security. The state's claim to autonomy, based on its capabilities, has been measured universally against a Western model of reconstruction, and development measured in terms of liberal political development and economic growth (Suhrke, 2007, p. 1929), which has been a basis of the critique of external reconstruction as neocolonial. Within the liberal peace paradigm, local deviation from this model is not understood as evidence of ineffectiveness of the model itself. Rather, it has served as a justification for initiating and maintaining the intrusive intervention, yet without resolving the contradiction of "benign autocracy".

Legitimacy

For the external actors, reconstruction of the state, which is legitimate in the eyes of its citizens (Ball, 2001), is expected to produce dividends in terms of endorsement of their state-building project. Legitimacy rests on a "belief in a government's right to govern" (Barker, 1990, p. 27) and, based on this, acceptance of a given political order, manifested as active compliance with rules that underwrite the reproduction of that order. Students of legitimacy identify different forms of legitimation (Kaldor, 2009, pp. 184–188; Holsti, 1996, pp. 92–98; François and Sud, 2006). These correspond broadly to "input-oriented" legitimacy, reflecting the sense of cultural and political community, and "output-oriented" legitimacy derived from the capacity to solve problems and provide public goods (Scharpf, 1999). Since legitimacy is not reducible to any one of its forms (Barker, 1990, p. 23), this creates a particular challenge in the state-building context of multiple sources, sites, and actors involved in the legitimation process.

Internationalized state-building presents the "dual legitimacy" problem that maps onto the dichotomy between external and internal, or international and domestic legitimacy (Rubin, 2005; Bhatia, 2007, p. 94; Knoll, 2008, pp. 294–298). International legitimacy derives from the operations of external actors and their takeover of the prerogatives of a sovereign state. It is linked to the legal and normative bases of their deployment. By contrast, the domestic conception of legitimacy is informed by the perceptions of the beneficiaries of the external state-building. Several scholars of comprehensive reconstruction have explored the relationship between international and domestic legitimacy, pointing to their positive correlation (Rubin, 2005, p. 103; Morphet, 2002).

Critics contend that the very illegitimacy of the state-building enterprise, derived from the denial of sovereignty, means there cannot be a legitimate outcome for either external state-builders or the local state (Ignatieff, 2003; Knaus and Martin, 2003; Bain, 2003; Chandler, 2006; Wilde, 2008). As a form of internationalized governance, which is "a 'dual-key governance' setting" (Knoll, 2008, p. 289), including external and domestic actors, post-conflict state-building and reconstruction expose the limited applicability of classical state-centered models of legitimacy (Stahn, 2008, p. 531). Accordingly, scholars have explored how political constraints, innate in state-building by external actors, can be overcome or compensated – one example is the use of discourse and communication to overcome the lack of an "input" validation for extraneous agents.

The distinction between external and internal legitimacy provides insight into normative and structural complexity of legitimation of external interventions in the affairs of states. It also offers a narrow understanding of legitimacy of the local state conceived entirely as a by-product of the legitimacy of external actors and their actions. Such a perspective denies the local state the Weberian "entitlement claim" to legitimacy. The study of resistance to external liberally framed intervention in post-conflict states has directed attention to the agency of local actors. While such a reversal of the perspective explains why a Western state cannot be implanted in a "non-Western context" (Bliesemann de Guevara, 2010), it falls short of offering an alternative to the rational-institutional Weberian state as a desirable norm and as an ultimate source of legitimacy for domestic constituency. However, as Kaldor (2009, p. 193) points out, in a global era the notion of "legitimate political authority" may refer either to a state, a municipal or regional government, or even an international administration. According to her, key to forging a relationship on the basis of trust, which underpins legitimacy and ensures compliance with rules, is the cosmopolitan outlook that "respects both human equality and the different ways of being human".

Accountability

External state-building and reconstruction interventions are characterized by the absence of formal accountability provisions available to local populations (Chesterman, 2004, p. 151). This applies to interventions that encompass the exercise of authority by external actors on behalf of, and in the benefit of, local populations (e.g. in Kosovo where the United Nations Interim Administration Mission in Kosovo, or UNMIK, effectively acted as a government in the immediate post-NATO intervention period), as well as those with a "light footprint" (e.g. in post-2003 Liberia where formal executive authority remained with the Liberian authorities but did not constrain international intrusion in policy matters (cf. Andersen, 2010, pp. 129–135)). Not unlike considerations of legitimacy, accountability becomes a problem because of an indirect relationship between foreign governors and local constituencies, despite a direct impact of policies pursued by international actors. As Sperling (2009, pp. 8–17) points out, globalization has altered accountability relationships, which are traditionally conceived as a relation between "agents" (elected officials) and "principals" (voters). In the context of global governance, and what Borowiak (2011, p. 152) calls the "unwinding of sovereign accountability", questions have been raised as to whom representatives of international institutions should be politically and criminally accountable and how.

For international actors, upward political accountability has taken precedence over the downward accountability toward those affected by their actions. For example, transitional administrators, as implementers of comprehensive reconstruction efforts, have been accountable upwards to bodies that appoint them (Caplan, 2005b). Thus, in Bosnia-Herzegovina, the High Representative is responsible to the Peace Implementation Council (PIC), the *ad hoc* international body of 55 states and organizations that oversees international administration in Bosnia-Herzegovina, and to the UN Secretary-General. When it comes to criminal accountability, a security dimension of comprehensive post-reconstruction efforts has highlighted the "fragmentation of responsibility" (Kearney, Botzios, and Hadden, 2011, p. 225) implicit in the established principle that any enforcement or disciplinary action for international police and military personnel remains a matter for the authorities of their home countries, rather than for international missions in which they serve. Difficulties in conducting proceedings far away from the site of the incident also reduce the likelihood of conviction, which in turn undermines the legitimacy of security structures amongst the local population. An illustrative case in point is the lack of sanction for UNMIK officers who shot two protesters at a rally for a civil society movement Vetëvendosje! (Kearney, Botzios, and Hadden, 2011, pp. 226–229). Meanwhile, other avenues, such as local and global civil society and media, or an office of an ombudsman, have been relied on to expose transgressions. Nonetheless, these alternative channels have remained only a substitute for formal accountability mechanisms, without the establishment of responsibility, due process, and punitive measures, which should be key defining features of international policymakers' democratic accountability (Borowiak, 2011, pp. 3–21).

Furthermore, local power holders nominally remain accountable to their publics for policies under their control, but this has not necessarily increased their responsibility. A maze of relationships between external and domestic actors has incentivized each side to take credit for popular outcomes, while allocating blame for unpopular ones to the others (Andersen, 2010, p. 148). In sum, accountability – a pillar of democratic legitimation and a means to building local capacity – has also led to abrogation of responsibility and delegitimation of international efforts. In fragile, often divided post-conflict societies, a lack of accountability has fuelled nationalist reactions that have further obstructed reconstruction efforts.

Ownership

Local ownership is an ultimate aim of the reconstruction effort, given that it represents a rationale for the exit and disengagement of external actors. However, rather than being a part of a solution, the concept of ownership has itself become a point of controversy in both the theory and practice of external state reconstruction because there is no coherent answer to the question "who owns what?" (Donais, 2012, p. 139).

First and foremost, the contestation concerns the nature of involvement and participation on the part of local actors. Ownership is variably interpreted in terms of consultation and inclusion of local actors in the policy process or as power and control over policy that "means a power shift, which goes far beyond existing practices" (Reich, 2006, p. 15). Suhrke (2007, p. 1292) responds by arguing that, regardless of a power shift, "local ownership means 'their' ownership of 'our' ideas, rather than the other way round." Neither is there any greater clarity about who is or should be the local subject. On the one hand, the dilemma of a local "owner" concerns the levels of local governing structures, including national, regional and sub-regional, or municipal authorities. On the other, consideration of the local owners of policy processes is more difficult in a fragmented post-conflict environment, characterized by deep ethnic, political, and geographic cleavages impacting upon both state and non-state spheres (Donais, 2012, pp. 40–77; Scheye, 2008, pp. 63–64). An additional challenge is the informal exercise of power behind the façade of formal institutions, which can be more legitimate in the eyes of the local populations (Reno, 2008, p. 145). Therefore, to the extent that the purpose of external reconstruction is to build a capable and sustainable state, the dilemma of re-balancing authority in favor of the locals in external interventions also carries the risk of empowering the spoilers (cf. Narten, 2009, pp. 260–262).

At the same time, the local ownership debate reflects a contested normative understanding of external reconstruction – either as a liberal or neocolonial project. The discourse of local ownership is intended to underwrite the liberal assumption of contemporary interventions as distinct from great power colonialism (e.g. Paris, 2002, p. 652). Chesterman argues that attempts to frame the concept of ownership as a means rather than an end of external state-building are misleading, given that the lack of capacity for self-government was the original reason for the introduction of an intrusive intervention (2004, p. 144). Consequently, the ideal is that the contradiction found in the simultaneity of external rule and local ownership is to be resolved through a gradual transition in the course of intervention. The concept of ownership also informs a critique of external state reconstruction as a neocolonial enterprise. Thus, for Chandler (2006, pp. 11–18), the language of ownership, and the related concept of empowerment of "locals", plays a key role in understanding state-building as "empire in denial", that is a hierarchical type of rule characterized by coercion despite its appearance of being consensual. This denial of capacities for autonomy, according to Hughes and Pupavac (2005), is related to the pathologization of local populations whose portrayal as dysfunctional has served to legitimize intrusive international intervention that is ostensibly functional.

Originating in the development literature, appropriated in the peacebuilding theorizing, the concept of ownership is associated with enhancing the effectiveness of international intervention. At a minimum, this rationale assumes that a local voice will ensure the appropriateness, and hence sustainability, of reconstruction as well as increase the local stake in an externally led project (cf. Egnell, 2010, p. 476). Tainted by a combination of a lack of clarity of its meaning and the challenges of its implementation, the concept of ownership has been a contributing factor to deeply fraught relationships between external and local actors (Martin *et al.*, 2012). Local populations' calls for the exit of outsiders has, paradoxically, been justified by undelivered promises of transfer of power to local authorities rather than enhancing local capacity, which is seen as a guarantee of security (cf. Caplan, 2012, p. 315).

In sum, tensions in external state-building, as discussed through the prism of sovereignty, legitimacy, accountability, and ownership, have proved irresolvable from the liberal perspective. They have fuelled the divide between proponents and critics of liberal peace, often set in "zero-sum" terms, resulting in the present crisis of theories and practice of external state-building. In particular, liberal frameworks have been challenged by the complexity of governance in the global context, including the multiplicity of actors in the global political space and the plurality of spaces/scales of politics.

New Emerging Alternatives: Hybrid and Post-Liberal Peace, the "Local", the "Everyday", and Beyond

As a means of confronting the previously described paradoxes and tensions, and the tendency for the liberal peace to be confronted by resistance, crisis-ridden peace and state-building efforts and, therefore, freshly reproduced forms of conflict in the wake of intervention and/or engagement, a number of scholars have demanded a shift in the study and policy frameworks of "peacebuilding". Taking their cue from postcolonial scholarship on hybridity and ambivalence (e.g. Bhabha, 1994), studies of the quotidian and everyday (e.g. De Certeau, 1984; Le Febvre, 1992; Heller, 1985) and pluralist conceptions of peace, these scholars seek a way out of what they see as the top–down and domineering frameworks of hegemonic liberalism towards what they frequently term "post-liberal" or "hybrid peace". An alternative emerging peace framework, which is more empathetic and emancipatory because it flows in the opposite direction to "liberal peace" (from the communities most directly affected by conflict), is partly a "bottom–up" approach that also emphasizes the interface between local and indigenous actors and the international spheres of liberal peace.

Consequently, these approaches seek to challenge the commonplace assumption that peacebuilding knowledge and practice must be based around liberal frameworks, such as reconstruction pursued through a particular model or template of (the Westphalian) state and (civil) society. Instead, the study of and engagement with local spaces, and the practices and strategies of diverse populations, directly locate agency for peace in the way that communities deploy everyday coping strategies for protection; for intra- and inter-community engagement; and access to resources for peacebuilding and development at local levels, often in ways that ward off, subvert, resist, or adapt hegemonic state-building frameworks and practices (Mac Ginty, 2011, pp. 84–90). Typical examples that have been cited include forms of everyday local community protection in Northern Ireland – what Audra Mitchell has termed "threatworks" (2010, pp. 19–22) – or the way in which non-liberal actors produce alternatives to the civic frames of liberal peace frameworks, such as Hezbollah in Lebanon (Mac Ginty, 2011, p. 181).

These models therefore frequently stress the local and everyday as a space of indigeneity, authenticity, tradition, and "feeling" that are typified by religious, ethnic, caste, gender, and status identities, and communities that are either disqualified or marginalized by liberal frameworks (Mac Ginty, 2011; Richmond, 2011). This is contrasted with the aforementioned rationalized, Westphalian, territorial, and governmental architecture of international order. These spheres meet to construct hybrid interactions, which can lead to co-option of local identities and communities within the dominant frame of liberal peacebuilders (e.g. the Loya Jirga in Afghanistan is a classic example – see Mac Ginty, 2011, p. 62) but can also lead to resistance and subversion on the part of local communities as well as dissonance and antagonism in the course of their engagement. However, as the hybrid peace scholars assert, it also provides the potential for an alternative (and more self-aware) hybrid interaction between international and local actors and structures, which is more open and attentive to the harnessing of local and everyday agency and to peace as a plural field rather than a monopoly of liberal universal frameworks (Van Leeuwen, Verkoren, Boedeltjer, 2012). In this way disqualified practices and the hitherto hidden script of local peacebuilding can be utilized, not to displace the role of international actors but to produce a greater sensitivity to and mobilization of local peacebuilding practices.

Indeed, the hybridity framework has been used to try and revitalize the centrality of the social contract within international state-building. Rather than adopting the top–down frameworks of civil societal reconstruction, democratization, and marketization, some scholars have argued for a social contract built out of the interactions of hybrid peace itself (e.g. Richmond, 2011, p. 15; Roberts, 2011, pp. 8–10). In this framework, the "social contract", so elusive in the aforementioned liberal frameworks, is instead constituted by a direct engagement between international and local actors. According to this approach, the focus on international engagement at the local level facilitates the bypassing of a number of obstacles and problems present in the liberal peace paradigm. For some authors, this evidently includes the ability to bypass the state and national elites who currently dominate the international–local interface and who co-opt or disrupt the potential for a more bottom–up, organic and direct interface in the construction of an international-to-local social contract. Here, the construction of an international–local social contract would provide a responsive relationship between communities and structures of governance and development at the local level. For other authors adopting a more traditional linear perspective, this can potentially serve as a first phase in the construction of more responsive governance structures that can be integrated into broader, more stable, traditional state structures (Roberts, 2011, p. 15). Clearly implicit in the overall contractarian emphasis approach is a search for "authenticity" in the social sphere, given the tendency for liberal peace frameworks to construct "civil society" through a very Eurocentric lens and to build the state from the "outside".

Despite the novelty and the utility of the critique that the "hybrid peace" approach provides, there are a number of pressing problems with the framework. The first is that despite its frequent self-description as post-liberal, it is more often a problem-solving critique of the liberal peace, as the aforementioned social contract frameworks indicate. Second, despite strenuous attempts to either claim that the framework's categorization of the local and international is purely descriptive or that the framework is deliberately seeking to avoid the romanticization of the "local", there is a tendency to portray local communities as "traditional" and pre-modern through the denial that frameworks of power that inhere in the international and Western sphere are at work in the locales of the East and South. As a result, the hybrid peace repeats the subjugatory categories of colonial and neocolonial power-knowledge. Third, the call for a closer international–local engagement, or even social contract, does not really address past critiques that have indicated the divide between the insurance and welfare frameworks of Western states and the lack of reciprocity and social responsiveness of international developmental and humanitarian engagement (Duffield, 2007, pp. 19–24). Moreover, it does not address the constant claim that the state structures created by international state-building are ultimately cosmetic, shell-like forms devoid of even rudimentary sovereignty (Chandler, 2010). Fourth, critics will point to the lack of alternatives to liberal peace and the fact that a focus on post-liberal, local, everyday, and facets of peace may end up privileging illiberal conduct through, for instance, the reinforcing of authoritarian and autocratic rule and/or repressive customary local practices (Paris, 2010, pp. 357–361; see also the acknowledgement of this risk by Mac Ginty, 2008, p. 150). Lastly, there is an obvious tendency in the "hybrid" peace and "everyday" peace approaches to neglect the way in which conflict is also hybrid and present in the world of everyday existence, so that a focus on hybrid peace must also acknowledge hybrid war more extensively than it currently does (Nadarajah and Rampton, 2012).

Conclusion

What is clear, therefore, is that the international state-building project, dominated as it has been by liberal frameworks, has been confronted by a series of challenges to its epistemic, conceptual, and practical frameworks, evident in the failures and limited successes that it has generated in the recent past. This crisis in the expansion of liberal order is, to a great degree, a result of what has been described as "input incongruence" arising from the multiplicity of actors and dynamics in contention with the impact upon state-building and the resistance it encounters in a globalized world (cf. Zürn, 2012). The response to this crisis has produced both a recent, emerging approach advocating a wider participatory hybrid, local, and quotidian peace, as well as a long-running powerful set of critiques from liberal institutionalist, and classical liberal, realist, and political economy perspectives. Yet in a sense, these approaches frequently privilege certain processes, institutions and/or local, and/or international actors that dominate the frameworks of their understanding of who should participate and how in state-building, whether through the state–society relation or through a social contract fashioned between the spheres of the local and international. What needs to be addressed, therefore, in a more fundamental way in both academic knowledge and policy frameworks is how a more holistic framework can be developed to encompass the complex, multipolar networked mesh of discourses, processes, actors, and identities – a framework that will have to encourage greater participation by avoiding the hierarchies of inclusion and exclusion characteristics of the liberal (or hybrid) peace whilst simultaneously avoiding the tendency for international state-building to generate the counterproductive illiberal effects it seeks to overcome. The development of such a framework will also have to involve the acknowledgement that solutions premised on a return to a (mythic) territorial, statist order cannot (by virtue of that order's epistemological framework) even begin to apprehend or engage with the profound complexity of the global and local actors and processes at work across conflict, peace- and state-building.

References

Allen, Daniel. 2010. "New Directions in the Study of Nation-building: Views through the Lens of Path Dependence." *International Studies Review*, 12: 413–429.

Andersen, Louise. 2010. "Outsiders inside the State: Post-Conflict Liberia between Trusteeship and Partnership." *Journal of Intervention and Statebuilding*, 4: 129–152.

Bain, William. 2003. *Between Anarchy and Society: Trusteeship and the Obligations of Power*. Oxford: Oxford University Press.

Ball, Nicole. 2001. "The Challenge of Rebuilding War-Torn Societies." In *Turbulent Peace: The Challenges of Managing International Conflict*, edited by Chester A. Crocker, Fen Osler Hampson and Pamela Aall, 719–736. Washington, DC: United States Institute of Peace Press.

Barakat, Sultan, and Steven A. Zyck. 2009. "The Evolution of Post-conflict Recovery." *Third World Quarterly*, 30(6): 1069–1086.

Barker, Rodney S. 1990. *Political Legitimacy and the State*. Oxford: Clarendon Press.

Bhabha, Homi. 1994. *The Location of Culture*. Abingdon: Routledge.

Bhatia, Michael. 2007. "The Future of the Mujahideen: Legitimacy, Legacy and Demobilization in Post-Bonn Afghanistan." *International Peacekeeping*, 14: 90–107.

Bliesemann de Guevara, Berit. 2010. "Introduction: The Limits of Statebuilding and the Analysis of State-Formation." *Journal of Intervention and Statebuilding*, 4(2): 111–128.

Bojicic-Dzelilovic, Vesna, James Kerr-Lindsay, and Denisa Kostovicova, eds. 2013. *Civil Society and Transitions in the Western Balkans*. Houndmills: Palgrave Macmillan.

Borowiak, Craig Thomas. 2011. *Accountability and Democracy: The Pitfalls and Promise of Popular Control*. New York, NY: Oxford University Press.

Brinkerhoff, Derick W. 2005. "Rebuilding Governance in Failed States and Post-conflict Societies: Concepts and Cross-cutting Themes." *Public Administration and Development*, 25: 3–14.

Call, Charles T. 2008. "Building States to Build Peace?" In *Building States to Build Peace*, edited by Charles T. Call with Vanessa Wyeth, 365–388. Boulder, CO: Lynne Rienner Publishers.

Calhoun, Craig. 2007. *Nations Matter: Culture, History, and the Cosmopolitan Dream*. Abingdon: Routledge.

Caplan, Richard. 2005a. *International Governance of War-Torn Territories: Rule and Reconstruction*. Oxford: Oxford University Press.

Caplan, Richard. 2005b. "Who Guards the Guardians? International Accountability in Bosnia." *International Peacekeeping*, 12: 463–476.

Caplan, Richard. 2012. "Policy Implications." In *Exit Strategies and State Building*, edited by Richard Caplan, 311–319. Oxford: Oxford University Press.

Chandler, David. 2006. *Empire in Denial: The Politics of State-Building*. Ann Arbor, MI: Pluto Press.

Chandler, David. 2010. *International Statebuilding: The Rise of Post-Liberal Governance*. London: Routledge.

Chesterman, Simon. 2004. *You, the People: the United Nations, Transitional Administration, and State-Building.* Oxford: Oxford University Press.

Cooper, Robert. 2004. *The Breaking of Nations: Order and Chaos in the Twenty-First Century.* New York, NY: Atlantic Monthly Press.

Cooper, Neil. 2007. "On the Crisis of the Liberal Peace." *Conflict, Security & Development*, 7(4): 605–616.

Cooper, Neil, Mandy Turner, and Michael Pugh. 2011. "The end of history and the last liberal peacebuilder: a reply to Roland Paris." *Review of International Studies*, 37(4): 1995–2007.

Crisp, Jeff. 2001. "Mind the gap! UNHCR, humanitarian assistance and the development process." *New Issues in Refugee Research*, UNHCR, No. 43, May, Geneva.

Duffield, Mark. 2007. *Development, Security and Unending War: Governing the World of Peoples.* Cambridge: Polity Press.

De Certeau, Michel. 1984. *The Practice of Everyday Life* [Translated by Steven Rendall]. Berkeley, CA: University of California Press.

Dillon, Michael, and Julian Reid. 2009. *The Liberal Way of War: Killing to Make Life Live.* Abingdon: Routledge.

Donais, Timothy. 2012. *Peacebuilding and Local Ownership: Post-Conflict Consensus-Building.* London: Routledge.

Duffield, Mark. 2001. *Global Governance and the New Wars: The Merging of Development and Security.* London: Zed Books.

Duffield, Mark. 2007. *Development, Security and Unending War.* Cambridge: Polity Press.

Egnell, Robert. 2010. "The Organised Hypocrisy of International State-Building." *Conflict, Security & Development*, 10: 465–491.

Etzioni, Amitai. 2007. "Reconstrucion: An Agenda." *Journal of Intervention and Statebuilding*, 1(1): 27–45.

Fearon, James D., and David D. Laitin. 2004. "Neotrusteeship and the Problem of Weak States." *International Security*, 28: 5–43.

François, Monika, and Inder Sud. 2006. "Promoting Stability and Development in Fragile and Failed States." *Development Policy Review*, 24: 141–160.

Fritz, Verena, and Alina R. Menocal. 2007. *Understanding State-building from a Political Economy Perspective: An Analysis and Conceptual Paper on Processes, Embedded Tensions and Lessons for International Engagement.* London: Overseas Development Institute.

Fukuyama, Francis. 2004. "The Imperative of State-building." *Journal of Democracy*, 25(2): 17–31.

Ghani, Ashraf, and Clare Lockhart. 2008. *Fixing Failed States: A Framework for Rebuilding a Fractured World.* Oxford: Oxford University Press.

Habermas, Jurgen. 2001. *Postnational Constellation: Political Essays* [Translated by Max Pensky]. Cambridge, MA: MIT Press.

Heller, Agnes. 1985. *Everyday Life.* London: Routledge and Kegan Paul.

Holsti, Kalevi J. 1996. *The State, War, and the State of War.* Cambridge: Cambridge University Press.

Hughes, Caroline. 2011. "The politics of knowledge: ethnicity, capacity and return in post-conflict reconstruction policy." *Review of International Studies*, 37: 1493–1514.

Hughes, Caroline, and Vanessa Pupavac. 2005. "Framing Post-Conflict Societies: International Pathologisation of Cambodia and the Post-Yugoslav States." *Third World Quarterly*, 26: 873–889.

Ignatieff, Michael. 2003. *Empire Lite: Nation-Building in Bosnia, Kosovo and Afghanistan.* London: Vintage.

Jackson, Robert R., and Carl G. Rosberg. 1982. "Why Africa's Weak States Persist: The Empirical and the Juridical in Statehood." *World Politics*, 35: 1–24.

Kaldor, Mary. 2009. "The Reconstruction of Political Authority in a Global Era." In *Persistent State Weakness in the Global Age*, edited by Denisa Kostovicova and Vesna Bojicic-Dzelilovic, 179–195. Aldershot: Ashgate.

Kearney, Jonathan A., Sofia Botzios, and Tom B. Hadden. 2011. "Addressing the Accountability Challenges in International Policing in Peace Support Operations." *Crime, Law and Social Change*, 55: 217–239.

Knaus, Gerald, and Felix Martin. 2003. "Travails of the European Raj." *Journal of Democracy*, 14: 60–74.

Knoll, Bernhard. 2008. *The Legal Status of Territories Subject to Administration by International Organisations*. Cambridge: Cambridge University Press.

Kostovicova, Denisa, and Vesna Bojicic-Dzelilovic. 2009. "Introduction: State Weakening and Globalization." In *Persistent State Weakness in the Global Age*, edited by Denisa Kostovicova and Vesna Bojicic-Dzelilovic, 1–16. Aldershot: Ashgate.

Kymlicka, Will. 2005. "Liberal Multiculturalism: Western Models Global Trends and Asian Debates." In *Multiculturalism in Asia*, edited by Will Kymlicka and Baogang He. Oxford: Oxford University Press.

Le Febvre, Henri. 1992. *Critique of Everyday Life Vol. 1* [Translated by John Moore]. London: Verso.

Mac Ginty, Roger. 2008. "Indigenous Peace-Making Versus the Liberal Peace." *Cooperation and Conflict*, 43(2): 139–163.

Mac Ginty, Roger. 2011. *International Peacebuilding and Local Resistance: Hybrid Forms of Peace*. London: Palgrave Macmillan.

Martin, Mary, Vesna Bojicic-Dzelilovic, Denisa Kostovicova, Anne Wittman, and Stefanie Moser [Policy Paper, Friedrich Ebert Stiftung]. 2012. "Exiting Conflict, Owning the Peace: Local Ownership in International Peace Operations." Accessed December 5, 2012 from http://www.owning-the-peace.eu/downloads/Policy_Paper_Local%20Ownership.pdf

Mansfield, Edward, and Jack Snyder. 2007. *Electing to Fight: Why Emerging Democracies Go to War*. Cambridge, MA: MIT Press.

Mitchell, Audra. 2011. "Quality/control: international peace interventions and 'the everyday'." *Review of International Studies*, 37(4): 1623–1645.

Moore, David. 2000. "Levelling the playing fields and embedding illusions: 'post-conflict' discourse and neo-liberal 'development' in war-torn Africa." *Review of African Political Economy*, 27(83): 11–28.

Morphet, Sally. 2002. "Current International Civil Administration: The Need for Political Legitimacy." *International Peacekeeping*, 9: 140–162.

Nadarajah, Sutha, and David Rampton. 2012. "Liberal Peace and Biopolitical War in Sri Lanka." Lecture given at the Department of Politics and International Studies Departmental Seminar, School of Oriental and African Studies, London, March 14.

Narten, Jens. 2009. "Dilemmas of Promoting "Local Ownership": The Case of Postwar Kosovo." In *Dilemmas of Statebuilding: Confronting the Contradictions of Postwar Peace Operations*, edited by Roland Paris and Timothy D. Sisk, 252–283. London: Routledge.

Ottaway, Marina. 2002. "Rebuilding State Institutions in Collapsed States." *Development and Change*, 33(1): 1001–1023.

Paris, Roland. 2002. "International peacebuilding and the 'mission civilisatrice'." *Review of International Studies*, 28(4): 637–656.

Paris, Roland. 2004. *Towards More Effective Peacebuilding: Institutionalization before Liberalization-Building Peace after Civil Conflict*. Cambridge: Cambridge University Press.

Paris, Roland. 2010. "Saving Liberal Peacebuilding." *Review of International Studies*, 36(2): 337–365.

Paris, Roland, and Timothy Sisk, eds. 2009. *Dilemmas of Statebuilding: Confronting the Contradictions of Postwar Peace Operations*. London: Routledge.

Pugh, Michael. 2004. "Peacekeeping and Critical Theory." *International Peacekeeping*, 11(1): 39–58.

Reich, Hannah. 2006. ""Local Ownership" in Conflict Transformation Projects: Partnership, Participation or Patronage?" Berghof Occasional Paper No. 27. Berghof Research Center for Constructive Conflict Management.

Reno, William. 2008. "Bottom–Up Statebuilding?" In *Building States to Build Peace*, edited by Charles T. Call with Vanessa Wyeth, 143–161. Boulder, CO: Lynne Rienner Publishers.

Richmond, Oliver P. 2006. "The problem of peace: understanding the 'liberal peace'." *Conflict, Security & Development*, 6: 291–314.

Richmond, Oliver. 2011. *A Post-Liberal Peace*. Abingdon: Routledge.

Roberts, David. 2011. "Beyond the metropolis? Popular Peace and Post-conflict Peacebuilding." *Review of International Studies*, 37(5): 2535–2556.

Rotberg, Robert I. 2007. "The Challenge of Weak, Failing, and Collapsed States." In *Leashing the Dogs of War: Conflict Management in a Divided World*, edited by Chester A. Crocker, Fen Osler Hampson, and Pamela R. Aall, 83–94. Washington, DC: United States Institute of Peace Press.

Rubin, Barnett R. 2005. "Constructing Sovereignty for Security." *Survival*, 47: 93–106.

Scharpf, Fritz. 1999. *Governing in Europe: Effective and Democratic?* Oxford: Oxford University Press.

Scheye, Eric. 2008. "Unknotting Local Ownership Redux: Bringing Non-State/Local Justice Networks Back." In *Local Ownership and Security Sector Reform*, edited by Timothy Donais, 59–81. Zurich/Berlin: Lit Verlag.

Sperling, Valerie. 2009. *Altered States: The Globalization of Accountability*. Cambridge: Cambridge University Press.

Stahn, Carsten. 2008. *The Law and Practice of International Territorial Administration: Versailles to Iraq and Beyond*. Cambridge: Cambridge University Press.

Suhrke, Astri. 2007. "Reconstruction as Modernisation: The 'Post-Conflict' Project in Afghanistan." *Third World Quarterly*, 28: 1291–1308.

Taylor, C. 1990. "Modes of Civil Society." *Public Culture*, 3(1): 95–118.

Van Leeuwen, Mathijs, Willemijn Verkoren, and Freer Boedeltjer. 2012. "Thinking beyond the liberal peace: From utopia to heterotopias." *Acta Politica*, 47(3): 292–316.

Wesley, Michael. 2008. "The State of the Art on the Art of Statebuilding." *Global Governance*, 14(3): 369–385.

Wilde, Ralph. 2008. *International Territorial Administration: How Trusteeship and the Civilizing Mission Never Went Away*. Oxford: Oxford University Press.

Williams, David, and Tom Young. 2012. "Civil Society and the Liberal Project in Ghana and Sierra Leone." *Journal of Intervention and Statebuilding*, 6(1): 7–22.

Wolff, Stefan. 2011. "Post-Conflict State Building: The debate on Institutional Choice." *Third World Quarterly*, 32(10): 1777–1802.

Woodward, Susan. 2001. "Compromised Sovereignty to Create Sovereignty: Is Dayton a Futile Exercise or an Emerging Model." In *Problematic Sovereignty: Contested Rules and Political Possibilities*, edited by Stephen D. Krasner, 252–300. New York, NY: Columbia University Press.

Woodward, Susan. 2009. "Measuring State Failure/Weakness: Do the Balkans Cases Fit?" In *Persistent State Weakness in the Global Age*, edited by Denisa Kostovicova and Vesna Bojicic-Dzelilovic, 151–165. Aldershot: Ashgate.

Zaum, Dominik. 2007. *The Sovereignty Paradox: The Norms and Politics of International Statebuilding*. Oxford: Oxford University Press.

Zürn, Michael. 2012. "Globalization and Global Governance." In *Handbook of International Relations*, second edition, edited by Walter Carlsnaes *et al.* London: Sage Publications.

Chapter 16

Strengthening Democratic Governance in the Security Sector: The Unfulfilled Promise of Security Sector Reform

Nicole Ball

Security sector reform (SSR) can play a critical role in helping governments and populations meet the multiple security challenges confronting their societies. In particular, it can help answer the questions of who primarily benefits from the existing security arrangements, what makes people insecure and what changes are necessary to deliver broad based security. SSR began to makes its way onto the policy agenda in the late 1990s. Now, over a decade later, there is growing acceptance of the concept of security sector reform at the policy level and some progress has been made in embedding these principles in the practical application of the "SSR" agenda. Yet there remains a considerable way to go before the SSR agenda can be effectively and reliably implemented.

This chapter begins by defining SSR and briefly reviewing the evolution of the concept and its application. It then considers four of the more important challenges currently facing the effective and reliable implementation of the concept: the international political and security climate, the degree to which reforming countries own SSR efforts, the ability of international actors to navigate the political waters of reforming countries, and the effectiveness of donor approaches to SSR. The chapter concludes by discussing the importance of greater attention to process in producing more successful SSR outcomes.

What is Security Sector Reform?

There are many definitions of SSR tailored to the needs of different governments and organizations. These definitions mostly derive, however, from the Organisation for Economic Co-operation and Development (OECD) Development Assistance Committee's (DAC) approach to SSR, which is built on four pillars:

The Handbook of Global Security Policy, First Edition. Edited by Mary Kaldor and Iavor Rangelov.
© 2014 John Wiley & Sons, Ltd. Published 2014 by John Wiley & Sons, Ltd.

- Developing a clear institutional framework for providing security that integrates security and development policy and includes all relevant actors and focuses on the vulnerable, such as women, children, and minority groups;
- Strengthening governance and oversight of security institutions;
- Building capable and professional security forces that are accountable to civil authorities and open to dialogue with civil society organizations; and
- Promoting the sustainability of justice and security service delivery (OECD, 2004a, p. 2; OECD, 2007).

As will be discussed next in more detail, the prevalence of the DAC definition reflects the fact that the conceptualization and implementation of the SSR concept has been primarily driven by the international community and specifically the development assistance community. Nonetheless, many of the fundamental underpinnings of the concept have been accepted by constituencies in non-OECD countries, particularly civil society organizations in many parts of the world, and by the African Union.

According to the DAC consensus, SSR should be: "People-centred, locally owned and based on democratic norms and human rights principles and the rule of law, seeking to provide freedom from fear" (OECD, 2004a). Moreover, although the original term of art was "security sector reform," it has long been recognized that effective justice systems are essential for the achievement of safe and secure environments. Both the literature and practitioners increasingly speak of "justice and security sector reform" (JSSR), security sector development (SSD), or security and justice work.

In addition to these core elements of SSR, programs that support disarmament, demobilization, and reintegration of former combatants (DDR) and reduce access to and/or control the use of small arms and light weapons (SALW) are part of many definitions of SSR. While DDR and SALW are often considered somewhat peripheral to SSR processes, they reflect real needs in many countries and some thought has been given to how to link them to SSR (United Nations Office of the Special Adviser on Africa, 2007; de Vries and van Veen, 2010; Donald and Olonisakin, 2007).

The Evolution of the Security Sector Reform Concept

SSR was developed as a response to one of the legacies of the Cold War era, the deficit of democratic accountability in the security and justice sectors throughout the world. The absence of democratic accountability has been a major cause of insecurity, above all for the world's poorest citizens (Ball and Hendrickson, 2009; Sedra, 2010). In particular, SSR was viewed as a means of complementing traditional security assistance, which had been focused on training and equipping security forces.

During the Cold War, security assistance was used to foster strategic relationships with key allies, often countries where the military played a central political role. It promoted security for the élites and authoritarian regimes at the expense of security for citizens, communities, and often even the state. Delivering security and justice for the entire population was not part of the agenda, or was it democratically accountable. Highly autonomous security services routinely thwarted the development of participatory forms of government, societies based on the rule of law and a strong civilian capacity to manage and monitor the security sector, including the justice system. Although these problems were clearly evident prior to 1990, it was only after the strategic priorities of the major powers shifted during the 1990s following the dissolution of the Soviet Union and the end of the Cold War that it became possible for democratic security sector governance and the impact of security sectors on development to be addressed, either within the developing world or by the international community. It was also only at that point that a shift was possible from an exclusively state- and regime-focused approach to security to a more inclusive approach to security and justice based on the needs and perceptions of the population at large. These were identified for example through the use of participatory poverty assessments that consistently identified a lack of security and inaccessible justice as a major concern for poor people and supported an effort to promote more equitable service delivery. The World Bank "Voices of the Poor" study was one of the first to reveal the extent to which the police and the official justice system cause insecurity and injustice and contribute to the impoverishment of people rather than acting as the guardians of "justice, peace and fairness" (Narayan, Chambers, and Petesch, 2000, p. 163).

The end of the Cold War brought other important changes in the non-OECD world that influenced the trajectory of the SSR concept. As the security assistance provided by the major powers decreased, many governments found themselves without the resources necessary to maintain unsustainably large security systems or to continue to pursue civil wars. The immediate post-Cold War period saw a number of civil wars come to an end, for example in Mozambique and El Salvador, and the amount of resources devoted to the security services decline. However, in many cases, the seemingly strong authoritarian states morphed into fragile states, where control over the means of violence fragmented, economies were weakened by years of structural adjustment and corruption, and the internal conflicts that had been suppressed during the Cold War turned violent.

Although there was input from non-OECD countries in developing the SSR concept, it was provided almost exclusively by civil society actors with limited means of influencing their governments in the short term. This meant that the international community became the leading force in the development and implementation of the SSR concept. Within the international community, it was primarily the development actors who engaged early on, and the objective was to offset the traditional approach to security assistance provided by foreign policy, security, and intelligence actors. The SSR concept was initially developed without much reference to these other actors and as a result an opportunity to begin to engage them in the SSR agenda at an early stage was lost.

Additionally, as the development donors began to devote an increasingly large share of their resources to fragile and conflict-affected states, they came to view SSR through that lens. Thus, while many countries would benefit from an SSR process, SSR essentially became a concept that was applied to the poorest, most conflict-ridden societies. Lastly, for the development actors to engage effectively, they needed to incorporate governance concerns (in all sectors, but particularly security and justice) into their approaches and to debate the appropriate role for development assistance in strengthening security. This took time and is in fact still a work in progress in the early twenty-first century.

The SSR concept, which emerged in the late 1990s, drew on three major strands of literature and experience: (1) civil-military relations; (2) reform efforts in non-OECD countries (particularly Eastern Europe, former Soviet Union, and Africa); and

(3) human security (Ball and Hendrickson, 2009, pp. 10–12). As a consequence, the SSR concept includes a diverse set of national, regional, and international actors. There are five major categories of national actors who influence security sector governance and therefore may be included in SSR activities: (1) bodies authorized to use force; (2) civil management and oversight bodies; (3) judicial and public security bodies; (4) non-state security force institutions; and (5) civil society bodies (Ball, Bouta, and van de Goor, 2003, pp. 32–33). To underscore the broad nature of SSR, the DAC speaks of "security system reform". Although then-DAC Chairman Richard Manning noted in his foreword to the DAC guidance on SSR that the security system includes "civil society" (OECD, 2004b, p. 4) and civil society is recognized as playing a central role in SSR, key DAC documents do not include the fifth category in their descriptions of security system actors.

In common with other types of reform processes, SSR will be sustainable to the extent it is led by national actors, has inputs from the broad range of national stakeholders, and reflects local context. While many non-OECD countries have continued to be interested in traditional forms of security sector assistance, often called "train and equip", there has been distinctly less interest overall in the democratic governance components of SSR. The African Union approved a continent-wide framework for security sector reform in 2013. This framework is grounded in many of the same principles as the OECD approach to SSR, in particular the development of effective security institutions that are accountable to democratic institutions. The framework also defines the security sector in much the same way as the OECD does. At the same time, it took a number of years for the AU framework to be negotiated and approved and the commitment of individual AU member states to the principles in the framework remains to be tested as of this writing. Some AU governments are known to continue to view the SSR concept with a degree of suspicion.

This relatively limited support for SSR in many parts of the world created a vacuum into which the international community has inserted itself. A number of OECD governments that provide either security or development assistance to partner countries have been among the strongest proponents of SSR to date and have funded activities that fall under the SSR rubric. Of these, the United Kingdom has been the strongest bilateral supporter of SSR, both conceptually and operationally, although other OECD countries have also supported justice and security work. The UK's strong engagement is linked to Department of International Development's (DFID) growing understanding, beginning in the late 1990s, that

> A military sector that is well tasked and managed can serve the interests of all, including the poor. A military sector that is inappropriately tasked, badly managed and undisciplined can undermine the interests of the poor and inhibit development – sometimes for decades. In many of the world's poorer countries, elements within the security sector are a major cause of insecurity, conflict and human rights abuse (Short, 1998).

United Nations peace support missions and agencies, notably United Nations Development Programme (UNDP), have also increasingly provided support. Other multilateral organizations, such as the World Bank, also have a role to play within the boundaries of their mandates that have yet to be fully exploited (Byrd and Guimbert, 2009; Ball and Holmes, 2002). At the regional level, actors as diverse as the inter-governmental AU, the various African regional economic commissions such as the Economic Community of West Africa (ECOWAS) or the Southern African Development Community (SADC), professional bodies such as the Southern African Regional Police Chief Council Organization (SARPCCO) and nongovernmental organizations (NGOs) like Africa Security Sector Network (ASSN) can support SSR efforts.

DFID's initial decision to make the Conflict and Humanitarian Affairs Department (now the Conflict, Humanitarian and Security Department, CHASE) the locus of DFID SSR activities, rather than the Governance Department (subsequently disbanded in an administrative restructuring) thus had important ramifications for the evolution of the SSR agenda. It reduced the influence of the initial impetus for SSR, improving security sector governance, although the governance underpinning of SSR remained strong at the rhetorical level (OECD, 2004a, p. 1). It split work on policing (overseen by the Governance Department, which developed a parallel policy on access to justice) from SSR, confirmed a focus on conflict-affected countries and set the stage for a major turf battle within DFID. It also delayed meaningful dialogue within the British government on how to address insecurity most effectively through the UK's foreign, defense, and development policies.

Over time, the United Kingdom has modified its approach to SSR in a number of important ways. Recognizing that SSR requires inputs from a range of actors, it has pioneered a joined up approach to SSR within the UK government. It has used pooled funding as a major tool to achieve this outcome, although evidence suggests that pooled funding is not a substitute for strong and consistent policy guidance (Ball, Biesheuvel, Hamilton-Baillie, and Olonisakin, 2007; Ball and van de Goor, 2008). In 2009, DFID declared that security and justice must be "a priority" if peace- and statebuilding are to be effective in conflict-affected and fragile states, a decision that appears to have survived the change of government in 2010. By 2012, CHASE continued to lead on SSR work with a "governance and security pillar" and "security and justice advisers". What is more, the Stabilisation Unit, a group that provides services to DFID, the Foreign Office, and the Ministry of Defence, is playing an increasingly important role in supporting security and justice work.

DFID's various decisions on its approach to SSR have also colored the way in which the international community has approached SSR. There are two main reasons for this. First the United Kingdom has been seen as the "market leader" in SSR and its innovations carry particular weight. Second, the United Kingdom has influenced and supported the DAC approach to SSR, and the DAC approach has influenced a wide range of actors, including security actors. Not all actors have followed the evolution of the UK's approach, however. For example, although the United Kingdom has increasingly sought to bring together its security and justice work, some actors – such as the World Bank – continue to see SSR as aimed exclusively at military security. Additionally, the debate on the relationship between SSR and justice system transformation is far from resolved. Objectively speaking, it is clear that the criminal justice system needs to be included in "SSR" work because the police, the judiciary, and the corrections system need to work in tandem to deliver effective services. However, concerns remain within the justice community about close engagement with the security services, in part because of worries that justice would be given lower priority than security if the two were combined in a "justice and security" concept.

While one might have wished for a better understanding of some key features of the SSR concept at an earlier stage, the fact that the United Kingdom has learned some lessons from its SSR efforts and incorporated those into its approach to SSR has had a positive influence on other actors. For example, to support a more uniform approach to SSR work and to begin to translate norms into operational activities, the DAC developed a handbook on SSR with UK support (OECD, 2007). While the handbook is not operationally oriented, it does lay out a number of key features of justice and security reform. It and other elements of the evolving SSR agenda have begun to influence to some degree the approach of security actors. For example, the US Army field manual on stability operations contains a chapter on SSR that closely mirrors the DAC approach (United States Department of the Army, 2007, chapter 6). The UK's efforts to work jointly across government departments inspired the US government to issue its own cross-departmental SSR guidelines in 2009 (USAID, US Department of Defense and US Department of State, 2009) and the Netherlands to pursue a joined up approach in designing and implementing the Security Sector Development (SSD) Program in Burundi.

Lastly, the funding of SSR-related activities through the tri-departmental conflict prevention pools and the creation of the tri-departmental Stabilisation Unit, which supports a good deal of UK SSR work, have highlighted the importance of achieving as much coherence as possible among national foreign, security, and development approaches to SSR. In reality, when a bilateral government perceives its strategic interests to be engaged, the governance and human security elements of the SSR agenda will be secondary, at best. Nonetheless, the UK experience indicates that it is important to have mechanisms through which the various players are required to negotiate a government-wide approach to SSR and, importantly, gives development officials a seat at the table when foreign policy and security issues are discussed.

The Challenges of Implementing the SSR Agenda

As the foregoing suggests, the SSR concept and agenda are slowly making their way into policy and even operational documents within the international community. Much less progress has been recorded in terms of institutionalizing that agenda and implementing it within the international community or promoting demand for SSR in countries in need of reform. While a growing amount of internationally supported SSR programs have been undertaken in developing countries, particularly those seeking to rebuild following war, all too often these programs have been old style security programs that are devoid of governance content but have been "rehatted" as "SSR" activities. Even where SSR principles are well represented in donor activities, there is often a serious lack of understanding of how to engage in processes that will effectively deliver better security and justice outcomes. From the perspective of the governments of reforming countries, SSR is frequently viewed not as a means of helping them to serve their populations better but as something imposed by international actors that challenges élite prerogatives.

There are a number of important factors that influence the effective implementation of the SSR agenda. Chief among these are the international political and security climate, the degree of the reforming countries own SSR efforts, the ability of international actors to navigate the political waters of reforming countries, and the effectiveness of the approaches that international actors employ.

International Political and Security Climate

Just as the end of the Cold War was a pivotal moment in the development of the SSR concept, the attacks of September 11, 2001, which inaugurated the "War on Terror", exerted a significant influence over the concept's evolution and operationalization (Sherman, 2010, pp. 61, 66–71; Ball and Hendrickson, 2009, pp. 30–35). The attacks occurred when the SSR concept was in its infancy. Overall, development assistance came under considerable pressure to make security the central foreign policy objective of donor countries, subordinating both development and trade as policy tools. This was less of a deviation in the United States where foreign and security policy objectives have dominated US foreign assistance since the end of the Second World War (Ball, 1988, pp. 237–294). For European countries, however, where poverty reduction and governance concerns shaped development agendas, this approach was deeply troubling.

The emphasis on counterterrorism in some OECD countries has placed the SSR agenda under considerable pressure. Demands from Western donors of security assistance – particularly, but not exclusively, the United States – to reshape the security services to meet the needs of the "War on Terror" have returned operational effectiveness to the top of the agenda, with efforts to develop democratic accountability and oversight mechanisms and behaviors taking a back seat. This has impinged on the intelligence services and internal security bodies the most but defense and policing bodies have also been affected.

Experience since 2001 suggests that the emphasis on counterterrorism may lead the interests of poorer countries to be conflated with the interests of richer countries, with the result that the security needs of the populations of the poorer countries and possibly also of the poorer countries themselves will not be met. Countries that are seen to harbor political elements that may be a threat to Western countries have received most attention, but even countries that are not obvious havens of potentially anti-Western groups can also be tempted to sign up to the "War on Terror." As one African analyst has noted: "the war on terror approach … is politically less demanding and may carry more tangible benefits" than the SSR approach for recipients of security assistance (Eboe Hutchful, personal communication, October 25, 2005).

Of the OECD countries, the United States has been particularly focused on the counterterrorism agenda and is particularly weak on the SSR agenda. Where US strategic interests are engaged, such as in Afghanistan and Iraq, there has been no pretense of support for broader SSR principles. What is more, security assistance for counterinsurgency objectives directly contradicts SSR goals. It enables the arming of abusive warlords, local militias, and other informal actors and runs the strong risk of creating formal security services that operate in counterinsurgency/counterterror mode without adequate countervailing accountability structures, as was the case with the security assistance provided by both East and West during the Cold War.

Even in other countries where US strategic interests are weaker, train and equip activities outweigh attention to governance-related activities. In Liberia, for example, it was the United States that drove the decision in 2005–2006 to create a 2000 person army without any strategic needs assessment. The long-term costs of maintaining this force (or any of the other parts of Liberia's security system) were not adequately integrated into the Liberian budget. The specter of the drawdown of the UN peacekeeping force, continued domestic insecurity, and insecurity related to refugees from Côte d'Ivoire caused attention to shift in 2011 to extending the reach of the police, immigration service, and justice system outside of the capital city, Monrovia, particularly to areas bordering on Côte d'Ivoire and to begin to assess how the state will pay for the provision of security and justice services. The proposed "hub" approach mirrors the United Nations Missions in Liberia (UNMIL) deployment, but it is not clear that this will effectively address security and justice needs of the entire population or that it will be fiscally sustainable.

However, it is not only the United States that influences the direction of SSR globally. Of the non-OECD donors of security assistance, the Chinese government has become increasingly active in many parts of the world. The strings attached to Chinese assistance are commercial in nature and thus more attractive to governments than the governance-related strings that can come with Western SSR support. To the extent that countries which could benefit from a governance approach to SSR have an alternative that is less challenging to the existing power structure, the governments of these countries have a strong incentive to accept that assistance, even if it ultimately undermines the sustainability of the country's economy.

While it has not had global reach, the series of popular uprisings known collectively as "the Arab Spring" has inaugurated substantial political changes throughout North Africa and the Middle East that have the potential to reshape the relationship between citizens and state security systems. The political turmoil unleashed in countries as diverse as Bahrain, Egypt, Libya, Syria, Tunisia, and Yemen have laid bare the essential relationships between political leadership and the security systems on which they depend for power, as well as the degree to which key security sector players benefit from the *status quo*. The Arab Spring has thus simultaneously underscored the urgent need for improved governance of the security sector throughout the region and demonstrated the enormous difficulties involved in confronting entrenched power and privilege (Kawakibi, 2012; Tanner and Ould Mohamedou, 2012; Mikail, 2012).

Ownership

It has become increasingly evident that without the commitment of national actors to development efforts, these efforts will not be sustainable. It has also become evident that such commitment is impossible in the absence of a strong leadership role on the part of national actors. Ownership is accordingly one of the five areas identified as particularly important for aid effectiveness in development contexts in the Paris Declaration and the Accra Agenda for Action (AAA) (High Level Forum, 2005; 3rd High Level Forum on Aid Effectiveness, 2008). Experience with efforts to implement SSR programs indicates that ownership is equally important for effective security and justice programming (OECD, 2009). What is more, the international Dialogue on Peacebuilding (comprised of the 19 fragile states known as the g7+, their development partners, and international organizations) identified the "weak alignment of donors behind a unified national plan" as one of the major impediments to the attainment of peacebuilding and statebuilding goals in the areas of legitimate politics, security, justice, economic foundations and revenues and services (International Dialogue on Peacebuilding and Statebuilding, 2010 and International Dialogue on Peacebuilding and Statebuilding, 2011, p. 2). While there are legitimate reasons for questioning the commitment of at least some of the g7+ governments and their development partners to the peacebuilding and statebuilding goals, there is no doubt that the Dialogue has provided a mechanism for injecting the priorities of the governments of fragile states into the OECD-led debate on development assistance. The emerging, non-traditional development donors appear to be skeptical of the Dialogue, viewing it as dominated and driven by the OECD countries, although they are not all necessarily hostile to the goals it enunciates.

Achieving ownership of donor supported security and justice activities has proven to be highly challenging, particularly in fragile and conflict-affected situations where the international community has placed much of its emphasis on promoting SSR. In part, this is because the concept is applied in various ways by different actors. While most development specialists would agree that ownership involves all relevant national stakeholders, governmental and nongovernmental, in practice external actors tend to focus primarily on the national authorities. Within that subset of national actors, there is a tendency, particularly on the part of security donors, to work with those actors charged with providing security or managing security affairs. Executive branch actors, such as finance or planning ministries, which should be engaged in setting priorities, are frequently not at the table or not adequately empowered to play the same role with security ministries as they do with, say, health ministries. Oversight actors such as parliaments, constitutional courts, and ombudsmen also tend not to obtain the sort of attention they (and the functions they are meant to fulfill) merit. Additionally, because the national authorities in many countries do not view civil society as a partner in either policymaking or policy implementation and frequently have contentious relations with civil society groups because of their critical appraisal of government actions, external actors may be loath to pressure governments to engage more closely with nongovernmental actors.

Equally important, external actors frequently tend to assume that ownership is impossible without the capacity to *implement activities*. In fact, national actors can exercise ownership by *leading reform processes*. Additionally, many international actors continue to confuse "ownership" with "buy in" to donor-defined activities. International actors often assume that ownership exists when local stakeholders are consulted about donor programs and appear to agree to engage on the basis of these programs (OECD, 2009, p. 14; Ball and van de Goor, 2011, p. 7). It is true that national actors, particularly in fragile and conflict-affected states, often do not have the capacity to assert "effective leadership" over policies and strategies or to coordinate the multiplicity of SSR-related activities ongoing in their country as foreseen in the Paris Declaration. Even more important, the political environment in many fragile and conflict-affected situations where political structures and relations are still in a state of flux makes it very difficult – if not impossible – to agree on priorities.

The answer, however, is not to bypass national actors or to make decisions for them; rather, it is to support national actors in developing the capacity to progressively exercise genuine leadership over decisions on policies and how to implement them. Meeting in Kinshasa in July 2008 prior to the adoption of the Accra Agenda for Action, a group of aid donors and their partner governments issued a statement underscoring the

> need for an adapted development partnership in situations of fragility and conflict. ... We support the resolution in the AAA to strengthen country owned development processes. However, we recognise that in situations of fragility and conflict, where realising full ownership can be challenging, government leadership over priorities and policy direction is an important first step towards ownership (Kinshasa Statement, 2008).

International actors supporting security and justice work have yet to make much progress on addressing this challenge, although in 2011 the International Network on Conflict and Fragility (INCAF) began a program of work aimed at improving the effectiveness of security and justice assistance that will examine, *inter alia*, methods of strengthening national ownership.

Thus far, there has been little ownership of the concept of SSR among reforming countries. SSR has generally been viewed as a requirement imposed by the international community without adequate consideration of local conditions or interest. Governments may appear to accede to donor pressure to engage in an SSR process but then fail to follow through on implementation because they have not been convinced of the desirability of engaging in SSR, as was the case, for example, with the Guinea–Bissau SSR Strategy in 2008 (Ball and van de Goor, 2011, p. 17).

Even when governments are willing to undertake SSR-related activities, they can find it difficult to gain control over programs supported by donors. This is in part a byproduct of the confusion in donor minds between "buy in" and "ownership." Most often donor-supported programs are structured around donor-conceived activities, rather than efforts to create an environment in which national actors can identify their own priorities and progressively assume leadership of SSR-related efforts. In part, the problem derives from insufficient capacity of national actors to develop strategies and plans (against which the needs can be prioritized), which are essential in fragile and post-conflict contexts where almost everything is an urgent need. Building capacity to allow local stakeholders to develop strategies and identify objectives takes time that the international community often does not have given its demand for quantifiable results that can be achieved rapidly. Under these circumstances, the tendency is to deploy advisers and consultants to help national governments prepare decisions. In principle, this assistance can build capacity. All too often, however, the time pressures imposed by donors create a situation in which the "adviser" is effectively making the decision (Ball and van de Goor, 2011, p. 12).

Additionally, donors can resist giving reforming governments full control over reform programs because they disagree with governmental priorities. This problem is not unique to security sector reform. It afflicts statebuilding work more broadly (OECD, 2011, p. 50). With regard to SSR, development donors are often concerned that train and equip programs for security forces take precedence over governance-related activities that are the core of SSR; however, experience suggests that train and equip assistance may be a useful entry point into improving the management and governance of the security and justice sectors precisely because this is the type of assistance governments want. By providing a modest amount of training or equipment (including non-lethal equipment), external actors may be able to develop the type of relationships with local actors necessary to convince them that well-managed and well-governed security and justice institutions are in their interest. Delivering such assistance requires, however, a well-calibrated multipronged approach that most donors are ill-prepared to deliver. Thus there is the tendency to try to engineer "buy in" to programs that are more palatable to the donors and that can, importantly, be delivered in a specific time frame.

Politics of Security Sector Reform

Decision-makers face similar political, policy, organizational, and delivery challenges in the area of security and justice to those in other areas of development. However, SSR is generally more political (and thus riskier) than traditional socio-economic development interventions. The instruments of security and justice (such as the military or the legal system) can be used to impose and enforce decisions with immediate impact on power relations, power distribution, and potentially the stability of a country. Additionally, the political rules of the game in many fragile and conflict-affected situations tend to be in a state of flux. In consequence, the political environment is subject to change on relatively short notice and it frequently is very difficult to agree on priorities.

This poses several challenges to SSR programming. First, external actors need to understand the complex political environment in which they are working. While many development activities can have important political consequence and require a solid understanding of the political environment, security and justice is *consistently* political. Most SSR programs are not built on a solid understanding of the local or regional political environment, largely because of the considerable difficulties that outsiders face in understanding the dynamics of power relations. Westerners in particular tend to look at formal structures and assume that power flows according to those structures, whereas power relations are much more fluid, particularly in fragile and conflict-affected environments. Limited language capacity contributes to this problem in no small measure. Insufficient attention has been given in the past to identifying culturally and politically sensitive field staff who can understand the nuances of local political conditions. Additionally, there is often a barrier between security and justice programs and donor political staff that prevents programs from adequately drawing on the political support necessary to overcome obstacles to sustainable change in the security and justice arenas. However, there is evidence that when donors are able to provide SSR programs with political support, these programs are more likely to be able to address political constraints facing them, as recent experience with the Burundi–Netherlands Security Sector Development (SSD) program illustrates.

In 2009, the governments of Burundi and The Netherlands signed an eight-year memorandum of understanding, setting in motion the SSD program. The program's overall objective is "to make the security sector in Burundi a set of organizations, institutions, and regulations that are transparent, democratically managed, financially sustainable and accountable, capable of effectively ensuring security and justice to the citizens of Burundi" (Mémorandum d'Entente, 2009). At times, the SSD program has encountered a lack of political will on the part of highly placed Burundian authorities to change attitudes and behavior of both political actors and security actors. Specific problems include an increase in extra-judicial killings by some members of the Burundian security forces following the 2010 elections, and questions surrounding the constitutionality of the structure of the Ministry of Public Security, which oversees the police. The Dutch Parliament has been particularly concerned about the former. The SSD program itself has flagged the problems associated with the structure of the Ministry. The Dutch Chargé d'Affaires, the ranking Dutch political officer in Burundi, has led a multidonor initiative to address these and related issues at a strategic level, while the political officer at the Embassy Office of The Netherlands has worked with representatives of the Burundian government and members of the SSD program to follow up on the strategic level engagement (Ball, Gasana and Nindorera, 2012, p. 48).

The second challenge is to promote a balance between state-centric approaches to SSR and people-centric approaches. One of the principles of SSR is that it is people-centered and that providing security and access to justice for all citizens should be a core objective of SSR work. To date, SSR programs have tended to focus on formal state institutions, particularly at the national level. Effective state institutions are, of course, essential for guaranteeing human security. In many countries, however, state security and justice institutions are weak, corrupt, and/or ineffective and fail to provide either security or access to justice for the vast majority of the population. Often these central state bodies are not deployed beyond the capital city or other major cities and towns. National-level security and justice actors may also not be trusted for a variety of reasons (corruption, repression, ethnic/religious/regional/political affiliations, and so on) and there is always the danger that train and equip programs can exacerbate this problem. Access to formal justice systems may be also limited by cost, language, or location.

In addition and in consequence, there are many local actors that provide varying degrees of security and justice for populations. Most people obtain security and justice from local security and justice providers, many of whom are in fact linked to the state system and have the legal authority to provide justice or security services (Baker, 2010, p. 601). Others are non-state actors without legal standing but who nonetheless dispense justice or security (Scheye, 2011, p. 3). A focus on the formal, central institutions of state generally obscures the roles played by these locally based actors and they have been poorly integrated into SSR programming. Partly as a result, SSR programming has had too little impact on the security of ordinary people. Additionally, even when efforts are made to include local providers in internationally funded programs of support, national actors may object to a pluralist approach because that runs the risk of undermining their objective of gaining centralized control over the provision of security and justice.

The third challenge is to balance political and technical approaches to SSR. Security and justice work is highly political. At the same time, security and justice work focuses on effective service delivery and this makes it a technical process as well. All too often, however, the emphasis in program design and implementation is on the technical side because it is "easier". Programs can be designed and the risk of inadequate national commitment to the program can be acknowledged and then the program can be implemented as if these political constraints do not exist.

Furthermore, developing programs that take into account political realities also requires a recognition of the fact that political elites have their own agendas and that these agendas may not accord fully with funder agendas or with the needs of local populations. Experience indicates that it is important to move slowly to address politically sensitive issues rather than only focusing on what is technically possible. Local actors have to be convinced of the added value of engaging in a particular type of work. In simple terms, this involves showing them that there is "something in it for me/us". In South Sudan, for example, the United Kingdom was interested in the possibility of supporting work with local actors but realized that senior South Sudanese political leaders were not comfortable with a decentralized approach. The UK officials believed that considerable dialogue with officials in Juba would be necessary to prepare the political terrain. They therefore decided to begin by working on police development and, subsequently, to examine how formal and informal institutions interact at the state level, identify linkages, and over time figure out how to exploit these linkages to improve the delivery of security and justice services (Ball and van de Goor, 2011, pp. 25–26).

Effectiveness of Donor Approaches to Security Sector Reform

The modes of operation and operating procedures that international actors have applied to SSR suffer from a number of weaknesses that limit the effectiveness of their assistance. These weaknesses are not unique to security and justice work. To a large extent, they mirror problems that have afflicted their support to fragile and conflict-affected countries since the early 1990s. While development donors in particular have made progress in adapting to fragile and conflict-affected states, their modes of operation and operational procedures are still not tailored for environments where the political rules of the game are contested, control over the security sector is a major component of political power, and capacity at all levels is frequently weak. Security donors have even greater problems in these respects. While there is a growing awareness of these shortcomings, finding solutions to them has lagged.

In general, development and security donors continue to face difficulties in: (1) adapting their programming to local conditions; (2) using the SSR concept as an analytic framework rather than a programming tool; and (3) being realistic about the ability of their SSR support to create "ideal-type" conditions in a short period of time. (The way in which some providers of security and justice assistance have sought to ameliorate these problems is discussed in Ball and van de Goor, 2011.) Underlying these problems are donor/international community timeframes, the relative inflexibility of the program planning process, and a growing need for concrete, measurable results.

Experience in implementing the SSR agenda underscores the need for a lengthy timeframe when making significant changes in a country's security and justice systems. Time is needed to develop relationships of trust between local and international actors, an understanding of local and regional political relations, and local actors' capacity for identifying priorities and developing policies and plans, as well as to embed reforms. This is no different from effecting any type of institutional change. A study carried out for the World Bank found that the fastest reformers in the twentieth century required, on average, seventeen years to remove the military from politics, twenty-seven years to control corruption, and forty-one years to institute effective rule of law (World Bank, 2011, p. 11).

Both development and security donors, however, are under pressure to deliver results rapidly. Even when donors attempt to slow down the process, their time-frames can still appear too rapid for local stakeholders. The Netherlands, for example, decided to explore the possibility of providing SSR assistance to Burundi in 2008. It took approximately eight months to negotiate a memorandum of understanding with the Burundian government for what became the SSD program. For the Dutch government, this was a lengthy process. The Burundians, however, reportedly felt "rushed". In view of the fragile political environment in Burundi and the newness of the concept, one can understand why the Burundians might have wanted to proceed with caution. At the same time, at some point it is necessary to agree in principle to proceed and to develop a process whereby decisions can be made on a rolling basis. This is why it is extremely important for the parties to develop a strong relationship built on trust.

International actors also face pressure to spend allocated funds within specified timeframes (generally three to five years) on well-defined programs that have measurable outputs and outcomes. While there is often an effort to be flexible within the limits of agreed programs and to develop program objectives in collaboration with local partners, very few security and justice programs are based on an iterative approach to identifying needs, devising workable responses, and adjusting course as necessary. Rather, most programming occurs in a linear manner: assessments are carried out (generally by international consultants) and programs are then developed (again generally by international consultants) for specific amounts of money. These programs have log-frames and results frameworks that guide their implementation and define what activities will take place. This does not leave adequate room for a process of discussions and negotiations and an evolutionary approach to determining exactly what activities will take place. Local stakeholders, however, work more slowly, not necessarily because they do not want to make a decision or do not have the capacity to make a decision – it frequently takes a long time to develop the political backing for any particular course of action in fragile and conflict-affected countries.

Becoming More Effective: Giving More Attention to Process

In 1994, South Africa began its transition to multiparty rule. As part of that process, the new government began to formulate a number of policies in the security and justice area. Individuals involved in these efforts subsequently stressed the importance of process in achieving the desired outcomes. For them, a good process (one that was transparent, inclusive, brought stakeholders together, and found compromises for difficult issues) was more important than a technically perfect product (such as a defense or public safety and security white paper). The process was a vehicle for navigating the complex political waters of change in post-apartheid South Africa and developing the relationships that are necessary to make fundamental changes in the attitudes and behaviors of key stakeholders and institutions.

Unfortunately this important insight has largely failed to influence international approaches to SSR to date. This should not be surprising because development practice more broadly has failed to adequately incorporate process into programming approaches, despite some evidence that it can be beneficial in achieving positive results. According to Barakat and Chard, development practitioners and implementing agencies generally agree they should transform,

> practice from a top down "blueprint" to a participatory "learning-process" approach building on existing institutions and capacities. [Nonetheless] records of actual practice over the past three decades show that, with few exceptions, there has been remarkably little change: inappropriate "blue-print" strategies and approaches identified in the late 1970s and again in the early 1990s are still in evidence today. (Barakat and Chard, 2002, p. 818)

In line with this observation, most SSR programming tends to follow standard programming approaches that rely on log-frames, results chains, and pre-established results that give preference to output measurements – all defined largely by external actors. Donors also tend to take the ideal state as the starting point, do an assessment, identify deficits between the programming environment and the ideal state and develop programs to remove the deficits as soon as possible.

However, work conducted under the auspices of the INCAF in 2011 and early 2012 has identified a number of process-related factors that appear to increase the effectiveness of external support to SSR. These include (1) engaging politically at all levels and on a daily basis; (2) establishing results progressively; (3) working iteratively at every stage of the program cycle with an increasingly central role for local stakeholders; (4) being flexible in using resources; and (5) having a time horizon commensurate to ambition and environment (Ball and van de Goor, 2011; and Ball, Gasana, and Nindorera, 2012).

It is not realistic to assume that the donors' approach or toolkits will change overnight. Log-frames and results frameworks will be with us for some time to come, even if they lend a false certainty to programming. Nor is it likely that donors will begin to accept ten to twenty-year programming timeframes; however, it should be possible to develop an evidence-base of what works within the existing programming constraints and to develop compelling indicators to measure results based on the support of a more open-ended, process-oriented approach. For example, the UK Serious Organized Crimes Agency has worked on the basis of five-year rolling timeframes for its programs in Afghanistan, with a clearly defined exit strategy should conditions change. It has adopted a "two-speed" approach, with short-term projects with tangible outcomes. It has also worked to manage the expectations of senior officials and politicians by keeping them well informed of progress (or lack thereof) and sponsoring study visits to Afghanistan so that superiors are cognizant of the difficulties faced by programming in such environments.

It should also be possible to provide more political support to SSR programs. As noted earlier, political support from donors can make SSR programs more able to address political constraints facing them and thus to become more effective, as in the case of the Burundi–Netherlands SSD program. Of all of the process elements identified by the INCAF work, the ability to engage politically at multiple levels may bring the most benefits in terms of increased effectiveness of international engagements because the political blockages are the most fundamental. Unless they are addressed, SSR will only be able to tinker around the edges.

References

Baker, Bruce. 2010. "Linking State and Non-State Security and Justice." *Development Policy Review*, 28(5): 597–616.

Ball, Nicole. 1988. *Security and Economy in the Third World*. Princeton, NJ: Princeton University Press.

Ball, Nicole, and Dylan Hendrickson. 2009. "Trends in Security Sector Reform (SSR): Policy, Practice and Research." *CSDG Papers No. 20*. London: King's College London. Accessed December 4, 2013 from http://www.securityanddevelopment.org/pdf/CSDG%20Paper%2020.pdf

Ball, Nicole, and Malcolm Holmes. 2002. "Integrating Defense into Public Expenditure Work." Commissioned by the UK Department for International Development. Accessed December 4, 2013 from http://www.gsdrc.org/docs/open/SS11.pdf

Ball, Nicole, and Luc van de Goor. 2008. *Promoting Conflict Prevention through Security Sector Reform: Review of Spending on Security Sector Reform through the Global Conflict Prevention Pool*. London. Accessed December 4, 2013 from http://www.ssrnetwork.net/documents/Publications/PromConfPrevThruSSR/GCPP%20SSR%20Report%20Final%209Apr08.pdf

Ball, Nicole, and Luc van de Goor. 2011. 2013. *The challenges of supporting effective security and justice development programming*, OECD Development Co-operation Working Paper WP10/2013. Accessed December 4, 2013 from http://www.oecd-ilibrary.org/development/the-challenges-of-supporting-effective-security-and-justice-development-programming_5k49dffl6bmq-en

Ball, Nicole, Tsjeard Bouta, and Luc van de Goor. 2003. *Enhancing Democratic Governance of the Security Sector: An Institutional Assessment Framework*. Prepared by the Clingendael Institute for the Netherlands Ministry of Foreign Affairs. The Hague. Accessed December 4, 2013 from http://www.clingendael.nl/sites/default/files/20030800_cru_paper_ball.pdf

Ball, Nicole, Piet Biesheuvel, Tom Hamilton-Baillie, and 'Funmi Olonisakin. 2007. "Security and Justice Sector Programming in Africa." *DFID Evaluation Working Paper No. 23*. London. Accessed December 4, 2013 from http://webarchive.nationalarchives.gov.uk/+/http://www.dfid.gov.uk/aboutdfid/performance/files/sjr.pdf

Ball, Nicole, Jean-Marie Gasana, and Willy Nindorera. 2012. "From Quick Wins to Long-Term Profits? Developing better approaches to support security and justice engagements in fragile states: Burundi case study." Prepared for the INCAF Peacebuilding, Statebuilding and Security Task Team. Accessed December 4, 2013 from http://www.ciponline.org/images/uploads/publications/290312_Report_SJ_Burundi_final.pdf

Barakat, Sultan, and Margaret Chard. 2002. "'Rhetoric and Practice: Recovering the Capacities of War-Torn Societies." *Third World Quarterly*, 23(5): 817–835.

Byrd, William, and Stéphane Guimbert. 2009. "Public Finance, Security, and Development: A Framework and an Application to Afghanistan." *Policy Research Working Paper 4808*. Washington, DC: World Bank. Accessed December 4, 2013 from http://siteresources.worldbank.org/SOUTHASIAEXT/Images/223545-1144956091324/2443614-1238182344763/AfghanFin.pdf

de Vries, Hugo, and Erwin van Veen. 2010. "Living Apart Together? On the Difficult Linkage between DDR and SSR in Post-Conflict Environments." *CRU Policy Brief #15*. Den Haag: Conflict Research Unit/Clingendael Institute. Accessed December 4, 2013 from http://www.ssrresourcecentre.org/wp-content/uploads/2010/09/CRU-policy-brief-Living-apart-Together.pdf

Donald, Dominick and 'Funmi Olonisakin. 2007. "Security sector reform and the demand for small arms and light weapons." Project Ploughshares Briefing 01/7. Accessed December 4, 2013 from http://www.ssrnetwork.net/uploaded_files/4000.pdf

High Level Forum. 2005. "Paris Declaration on Aid Effectiveness: Ownership, Harmonisation, Alignment, Results and Mutual Accountability." March 2.

International Dialogue on Peacebuilding and Statebuilding. 2010. "Dili Declaration: A New Vision for Peacebuilding and Statebuilding." April 10. Accessed December 4, 2013 from http://www.pbsbdialogue.org/documentupload/44927821.pdf

International Dialogue on Peacebuilding and Statebuilding. 2011. "A New Deal for engagement in fragile states." Busan, December. Accessed December 4, 2013 from http://www.pbsbdialogue.org/documentupload/49151944.pdf

Kawakibi, Salam. 2012. "La 'Securitocratie' dans la tourmente des révolutions arabes," *EuroMeSCO*, Brief No. 45. Accessed December 4, 2013 from http://www.euromesco.net/images/briefs/euromescobrief45.pdf

Mémorandum d'Entente entre le Gouvernement de la République du Burundi et les Ministres des Affaires Etrangères, de la Coopération au Développement et de la Défence des Pays-Bas sur le Développement du Secteur de la Sécurité, 9 April 2009.

Mikail, Barah. 2012. *The Future of Security Sector Reform in the MENA Region.* Accessed December 4, 2013 from http://www.opendemocracy.net/opensecurity/barah-mikail/future-of-security-sector-reform-in-mena-region

Narayan, Deepa, Robert Chambers, Meera K. Shah and Patti Petesch. 2000. *Voice of the Poor: Crying Out for Change,* Oxford: Oxford University Press. Accessed December 4, 2013 from http://siteresources.worldbank.org/INTPOVERTY/Resources/335642-1124115102975/1555199-1124115201387/cry.pdf

Organisation for Economic Co-operation and Development (OECD). 2004a. *Security System Reform and Governance.* Policy Brief. Paris. Accessed December 4, 2013 from http://www.oecd.org/dac/31642508.pdf

Organisation for Economic Co-operation and Development (OECD). 2004b. *Security System Reform and Governance: Policy and Good Practice.* Paris. Accessed December 4, 2013 from http://www.oecd.org/dac/incaf/31785288.pdf

Organisation for Economic Cooperation and Development (OECD). 2007. *OECD DAC Handbook on Security System Reform: Supporting Security and Justice.* Paris. Accessed December 4, 2013 from http://www.oecd.org/development/incaf/38406485.pdf

Organisation for Economic Co-operation and Development (OECD). 2009. *Security System Reform: What have we learned?* Paris. Accessed December 4, 2013 from http://www.oecd.org/dac/incaf/44391867.pdf

Organisation for Economic Co-operation and Development (OECD). 2011. *Supporting Statebuilding in Situations of Conflict and Fragility: Policy Guidance.* Paris. Accessed December 4, 2013 from http://www.oecd-ilibrary.org/docserver/download/4311031e.pdf?expires=1386171996&id=id&accname=guest&checksum=28D6C616D1B039D678CD4719D8D4E1B6

Scheye, Eric. 2011. *Local Justice and Security Development in Burundi: Workplace Associations as a Pathway Ahead.* The Hague: Clingendael Institute/Conflict Research Unit. Accessed December 4, 2013 from http://www.clingendael.nl/sites/default/files/20111000_burundi_scheye.pdf

Sedra, Mark, ed. 2010. *The Future of Security Sector Reform.* Waterloo, ON: Centre for International Governance Innovation. Accessed December 4, 2013 from http://www.cigionline.org/sites/default/files/The%20Future%20of%20Security%20Sector%20Reform.pdf

Sherman, Jake. 2010. "The 'Global War on Terrorism' and its Implications for US Security Sector Reform Support." In *The Future of Security Sector Reform,* edited by Mark Sedra, 59–72. Waterloo, ON: Centre for International Governance Innovation.

Short, Clare. 1998. "Security, Development and Conflict Prevention." Speech to the Royal College of Defence Studies, London. Accessed December 4, 2013 from http://webarchive.nationalarchives.gov.uk/+/http://www.dfid.gov.uk/news/speeches/files/sp13may.html

Tanner, Fred, and Mohammad-Mahmoud Ould Mohamedou. 2012. "The Imperative of Security Sector Reform After the Arab Spring." *EuroMeSCO, Brief No. 43.* Accessed December 4, 2013 from http://www.euromesco.net/images/briefs/euromescobrief43.pdf

3rd High Level Forum on Aid Effectiveness. 2008. "Accra Agenda for Action." September 4.

United Nations Office of the Special Adviser on Africa. 2007. *Linkages between DDR and SSR.* Accessed December 4, 2013 from http://www.un.org/africa/osaa/speeches/ddr-ssr.pdf

United States Department of the Army. 2007. *Stability Operations.* Field Manual 3-07. Accessed December 4, 2013 from http://usacac.army.mil/cac2/Repository/FM307/FM3-07.pdf

USAID, US Department of Defense and US Department of State. 2009. *Security Sector Reform.* Washington, DC. Accessed December 4, 2013 from http://www.state.gov/documents/organization/115810.pdf

World Bank. 2011. *Conflict, Security and Development: World Development Report 2011.* Washington, DC: World Bank.

Chapter 17

Diplomacy and Mediation

Àlvaro de Soto

In his introductory chapter to the 2009 edition of the indispensable *Satow's Guide to Diplomatic Practice*, Sir Ivor Roberts defines diplomacy as "the application of intelligence and tact to the conduct of official relations between the governments of independent states," and quotes the Duc de Broglie to the effect that diplomacy is "the best means devised by civilization for preventing international relations from being governed by force alone" (Roberts, 2009).

There have been diplomats since time immemorial, but diplomacy as we know it began to take shape with the 1648 Peace of Westphalia. What we refer to loosely as the Westphalian system, including the bedrock notion of the sovereignty of states, remains the framework within which diplomacy is conducted. The Congress of Vienna, almost two centuries later, codified the basis for diplomatic representation in its *Règlement de 1815*, and with it the practice of diplomacy as a distinct profession.

Like World War I, World War II represented a catastrophic failure of the system. The repair work began early in the War, and the centerpiece that emerged was the collective security system as embodied in the United Nations. The dream was spoiled soon after its creation with the onset of the Cold War, which left the collegiality of the five permanent members of the Security Council on which it was premised in tatters. Yet the near-universal instrument that now regulates the conduct of diplomacy, the Vienna Convention on Diplomatic Relations, was drawn up under the aegis of the United Nations in 1961. The fact that it came into force in the depths of the Cold War bears testimony to the shared desire to preserve forms and keep channels open, even in bleak times.

If normal relations between states survived throughout the Cold War, diplomacy, as a tool for conflict resolution, as well as mediation and other diplomatic conflict resolution techniques, was all but paralyzed.

Another casualty of the Cold War was the UN Secretary-General as a major diplomatic player. Dag Hammarskjold showed some of the potential of the office in the

The Handbook of Global Security Policy, First Edition. Edited by Mary Kaldor and Iavor Rangelov.
© 2014 John Wiley & Sons, Ltd. Published 2014 by John Wiley & Sons, Ltd.

hands of an independent-minded player who was prepared to push the envelope. But the Secretary-General was mostly left on the margins, except for isolated cases: his successor U Thant helped to defuse the perilous standoff over Soviet missiles in Cuba in October 1962 in a role initiated and carefully scripted by the superpowers. The Secretary-General's ministrations were not welcome in proxy wars between superpowers in Africa, Asia, and Latin America.

When the Cold War began to thaw, the threat of global nuclear conflagration receded, the competition for spheres of influence waned, and diplomatic opportunities previously out of reach began to open, gradually, tantalizingly. In the late 1980s and the early 1990s, the fifth Secretary-General, Javier Pérez de Cuéllar, quietly slipped out of the Cold War's straitjacket and into the peacemaker's garb. He and others operating in the UN framework conjured solutions to various conflicts: Soviet troops withdrew from Afghanistan, the carnage between Iran and Iraq ended, the withdrawal of foreign combatants from Angola enabled the self-determination and independence of Namibia, wars in Cambodia and Mozambique wound up through negotiation, and solutions were brokered to the conflicts in Nicaragua and El Salvador and initiated in Guatemala. Pérez de Cuéllar ended his term in office with a flourish, initialing an agreement on the UN-mediated El Salvador peace accord at the stroke of midnight on his last day, heralding what appeared to be a new era of peacemaking.

One month later, on 31 January 1992, the UN Security Council met at the level of Heads of Government for the first time in its history. The whiff of hubris, faint but unmistakable, was in the air. There was a sense that a turning point had been reached. Was the United Nations, with the Council as its flagship, at last coming into its own as envisaged by the founders? The leaders issued an upbeat statement and asked the new Secretary-General, Boutros Boutros Ghali, to present a blueprint to strengthen the UN's capacity for peacemaking, peacekeeping and preventive diplomacy. In June 1992, Boutros Ghali produced the requested blueprint in the celebrated *An Agenda for Peace*, which contained a number of suggestions, some new, many recycled.

Boutros Ghali, more guarded than the Council, introduced his report with a note of caution:

"While my report deals with ways to improve the capacity [of the UN] to pursue and preserve peace, it is crucial for member states to bear in mind that the search for improved mechanisms and techniques will be of little significance unless [the] new spirit of commonality is propelled by *the will to take the hard decisions demanded at this time of opportunity*" (my italics) (Boutros Ghali, 1992).

Before long, as if to punish world leaders for their presumption, a veritable Pandora's box cracked open, releasing, like so many serpents and dragons, horrendous crises in the former Yugoslavia, Somalia, and Rwanda. Post-Cold War expectations were unceremoniously dashed, exposed almost in real time by the scrutiny of a newly empowered and intrusive press. All three crises are frequently held up as models of incoherence, aimlessness, fecklessness, foot-dragging or worse.

In 1995, Boutros Ghali (1995) issued a Supplement to *An Agenda for Peace*, designed to set the stage for discussion by leaders at the General Assembly's 40th anniversary session. It was cloaked in tones far more grey than the original, with nary a hint of hubris. In several speeches, Boutros Ghali had challenged member states to focus on the new set of dangers emerging with the end of the Cold War, which he saw as a historical moment as transcendental as the end of the Napoleonic Wars and World Wars I and II. Each of these, he emphasized, had been followed by a concerted effort to rearrange world order – the 1815 Congress of Vienna, the 1919 Paris Conference and the careful preparation that culminated at the 1945 San Francisco conference. No equivalent reassessment of whether the international community was properly organized to deal with the new situation was being made.

Under pressure to carry out reforms in the Secretariat at this incongruous moment, he compared himself to the driver of a vehicle undergoing repairs while hurtling over rugged terrain at high speed, with no one on hand with the appropriate tools and spare parts to get the job done. One began to hear murmurs of nostalgia for the stability and predictability of the Cold War. I recall a touchingly candid senior official from Central Europe remarking to the Secretary-General that his government had no institutional memory to help it cope with the crises emerging in his part of the world: the KGB used to sort those out with a minimum of fuss. Elsewhere, African leaders, no longer courted by competing powers, were feeling a new vulnerability.

The first half of the 1990s represented the high point of conflict. After Rwanda (1994) and the Dayton agreement (1995) the number of conflicts decreased significantly, many coming to an end by negotiation. New opportunities for diplomacy and mediation as tools for conflict management or resolution were indeed emerging, but they were of a new breed.

The Post-Cold War Issues

In addition to the headline-grabbing crises that sent the Security Council reeling in the early 1990s, a plethora of new issues have emerged as a result of the prevalence of internal conflict in the aftermath of the Cold War. These issues confront would-be conflict resolvers with complex, difficult, new, and unscripted challenges, as well as some serious dilemmas. Below are a few of these new challenges and a brief explanation of the issues.

If there is a common thread running through these challenges it is that those who seek to deal with them – to whom I shall turn in the next section about the post-Cold War actors – are forced to make choices that are rarely straightforward.

The Tension between Accountability and Peace

There can be no doubt that the 2002 establishment of the International Criminal Court (ICC), long in the making, is a major milestone in the pursuit of accountability and justice. The fact that many states are still not parties to the 1998 Rome Statute that led to its creation does not diminish this fact; it merely underscores that it is still a work in progress. However, the advent of the ICC has not put an end to the two-decade old debate about how to reconcile the equally worthy goals of peace and justice, which arises when conflict parties will only agree to make peace if they are ensured immunity from prosecution. In that debate, one side argues that the main source of injustice is war itself: the fighting must be stopped even at the expense of justice and accountability. The other side counters that unless accountability is part and parcel of peace, it will be built on shaky ground. Previously, amnesties or other *ad hoc* arrangements were used as a tool for defusing crises, solving conflict, or removing an abusive autocrat – more than one friendly dictator who had exceeded acceptable levels of thuggery found safe haven on one Riviera or another. With the establishment of the ICC this has become much harder. Today's peacemakers will balk at using such a tool. Stark choices must be made in the contest between peace and justice – both fundamental human values.

Under the Statute, the Security Council, though not itself a mediator or a party as such, has the authority to refer to the ICC cases occurring in states that are not parties. Thus even though three permanent members are not parties, they play a decisive role at the point where the pursuit of accountability and the imperative of stopping bloodshed intersect. An early such case was the Council's referral of Sudanese leader Omar al-Bashir and his indictment in 2008. More recently, the Council, at a surprisingly early stage in the Libya crisis, referred it to the ICC Prosecutor. This may have been consistent with the centerpiece of the Council's action – to authorize all necessary measures to protect civilians – but it closed off any possibility of a negotiated exit from power for Muammar Qaddafi, thereby possibly contributing to prolongation of the bloodshed for an agonizing number of months – until Qaddafi's capture by a lynch mob and thereafter. Questions have also been raised as to why the Council takes action in some cases and not others.

For parties to the Rome Statute or mediators acting on their behalf, it is not a matter of choice: they are bound by it. Well before the Statute entered into force, Secretary-General Kofi Annan issued guidelines to his envoys to oppose blanket amnesties for war crimes, crimes against humanity, or genocide. The United Nation is the quintessential normative mediator: it has a certain responsibility to uphold the body of laws that has developed under the aegis of the Organization. On the basis of those guidelines, when the Lomé Agreement ending the conflict in Sierra Leone provided "absolute and free pardon" for Foday Sankoh, the monstrous rebel leader, the United Nations reserved its position, thus making it possible later for the United Nations and the government of Sierra Leone to establish the Special Court that sentenced Charles Taylor to 50 years in prison in May 2012.

Judging from his role in the Yemen question, however, Annan's successor, Ban Ki-moon, does not seem troubled by blanket amnesties. Despite the call by the members of the Security Council for those responsible for human rights violations to be held accountable, Ban and the Security Council endorsed the 2011 GCC initiative on the transfer of power in Yemen, under which outgoing President Saleh and those who served under his rule are granted "immunity from law and judicial prosecution" (sic). Both the Council and the Secretary-General seem to be groping.

Dealing with the Past

The roots of internal conflict, particularly if ethnic groups are in confrontation, can run deep, and if they are not properly processed, they can bedevil the aftermath. On the other hand, some argue that it is better to let bygones be bygones and focus on the future. After wrenching internecine conflict, is it better to air past grievances or to turn the page? There are examples of both: in Spain after the death of Franco it became possible to establish a thriving democracy only when it was agreed not to reopen the wounds that resulted from the 1936–1939 Civil War and its aftermath. In Mozambique, a 15-year conflict ended in 1992 with no provision for a reckoning with the past. Conversely, one of the first acts of President Nelson Mandela after the abolition of *apartheid* was the appointment of a Truth and Reconciliation Commission combining judicial processes and restorative justice. In El Salvador, the parties agreed to establish a Truth Commission because it was judged that in order to overcome the trauma of the past, society needed to go through the catharsis of facing the truth about it.

The decision whether to confront the past or move on is separate from the decision to pursue accountability. Though the temptation may arise to opt for a truth-clarifying exercise in the hope of avoiding accountability, these are different paths addressing discrete needs.

Managing Diversity in an Age of State Fragmentation

In the face of ethnic strife or other sources of internal division, the inclination of our state-centered Westphalian system has been to encourage states to manage their problems in ways that promote coexistence and avoid state breakup. Thus under the UN Charter, the right to self-determination is set in the context of decolonization. There are good, objective reasons for this, including the risk of spreading instability and the growing unmanageability of a world of close to 200 states and still counting. Decentralization, autonomy, federalism, and combinations thereof have been standard tools in the management of diversity.

The breakup of the USSR may have been unavoidable at the end of the Cold War. The splitting apart of Yugoslavia brewed for years after the death of Tito and picked up speed at the end of the Cold War, accompanied by shocking violence and ethnic cleansing in Croatia and Bosnia, paving the way for the dismemberment of Serbia and Montenegro and the secession of Kosovo from Serbia.

Sub-Saharan Africa embodies a separate and distinct problématique rooted in historical decisions in which Africans had no say but which they can't easily undo. Borders between colonies drawn by colonial powers left ethnic and tribal groups straddling two or more states. At the time of decolonization, an attempt to re-draw borders would have courted disaster and put off independence. After independence, highlighting demographic faultlines is no way to gain acceptance and legitimacy and viability as a self-standing state – investors dislike turmoil. Despite their abhorrence of the colonial borders, therefore, when newly independent African states created the Organization of African Unity, they specifically agreed that borders between them would not be touched. That position has by and large remained in place for over four decades.[1]

African colonial borders are, however, no longer intangible – Eritreans warred against annexation by Ethiopia until they gained separation in 1991. The civil war in Sudan raged from 1983 until 2005 when the warring parties agreed to a truce for six years, at the end of which the South would hold a referendum on whether to remain in Sudan or become independent. In the 2011 referendum, the South Sudanese overwhelmingly chose independence.

The centrifugal forces unleashed reverberate far. In the wake of the fall of the Berlin Wall, the international community's adherence to the preservation of state unity is wavering. It is today more difficult to tell a separatist leader in a state suffering internal strife that the international community would be averse to a split; efforts to conceive arrangements, short of separation or secession, that address concerns of minorities have been complicated by knowledge that there is an alluring alternative script in which they end up leading their own statelet. I vividly recall the separatist Turkish Cypriot leader Rauf Denktash rhapsodizing about the impending split of Montenegro from Serbia.[2]

Making Peace Sustainable after Intrastate Conflict

The prevalence of internal conflict in the wake of the Cold War brings with it a set of challenges that affect the conduct of diplomacy and mediation as a device to ensure global as well as regional security.

If after an international conflict armed forces separate and disengage and each goes back to its own territory, the greatest immediate source of relapse into conflict is defused. This is not the case in an internal setting because combatants don't withdraw to another country after the fighting stops: they are already home, cheek to jowl with yesterday's mortal enemies, and the potential for friction is likely to remain until all sides see their grievances addressed. It is only by moving in this direction that we can hope that uneasily separated combatants will gradually learn to co-exist.

It follows that a new, inescapable responsibility falls on a mediator trying to solve internal conflict: he must plan for the aftermath and pave the way for implementation and strive to ensure that mechanisms and institutions for the solution of future disputes by peaceful means are in place. This may involve major governance reform, as was the case in El Salvador. In order to help national actors see through the implementation of such plans, international involvement, frequently an indispensable spur, may extend over a long time. At this stage, it may be advisable to involve sectors of society that did not participate in the violent conflict or in the negotiation to solve it, but can provide a wider sampling of views as to what is desirable and help strengthen support for emerging agreements. Such an exercise is not without pitfalls, however. The temptation to broaden participation is understandable, but the mediator mustn't lose sight of the bedrock fact that his margin for maneuver derives from the confidence of the warring parties who hold the capacity to decide whether the conflict will continue or not. It is therefore prudent to make a distinction between the negotiating role of the warring parties and the consultative role of other players.

Even when a conflict ends in a clear-cut victory rather than a negotiated outcome, if there is substantial support for the demands for which the defeated forces fought – often the case where the defeated army represented an ethnic or other minority – their grievances need to be addressed lest they reappear, even years later, from the ashes. Think Sri Lanka.

Frequently after prolonged conflict, adjustments in the tools of economic governance are required to compete in a globalized world. Growth and productive employment are necessary features of sustainability. Thus the challenge may involve more than moving from war to peace, difficult enough in and of itself; it may entail a multiple transition, institutional, systemic, and economic, and the goals of one transition may clash with those of another and must be reconciled. There are no fixed formulas. In the case of Africa, the emphasis on institutions of good governance, "premised on the fallacy that a state even existed there," is considered misplaced by some authors, who believe "the key to sustained peace is perhaps more cogently based on security and sustained and distributed economic growth" (Ayangafac and Cilliers, 2011).

In *An Agenda for Peace*, Boutros Ghali called the set of activities in such multipronged, multilayered transitions "post-conflict peace-building." He defined it as the set of actions needed to ensure that a conflict will not recur. He emphasized that the concept was different in nature from traditional peacekeeping, and more complex, not least because it would involve, beyond the familiar blue berets and helmets, small armies of civilian technocrats to assist in carrying out these activities. Rallying the wide array of players round the overarching goal and ethos of preventing the recurrence of conflict requires an adjustment in policies of some of those players.[3]

UN policy drifted after Boutros Ghali's 1992 conceptual breakthrough in the *Agenda*. The Security Council was reluctant to embrace post-conflict peacebuilding as an inherent part of its responsibilities for the maintenance of peace and security under the Charter. It is debatable whether the joint creation, by the General Assembly and the Security Council, of the Peace-Building Commission (PBC), agreed at the World Summit of 2005, remedies the drift. The PBC only takes on cases with which the Security Council is not seized. Arguably, it provides an alibi for the Security Council, admittedly overworked, to avoid taking the central role, which it should be taking in this area.

Managing Complex, Multilayered Transitions

The variety of tasks to be performed after conflict may require a wide spectrum of specialists, all operating in the same geographical space and competing for the attention of national leaders who must perforce play the decisive role. There is a strong potential for disarray in any setting in which a multiplicity of organizations, and possibly also individual states and nongovernmental organizations (NGO), are acting. We normally look to the United Nations to lead such operations, and specifically to the person at the head, who usually carries the lofty title of Special Representative of the Secretary-General (SRSG) – which usually presumes a mandate from the Security Council.

The fact is that the UN System, as it emerged from World War II, is not structured in a way that allows the SRSG to get the various agencies to accept its lead. This is particularly the case of agencies such as the World Bank and the International Monetary Fund (which are only loosely associated with the UN System) who are key players and far better endowed and powerfully staffed than the UN Secretariat itself. It is also the case of other agencies that are part of the UN System but, like the World Bank and the International Monetary Fund, are the creation of and answerable to corresponding branches of national governments, such as the FAO, WHO, ILO, etc – almost as tenuous is the Secretary-General's control over UN programs such as the UN Development Programme (UNDP). Although the Secretary-General proposes the appointment of the Administrator to the General Assembly, he does not exercise operational control over its activities; thus, he must rely heavily on persuasive leadership in the field.

Dealing with Groups Labeled as Terrorists

The "Global War On Terror" that followed the attacks of September 11, 2001 against US targets, ongoing even if the GWOT moniker has been retired, has lastingly stigmatized dealing with groups and persons labeled as terrorists on official lists. The feral nihilists of Al Qaeda kill unarmed civilians indiscriminately; they want to do away with the state system and take us back to the pre-Westphalian era; they have no perceptible constituency; and they show no interest in negotiating their grievances. Few groups on official lists meet such rarefied qualifications. On the other hand, they include groups and organizations whose goals are not necessarily outrageous and who, however condemnable their methods, speak to legitimate grievances, enjoy strong support, and cannot be circumvented if peace is to be negotiated. A blanket refusal to engage them may actually prolong conflict. Indiscriminate stigmatization is a serious handicap to conflict resolution, which has hampered, up until now, important players in conflict resolution, including the United States and all members of the European Union. The drawbacks of stigmatizing engagement with those who must be engaged to make peace should be perfectly clear: yes, terrorist acts are unacceptable, but not all those who commit such acts need to be treated like Al-Qaeda. Even the United Nations, which had long engaged all parties in the framework of peacemaking and peacekeeping, has buckled under the pressure, the most notorious case being its complicity in the ostracism of Hamas, the victor of the most recent Palestinian elections, arguably putting a negotiated solution to the Israeli–Palestinian conflict beyond reach or making it impracticable. I still find it hard to believe that the intention behind this sweeping policy was knowingly to foreclose negotiations with other organizations without whom conflict can't be solved. It is past the time to revisit the issue.

The Proliferation of Would-Be Mediators

The characteristics, advantages, and disadvantages of the various actors are examined in the next section, the post-Cold War actors. The United Nations is a big player, but some regional organizations are coming into their own as well. Some states have always been significant players; new ones are appearing on the scene. Conflict-resolution NGOs are a very interesting new feature of the peacemaking landscape, as are eminent and experienced individuals.

During the Cold War would-be peacemakers were not welcome in parts of the globe where superpowers competed for influence. With the Cold War receding, political constraints on would-be conflict managers or resolvers disappeared, and would-be peacemongers who would otherwise have abstained began to feel the temptation to engage in mediation, a low-tech field of endeavor potentially rich in domestic political dividends. Thus, we have today a surfeit of competing would-be conflict managers or resolvers and no rules or criteria to decide who is best suited in each case. The question of who will take on this or that conflict encourages "forum-shopping" by conflict parties. It has become one of the challenges to post-Cold War peacemaking.

One could already feel the trend in the late 1980s. Pérez de Cuéllar was of the view that competition between would-be mediators was something to be avoided, and if others were engaged he would refrain from offering his services. Thus he bided his time, as in the South Atlantic and Central America, while the US Secretary of State and the Contadora Group, respectively, took the crises in hand. When the Contadora Group passed him the baton on Central America, we put together a group of "friends" of the Secretary-General whom we brought into our confidence so as to use their energy and knowledge and contacts with both sides and, in the process, discourage any temptation to initiate a rival effort.

We asked them to intervene with one or the other of the parties only at our request and to follow guidelines that we would provide them. We remained in frequent contact with them, and they reciprocated by letting us know when opportunities to engage the parties arose in their capitals or elsewhere. There was one isolated episode where a "friend" could not control the temptation to take on his own a diplomatic initiative, but it was quickly quashed by one of the parties in the negotiation and repudiated by the other "friends". They played their role with ability and loyalty, and they shared in the success of the effort when it came.

The formula has been widely used since, with varying success. The central feature is that it is a way to involve would-be mediators without undermining the need to ensure that control remains with whoever is charged with it. The usefulness of such a mechanism is that it encourages the ethos that peacemakers shouldn't intervene where others are involved, and that there must be a single person or institution in charge – others wishing to play a role should accept to assist as "friends" of whoever is in the lead, and refrain from acting except at the behest of the leader and according to his specifications.

The Post-Cold War Actors

I said at the outset that the diplomat and the mediator's tools are, by and large, those that have been in use since the inception of the Westphalian system of states. In the previous section, I have attempted to provide a taste of the challenges in the new, uncharted era that followed the Cold War, as well as of the new burdens, substantive and managerial, piled onto the practitioner. The essence of how a mediator goes about his task, and the general rule that impartiality lies at the core of it, has not changed.

In a conflict situation, the mediator's core responsibility remains to assist warring parties, who are willing to bring it to an end but are unable to do so alone. The precise nature of the mediator's role depends on the issues and on whether any progress has been made in earlier efforts to address them, as well as on the degree of confidence, if any, between the parties. Even if the mediator writes all the texts, the negotiation belongs to the parties. The parameters within which the mediator operates are determined by the parties. Ideally, they can be set out in writing; failing that, the mediator will gradually ascertain the boundaries by probing the limits. The range is considerable. At one end, a third party may be required simply because the parties cannot be seen to make concessions to each other, but can do so to a third party – U Thant in the Cuban missile crisis is a case in point. At the other end of the intrusiveness spectrum, a third party may be required because the level of distrust is so high that they can't even bring themselves to meet except in the presence of a third party, and cannot budge (or be seen to budge) from well-known positions. They may automatically reject any proposal made by the other side simply because it is presented by the other side; in that case the third party must play a proactive role in proposing ways out – as in the UN's role in El Salvador. The more intrusive the role, the greater the possibility for the third party to make suggestions for actions that, in his judgment, could enhance the chances of success of the agreements that they reach.

The range of inputs that a third party can make may thus be very wide and deep, or very narrow and accessorial. But the mediator must never lose sight of the basic premise that his primary goal is to work out terms for a peace agreement that will withstand the test of time and future disputes. He should, if he believes this will enhance the sustainability of a settlement, encourage the parties to include provisions that will broaden support for the agreement. But in doing so, it would be unwise to put at risk the support of those without whose support the conflict will continue – the warring parties. It is the parties at war that must make peace, and only a reckless mediator would presume to question the warring parties' decision as to who should have a say.

These caveats aside, the mediator's task remains the same. What has evolved, sometimes dramatically, is the set of issues that a mediator (these days mostly involved in conflict management or resolution in an intrastate context) has to tackle with a view to achieving solutions that will endure.

It is tempting to think that, given the variety of skills that have to be marshaled during and after, mediation can somehow be farmed out, subcontracted, subdivided, delegated, or otherwise apportioned or shared. I will refer to a developing trend in this direction in the final section of this chapter. For now, I will only say that this temptation must be resisted. Mediation remains best discharged by a single authoritative individual who is, and is known to be, in control. The idea that two or more mediators joining forces can somehow be beneficial to mediation is mistaken. Simple arithmetic doesn't apply: in fact, adding players *subtracts* efficacy of strategy and efficiency of execution. If more players are involved, they have to compromise with each other, which will blunt strategy and increase the risk that they will be played off against one another by the negotiating parties. The need for tight focus of responsibility in a single pair of hands increases the higher the stakes involved. Compare mediation in a peace negotiation to driving a bus full of passengers along a narrow, slippery cliff-side road in the fog: the person holding the wheel must also control the pedals and the brake.

These considerations should be borne in mind in considering the various actors involved in mediation today, which fall into four broad categories: the UN Secretary-General; regional organizations; states; and NGOs and eminent individuals. Their advantages and disadvantages should be weighed in light of the complex agenda earlier discussed. As the reader will see, the choices on offer are far from simple.

All are confronted with difficult conundrums; all face difficult dilemmas; all have to make difficult choices. They are doing so in an environment that is severely straining the structures of the international community as it is organized, if that is the word, today.

The United Nations Secretary-General

Since the end of the Cold War, the number of UN envoys in a third party role has risen dramatically. There are about twenty envoys listed on un.org at the time of writing this chapter, as compared to the half dozen or so reporting to Pérez de Cuéllar 20 years ago.

This growth may give the impression that the UN Secretary-General is something like the world's default peacemaker, with the power to pick his peacemaking assignments. Not so. Granted, he has broader powers than his League of Nations predecessor, and plenty of exploratory latitude, but there is no blanket mandate for the Secretary-General's good offices in the Charter or in any other UN legislative decision. To take on a good offices role he must have, in addition to the consent of the parties concerned, the assent of an intergovernmental UN body with the power to confer it – usually the Security Council, exceptionally the General Assembly. This must be obtained case by case.

The Secretary-General has a certain number of advantages over other peacemakers. The first is quite simply the stature of his office. The second is the UN's institutional memory. The third is the presumption of impartiality – of not having a stake in the outcome. The fourth is that the Secretary-General is uniquely placed to mobilize expertise available throughout the United Nations System. The fifth, already mentioned, is the freedom to engage any interlocutor of his choice. The sixth is the global perspective that informs the UN's work, protected under chapter VIII of the UN Charter. Some of these advantages are potential disadvantages, or must be subjected to a large caveat. Each advantage point will be discussed next.

The UN's elevated stature – on the surface, the highest instance in the world – is not necessarily desirable in all cases: one or more parties in a conflict may prefer that it be dealt with at a lower level. They may be concerned about interference from members of the Security Council, by couching his mandate in a prejudicial way. Once a matter comes before the Council, it may prove difficult for a recalcitrant, or even merely skittish, party to a conflict to extricate itself. A government party may also prefer to approach a regional body where empathy from peers might be more forthcoming. An NGO operating out of the public eye, without the unwanted scrutiny of meddling outside powers or the legitimization of rebels, is another option.

The UN's institutional memory is still more desideratum than reality. There isn't yet evidence that it has mastered its reporting and lessons-learning abilities to the extent desirable. Institutional memory and the rich background of experience that can be drawn from it, is only useful to the extent of UN envoys' ability to marshal and process it. In the early phase of the UN's peacemaking revival, Secretary-General Pérez de Cuéllar chose envoys from among people he knew and trusted and had personally worked with, but they were only a handful. With the peacemaking boom since, and the creation of a Department of Political Affairs, such appointments have come under closer scrutiny and procedures have been laid down, narrowing the Secretary-General's ability to choose. It is in the nature of things that envoys are frequently pressed into service on exceedingly short notice and there is very little time for indoctrination.

In an internal conflict setting, impartiality isn't necessarily seen as a virtue by the government party to a conflict. Nothing in the Charter prevents the Secretary-General from involvement as a third party in an internal conflict, but the United Nations was not really designed for such a purpose: it is an organization of states, and governments represent those states. It should come as no surprise that governments balk at an arrangement that appears to legitimize rebel groups. The other side of this coin is the fear of those rebel groups that the United Nations will tilt in favor of the governmental party. A third aspect is that the Security Council, which is composed of states, may try to micromanage the Secretary-General's efforts by building into his mandate elements that favor one or the other side. To counter this, when the Secretary-General's good offices in a conflict are at stake, he must master the elusive art of interacting with the Council. He must remain a few steps ahead and keep it informed enough so that it feels confident in his handling of the issue, but not so much that it will be tempted to micromanage his effort.

I have already dealt with the challenges to the Secretary-General's capacity to mobilize expertise that exists in the UN System earlier, under the heading *Managing Complex, Multilayered Transitions*.

The member states have traditionally accepted the UN Secretary-General's freedom to engage any interlocutor of his choice, which is implicit in Article 99,[4] protected by Article 100 of the Charter and grounded in decades of practice. The "Global War on Terror" that followed Al-Qaeda's September 11, 2001 attacks against the United States created a climate in which dealings with any and all groups or persons on lists of persons or groups labeled as terrorists – discussed earlier under "*Dealing with Groups Labeled as Terrorist*" – were severely frowned upon. Starting with the victory of Hamas in Palestinian Authority legislative elections in January 2006, the Secretary-General stopped dealing with the Palestinian Authority leadership and later extended the no-contact policy to persons indicted by the ICC. The ability of the Secretary-General to play a useful role in the Israeli–Palestinian conflict, in Somalia, and in Sudan has suffered as a result. By compromising longstanding practice, the Secretary-General has arguably diminished the office itself.

Under Chapter VIII of the Charter, regional arrangements are encouraged to resolve threats to peace. They are, however, not obliged to do so, and in any case this is without prejudice to the right of the United Nations to be seized of any issue. The UN Secretary-General does not aspire to deal with all matters and indeed welcomes it when regional arrangements tackle them. But the broader interest of the international community as embodied in the United Nations is served by ensuring that principles and norms are not reinterpreted or diluted or distorted regionally, and to that end the global perspective (the sixth advantage) that comes with the UN's involvement brings an added value. The assumption that proximity to the conflict area makes for better understanding of the issues argues in favor of addressing it at the regional level, but conversely geographical distance gives detachment and lowers the risk of partiality. Thus, the United Nations has by and large preferred to use envoys from as far away as possible so as to avoid even a suspicion of partiality, e.g. the long list of Latin Americans, a Canadian, a Korean and now an Australian who have led efforts to solve the Cyprus problem.[5]

Regional Organizations

Soon after the end of the Cold War, Secretary-General Boutros Ghali reached out to the heads of regional organizations, via collective gatherings, with a clear message: the United Nations, with its hands full, would welcome all the help that it could get. The Panamerican Union, predecessor of the Organization of American States (OAS), existed long before the United Nations. The Organization of African Unity, now rebranded as the African Union (AU), was created in 1964. The European Union (EU), whose origins are in the late 1950s, has in recent decades shown a vocation for conflict resolution. Then there is the Organization for Security and Cooperation in Europe (OSCE), which had its origins in the Cold War-era Helsinki agreements. There are various subregional organizations in Africa, Asia (most notably the Association of Southeast Asian Nations), and in the South Pacific but there is no regional organization encompassing the whole of Asia.

The lack of symmetry or uniformity of regional approaches and also the wide divergences in the nature and capabilities as well as the institutional and financial strength of regional arrangements are striking. Only a few of these organizations have a peacemaking vocation that might be considered analogous to that of the United Nations. In fact, it can be narrowed down to the European Union and OSCE, the African Union, and several African subregional organizations, and in a limited way to OAS. The OSCE is first and foremost a diplomatic actor, somewhat constrained by the fact that it takes its decisions by consensus, and includes every country in the northern hemisphere, from the Bering Strait in the West to China's western border in the East. The African Union and the main African subregional organizations have drawn up a complex "African Peacemaking Architecture" that emphasizes coordination and cooperation rather than integration or choice of leadership. Subregional organizations, notably the Economic Community of West African States (ECOWAS), have played an enforcement role in the West African region, which they rather loosely describe as peacekeeping. With the OAS, diplomatic action is most visible in cases where the constitutional order in a member state has been interrupted.

The European Union has a stated vocation for peacemaking, and High Representative for Common Foreign and Security Policy Javier Solana, an engaging and experienced diplomatic player, multiplied himself by playing, grandmaster-like, on many chessboards at one time. He had an experienced team of envoys and advisers who were influential not least because of their capacity to mobilize resources to tackle problems. The EU's ability to assert a role that would reflect its mammoth economic weight and translate it into sharply focused, strategic mediation has been hampered by the lingering reluctance of some of the EU's members to relinquish their sovereign power to continue to act as self-standing diplomatic players. It is not clear that this threshold will be crossed any time soon. In the meantime, the European Union has not yet reached the point where joint action in the peacemaking field produces results that go beyond what one could expect from the sum of its parts. The jury is still out on whether the restructuring agreed at the 2009 Lisbon Euro Council will improve the EU's capacity as a peacemaking power.

As stated under the previous heading, there is a case to be made for tackling regional crises at the regional level if there is machinery to do so, as well as a counter case. There are no agreed criteria for deciding which is more suitable. In recent years, the slogan "African solutions for African problems" has acquired currency in that part of the world, but some observers view this as a cynical ploy by dictators to shield themselves from international scrutiny (Ayangafac and Cilliers, 2011, p. 116). Sometimes the United Nations and the African Union work together with separate envoys or, as in Sudan today, a single agreed envoy. An exceptional collaboration was that between the United Nations and the European Union in the former Yugoslavia, where separate envoys working with unusual synchronicity produced a formula for the cantonization of Bosnia, which did not find favor at the time but, many today believe, would have led to a situation less fractured and polarized than the one that emerged from the famously unfinished 1995 Dayton agreement.

States

There are many states that dabble sporadically in mediation because the leader of government or the foreign minister at the time is personally inclined to do this or well placed to assist in tackling a given dispute or conflict. Some states play this role more systematically as a matter of policy. This can be because they believe it is in their general interest to promote stability, because they see it as part of their general responsibility, or because they have a national policy of promoting peace as a desirable goal in itself without regard to national interests.

Major Powers   I don't wish to diminish the ability or imagination of US diplomats, but the advantage of major powers as mediators that stands out is their ability and readiness to exercise leverage not available to others. About other such powers little information is available. One well-known example of what the United States can do is the Egypt–Israel Peace Treaty of 1979, brokered by US President Jimmy Carter, which came with incentives in the form of substantial annual grants and aid packages to both countries which continue to this day. Another example, of leverage through coercion, was NATO's bombing of Serb targets in Operation Deliberate Force in the summer of 1995, a key factor in bringing about the US-brokered Dayton Agreement that ended the war in Bosnia-Herzegovina in December of the same year.

The United States is widely seen as the indispensable player in the elusive search for a solution to the Israeli–Palestinian conflict. Given the strength of the bonds that tie the United States and Israel, this is something of an oddity because the United States makes no claim to being impartial. Even though Israel prefers to negotiate with its adversaries without intermediaries, it accepts the United States in a third party role in the confidence that the United States "has its back", in the words of President Obama, and won't present proposals that run counter to Israel's interests – indeed, it will consult Israel before making any proposals at all, as strategic allies do. Israel's comfort with the United States playing this *sui generis* role is hardly surprising. What is remarkable is that the Palestinian side – the Fatah-led Palestine Liberation Organization (PLO) rather than the Palestinian Authority – not only accepts the US role, but prefers it to other would-be third parties because it reasons that only the United States can "deliver" Israel – if anyone can.

Middle Powers   Two European countries, Norway and Switzerland, epitomize the state, which as a matter of non-partisan policy, devotes significant efforts and resources to the disinterested search for peace in far-flung points of the globe. Neither is constrained by EU membership, which includes restrictions on contacts with proscribed groups.

Switzerland, which has not fought in a war for almost two centuries, holds its neutrality dear. The prestigious International Committee of the Red Cross, a Swiss creation, is headquartered in Geneva, its most international city, seat of the League of Nations after World War I. In addition to the headquarters of a large number of international organizations, it is the venue for countless international diplomatic conferences. The highly respected and supremely professional Swiss Foreign Ministry has a section entirely devoted to peacemaking efforts in many conflicts with uniquely Swiss discretion.

Like Switzerland, Norway has no past as a colonial power. It is the largest donor of aid to developing countries in the world on a per capita basis and, fabulously rich from North Sea oil, a prominent one in absolute terms. As a NATO member, Norway doesn't qualify as neutral, but this has not been an obstacle for its commitment over twenty years ago, uninterrupted with changes of government, to help solve conflict in many parts of the world, without shying away from the perennial or frozen ones. The accession to the European Union of Sweden, which during the Cold War played an important part, has facilitated Norway's new role. Partnering with Norwegian Church groups, Norway set in motion the UN-mediated process that ended the war in Guatemala. It brokered the breakthrough negotiations that led to the Israeli–Palestinian Oslo Accords signed on the White House lawn in 1993. It led the initially promising but ill-fated effort to find a negotiated solution to the conflict opposing the Liberation Tigers of Tamil Eelam (LTTE) to the government of Sri Lanka, and worked hard to end the civil war in Sudan.

International pressure helped bring down apartheid in South Africa, and African National Congress (ANC)-led South Africa, starting with the presidency of iconic leader Nelson Mandela, has paid back with peacemaking efforts both in sub-Saharan Africa and in geographically more distant conflicts, such as Western Sahara and Palestine. His successor Thabo Mbeki continued to play a prominent role in African peace efforts after his presidency and there is a small but significant NGO peace community based in South Africa.

Qatar and Turkey have burst onto the peacemaking scene in recent years. The position that Qatar has carved out for itself, given its geostrategic position and internal demographics, is in and of itself a bold balancing act: it hosts a major US military presence while giving support to Islamist movements in many places; it has maintained a fluid relationship with both Iran and Israel; and it has created the influential Al Jazeera, a communications powerhouse not just in Arabic but also in the English-speaking world and plans to expand to places which Western news channels neglect. Supported by immense hydrocarbon wealth and free of the turmoil that has affected many North African and Middle Eastern countries since the beginning of 2011, the maverick Emir played a pragmatic hand in helping to defuse a looming internal confrontation in Lebanon. More recently, it has taken a clear-cut stance against the Assad régime in Syria. It is not clear whether Qatar plans to go beyond crises where a suitable opportunity arises. It is too soon to tell whether its viability will be affected by its recent militance on Syria.

With its unique location at several crossroads, Turkey is and will remain an important player. After World War I, Turkey threw its lot unequivocally with the West and possesses the second largest armed forces in NATO at a time when European military establishments are dwindling. There is a dissonance between the importance of Turkey's role at Europe's Eastern flank and Europe's equivocal policy toward Turkey. The European Union invited Turkey to start EU accession negotiations, but then some members backtracked. Yet it was the prospect of European accession down the road that put Turkey on a track of internal reforms that have accelerated its democratization. Under AKP, Turkey has finally faced down the armed forces. Turkish entrepreneurs have taken advantage of opportunities in new markets, including Russia, Central Asia, and the Arab world with goods and services. The AKP government prides itself on speaking to everyone and has parlayed this into a key role in a complex and volatile region (thereby flaunting its indispensability to Europe). Notwithstanding Turkey's continuing military presence in Cyprus and pending issues over the Aegean, it has very good relations with Greece, but EU accession talks are at a standstill, blocked by Greek–Cypriot-led Cyprus and others. Decades of close relations with Israel have come under strain because of Turkish participation in protests against Israel's treatment of Gaza. That and strong support of popular insurgencies have earned Turkey an influential role in the region, where its Islam-inspired but secular dispensation is proclaimed as a model. Its Kemalist slogan "zero problems with our neighbours" is being challenged by the developments of 2011–2012 in Syria, where Turkey tried very hard to bring around the Assad régime before finally giving up on him and offering sanctuary not just to refugees and diaspora leaders working from abroad to bring about the downfall of the régime but also, along its borders, to fighters who make no pretense of using nonviolent methods. Turkey sits in a rough neighborhood, but its diplomatic pedigree rests on centuries of history. Like diplomatic establishments everywhere, Turkey is having to adapt to the new set of circumstances and the range of new players that have emerged in the wake of the Cold War.

Nongovernmental Organizations

NGOs as peacemakers have come of age since the end of the Cold War.

They are not an entirely new phenomenon. The Atlanta-based Carter Center and Jimmy Carter himself, in his long and glittering post-presidency career, have been active in peacemaking diplomacy for decades. Many have labored at "Track II" – non-official contacts between members of civil society – in places like Nicosia and Palestine where the official variant – Track I – has failed to bear fruit.

Perhaps the most spectacular story of NGO peacemaking is that of the Comunità di Sant'Egidio, a Catholic Church public lay association in war-ravaged Mozambique. In 1990, FRELIMO, in government, and RENAMO, a rebel group promoted by *apartheid* South Africa and others, agreed to Sant'Egidio's mediation and, to everyone's astonishment, brought about an agreement, signed in Rome on October 4, 1992, to end a war of extraordinary cruelty that had raged there since soon after its 1975 independence.

The fact that in the final stretch Sant'Egidio sought the assistance of various leaders and of the United Nations so as to close the deal and make sure it was properly designed does not diminish the magnitude of their accomplishment; rather, it bears testimony to their good sense because it reveals one of the most important limitations of NGO peacemaking: they don't have the institutional capability to carry a peace negotiation through to implementation, or to help a country coming out of war navigate the shoals of consolidating peace and ensuring that it will last. For Mozambique, the United Nations created a mission led by Aldo Ajello, who set the gold standard for post-Cold War Special Representatives.

The name of the premier conflict resolution NGO today, Humanitarian Dialogue (HD), reveals that it came to its role in a roundabout way, a bit like Sant'Egidio in Mozambique – aid workers turned peacemakers. According to its website, HD began operations in August 1999 following discussions "among those who had a practical impact on humanitarian policy and practice". HD's aim is "to help alleviate the suffering of individuals and populations caught up in both high-profile and forgotten conflicts, *by acting as mediators and by providing other mediators with the support they need to work effectively*" (emphasis added). The task of humanitarians is not to stop wars but to care for its victims: they could settle for the first part of the stated aim, up to the word "conflicts", but the operative part is the bit in italics after the comma.

It is almost as if HD was born of the impatience of humanitarians with the work of peacemakers – an understandable impulse. Humanitarian workers turned peacemakers? Well, some – such as the first director – have experience as humanitarian workers, but there are a number of seasoned diplomats and mediators at the top of HD. This is a very professional outfit. Since they work under the radar, they can escape the post-9/11 inhibitions of many organizations and states and deal with interlocutors who are suspected or guilty of terrorist acts but without which it is not possible to solve conflicts viably.

An indication of HD's professionalism is that when asked what cases or issues they are dealing with, they may coyly cite the number of such cases or issues, but will not say which they are. They will only admit to dealing with a given issue if the parties involved have made this public. The only such case, to my knowledge, is the revelation some years ago by both the Spanish government and ETA that they were in talks – with HD in the middle.

HD's adherence to confidentiality may not be helpful for the purposes of outsiders examining their work, but it is reassuring for parties to conflict who are considering a negotiated solution but don't want this to be known. In an age where it is difficult to keep anything out of the public eye, confidentiality is desirable because it is only in a confidential environment that parties to a conflict groping for a way out can freely test ideas and probe formulas. UN envoys are hard pressed to protect bits of information, such as their travel schedule, which can reveal their movements and lead to noisome speculation. Agents for a small organization like HD are better able to stay out of the limelight than envoys from an international or regional organization or a state who must follow procedures and remain accountable and are therefore leak-prone. It is no surprise that Norway and Switzerland are strong supporters of HD.

Eminent Individuals

Kofi Annan came away from his decade as Secretary-General with the Nobel Peace Prize, worldwide name and face recognition, and a glowing aura. The difficulties he faced in his second term have been largely forgotten. He is active on various issues, including food security in Africa and membership in The Elders, in addition to the work of the Geneva-based foundation that bears his name.

He has not entirely eschewed public service, however. In Kenya, he brokered the February 2008 power-sharing agreement that ended the violent crisis that ensued after manipulation of the results of the Presidential election.

More recently, in February 2012, as the crisis in Syria that began in March 2011 aggravated, with the Security Council in deadlock and with little common ground between either the Assad régime and the opposition or the West, and Russia and China as well as growing casualties and outrage in the West, the United Nations and Arab League Secretaries-General announced Annan's appointment as their joint envoy for Syria. This has proven to be a risky undertaking, with success far from certain.

Martti Ahtisaari made his mark when he led the UN's oversight of Namibia's self-determination and independence. He later worked on Bosnia during the war years in the early 1990s, and was instrumental in persuading Serb leader Slobodan Milosevic to release control of Kosovo. He went into politics and was President of Finland from 1994 to 2000. He has since played important roles in the implementation of the Good Friday agreements in Northern Ireland and as UN Envoy on the Status of Kosovo. He received the Nobel Peace prize in 2008.

Besides their UN background and experience, Annan and Ahtisaari have in common the ability to straddle various levels and fora, from the NGO through regional organizations and state initiatives up to and including the United Nations, and combinations of these. Because of who they are their role must inevitably be public. They are careful about what they take on but not entirely risk-averse. Given their stature, the value they add is the difficulty for most interlocutors to refuse them and remain unscathed. Neither seeks further personal or other gains. Both can stand up to major power pressure. In diplomacy, this is heavy artillery: even a major power wants to avoid one of them walking out and making public why.

Post-Cold War Trends

I have not addressed certain worrisome phenomena and trends including conflict persistence or recurrence and the expansion of the sources of violence, even though they are shaking the paradigms to which we are accustomed. In my view, this would have exceeded what could be expected in a chapter on diplomacy and mediation – important tools and techniques but ultimately only that. The exception is where I have touched on, indeed strongly emphasized, one aspect in which good diplomacy and mediation can make a difference: the proper design and implementation of peace agreements precisely so as to ensure that they deal with root causes and provide avenues and institutions to address these causes and future conflicts peacefully. The trend toward recurrence and collapse of agreements, of persistent conflict, is a policy matter that exceeds the capacity of diplomacy and mediation. One wishes that world leaders had been paying attention when Boutros Ghali sounded the alarm and queried whether the world peace architecture was suited to the alarming new challenges. Kofi Annan used to speak of "problems without passports" – a post-Westphalian set of issues that represents a major challenge for our Westphalian architecture.

The panorama I have sketched combines a considerably more complex set of challenges for peacemakers having to deal with internal conflict, which dominates the agenda; restrictions on their ability to speak to proscribed groups; and, paradoxically, a growth in the numbers of actors wishing to play a role. I have dwelt at length with the first two phenomena. In this concluding section, I will touch upon the third.

In 2008, remarks later published as an article, Chester Crocker (2011) described a conflict management world rife with crisscrossing, competing would-be mediators with little regard for each other or for the effects that their disparate actions might have on the chances of attainment of the goals they profess to seek.

More recently, the United States Institiure of Peace published *Rewiring Regional Security in a Fragmented World* (Crocker, Osler Hampson, and Aall, 2011), also involving Chester Crocker. This is a comprehensive review of conflict management at the global and regional levels by an encyclopedic array of authors. The editors identified "new patterns of cooperative international behavior that combine conflict management capabilities at both the regional and global levels and that may provide an appropriate model for global conflict management in the twenty-first century" in order to deal with devastating threats to peace for which, absent "politically sustainable and doctrinally coherent strategies," there is "no clear assignment of responsibility" and "little sign of the emergence of a global consensus on which powers or institutions should be held responsible" (2011, pp. 530–531).

The editors refer to the various alternative mechanisms that are emerging to fill the vacuum as "collective conflict management" (CCM), a phenomenon with "no organizational center or universal rules of the road" involving, rather, "improvised strategies of collective action" that are "informal, improvised, ad hoc, and opportunistic." "Pragmatism reigns, sometimes at the expense of the norms embodied in formal charters or alliances ... influenced by a convergence of threat perceptions at the regional level" (Crocker, Olser Hampson, and Aall, 2011, p. 545). There is no certainty regarding whether the disparate regional initiatives "will join with each other and/or with international and other actors to form new models of multilateral conflict management" (2011, p. 532). Another aspect is the growing normative differentiation, from region to region and between regions and the global level.

Among the examples of CCM cited are the joint AU–UN operations in the Horn of Africa and the Philippines' International Contact Group to support the peace talks between the government and the Moro Islamic Liberation Front.

The editors of *Rewired* merely identify collective conflict management as an emerging trend – they do not advocate it as their preferred approach. They see in it a positive glimmer merely because, amid the surrounding disorder, it represents an effort to minimize bumping into each other. They are under no illusion of the pitfalls involved.

This is a troubling trend. There must be a better way to manage sensitive processes than to simply embark every volunteer in it. The stakes of the work of peace are too high to be trifled with – as I said earlier, sharing responsibility tends to blunt strategy and dilute responsibility. I find it hard to accept that anyone with even passing experience in the field would see merit in this trend. I must therefore conclude, with sadness and dismay, that it has developed haphazardly rather than by design. In the absence of rules, a code of conduct, and some general criteria, let alone someone to enforce them, the various candidates for the role, unable to agree which is better suited for a particular endeavor at a given time and reluctant to defer to one another in an institutional competition, end up joining forces and thereby, instead of creating something more and better than those whose forces have been joined, produce a collegial arrangement that is weak by nature. Current trends represent a step back in the organization of human affairs, a failure of leadership and a disservice to those who hope to be freed from the ravage of war. It is a symptom of the desuetude of global security machinery.

Notes

1. For an examination of the historical background, see Touval (1967).
2. See Wolff and Yakinthou (2012).
3. For a thorough examination of this challenge, based on comparative field experience, see Graciana del Castillo (2008), as well as Berdal and Dominik Zaum, (2013).
4. Under Article 99 of the UN Charter, "the Secretary-General may bring to the attention of the Security Council any matter which in his opinion may threaten the maintenance of international peace and security." However, he does not have the means, in the form of personnel in the field, to inform himself independently, and must therefore rely on publicly available information and analysis and such intelligence as states are willing to share with him.
5. I have discussed only the Secretary-General and his envoys, not the Security Council, a principal organ of the United Nations, which I have frequently mentioned. The fact that the Security Council does not perform a diplomatic role *per se* does not mean that what it does or refrains from doing has no bearing on the conduct of a mediation either by the UN Secretary-General or any other player. It does, and it can be very far reaching and make the task of the mediator much more difficult or far easier.

References

Ayangafac, Chrysanthus, and Jakkie Cilliers. 2011. "African Solutions to African Problems." In *Rewiring Regional Security in a Fragmented World*, edited by Chester A. Crocker, Fen Osler Hampson and Pamela Aall, pp. 123–124. Washington, DC: United States Institute of Peace Press.

Berdal, Mats, and Dominik Zaum, eds. 2013. *Political Economy of Statebuilding: Power after Peace*. London: Routledge.

Boutros Ghali, Boutros. 1992. *An Agenda for Peace: Preventive Diplomacy, Peacemaking and Peace-keeping*. Report of the Secretary-General (pursuant to the statement adopted by the Summit Meeting of the Security Council on 31 January 1992). A/44/277 – S/24111, June 17, 1992, New York, Department of Public Information, United Nations, 1992.

Boutros Ghali, Boutros. 1995. *Supplement to An Agenda for Peace: Position Paper of the Secretary-General on the occasion of the Fiftieth Anniversary of the United Nations*. Document A/50/60 – S/1995/1, January 3, 1995, New York, NY: Department of Public Information, United Nations.

del Castillo, Graciana. 2008. *Rebuilding War-Torn States: The Challenge of Post-Conflict Economic Reconstruction*. Oxford: Oxford University Press.

Crocker, Chester. 2011. "Thoughts on the Conflict Management Field after 30 Years." *International Negotiation*, 16(1): 1–10. DOI: 10.1163/157180611x553845.

Crocker, Chester, Fen Osler Hampson, and Pamela Aall, eds. 2011. *Rewiring Regional Security in a Fragmented World*. Washington, DC: United States Institute of Peace Press.

Roberts, Ivor. 2009. *Satow's Diplomatic Practice, Sixth Edition*. Oxford: Oxford University Press.

Touval, Saadia. 1967. "The Organization of African Unity and African Borders." *International Organization*, 21(1): 102–127. DOI: 10.1017/S0020818300013151.

Wolff, Stefan, and Christialla Yakinthou. 2012. *Conflict Management in Divided Societies: Theories and Practice*. New York, NY: Routledge.

Chapter 18

Global Security and International Law

Richard Falk

A Conceptual Introduction

Addressing the General Assembly on September 25, 2012 President Barack Obama made the following unqualified observation: "We know from painful experience that the path to security and prosperity does not lie outside the boundaries of international law and respect for human rights." In my judgment, this is a perceptive historical assessment of the contemporary situation, but unfortunately it is only inconsistently reflected in the foreign policy of the United States and many other leading countries. As descriptive, perhaps, is the cynical observation of Henry Kissinger, contained in a Wikileaks document: "the illegal we do immediately; the unconstitutional takes a little longer." Somewhere between these two extremes is situated the complex link between global security policy and adherence to international law, part respect, part interpretative manipulation, part expedient violation.

In effect, there is a wide gap between the public *rhetoric* of respect for or neglect of international law and human rights and the *behavior* of states within and beyond their borders undertaken on behalf of national and global security. The extent of this gap is one way of depicting the contours of global insecurity that exist in this histori- cal era (see Mittelman, 2010).[1] The shortcomings of response to global insecurity are particularly evident in the inability of international law to implement restraints on threats and uses of force and to establish an agreed framework of obligatory limits on greenhouse gas (GHG) emissions.

The essential explanation of these failures to achieve acceptable levels of global security, as measured by the public common good, relates to the structure of world order as continuing to be state-centric in relation to the global policy agenda. Despite acknowledging the relevance of globalization, most governments continue to proceed on the basis of maximizing their national interests, whether or not such actions can be reconciled with the promotion of global interests, especially when perceived security

The Handbook of Global Security Policy, First Edition. Edited by Mary Kaldor and Iavor Rangelov.
© 2014 John Wiley & Sons, Ltd. Published 2014 by John Wiley & Sons, Ltd.

interests or economic growth are at stake. So ingrained is this nationalist outlook on the shaping of foreign policy that deference to a global perspective is rarely even considered when weighing decision options. Due to the unevenness of sovereign states, with respect to capabilities, size, resource endowments, stage of development, perceptions, information, and policy priorities, it is usually difficult to achieve a multilateral agreement on appropriate behavior if vital national interests are engaged. Because the absence of constraints has had such a devastating effect in the recent past and threatens grave dangers in the future, there is a deceptive engagement with rhetoric that acknowledges the requirements of global security, but no commensurate willingness to do what is necessary to make the standards operative as effective regulators of behavior. Thus such legal instruments as the Universal Declaration of Human Rights (UDHR) or the United Nations Charter set forth lofty goals that are ritualistically endorsed by governments, but there are often many strings attached in the form of interpretative loopholes, making the whole far less than the sum of its parts. For instance, the UDHR was expressed in declaratory form so as to give governments an assurance that no enforcement was intended, leaving respect for human rights where it had been for decades, if not centuries, at the less-than-tender mercies of the territorial sovereign state. The same pattern of promising without performing can be associated with the refusal to deliver on the pledge by nuclear weapons states in Article VI of the Nuclear Nonproliferation Treaty to pursue in good faith nuclear disarmament or in acting to uphold the grand commitment of the UN Charter "to save succeeding generations from the scourge of war."

State-centricism is built into the constitutional structure of the United Nations, especially by way of giving the victorious powers in World War II permanent membership in the UN Security Council with a right of veto. If we appreciate that the Security Council is the only organ within the UN System that possess a power of decision, it becomes clear that the pursuit of global security is made subject to the approval of those few states playing geopolitical roles in the shaping of world history. These states, or at least some of them, have their own grand strategies for projecting influence and upholding a particular version of world order, but this orientation is not shaped by any sense of allegiance to human security or to the promotion of the human interest, which at most are claimed as incidental benefits of a benevolent pursuit of national interests. Depending on the vagaries of national leadership and shifting domestic public opinion, these patterns may be more or less congenial with the imperatives of global security. For instance, the presidency of George W. Bush was more destructive of global security (and also the national security of the United States) than has been that of Barack Obama, although neither leader showed any willingness to defer national policy to assessments of what would most benefit humanity in the long run or to show consistent respect for international law (Sands, 2005; Cohn, 2007).[2]

Putting the issue more abstractly, state-centric problem-solving mechanisms are not consistently capable of promoting the collective good of humanity as a whole at this stage of history. In earlier periods of less global interdependence, such concerns mattered less as global interests were seldom at issue. Such a lack would still not be of great concern if there had not arisen a strongly felt need for the protection of a variety of specific collective goods. The development of nuclear weaponry highlights both the importance of a global perspective and the difficulty of implementing the vision of a world without nuclear weapons, articulated from time to time by world leaders as morally imperative and politically prudent.[3] Arguably, with nuclear weapons, even national security interests are held hostage to entrenched bureaucratic and economic interests, what Eisenhower evidently had in mind when he warned about the insidious influence of "the military-industrial-complex" half a century ago. What was done to address the dangers posed by the existence of nuclear weapons is deeply revealing and disturbing. Instead of eliminating these weapons of mass annihilation, their possession was confined to powerful state actors with the security of other states tied to the mast of non-proliferation. In the resulting two-tier, discriminatory system of global security, nuclear weapons states adapted balance of power logic to the new situation by relying on a sophisticated rendering of "deterrence", while using their leverage to keep the weaponry from falling into unwanted hands, an approach with its own pattern of inconsistencies known as "non-proliferation".

In other words, the people of the world have been burdened by a geopolitical definition of global security that struck an unstable compromise between the dangers posed by these weapons and the refusal of the most powerful sovereign states to give up some formidable instruments of destruction and deterrence. In the last analysis, the threat to global security posed by the retention of nuclear weapons, with hundreds still kept on alert status by the United States and Russia, and maybe other states, is one of catastrophic warfare, with spillover effects of radioactivity and clouds of smoke causing "nuclear famine" on earth for as long as a decade. As world order is structured, despite a widespread acknowledgement of these risks, no major steps beyond the limits of the geopolitical consensus have ever been taken.[4] The fact that none of these weapons have been used in warfare since 1945 has contributed to complacency about the risks, as well as a normalization of the morally intolerable idea of resting the security of large states on their credible willingness and capacity *at their discretion* to kill tens of millions of innocent persons living elsewhere.

But the other side of the conflict spectrum is almost equally unable to address the problems of sustained violence and abuse by governments in relation to their own people or to persecuted minorities trapped within national borders. As Ken Booth (1993) influentially pointed out twenty years ago, the Westphalian state has for several centuries provided a sanctuary for "human wrongs". The rise of international rights since 1945 is a notable achievement, but as with nuclear weaponry, compliance is more a function of geopolitics than of the recognition that global security would be strengthened by governments that effectively, comprehensively, and uniformly implemented agreed standards of international human rights. As matters now stand, even the most extreme patterns of abuse, associated with persistent and massive Crimes Against Humanity, are not addressed unless the geopolitical climate is sufficiently unified to support a shared response, and even then it is not likely to alter the behavior of a large state ("too big to regulate"). The international law approach of treating equals equally is not operative when it comes to taking constraints on territorial governance seriously. It is notable that Nazi and Japanese war criminals were prosecuted after World War II, an apparent challenge to the impunity of leaders of sovereign states, and a potential precedent for the future, but experience has abundantly demonstrated that criminal accountability is still confined to the weak and defeated, and is not invoked to address the crimes of the large states that, from a global security perspective, pose the most dangerous threats and do the most serious harm to their own populations and to others.

The organized international community in the aftermath of the Kosovo War of 1999 tried to come up with a new approach to the balance between protecting vulnerable populations from humanitarian catastrophes and respecting sovereign territory. The response to the threat of ethnic cleansing in Kosovo was controversial for several reasons, including the absence of a UN Security Council mandate, but the fact that "a coalition of the willing" had the backing of NATO and almost the whole of Europe, as well as the background of Serbian genocidal tactics in Bosnia, gave the intervention on behalf of the endangered Albanian majority population widespread support, but also occasioned sharp criticism.[5] The most influential result of this debate was the formulation of a Responsibility to Protect (R2P) norm, endorsed by the UN Security Council, and operationalized to an extent when in March 2011 the UN Security Council authorized NATO to conduct limited military operations in Libya. What emerged remains controversial. R2P is subject to a geopolitical veto, as well as to the Security Council procedures, which means that some highly vulnerable people are outside the orbit of international protection (e.g. Palestinians under occupation, Chechens, Kurds) regardless of abuses experienced or the severity of threats directed at them (Orford, 2013). What it is possible to affirm is that the normative and psycho-political global setting can no longer shut itself off from "new wars" that are waged within territorial boundaries by invoking earlier Westphalian conceptions of unconditional territorial sovereignty, but neither can such concerns be consistently addressed due to the persisting primacy of geopolitics (Kaldor, 2006).[6] As a result, the nature of global security in relation to these conflict patterns occupies a law/no law space that is subject to contradictory interpretations.

There are new questions being asked about the role of civil society in producing global security. Can humanitarian nongovernmental organizations (NGO) promote conflict resolution in situations where traditional statecraft, even as abetted by the United Nations, is at a loss? The war in Syria that has raged since early 2011 is illustrative of this potentiality, suggesting possible multiple civil society roles, ranging from the delivery of food and medicine to the civilian population, providing auspices for the negotiation and maintenance of local ceasefire arrangements, compiling the evidence to support charges of war crimes and crimes against humanity, and offering antagonists ideas for limiting or ending the violence (see Beebe and Kaldor, 2010). States, despite their sense of futility in relation to such conflicts, are reluctant to yield political space to civil society initiatives, and jealously guard traditional diplomatic prerogatives exclusively reserved for states. Even the United Nations has not accommodated the rise of global civil society by giving non-state actors more influential and meaningful roles within the organization.

Global Security, Use of Force, and International Law

Much of the controversy and uncertainty about the relevance of international law to the foreign policy of sovereign states has over the years involved threats and uses of force, and related issues associated with the application of law to war and its aftermath. Due to such preoccupations we tend to forget how dependent the peoples and nations of the world are upon the generally reliable legal framework that governs routine transnational relations, whether in trade, diplomacy, maritime and air safety, tourism, communication, and transportation. There is a widespread recognition among governments and more sophisticated citizens that international law is crucial to the reliability of routine cross border stability that is of great benefit to all peoples and establishes relatively high standards of global security under *normal* conditions. International law reinforces this framework of stability by providing participants in international life with flexible dispute settlement procedures by way of mediation, arbitration, and adjudication that generally keep conflicts within bounds similar to those that exist in well-ordered domestic societies. Where the society is poorly governed and internally lawless, then the maintenance of stability for transnational relations of all kinds with outsiders is likely to be seriously compromised.

Why then the inability to find solutions for the governance of the use of force? After World War II, the political leaders of the victorious countries were unusually receptive to developing restraints on recourse to the military option because they were at that moment acutely conscious of how devastating a future war was likely to be in the aftermath of the atomic bombings of Hiroshima and Nagasaki. The founding states of the United Nations were able to agree on four far-reaching ideas: (1) the creation of the United Nations based on a UN Charter that unconditionally prohibited threats and uses of force except in instances of self-defense narrowly defined; this prohibition was supplemented by (2) a responsibility of the organized world community to protect states that were victims of aggression by sufficient measures of collective security; (3) the imposition of individual criminal responsibility on leaders who waged, and even threatened, "aggressive wars"; and (4) the norm that territory could no longer be validly acquired by force.[7] We must inquire, as carefully as possible, why this seemingly humane and sensible constitutional framework was never fully implemented. The result has been a confusing tension between constitutional guidelines for the maintenance of international peace and security provided by international law and the continued reliance by states on self-help mechanisms (defense capabilities, alliances) restrained by countervailing power and prudence rather than by an acceptance of the constraints of international law. When George W. Bush told the US Congress that the United States would never seek a permission slip from the United Nations to use force when its security interests were at stake, it was both an assertion of American exceptionalism and an expression of hard power defiance of a global leader repudiating the authority of law, which is the essence of soft power. It was also a reminder to the world body that leading states consider their geopolitical status as conferring discretion that takes precedence over accountability to law in relation to its security agenda. Although the United States is the most outspoken among the current group of leading states, all of these first tier governments in practice treat their national security priorities as overriding contrary legal obligations. Of course, when international law supports a security claim of a geopolitical leader, or undercuts the behavior of an international adversary, then it will be invoked with the solemnity of a church preacher. The realist orientation of government respects international law governing force so long as it is convenient to do so, and departs as necessary without many qualms, although almost always disguised at home by reliance on elaborate public rationalizations for recourse to force or war couched in legal language.[8] For instance, when the US government in the aftermath of the

9/11 attacks authorized "torture" unconditionally prohibited by international law, government lawyers called torture "enhanced interrogation techniques".[9]

Two broad lines of assessment can deepen our understanding of the character of global security: ideological and structural. Governments, especially of leading countries, continue to be mainly guided by *ideological* adherents of political realism who believe that history is shaped by the outcome of military confrontations, that military superiority is positively correlated with national and global security, and that neither nuclear weapons nor international law have changed this fundamental situation.[10] The structure of world order reinforces this realist consensus by fragmenting political consciousness on the basis of separate and distinct sovereign states that are oriented around the promotion of *national* interests at the expense of *global* interests (Johansen, 1980). Beyond this, there is a challenge to territorial sovereignty that combines the emerging authority of human rights with the geopolitical capability and willingness to intervene selectively to protect human rights. There exists a widespread view, especially influential in the West, that in an interconnected world, the insulation of the internal political life of sovereign states should not be exempt from international accountability under extreme circumstances that put the people of a country at great risk due to governmental abuse or incompetence. The structural perspective continues to mean that global security is achieved or not, at the level of the state, and that reliance on collective security mechanisms depends principally on alliance relationships and pragmatic calculations rather than on the rule governed by the undertakings of the United Nations and regional actors.[11]

Nuclear Weapons

The interplay of these factors produces a distinctive diplomacy that is more complicated than what existed until the last half of the twentieth century. The existence of nuclear weaponry makes war avoidance among powerful states a high priority for realists, but their choice is not the renunciation of the weaponry but its "use" in a threat mode called "deterrence". The efforts to challenge such reliance on massive threats of indiscriminate warfare produced an Advisory Opinion by the International Court of Justice whose majority of judges concluded that this weaponry could be provisionally retained despite the seeming inability to find lawful uses for it in warfare, except conceivably if the survival of a state was being credibly threatened in a crisis situation. Unanimously, also, the International Court of Justice contended that the nuclear weapons states had a treaty obligation to enter nuclear disarmament negotiations in good faith (see International Court of Justice, 1996). What is most revealing is that this carefully reasoned assessment of the status of nuclear weapons has had no discernible impact on the behavior of those governments that possess nuclear weapons. It confirmed, on this matter of the greatest potential relevance for global security, that there is no willingness whatsoever to allow international law to supplant geopolitical control and discretion.

When it comes to what can be identified as "second order legality", then international law is employed to manage the geopolitical regime by way of the Nonproliferation Treaty (NPT) and its implementation.[12] The NPT relies on the authority of an international treaty instrument to obligate non-nuclear states that become parties to forego the weapons option in exchange for receiving assurance of gaining the benefit of peaceful uses of nuclear energy. The recent diplomacy adopted by nuclear weapons states toward those states accused of seeking to obtain nuclear weaponry, including Iraq, North Korea, and Iran, is suggestive of geopolitical procedures put to work in the service of *de jure* nonproliferation obligations.[13] The Iraq War of 2003 was allegedly undertaken, in part, as a means of preventing a future acquisition of such weaponry, creating a geopolitical claim to override the constraints of international law. By way of contrast, Israel, and to an extent India and Pakistan, (states that remained outside the NPT framework), were given a pass to enter the club. An initial discomfort about India and Pakistan was exhibited by the US government and at the United Nations, but it was never more than an expression of displeasure and, in the case of India, even this was quickly overtaken by entry into commercially attractive nuclear technology sharing arrangements with the United States. Israel has been treated even more preferentially, being allowed to fly under the radar while acquiring and developing an arsenal of nuclear weapons. In other words, international law is appropriated to make effective a legal regime that reflects an approach to nuclear weaponry that rejects the fundamental legal principle of treating equals equally. It institutionalizes a treaty regime that is delegitimized by the application of double standards and it is relied upon to validate a violent geopolitics that has meant in the aftermath of nuclear weaponry a dubious connection between genocidal threats and global security, as conceptualized during the Cold War in the doctrine of deterrence, and since then by threats and recourse to military intervention as with Iran and Iraq.[14]

Recourse to Threats and Uses of Force

The core commitment of the UN Charter is contained in Article 2(4) of the UN Charter: "All Members shall refrain in their international relations from the threat or use of force against the territorial integrity or political independence of any state." It is important to note that in the Charter threats are as prohibited as are uses of force, which in effect legally disallows what is sometimes called "coercive diplomacy" (Falk, 2013). But in state practice, actual uses of force are at least scrutinized, as was the case in relation to the 2003 attack on Iraq, but threats are not registered on the regulatory radar screen. For instance, the frequent allusions by the United States to keeping the military option "on the table", Israeli-leaked stories about war games involving attack scenarios on the Iranian nuclear facilities, and speculation about the location of red lines with respect to the Iranian nuclear program are clearly articulated in the form of "threats" that would, on the face of it, violate the prohibition in Article 2(4). But here the legal sphere defers without objection to the political sphere, and threats seem to be an acceptable mode of diplomatic interaction that accords *de facto* deference to prevailing patterns of geopolitics. Again the efforts of international law to confine reliance on force to situations of genuine self-defense have not been integrated into responsive behavioral patterns.

Since the United Nations was established in 1945, the prohibition on force as means of territorial expansion has been reasonably well respected, and even implemented, when massively violated. The United Nations responded to the North Korean attack of South Korea in 1950; the Suez Operation of France, Israel, and the United Kingdom in 1956; and the Iraqi attack on Kuwait in 1990. In all of these instances, norm prohibiting aggressive warfare was upheld, although some degree of controversy exists in each setting as to the degree of compliance. The 1967 war between Israel and its Arab neighbors resulted in the expulsion of Jordan from its administrative role in the West Bank and East Jerusalem, and the prolonged occupation of these portions of historic Palestine by Israel, although without the seal of international legitimacy. The United Nations Security Council Resolution 242 (1967) set forth the expectations that Israel would withdraw forthwith from Occupied Palestine, invoking explicitly the norm against the acquisition of territory by force of arms. More than 46 years later, these expectations, generally considered expressive of international law, have not been fulfilled; on the contrary, Israel has taken steps by way of establishing large settlement cities, building a network of settler roads, constructing a separation wall that encroaches on Occupied Palestine, and shows no signs that it has any intention of ever implementing the withdrawal obligation at the center of Resolution 242.[15] In this regard, occupation of Palestinian territories has shielded an actual policy of creeping annexation by Israel, the occupying power. This clearly violates the spirit and substance of the 4th Geneva Convention, but the political will in the international community to challenge Israel's unlawful conduct is absent.

Another important situation arose in 1974 when Turkey intervened in Cyprus, supposedly for the protection of the threatened Turkish minority, with a resulting division of the island. The Turkish intervention was censured at the United Nations and denied any legal effect. Turkish Cyprus remains diplomatically isolated after almost 40 years. Several attempts have been made by third parties to negotiate a solution of Cyprus that would reunify the island, most notably the so-called UN-backed "Annan Plan" that was approved by a referendum in Turkish Cyprus, but rejected by the population of Greek Cyprus. Turkish Cyprus remains in a twilight zone of legality, with formal recognition being given only by Turkey, and a strong conviction on the Greek side that Turkey had unlawfully seized territory by force without suffering adverse consequences. Again, geopolitics probably helps explain the neutralization of international law: the United States, in particular, was caught between its positive relationship with these two members of NATO, and Turkey, the transgressor state in the eyes of the world, was particularly critical to Western strategy in the Cold War era.[16]

Although the record of compliance with the prohibition of aggression is on balance impressive, the story is somewhat more clouded in relation to the use of force to carry out military interventions designed to alter the dynamics of self-determination within the borders of sovereign states. The norm of self-determination is not made obligatory in the UN Charter, which, when drafted, did not challenge the legitimacy or legality of European colonial rule. As decolonization became the next wave of global history, the United Nations changed its tune, and self-determination was proclaimed as such a fundamental principle of international law as to be inalienable. Respect for self-determination was one of seven principles set forth in the still influential 1970 UN General Assembly Resolution 2625, which has the title Declaration of Principles Concerning Friendly Relations and Co-operation Among States, as well as being affirmed in common Article 1 of the two major UN human rights covenants signed in 1966.[17]

Interventions to achieve regime change tend to be justified either by humanitarian claims or to protect the international community from dangers associated with the acquisition of nuclear weapons by states branded as "outlaw states".[18] Despite a major effort by the US government to obtain authorization for the use of force in 2003, the Security Council refused to grant it, and the subsequent American invasion and occupation of Iraq was widely viewed as unlawful under the UN Charter and international law.[19] The perspectives of international law were only clearly developed by the Iraq War Tribunal, a civil society initiative organized on a worldwide basis and culminating in Istanbul in a 2005 session (for the proceedings and expert testimony, see Sokmen, 2008). Ever since the Vietnam War, civil society actors have tried to fill the void left by the refusal of geopolitical actors to abide by international law, having organized essentially *symbolic* events in the form of people's tribunals, which have no *substantive* capacity to implement their findings. At the same time, the proceedings of these tribunals have often provided the most comprehensive and trustworthy legal assessments of the challenged behavior of geopolitical actors.[20] The mainstream media tends to ignore these civil society events because they are seen as without legal weight as they are not backed by governmental or inter-governmental authority. In a few instances, the findings of such undertakings have had a mobilizing effect on public opposition to authoritarian governance, as was the case in relation to the authoritarian regime of Ferdinand Marco in The Philippines.

Humanitarian intervention or R2P is more controversial, and as suggested earlier, is widely viewed with suspicion in the non-Western world where vivid bad memories of colonialism remain. The underlying legal appreciation of national sovereignty is expressed by respect for the norm of non-intervention, which *legally* insulates states from coercive encroachment. This principle is also asserted in Article 2(7) of the UN Charter, which affirms that there is no authorization for "the United Nations to intervene in matters which are essentially within the domestic jurisdiction of any state or shall require Members to submit such matters to settlement under the present Charter." This principle of international law is a central provision of the social contract struck between sovereign states and the United Nations, and is, in effect, a commitment to respect the internal authority of small states. Larger states, due to their size and capabilities, are practically not subject to intervention, nor are smaller states that enjoy firm geopolitical backing. Russia, China, the United States, and Brazil are examples of global adherence to non-intervention on the basis of size, while Israel, Turkey, and Bahrain illustrate the same phenomenon on the basis of geopolitical patronage and military capabilities. Deference to non-intervention has been eroded by the rise of human rights as a challenge to unconditional sovereignty, by a global media that calls attention in real time to crimes against humanity and other humanitarian catastrophes, and by some moves in the direction of reformulating sovereign rights by reference to "responsible sovereignty" (see Deng *et al.*, 1996).

The struggle in Syria dramatically demonstrates the dilemmas of intervention and non-intervention. As the French statesman, Talleyrand, insisted long ago, non-intervention is indistinguishable from intervention in relations to some situations of internal strife. This is especially true, as in Syria, where other states are lending material support to both sides in an ongoing civil war, creating a second layer of conflict known as "proxy war". There is an underlying rule of world order that legally allows states to discriminate in favor of the established government faced with a domestic insurgency. But what if the government is guilty of atrocities or unable to protect its population from famine and disease? In effect, governments have wide discretion to determine their relations to internal conflict in foreign countries, and the UN responses to such conflicts depends on whether a geopolitical consensus can be achieved and sustained. The authorization to use force in Libya reflected such a consensus, although a weak one, while the inability of geopolitical rivals to agree about the situation in Syria has effectively neutralized the United Nations, limiting its role to seemingly futile pleas for compromise and negotiations put forward by UN/Arab League Special Envoys. In effect, international law is flexible, but dependent on a political climate that generates a consensus. The political climate tends to reflect the frequently antagonistic views of geopolitical rivals and the world order tensions of a post-colonial global setting.

There are also issues involving capabilities and tactics. Military intervention, especially if carried out to minimize the human costs to the intervening side, is a very crude instrument, and unless reinforced by a lengthy commitment to economic and political reconstruction, can lead to political frustration and peacekeeping fatigue even if overwhelming military superiority brought initial success. This questionable efficacy of military superiority to offset the dynamics of self-determination should have been one of the primary lessons of the Vietnam War, rather than overcoming the "Vietnam Syndrome" by the redesign of counterinsurgency warfare (see Kaplan, 2013). The United States has had further negative experiences along similar lines in relation to Iraq and Afghanistan, but shows little willingness to rethink the viability of the underlying mission. The latest move is to shift from traditional combat operations to a mixture of covert undertakings by "special forces" and reliance on attack drones, both highly interventionary tactics without any foundation in international law, but adaptations to the non-territorial nature of the long war carried out against AlQaeda and its affiliates on a global battlefield that seeks "consent" from the territorial government but, when it is not formally forthcoming (as in Pakistan), goes ahead with its attacks in any event.[21]

The opportunities for civil society interventions in ongoing internal wars is an underexplored subject matter that relates ambiguously to the role of international law in relation to global security. Part of the difficulty is the reluctance of governments to cede space to civil society actors with respect to conflict-mitigation and conflict resolution. Where trust is absent within sovereign states, there would seem to be important opportunities for independent civil society actors to propose compromises to both sides, to establish a neutral presence in areas under the control of opposition forces, and to provide the kind of monitoring capabilities that could help to sustain a truce, facilitate a transition from war to peace, and offer parties a means of indirect communication that tests whether grounds for agreements exist. Should international law venture onto this hitherto off-limits terrain? One can imagine an agreed code of conduct for civil society activities in internal war situations that was formulated and agreed upon by an assembly of civil society actors. Such a development, although seemingly a challenge to state-centric lawmaking, would be innovative in the best sense, an instance of international law perhaps better understood as "global law", negotiated from below and responsive to gaps in the effectiveness of international humanitarian law.

Climate Change and Other Global Challenges

As earlier suggested, state-centric international law has been remarkably successful in providing a stable framework for a wide spectrum of transnational relations. It has had a measure of success in addressing global collective goods problems in the past, including management of the global commons and providing global public order for polar regions. Perhaps, the most impressive achievement along these lines is the Law of the Seas Treaty (1982) negotiated over the course of a decade and involving significant tradeoffs and compromises for the sake of reaching a maximum level of agreement. Ironically, the United States was instrumental in brokering the process, but to this day has been unwilling to ratify the treaty due to opposition from the extreme sovereignty oriented membership of the US Senate. Global security has on balance benefitted by these arrangements, and it is suggestive of the degree to which global leadership by dominant states can put the lawmaking process beyond the scope of narrowly conceived national interests. Management of the global commons for the sake of the common good suggests that in some situations national interests and global interests are perceived to converge, even by realist-oriented representatives of government.[22]

Yet there are important instances where national and global interests diverge, and these concerns have become more serious under contemporary conditions. I have earlier referred to the inability to work out an agreed scheme of nuclear disarmament, which actually willfully disregards the NPT legal obligation to do just that. In the setting of hard power, the divergence is too great in situations where perceived security interests are at stake, and is heightened by the over-estimation of the use value of hard power in the present global setting.[23] Although nuclear weapons have not been used since 1945, the apocalyptic effects of some future use together with the error-prone nature of governmental institutions and the suicidal character of extremist politics, suggests that over time humanity is irrationally subjecting itself to a risk of immeasurable gravity by not taking all possible steps to eliminate nuclear weaponry. The failure to do so underscores a fundamental crisis of world order associated with insufficient mechanisms for the promotion and protection of basic global and species interests.

Climate change highlights this deficiency in world order because it has proved impossible to find a sufficient response to the challenge of global warming to protect either global security or the human interest. This deficiency is already causing severe harm to some societies and to the overall environment, and is unresponsive to the warnings issued by a well-documented consensus among climate scientists.[24] Why has international law been so unable to move toward establishing a regulatory framework that protects the human interest, given its ability to do so in other domains of concern?[25] There are several reasons for this world order failure that help us understand its underlying nature. First of all, states are pursuing national interests in a setting where restraints on GHG emissions are seen as impediments to economic growth, which is the highest priority of almost every government. This impediment is made more serious because states disagree about the proper way to apportion responsibility for the buildup of greenhouse gases: aggregate present volume of emissions, historical contributions dating to the Industrial Revolution, per capita level of current emissions. These complications are further aggravated by a well-funded campaign of climate skeptics, those scientists, many of whom are funded by special interests, who question whether allegations of global warming is occurring and are a result of GHG emissions or just reflect natural cyclical weather behavior (Oreskes and Conway, 2010). Such well-financed challenges to the scientific consensus create public confusion, especially in the pro-capitalist United States, strengthen the position of rightest opposition to environmental and other forms of international regulation, which in turn erodes the global leadership role of the United States, and makes the negotiation process problematic, and tend to produce fruitless negotiations that degenerate into the pursuit of contradictory perceptions of national interests. Under these circumstances, it is hardly surprising that international law has not been able to respond to the challenge, and seems unlikely to do so until tipping points have been passed that make the restoration of favorable climate conditions almost impossible (see Giddens, 2009, pp. 2–3).[26] While climate science seems clear that average earth temperature rises of 2°C at the very most would likely remain manageable, although even so with some disruptive developments (increases in extreme weather, polar melting, ocean acidification), the dynamics of expanding energy use, rising standards of living, increasing population are producing conditions that seem likely to result in the unambiguously disastrous result of a 4°C or greater average temperature rise.

Concluding Comment

In effect, the mechanisms of lawmaking to serve the global interest exist, as does the diplomatic rhetoric that acknowledges the gravity of global challenges, yet the structures of world order create a situation in which the policy outcomes remain unresponsive and dysfunctional from the perspective of achieving sustainable development. It does not seem coincidental that Europe, by way of the European Union, has been the most forthcoming political actor in relation to climate change because its regional policies seem less beholden to divergent national interests. On a global level, international institutions are too weak to overcome the effects of political fragmentation with respect to climate change, and the system depends on a benevolent hegemon to overcome the authority deficit. The United States played this role to a certain extent in the last half of the twentieth century, but not in relation to nuclear weaponry, always with certain limitations, and less and less so.[27]

As scholars in international relations have argued, the plural order of sovereign states was capable of promoting cooperative relations and maintaining order that served the community of states until the twentieth century, but even then with the high moral costs for the majority of people on the planet due to the exploitative nature of Western colonial hegemony. It became evident that the military technology was undermining the viability of such a decentralized world order a century ago with the mutually destructive costs of World War I. From that mutually destructive experience of warfare, Western efforts were made to strengthen international law, weaken sovereignty, and construct international institutions dedicated to global security and the human interest. But the political will on the level of the state to make those institutions effective enough to cope with global challenges of great magnitude has not been forthcoming. The United Nations has in some respects been far more successful than its predecessor, the League of Nations. It has achieved universal membership, presided over the dismantling of colonialism, facilitated the rise and implementation of human rights, facilitated economic development for many regions of the world, and helped to promote peaceful resolution of many conflict situations. At the same time, it has not been able to protect many vulnerable peoples from abuse by territorial governments, rid the world of nuclear weapons, establish an obligatory framework for constraints on GHG emissions, and demilitarize the global commons. One way of expressing this limitation on international law is to insist that *some* global challenges require mechanisms of "global law", and these are not available.

The Plan B of world order is reliance on what used to be called Great Powers as playing managerial roles that combined self-interest with the promotion of global security. This has been most evident in relation to the global commons, especially the oceans. Here there were early tensions between advocates of the territorializing of the oceans and those states supportive of "freedom of the high seas", which was of greatest benefit to maritime states with strong navies. Shared interests were strong enough to create generally tolerable conditions in the global commons until recently, and lent support to the view that a plural structure of world order was preferable to a unified structure that posed risks of global tyranny, and the like.[28] With the competition to control undersea resources, there are increasing pressures on the present international law framework.

The emergence of a unipolar world after the collapse of the Soviet Union created an opportunity for the United States to use its dominance on behalf of global security for the sake of sustainable development and world peace and justice. Instead, it emphasized a predatory form of neoliberal globalization that accentuated inequality and environmental irresponsibility, without seeking to diminish the role of military power and building up the capabilities of the United Nations (Falk, 1999). After 9/11 there occurred a major resecuritization of the global agenda, and American leadership relating to the global common good essentially evaporated.[29]

The Plan C of world order is associated with the global multilateralism as by way of the UN General Assembly and related activities. For instance, the mechanisms for addressing climate change is through the UN Framework Convention on Climate Change, which organizes annual meetings of all parties to produce global policy that will protect the peoples and states of the world from the ravages of global warming. Such a mechanism has proved unwieldy when important and divergent economic interests are at stake, especially if there is no strong leadership by geopolitical actor(s) that perceive a strong enough self-interest to press for a regulatory approach that will uphold global security. At the 2009 Copenhagen UN Conference on Climate Change, the United States undermined the multilateral approach seeking obligatory controls over GHG emissions by proposing a voluntary approach based on national pledges that are at most unilaterally determined statements of good faith.

The Plan D of world order is associated with the degree to which transnational civil society activism can mobilize a constituency for the promotion of global security by way of the development and implementation of international law (see Keck and Sikkink, 1998). There is no doubt that such civil society activism has been effective in a number of specific contexts, including exerting pressures supportive of lawmaking in relation to human rights, some forms of environmental protection, prohibition of antipersonnel landmines, and the establishment of the International Criminal Court. But as has been obvious at the level of implementation, the *vertical* dimension of the state system means that implementation will be subject to geopolitical control, with resulting double standards. For instance, patterns of criminal accountability are illustrative: for losers in conflicts or for weak and marginal non-Western countries, with impunity for Western leaders.[30]

Civil society initiatives have sought to overcome the failure of international law to protect the human interest in relation to criminal accountability, climate change, and nuclear disarmament, but have not had the capability to generate global law responsive to the challenge or to alter the understanding of national interests on the part of dominant states. For instance, I would argue that the US government would better serve its national interests by adhering to international law. Such adherence would have avoided the disastrous involvements in interventionary diplomacy ever since Vietnam, but such a view is not influential at the level of governmental policymaking where traditional realist thinking prevails, as reinforced by an array of special interests.

Notes

1. Also for the limits of law in relation to uses of force, see Glennon (2001).
2. Sands (2005) and Cohn (2007) explicate the refusal of the Bush presidency.
3. Barack Obama, early in his presidency, articulated such a vision, but took few steps to exhibit an intention to bring it about. Prague, June 2009.
4. See the warnings of Jonathan Schell and many others in Schell (1982); also Falk and Krieger (2012).
5. See Noam Chomsky (1999); for an analysis and argument in support, see the *Kosovo Report* by the Independent International Commission on Kosovo (2000); for a more general critique of humanitarian intervention, see Anne Orford (2003).
6. For a well documented argument that territorial sovereignty has always been conditional and frequently encroached upon throughout the entire Westphalian era, see Stephen Krasner (1999).
7. It is useful to recall that prior to the outlawry of aggressive war that peace treaties validated territorial expansions resulting from the use of force; there are still arguments about whether territory acquired in the course of exercising a right of self-defense must be relinquished. Security Council Resolution 242, adopted after the Six Day War in 1967, decided that Israel must withdraw from the territory it had acquired. The fact that Israel has failed to do so is illustrative of the gap between international law and its implementation in situations where geopolitical factors support non-implementation.
8. For an exposition of such realist orientations, see Kissinger (1994) esp., pp. 218–245; Kennan (1952). For realism from the perspective of international law experts, see Arend and Beck (1993); Weisburd (1993); McDougal and Feliciano (1961).
9. For an excellent overview, see Hajjar (2013). The issues are usefully explored in Danner (2004). For a range of views, see Levinson (2011); Cohn (2011).
10. I have tried to challenge this presumption on empirical and normative grounds, contending that respect for international law rules governing the use of force is more likely as of the twenty-first century to serve the national interest than is their rejection. See Falk (2008).
11. There is legal ambiguity as to whether regional actors can undertake "enforcement" without receiving the prior approval of the UN Security Council. Article 53 of the UN Charter has some rather clear language to the effect, "no enforcement shall be taken under regional arrangements or by regional agencies without the authorization of the Security Council." But what is "enforcement"? And is NATO an alliance or a regional organization?

12. First-order legality refers to rules governing the weaponry itself, not agreements that prohibit access; in contrast to nuclear weaponry, biological and chemical weapons are prohibited to all states as a result of first-order treaty law regimes.

13. Categorizing these states as an "axis of evil" was particularly provocative and self-serving, as well as misleading; North Korea and Iran and Iraq have no linkages, much less an "axis".

14. In the NPT, there is a nod toward a negotiated bargain based on "sovereign equality" in Article VI mandating nuclear disarmament, but its implementation was left to the good will of the nuclear weapons states, while the nonproliferation obligations are enforced, although selectively, by geopolitical managerial procedures.

15. These encroachments on occupied Palestinian territories also seem in direct violation of Article 49(6) of the Fourth Geneva Convention (1949) governing occupation in accord with international humanitarian law.

16. It should also be observed that the Turkish narrative of the case for intervention due to the imminent threat directed at the Turkish minority has not received as much sympathetic attention as it deserves.

17. There are significant ambiguities regarding the principle of self-determination, including the idea that its exercise should not have the effect of fragmenting the unity of existing states; in other words, the idea of self-determination was formulated with the primary idea of supporting movements against alien rule, most prominently the European colonial system, but it was *formally* intended to encourage minorities to seek political independence by challenging the territorial unity of an established state. The Kosovo case is controversially situated at the interface because, arguably, Serbian rule was "alien", but the result was the dismemberment of Serbia, a UN member. In the background is the question as to whether Serbia forfeited sovereign claims by gross violations of human rights. In *practice*, claims of self-determination are validated if the movements so dedicated are successful, regardless of whether dismemberment occurs, as happened after the collapse of Yugoslavia and the Soviet Union – the political outcomes create legitimate secessionist states as long as the result is endorsed by the international community, especially reflected in membership in the United Nations.

18. The Bush presidency developed two related ideas that were relied upon to justify the attack on Iraq in 2003: that Iraq possessed chemical weapons of mass destruction and was pursuing a program to acquire nuclear weapons, and that force could be used preemptively and preventively to avert a future credible threat, given the realities of the post-9/11 world.

19. Ambiguity surrounds the legal status of the Iraq War because the United Nations, immediately after the fact, cooperated with the American-led occupation of Iraq and failed to condemn the attack or to make any effort to protect a state threatened by aggressive war.

20. For the proceedings of the Russell Tribunal, see Duffett (1968).

21. See the important, if incoherent, position of Philip Bobbitt (2008) to the effect that the nature of warfare changes in response to the identity and tactics of conflictual adversaries. It seems incoherent because Bobbitt both argues that belligerent behavior must adapt to new configurations of conflict but also that democratic states must not relinquish their respect for international law.

22. See related argument on disaggregated sovereignty in Slaughter (2004). Another important example is the Antarctica Treaty suspending sovereignty claims and foregoing mining operations. I would maintain that refusing to challenge freedom of the high seas for naval operations represents a major concession to the *vertical* dimension of Westphalian world order, that is, conceding management roles to major states.

23. In the nineteenth century, hard power was a rational instrument for territorial gains and access to resources, but that changed in the mid-twentieth century with the normative rise

of self-determination, reinforced by renewed confidence in the combination of soft power and national resistance.

24. See, for example, the IPCC World Bank Report (2012) "Turn Down the Heat: Why a 4°C Warmer World Must be Avoided". For a view that corporate obstruction of climate change adaptation is endangering the human future, see McKibben (2012).

25. For example, agreements to sustain depleted fisheries, protect whales, and ozone depletion.

26. Especially the "Giddens Paradox", which suggests that by the time a political will sufficient to address climate change exists, it will be too late to take effective action. For a helpful overview of the potential political consequences of global warming, see Dyer (2010).

27. For instance, the United States has failed to ratify the Law of the Sea Treaty, despite its strong support from national interest perspectives by the Executive Branch because of sovereignty-oriented concerns and its overriding interest in maintaining freedom of navigation for naval vessels.

28. Perhaps, most compellingly argued by Bull (1977).

29. Obama made some idealistic statements in 2009, relating to nuclear weapons, Palestine/Israel but was revealingly unable to deliver on such promised initiatives, and basically abandoned even their advocacy.

30. The horizontal dimension of world order is based on juridical equality, while the vertical dimension of world order reflects the hierarchy of political influence and the exercise of geopolitical leverage.

References

Arend, Anthony C., and Robert J. Beck. 1993. *International Law & the Use of Force: Beyond the UN Charter Paradigm*. London: Routledge.

Beebe, Shannon, and Mary Kaldor. 2010. *The Ultimate Weapon is No Weapon: Human Security and the New Rules of War and Peace*. New York, NY: Public Affairs.

Bobbitt, Philip. 2008. *Terror and Consent: The Wars for the Twenty-First Century*. New York, NY: Knopf.

Booth, Ken. 1993. "Human Wrongs and International Relations." *International Relations*, 71(1): 103–126.

Bull, Hedley. 1977. *The Anarchical Society: A Study of Order in World Politics*. New York, NY: Colubmia University Press.

Chomsky, Noam. 1999. *The New Military Humanism: Lessons from Kosovo*. Monroe, ME: Common Courage Press.

Cohn, Marjorie. 2007. *Cowboy Republic: Six Ways the Bush Gang Has Defied the Law*. Sausalito, CA: PoliPoint Press.

Cohn, Marjorie, ed. 2011. *The United States and Torture: Interrogation, Incarceration, and Abuse*. New York, NY: New York University Press.

Danner, Mark. 2004. *Torture and Truth: America, Abu Ghraib, and the War on Terror*. New York, NY: New York Review of Books.

Deng, Francis, Sadikiel Kimaro, Terrences Lyons, Donald Rothchild, *et al.* 1996. *Sovereignty as Responsibility: Conflict Management in Africa*. Washington, DC: Brookings.

Duffett, John, ed. 1968. *Against the Crime of Silence: Proceedings of the International War Crimes Tribunal*. New York, NY: Simon & Schuster.

Dyer, Gwynne. 2010. *Climate Wars: The Fight for Survival as the World Overheats*. Oxford: Oneworld Publications.

Falk, Richard. 1999. *Predatory Globalization: A Critique*. Cambridge: Polity Press.

Falk, Richard. 2008. *The Costs of War: International Law, the UN, and World Order after Iraq*. New York. NY: Routledge.

Falk, Richard. 2013. "Threat Diplomacy in World Politics: Legal, Moral, Political, and Civilizational Challenges." In *The Ethics of Preventive War*, edited by Deen Chaterjee. Cambridge: Cambridge University Press.

Falk, Richard, and David Krieger. 2012. *Path to Zero: Dialogues on Nuclear Danger*. Boulder, CO: Paradigm.

Giddens, Anthony. 2009. *The Politics of Climate Change*. Cambridge: Polity Press.

Glennon, Michael J. 2001. *Limits of Law: Prerogatives of Power: Intervention After Kosovo*. New York, NY: Palgrave.

Hajjar, Lisa. 2013. *Torture: A Sociology of Violence and Human Rights*. New York, NY: Routledge.

Independent International Commission on Kosovo. 2000. *Kosovo Report*. Oxford: Oxford University Press.

International Court of Justice. 1996. *Legality of the Threat or Use of Nuclear Weapons, Advisory Opinion*. ICJ Reports.

IPCC. 2012. "Turn Down the Heat: Why a 4°C Warmer World Must be Avoided." *A Report for the World Bank by the Potsdam Institute for Climate Impact Reseach and Climate Analytics*. November 2012. Washington, DC: The World Bank.

Johansen, Robert C. 1980. *The National Interest and the Human Interest: An Analysis of US Foreign Policy*. Princeton, NJ: Princeton University Press.

Kaldor, Mary. 2006. *New & Old Wars: Organized Violence in a Global Era (2nd edition)*. Stanford, CA: Stanford University Press.

Kaplan, Fred. 2013. *The Insurgents: David Petreus and the Plot to Change the American Way of War*. New York, NY: Simon & Schuster.

Keck, Margaret E., and Kathryn Sikkink. 1998. *Activists Beyond Borders: Advocacy Networks in International Politics*. Ithaca, NY: Cornell University Press.

Kennan, George F. 1952. *American Diplomacy, 1900–1950*. New York, N: New American Library.

Kissinger, Henry. 1994. *Diplomacy*. New York, NY: Simon & Schuster.

Krasner, Stephen. 1999. *Sovereignty: Organized Hypocrisy*. Princeton, NJ: Princeton University Press.

Levinson, Sanford, ed. 2008. *Torture: A Collection*. Revised paperback edition. New York, NY: Oxford University Press.

McDougal, Myres S., and Florentino P. Feliciano. 1961. *Law and Minimum World Public Order*. New Haven, CT: Yale University Press.

McKibben, Bill. 2012. "Global Warming's Terrifying New Math." *Rolling Stone*, July 19.

Mittelman, James H. 2010. *Hyperconflict: Globalization and Insecurity*. Stanford, CA: Stanford University Press.

Oreskes, Naomi, and Erik M. Conway. 2010. *Merchants of Doubt: How a Handful of Scientists Obscured the Truth on Issues from Tobacco Smoke to Global Warming*. New York, NY: Bloomsbury Press.

Orford, Anne. 2003. *Reading Humanitarian Intervention: Human Rights and the Use of Force in International Law*. Cambridge: Cambridge University Press.

Orford, Anne. 2013. "International Authority and the Responsibility to Protect." In *Norms of Protection: Responsibility to Protect, Protections of Civilians and their Interaction*, edited by Angus Francis, Vesselin Popovski, and Charles Samford. Washington, DC: Brookings.

Sands, Phillipe. 2005. *Lawless World*. New York, NY: Viking.

Schell, Jonathan. 1982. *Fate of the Earth*. New York, NY: Knopf.

Slaughter, Anne-Marie. 2004. *The New World Order*. Princeton, NJ: Princeton University Press.

Sokmen, Muge Gulrsoy, ed. 2008. *World Tribunal on Iraq: Making the Case against the war*. Northampton, MA: Olive Branch.

Weisburd, A. Mark. 1993. *Use of Force: The Practice of States since World War II*. Philadelphia, PA: University of Pennsylvania Press.

Chapter 19

Transitional Justice

Iavor Rangelov and Ruti Teitel

Introduction

Since 1945, and more recently in the post-Cold War period, a growing number of efforts for addressing large-scale human rights violations have given rise to transitional justice as a distinctive field of policymaking and interdisciplinary inquiry. The term "transitional justice" was coined in 1991 by Ruti Teitel in her scholarly and advisory work on transitions from military juntas to democracy across Latin America and other transitional processes such as those emerging from the collapse of the Soviet Union (see Luban, 2006; Kritz, 1995). In her path-breaking book, *Transitional Justice* (2000), Teitel further elaborates the terms and advances a new conception of justice that pertains to such periods. The phenomena included developments across a range of transitional societies throughout Latin America, Eastern Europe and the former Soviet Union, and parts of Africa, which had overthrown military dictatorships and totalitarian regimes and were undergoing processes of democratization and liberalization.

In these periods of political movement away from illiberal rule, a number of questions arose: how should societies deal with their repressive pasts? What, if any, is the relation between a state's response to its repressive past and its prospects for creating a "liberal" order? What is law's potential for ushering in liberalization? "Transitional justice" was defined to account for the self-conscious construction of a distinctive conception of justice associated with periods of radical political change following past oppressive rule.

With the end of the Cold War and the collapse of Communism, and in the context of the East European transitions, it appeared that political exceptionalism constituted the preeminent characteristic of transitional justice: namely, that the structure of the state's transitional response was shaped by its distinctive circumstances, the legacy of repression inherited from the previous regime, and the parameters of the political

The Handbook of Global Security Policy, First Edition. Edited by Mary Kaldor and Iavor Rangelov.
© 2014 John Wiley & Sons, Ltd. Published 2014 by John Wiley & Sons, Ltd.

conditions associated with the transition itself. Justice in such times, one could say, was both a driver and a product of the transitional political context and therefore might well not reflect an ideal fitting for a steady-state legitimate regime. And, moreover, in such moments of political flux we learned that the law was operating differently, and often was incapable of meeting all of the traditional values associated with the rule of law, such as general applicability, procedural due process, as well as more substantive values of fairness or analogous sources of legitimacy.

In the late twentieth century, it was helpful to conceptualize transitional justice phenomena in terms of its diverse political contexts and varying related aims and purposes. It was also useful to conceptualize transitional justice in terms of its various modalities: the diverse forms associated with transitional responses and justice-seeking, such as constitution-making and institutional reform, criminal trials, truth commissions, reparations. Indeed, for practitioners working in this area, this modalities-based approach appears to have become a salient feature (e.g. the International Center for Transitional Justice) and has sometimes become collapsed with the idea or process or meaning of justice itself.

In periods of political transition, often the focus was on exclusion of perpetrators from the new regime, for instance by emphasizing the retributive response; here, one thinks of the sharp debates over punishment versus impunity in later twentieth-century post-military rule Latin America (see, e.g. Huntington, 1991; Zalaquett, 1992). Nevertheless, we can see that in the immediate successor regime, compromised conditions of justice often prevail. As a result, under such conditions, the criminal sanction tends to be limited in nature or avoided altogether, and clemency measures are more likely to prevail. At such times, there is often a turn to diverse responses that go beyond punishment to incorporate a variety of administrative measures, vetting or lustration policies, civil actions, historical inquiries, and other forms of systemic institutional reform, such as constitutionalism. In South Africa, for example, the very basis of the amnesty trade-off was set out in the country's constitutional process. These diverse forms constitute the distinctive phenomena that have been characteristic of transitional justice deliberations. In the early transitions from dictatorship to democracy, wherever the criminal justice response was compromised or otherwise limited, states often drew a line in response to the predecessor regime's repressive rule, where such alternatives could develop capacities for advancing the rule of law that were particular to the country's political and legal traditions.

The legal phenomenology that characterizes modern periods of political flux could be seen as giving rise to a transitional paradigm. While the modalities of justice-seeking during transformative periods may appear diverse – retributive, reparatory, bureaucratic, constitutional, and historical, across plural legal responses, there are distinctive processes associated with political change. Across legal categories, a paradigm of law emerges that is best understood as a form of "transitional jurisprudence". At its core are the questions of what is deemed fair and just in these extraordinary political circumstances, and how is this determined from the perspective of the transitional position. The transitional phenomenon over the years reflects how the appropriate regime transition has often been contingent on a number of factors – the affected society's legacies of injustice, its legal culture, and political traditions – as well as upon the exigencies of its transitional political circumstances, country and regional context. How evolved the process was depended on commitment to change and other issues of capacity, both legal and political. Ultimately, the success of a state's transitional justice often depends on the nature of its substantive commitments to liberalization, democratization, and human rights as well as the legitimacy of those actors and institutions that become involved in justice processes.

The Evolution of Transitional Justice

How has transitional justice changed from the early period of this idea's development? The major change has been the normalization and related legalization of these issues, which has gone hand-in-hand with the rise of the individual as a subject and agent. As in other areas of international law, in the post-Cold War moment we can see a number of areas where there has been a move in international law and affairs from the protection of states and focus on international conflict to internal and transnational conflict and the protection of persons and peoples (Teitel, 2011). In recent years, it has become increasingly apparent that transitional justice is evolving beyond the earlier central focus on the state's political transition to restoration and repair of individual and society. These purposes relate in important ways to shifting security concepts: the early debates about state security; the shift to international peace and security in the 1990s; and, increasingly, human security (see Kaldor, Chapter 5 in this volume).

The shift can be seen in the response to the war in Bosnia, where an international court was created – the International Criminal Tribunal for the former Yugoslavia (ICTY) – to address international security needs: no longer the political project of any one state, but rather international peace and security. Twenty years later, the view is that such processes could advance security and peace more generally and they even have been linked up to goals such as victim's repair, for example trust funds in the International Criminal Court (ICC).

With these changes, transitional justice has burgeoned into a field of both scholarship and practice (Bell, 2009), with connections to international criminal law as well as the law of war, where there is an evolving scholarship on the relationship of transitional justice to *jus post bellum* (Teitel, 2013). Part of this relates to changes in the character of prevailing forms of organized violence, in particular the proliferation of persistent conflict and "new wars" (Rangelov and Kaldor, 2012; Kaldor, 2012), as well as to recognition of those previously excluded from the legal framework – persons and peoples. To be sure, this means not displacing the state but rather supplementing the prior classical framework that was virtually exclusively state-centric, as well as rationalizing transitional justice in those terms.

While we can see the evidence in continuing national debates that persist over a long period of time in places like Latin America and South Asia, as well as prominently in the current political transitions in the Middle East and elsewhere, the debates over transitional justice have changed in significant ways. While transitional justice remains a subject of politics, it is also increasingly a subject of law, often judicialized not just in domestic courts, but also via diverse judiciaries of transnational nature, and ultimately giving rise to an emerging transnational law of transitional justice. In fact, with growing supervision of transitional justice processes by structures of transnational judiciary, one can see that the issues themselves are being globalized, and often articulated and negotiated in terms of human rights.

Over the past several decades, we have become increasingly aware that while political context plays one role during the transition, often there would be other subsequent contexts of transitional justice, for example following successive regime change, where these issues have either returned or persisted until they are addressed. Recent years have seen the ongoing proliferation of transitional justice processes throughout Latin America, most evidently in countries like Argentina and Peru, as well as the revival of postponed justice-seeking efforts in a great variety of countries from Morocco to Cambodia. These developments have led some scholars to recommend different modalities at different stages (e.g. Snyder and Vinjamuri, 2003/4), although it is far from clear that the earlier sequential understanding of "transition" inherited from the "third wave" of democratization (Huntington, 1991) can be useful in many contemporary cases of democratizing and conflict-affected states, where the overall direction of peace and transitional processes is often ambiguous and uncertain (Carothers, 2002; Rangelov, forthcoming).

Moreover, one can also see in current international affairs the pervasive instances of conflict, particularly ethnic and sectarian violence, giving rise to a related generation of post-conflict responses and raising questions about the relationship between transitional justice and post-conflict justice. These questions have become more and more pertinent and controversial with the persistence of conflict (Rangelov and Kaldor, 2012), and particularly with the growing attention to terrorism and a related counterterror campaign. One can also see that with the rise of victims' rights, there has been an apparent aim to entrench and normalize a number of limited legal responses which appear, until now, to have been associated primarily with provisional regimes. Hence, more and more it appears that transitional justice implies an emerging "right to accountability", including right to truth, to reparations, as well as to prosecutions, which is evolving from the judicialization of transitional justice claims in the human rights adjudication arising out of dirty war disappearances in Latin America (see, e.g. Velasquez Rodriguez, 1988) but also in the jurisprudence of the European Court of Human Rights.

Given these ongoing developments, transitional justice often becomes enmeshed in broader dynamics, from the rise of an international humanitarian legal regime associated with and responding to globalization, to the emergence of weak and failed states and often-related processes of political fragmentation. At some level, these developments have led to the entrenchment of certain rights claims in international law, often giving rise to and reflecting salient tensions and contradictions. At present, transitional justice often involves a host of competing aims and aspirations (Leebaw, 2008) that are increasingly relating to fragile and conflict-affected environments, such as promoting stability and security, but also a larger range of regime and constitutional change.

In this political context of increased sense of pervasive violence and vulnerability, the demand for transitional justice plays a number of roles. At present, we find ourselves in a "global phase" of transitional justice, where justice-seeking processes have become normalized and entrenched (Teitel, 2003). The global phase is defined by three important characteristics: first, the move from exceptional transitional responses to a "steady-state" justice, associated with conflict and post-conflict related phenomena that emerge from a state of persistent conflict, including regional conflict, ethnic and sectarian violence, terrorism and counterterror; second, a shift from a focus on state-centric obligations to the far broader array of interests pertaining to non-state actors associated with globalization; and, lastly, we are witnessing an expansion of the law's role from advancing democratization and state-building to the more complex role of transitional justice in the broader purposes of promoting and maintaining peace and human security.

These ongoing changes do not necessarily work in a linear or harmonious direction; instead, they may well result in chaotic developments and clashes in the multiple rule of law values involved in the protection of the interests of states, persons, and peoples. Hence, the now historical "punishment vs. impunity" debate has given way to a marked demand by diplomats and legal scholars for more judicialization and tribunalization at the transnational level. Complex forms of accountability are emerging that are often associated with the rise of private actors implicated in violent conflict, both as perpetrators – for example, paramilitaries, warlords, or military contractors – and as victims, as we see the ever greater toll borne by civilians in contemporary situations of conflict and violence.

Accordingly, in light of this mix of goals, relating to both the individual and the collective, one can see that there is also an array of institutions and actors involved in the business of transitional justice beyond the state, in addition to a myriad of local responses. Inevitably, these changes affect the normative outcome of transitional justice processes (Teitel, 2003; Rangelov and Teitel, 2011). Still in operation are the United Nations special tribunals – the so-called *ad hoc* international criminal tribunals for the former Yugoslavia and Rwanda, set up pursuant to the UN Security Council's Chapter VII peacemaking powers in the midst of ethnic cleansing in Bosnia, and in response to the genocide in Rwanda. In addition to these *ad hoc* courts, there are a number of hybrids or mixed international–domestic courts, such as those in Bosnia, Cambodia, Sierra Leone, and East Timor, as well as the permanent International Criminal Court with its defined mandate of jurisdiction regarding the most serious international crimes on a "complementarity" basis. Given the nature of the crimes prosecuted in these courts and tribunals, the judicial processes often overlap with the purposes of transitional justice, giving rise to tensions and dilemmas. But clearly these developments are also tied to other institutions of global governance, such as the European Union and the United Nations (Rangelov, 2014; United Nations, 2004), and playing a role in political processes such as the European integration of the post-Yugoslav states or UN-led transitional governance, as well as in monitoring and standard-setting with respect to new democracies.

The Justice Dilemma and its Critics

The "justice dilemma" refers to a set of perceived tensions that arise in pursuing justice policies in peace and transitional processes, which are often framed as a choice between promoting normative commitments, such as human rights and democracy, and strategic considerations like the advancement of peace and stability (Rangelov, forthcoming). The iterations of the justice dilemma have followed closely the shifting articulation of transitional justice processes since the Second World War, emphasizing certain security risks associated with the pursuit of justice and accountability in a variety of historical and political contexts. Already in the aftermath of the Nuremberg and Tokyo Trials, observers expressed concerns about the dangers of treating enemy leaders as war criminals: "Would statesmen yield before having exhausted every means of resistance, if they knew that in the enemy's eyes they are criminals and will be treated as such in case of defeat?" (Aron, 2003, p. 115). At that time, however, the significance of such anxieties was diminished by the decisive military victory of the Allies and the fact that international prosecutions were conducted in countries under occupation.

In the post-war decades, the justice dilemma reappeared in a growing number of countries transitioning from dictatorship to democracy. From the start, the question how to deal with the legacies of past human rights abuse in new democracies was framed as a policy dilemma: "Forgive and forget, or prosecute and purge?" (Herz, 1978, p. 560). The traction of the dilemma in scholarly and policy discussion can be attributed to its perceived implications for security and stability: the pursuit of justice was associated with a high risk of destabilization and the prosecution of members of the old regime, in particular, was seen as highly disruptive of democratic transitions and potentially derailing them altogether. In this environment, some observers were sympathetic to the normative arguments for justice-seeking but even they often acknowledged demands for justice only in order to dismiss them, suggesting that the pursuit of accountability for "state crimes" of previous regimes, at best, "may not necessarily be suicidal" (O'Donnel and Schmitter, 1986, p. 32).

Samuel Huntington provides the most systematic examination of the justice dilemma in the "third wave" of democratization, which affected thirty countries in the period from 1974 to the early 1990s. He argues that the justice issue presented one of the key problems of democratic consolidation for these states: "How should the democratic government respond to charges of gross violations of human rights – murder, kidnapping, torture, rape, imprisonment without trial – committed by the officials of the authoritarian regimes? Was the appropriate course to prosecute and punish or to forgive and forget?" (Huntington, 1991, p. 211). The decisive factor shaping the justice response of the state (or lack thereof) was the nature of the transition. In most "third wave" cases, reformers from the previous regime played a key role in the transition to democracy, which meant that prosecution was not really an option – either feasible or desirable. In such contexts, amnesties became the preferred response to the criminal legacies of the past. In a few cases, like Argentina and Greece, where the authoritarian regime was weakened or collapsed, trials were conducted with mixed results. The experience of Argentina provided a paradigm for interpreting the tensions between human rights and stability in the justice domain, demonstrating the destabilizing potential of criminal trials: "For several years after Alfonsin came to power, the issue of how to handle human rights violations agitated and at times convulsed Argentine politics, stimulating at least three military coup attempts" (Huntington, 1991, 220). The analysis of the "third wave" of democratization reinforced the idea of tensions and trade-offs between accountability and stability, and Huntington's answer to the justice dilemma distilled the main lessons in the following way: "do not prosecute, do not punish, do not forgive, and, above all, do not forget" (Huntington, 1991, 231).

Since the end of the Cold War, the justice dilemma has been rearticulated yet again, in the context of the far-reaching changes associated with the "global" stage of transitional justice. Its current framings reflect in particular the shift from democratization to conflict (and mixed) scenarios and the ongoing proliferation of transitional justice sites, instruments, and actors. As the field is coming of age, debates over justice engage a multiplicity of well-established instruments and mechanisms, such as criminal trials, truth commissions, reparations, and vetting, in a variety of political contexts and geographies (see, e.g. Ambos, Large and Wierda, 2009; Hayner, 2010; Kerr and Mobekk, 2007; Lutz and Reiger, 2009). The justice dilemma has been reframed to reflect these important changes, while retaining the central notion that there are tensions and trade-offs between the normative commitments and strategic considerations of policymakers. In situations of active conflict and peace processes, the dilemma has been endlessly debated in the so-called "justice vs. peace" debate (Sriram, 2004; Sriram and Pillay, 2009), occasioned by the establishment of the ICTY in the midst of the war in Bosnia and fuelled by subsequent interventions of the ICC in African conflicts (Akhavan, 1998; Allen, 2006; Mamdani, 2009; Vinjamuri, 2010). Another version of the dilemma currently in circulation emphasizes a choice between principle and pragmatism, suggesting that ethical and legal arguments for the pursuit of justice should be evaluated against the danger of destabilization and backlash from spoilers (Snyder and Vinjamuri, 2003/4), thus closely mirroring the dominant framing in "third wave" debates (see, e.g. Zalaquett, 1992).

One answer to the justice dilemma prevalent in the literature emphasizes the importance of timing and sequencing. The argument is that in conflict-affected and transitional states, the consolidation of peace and democracy is the main priority: justice should be postponed until these key goals are achieved and the risk of destabilization and radicalization diminishes. In situations of active conflict, for example, it is often critical to contain spoilers and the prospect of putting them on trial may complicate the emergence of peace through negotiations (Grono and O'Brien, 2008). Snyder and Vinjamuri (2003/4, p. 6) put the issue starkly: "Justice does not lead; it follows." This framing reflects two assumptions that underpin the justice dilemma and the sequencing paradigm offered as a solution: a clear demarcation between "conflict" and "peace" and a more or less predictable and progressive direction of stabilization and democratization processes. Critics, however, increasingly call into question these assumptions, suggesting that they cannot withstand critical scrutiny.

One problem is the persistence of contemporary conflicts. The World Bank estimates that 1.5 billion people are affected by new forms of conflict and violence that don't fit easily the conventional distinction between "war" and "peace", and emphasizes in particular the risk of repeated cycles of violence (World Bank, 2011). A key factor that accounts for the high recurrence rates of today's conflicts concerns their inconclusive endings: violence often stops without either a victory or negotiated settlement, making conflict recurrence much more likely (Merz, 2012; see also Kaldor, 2010). The "persistent conflict" literature highlights the diminishing utility of policy approaches that are premised on a clear demarcation between conflict prevention, crisis management, and post-conflict reconstruction (Rangelov and Kaldor, 2012). Similar concerns are expressed in the literature on democratization. Scholars have unraveled the assumption that transitions to democracy unfold as a sequence of phases (opening, breakthrough, consolidation), leading one prominent analyst to declare "the end of the transition paradigm" (Carothers, 2002). The unpredictable logic and sequence of contemporary conflicts and transitions raise serious concerns about the framing of the justice dilemma and the ability of the sequencing paradigm to provide a reliable guide for policymakers, who increasingly confront the challenge of developing justice policies in societies caught in a "grey zone" between conflict and peace, repressive and democratic rule (Rangelov, forthcoming).

Another set of criticisms of the justice dilemma emerge from empirical studies of the "impact" of transitional justice. Assessing the impact of justice policies and instruments has proven to be extremely difficult for social scientists across the qualitative–quantitative divide, and attempts to measure their effects are often fraught with analytical and methodological problems. The authors of one study that takes stock of these efforts concluded that there is little conclusive evidence about the positive or negative effects of transitional justice: "Given the paucity and contradictory nature of the empirical findings to date, there appears to be an urgent need for more sustained, systematic, comparative analysis, and for greater attention to fact-based rather than faith-based claims" (Thoms, Ron, and Paris, 2010, p. 354).

Nevertheless, a number of challenges to the justice dilemma can be detected in the empirical literature. One concern is that the purported tensions between normative and strategic goals, which are at the heart of the justice dilemma, may be overstated. Some studies find little evidence for the claim that transitional justice mechanisms have uniquely destabilizing effects on affected societies (Dancy, 2010), or call into question the idea of simple trade-offs and suggest that among various justice options, the combination of amnesties and accountability processes may be the one most clearly correlated with improvement in human rights and democracy measures (Olsen, Payne, and Reiter, 2010). Other critics highlight the risks associated with impunity and incorporation of perpetrators of human rights abuses in power structures, particularly in environments where it is difficult to draw the line between political violence, criminal violence, and human rights violations, and where perpetrators are often key nodes in the very networks that sustain the predatory political economy of conflict and insecurity (Nadery, 2007; Rangelov and Theros, 2012; Rangelov, 2014). Finally, a growing number of studies examine the contributions of transitional justice to peace and democracy, highlighting the potential of justice instruments to help sideline peace spoilers, deter atrocities, and promote human rights and the rule of law (Akhavan, 1998; Kim and Sikkink, 2010; Sikkink, 2011).

Beyond the State: Challenges for Scholars and Policymakers

At the current juncture, some of the key challenges for transitional justice policy and scholarship concern the need to move beyond conventional approaches that focus almost exclusively on the state as the key reference point and basic unit of analysis. There are several avenues available to researchers and policymakers that can be harnessed productively to address – and move beyond – the state-centricity that has dominated the justice field, by engaging alternative normative frameworks, geographies, and sources of agency and legitimacy. In this section, we examine the productive potential of three such areas: the rise of humanity law and human security, the regional dimension of justice processes and mechanisms, and the growing role of civil society at local and global levels.

Much contemporary advocacy, as well as scholarly and policy work regarding transitional justice, seems to take for granted that one can take the models and mechanisms associated with transitional justice in the later twentieth century and assume that these approaches and responses inure to the benefit of human security (see UN

General Assembly Resolution on Rule of Law, United Nations A/RES/64/116, 15 January 2010), for example the changing UN approach to transitional justice that sets out as a formula state adherence to the "four pillars of transitional justice". Indeed, such formulas are often urged by various non-state actors as well. At the same time, the ICC as an institution, as well as the framing documents of the *ad hoc* international criminal tribunals for the former Yugoslavia and Rwanda, appear to assume that a broad range of purposes, namely the pursuit of justice and the promotion of international peace and security, can be easily reconciled. Indeed, the most illustrative case may be the ICTY, which was established by the UN Security Council during the war in Bosnia and Herzegovina and was explicitly justified in terms of contributing to the objective of "restoration and maintenance of peace" (UN Security Council Resolution 808, S/RES/808, 22 February, 1993).

But these and similar claims set out in a number of texts, with varying degrees of legitimacy, often gloss over important tensions that arise when one shifts the analytical lens and normative framework for debating, pursuing, and evaluating transitional justice. It matters a great deal whether the starting point is provided by emphasizing state security, conventionally understood as public order and political stability; by concerns for international peace and security, as they are set in the framing documents of the United Nations; or by demands for human security, defined as "freedom from want" and "freedom from fear", which places individuals and communities at the heart of security thinking and policies. As discussed in the previous section, the growing body of transitional justice scholarship and practice tends to be shaped by concerns for state-centric conceptions of security, which emphasize stability, public order, and peace. Human security is rarely employed as an analytical lens and a normative framework in these debates, and it remains to be seen how transitional justice policy may be reconsidered and reformulated from the perspective of the security of affected individuals and communities. One impetus for such reorientation of transitional justice scholarship and policymaking is provided by ongoing changes in the international legal regime, notably the emergence of persons and peoples as subjects of international law: the normative changes associated with the rise of "humanity law" that can be detected in a variety of recent developments in international human rights law, international humanitarian law, and international criminal law (Teitel, 2011).

To what extent does the work of tribunals that seek to individualize responsibility for atrocities and abuses advance the goals of human security on the ground? Is this even the lens by which these institutions and related processes are currently evaluated by scholars and policymakers? What normative principles can do the work to reconcile or harmonize diverse understandings of security – state-framed or national security, international peace and security, and human security – and in turn their relationship to transitional justice? What role can the conception of justice in transition play in promoting the security of affected individuals and communities? We know that the traditional view of the relationship of transitional justice and (state) security tends to frame them in dichotomous terms, but we know very little about the relationship of transitional justice and human security, and how the dilemmas of transitional justice may be recast and reconciled from that perspective.

Another important avenue for addressing the state-centric bias of transitional justice as a field of study and practice would involve placing a greater emphasis on the role of non-state actors across processes of claims-making, advocacy, and adjudication. While the state looms large in the academic and policy debates over justice-seeking, civil society is rarely engaged and taken seriously as an agent and source of legitimacy in transitional justice processes. And yet, civil society raises a number of important questions, both theoretical and empirical in nature, for the field of transitional justice. This is evident in those accounts that examine civil society primarily in relation to the state (e.g. Brysk, 1994; Crocker, 2000; Backer, 2003; Katz, 2011), as well as in the literature that investigates the role of civil society in the emergence and operation of justice norms and structures at the international level (Glasius, 2006; Hill, 2008; Clarke, 2009; Boesenecker and Vinjamuri, 2011; Haslam, 2011).

A mapping study of the engagement of global civil society in transitional justice processes around the world identified three main characteristics of these pervasive interactions at the current juncture:

> First, civil society includes a broad range of actors and forms of engagement in transitional justice and its scale of operation and organization extends from the local and national to the regional and global. Second, in the current period civil society relates to a polycentric framework of governance and interacts with increasingly internationalized structures and processes of transitional justice. Finally, civil society advances plural and often conflicting conceptions of justice and serves as an arena where the discourse and practice of transitional justice are contested and negotiated, both within and beyond the state. It is the combination of these three features that distinguishes the "global" character of civil society and its role in contemporary transitional justice. (Rangelov and Teitel, 2011, p. 170)

These findings underscore the growing significance of civil society in transitional justice in a variety of different contexts. And yet, in thinking about what forms justice should take and what its goals and effects may be, there is a tendency to focus on the state and other elite actors, thus taking for granted that a top–down approach to addressing past and ongoing human rights violations will work and deliver as intended. The challenge is to "democratize" transitional justice by opening it up, not only to civil society contestation and critique, but also to meaningful forms of civil society participation at all stages of the deliberation, design, and implementation of specific justice processes and responses. There is much to be gained if a bottom–up approach is taken seriously and pursued as a matter of priority, not only in terms of legitimating transitional justice, but also by harnessing the creative potential of civil society actors to promote experimentation and innovation in this important policy arena.

Finally, it is becoming increasingly apparent that the conventional statist conception of transitional justice cannot provide an answer to the growing regionalization and transnationalization of the underlying violence and abuses, which justice responses are supposed to address. Few contemporary conflicts are contained within state borders; instead, we are witnessing how the regional spillovers and dimensions of conflict are becoming more prominent: refugee flows, transnational criminal networks that feed off and finance the violence, or the role of neighboring countries in supplying arms, bases, or fighters. From the Balkans to the Great Lakes and the Middle East, the regional character of organized violence has prompted scholars to draw attention to the regional aspects of conflict and to develop new analytical lenses, such as "regional conflict complexes" and "regional war economies" (Wallenstein and Sollenberg, 1997; Pugh, Cooper, and Goodhand, 2003). There is also the challenge of transnational crime and terrorism and the range of interventions and practices associated with the "War on Terror" – a global campaign that has produced its own legacies of abuse, which cannot be easily reconciled with the classic state-centric framework of war and also call into question accepted distinctions such as those between internal and international armed conflict, criminal and political violence, or war and peace. These new forms of conflict and violence, rather than being the exception, are increasingly becoming the rule and are currently estimated to affect the lives of 1.5 billion people who live in situations of fragility, conflict, or extreme criminal violence (World Bank, 2011).

And yet, the regional and transnational character of the underlying conflicts and legacies of abuse has been largely neglected by transitional justice scholars and policymakers (Rangelov, forthcoming). While the tensions are coming to the fore in a variety of contexts, they have been particularly challenging for transitional justice in places like the Balkans. In the post-Yugoslav space, any transitional justice response confronts the problem that victims, perpetrators, witnesses, and evidence, are often on different sides of today's borders. In fact, the regional dimension of the politics and practice of transitional justice is arguably its most salient feature and the most significant obstacle for dealing with the legacies of the wars in the 1990s across the region. Similar problems are encountered in parts of Africa, where scholars highlight how the mismatch between the transnational character of conflicts and crimes and the state-centricity of transitional justice and international law produces "zones of impunity" (Sriram and Ross, 2007). In places like Afghanistan and Iraq, we are seeing at play both the regional aspect (e.g. the role of Pakistan-based actors in atrocities committed on the territory of Afghanistan and targeting Afghan citizens) and the need for reckoning with abuses committed by international forces and security contractors and their local counterparts in the US-led counterterror and counterinsurgency operations over the past decade, such as civilian casualties of airstrikes and night raids, detention without trial, torture, etc.

While these challenges are significant and require sustained efforts to confront them head-on, they are not necessarily insurmountable. There are interesting experiments in moving beyond the state that are already underway in different parts of the world, which are gesturing towards developing new ways of thinking and providing tentative answers to some of the tensions and contradictions associated with the dominance of the state-centric framework of justice for mass atrocity and human rights abuse. One example from the Balkans is the civil society initiative for the establishment of RECOM, a regional commission to establish the facts of war crimes and human rights violations committed on the territory of the former Yugoslavia between 1991 and 2001, and to address the problem of the remaining 15,000 missing persons in the region. The Coalition for RECOM, which has more than one thousand members from all post-Yugoslav states (NGOs, associations of victims and war veterans, women's and youth groups, religious actors, media and public intellectuals) is an illustration of the potential of civil society to offer an innovative approach that is both bottom–up and regional in character, and places the security of individuals and communities, rather than states, at the heart of transitional justice (Chinkin and Rangelov, 2011). Since 2008, the Coalition has organized an extensive process of civil society consultations at local, national, and regional levels with a variety of constituencies, drafted a statute of RECOM, and collected more than half a million signatures from citizens in support of the initiative. At the time of writing, it remains to be seen whether the governments in the regional and key international actors, such as the European Union, will begin formal negotiations for establishing RECOM. Nevertheless, it could be argued that the RECOM process itself has been significant, not only for transitional justice in the region, but also as an experiment in bottom–up, regional, and human security-focused transitional justice.

Conclusion

The proliferation of transitional justice in recent decades draws attention to the emergence of new dynamics and actors, which are currently shaping both justice processes and their complex relationship to security. The key characteristics of contemporary transitional justice suggest both an expanded range of contexts, including past and ongoing conflict alongside situations of post-authoritarian and mixed transitions, and an array of private actors that are often enmeshed alongside public actors in processes of claim-making, advocacy, and adjudication.

This chapter has traced the evolution of transitional justice over the past three decades from its origins in the "third wave" of democratization, associated with exceptional periods of political change, to the current "global phase" of normalized and entrenched transitional justice. While scholars and policymakers often frame the relationship between justice and security in terms of clear tensions and trade-offs – prosecute and punish vs. forgive and forget, justice vs. peace, principle vs. pragmatism – the empirical evidence is mixed and often suggests that their relationship is much more complex, calling into questions the assumption that normative and strategic dynamics are working in cross-purposes in the justice arena. Addressing the main challenge for transitional justice at the current juncture – going beyond the state in terms of normativity, actors, and geographies – may further complicate and unravel some of the accepted understandings that circulate in the field and frame much of the debate over justice and security.

At a time of persistent conflict and volatile transitions, of global interdependence without political integration, there is a surging demand for accountability: from the political upheaval across the Arab world to the Mothers of Latin America and the involvement of the Security Council in the crisis in Libya. Notwithstanding the multiplicity of sites, actors, and institutions, it is clear that in the changing security context of the twenty-first century, the contribution of transitional justice to global security is predicated on commitment to processes that draw as much as possible upon shared norms and discourse contributed by law and concerned with meaningful recognition of human rights abuse as a necessary basis for societal repair.

References

Akhavan, Payam. 1998. "Justice in The Hague, Peace in the former Yugoslavia? A Commentary on the United Nations War Crimes Tribunal." *Human Rights Quarterly*, 20(4): 737–816.

Allen, Tim. 2006. *Trial Justice: The International Criminal Court and the Lord's Resistance Army*. London: Zed Books.

Ambos, Kai, Judith Large, and Marieke Wierda, eds. 2009. *Building a Future on Peace and Justice: Studies in Transitional Justice, Conflict Resolution and Development*. Berlin: Springer.

Aron, Raymond. 2003. *Peace & War: A Theory of International Relations*, 2nd ed. New Brunswick, NJ: Transaction Publishers.

Backer, David. 2003. "Civil Society and Transitional Justice: Possibilities, Patterns and Prospects." *Journal of Human Rights*, 2: 297–313.

Bell, Christine. 2009. "Transitional Justice, Interdisciplinarity and the State of the 'Field' or 'Non-Field'." *International Journal of Transitional Justice*, 3(1): 5–27.

Boesenecker, Aaron P., and Leslie Vinjamuri. 2011. "Lost in Translation? Civil Society, Faith-Based Organizations and the Negotiation of International Norms." *International Journal of Transitional Justice*, 5(3): 345–365.

Brysk, Alison. 1994. *The Politics of Human Rights in Argentina: Protest, Change and Democratization*. Stanford, CA: Stanford University Press.

Carothers, Thomas. 2002. "The End of the Transition Paradigm." *Journal of Democracy*, 5(1): 5–21.

Chinkin, Christine, and Iavor Rangelov. 2011. "A Bottom–up Approach to Redressing Past Human Rights Violations." In *Bottom–up Politics: An Agency-Centred Approach to Globalization*, edited by Denisa Kostovicova and Marlies Glasius. Basingstoke: Palgrave Macmillan.

Clarke, Kamari Maxine. 2009. *Fictions of Justice: The International Criminal Court and the Challenge of Legal Pluralism in Sub-Saharan Africa*. New York, NY: Cambridge University Press.

Crocker, David A. 2000. "Truth Commissions, Transitional Justice, and Civil Society." In *Truth v. Justice: The Morality of Truth Commissions*, edited by Robert I. Rotberg and Dennis Thompson. Princeton, NJ: Princeton University Press.

Dancy, Geoff. 2010. "Impact Assessment, Not Evaluation: Defining a Limited role for Positivism in the Study of Transitional Justice." *International Journal of Transitional Justice*, 4: 355–376.

Glasius, Marlies. 2006. *The International Criminal Court: A Global Civil Society Achievement*. Abingdon: Routledge.

Grono, Nick, and Adam O'Brien. 2008. "Justice in Conflict? The ICC and Peace Processes." In *Courting Conflict? Justice, Peace, and the ICC in Africa*, edited by Nicholas Waddell and Phil Clark. London: Royal African Society.

Haslam, Emily. 2011. "Subjects and Objects: International Criminal Law and the Institutionalization of Civil Society." *International Journal of Transitional Justice*, 5(2): 221–240.

Hayner, Priscilla. 2010. *Unspeakable Truths: Transitional Justice and the Challenge of Truth Commissions*. New York, NY: Routledge.

Herz, John H. 1978. "On Reestablishing Democracy after the Downfall of Authoritarian or Dictatorial Regimes." *Comparative Politics*, 10(4): 559–562.

Hill, Gina E. 2008. "A Case of NGO Participation: International Criminal Court Negotiations." In *Critical Mass: The Emergence of Global Civil Society*, James Walker and Andrew Thompson, eds. Waterloo, ON: Wilfrid Laurier University Press.

Huntington, Samuel. 1991. *The Third Wave: Democratization in the Late Twentieth Century*. Norman, OK: University of Oklahoma Press.

Kaldor, Mary. 2010. "Inconclusive Wars: Is Clausewitz Still Relevant in These Global Times?" *Global Policy*, 1(3): 271–181.

Kaldor, Mary. 2012. *New and Old Wars: Organized Violence in a Global Era*, 3rd ed. Cambridge: Polity Press.

Katz, Paul. 2011. "A New 'Normal': Political Complicity, Exclusionary Violence, and the Delegation of Argentine Jewish Associations during the Argentine Dirty War." *International Journal of Transitional Justice*, 5(3): 366–389.

Kerr, Rachel, and Eirin Mobekk. 2007. *Peace and Justice: Seeking Accountability after War*. Cambridge: Polity Press.

Kim, Hunjoon, and Kathryn Sikkink. 2010. "Explaining the Deterrence Effect of Human Rights Prosecutions for Transitional Countries." *International Studies Quarterly*, 54(4): 939–963.

Kritz, Neil. 1995. *Transitional Justice: How Emerging Democracies Reckon with Former Regimes*. Washington, DC: United States Institute of Peace Press.

Leebaw, Bronwyn Anne. 2008. "The Irreconcilable Goals of Transitional Justice." *Human Rights Quarterly*, 30(1): 95–118.

Luban, David Jay. 2006. "Book Review: Transitional Justice in Historical Perspective." *Ethics*, 116: 409–412 (reviewing Jon Elster, *Closing the Books: Transitional Justice in Historical Perspective*. Cambridge: Cambridge University Press, 2004).

Lutz, Ellen L., and Caitlin Reiger, eds. 2009. *Prosecuting Heads of State*. Cambridge: Cambridge University Press.

Mamdani, Mahmood. 2009. *Saviors and Survivors: Darfur, Politics, and the War on Terror*. New York, NY: Pantheon Press.

Merz, Sebastian. 2012. "Less Conflict, More Peace? Understanding Trends in Conflict Persistence." *Conflict, Security & Development*, 12(3): 201–226.

Nadery, Ahmad Nader. 2007. "Peace or Justice? Transitional Justice in Afghanistan." *International Journal of Transitional Justice*, 1(1): 173–179.

O'Donnel, Guillermo, and Philippe C. Schmitter. 1986. *Transitions from Authoritarian Rule: Tentative Conclusions about Uncertain Democracies*. Baltimore, MD: Johns Hopkins University Press.

Olsen, Tricia D., Leigh A. Payne, and Andrew G. Reiter. 2010. "The Justice Balance: When Transitional Justice Improves Human Rights and Democracy." *Human Rights Quarterly*, 32: 980–1007.

Pugh, Michael, and Neil Cooper with Jonathan Goodhand. 2003. *War Economies in a Regional Context: Challenges of Transformation*. Boulder, CO: Lynne Rienner Publishers.

Rangelov, Iavor. Forthcoming. "Democracy or Stability? European Approaches to Justice in Peace and Transitional Processes." *Global Policy* (early view).

Rangelov, Iavor. 2014. *Nationalism and the Rule of Law: Lessons from the Balkans and Beyond*. New York: Cambridge University Press.

Rangelov, Iavor, and Mary Kaldor. 2012. "Persistent Conflict." *Conflict, Security & Development*, 12(3): 193–199.

Rangelov, Iavor, and Ruti Teitel. 2011. "Global Civil Society and Transitional Justice." In *Global Civil Society 2011: Globality and the Absence of Justice*, edited by Martin Albrow and Hakan Seckinelgin. Basingstoke: Palgrave Macmillan.

Rangelov, Iavor, and Marika Theros. 2012. "Abuse of Power and Conflict Persistence in Afghanistan." *Conflict, Security & Development*, 12(3): 227–248.

Snyder, Jack, and Leslie Vinjamuri. 2003/4. "Trials and Errors: Principle and Pragmatism in Strategies of International Justice." *International Security*, 28(3): 3–44.

Sriram, Chandra Lekha. 2004. *Confronting Past Human Rights Violations: Justice vs. Peace in Times of Transition*. London: Frank Cass.

Sriram, Chandra Lekha, and Amy Ross. 2007. "Geographies of Crime and Justice: Contemporary Transitional Justice and the Creation of 'Zones of Impunity'." *International Journal of Transitional Justice*, 1(1): 45–65.

Sriram, Chandra Lekha, and Suren Pillay, eds. 2009. *Peace versus Justice? The Dilemma of Transitional Justice in Africa*. Scottsville, South Africa: University of KwaZulu Natal Press.

Sikkink, Kathryn. 2011. *The Justice Cascade: How Human Rights Prosecutions are Changing World Politics*. New York: W.W. Norton & Co.

Teitel, Ruti. 2000. *Transitional Justice*. New York, NY, NY: Oxford University Press.

Teitel, Ruti. 2003. "Transitional Justice Genealogy." *Harvard Human Rights Journal*, 16: 69–94.

Teitel, Ruti. 2011. *Humanity's Law*. New York, NY: Oxford University Press.

Teitel, Ruti. 2013. "Rethinking Jus Post Bellum in an Age of Global Transitional Justice: engaging with Michael Walzer and Larry May." *European Journal of International Law, Symposium Issue*, 24 (1): 335–342.

Thoms, Oskar N.T., James Ron, and Roland Paris. 2010. "State-Level Effects of Transitional Justice: What Do We Know?" *International Journal of Transitional Justice*, 4: 329–354.

United Nations. 2004. "The Rule of Law and Transitional Justice in Conflict and Post-Conflict Societies." UN Doc. S/2004/616.

Velasquez Rodriguez Case, Judgment of July 29, 1988, Inter-Am.Ct.H.R. (Ser. C) No. 4 (1988).

Vinjamuri, Leslie. 2010. "Deterrence, Democracy, and the Pursuit of International Justice." *Ethics & International Affairs*, 24(2): 191–211.

Wallenstein, Peter, and Margareta Sollenberg. 1997. "Armed Conflict and Regional Conflict complexes, 1989–1997." *Journal of Peace Research*, 35(5): 621–634.

World Bank. 2011. *World Development Report 2011: Conflict, Security, and Development*. Washington, DC: World Bank.

Zalaquett, José. 1992. "Balancing Ethical Imperatives and Political Constraints: The Dilemma of New Democracies Confronting Past Human Rights Violations." *Hastings Law Journal*, 43: 1425–1438.

Part IV   Global Security Actors

Reframing the Use of Force: The European Union as a Security Actor

Mary Martin

Introduction

In December 2012, the Nobel Peace prize was awarded to the European Union in recognition of its six decades of work promoting "peace and reconciliation, democracy and human rights". The award attracted controversy in part because it occurred in a year when the European Union had never appeared so divided, its common currency under attack, and deep tensions arising between debtor nations such as Greece, Spain, Portugal, and Italy, on one side, and those who were called upon to bail them out, principally Germany, on the other. The politics of austerity produced street protests in European cities as citizens resisted their own politicians, as well as the demands of Brussels policymakers for budget cuts as they sought to prevent the collapse of the European single currency. The appearance of far right parties, and a new wave of Euroscepticism in Member States, such as the United Kingdom, signaled schisms of a further kind. The Nobel committee president, Thorbjoern Jagland, praised the EU's role in transforming a European "continent of war" into a "continent of peace", yet events across Europe appeared to make a mockery of such accolades.[1]

Although European security has been at the heart of the integration of the EU's nation states since the genesis of collective policymaking, and predates even the founding of the European Union in 1957, the region's security identity has never been settled during this period. The European project originated in the explicit attempt to ban war, and end centuries of fratricide that culminated in total war, genocide, terror, and totalitarianism from 1914 to 1945. The pragmatic decision to merge the strategic resources of France and Germany in the European Coal and Steel Community in 1950 sought to make impossible the return of Europe's "great civil war" (Kaldor, 2010). Similarly, an attempt in 1954 to establish a European Defence Community

The Handbook of Global Security Policy, First Edition. Edited by Mary Kaldor and Iavor Rangelov.
© 2014 John Wiley & Sons, Ltd. Published 2014 by John Wiley & Sons, Ltd.

(EDC) envisaged an integrated European army, placed under the responsibility of a common Defence Minister, and controlled by a European assembly. The EDC Treaty was rejected by the French Parliament in 1954 as a step too far. The French veto had profound political consequences in Europe, relegating the question of a common security policy for the next three and a half decades. In its absence, the development of NATO and the transatlantic alliance took responsibility for European security, while economics rather than "high politics" defined the nature of European integration. Later attempts, such as European Political Co-operation (EPC) and the Fouchet Plan to systematize EU external relations, had limited results, and it was not until after the Cold War that security would re-emerge as a domain of shared policy making. Meanwhile, technocratic integration in other policy areas cemented Europe's new-found unity, rather than grand visions or existential issues.

Security evolved as an ambiguous concept, in both a geographic and political sense, becoming "of Europe" rather than "for Europe". It involved a challenge both to traditional ideas of sovereignty and to the use of classic instruments. Compared to conventional ideas of security that had prevailed before 1945, it was therefore an anomaly.

The *pax americana*, which ruled Europe after 1945, relied on NATO and large numbers of US and Allied troops on European soil to guarantee the security of the region, not only to keep the peace between European nations, but on a global level to protect them from aggression by external powers, principally the Soviet Union. With its territorial defense provided by others, the European Union was able to avoid security as a policy domain for collective decision-making, although individual Member States continued to practice traditional foreign and security policies, maintain armies, and extend the capability of their military resources, including nuclear weapons.

The concept of security applied to the European Union also took unusual forms. When security did become part of EU collective policymaking after the end of the Cold War, it did not follow classic definitions: there was no European army and the European Union relied on non-military forms of power to exercise influence regionally and globally. The story of the European Union as a security actor has therefore been one of exceptionalism, and a concept of security disconnected from traditional notions of sovereignty and power.

This chapter explores this exceptionalism and how it has shaped firstly the emergence of the European Union as a global security actor, capable of projecting its power and identity outwards onto the world stage; and second how it has come to shape ideas of what is normal in international politics, in other words how Europe's exceptional experience attempted to become mainstream. To understand the meaning of security in EU terms and to analyze Europe's security role in global politics, this chapter adopts three perspectives: first the integration project itself, how it developed between 1948 and 2008, and the architecture and institutions that gave rise to collective policymaking. The second perspective looks at norms and values that make up the highly specific identity of the European Union, which it projects in its external relations. Finally, European security is defined in terms of the EU's capacities for action. These consist of not only the very concrete resources it can command to implement its external policies but also how it has deployed them in external missions.

Integrated Security

In the Cold War context, foreign and defense policies sat awkwardly in the European approach: they were not "sectoral" policies but belonged to high politics – an area that European integration had specifically eschewed in going down the route of establishing first the Coal and Steel Community, and then the customs union, which was the basis of the European Economic Community in 1957. High politics (Hoffmann, 1966) were the bastion of national interests that the founding fathers of Europe, such as Jean Monnet and Robert Schumann, attempted to restrain. Thus foreign and security policies were the least integrated in the European framework. Before the Single European Act of 1987, foreign policy was not even included in the European treaties; however, the history of European integration is a series of complex dialectics between voluntary construction and spontaneous emergence, grand design, and incremental progress and between a process of institution building and decision-making driven by Member States on the one hand and an evolving supranational polity working both above and below the level of the nation state on the other (Schméder and Martin, 2011). After the failure of the European Defence Community, France made a second attempt at political integration in 1961 when President Charles De Gaulle proposed the Fouchet Plan to form a new "Union of States", representing an intergovernmental arrangement for decision-making. The plan was an attempt to wrest back control from the supranational institutions of the European Community and to keep the balance of power in France's favor. The proposed "Union" of states had two major aims: a common foreign policy and a common defense policy. Other aims of the Union were the development of the "common heritage" of the member states and "the protection of the values on which their civilization rests".[2] The Fouchet Plan, like the EDC before it, failed because it was overtly political. Member States worried that it would undermine the character and process of integration by the Monnet method, which depended on the establishment of supranational Community institutions. Germany and The Netherlands, in particular, were opposed because they saw the Fouchet Plan as a threat to NATO, and the US security guarantee.

The next attempt to introduce a security dimension to EU integration came in 1970 with the establishment of European Political Co-operation, a network of collective diplomacy, intended to produce a common, or at least harmonious, voice among EU Member States on global political issues, such as the Middle East crisis, or East–West relations between the superpowers. EPC was outside Community structures and provided a framework for discussion, if not decision, between EU foreign ministers. It was described as having "a scope of action so indeterminate that it threatened to invite more conflict than co-operation", mechanisms that were "feeble and peculiar", rules that were vague, and few instruments. "Preoccupation with procedures ... served as a substitute for policy" (Forster and Wallace, 1996, p. 411; Smith, 2004). One of the few areas of agreement among participants was that security and defense matters were not appropriate subjects for discussion (Smith, 2004, p. 1). Despite this, EPC managed to last until the formation of the European Union, under the 1992 Maastricht Treaty, inaugurated security as a policy domain not just for cooperation but formal, collective European decision-making. Until the birth of the Common Foreign and Security Policy (CFSP), any attempt that envisaged EU Member States cooperating in foreign policy issues as part of its external relations attracted profound political disagreement within and among Member States, and were seen as "a pretentious waste of time or even a failure" and a nuisance (Smith, 2004, p. 3). External relations were dominated not by security policies, but by trade and enlargement. In other words, the European peace project was exported for the first 40 years of integration, either through Europe's trade relations, or through negotiations to extend the membership of the European Community (initially, beyond the original six states to include the United Kingdom, Scandinavia and Denmark, Austria, Spain and Portugal; and after the end of the Cold War, to the newly liberated states of Eastern Europe). "The benign effect" of integration was intended as the means by which an enlarged European Union would strengthen the stability of the European continent (Solana, 2001).

The Western European Union (WEU), formed in 1948, which included a mutual assistance clause among members in the event of external aggression, also attempted to plug the gap in European security politics by providing a framework for consultation, which went beyond the economic aspects of security issues. In 1984, the WEU's Rome Declaration allowed its members to "consider the implications for Europe of crises in other regions of the world". It envisaged the creation of a European security identity and gradual harmonization of members' defense policies (WEU, 1984).

Events after 1989 forced the pace of change, pushing the European Union to adopt policies that went closer to the heart of classic politics of sovereignty and state power. The technocratic approach to integration, which had "spilled" over into foreign policy, was overridden by a much more ambitious agenda that led to the crafting of a Common Foreign and Security Policy and a security dimension for the European Union. The ingredients in this change of political will were the need to deal with a newly reunited Germany and the desire to constrain any resurgence of German power, and the dissolution of the Soviet Union, which was preceded by tensions between Soviet forces and nationalists in the Baltic States. Even more decisive was the break up of Yugoslavia after June 1991 and the conflicts that resulted in Bosnia and then Kosovo. These events required a united response from the European Union, which until then had lacked both the political will and the institutions to achieve systematic consensus on foreign policy issues. In a rapidly changing international context, the European Union had to adopt a new policy framework, as well as developing policy content.

The liberation of the former Soviet bloc also made it unfeasible that individual Member States should continue to pursue exclusively bilateral relations with the newly independent countries of Eastern Europe. The timing and content of an embryonic EU foreign policy also owed much to US intervention and its own policy preferences in regard to Europe and the NATO alliance after the fall of the Berlin Wall. US Secretary of State James Baker, in a speech in Brussels in December 1989, proposed a new transatlantic bargain to reflect the end of American security dominance in Europe. The new security agenda should include not only political and military issues, but also economic and environmental concerns.[3] EU policy towards the new Eastern European democracies was also heavily skewed towards economic relations and rebuilding market economies (Piening, 1997, p. 38; White, 2001, p. 95).

Meanwhile, changes to the understanding of what constituted security were taking place not only in Europe, but also globally. New conceptualizations of security were most evident within the United Nations. The 1994 UN Development Report mainstreamed the expression "human security" to reflect a shift in the perception of security threats, as well as the referent object of security policies. The focus was no longer exclusively states and interstate relations, but included individuals and groups. In 2000, Secretary-General Kofi Annan championed ideas of human security and individual empowerment in *We the people* (Annan, 2000), which challenged traditional norms of state sovereignty (Newman, 2001, 2014; Martin and Owen, 2010, p. 3). The academy was also revising studies of security. Buzan and Waever's theories on security policy (which became known as the Copenhagen School) questioned the primacy of military approaches, and therefore the predominance of state-centered views of security. They suggested a multisectoral approach to dealing with security threats and, crucially for the development of a new European discourse, they also highlighted how security decisions were essentially political acts, at the extreme end of a range of policy options. They defined security as:

> the move that takes politics beyond the established rules of the game and frames the issue either as a special kind of politics or above politics … In theory any public issue can be located on the spectrum ranging from non-politicised … through politicized … to securitized, meaning the issue is presented as an existential threat requiring emergency measures and justifying actions outside the bounds of political procedure. (Buzan, Waever, and de Wilde, 1998, pp. 23–24)

Europe's integration project could no longer ignore security and defense as a sphere for collective action. Security policy began to be seen as a logical continuation of Member States' willingness to pool their sovereignty and create an institutional framework for joint decision-making. The question was how to do this in a way that took account of other more powerful institutions already active in the field of European security, in particular NATO, and not undermine them. The question of an EU security role also had to navigate a complex mosaic of different cultural, historical, and legal traditions of Member States.

The Western European Union's Petersburg Declaration of 1992 attempted to set out Europe's responsibilities in terms that reflected both these constraints. The declaration speaks of "soft security" as being an essential companion to military capability. Soft security was defined as dealing with social and economic inequality, environmental risks, and transborder crime (WEU, 1992; Sjursen, 2004, p. 65). The response to these types of threats was spelled out as supporting:

> on a case-by-case basis and in accordance with our own procedures, the effective implementation of conflict-prevention and crisis-management measures, including peacekeeping activities of the CSCE or the United Nations Security Council. (WEU, 1992)

The CFSP inaugurated under the EU's Maastricht Treaty of 1992 codified this emerging global vision. It established a three-pillar structure, which was to move the integration project towards a political union. The first pillar consisted of the original Community institutions and policy areas, such as agriculture, fisheries, and trade. In the first pillar, decisions would be taken by the "Community method", under which the European Commission would propose policy, the Council and the European Parliament would have rights of decision, and the Court of Justice would be responsible for monitoring compliance with Community law.

Title V of the Treaty establishing CFSP constituted the second pillar and allowed Member States to take joint action in the field of foreign policy, on the basis of unanimous votes. Although Member States were in the driving seat of foreign policy through the European Council, the Maastricht Treaty allowed a "modest" role for the European Commission in developing a proactive role for the European Union in global issues (Smith, 2003, p. 38). The role of the parliament was initially almost invisible and the Court of Justice had no presence at all in the new second pillar.

Thus foreign policy was an example of how the institutional machinery of integration ensured that the European Union became a distinctive kind of global actor. Foreign policy processes were both complicated and often contradictory, with different and sometimes clashing agendas of the Council on the one hand, and the Commission on the other. Decisions were the result of a number of different processes occurring, often simultaneously. These included intergovernmental bargaining between EU Member States within the Council framework, where outcomes reflected the relative power of actors with fixed preferences (Sjursen, 2004, p. 59; Moravscik, 2003); supranational deliberations within Community institutions, such as the Commission, and gradually also the European Parliament; and bilateral coordination between individual Member States, as well as unilateral action by single Member States. At the same time, the pursuit of security was increasingly seen as being through multilateral institutions such as the United Nations and NATO, rather than through the traditional means of military alliances that had dominated European politics for centuries. Europe's new security concept was therefore predicated first on the ability of Member States to agree unanimous positions on key issues, or even to admit them to the collective agenda, and second on how the European Union could work with and be subordinate to more established multilateral actors. The European Union could play a useful role in crisis response situations to suit the agendas of established global players (Bailes, 2008). Collective security policies were also a vehicle for reshaping the international security and defense architecture.

France and Britain saw that a European Security and Defence Policy (ESDP) could suit their national interests in either balancing against the United States (in the case of France), or bridging between it and Europe (in the case of the United Kingdom) (Matlary, 2008, p. 131). A bilateral declaration by the United Kingdom and France at their summit in St Malo in December 1998 committed the two countries to steering the European Union towards autonomous action, backed up by credible military forces, in order to respond to international crises when the Atlantic Alliance was not involved. The difference between the Petersburg Declaration six years earlier and the agreement at St Malo was that the latter paved the way for the European Union to institutionalize a security identity that was explicitly military. The new impetus behind ESDP was also the EU's experience during the wars in Bosnia and Kosovo. Not only did these conflicts thrust the European Union into playing a major role in rewriting security in Europe, but the failure of early warning systems to avert bloodshed in the Balkans, the weakness of European diplomacy, and the lack of means to confront the unfolding violence in Bosnia and then Kosovo meant that European leaders depended on US force and diplomatic power to address the crises. The crisis in Yugoslavia revealed the inadequacies of the CFSP as a long-term conflict prevention mechanism, at a time when crisis response was required (Smith, 2004, p. 196). The brutality of a war in the EU's own backyard, combined with US reluctance to engage first in Bosnia (Secretary of State James Baker famously declared "We do not have a dog in this fight") and then to put troops on the ground in Kosovo, confirmed to European leaders the relevance of providing the European Union not just with an autonomous capability, but one that made collective policymaking more fit for purpose. The EU's tools for conflict resolution, even after the Dayton Agreement ending the war in Bosnia and the removal of Serb aggression in Kosovo, were shown to be inadequate in providing a sustainable underpinning to peace or delivering multiethnic societies in these countries. The European Union spent €17 billion in the Balkans between 1991 and 2000, but the combination of "chequebook conflict management" and the promise of enlargement of the European Union failed to transform it into a convincing regional security guarantor (Hughes, 2009, pp. 300–301; Independent International Commission on Kosovo, 2000, p. 285).

A different kind of milestone was reached in 2003 when the European Security Strategy (ESS) was published by the European Council. The ESS was produced in response to the deep schism within the European Union caused by different reactions to the US invasion of Iraq. By stating the EU's goals and approaches as a collective security actor, the ESS sought to override the political disagreements between Member States that the Iraq war had produced (Solana, 2014; Biscop and Andersson, 2008).

Norms and Values

The ESS was also significant in setting out the norms that underpinned Europe's willingness to act on a wider stage. The text emphasizes "effective multilateralism" and cooperation (the Strategy never refers to the "enemy"). It asserts the ultimate authority of the United Nations and that military methods must be used only as a last-resort adjunct of other "peaceful", diplomatic, political, economic, and humanitarian measures (ESS, 2003).

Some of the rhetoric of the ESS expands on Article 6 of the Maastricht Treaty of the European Union (repeated in Article 2 of the Lisbon Treaty), which states:

> The Union is founded on the values of respect for human dignity, freedom, democracy, equality, the rule of law and respect for human rights, including the rights of persons belonging to minorities. These values are common to Member States in a society in which pluralism, non-discrimination, tolerance, justice, solidarity and equality between men and women prevail. (European Union, 1992)

This is the ideational bedrock on which the EU's foreign and security policy was built. EU values and norms were not made explicit in the early days of the integration project. They were assumed, rather than articulated openly. It was only after the end of the Cold War, and the possibility that Europe should develop a role as a global political actor, alongside its economic influence, that a debate got underway about what the European Union stood for.

The success of the Single Market and the integration of new democracies from Spain and Portugal, and then the former Eastern bloc countries, had helped to reverse Europe's image from a war-prone to a "civilian" figure, defending virtues of civility, tolerance, and nonviolence. Francois Duchêne saw the European Community as heralding a "new stage in political civilization", a polity that was capable of exercising a civilizing influence in international affairs through "essentially civilian forms of power" (Duchêne, 1973, p. 19). The key elements of civilian power were that its holder deployed primarily non-military foreign policy instruments, especially economic ones, and worked with other states and through multilateral institutions to manage international problems (Maull, 1990, 2005).

The adoption of a civilian power identity was regarded skeptically by some who viewed it as a necessary tactic, rather than a deliberate choice. It reflected how Member States used the European Union to advance their commercial and trading interests through its established collective economic power, or treating the European Union as the repository for a set of human rights and other second-order normative concerns, which traditionally had no place in member states' foreign and defense policies (Hyde-Price, 2008, p. 31). The realist reading of the EU's civilian power was that it was a product of the EU's failure to respond coherently to foreign and security issues, particularly in the case of violent conflict in the Balkans, as well as by its lack of hard instruments to back up its policy declarations.

Whatever the combination of motivations, this sense of limited or constrained acting in global politics was stronger in some Member States, such as Germany, than those with long military cultures, such as Britain and France. Europe's emerging security identity was therefore as much a point of difference as a consolidating force. References to a shared history of the twentieth century belied different perspectives from that history, and the fact that, by the second half of the twentieth century, it gave rise to quite incompatible forms of strategic culture. As Hyde-Price notes, Germany's Bundeswehr regarded the prospect of firing a shot in anger as a failure, while France believed it needed to increase military capability to defend and protect her national interests (Hyde-Price, 2000, p. 139), and Britain saw in the Allied victory confirmation of the effectiveness of its armed forces.

In one important respect, however, Europe's civilian power concept became a significant marker in that it distinguished it from the United States. Robert Kagan's "Weakness and Power" first published in June 2002[4], gained notoriety for its epithet: "Americans are from Mars, Europeans are from Venus". The gulf in strategic culture led Kagan to summarize his argument thus:

> It is time to stop pretending that Europeans and Americans share a common view of the world, or even that they occupy the same world. On the all important question of power ... American and European perspectives are diverging. Europe is turning away from power ... it is moving beyond power into a self-contained world of laws and rules and transnational negotiation and co-operation. It is entering a post-historical paradise of peace and relative prosperity, the realization of Immanuel Kant's "perpetual peace". Meanwhile the United States remains mired in history, exercising power in an anarchic Hobbesian world ... that is why on major strategic and international questions today, Americans are from Mars and Europeans are from Venus. (Kagan, 2003)

This was illustrated by the war in Kosovo in 1999 when US tactics for dealing with Milosevic had clashed with a "European approach to warfare", which favored less aggressive bombardment of Serbian targets as part of the NATO offensive. As NATO commander, General Wesley Clark wrote in his account of the campaign, "On some issues there were almost as many viewpoints as there were nations" (Clark, 2001, p. xxvii).

Kagan's thesis not only highlighted the difference in outlook and capabilities that separated Europe from the United States in security issues, but also tapped into cultural logics that departed from the sovereign interests, which predominated in studies of international order. The civilian power identity that Europe had assumed after World War II and through the Cold War, drew on German and Nordic concepts, which eschewed the use of force in favor of economic or diplomatic power. Not only did these ideas provide the states with a niche role in world politics, but they also appeared increasingly relevant in terms of contemporary forms of conflict. A civilian approach to violence gained credence from the belief that the "long history of great power conflict and security competition was over and that a new era of international peace and cooperation – a 'new world order,' with a peaceful Europe at its core – was dawning" (Hyde-Price, 2004).

The contrast with the United States became more marked in the first decade of the twenty-first century. Its rejection of the Kyoto Treaty on emissions to address climate change, its refusal to sign up to the International Criminal Court, and finally its resort to military invasion in response to the 9/11 attacks, became a driver in cementing European security norms (Martin, 2005). The ESS attempted to rally Member States to rediscover their collective interests in security in contrast to the preemptive defense doctrine contained in the US National Security strategy of 2002, which provided the policy script for the invasion of Iraq a year later.

Meanwhile, examples such as Charles Grant's *Powerless Europe* (Prospect March, 2002), Steven Evert's Centre for European Reform booklet *Shaping A Credible EU Foreign Policy* (CER February, 2002) and Kori Schake's *Constructive Duplication* (CER January, 2002), built on the discourse of difference and the forging of a distinct identity for the European Union.

One EU diplomat recalls that discussions about global norms were far from dominant in attempts to build ESDP:

> People were thinking about the good of *Europe*: shocked by the events in Kosovo and the Europeans' lack of capacity to master that crisis, they sought new crisis management capabilities for Europe to use on its own chosen ground and under its own control in future. Many others were thinking of the good of NATO and US–European relations, convinced that Atlantic ties would in the last resort be stronger if Europeans shouldered more of the burden of their own security. Some were simply hoping to get the Germans to make more effort in defence. There was remarkably little public debate on the initiative, and even less about the ethical implications of what the EU was doing. (Bailes, 2008, p. 115)

More salient was the EU's sense of powerlessness during the Balkan wars: first over the nationalist and ethnic strife in Bosnia, and then in the face of Slobodan Milosevic's ethnic cleansing in Kosovo. The European Union had an alternative discourse, which had emerged out of the Helsinki Accords and the post-Cold War era, of human rights and civilian, rather than military responses, coupled with an imperative of multilateral intervention in place of classic sovereignty to relieve suffering – but prior to 1999, it had trouble translating this into effective action.

The EU's normative purpose, sharpened as a result of the Balkan wars, culminated in initiatives such as the St Malo agreement, which attempted to fashion ESDP as a novel form of security framework. It also happened to coincide with the policy preferences of EU leaders, such as Tony Blair, to reinforce the UK's European perspective, a preference that was to change abruptly after 9/11 in favor of solidarity with the United States.

Not only was the EU's distinctive identity becoming significant, it also opened up a form of actorness in the shape of norm diffusion. Ian Manners's "Normative Power Europe" thesis encapsulated this aspect of the EU's role in global politics, that the ideational force of the European Union consisted in "its ability to shape conceptions of 'normal' in international relations" in line with its unique normative basis, which is rooted in its *sui generis* history and character as a post-sovereign or post-Westphalian entity. Displaying "a willingness to disregard Westphalian conventions", Manners argued that the EU's international presence and value-rational conduct in foreign policy led to it spreading universal values such as peace, democracy, the rule of law, and human rights. This represented a "care for the 'other', an expression of border-crossing solidarity with less fortunate people that is grounded not in self-interest but in normative convictions" (Manners, 2002, p. 239).

The EU's increasing activity in ensuring global security after September 11, 2001 was driven not only by the need to develop a collective response to intra-state crises in Asia, Africa, neighborhoods in North Africa, the Middle East, the Balkans and the Caucasus, and to the threat posed by international terrorism; it also sought to demonstrate that it could mount a distinctive form of action. As a peace project rather than a nation state, the European Union could act without the classical motivations of defending borders and territorial rights, offering security through negotiation, governance assistance, rule of law measures, and economic aid (Solana, 2014).

Part of the public consensus that allowed integration to proceed and expand during the 1960s and 1970s was based on a perception that in the fields of human rights and security, European integration had been a positive development (Schmeder and Martin, 2011).

Yet this actorness had to resolve a fundamental dissonance between Europe as a "peace project" and the militarization, which was a cornerstone of the post-World War II order. Moreover, the European approach to security remained very traditional and top–down, focusing on interstate relations. Most European countries financed large standing armies and substantial military means. The idea of a peace project also implied a bottom–up phenomenon involving – passively if not actively – European citizens, while the reality for much of the post-war period was that the policies implementing the peace project were heavily directed from the top. Security was a "domaine reserve" for experts, and focused on interstate relations, not mass engagement, with civil society marginalized.

Despite Raymond Aron's assertion that "there were no such animals as 'European citizens'" (Aron, 1974), the mobilization of European publics in protest against the siting of nuclear weapons on European soil during the Cold War revealed the existence of a "cosmopolitan" citizenry within national identities, whose claim for a "civilian Europe" challenged the traditional relationship between citizen, nation, and territorial state.

This side to European perceptions of peace and security resurfaced after the end of the Cold War, for example in the Barcelona Report of 2004 on the EU's security capabilities, commissioned by the High Representative. The report gained attention not for its recommendations on the resources that the European Union should deploy as a global actor (although one of the least noticed aspects of the report argued for a bespoke "human security response force"), but for what it had to say about the EU's values in the area of foreign and security policy. It urged the European Union to adopt a doctrine of human security for reasons of universalist morality, legal obligation, and enlightened self-interest (Barcelona Report, 2004, p. 5).

Human security expressed much of what the European Union was struggling to institutionalize as both a distinctive and active actor in world politics. It embodied a holistic approach to security that stressed civilian as well as military capabilities; the integration of security and development concerns; dealing with "freedom from fear as well as freedom from want"; and a normative concern based on cosmopolitan ethics expressed in the ESS paper called "A Secure Europe in a Better World". The EU's approach to security through crisis management and conflict prevention contained much that was implicitly about human security. Under the leadership of Benita Ferrero-Waldner as the commissioner in charge of external relations from 2004–2009, human security was an explicit policy goal; however, it remained a contested idea within EU policymaking (Kaldor, Martin, and Selchow, 2007; Matlary, 2008; Martin and Owen, 2010). It was not until 2008 that the concept formally found its way into official documents, such as the implementation report of the ESS.

European Security Capabilities

In 1994, Christopher Hill wrote an influential article referring to the EU's "capability-expectations" gap, which predicted a flaw in the arrangements of the Maastricht Treaty setting up CFSP. His argument was that the brave rhetoric of EU treaties could not be matched by the reality of a Europe that was poorly equipped and politically divided in taking on a bigger role in international politics (Hill, 1993, 1998).

The European Union took two steps in particular to address its perceived weakness after 2000: it reinforced its security capabilities, in particular developing for the first time an autonomous military capability; and through the Lisbon Treaty of 2007, it attempted to change the institutional arrangements for foreign policy to improve the coherence between its different policy paths and resources. Yet perhaps the biggest change came through the deployment of EU missions on the ground in crisis zones, not only in its own backyard in the Balkans and the Caucasus, but in Asia and Africa.

Two of the first EU operations were taken over from NATO and were in the Balkans. Local populations may have had misgivings about whether the Europeans were indeed up to the task, but the use of NATO assets meant that in many ways the early missions were simply rebranded peacekeeping missions of traditional actors. The European Union's first non-European mission, Operation Artemis in the Democratic Republic of the Congo in 2003, was placed in a classic peacekeeping context involving close cooperation with the United Nations (Bailes, 2008, p. 116).

The NATO summit of 1994 had authorized the WEU to undertake autonomous action using NATO assets, and established a strategic partnership between the two organizations in crisis management. The permanent arrangements became known as the Berlin Plus arrangements and provided for European Union access to NATO planning resources, assets, and capabilities, and the exchange of classified information.

The development of autonomous EU capabilities after 2003 through ESDP were controversial because the addition of military resources not only undermined for some the EU's hallmark civilian power (Smith, 2000; European Peacebuilding Liaison Office, 2009; cf. Mitzen, 2006) but created an ambiguous idea of security. In fact, most of the missions that the European Union has undertaken – a total of more than 20 between 2003 and 2009 – are civilian in nature, offering rule of law assistance, such as its largest deployment of over 3000 people in Kosovo, border control (in Gaza and Moldova), policing in the Balkans and Afghanistan, and security sector reform (in the Democratic Republic of the Congo). Military deployments, such as to the Democratic Republic of the Congo in 2006, have been the exception, and even then have been distinctive in the way troops have been deployed and combined (Martin, 2007). However the ambition to be able to use coercive force accompanied by the accretion of capabilities, such as a military committee, military planning and the European Defence Agency to support the development of defense technologies, dominated the growth of ESDP until 2009, and altered the character of European security. Thus in 2004, the European Union set itself headline goals to be achieved by 2010 to structure the targeted contributions it sought from Member States, both in terms of military and civilian resources. In 2007, the first EU Battlegroups became operational, with the aim of enabling the European Union to engage in rapid response crisis management operations, and also to encourage Member States to restructure their armed forces in ways consistent with the ability to operate internationally, autonomously from NATO (Major and Mölling, 2011).

The military dimension not only raised issues about the true nature of European security under CFSP; it also prompted questions about the circumstances under which the European Union would use kinetic power, and how it would be deployed within a comprehensive concept of sustainable security, including the balance at both strategic and operational levels, between military expertise and civilian resources. It also changed the relationship between the European Union and other actors such as NATO and nation states.

> "A European security policy seen through the lens of its potential to deploy armed force looks quite different from one which deploys judges, police, economists and border monitors. ... It mitigates the distinctiveness of a European way." (Martin and Kaldor, 2008, p. 7)

On the other hand, criticisms focused not on the normative puzzle of whether militarization is appropriate for the European Union, but whether the European Union was any more effective as a result of the commitment to deploy a full range of security tools (Menon, 2009).

Meanwhile the European Union struggled to manage the rapid growth and enlargement of its security apparatus. As well as the development of CSFP, which was managed by the Council as an intergovernmental process, the European Commission developed instruments such as democracy and human rights protection as part of its remit in the security sphere. Coordinating multiple policy silos required further institutional change. The Lisbon Treaty of 2007 was meant to achieve a more streamlined architecture for security and defense, doing away with the old pillar structure of policy competences to meet its commitment to "promote peace, its values and the wellbeing of its peoples" (Article 3.1) and to "preserve peace, prevent conflicts and strengthen international security" (Article 21.2(c)).

In the area of security, the most notable innovation of the Lisbon Treaty was the European External Action Service (EEAS), a new diplomatic service headed by the High Representative who was to report to the Council, but also occupy a role as deputy president of the European Commission. At the time of writing, the EEAS has had a difficult birth since it began work in 2011 (EPLO, 2012). Personnel difficulties, a failure to be active in key international crises and turf wars have dogged the new service, alongside criticisms of the leadership of Cathy Ashton, the High Representative/Vice President who succeeded Javier Solana. The dynamic drive to increase capabilities and, in parallel, to develop a narrative of European security in the decade from 1999 to 2009 has since stalled dramatically. Leadership failures, institutional confusion, and a persistent deficit of legitimacy that the euro crisis compounded after 2011, have stripped EU security policy of its once ambitious horizons. Collective policy has under delivered in key international crises, such as Afghanistan, or failed to materialize in the Syrian civil war. The 2013 intervention in Mali was undertaken by France rather than an EU military force.

Conclusion

The European Union has marked successive anniversaries and milestones – its 50th birthday, 10 years of ESDP, and its award of the Nobel Peace Prize as well as the passing of new foundational treaties – while struggling to set out, definitively, a vision of security for itself. The ambition of EU policymakers is to devise a *sui generis* form of external action, which is simultaneously appropriate and relevant to a different kind of polity, effective in a world of rapidly changing security challenges, and which is seen as legitimate both by EU citizens and third party populations, including those on the receiving end of its security démarches.

It is buffeted by different types of criticism: that it is an irrelevance on the global stage on the one hand and that it overreaches itself on the other hand. Although the European Union is a regional security actor, the impact of its security policies has been minimal in terms of safeguarding its own citizens against traditional existential threats (although it engages in new areas such as cybercrime, and transnational crime, as well as terrorism). Its effects on global security have been highly targeted, such as supporting a peace process in Indonesia or addressing chronic conflict in central Africa, and sometimes poorly received, as in Afghanistan. It has had limited success in its neighborhood, including the Balkans and the Caucasus, and it relies heavily on its power of attraction either through membership, or preferential association agreements for non-member states. In 2013, its persistence in seeking to broker an agreement between Kosovo and Serbia paid off when Serbia proved willing to compromise over territorial control of northern Kosovo in order to open accession talks. Whether this agreement can be sustained is unclear, but in any case enlargement is a diminishing part of the EU security toolkit, with the prospect of further accessions highly unlikely in a European Union that is struggling to keep even its existing members on board.

Its ambition to represent a new form of collective security, underpinned by norms and values, and by an extensive investment in new institutional architecture and resources has most often been undermined – as at the beginning of its security journey in the first decade after World War II – by the rival claims and capabilities of nation states. Thus, when challenged by insecurity on its doorstep in north Africa, first with the Libyan uprising of 2011, the Syrian civil war, or insurgency in Mali and the Sahel in 2013, it has had to rely on the political will and resources of traditionally powerful member states, such as France and Britain, to do the heavy lifting.

Notes

1. http://www.guardian.co.uk/world/2012/dec/10/eu-receives-nobel-peace-prize   [accessed December 28, 2012]
2. http://www.cvce.eu/viewer/-/content/485fa02e-f21e-4e4d-9665–92f0820a0c22/en; jsessionid=441BD693160E8706492434D58977AEB5 [accessed January 2, 2013]
3. "A new Europe, a new Atlanticism: Architecture for a new Era", speech to the Berlin Press Club, December 12, 1989 [cited in Forster and Wallace, 1996, p. 420).
4. The original article in *Policy Review* No. 113, June 2002 was subsequently part of *Paradise and Power*, a book on the thesis.

References

Annan, Kofi. 2000. *We the People*. Report of the Secretary-General. New York, NY: United Nations.

Aron, R. 1974. "Is Multinational Citizenship Possible?" *Social Research*, 41(4): 638–656.

Bailes, A. 2008. "The EU and a "Better World': What Role for the European Security and Defence Policy?" *International Affairs*, 84(1): 115–130.

Barcelona Report. 2004. "A human security doctrine for Europe: the Barcelona Report of the Study Group on Europe's Security Capabilities." Accessed December 12, 2013 from http://eprints.lse.ac.uk/40209/

Buzan, B., O.Waever, and J. de Wilde. 1998. *Security, a New Framework of Analysis*. Boulder, CO: Lynne Rienner.

Biscop, S., and J-J Andersson eds. 2008. *The EU and the European Security Strategy*. Abingdon: Routledge.

Duchêne, F. 1972. "Europe's role in World Peace." In *Europe Tomorrow: 16 Europeans Look Ahead* edited by R. Mayne. Fontana, CA: Collins.

European Peacebuilding Liaison Office (EPLO). 2009. "EPLO Statement on Civilian-Military Integration in European Security and Defence Policy." Accessed January 20, 2013 from http://www.eplo.org/assets/files/2.%20Activities/Working%20Groups/CSDP/EPLO_Statem ent_Civilian-Military_Integration_in_European_Security_and_Defence_Policy.pdf

European Peacebuilding Liaison Office (EPLO). 2012. "The EEAS and Peacebuilding One Year on." Accessed January 20, 2013 from http://www.eplo.org/assets/files/2.% 20Activities/Working%20Groups/EEAS/EPLO_Statement_EEASPeacebuildingOneYearOn. pdf

European Security Strategy (EES) (European Council Brussels). 2003. "A Secure Europe in a better world: European Security Strategy." Accessed December 12, 2003 from http://www. consilium.europa.eu/uedocs/cmsUpload/78367.pdf

European Union. 1992. Maastricht Treaty. Accessed December 12, 2013 from http://www.
eurotreaties.com/maastrichtec.pdf

Evert, S. 2002. "Shaping a Credible EU Foreign Policy." Accessed December 12, 2013 from
http://www.cer.org.uk/publications/archive/report/2002/shaping-credible-eu-foreign-policy

Forster, A., and W. Wallace. 1996. "Common Foreign and Security Policy: A New Policy or
Just a New Name?" In *Policy-making in the European Union*, 3rd ed., edited by H. Wallace
and W. Wallace. Oxford: Oxford University Press.

Grant, C. 2002. Powerless Europe, *Prospect*, March 20, 2002. Accessed December 12, 2013
from http://www.prospectmagazine.co.uk/magazine/powerlesseurope/#.Uqmm2PRdV8E

Hill, C. 1993. "The Capability-Expectations Gap, or Conceptualising Europe's International
Role." *Journal of Common Market Studies*, 31(3): 305–328.

Hill, C. 1998. "Closing the Capability- Expectations Gap." In *A Common Foreign Policy for
Europe? Competing Visions of the CFSP*, edited by J. Peterson and H. Sjursen. Abingdon:
Routledge.

Hoffmann, S. 1966. "Obstinate or Obsolete? The Fate of the Nation State and the Case of
Western Europe." *Daedalus*, 95: 862–915.

Hughes, J. 2009. "Paying for Peace: Comparing the EU's Role in the Conflicts in Northern
Ireland and Kosovo." *Ethnopolitics*, 8(3–4): 287–306.

Hyde-Price, A. 2000. "Reflections on Security and Identity in Europe." In *Security and Identity in Europe: Exploring the New Agenda*, edited by L. Aggestam and A. Hyde-Price.
Basingstoke: Macmillan.

Hyde-Price, A. 2004. "European Security, Strategic Culture, and the Use of Force." *European
Security*, 13(4): 323–343.

Hyde-Price, A. 2008. "A 'Tragic Actor'? A Realist Perspective on 'Ethical Power Europe'."
International Affairs, 84(1): 49–64.

Independent International Commission on Kosovo. 2000. *The Kosovo Report: Conflict, International Response, Lessons Learned*. Oxford: Oxford University Press.

Kaldor, M. 2010. "The EU needs to return to its roots." *The Guardian*. Accessed December 12,
2013 from http://www.theguardian.com/commentisfree/2010/feb/27/eu-return-roots-peace

Kaldor, M., Martin, M., and Selchow, S. 2007. "Human Security: A New Strategic Narrative
for Europe," *International Affairs*, 83(2): 273–288.

Kagan, R. 2002. "Power and Weakness." *Policy Review*, 113: 3–28.

Kagan, R. 2003. *Paradise and Power*. London: Atlantic Books.

Manners, I. 2002. "Normative Power Europe: A Contradiction in Terms?" *Journal of Common Market Studies*, 40(2): 235–258.

Martin, M. 2005. "Europe's Other. How a Gap Became an Ocean in Transatlantic Relations."
Bologna Center Journal for International Relations, 50th Anniversary Issue.

Martin, M. 2007. "The European Union in the Democratic Republic of Congo – a Force for
Good?" In *The European Union and Human Security*, edited by M. Martin and M. Kaldor.
Abingdon: Routledge.

Martin, M, and M. Kaldor (eds.). 2009. *The European Union and Human Security: External
Interventions and Missions*. Abingdon: Routledge.

Martin, M., and T. Owen. 2010. "Second Generation Human Security. Lessons from the EU
and UN Experiences." *International Affairs*, 86(1): 211–224.

Matlary, J-H. 2008. "Much Ado about Little: the EU and Human Security." *International
Affairs*, 84(1): 131–143.

Major, C. and C. Mölling. 2011. "EU Battlegroups: What Contribution to European
Defence?" SWP Research Paper, June 8. Accessed January 20, 2013 from http://www.swp-
berlin.org/fileadmin/contents/products/research_papers/2011_RP08_mjr_mlg_ks.pdf

Maull, Hanns W. 1990. "Germany and Japan: The New Civilian Powers," *Foreign Affairs*,
69(5): 91–106.

Maull, Hanns W. 2005. "Europe and the New Balance of Global Order," *International Affairs*, 81(4): 775–799.

Menon, A. 2009. "Empowering Paradise? The ESDP at Ten." *International Affairs*, 85(2): 227–246.

Mitzen, J. 2006. "Anchoring Europe's Civilizing Identity: Habits Capabilities, and Ontological Security." *Journal of European Public Policy*, 13(2): 270–285.

Moravcsik, A. 2003. *The Choice for Europe*. Abingdon: Routledge.

Newman, E. 2001. "Human Security and Constructivism." *International Studies Perspectives*, 2: 239–251.

Newman, E. 2014. "The United Nations and Human Security: Between Solidarism and Pluralism." In *Routledge Handbook of Human Security* edited by M. Martin and T. Owen. Abingdon: Routledge.

Piening, C. 1997. *Global Europe*. Boulder, CO: Lynne Riener.

Schake, C. 2002. "Constructive duplication: Reducing EU reliance on US military assets," Centre for European Reform, 4 January, 2002. Accessed December 12 2013 from http://www.cer.org.uk/publications/archive/working-paper/2002/constructive-duplication-reducing-eu-reliance-us-military-as#sthash.UnpUf8Vw.dpuf

Schmeder, G., and M. Martin. 2011. "Peace and the People: How the European Union Rewrites Security." In *Bottom–Up Politics: An Agency-centred Approach to Globalisation*, edited by D. Kostovicova and M. Glasius. Basingstoke: Palgrave Macmillan.

Sjursen, H. 2004. "Security and Defence." In *Contemporary European Foreign Policy* edited by W. Carlsnaes, H. Sjursen, and B. White. London: Sage Publications.

Smith, K.E. 2000. "The End of Civilian Power EU: A Welcome Demise or Cause for Concern?" *International Spectator*, 35(3): 11–28.

Smith, K.E. 2003. *European Union Foreign Policy in a Changing World*. Cambridge: Polity Press.

Smith, M.E. 2004. *Europe's Foreign and Security Policy*. Cambridge: Cambridge University Press.

Solana, J. 2001. "Some thoughts about the European Union's new approach towards Central and Eastern Europe." Speech to Conference of the German–Poland Institute and the Germany and Northern Europa Institute, Brussels, June 26.

Solana, J. 2014. "The Making of a Global Security Actor." In *Routledge Handbook of Human Security* edited by M. Martin and T. Owen. Abingdon: Routledge.

WEU. 1984. "Rome Declaration." Council of Ministers, October 24.

WEU. 1992. "Petersburg Declaration." Council of Ministers, Bonn, June 19.

White, B. 2001. *Understanding European Foreign Policy*. Basingstoke: Palgrave Macmillan.

Chapter 21

China

May-Britt U. Stumbaum and Sun Xuefeng

Introduction

"China is a sleeping giant. And if it awakes, the world will tremble" – these words, assigned to Napoleon Bonaparte, describe well the process that the international system is currently experiencing: the rise of a power that, by its sheer size and accumulated economic power, is increasingly impacting international affairs and has started to co- and re-shape the forms of interaction in international initiatives to address today's challenges. Reading the *Chinese Concept Paper on the New Security Notion* (Ministry of Foreign Affairs of the People's Republic of China, 2002), the key threats mentioned resemble those acknowledged in the European Security Strategy and in national security documents such as the United States', the British, the French or the German White Papers and security strategies. With China (PRC) being located in an environment that is characterized still by unresolved border and territorial disputes, as well as a very low level of regional integration, perceived security threats are still dominated by traditional threats, although nontraditional threats ranging from terrorism to climate change and pandemics also play a role. Yet, China remains a special case, not only because of its unprecedented development and its potential impact on changing the international system. China also represents a country that faces rapid change and expansion of its security concerns alongside its impressive economic growth. Concurrently, there is a vivid debate in China about what China's security interests actually are and what its responses should be, with a simultaneously evolving body of scholarship on international relations as such, culminating in discussions of questions such as – *whether there is* a "Chinese International Relations Theory". The remainder of this chapter will provide an overview of the debates within and outside of China on the country's security concerns, its capabilities to meet them, the approaches that have been chosen, and the debates among scholars and policymakers about where China is and should be heading.

The Handbook of Global Security Policy, First Edition. Edited by Mary Kaldor and Iavor Rangelov.
© 2014 John Wiley & Sons, Ltd. Published 2014 by John Wiley & Sons, Ltd.

Part I

Part one will provide an overview of the Chinese definition of what "security" is – traditional security challenges are still predominant in the Chinese paradigm, while nontraditional security threats (NTS) are also playing an increasing role. Part one concludes with an outlook on China's capabilities to meet those challenges.

Defining Security

A classical Chinese dictionary explains "security" in terms of "no danger", "no threat", and "being free of incidents"(CASS, 2005). According to Yan Xuetong, security is based on the ability to reject the demands of adversaries. If a state lacks the ability to effectively refuse those demands, it does not enjoy sound security. However, in the real world absolute security will not exist because dangers, threats, and incidents cannot be completely removed. As a result of the unattainability of absolute security, peace is always maintained with a certain degree of insecurity (Yan and Zhou, 2004).

Yan Xuetong's analysis further shows that peace is not equivalent to security. First, peace only means the non-existence of armed conflict. Nations at peace still face dangers of military threat, armed conflict, or war. Second, the degree of national and international security can differ during times of peace. In the same period of peace, the degree of security varies from country to country. Third, in terms of the degree of national security, a nation at peace may have less of it than a country at war (Yan and Zhou, 2004, p. 10).

Challenges – Security Threats that China is Facing

Concurrent with the expansion of Chinese interests on a global scale and an intensifying debate about China's role in the world, the definition of what are China's core security interests has been ever more vivid. In a speech in 2004, then Chinese President Hu Jintao outlined the core tasks, which the People's Liberation Army (PLA) needed to prepare for, and called them the "Four New Historic Missions". Those four missions included ensuring military support for continuing the rule of the Chinese Communist Party (CCP); defending China's sovereignty, territorial integrity, and national security; protecting China's expanding national interests; helping to ensure a peaceful global environment and promote mutual development (Hartnett, 2009).

Traditional Security Threats   Characteristically for threats faced by nations in the twenty-first century, China's threats fall into two major categories – traditional and nontraditional security threats (NTS). According to Craig (2007), traditional threats can be "characterized loosely as threats to a nation emanating from other nations and involving a military component". China's security outlook is shaped by 14,000 miles of land border and 9,000 miles of coastline, bordering 14 countries as diverse in terms of size, military power, and regional and global influence as Bhutan and Russia. Not being a member of any bi- or multilateral military alliance, China finds itself in a geopolitical scenario that is characterized by still unresolved border conflicts on land, for example with India over Arunachal Pradesh, or in the East and South

China Seas, where China disputes with neighboring countries such as the Philippines, Vietnam, and Japan over the control of several groups of islands and has frequently clashed with these countries, most recently in 2012 over the Scarborough Shoal and the Diaoyu/Senkaku Islands (Japanese and Chinese coast vessels) (Scobell and Nathan, 2012, p. 3). The tensions between China and Japan have also flared, for instance following Japan's arrest of the captain of a Chinese fishing boat in waters near the Diaoyu Islands in September 2010, and when the Japanese central government bought the Diaoyu Islands from private Japanese owners in September 2012 *(New York Times, 2012)*.

A core and defining issue for the PLA remains achieving and maintaining national unity, the foremost concern being the statehood and future of Taiwan. In the PRC's "Anti-Secession-Law" of 2005, the Chinese leadership reiterated its resolve to prevent a formal independence of Taiwan by threatening the use of force should Taiwan declare independence. As the United States has pledged aid to Taiwan in case of an attack from the PRC in the 1979 Taiwan Relations Act, developments in the Taiwan Strait have the potential to trigger war between the PRC and the United States, thereby affecting the whole region and consequently the world. The past two decades witnessed an increasing pro-independence sentiment and practice on the island. On July 9, 1999, former President of Taiwan Lee Teng-hui defined the relations between the PRC and Taiwan as "special state to state" relations (Embassy of the People's Republic of China, 2003). Three years later, then President of Taiwan Chen Shui-bian proclaimed that he backed legislation on a referendum to decide whether Taiwan should declare independence and stated that each side (of the Taiwan Straits) is a country. By the end of 2007, Chen Shui-bian had put forward the United Nations membership referendum and pledged to push for a new constitution for Taiwan.

Many officials, policy analysts, and academic pundits were pessimistic about maintaining peaceful conditions in the Taiwan Straits in the eventuality of the pro-independence Democratic Progressive Party (DPP) candidate winning the election in March 2008 (GlobalSecurity.org, 2011). The election of President Ma Ying-jeou was seen as having a de-escalating effect on the crisis. Since 2008, mainland China and Taiwan have enjoyed ever-closer economic cooperation, leading to the signing of the Economic Cooperation Framework Agreement (ECFA) in June 2010. The Early Harvest in the ECFA entered into force from January 1, 2011 (Ministry of Foreign Affairs, 2011). Thanks to the ECFA, trade volume between the two sides of the Taiwan Straits exceeded US$168.9 billion in 2012 (People's Daily Online, 2013).

However, public opinion on Taiwan's status and Taiwanese identity has been more favorable to the independence forces since 2008. According to a survey conducted by the Taiwan Chengchi University about Taiwanese identities, the percentage of those seeing themselves as Taiwanese increased from 48.4% in 2008 to 54.3% in 2012, while the percentage of those identifying as Chinese decreased from 4% to 3.6% in the same period (Zhou, 2012).

At the same time, some sections of the political elite in Taiwan denied or held more negative views on the 1992 Consensus or One China Principle. Tsai Ing-wen, chairwoman and the presidential candidate of the DPP, refused to acknowledge the 1992 Consensus on her China policy platform (WantChinaTimes, 2011). Also Ma Ying-jeou responded to the perceived voters' opinion on Taiwan's status. On July 11, 2011, Ma Ying-jeou claimed, "I identify with Taiwan in terms of my identity.

I fight for Taiwan and I am Taiwanese; in nationality, I am a Republic of China [ROC] citizen and I am the president of the ROC" (*Taipeh Times*, 2011).

These trends imply that Taiwan's independence movement may regain momentum at any time, especially in Taiwanese presidential election campaigns. China's top leaders will continue to be wary of trends towards independence and the level of perceived external support to the independence movement. The three major crises in 1999, 2004, and 2008 illustrate the impact of US policy on China's assessments of its use of force in the dispute. In these cases, the United States also contributed to a de-escalation by indicating that it did not politically support Taiwan's efforts to move toward formal independence (Fravel, 2007/08; Wu, 2008). A majority of scholars in China today argue that mainland China will not resort to the use of force to contain Taiwan's independence forces in the coming decade if the United States does not support the independence movement in Taiwan because they pose a fundamental challenge to the current status quo in Taiwan Straits (Sun and Huang, 2012).

Nontraditional Security Threats   Nontraditional security threats (NTS) are defined as those that "transcend national boundaries, go beyond the military sphere, are unpredictable and/or unexpected, have both internal and external elements and ramifications, and are frequently interwoven with traditional security threats" (Craig, 2007, p. vii). The NTS facing China include as disparate issues as the Avian Flu, AIDS, terrorism, proliferation, climate change, water scarcity/desertification, drug trafficking, and piracy. China, with its 55 ethnic minorities that the PRC officially acknowledges in addition to the Han majority, also experiences the tension of ethnic conflicts as seen by the riots in Xinjiang and Tibet (*Guardian*, 2011; Xinhuanet, 2011). Environmental problems have also gained increasing attention. As a victim of climate change, as well as of the consequences of its rapid industrialization, China faces severe deforestation and desertification: North of Beijing, the Gobi Desert currently expands by about 2500 km^2 annually, which will eventually lead to sand storms in the capital. Another potentially transboundary challenge is air pollution – according to the World Bank, 16 of the world's 20 most polluted cities are in the PRC (World Bank, cited in CBSNews, 2010). Measurements of the Beijing air quality showed 755 micrograms per cubic meter in January 2013 on the Air Quality Index (AQI). This index, based on revised standards of the American Environmental Protection Agency (EPA), deems an AQI of 100 as "unhealthy for sensitive groups" and anything above 400 as "hazardous" for all (*Economist*, 2012; Han, 2006). The Chinese government has responded with initiatives such as the "Green Wall" against the desertification and efforts to limit car traffic in cities. Many international projects, for example by the European Union, are also targeting "green projects". These concerns harbor the possibility of a growing international cooperation and the involvement of non-state actors, such as big environmental organizations like the US nongovernmental organization (NGO) Nature Conservancy and others.

An official international definition of NST is still lacking, which makes them difficult to identify and prioritize, and adequate institutions to cope with them are also nascent at best. The appearance of NTS and their transboundary nature, however, seems to offer more opportunities for joint action than confrontation between states (Morton, 2011) – a shift in paradigm that is also identified in China's Position Paper of the New Security Concept (CPP) of 1996 (Ministry of Foreign Affairs of the People's Republic of China, 2002). Comparable with other national security concepts of the post-Cold War era, the CPP emphasizes traditional as well as nontraditional security challenges and underlines the conviction that the use of force alone will not fundamentally resolve disputes in the long term. According to the document, China, having over the last decade become a power with global political and economic influence, considers the current international security environment as an opportunity to "discard the old way of thinking and replace it with new concepts and means to seek and safeguard security" (Ministry of Foreign Affairs of the People's Republic of China, 2002). Similarly to Western national security strategies (European Council, 2003; Federal Ministry of Defense, 2012; HM Government, 2010; Présidence de la République, 2008), CPP points out the changing nature of risks and threats in the twenty-first century, underlining the preeminence of international terrorism, the influence of non-governmental actors and the asymmetrical nature of new confrontations. They also include challenges that go far beyond purely military concerns, including demographic shifts, pandemics, and the securing of natural resources. They agree that the challenges of today are global in nature and require concerted responses by the international community. In other words, they necessitate extensive international cooperation. The "new security concept" as laid out by the Chinese government even insists that in this "world of diversity […] security cooperation is not just something for countries with similar or identical views and modes of development, it also includes cooperation between countries whose views and modes of development differ" (Ministry of Foreign Affairs of the People's Republic of China, 2002).

Capabilities: China as a Security Actor

Concurrently with the impressive development of China's economic performance in the framework of China's "peaceful rise" (Guo, 2006), its defense budget has steadily increased by an average of 10% during the last two decades and totaled around US$111 billion in 2012, according to official Chinese figures (Buckley, 2012; Guo, 2006; SIPRI, 2012). Amounting to a seventh of the US defense budget in 2012, the Chinese defense budget funds the Chinese version of a revolution in military affairs (RMA) of the Chinese PLA. This modernization process aims to enable the PLA to fight "local wars under conditions of informatization" or "high-intensity, information-centric regional military operations of short duration" and to fulfill the "New Historic Missions" (Federal Ministry of Defense, 2012).

Chinese economic development has created interests overseas in terms of protection of expanding imports, direct investment, and the dispersion of Chinese civilians all around the world. According to Chinese official statistics, more than 70 million Chinese citizens traveled abroad in 2011 alone (Xinhuanet, 2012b). In the same year, there were more than 18,000 Chinese overseas enterprises and China's FDI in the stock increased to US$380 billion (Sina, 2012). From 2007 to 2011, the Chinese Ministry of Foreign affairs coordinated to handle more than 160,000 consular protection incidents and provided assistance to more than 1 million Chinese (Embassy of the People's Republic of China, 2012).

China's growing global interests demand that the Chinese military be capable of going global and that it possess long-range delivery capability. As President Hu

Jintao stated, China needs to build effective national economic security systems, early-warning crisis response and the capacity to protect our interests and the safety of our citizens abroad (Xinhuanet, 2007). In December 2008, China sent an antipiracy task force to Somalia. It was China's first potential combat mission beyond its territorial waters in centuries (Harmsen, 2008). China's first aircraft carrier was delivered and commissioned to the PLA Navy in September 2012 after years of refitting and sea trials (Xinhuanet, 2012a).

China's naval build-up has led to the mounting distrust and balancing against China in the United States and East Asian countries. Responding to China's naval build-up, the United States and partners and allies in the region, such as Japan and India, are also expected to resort to increased naval spending and intensified build-up of their own maritime capabilities (Holslag, 2009). From 2009–2012, bilateral disputes continued to emerge between China and Vietnam, and also China and the Philippines (International Crisis Group, 2012a).

Apart from extensive investments in modernizing the PLA, the PRC is also increasingly participating in multilateral organizations – first of all in the United Nations, where China, as one of the "Permanent Five", is a veto-holder in the UN Security Council and has since 1992 increasingly participated in and contributed to UN peacekeeping missions. In early 2013, China had deployed more than 2000 peacekeepers in 12 UN missions from Haiti to Sudan and participated in the antipiracy operations in the Gulf of Aden (International Crisis Group, 2009). Participating in international peacekeeping operations provides a sign of Chinese goodwill, transparency, and an increase in influence in international negotiations, but also operational experience – because China is not a member of any military alliance and in the absence of waging war, peacekeeping is a much needed access point to operational know-how. Beyond the United Nations, China has also been increasingly involved in regional multilateral fora, such as the East Asian Summit, the ASEAN+3 (Association of South-East Asian Nations plus South Korea, Japan, and China) and the ASEAN Regional Forum (ARF), and the ASEAN Defence Ministers' Meeting PLUS (ADMMPlus). It has furthermore established the Shanghai Cooperation Organization (SCO) that combines China, Russia, Kazakhstan, Kyrgyzstan, Tajikistan, and Uzbekistan plus Observers, dialogue partners, and guest attendance – neither the United States nor the European Union (or any of its Member States) participates in the SCO gatherings.

As in many other countries, domestic institutional interests have an influence on Chinese security policymaking; however, because decision-making procedures are not accessible from the outside, there has been a still nascent field of literature of particularly non-Chinese scholars looking to identify the impact of domestic institutional interests (International Crisis Group, 2012b; Knox and Jakobson, 2010).

Part II: China's Role in Global Security

Part two will deal with China's role in global security – as discussed within China as well as abroad. With China's increasing influence in global affairs due to its unprecedented economic growth and expansion of its interests in resources worldwide, there has been a louder call for China to play a greater role in coping with today's global security challenges. Although politicians and experts in the "West" call for China to become a "responsible global power", there is concurrently a vivid debate within

Chinese policy circles about the role for China in global security – and about core principles that should guide Chinese foreign and security policy, as well as on the question of which theoretical approach can capture China's security outlook and options best.

Chinese Perspective and Debates

Concurrently with the debate about China's role in international security, a lively theoretical debate on security and international relations is evolving, with scholars like Qin Yaqing and Yan Xuetong arguing for a "Chinese IR theory" (Qin, 2009). The following section will focus on two ongoing debates that exemplify the ongoing simultaneous process of international relations (IR) theory evolution and China's changing policies due to its increasing impact on world affairs.

On Theory: Security Dilemma vs. Dilemma of Rising Powers

Many Chinese IR scholars believe that China's major security challenge in East Asia is rooted in its security dilemmas with its neighbors, including the United States (Christensen, 1999; Shi, 2000; Wang, 2012; Zhu, 2007). However, some scholars emphasize that the theory of the security dilemma cannot be applied to the security competitions between China and East Asia states, especially between China and the United States.

One necessary condition for the security dilemma theory is that the strategic intentions of all relevant states are benign, i.e. that they do not purposely damage the security of their interlocutors (Jervis, 2011; Tang, 2010b). For this reason, there is a need to carefully discuss the intentions of China and other states in each specific context.

First, the US security objective is perceived by many Chinese scholars as about achieving absolute security in East Asia. In this view, the configuration of power in East Asia changed from balance to asymmetry after the Cold War. American unipolarity has been strengthened, rather than undermined in East Asia, mainly due to the foreign policies pursued by the Obama administration (Zhang, 2012a). In an asymmetric power structure, the United States raises its goal to absolute security and looks for strategic expansion to maintain its regional dominance in East Asia (Yan and Zhou, 2004).

Second, following the conclusion of the Cold War, the rapid rise of Chinese power has been accompanied by a gradual expansion of China's security interests. Whether China's behavior is intentionally damaging the security interests of its neighbors in this endeavor to pursue its rapidly expanding security interests is difficult to determine. The debate about China's construction of its first aircraft carrier is a typical case in point (Ross, 2009).

Third, as Chinese capabilities continue to increase, China's territorial disputes in East Asia continue to become the most salient security contradictions in its bilateral relations throughout the region. Central to a territorial dispute is that both parties to the dispute do not recognize the territorial claims advanced by the other party. Such behavior inherently implies that both parties to the dispute purposely threaten one another's security and, as such, the necessary condition of the security dilemma is not met. In other words, the security dilemma approach does not apply to explain security disputes over sovereign territory between China and its neighbors.

Consequently, scholars in China have been developing a complementary theory – the theory of the "dilemma of rising powers" – in order to explain China's regional security challenges. The dilemma of rising powers consists of two indispensable dynamics (Glosny, 2009; Ross, 2009; Sun, 2005, 2011). On the one hand, the rising powers have to translate their new acquired capabilities into the greater national influence to safeguard their expanding national interests; on the other hand, the efforts to increasing national influence always lead to the containment and balancing of the dominant power and neighboring states, which set obstacles for the rising powers to maintain their further growth in national power. That means that the rising powers always face, to varying degrees, dilemmas in maintaining their rising momentum and shaping the relatively favorable external environment. Accordingly, some scholars view China as being locked into the dilemma of rising powers, i.e. China must manage to enhance its material capabilities to protect its expanding interests while preventing the balancing measures of the United States and major Asian powers and avoiding unnecessary tensions and conflicts with them (Sun, 2012).

On Strategy: The Non-Alignment Debate   The widely discussed "pivot to Asia of the United States", the US policy initiatives in Asia–Pacific and that of its regional allies to respond to China's rise, have fuelled Chinese domestic discussions on rethinking its non-alliance policy that has been a guiding foreign policy principle since the 1980s.

Yan Xuetong took the lead in publicly criticizing China's non-alignment strategy. He contends that the non-alignment policy has been serving China's paramount goal of domestic economic development over the past three decades, but has gradually become a major flaw in its foreign policy, with China's security interests outweighing its economic interests. China's non-alignment policy would not only fail to reduce its regional neighbors' strategic concerns over China's rise, but is also becoming an obstacle to winning their support when China faces maritime disputes in East Asia. In addition, China's lack of allies would have weakened its moral authority and strategic credibility (Yan, 2011; Zhang, 2012b).

Since early 2010, Yan has thus repeatedly advocated for China to abandon its long-cherished policy of non-alignment. Tang Shiping also urges that China should consider all strategies that can advance its interests because China's denial of alliance-making has led regional neighbors to believe China has been glossing over the importance of alliances in China's own foreign-policy history (Tang, 2010a; Zhang, 2012b).

For those scholars who oppose the non-alignment strategy, Russia is held as one of the most important potential partners for a strategic alliance. As Zhang Wenmu stresses, a Sino–Russian alliance will defend the legitimate interests of China and Russia against a perceived American encroachment and prevent a worsening of China's strategic environment. With China now enjoying comprehensive capabilities, an alliance with Russia would also no longer pose a risk for China (Zhang, 2012b).

However, many Chinese scholars and analysts disagree with the idea of abandoning the non-alignment policy. Zhu Feng emphasizes that it will be extremely hard for China to persuade other countries to ally with China. Wang Jisi also believes that there is almost no country in the world that is willing to construct a long-term, anti-US alliance with China (Wang, 2011; Zhang, 2012b). As for the alliance with

Russia, they believe a China–Russia alliance is unlikely to solve intractable problems in China's foreign policy, such as territorial disputes.

Thus, Wang Jisi emphasizes a good relationship with the United States should remain China's primary policy objective. Zhu Feng even concludes that it will be simply a strategic folly if the goal of an alliance strategy is to seek a Sino–US confrontation (Zhang, 2012b; Zhu Feng, 2012). These arguments have resonated in the Chinese government's stance in a way that continues with the non-alignment policy: the 2011 White Paper "China's Peaceful Development" reaffirmed that China would not align with any country or group of countries (Gov.cn, 2012).

The Non-Interference Debate   China's impressive economic rise has resulted in the growing expectations for China to take on more responsibilities in international security issues, and Western great powers, especially the United States, have called on China for a more active role in international conflict responses. Keeping the difficulties and risks in mind, Chinese leaders and scholars alike have been addressing the growing international expectations on China to take on global responsibilities.

China, contributing the largest number of peacekeepers to UN missions among the Permanent Five (P5) Members of the UN Security Council, has altogether sent over 10,000 peacekeeping personnel to 24 UN peacekeeping missions, including over 2100 who are currently performing peacekeeping duties (Yang, 2010). To date, Chinese peacekeeping troops encompass medical and logistical staff. Beyond sending troops, China also supports the processes in conflict-ridden countries by financial means. In March 2008, it was the first country to make a donation to settle the Darfur issue, with the Chinese government donating US$500,000 to the UN Trust Fund for the Political Process of Darfur (Ministry of Foreign Affairs of the People's Republic of China, 2008).

Meanwhile, competing principles of intervention and non-intervention are dominating the international debate among policymakers and scholars alike. The principle of non-interference in the internal affairs has been challenged by the changing definition of internal affairs and the emerging principle of the "Responsibility to Protect" (R2P) (Yang, 2012). Many developing countries are now adopting the norm of intervention. In response to the Syrian domestic military conflicts, the Arab League suspended Syria's membership in the body and imposed economic sanctions on it in December 2011. In the same month, 33 countries in Latin America and the Caribbean agreed the Caracas Declaration, which commits all signatories to intervene in other states in cases of regime change through a military coup (Yan, 2012). Yan Xuetong argues that although the non-intervention principle persists as the dominant norm, the principle of intervention now has a chance to emerge as the new international norm (Yan, 2012).

The emerging new norm of intervention has triggered the reflections on China's principle of non-interference among Chinese scholars and policy analysts. According to Yuan Peng, China has to take into consideration the tremendous changes in international norms and adopt the more flexible and open attitudes to the new principles of intervention (Yuan, 2012). Yang Zewei also urges that China should rethink and modify the principle of non-interference in internal affairs. The protective intervention will be China's new and smart strategy to tackle the challenges for the principle of non-intervention in internal affairs (Yang, 2012).

Chen Qi and Huang Yuxing emphasize that it is in China's interests to support the legitimate intervention. The legitimate interventions are characterized by the multilateral approach approved by the United Nations and the balance between the coercive measures and the desired results. Meanwhile, these interventions should not undermine the regional orders and export the specific political ideologies and institutions (Chen and Huang, 2009).

However, there are still strong voices to defend the principles of non-interference. Li Anshan has argued that external forces do not have the right to intervene in the choice of politic institutions by a sovereign state – it should be decided by the sovereign state independently (Li, 2006). Zhu Wenqi also rejects the justification of international inventions through preventing the violations of human rights because these external interventions may cause more damage and disasters (Zhu Wenqi, 2012).

Chinese government also reiterates the adherence to the principle of non-interference. China opposes what is perceived as an attempt by some countries to interfere in other countries' internal affairs and impose their model of development on others in the name of democracy and good governance (FOCAC, 2012). In an article published in 2012, Yang Jiechi, Minister of Foreign Affairs, argued that by observing the principle of non-interference in others' internal affairs, China respected and supported the efforts of west Asian and north African countries to handle their internal affairs on their own, and determined China's principled position on Libya and Syria on the basis of the situation on the ground (Ministry of Foreign Affairs, 2012).

It still needs to be seen how the debates on the principle of non-interference will shape the practice of Chinese government. China faces daunting challenges and faces the necessity to adjust key domestic and foreign policies adopted in the past thirty years. China's reluctance or failure to undertake her international responsibilities is seen as potentially damaging to China's strategic reputation and intensifying other middle and small powers' distrust of China's positive role in the world. Without the support from the developing world, there is a view among scholars that China will suffer more difficulties in legitimizing its strategic measures to ease the dilemma of rising powers and shape the further reform of international norms (Sun, 2012).

Non-Chinese Perspectives

Debates on the desired role for China in global security differ between Europe and the United States. While the strategic implications of China's rise – and hence the impact on security policy – have always been an integral part of the American debate, the European debate has long suffered from "the tyranny of distance" and the "primacy of trade" of a "secondary relationship" between Europe and China, as Yahuda called it (Yahuda, 1995, 2001). In the policy world, both the United States and the European Union, see China as a crucial actor in coping with today's challenges, without which neither climate change nor non-proliferation initiatives will be successful (Solana, 2004; Stumbaum, 2007). Both sides are calling on China to get ever more involved in addressing global security challenges, as well as becoming more transparent about its military modernization and strategic intentions.

After assuming her position as the EU's High Representative for Foreign and Security Policy, Baroness Catherine Ashton emphasized the importance of China as a strategic partner (Rettman, 2010). Already in 2007, the European Council stated that,

> the policy choices of China, now emerging as a global player, are of strategic importance to the EU. [...] The EU has a big interest in encouraging China to take on its global responsibilities, notably in the political, economic, commercial and monetary fields as well as to play a constructive role in the promotion of effective multilateralism and the resolution of international and regional issues. (Council of the European Union, 2007)

The evolution of the US government's attitude towards China illustrates the uncertainty about China's strategic intentions – from attempted containment policies under the early George W. Bush Administration, to "hedging" and engaging China to become a "responsible stakeholder" later on in the Bush Administration, and a "responsible power" under US President Obama. The Obama Administration hardened their stance vis-à-vis China again with its recalibration of US policy towards the Asia–Pacific, often labeled the "US' pivot to Asia" (*New York Times*, 2012; Zoellick, 2005). Former US Secretary of Defense Robert Gates stated in the National Defense Strategy of June 2008 that "our strategy seeks to encourage China to make the right strategic choices for its people, while we hedge against other possibilities", including the ever more prominent challenge of cyber security in times of information warfare (Lynn, 2008). With the United States refocusing on East Asia, a new spirit of cooperation between the United States and the European Union on Asia–Pacific can be observed with former US Secretary of State Hillary Clinton and EU High Representative Ashton issuing a "Joint EU–US statement on the Asia–Pacific region" on occasion of the 2012 ASEAN Regional Forum in June 2012 (Council of the European Union, 2012).

The security debate in the United States is driven by think tanks and the defense pundits primarily based in Washington DC, while the academic debate spans from Harvard on the East Coast to San Diego and San Francisco on the West Coast. China's role in global security is seen as an aspiring actor with still opaque intentions, and labeled as a possible "strategic competitor". During the past years, the atmosphere has changed from a division of "panda huggers" and "dragon slayers" to a widespread unease about China's intentions in security policy (see, e.g. Ross, Tunsjø, and Zhang, 2012; Scobell and Nathan, 2012). While both sides – Chinese and United States – see each other as the top foreign policy priority, a "strategic distrust" remains in which the Chinese side suspects that the US side aims to undermine its ascendance, while the US side sees the Chinese actions as increasingly threatening its own interests. A 2012 joint Brookings report by Lieberthal and Wang illustrates how the mutual "strategic distrust" is growing (Lieberthal and Wang, 2012).

The debate in Europe on China's role is growing, but still relatively nascent. While there are some edited books that cover EU–China relations in a comprehensive fashion ranging from economics to political issues and security (Ross, Tunsjø, and Zhang, 2012; Shambaug, Sandschneider, and Zhou, 2008), there is a more lively debate among think tank publications (see SWP [Shambaug and Wacker, 2008]; GIGA [Noesselt, 2012]; ECFR [Fox and Godement 2009]; Clingendael). Holslag puts the argument forward that there is also a disconnect between China and the European

Union that prevents real cooperation on strategic issues – he calls it a "normative disconnect" (Holslag, 2010).

Conclusion

The world has started to tremble since China has started to turn its increasing power into influence in the international system – no conflict solution and no collective international response to today's global challenges ranging from proliferation to climate change can be thought through without involving China at some point. At the same time, China is under heavy pressure to adjust its growing security interests within an increasingly skeptical, partly hostile environment and in a regional context that is still shaped by unresolved border and territorial disputes, prevailing historical memories, and a low-level of regional integration or deep regional institution building. Starting out with a Chinese definition of security, the chapter first provided an overview of security challenges facing China – where traditional threats are still predominant and the question of Taiwan still has a great impact on Chinese security considerations. Part one concluded by summarizing the capabilities that China has been acquiring to meet these challenges. Part two gave an overview of the major debates going on within and outside of China on its new role in the international community on issues concerning security and global security, the ongoing debates on core principles such as non-alignment and non-interference, and the concurrent evolution of IR theory in Chinese debates. Comparing the debates within and outside of China, it can be noticed that the debate outside of China can be divided into the US debate that sees China as a strategic competitor and in a rather realist paradigm, and debates from the European side on strategic aspects which are still nascent. Within China, the dominant feature of debates seems to be the endeavor to conceptualize China's new role, its interests, and its approaches – and finding the right theory to grasp China's new role in global security.

References

Buckley, Chris. 2012. "China boosts defense budget 11 percent after US 'pivot'." *Reuters*, March 4.

CASS. 2005. *A Modern Chinese Dictionary* (Xiandai hanyu cidian).

CBSNews. 2010. "The Most Polluted Places On Earth." Accessed February 6, 2013 from http://www.cbsnews.com/8301-18563_162-2895653.html

Chen, Qi, and Huang, Yuxing. 2009. "The Normative Dimension of International Interventions (Guoji ganshe de guifan weidu)." *World Economics and Politics (Shijie jingji yu zhengzhi)*, 4: 12–14.

Christensen, Thomas J. 1999. "China, the US–Japan Alliance and the Security Dilemma in East Asia." *International Security*, 23(4): 49–80.

Council of the European Union. 2007. "Guidelines on the EU's Foreign and Security Policy in East Asia." Accessed February 13, 2013 from http://eeas.europa.eu/asia/docs/guidelines_eu_foreign_sec_pol_east_asia_en.pdf

Council of the European Union. 2012. "Joint EU–US statement on the Asia–Pacific region, (A 328/12)." Accessed January 17, 2013 from http://www.consilium.europa.eu/uedocs/cms_Data/docs/pressdata/EN/foraff/131709.pdf

Craig, Susan L. 2007. "Chinese Perceptions of Traditional and Nontraditional Security Threats." Accessed February 13, 2013 from http://www.strategicstudiesinstitute.army.mil/pdffiles/pub765.pdf

Economist, The. 2012. "Beijing's air pollution, Blackest day." January. Accessed February 6, 2013 from http://www.economist.com/blogs/analects/2013/01/beijings-air-pollution

Embassy of the People's Republic of China (in the United States of America). 2003. Spokesman on Lee Teng-Hui's Separatist Malice. Accessed January 23, 2013 from http://www.china-embassy.org/eng/zt/twwt/t36718.htm

Embassy of the People's Republic of China (in the United States of America). 2012. "The Foreign affairs minister Xie Hang Sheng talks about employment protection: people-oriented, foreign affairs for the people, the powerful defend principle rights of the overseas Chinese and legal people (Waijiabu fubuzheng Xie Hang Sheng tan lingshi baohu gongzuo: yirenweiben waijiao wei min youli weihu haiwai Zhongguo gongmin he faren zhengdang quanli)." Accessed January 23, 2013 from http://www.china-embassy.org/chn/jbwzlm/2011/zt/2012quanguolianghui/t913278.htm

European Council. 2003. "A Secure Europe in a Better World – European Security Strategy." Accessed November 17, 2013 from http://www.consilium.europa.eu/uedocs/cmsUpload/78367.pdf

Federal Ministry of Defense (Germany). 2012. "White Paper 2006 on German Security Policy and the Future of the Bundeswehr." November 17. Accessed February 13, 2013 from http://www.bmvg.de/resource/resource/MzEzNTM4MmUzMzMyMmUzMTM1MzMyZTM2MzEzMDMwMzAzMDMwMzAzMDY3NmE2ODY1NmI3ODDc4MzIyMDIwMjAyMDIw/W%202006%20eng%20DS.pdf

FOCAC, Forum on China–Africa Cooperation. 2012. "How to uphold and expand common interests of china and Africa under new circumstances." Accessed December 18, 2013 from http://www.focac.org/eng/zfgx/t984735.htm

Fox, John, and Godement, Francois. 2009. "A Power Audit of EU–China Relations." Policy Report EFCR 2009. Accessed 18 December 2013 from http://ecfr.eu/page/-/ECFR12_-_A_POWER_AUDIT_OF_EU-CHINA_RELATIONS.pdf

Fravel, Taylor. 2007/2008. "Power Shifts and Escalation Explaining China's Use of Force in Territorial Disputes." *Muse Volume*, 32(3): 44–83.

GlobalSecurity.org. 2011. "Taiwan Confrontation – Introduction." Accessed January 23, 2013 from http://www.globalsecurity.org/military/ops/taiwan-intro.htm

Glosny, Michael. 2009. *Grand Strategies of Rising Powers: Reassurance, Coercion, and Balancing Responses.* Dissertation, Cambridge University, UK.

Gov.cn. 2012. "Full Text: China's Peaceful Development." Accessed January 23, 2013 from http://www.gov.cn/english/official/2011-09/06/content_1941354_4.htm

Guardian, The. 2011. "China closes Tibet to tourists for anniversary of riots." March 7. Accessed February 6, 2013 from http://www.guardian.co.uk/world/2011/mar/07/china-closes-tibet-tourist-visas

Guo, Sujian ed. 2006. *China's Peaceful Rise in the 21st Century: Domestic and International Conditions.* Farnham: Ashgate.

Han, Jun. 2006. "Effects of Integrated Ecosystem Management on Land Degradation Control and Poverty Reduction." Workshop on Environment, Resources and Agricultural Policies in China. June 19–21, 2006, Beijing, China. Accessed February 6, 2013 from http://www.oecd.org/agriculture/agriculturalpoliciesandsupport/36921383.pdf

Harmsen, Peter (Inquirer.net). 2008. "Chinese navy off on anti-piracy mission." Accessed January 23, 2013 from http://globalnation.inquirer.net/news/breakingnews/view/20081226-180067/Chinese-navy-off-on-anti-piracy-mission

Hartnett, Daniel M. 2009. "The PLA's Domestic and Foreign Activities and Orientation, Testimony by Daniel M. Hartnett." US–China Economic and Security Review Commission,

Washington DC, March 4. Accessed December 18, 2013 from http://www.uscc.gov/sites/default/files/3.4.09Hartnett.pdf

HM Government. 2010. "The National Security Strategy – A Strong Britain in an Age of Uncertainty." Accessed November 17, 2012 from https://update.cabinetoffice.gov.uk/sites/default/files/resources/national-security-strategy.pdf

Holslag, Jonathan. 2009. "Embracing Chinese Global Security Ambitions." *Washington Quarterly*, 32(3): 109–112.

Holslag, Jonathan (Europe'sWorld). 2010: "Europe's normative disconnect with the emerging powers." Accessed December 18, 2013 from http://www.vub.ac.be/biccs/site/assets/files/apapers/2010301 - Normative disconnect.pdf

International Crisis Group. 2009. "China's Growing Role in UN Peacekeeping." Accessed February 13, 2013 from http://www.crisisgroup.org/~/media/Files/asia/north-east-asia/166_chinas_growing_role_in_un_peacekeeping.pdf

International Crisis Group. 2012a. "Stirring up the South China Sea (II): Regional Responses." *Crisis Group Asia Report*, No. 229.

International Crisis Group. 2012b. "Stirring up the South China Sea (I)." April 23. *Crisis Group Asia Report*, No. 223.

Jervis, Robert. 2011. "Dilemmas About Security Dilemmas." *Security Studies*, 20(3): 416–423.

Knox, Dean, and Linda Jakobson. 2010. "New Foreign Policy Actors in China." *SIPRI Policy Paper No. 26*.

Li, Anshan. 2006. "China–African Relations in the Discourse on China's Rise (Lun Zhongguo jueqi yujing xia de Zhong Fei guanxi)." *World Economics and Politics*, 11.

Lieberthal, Kenneth, and Wang, Jisi. 2012. *Addressing US – China Strategic Distrust*. John L. Thornton China Center Monograph Series No. 4. Washington DC.

Lynn, William J. 2008. "National Defense Strategy of the United States of America, Speech on Cyber Security at the Center for Strategic and International Studies." Department of Defense, Center for Strategic and International Studies.

Ministry of Foreign Affairs of the People's Republic of China. 2002. "China's Position Paper on the New Security Concept." Accessed December 18, 2013 from http://www.fmprc.gov.cn/ce/ceun/eng/xw/t27742.htm

Ministry of Foreign Affairs of the People's Republic of China. 2008. "China Made Donation to the UN Trust Fund for the Political Process of Darfur Issue (Zhongguo xiang Lian-heguo Daerfuer wenti zhengzhi jincheng xintuo jijin juankuan)." Accessed February 6, 2013 from http://www.fmprc.gov.cn/mfa_chn/wjdt_611265/sjxw_611273/t420053.shtml. [English version: http://www.chinadaily.com.cn/china/2010-12/23/content_11745193.htm (accessed December 18, 2013)].

Ministry of Foreign Affairs, of the People's Republic of China. 2011. "Premier Wen Jiabao Meets the Press." Accessed December 18, 2013 from http://me.china-embassy.org/mon/xwdt/t807599.htm

Ministry of Foreign Affairs, of the People's Republic of China. 2012. "Serving the Nation with Vigorous Steps: China's Diplomacy in 2011." Accessed January 23, 2013 from http://www.fmprc.gov.cn/eng/wjb/wjbz/2461/t896194.htm

Morton, Katherine. 2011. "China and nontraditional security: Toward what end?" Accessed December 18, 2013 from http://www.eastasiaforum.org/2011/03/31/china-and-non-traditional-security-toward-what-end/

New York Times. 2012. "More Protests in China Over Japan and Islands." Accessed January 23, 2013 from http://www.nytimes.com/2012/09/19/world/asia/china-warns-japan-over-island-dispute.html

Noesselt, Nele. 2012. "Chinese Perspectives on International Power Shifts and Sino–EU Relations (2008–2011)." GIGA Working Paper No. 193. Hamburg, 04/2012.

People's Daily Online. 2013. "General Administration of Costums (GAC): The bilateral volume trade of last year reaches 168,900 000 000 US Dollar (Haiguanzongshu: qunian liangan maoyie da 1689 yi meiyuan)." Accessed January 23, 2013 from http://finance.people.com.cn/n/2013/0110/c1004-20161818.html

Présidence de la République. 2008. "The French White Paper on defence and national security." Accessed November 17, 2012 from http://www.ambafrance-ca.org/IMG/pdf/Livre_blanc_Press_kit_english_version.pdf

Qin, Yaqing. 2009. "Development of International Relations Theory in China." *International Studies*, 46: 185.

Rettman, Andrew. 2010. "Ashton Designates Six New 'Strategic Partners'." *EUObserver*. Availabel from http://euobserver.com/institutional/30828

Ross, Robert. 2009. "China's Naval Nationalism: Sources, Prospects, and the US Response." *International Security*, 34(2): 46–81.

Ross, Robert, Øystein Tunsjø, and Tuosheng Zhang, eds. 2012. *US–China–EU Relations: Managing the New World Order*. London: Routledge.

Scobell, Andrew, and Andrew J. Nathan. 2012. *China's Search for Security*. New York: W.W. Norton & Co.

Shambaugh, David, and Wacker, Gurdrun. 2008. "American and European Relations with China." SWP Research Paper 03/2008, Berlin, June 2008. Accessed 18 December 2013 from http://www.swp-berlin.org/fileadmin/contents/products/research_papers/2008_RP03_shambaugh_wkr_ks.pdf

Shambaug, David, Eberhard Sandschneider, and Hong Zhou, ed. 2008. *China–Europe Relations: Perceptions, Politics and Prospects*. New York, NY: Routledge.

Shi, Yinhong. 2000. "East Asia's 'Security Dilemma' and Paths Forward (Dongya de 'anquan liangnan' yu chulu)." *Journal of PLA, Nanjing Institute of Politics*, 6: 48–51.

Sina. 2012. "At the end of 2011, our country reaches foreign investment reserves of 380 000 000 000 US Dollar (2011 nian di woguo duiwai touzi cunliang da 3800 yi meiyuan)." Accessed January 23, 2013 from http://finance.sina.com.cn/china/20120826/115612955997.shtml

SIPRI (Sam Perlo-Freeman). 2012. "China increases defence budget for 2012 by 11.2% to 670.3 billion Yuan." Accessed February 6, 2013 from http://www.sipri.org/media/expert-comments/exp1

Solana, Javier. 2004. "EU and China, strategic partners with global objectives." Accessed February 13, 2013 from http://www.consilium.europa.eu/uedocs/cms_data/docs/pressdata/en/sghr_int/79739.pdf

Stumbaum, May-Britt. 2007. "Common Threats – Common Action? Opportunities and Limits of EU–China Security Cooperation." *The International Spectator*, 42(3): 351–370.

Sun, Xuefeng. 2005. *Strategic Choice of the Rising Powers and Its Political Consequence (1816–1991)*. Dissertation, Tsinghua University, Beijing.

Sun, Xuefeng. 2011. *The Dilemma of China's Rise (Zhongguo jueqi kunjing)*. Beijing: Social Science Academic Press China.

Sun, Xuefeng. 2012. *The Dilemmas of the Rise of China*. Madrid: Elcano Royal Institute.

Sun, Xuefeng, and Yuxing Huang. 2012. "Revisiting China's Use of Force in Asia: Dynamic, Level and Beyond." *Pacific Focus*, 27(3): 413–414.

Taipeh Times. 2011. "Veteran advocate Koo backs Tsai's 'Taiwanese' line." Accessed January 23, 2013 from http://www.taipeitimes.com/News/taiwan/archives/2011/07/20/2003508679

Tang, Shiping. 2010a. "Alliance Politics and China's Security Strategy (Lianmeng zhengzhi he Zhongguo de anquan zhanlüe)." Accessed February 6, 2013 from http://21ccom.net/articles/qqsw/zlwj/article_2010113025525.html

Tang, Shiping. 2010b. *A Theory of Security Strategy for Our Times: Defensive Realism.* New York, NY: Palgrave Macmillan.

Wang, Jisi. 2011. "Transformations in World Politics and Thoughts on China's Foreign Strategy (Shijie zhengzhi bianqian yu zhongguo duiwai zhanlüe sikao)." In *China's International Strategy Review 2011 (Zhongguo guoji zhanlüe pinglun 2011),* edited by Jisi Wang. Beijing.

Wang, Jisi. 2012. "China's Grim International Environment." In *China 3.0,* edited by Mark Leonard. London: European Council on Foreign Relations.

WantChinaTimes. 2011. "Tsai's denial of 1992 Consensus would hurt Taiwan." Accessed January 23, 2013 from http://www.wantchinatimes.com/news-subclass-cnt.aspx?cid=1701& MainCatID=&id=20110825000093

Wu, Xinbo. 2008. "US Influence on Taiwan Affairs: Now and After (Meiguo dui Taiwan shiwu de yingxiang: xianzhuang yu zouxiang)." *Contemparary International Relations,* 6: 17–18.

Xinhuanet. 2007. "Hu Jintao Stresses the Need to Implement the Basic National Policy of Opening Up(Hu Jintao qiangdiao: jiandingbuyi di jianchiduiwaikaifang de jibenguoce)." Accessed February 6, 2013 from http://news.xinhuanet.com/newscenter/2007-09/29/content_6815036.htm

Xinhuanet. 2011. "Han Chinese proportion in China's population drops: census data." Accessed February 6, 2013 from http://news.xinhuanet.com/english2010/china/2011-04/28/c_13849933.htm

Xinhuanet. 2012a. "China's first aircraft carrier commissioned." Accessed January 23, 2013 from http://news.xinhuanet.com/english/china/2012-09/25/c_131871538.htm

Xinhuanet. 2012b. "Xie Hang Sheng: The powerful defend the principle rights of the overseas Chinese citizens and legal persons (Xie Hang Sheng: youli weihu haiwai Zhongguo gongmin he faren de zhengdang quanyi)." Accessed January 23, 2013 from http://news.xinhuanet.com/politics/2012lh/2012-03/11/c_111637217_2.htm

Yahuda, Michael. 1995. "China and Europe: The Significance of a Secondary Relationship." In *Chinese Foreign Policy: Theory and Practice,* edited by T.W. Robinson and D. Shambaugh. Oxford: Oxford University Press.

Yahuda, Michael. 2001. "The European Union: A Separate Voice." In *Making China Policy: Lessons from the Bush and Clinton Administrations,* edited by Ramon H. Myers, Michel C. Oksenberg, and David Shambaug. Lanham, MD: Rowman & Littlefield.

Yan, Xuetong. 2011. *Ancient Chinese Thought, Modern Chinese Power.* Princeton, NJ: Princeton University Press.

Yan, Xuetong. 2012. "The Weakening of the Unipolar Configuration." In *China 3.0,* edited by Mark Leonard. London: European Council on Foreign Relations.

Yan, Xuetong, and Fangyin Zhou, eds. 2004. *Security Cooperation in East Asia.* Beijing: Peking University Press.

Yang, Jiechi. 2010. "A Changing China in a Changing World." *Munich Security Conference,* February 5. Accessed December 18, 2013 from http://np.china-embassy.org/eng/zgwj/t656781.htm

Yang, Zewei. 2012. "Democracy and Rule by Law in International Societies and Protective Intervention (Guoji shehui de minzhu he fazhi jiazhi yu baohuxing ganyu)." *Science of Law,* 5: 42–44.

Yuan, Peng 2012. "Reflections on the Characteristics of New Era and China's Grand Strategy." *Contemporary World and Socialism,* 4.

Zhang, Feng. 2012a. "China's New Thinking on Alliances." *Survival: Global Politics and Strategy,* 54(5): 129–148.

Zhang, Wenmu. 2012b. "The Limit, Objective and Significance of a Sino–Russian Alliance (Zhong'E jiemeng de xiandu, mubibao he yiyi)." *Social Outlook (Shehui guancha),* 3: 7–84.

Zhou, Lihua. 2012. "Changes in Taiwanese/Chinese Identity of Taiwanese 1992–2012 (Taiwan mingzhong Taiwanren/Zhongguoren renting qushi fenbu)." Accessed February 6, 2013 from http://esc.nccu.edu.tw/modules/tinyd2/content/TaiwanChineseID.htm

Zhu, Feng. 2007. *International Relations Theory and East Asian Security (Guoji guanxi lilun yu dongya anquan)*. Beijing: Renmin University of China Press.

Zhu, Feng. 2012. "Seeking Confrontation with America is Strategic Folly (Qiu meiguo yu Zhongguo duikang shi zhanlüexing yuchun)." *Global Times*. Accessed January 13, 2013 from http://opinion.huanqiu.com/roll/2012-01/2352598.html

Zhu, Wenqi. 2012. "China and International Laws in the Turmoil in Northern Africa and Middle East (Zhongguo yu Beifei Zhongdong bianju zhong de guojifa)." *Science of Law*, 4.

Zoellick, Robert. 2005. "Statement on Conclusion of the Second US–China Senior Dialogue." US Department of State.

Chapter 22

India as a Global Security Actor

Jivanta Schöttli and Markus Pauli

Introduction

Since India gained independence in 1947 it has faced a number of military and security challenges from within South Asia and the neighboring region. One of the least economically integrated areas in the world,[1] South Asia hosts three nuclear weapon states: China, India, and Pakistan. After four wars (in 1947, 1965, 1971, and 1999) and a number of brinkmanship-style crises, India–Pakistan relations continue to be acrimonious, with some describing the rivalry as "conflict unending" (Ganguly, 2002). Despite the unstable regional environment,[2] India sought and succeeded in casting an international profile for itself.

India's international aspirations have an important pre-history, which will be covered in the first section, where the idea and practice of non-alignment is explored to highlight and explain its enduring significance in India. India's relevance as a security actor will then be assessed in terms of its activities and capacity to influence developments within two security zones of major contemporary importance: Afghanistan and the Indian Ocean. Finally, a section on constraints and challenges examines India's ability to navigate a multipolar world, the fallout and gains of nuclearization, the 2008 US–India civil nuclear agreement as well as "weaknesses from within" in terms of human security. With sustained economic growth and key investments in military capabilities (see Tables 22.1 and 22.2 for a comparative overview), India will face growing internal demands as well as from the international community to play a greater role in global security affairs. Nonetheless, there are a number of important impediments to India's readiness and ability to take on responsibilities or to influence matters of global security.

India is among the anointed ascendant powers also known as the BRICS countries,[3] of which China and Russia are also examined in this volume. The diffusion of power across the world tends to be identified through figures such as

The Handbook of Global Security Policy, First Edition. Edited by Mary Kaldor and Iavor Rangelov.
© 2014 John Wiley & Sons, Ltd. Published 2014 by John Wiley & Sons, Ltd.

Table 22.1 Military capabilities 2012 – India, Pakistan, China, and United States.

		India	Pakistan	China	United States
Nuclear	Nuclear weapons[a] (total: deployed and other)	80–100	90–110	240	8500
Army	Main battle tanks[b]	3233	2411	7400	5855
Navy	Submarines[c]	15	8	71	71
	Principal surface combatants[c] (aircraft carriers, cruisers, destroyers, frigates)	21 (1, 0, 10, 10)	10 (0, 0, 0, 10)	78 (0, 0, 13, 65)	114 (11, 22, 61, 20)
Air Force	Aircraft (combat capable)[d]	798	453	1693	1435
Troops	Active troops (rounded)[e]	1,325,000	642,000	2,285,000	1,569,000
	Paramilitary (rounded)[e]	1,301,000	304,000	660,000	–
	Manpower fit for military service (rounded)[f]	489,572,000	75,327,000	618,589,000	120,022,000

[a] Approximate estimates as of January 2011 (Stockholm International Peace Research Institute (SIPRI), 2011).
[b] International Institute for Strategic Studies (2012, pp. 56, 234, 244, 272).
[c] International Institute for Strategic Studies (2012, pp. 57, 235–236, 244–245, 273).
[d] International Institute for Strategic Studies (2012, pp. 63, 238, 246, 274).
[e] International Institute for Strategic Studies (2012, pp. 54, 233, 243, 272).
[f] Combined "number of males and females falling in the military age range for a country (defined as being ages 16–49) and who are not otherwise disqualified for health reasons; accounts for the health situation in the country and provides a more realistic estimate of the actual number fit to serve." (Central Intelligence Agency, 2012), 2010 estimates.

Table 22.2 Military spending 1989–2011, India, Pakistan, China and United States.

Country	US$ billion (in constant 2010 US$)				% of GDP			
	India	Pakistan	China	United States	India	Pakistan	China	United States
1989	17.8	3.7	16.6	534.9	3.5	6.0	2.5	5.5
1990	17.6	3.9	17.9	511.0	3.2	5.8	2.5	5.3
1991	16.4	4.1	18.9	448.8	3.0	5.8	2.4	4.7
1992	15.7	4.4	22.9	474.2	2.8	6.1	2.5	4.8
1993	17.7	4.4	21.2	449.3	2.9	5.7	2.0	4.5
1994	17.8	4.3	20.3	421.9	2.8	5.3	1.7	4.1
1995	18.3	4.3	20.9	399.0	2.7	5.3	1.7	3.8
1996	18.7	4.3	23.0	377.3	2.6	5.1	1.7	3.5
1997	20.7	4.1	23.8	375.4	2.7	4.9	1.6	3.3
1998	21.5	4.1	27.1	366.9	2.8	4.8	1.7	3.1
1999	25.0	4.2	31.2	367.8	3.1	3.8	1.9	3.0
2000	25.8	4.2	33.5	382.1	3.1	3.7	1.9	3.0
2001	26.7	4.5	41.2	385.1	3.0	3.8	2.1	3.0
2002	26.7	4.8	47.8	432.5	2.9	3.9	2.2	3.4
2003	27.3	5.1	52.0	492.2	2.8	3.7	2.1	3.7
2004	31.7	5.4	57.5	536.5	2.8	3.6	2.1	3.9
2005	33.7	5.6	64.7	562.0	2.8	3.4	2.0	4.0
2006	34.0	5.6	76.1	570.8	2.5	3.3	2.0	3.9
2007	34.4	5.7	87.7	585.7	2.3	3.0	2.1	4.0
2008	39.0	5.3	96.7	629.1	2.6	2.8	2.0	4.3
2009	45.9	5.5	116.7	679.6	2.9	2.8	2.2	4.8
2010	46.1	5.7	121.1	698.3	2.7	2.8	2.1	4.8
2011	44.3	5.7	129.3	689.6				

Source: Stockholm International Peace Research Institute (SIPRI) (2012a).

economic growth, trade balance, and foreign exchange reserves (see for example, National Intelligence Council, 2012). Burgeoning centers of production in Asia, the rise of globally competitive companies from Asia are contrasted with sluggish economies in the United States and Europe, prompting scholars, analysts, and policymakers to identify a tectonic shift in the global system. Publications have proclaimed the twenty-first century to be the Asian century (e.g. Asian Development Bank, 2011). Others have explored sources of resilience in Western ideas and institutions (Fukuyama, 2012; or Ferguson, 2012) or have depicted change as the "rise of the rest" (Zakaria, 2012). Neorealists are concerned with the implications of shifts in polarity (Ikenberry, Mastanduno, and Wohlforth, 2009) and the instability caused during a power transition. The liberal institutionalists instead highlight the challenges to finding a new global consensus on universal norms and codes of conduct (Moravcsik, 2012). The former emphasizes security as a hard concept of military preparedness, whilst the latter draws attention to human security concerns related to terrorism, unsustainable development, internal conflict, and humanitarian crises. India is central to both perspectives given its growing economy, the critical significance of India's strategic behavior for the wider region, the strength but also weakness of the Indian state in the face of internal challenges, and the resilience of its political system.

India's Worldview

Early Foundations of Independent India's Foreign Policy

Jawaharlal Nehru, India's first Prime Minister, who led the country from 1947 to 1964 and simultaneously was external affairs minister, is considered the architect of independent India's foreign policy. As a young man, Jawaharlal travelled widely and read and wrote extensively, especially during his long prison sentences in India, stimulating a strong interest in world politics and history (Nehru, 1934). The violent partition that accompanied India's independence, the first India–Pakistan war of 1947/1948 and subsequent impasse over Kashmir, were early shocks for the newly established nation.[4] While the relationship with Pakistan worsened, Nehru invested all his energies in improving relations with the newly established People's Republic of China.

Panchasheela or the five principles of peaceful coexistence were enshrined in an agreement between India and China in 1954. Nehru regarded this a crowning achievement of his diplomacy, earning him the credit of negotiating the first major international treaty with the People's Republic of China (Schöttli, 2012, Chapter 6). While the treaty contained a preamble pertaining to Panchasheela it mainly succeeded in making India rescind all interests, claims, or rights to Tibet and securing Indian recognition of Chinese suzerainty over Tibet. "Peaceful coexistence" between the two giants enabled a brief phase of amity known as "Hindi–Chini Bhai Bhai" ("Indians and Chinese are brothers") but was unable to prevent the 1962 border war, and generated a Chinese claim over 33,000 square kilometers of land under Indian jurisdiction.

Non-alignment, the central pillar of India's Cold War foreign policy, can be linked to Mahatma Gandhi's ideas of self-reliance, non-violence, and the pursuit of truth as the basis for action (Nehru, 1963). In his statements and speeches, Nehru argued this was India's only way of maintaining independence in a bi-polar global conflict. Non-alignment was not only driven by normative principles but also enabled India to receive aid from both the United States and the Soviet Union.[5] It is debatable whether non-alignment protected India and prevented South Asia from becoming a more contested arena. India's desire to keep out the superpowers failed early on when Pakistan concluded a mutual defense treaty with the United States in 1954, nurturing close relations with both the United States and China. By 1971, Indira Gandhi signed a Treaty of Friendship with the USSR, which was to become India's most reliable ally, calling into question India's "neutrality", especially during the Vietnam War and the Soviet invasion of Afghanistan in 1979.

Within India, non-alignment served another important purpose of keeping the military in check. In reaction to Britain's use of Indian armed forces during the nineteenth century and the two World Wars, independent India inherited an ambivalent attitude towards the use of physical power and force. Given Nehru's solidarity with anticolonial struggles,[6] it was important to demonstrate India's credentials as peace loving and non-hegemonic. The defense budget was kept minimal and defense planning was non-existent, enabling China to quickly overrun Indian forces in 1962. Nonetheless, the decision to maintain a professional armed force (also a valuable employer) was never questioned and India early on became one of the biggest contributors to United Nations Security Council-mandated peacekeeping operations (Nambiar, 2009).

It could be argued that both non-alignment and Panchasheela were a failure given the inability to prevent major wars with India's neighbors. In neither case did the Non-Aligned Movement play a role. Nor did Panchasheela earn India the trust and amity of smaller neighbors with whom relations remained troubled and tense throughout the 1980s and even into the 1990s. Despite this, non-alignment and Panchasheela continue to resonate with the Indian and even international publics. In a post-Cold War world, India persists in promoting the Non-Aligned Movement[7] and Panchasheela is mentioned in major speeches and at keynote events.[8] Some have argued that India suffers from a lack of strategic thinking (Tanham, 1992) and unwillingness to assume a proactive foreign policy. Instead, India's political culture predisposes the country to "muddling through" or a preference for strategic ambiguity (Chaulia, 2011, pp. 27–28).

Non-alignment 2.0: Framing India's Grand Strategy

In January 2012, an unusual document was released in India entitled, "Non-alignment 2.0", written by eight high-profile and influential thinkers – Sunil Khilnani, Rajiv Kumar, Pratap Bhanu Mehta, Lt Gen (Retd) Prakash Menon, Nandan Nilekani, Srinath Raghavan, Shyam Saran, and Siddharth Varadarajan. "Non-alignment 2.0" seeks to identify the "basic principles" guiding India's foreign and strategic policy and to present a "re-working" of the "fundamental principle" of non-alignment. In their words,

> The core objectives of Non-Alignment were to ensure that India did not define its national interest or approach to world politics in terms of ideologies and goals that had been set elsewhere; that India retained maximum strategic autonomy to pursue its own developmental goals; and that India worked to build national power as the foundation for creating a more just and equitable global order. (Khilnani et al., 2012, p. 8).

Strategic autonomy, the authors propound, has and continues to underpin, India's foreign and security policies (Khilnani et al., 2012, p. 6). However, why and whether "non-alignment" is an overarching banner or the foundation stone for India's policies in the twenty-first century is not explicitly investigated. After referring to non-alignment at the beginning, barely any mention of it is made in the report's seventy pages. No empirical evidence is provided of when and how effectively India has actually implemented non-alignment in the twenty-first century. Neither is the term examined in terms of its original application or theoretical potential as a normative framework for international relations more generally. Non-alignment is crucial to how the document is pitched, but the arguments do not rest on a conceptual, empirical, or theoretical application of the term.

Nonetheless, the document is instructive particularly with regards the relationship between security and development that the authors construe. Very early in the document, the authors propound that "the success of India's own internal development will depend decisively on how effectively we manage our global opportunities in order to maximize our choices – thereby enlarging our domestic options to the benefit of all Indians" (Khilnani et al., 2012, p. iii). In other words, development is projected as dependent on the success of India's foreign policy – a recognition that global opportunities need to be managed opportunistically to deliver benefits at home and a confirmation of the essential role that the state must play as mediator and manager of external events. At the same time, there is an additional dimension to India's performance lying in its ability to act as an example, to provide a developmental model combining economic growth, social inclusion, and political democracy.

Development and security are therefore tightly interlinked, one legitimating the other: "Enhance India's strategic space and capacity for independent action – which in turn will give it maximum options for its own internal development" is the justification offered by Khilnani *et al.* (2012). The treatise is a securitization of development because it proclaims how urgently developmental goals (not fully specified) must be pursued, how decisions taken now will have an irreversible impact on the future, and that nothing must steer India off its course. The document proclaims that India can and should be a different kind of power, one that "sets new standards for what the powerful must do". India's national power will thus act as the foundation for creating a more just and equitable global order.

The belief that India has an alternative to offer runs deep. Thanks to a legacy drawn from the freedom struggle, Mahatma Gandhi's ideas and leadership, combined with Nehru's extensive and erudite statements on international politics, India has actively sought to be a contributor to the ideas and practices of international politics. Non-alignment and Panchasheela are central examples, projected by Jawaharlal Nehru and his successors, but there are others such as Prime Minister Rajiv Gandhi's proposed Action Plan for Nuclear Disarmament in 1988.[9] Translated into measures of actual influence, India's room to maneuver on the global stage of diplomacy has been highly constrained not least because of a lack of hard power capabilities. Other factors include an unstable neighborhood which, for much of independent India's development, has been a primary security concern given that India shares borders with each of the South Asian countries, all of them post-colonial states (see Table 22.3 for an overview of wars, conflicts, and terrorist attacks affecting India).

With the fall of the Berlin wall and the Soviet Union's collapse, India was faced not only with having to manage a severe balance of payments crisis in 1991,[10] but also the diplomatic challenge of re-positioning itself in a newly configured global arena. To illustrate India's recalibration of options and opportunities, the following section examines India's response to two contemporary, global security challenges: how to stabilize and secure Afghanistan and the protection of sea lanes of communication and trade in the Indian Ocean.

India as a Global Security Actor

India in Afghanistan

The year 2011 marked a culmination in India's involvement in Afghanistan. The signing of an Afghanistan–India Strategic Partnership was the first of its kind for Afghanistan and, in November 2011, India attended the Turkey-hosted "Security and Cooperation in the Heart of Asia" conference with all regional stakeholders. The significance of these two events lies in India's involvement and efforts to gain, establish, and consolidate its foothold in Afghanistan to exert influence, not only within Afghanistan but also beyond, into Central Asia. Including provisions for India to

Table 22.3   Wars, conflicts, and terrorist attacks.

India versus Pakistan

2002	Crisis along the border: Operation Parakram
1999	Kargil War
1990	Kashmir Crisis
1987	Brass tacks Maneuvers
1984	Siachen Glacier
1971	Third India–Pakistan War
1965	Second India–Pakistan War
1947–1948	First India–Pakistan War
1947	Partition

Other international conflicts

1987–1990	Indian Peace Keeping Force (IPKF) in Sri Lanka
1962	China–Indian Border War

Internal conflicts

1988–	Kashmir
1983–2010	Assam
1983–1993	Punjab
1978–2009	Manipur
1978–2006	Tripura
1961	"Liberation" of Goa
1952–2007	Nagaland
1948	Hyderabad police action
1947	Junagadh Intervention

Terrorist attacks

2008	Terrorist Attacks on Mumbai
2008	Suicide bombing of the Indian Embassy in Kabul
2007	Samjhauta Express bombings
2001	Attack on the Indian Parliament

Source: Mitra (2011, p. 182) and Uppsala Conflict Data Program (2012).

train and equip Afghan security forces, the partnership agreement called for closer cooperation on national security issues and enhanced prospects for regional economic cooperation.

In recent years, India has strengthened bilateral relations with Afghanistan and bolstered its position within multilateral arrangements. This marks a new phase in Indian strategic behavior as Indian diplomats, negotiators, and decision-makers lobby across multiple fora including India's presence at the various international conferences that have taken place with Afghan leaders in European cities over the past decade, the 2012 Tokyo donors' conference, and within the South Asian Association for Regional Cooperation (SAARC), the Shanghai Cooperation Organization (SCO), the North Atlantic Treaty Organization (NATO), and the United Nations.

India's role and interests have often been sidelined, despite pledging almost US$2.0 billion on various projects to emerge the fifth largest bilateral donor to Afghanistan.

For instance, at the 2011 London conference, the initiation of negotiations with the Taliban was announced, based on the ability to distinguish between "good" and "bad" Taliban members. This was a policy turn that India was not in favor of, but which, in the end, it was forced to accept. Past US policy has regarded India to be a destabilizing factor given the suspicion and resentment aroused in Pakistan by every move and indication of Indian involvement (Hanauer and Chalk, 2012, p. x). India's efforts to become a full member (currently it has observer status) within the SCO have also been blocked by smaller members, such as Kazakhstan and Uzbekistan, expressing concern that India's entry would require Pakistan's and that the bitter rivalry would stymie the organization's work. Numerous observers and analysts agree that the distrust and hostility between India and Pakistan is a major obstacle to India consolidating its position in Afghanistan, a step that Pakistan regards in zero-sum terms.[11]

India's strategy towards Afghanistan has been two-fold: the use of soft power to win "hearts and minds" and to integrate Afghanistan into a regional network of trade and transport. Indian companies and the Indian government are building roads, providing medical facilities, and spearheading educational initiatives. Projects like these are not without strategic interest, such as the construction of the 218-kilometer long Zaranj–Delaram highway, enabling Afghanistan's access to the sea via Iran and providing a shorter route for Indian goods to Afghanistan. India's Border Roads Organization completed this major project in 2008. India was also the major promoter behind the initiative to make Afghanistan a full member of SAARC in 2007. Reflecting a general effort to enhance its soft power profile, the recently launched Indian Agency for Partnership in Development is slated to manage more than US$11 billion in aid transfers to countries such as Burma and Bangladesh over the next five to seven years.

While the consensus so far has been to avoid deeper engagement in Afghanistan, there are those who advocate a more assertive role, especially in order to secure the country's single-most crucial goal, preventing Pakistan from regaining a central role in Afghan affairs (Pant, 2011). Nevertheless, the likelihood of Indian military engagement is remote. India is far more likely to intensify diplomatic efforts to enhance its influence, in particular through regional players such as Iran and Russia. In this respect, India has shown persistence and skill in developing a wider Afghanistan policy to the extent that recently it hosted Secretary of State Hillary Clinton and an Iranian trade delegation on the same day in New Delhi.

Turning to the Indian Ocean Region, one notices in India's activities a similar ability to negotiate and navigate a variety of configurations.

The Indian Ocean Region: Maritime Reorientations

With the largest navy in the Indian Ocean Region (IOR), India has taken important steps to consolidate its naval capabilities through strategic exercises, as well as diplomatic initiatives (Brewster, 2010). These include the decision to establish a central command on the Andaman Nicobar Islands, providing India with a stepping-stone into South East Asia (see Map 22.1). More recently, plans have been implemented to develop new ports along the eastern coast, and in 2009 India unveiled its first indigenously designed and built ballistic missile submarine, the *INS Arihant*. The Indian

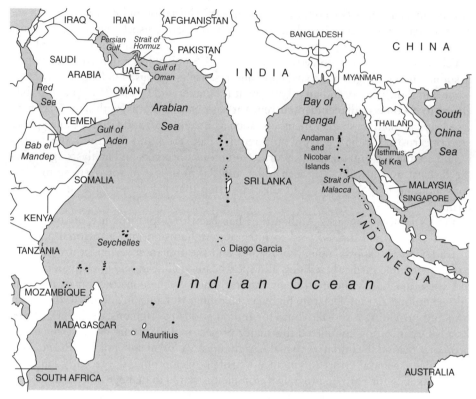

Map 22.1   Indian Ocean Region.

navy has been active in humanitarian and rescue operations, participating significantly in relief missions following the 2004 Tsunami disaster. In 2006, naval vessels evacuated more than 2000 Indian, Sri Lankan, and Nepali expatriate nationals from Lebanon during its war with Israel and 16,000 Indians from Libya in 2011. Furthermore, the navy has been involved in counterpiracy operations since 2008, with substantial deployments to the EU-led Operation *Atalanta* in the Gulf of Aden and the Somali Basin.

India's new activism is understandable given that almost 90% of India's oil needs are imported via the sea. Equally important, the sea-lanes to the Persian Gulf, Europe, and East Asia are vital for the country's exports. While China makes forays into the Indian Ocean Region through a rapid expansion of commercial and maritime ties with Bangladesh, Iran, Kenya, Myanmar, Pakistan, and Sri Lanka, India has activated naval ties with Mozambique, Mauritius, and the Seychelles. As part of its outreach to South East Asia during the 1990s (known as the "Look East Policy"), the *Milan* multilateral exercises were initiated in 1995 and since then institutionalized into a bi-annual event involving fourteen countries. In 2008, India proposed and launched the *Indian Ocean Naval Symposium*, which meets regularly and brings together navy chiefs from within the Indian Ocean Region. Complementing India's new maritime thrust, in 1996 India was invited to join the security forum of the Association of

Southeast Asian Nations (ASEAN), the ASEAN Regional Forum (ERF), and, in 2005, the East Asia Summit process that focuses on political and security issues in Asia. In 2010, India participated in the first expanded gathering of the ASEAN Defense Ministers' Meeting.

To date, India has been welcomed into multilateral arrangements and operations concerning the Indian Ocean Region. India has taken the initiative to create new institutions as well as to breathe new life into existing ones, such as the Indian Ocean Rim Association for Regional Cooperation (IOR-ARC), committed to upholding a system of open regionalism. However, as in the case of Afghanistan, Indian policymakers will have to make critical decisions about how to balance growing demands for Indian involvement with the reticence about displaying and exerting military power abroad as India develops global interests. Analysts have pointed out that, to operate in distant waters, the Indian Navy will ultimately need operational facilities requiring special political relationships and military partnerships with the countries concerned. These were precisely the arrangements that Indian security advisors rejected during the Cold War and to which India objects when China seeks nodes of access into the Indian Ocean.

India has shown its eagerness to participate in existing multilateral security initiatives in the Indian Ocean Region and the capacity to lead new ones. As in the case of Afghanistan, Indian diplomats can draw upon long traditions of historical interaction across a broad swathe of regions, from Central Asia to the expanse of littoral states within the Indian Ocean where India is generally regarded as a benign power (Brewster, 2010, p. 16). India's success at sustaining democracy helps to project India's non-hegemonic image and the political values of inclusion, consensus and pluralism that India has embraced. Undoubtedly, these are in need of continuous reaffirmation at home but act as compelling principles for India's inter-state interactions.[12]

Challenges and Opportunities

India in a Multi-polar World

India's ability to act on the global stage is molded as much by its will and worldview as by opportunities and constraints arising from developments within the country as well as externally. Integration into a globalizing world economy and the shedding of ideological determinants of foreign policy opened up new avenues of influence and interest for India. India's economic reforms and thrust towards liberalization in the 1990s unleashed an economic dynamism enabling Indian companies to do business abroad and to attract foreign investments in India. Economic relations have become interlinked with security considerations as India's trade balance (see Table 22.4) and energy needs have grown over time. As a result, while relations with major trade partners, such as China and the United States, have drastically improved over the last two decades, they have also been susceptible to critique and concerns within the domestic political arena.

Washington has emerged as India's major defense partner, and India conducts more military exercises with the United States than with any other country. During the Cold War, India refrained from purchasing weapons from the United States but has, since 2005, become a major buyer. The 2005 framework agreement, which

Table 22.4 Socio-economic indicators for India, Pakistan, China, and United States.

2011	India	Pakistan	China	United States
Gross Domestic Product (billion US$)	1848	211	7298	15,094
GDP growth (annual %)	6.9	2.4	9.1	1.7
GDP per capita (current US$)	1489	1194	5430	48,442
Inflation, consumer prices (annual %)	8.9	11.9	5.4	3.2
Foreign direct investment 2010 net inflows (billion US$)[a]	24.2	2.0	185.1	227.9
Trade in 1992 (% of GDP)	18.1	30.5	36.1	20.8
Trade in 2010 (% of GDP)	54.5	32.3	55.8	29.0
Life expectancy at birth (in years)	65.4	65.4	73.5	78.5
Human development index rank (out of 179)	134	145	101	4
Gender inequality index rank (out of 179)	129	115	35	47
Multidimensional poverty index headcount of poor (%)[b]	53.7	49.4	12.5	–[c]
Territory (in thousand sq km, rounded)	3287	796	9597	9827
Population (in millions, rounded)	1241	177	1344	312

[a]In current US$ (balance of payments).

[b]Percentage of population in multidimensional poverty. Data refer to 2003 (China), 2005 (India), and 2007 (Pakistan).

[c]The multidimensional poverty index is not available for states in the top 20 of the Human Development Index.

Sources: Life expectancy, human development index, gender inequality index, and multidimensional poverty index data from United Nations Development Programme (2012); territory from Central Intelligence Agency (2012); all other data from World Bank (2011).

laid the foundations for the 2008 Civilian Nuclear Deal, defined a number of areas for cooperation including peacekeeping, humanitarian relief, and maritime security – a departure from previous defense engagements that never specified joint political missions. Economic relations have steadily improved, although bilateral negotiations are blocked on a number of controversial issues such as market access, intellectual property rights, high-technology export controls, and the US farm subsidy program. Despite a turnaround in Indo–US relations and the highly influential role that the Indian diaspora in the United States played in this process, the Indo–US relationship remains a politically sensitive issue within India. The Congress Party, the main constituent of the ruling coalition United Progressive Alliance II, has not been able to develop a united position on relations with the United States. Tensions within the domestic political arena were high when the Indo–US civilian nuclear deal was being negotiated, with parties on the Left and Right arguing that the deal threatened to curtail India's freedom of action. Prime Minister Manmohan Singh threatened to resign when the Congress Party appeared to waver on the deal (Chari, 2009, pp. 1–17).

Relations with China have witnessed an equally drastic transformation thanks to trade and economic interaction. Bilateral trade between India and China grew to US$73 billion in 2011, up from US$63 billion in 2010 and less than US$3 billion in 2000. Both countries are targeting US$100 billion by 2015. However, in recent times, India's burgeoning trade deficit with China, which is estimated to reach

US$60 billion by 2014–2015, up nearly three-fold from US$23 billion in 2010–2011, has been receiving more critical attention. China is perceived as a "manufacturing threat" to India and seen to be dragging its feet on enabling a diversification of Indian exports to China, especially in the areas of information technology, pharmaceuticals, and engineering. Alarming figures are regularly published, such as a recent National Security Council (NSC) report, which projected that by 2014–2015 over 75% of India's manufacturing will depend on China. In December 2011, the NSC and Ministry of Commerce initiated an action plan involving inter-ministerial consultations from the ministries of industry, external affairs, telecom, information technology, pharmaceuticals, power, and agriculture to produce a China-specific strategy.

There is growing recognition that India must explore ways to enhance its leverage over China. An on-going border dispute, which receives constant media attention, producing at times over-hyped reports, serves as a constant reminder of the national security threat that China could pose. It is not coincidence that in recent years, India has reached out to enhance economic ties with a number of South East and East Asian countries. In 2009, a Comprehensive Economic Partnership Agreement (CEPA) was signed between India and the Republic of Korea, and in 2011, a CEPA was signed with Japan. At the same time, India has renewed efforts to woo South Asian neighbors. Following the success of the Sri Lanka–India Free Trade Agreement (in operation since 2000), concerted effort is underway to improve trade infrastructure and connectivity with Bangladesh (Government of India, 2012). Further to the east, Myanmar is a priority area for Indian investment in infrastructure and energy resources. On the occasion of Manmohan Singh's visit to Myanmar in May 2012, the first Indian Prime Minister to do so in 25 years, twelve agreements were signed on diplomacy and trade.

As India seeks to boost its exports, secure energy supplies, and sustain economic growth, New Delhi will have to manage external relations in a way that does not stoke or succumb to nationalist sentiments. Relations with China and the United States have the capacity to produce strong political and public reactions. Apart from the domestic arena, India faces the opportunities and challenges of being labeled a "swing state" in the emerging international order (Mohan, 2006). Most recently, in June 2012, American Secretary for Defense Leon Panetta told a Delhi-based think tank that India is the "lynchpin" for America's re-engagement with Asia (*The Times of India*, 2012). Meanwhile, at the SCO meeting in Beijing, Chinese Vice Premier Li Kequian, widely expected to be China's next Premier, told Indian Foreign Minister S.M. Krishna that Sino–Indian ties would be the most important bilateral relationship in the twenty-first century (Pandit and Parashar, 2012). While supporting multilateralism and a multipolar world system would appear to be India's first-order preferences, it remains to be seen how India plays its cards with regards the competitive rivalry between the United States and China.

India – A Revisionist Power? Nuclearization and the Non-Proliferation Treaty

Although most analysts and observers tend to portray India as a benign and generally stabilizing force, the decision to go nuclear in 1998 and the 2008 Indo–US nuclear deal were regarded as dangerous and revisionist. Following the May 1998 nuclear tests, the Clinton regime responded by imposing economic and technological sanctions mandated by the Nuclear Non-Proliferation Act of 1994 and simultaneously initiated high-level talks to discuss possibilities of convergence in Indo–US economic and political interests. The timing of the tests has been as much debated as the consequences. With the Bharatiya Janata Party (BJP) in power at the time, the nuclear tests were seen as a statement of strength and defiance by a resurgent Hindu-nationalist government. However, relegating the tests solely to the logic of domestic political gain and nationalism unfairly neglects the strategic context within which India took this decision and makes light of the underlying cost-benefit calculations. Pakistan, with a clandestine nuclear program, and China, with full-blown nuclear capability, represented a highly asymmetric strategic environment for India. Furthermore, by 1996 the Comprehensive Test Ban Treaty (CTBT) was ready for signature, adding pressure on India to sign a treaty, which it perceived as unfair and incomplete with no time-bound framework for a complete elimination of nuclear weapons (Pande, 1996).

The 1998 nuclear tests were immediately followed by Pakistan's own tests and shortly thereafter, the Kargil War on May 3 and ending on July 26, 1999. Fighting at very high altitudes along the Line of Control between India and Pakistan, casualties were sustained by both, with ultimately no physical change of positions and India resuming control over its territory. Whether or not nuclearization encouraged Pakistan to act rashly or proved to India that it could still win a conventional war as a nuclear weapon state, is the subject of much discussion and debate (Krepon, 2003). Since 1998, relations between the two countries have remained poor, with intermittent crises caused by acts of terrorism, such as the 2001 attack on the Indian parliament leading India and Pakistan to mobilize almost a million troops on the border. Despite high volatility, both sides have developed Confidence Building Mechanisms to deal with their nuclear weapons and, following the most recent terror attack on Mumbai in 2008, New Delhi's response was characterized by marked restraint.

The 2008 Nuclear deal included an agreement by India to have all its civil nuclear facilities safeguarded by the International Atomic Energy Agency (fourteen existing thermal power reactors and all future civil reactors and breeders) until 2014. In return, the United States agreed to relax the existing restrictions on export of technologies and materials (in place since India's first test in 1974) for India's civil nuclear program. Furthermore, Washington promised to lobby within the Nuclear Suppliers Group (NSG) to generate an "India-specific exemption", a waiver that was subsequently approved in September 2008. All forty-six NSG member states are now allowed to engage in civil nuclear business with India.

Three major criticisms were launched against the waiver: that it would trigger a new nuclear arms race in South Asia; that it undermined global nuclear disarmament efforts; and irreversibly damaged the Non-Proliferation regime. However, from an Indian perspective, the Non-Proliferation treaty was an inherently unequal treaty. Furthermore, both China and the United States, who have yet to ratify the CTBT that outlaws nuclear testing, were two countries India had reason to be wary of given that it fought a war with China in 1962 and the United States' close support of Pakistan. With India's clean record on proliferation, it has also been pointed out that the safeguards included in the nuclear deal could help India grow accustomed to international controls, paving the way to a less principled opposition to the

Non-Proliferation treaty (Rauch, 2010). Analysts have further argued that while India is dissatisfied with key elements of the Non-Proliferation regime, it does not fundamentally oppose it (Paul and Shankar, 2007).

South Asia remains a strategically unstable area thanks to the India–Pakistan conflict, the border issue with China, and the evolving situation in Afghanistan. Through its "all-weather friendship" with Pakistan, China is party to the South Asian security dilemma whilst India and China have not made headway on reaching a sustainable resolution. China's activities in India's near neighborhood, such as developing the Pakistani port of Gwadar into an access point for the Indian Ocean and infrastructure investments in Burma, are regularly referred to as China's "string of pearls strategy" in Delhi. More recently, there have been reports of Chinese attempts to persuade the King of Bhutan to concede territory that would threaten India at its strategically important Siliguri corridor. The decision to develop and test missiles – most recently Agni V in April 2012 and India's first intercontinental ballistic missile – and India becoming the largest importer of arms[13] have to be seen in the context of India's difficult strategic environment and as part of an effort to fast-track modernization of the armed forces.[14]

Human Security at Home: India's Achilles' Heel?

Terrorist attacks and inter-community conflict continue to occur and represent a major concern for the Indian government, leading some analysts to label India a "soft state". However, India's diversity is well represented through 22 official languages recognized in the Constitution and the 28 states that contain numerous crosscutting ethnic and religious identities. A carefully designed and flexible federal system has helped New Delhi to contain and address subnational grievances. Nevertheless, there have been controversies over the abuse of security provisions, for example over the Prevention of Terrorism Act, 2002. Further potential for instability arises from instances where internal migrant communities have been made targets of politically motivated attacks (for example the anti-Northern campaign in Maharashtra or recent anti-Muslim violence in the North Eastern State of Assam). While these have generally remained isolated outbreaks, they are a threat to law and order, requiring a calibrated response from state authorities to avoid escalation or retribution in other parts of the country.

Alongside India's high growth rates are a number of dismal facts relating to human development. Whilst India's democracy has proven its resilience over the past six decades and an impressive ability to accommodate diversity while granting an array of freedoms, it has not been effective in tackling a number of governance-related problems. Regarding the human development index (HDI) with its three dimensions of health, education, and living standard, India performs worst compared to its BRICS peers.[15] In several indicators for health, education, and living standard, the poorest Indian states are comparable to states in sub-Saharan Africa. Then again, one has to keep in mind the immense diversity of India as a subcontinent. Table 22.5 illustrates the range of human development – from the impressive human development achievements of states like Kerala to the specific needs (e.g. child school attendance, mortality, nutrition, or sanitation) in mega-states like Uttar Pradesh (with nearly 200 million citizens) or Bihar (with more than 100 million citizens).

Table 22.5 Multidimensional poverty index for Indian states.

MPI rank	State	Population (millions) 2011	Multidimensional poverty index	Proportion of poor (in %)[a]	Education		Health		Standard of living					
					Schooling	Child school attendance	Mortality	Nutrition	Electricity	Sanitation	Drinking water	Floor	Cooking fuel	Assets
1	Delhi	16.8	0.062	14	4	9	7	9	0	10	3	2	5	6
2	Kerala	33.4	0.065	16	1	7	4	12	5	4	9	3	15	11
3	Goa	1.5	0.094	22	4	9	4	16	2	16	10	12	17	12
4	Punjab	27.7	0.12	26	8	13	9	17	2	20	1	16	23	11
5	Himachal Pradesh	6.9	0.131	31	4	7	9	25	1	28	8	15	29	20
6	Tamil Nadu	72.1	0.141	32	9	8	11	21	7	31	5	12	30	24
7	Uttarakhand[b]	10.1	0.189	40	8	10	15	30	15	33	8	30	37	27
8	*Maharashtra	112.4	0.193	40	8	15	14	30	13	36	10	27	34	28
9	Haryana	25.4	0.199	42	8	20	15	30	8	34	8	24	39	25
10	Gujarat	60.4	0.205	42	12	13	17	33	9	36	10	24	36	29
11	Jammu & Kashmir	12.5	0.209	44	8	22	16	27	5	40	17	28	39	27
12	*Andhra Pradesh	84.7	0.211	45	19	13	16	29	8	41	6	19	42	35
13	*Karnataka	61.1	0.223	46	12	21	17	33	8	41	12	19	42	32
14	Eastern States[c]	45.6	0.303	58	19	21	19	37	41	45	23	50	55	42
15	*West Bengal	91.3	0.317	58	25	23	19	42	41	47	7	48	57	43
16	*Orissa	41.9	0.345	64	23	19	24	45	43	62	20	51	63	49
17	Rajasthan	68.6	0.351	64	21	32	28	44	31	60	24	36	61	47
18	*Uttar Pradesh	199.6	0.386	70	18	36	37	46	48	62	7	58	66	41
19	*Chhattisgarh	25.5	0.387	72	21	29	31	52	24	69	22	64	70	48
20	*Madhya Pradesh	72.6	0.389	70	22	32	31	50	25	65	31	57	67	52
21	*Jharkhand	33	0.463	77	26	45	30	56	55	73	42	63	76	55
22	*Bihar	103.8	0.499	81	35	52	35	61	65	74	4	70	79	57
	India		0.296	54	18	25	23	39	29	49	12	40	52	38

*States with "Left Wing Extremist"-affected districts included under Security Related Expenditure (SRE) Scheme (Ministry of Home Affairs, Government of India, 2010).

[a]The proportion of multidimensional poverty index poor population is estimated using the Demographic and Health Surveys (DHS) dataset 2005–2006, which has a slightly different distribution of population across states (OPHI, 2010, p. 6).

[b]Until 2006, it was called Uttaranchal.

[c]Eastern States include Assam, Arunachal Pradesh, Manipur, Meghalaya, Mizoram, Nagaland, Sikkim, and Tripura (OPHI, 2010, p. 6)

Sources: all MPI data from Alkire and Santos, 2010, pp. 124–125; population figures from Ministry of Home Affairs, Government of India, 2012.

The Indian case implies a clear link between human development and security. The majority of the states with so called "Left Wing Extremist" (LWE)-affected districts, meaning districts with Naxalite operations, are in the lower part of the human development spectrum, with proportions of people living in multidimensional poverty of up to 81% in the case of Bihar (see states marked with * in Table 22.5). Prime Minister Manmohan Singh declared that the Maoists constitute "the single biggest internal security challenge ever faced by our country." This led to the Integrated Action Plan (IAP) to foster development in 60 tribal and backward districts in LWE-affected regions. A special LWE scheme was introduced within the Security Related Expenditure (SRE). Under this scheme, financial resources spent in states on anti-naxalite operations and improvement of security-related infrastructure, are reimbursed by the Indian government (Government of India, Ministry of Home Affairs, 2010).

Conclusion: India's Emerging Global Profile

Both of India's major political parties, the Indian National Congress and the opposition, the Bharatiya Janata Party have endorsed the aspiration to great power status.[16] Economic growth, military modernization, and effective diplomacy have buttressed the country's ascent over the past two decades (see Table 22.4). The recognition of India's position and relevance is evident from the numerous official visits paid by leaders of major economies and the growing number of security-related agreements that have been signed. India has entered into numerous bilateral agreements, especially within South East Asia and enhanced its visibility and presence within multilateral organizations such as ASEAN and the East Asia Summit.

In terms of developing its role as a global security actor, India has the aspirations, and to a large extent the capabilities, but not yet the trappings of a great power. That India is not a permanent member of the United Nations Security Council is a fact that rankles, and various strategies have been adopted to push for reform. As a member of the "G4 nations", India worked together with Brazil, Germany, and Japan supporting each other's bids for permanent seats. Despite President Obama's support for India's candidature, announced during his visit in November 2010, India's efforts have been futile. Not willing to bandwagon with the United States, India maintains that the pursuit of "strategic autonomy" is the prime rationale behind its foreign policy.

Given India's commitment to the norms of peaceful international discourse, critics have pointed out that India is the only major democracy aside from the United States not to have ratified the Rome Statute of the International Criminal Court (ICC). This is a decision that reflects an innate Indian defensiveness regarding its sovereignty, but also a confidence in the strength of its own legal institutions. As India seeks to take on a greater global profile, the commitment to universal norms, of how to define them and when and how to uphold them, are bound to create situations and raise debates that will draw out ambiguities and tensions.[17] This was the case during the Libyan crisis, which occurred while India was a non-permanent member in the Security Council.

As the crisis developed in early 2011, India's first concern was for the safety of its citizens working in the region. On February 26, 2011, India voted in the UN Security Council for Resolution 1970, which condemned the use of force by the Gaddafi government against its own people and imposed international sanctions on Libya. Furthermore, the resolution unanimously referred Libya to the ICC. This appeared to mark a shift in Indian policy, one that hitherto had been critical of the ICC. However, on March 11, 2011, the Indian government appeared to revise its position when it abstained on UN Resolution 1973 providing the legal basis for military intervention in the Libyan war. Various interpretations have been offered of this decision. These included the need to avoid antagonizing Muslim sentiment (outside, but also crucially within India), practical arguments based on the lack of information available to the world at that point, claims that intervention in Libya was an act of Western neocolonialism, and even that India needed to curb its own great power aspirations so as not to appear as aligning too closely with the West. Each reflects sentiments and political positions that have developed within India over many years, drawing upon the country's historical experience and the dynamics of a difficult regional context.

This chapter has sought to highlight the particular worldview and pattern of external interaction that India has evolved over the last six decades. A nation state that is well accustomed to the need for accommodation and consensus – and one that is rightly proud of its institutions promoting participation, accountability, and legitimacy – India would ideally like to lead by virtue of its example. Recognizing the failings in its example, human security is a top priority and the object of manifold government-sponsored programs aimed at social and human development. Domestic stability and welfare, nevertheless, are therefore bound to be central concerns in New Delhi for many years to come.

Notes

1. Market integration in South Asia is the lowest in the world. Intra-regional trade between countries accounts for less than 2% of GDP for South Asia, compared with 40% for East Asia.
2. Following the 1971 War of Independence, Bangladesh was created out of the Eastern wing of Pakistan, and in the 1980s Sri Lanka was consumed by a virulent Civil War.
3. Coined by Goldman Sachs chief economist, Terence James O'Neill (2001) in his paper "Building better global economic BRICS", to depict the rapidly developing economies of Brazil, Russia, India, and China. Since then, South Africa was added to the group.
4. Having referred the Kashmir dispute to the United Nations in 1948, Jawaharlal Nehru felt betrayed when Security Council members showed sympathy for Pakistan's defense (Wolpert, 1996, pp. 433–435).
5. Despite leaning towards the Soviet Union through the friendship treaty of 1971, India avoided undertaking joint exercises or other service-to-service contacts with Moscow (Singh, 1986).
6. Nehru oversaw the Asian Relations Conference in Delhi (1947) and was a central promoter of the Bandung Conference of Afro–Asian Solidarity (1955).
7. See Ministry of External Affairs Annual Reports (http://mea.gov.in/annual-reports. htm?57/Annual_Reports accessed December 16, 2013).
8. A flurry of Panchasheela-related events occurred in 2004 to mark its fiftieth anniversary, despite the fact that the 1954 treaty lapsed in 1962 and has not been renewed.
9. Tabled at the United Nations, the Plan proposed a three-stage process of total disarmament via a regime that was global, universal, and non-discriminatory. It was one of the earliest initiatives for nuclear disarmament.

10. In 1991, the Government of India was close to a default and reportedly had enough foreign reserves to barely finance three weeks of imports. The crisis forced India to negotiate with the International Monetary Fund for an emergency loan and paved the way for a wave of liberalizing reforms of the economy.

11. In Afghanistan, India has been accused of aiding separatist movements amongst Balochi Nationalists. India has opened four consulates in Afghanistan: Herat, Mazar-e-Sharif, Jalalabad, and Kandahar, which Pakistan claims are not simply for visa-issuing purposes. Since 2006, India has deployed its own paramilitary force to guard its workers in Afghanistan, and opened negotiations to establish its first military airbase overseas in Tajikistan.

12. Sanjaya Baru, one-time media advisor to the Prime Minister, sought to develop what he termed the "Manmohan Singh Doctrine" based upon these principles (Baru, 2008).

13. According to the SIPRI report published in March 2012, India became the largest importer of arms during 2007–2011 (Stockholm International Peace Research Institute, 2012b).

14. See for instance, the fifteen-year Long Term Integrated Perspective Plan (LTIPP) and five-year Services Capital Acquisition Plan and Annual Acquisition Plan.

15. Human development index ranks of Russia (66), Brazil (84), China (101), South Africa (123), and India (134) (UNDP, 2012).

16. In 2006, Prime Minister Manmohan Singh expressed this in an interview: "Charlie Rose Interviews PM Manmohan Singh." *Council on Foreign Relations*, February 27, 2006. Accessed January 19, 2013 from https://secure.www.cfr.org/publication/9986/charlie_rose_interviews_indian_pm_manmohan_singh.html. In 2004, the Bharatiya Janata Party's election campaign explicitly pledged to make India a "great power" by 2020 (Bharatiya Janata Party, "Vision Document 2004," March 2004. Accessed January 19, 2013 from http://www.bjp.org/index.php?option=com_content&view=article&id=136&Itemid=548

17. For an example of India's position on the Responsibility to Protect, see Hall (2013).

References

Alkire, Sabina, and Maria E. Santos. 2010. "Acute Multidimensional Poverty: A New Index for Developing Countries." Accessed August 18, 2012 from http://www.ophi.org.uk/wp-content/uploads/ophi-wp38.pdf

Asian Development Bank. 2011. *Asia 2050: Realizing the Asian Century*. London: Sage Publications.

Baru, Sanjaya. 2008. "India and the World–Economics and Politics of the Manmohan Singh Doctrine in Foreign Policy." *ISAS Working Paper* No. 53, National University of Singapore.

Brewster, David. 2010. "An Indian Sphere of Influence in the Indian Ocean?" *Security Challenges*, 6(3): 1–20.

Central Intelligence Agency (CIA). 2012. "The World Fact Book." Accessed August 20, 2012 from https://www.cia.gov/library/publications/the-world-factbook/index.html

Chari, P.R. 2009. *Indo-US nuclear deal: Seeking synergy in bilateralism*. New Delhi: Routledge.

Chaulia, S. 2011. "India's 'Power' Attributes." In *Handbook of India's international relations*, edited by David Scott. 1st ed., 23–34. New York, NY: Routledge.

Ferguson, Niall. 2012. *Civilization: The West and the Rest*. New York, NY: Penguin Books.

Fukuyama, Francis. 2012. *The Origins of Political Order: From Prehuman Times to the French Revolution*. New York, NY: Macmillan.

Ganguly, Sumit. 2002. *Conflict unending: Indo–Pakistani tensions since 1947*. Chichester, NY: Columbia University Press.

Government of India, *Ministry of Home Affairs*. 2010. "Outcome Budget 2010–2011." Accessed December 16, 2013 from http://mha.nic.in/hindi/sites/upload_files/mhahindi/files/pdf/OB%28E%292010-11.pdf

Government of India, *Ministry of Commerce and Industry*. 2012. "Annual Report 2011–2012: Chapter 7: Commercial Relations and Trade Agreements."

Hall, Ian. 2013. ""Tilting at Windmills?" The Indian Debate over the Responsibility to Protect after UNSC 1973." *Global Responsibility to Protect*, 5(1): 84–108.

Hanauer, Larry, and Peter Chalk. 2012. "India's and Pakistan's Strategies in Afghanistan: Implications for the United States and the Region." Accessed August 20, 2012 from http://www.rand.org/content/dam/rand/pubs/occasional_papers/2012/RAND_OP387.pdf

Ikenberry, G. John, Michael Mastanduno, and William C. Wohlforth. 2009. "Unipolarity, State Behavior, and Systemic Consequences." *World Politics*, 61(1): 1–27. DOI: 10.1017/S004388710900001X

International Institute for Strategic Studies (IISS). 2012. *The Military Balance*. London: Routledge.

Khilnani, Sunil, Rajiv Kumar, Pratap B. Mehta, Prakash Menon, Nandan Nilekani, Srinath Raghavan, Shyam Saran, and Siddharth Varadarajan. 2012. "Non-alignment 2.0: A Foreign and Strategic Policy for India in the Twenty First Century." Accessed August 20, 2012 from http://www.cprindia.org/sites/default/files/NonAlignment%202.0_1.pdf

Krepon, Michael. 2003. "The Stability–Instability Paradox, Misperception, and Escalation Control in South Asia." Accessed August 20, 2012 from http://www.stimson.org/images/uploads/research-pdfs/ESCCONTROLCHAPTER1.pdf

Ministry of Home Affairs, Government of India. 2010. "List of 83 Left Wing Extremist affected districts included under SRE Scheme." Accessed December 16, 2013 from http://mha.nic.in/sites/upload_files/mha/files/NM%20Div.7.pdf

Mitra, Subrata K. 2011. *Politics in India: Structure, Process and Policy*: London: Routledge.

Mohan, C.R. 2006. "India and the Balance of Power." *Foreign Affairs*. July/August.

Moravcsik, Andrew. 2012. "Liberal Theories of International Law." In *Interdisciplinary Perspectives on International Law and International Relations: The State of the Art*, edited by Jeffrey L. Dunoff and Mark A. Pollack. Cambridge: Cambridge University Press.

Nambiar, Satish. 2009. *For the Honour of India: A History of Indian Peacekeeping*. New Delhi: United Service Institution of India.

National Intelligence Council. 2012. *Global Trends 2030: Alternative Worlds*. Accessed on January 18, 2013 from http://www.dni.gov/files/documents/GlobalTrends_2030.pdf

Nehru, Jawaharlal. 1934. *Glimpses of World History*. 2004th ed. New Delhi: Penguin Books.

Nehru, Jawaharlal. 1963. "Changing India." *Foreign Affairs*, 41(3): 453–465.

O'Neill, Terence James. 2001. "Building better global economic BRICS." *Global Economics Paper* No. 66 (66). Goldman Sachs & Co.

OPHI. 2010. "Country Briefing India." Accessed August 19, 2012 from http://www.ophi.org.uk/wp-content/uploads/Country-Brief-India.pdf

Pande, Savita. 1996. *CTBT: India and the Nuclear Test Ban Treaty*. New Delhi: Siddhi Books.

Pandit, Rajat, and Sachin Parashar. 2012. "US, China woo India for control over Asia–Pacific." *The Times of India*, June 7.

Pant, Harsh V. 2011. "The Afghanistan Conflict: India's Changing Role." *Middle East Quarterly*, 18(2): 31–39.

Paul, T.V, and Mahesh Shankar. 2007. "Why the US–India Nuclear Accord is a Good Deal." *Survival*, 49(4): 111–22. DOI: 10.1080/00396330701733951.

Rauch, Carsten. 2010. "Hushed Hope–India, the Nuclear Deal, and Nonproliferation." *PRIF Working Paper*, Issue 7. Frankfurt: Peace Research Institute.

Schöttli, Jivanta. 2012. *Vision and strategy in Indian politics: Jawaharlal Nehru's policy choices and the designing of political institutions*. London: Routledge.

Singh, S.N. 1986. *The yogi and the bear: Story of Indo–Soviet relations*. New Delhi: Allied Publishers.

Stockholm International Peace Research Institute (SIPRI). 2011. "Yearbook 2011–Chapter 7 World nuclear forces." Accessed August 20, 2012 from http://www.sipri.org/yearbook/2011/07

Stockholm International Peace Research Institute (SIPRI). 2012a. "Military Expenditure Database." Accessed August 20, 2012 from http://www.sipri.org/databases/milex

Stockholm International Peace Research Institute (SIPRI). 2012b. *Yearbook 2012: Armaments, Disarmament and International Security:* Oxford: Oxford University Press.

Tanham, George K. 1992. "Indian Strategic Thought: An Interpretive Essay." Accessed August 19, 2012 from http://www.rand.org/pubs/reports/2007/R4207.pdf

The Times of India. 2012. "Leon Panetta in Delhi, says India 'linchpin' for American strategy in Asia." *Times of India*, June 6.

United Nations Development Programme (UNDP). 2012. "Indices & Data: Human Development Reports (HDR)." Accessed August 20, 2012 from http://hdr.undp.org/en/statistics/

Uppsala Conflict Data Program (UCDP). 2012. "Database: Asia–India." Accessed August 19, 2012 from http://www.ucdp.uu.se/gpdatabase/gpcountry.php?id=74&regionSelect=6-Central_and_Southern_Asia

Wolpert, Stanley A. 1996. *Nehru: A Tryst with Destiny*. New York, NY: Oxford University Press.

World Bank. 2011. "Database." Accessed August 20, 2012. http://data.worldbank.org/

Zakaria, Fareed. 2012. *The Post-American World: Release 2.0*. New York, NY: W.W. Norton & Co.

Chapter 23

Security Agenda in Russia: Academic Concepts, Political Discourses, and Institutional Practices

Andrey Makarychev

Introduction

In one of his foreign policy pronouncements Vladimir Putin, campaigning for his third presidential term, claimed that the Western countries "have developed a peculiar interpretation of security that is different from ours".[1] Unfortunately, his pessimistic assessment seems to be fair enough. Russia on the one hand, and NATO and the European Union on the other, do indeed approach international security issues differently (like NATO enlargement, the deployment of American antimissile system in Central Europe, or the Syrian debate in the United Nations), as well as the key security concepts (in particular, in an effort to delegitimate Western policies, Putin lambasted "illegal instruments of soft power"). Russia accuses the West of bellicosity, in aggravating situations in countries subjected to humanitarian interventions, violating their sovereignty, and artificially keeping afloat obsolete stereotypes about Russia, etc. In response, Russia receives accusations from the West of neoimperial ambitions and unilateralism, in using energy weaponry against consuming countries, and so on.

One may agree that since the collapse of the Soviet Union, the US-led West has not been interested in strategic security partnership with Russia (Trenin, 2011) – perhaps to the same extent that Russia was not ready politically or technically for such a partnership. It is this complicated state of relations between Russia and the West that defines the nature of the problems I am going to tackle in this chapter. I will argue that there are two key issues for Russia in the security sphere. First, Russia is very much enmeshed in *defense* thinking (which is reactive and military-based), and lacks a more comprehensive *security* thinking to embrace a wider gamut of social threats, risks, and vulnerabilities. The second problem is the lack of fully fledged international acceptance of Russia's security posture, which stems not from a normative dissonance between Russia and the West (Russia's foreign and security

The Handbook of Global Security Policy, First Edition. Edited by Mary Kaldor and Iavor Rangelov.
© 2014 John Wiley & Sons, Ltd. Published 2014 by John Wiley & Sons, Ltd.

policies are simply short of any normative messages), but from the West's vision of Russia as an untrustworthy international actor with corrupt political and economic systems, which certainly has direct security repercussions (Rotberg, 2009).

In this chapter, I will demonstrate how the Russian security agenda is formulated, and how Russian security messages are communicated to the outside world. In doing so, I will employ the concept of securitization, which in my view, catches the immanent variety and changeability of discourses on security, their correlation with academic concepts and political narratives, and their institutional effects. Being a complicated combination of academic and political discourses, embedded in various institutional contexts, the security agenda in Russia is very sensitive to communication frameworks and information flows. There is a wide spectrum of questions that are intensely debated both academically and politically: who are the most prospective allies for Russia – semi-peripheral countries (such as Venezuela, Iran, Belarus, Kazakhstan, etc.) or core security actors belonging to the Euro–Atlantic security community? Which security role is the most appropriate for Russia – that of a "normal" power capable of taking on commitments, or that of an exceptional country unfit for membership in military alliances? What are the most important sources of threats for Russia – domestic or external?

I will start this chapter with a section on methodology to explain how the concept of securitization can be used for the analysis of Russian security-making. In the following two sections, I will flesh out the key milestones in Russia's domestic and international security discourses, which appear to be in sharp contrast with one another. In the final section, I will discuss the repertoire of Russia's security roles that it plays internationally, as well as domestically.

Methodological Remarks

The constantly changing and inherently fluid nature of security-making is convincingly reflected in the concept of securitization, widely known among academic experts due to the Copenhagen school. In this chapter, I understand securitization as

> an articulated assemblage of practices whereby heuristic artefacts (metaphors, policy tools, image repertoires, analogies, stereotypes, emotions, etc.) are contextually mobilized by a securitizing actor, who works to prompt an audience to build a coherent network of implications (feelings, sensations, thoughts and intuitions) about the critical vulnerability of a referent object. (Balzacq, 2011, p. 3)

What this broad and complicated definition implies is that there are four elements important in the securitization process. First, this process is initiated by securitizing actors, which are in many cases, but not necessarily, states. For example, the Russian government is confronted by a variety of non-state securitizing actors, such as terrorist groups operating in the North Caucasus.

Second, there should be a referent object of security discourse, i.e. something that is viewed as being under danger of extermination. The strongest cases of securitization usually imply threats to one's collective identity. Ultimately, it was the identity of Russia – articulated through such categories as national dignity in the case of the war against Georgia in August 2008, or the sanctity of the memories of the Second

World War in the case of the bitter tug-of-war with Estonia over the monument to Soviet soldiers removed from downtown Tallinn – that constituted the referent object of the most divisive and conflictual securitization practices of recent years.

Third, speeches by securitizing actors ought to be addressed to a specific audience, who is key for their social acceptance and legitimacy. Since securitization is an inter-subjective practice of persuading target audiences of the immanence and authenticity of threats, "securitizing moves in popular, elite, technocratic, and scientific settings are markedly different – they operate according to different constitutions of actor and audience" (Balzacq, 2011, p. 7). I will illustrate the audience-dependent character of Russian security discourses by showing essential differences between their domestic and international contexts, as well as *within* various international contexts.

Fourth, securitization is articulated by a variety of discursive and communicative tools. Securitization does not necessarily result from a rational design, thus

> the 2009 National Security Strategy of Russia does not cite NATO as a security threat but, paradoxically, presents Ukraine's and Georgia's membership in these terms. Similarly, the 2010 Russian Military Doctrine cites NATO enlargement as well as the movement of military infrastructure closer to Russia as the first of eleven main military dangers, while NATO as such is presented as a partner with which it is worth developing relations. (Bogomolov and Lytvynenko, 2012, p. 4)

Since security practices are usually results "of struggles among agents to define reality" (Pouliot, 2010, p. 45), much depends upon vocabularies (frames, storylines, and rhetoric tools such as analogies, metaphors, emotions, stereotypes), communication strategies, as well as contexts, which could be proximate (specific situations in which a security issue is embedded) and distal (socio-cultural milieu). Language games are an important component of security interaction, which is certainly the case of Russia's relations with its major Western partners.

A good example of the inherent interrelatedness of all components of the securitization process is Russia's proposal on a new European security treaty and the international reaction to this initiative. As a securitizing actor, Russia pointed to the obvious deficiency and vulnerability of the existing mechanisms of security that failed to prevent a series of violent conflicts, basically resulting from states' disintegration and secession of breakaway territories. Russia certainly had a point in raising the issue of conflict prevention, but the efficiency of the Russian proposal was hampered by at least two factors.

The first was Russia's reluctance to engage in a dialogue on the issue of security with its major security partners in the West. In particular, Moscow remained relatively indifferent to the 2010 "Helsinki Plus" report (Kaldor and Jordi, 2010) by the European Union–Russia working group (chaired by Javier Solana), as well as to the Euro–Atlantic Security Initiative (EASI), which became one of the key reference points for NATO's security vision.[2] These papers reveal deep conceptual gaps in security perceptions of Russia on the one hand, and the European Union and NATO on the other. The Western approach rejects a formal negotiated treaty with Russia and instead welcomes a gradual confidence-building process with transparency as its cornerstone. Along with military security, both the European Union and NATO strongly advocate for the adoption of a human security perspective, although it might be understood in different ways – as encompassing historical reconciliation between former enemies,[3] or as the focusing on the needs of populations rather than the interests of states. The unwillingness to seriously discuss the human security concept obviously weakens the Russian position in communicating with the West.

Second, what only exacerbates the weakness of the Russian stand is the lack of support from countries that Russia itself considers allies – the members of the Collective Security Treaty Organization (CSTO) and also the Shanghai Cooperation Organization (SCO). There is no evidence that Moscow has even tried to coordinate the drawing up of the European Security Treaty with any of them, which turns the whole idea into an individual speech act that resonates neither with Russia's neighbors nor with its Western interlocutors. Moscow's attempts to present the lukewarm reception by the West of this widely propagated security initiative as proof of its disinterest in partnership with Russia, only underpins the existence of profound perceptual gaps between Russia and the West.

Yet the application of the concept of securitization not only sheds light on the mechanisms of miscommunication between security actors, it also helps to unveil the flexibility of relations of friendship and enmity among nations whose roles and identities are not necessarily well established. Countries constantly securitize and desecuritize each other. Perhaps, the most notorious examples of countries securitized by Russia are Georgia (the military conflict between Moscow and Tbilisi in August 2008) and Estonia (the conflict caused by the removal of the Bronze Soldier monument from downtown Tallinn to a military cemetery in 2007). Both cases demonstrate that securitization can be driven by both material and ideational factors, and always includes a strong symbolic dimension.

In the meantime, several examples of more or less successful desecuritization can be given, as epitomized by Russia's improved relations with Poland and Norway. In both cases, the old conflicts, which were more politically pronounced in Poland's case due to the Polish dissatisfaction with the Russian unwillingness to unequivocally take responsibility for the Katyn affair,[4] and more technical in the relations with Norway, were transformed into a cooperative type of relationship. Both cases of desecuritization have led to the conclusion of bilateral agreements on visa-free border-crossing procedures for residents of adjacent areas, which is a good starting point for visa-free negotiations between Russia and the European Union. The fact that both Poland and Norway are NATO members clearly suggests that Russia's relations with this military bloc are in no way destined to mutual enmity and can be effectively redressed.

Desecuritization has to be distinguished from under-securitization or playing down the importance of security threats emanating from other actors. China is perhaps the best example of a country under-securitized in the Russian political discourse. This means that potential security threats from the largest of Russia's neighbors (including illegal migration, illicit trans-border trade, environmental issues, etc.) are either neglected or underestimated by policy makers in Moscow for the sake of hammering out a partnership with China within the frameworks of organizations such as BRICS and SCO. It is only within academic discourses, including those unfolding in Russia's far east, that these threats are properly acknowledged.

Yet, there is a much larger group of countries that are bereft of a more or less precise role in the Russian security imagery. The most important among these "moving targets" is the United States, which was perceived as an important ally for Russia in the beginning of 1990s, but turned into a major source of security threats to Russian interests by the end of the century. Even within a relatively short period of time, under the presidencies of Medvedev and Obama, Russian–American relations evolved from a desecuritized "reset" to the explicitly securitized Kremlin rebuff of the US antimissile system in Europe. The highly emotional reaction of the Kremlin to the meeting of a group of oppositional politicians with the US Ambassador Michael McFaul in the aftermath of the December 2011 election to the State Duma is one of the most recent indications of the on-going securitization of bilateral relations by the Moscow officialdom.

By the same token, Iran, which is deeply securitized by the United States, is another country that may have found itself in a role as either Russia's political ally (in a global resistance to US domination), or as a country developing its nuclear program, and thus inevitably posing a military threat to Russia. Iran may be considered as a possible power pole in the multipolar world order that Russia strives for, yet Moscow "has absolutely no interest in seeing Iran acquire nuclear weapons. Should that occur, the geopolitical balance from the Caucasus to Central Asia would shift dramatically against Moscow" (Trenin and Malashenko, 2010, p. 22). This makes Russia's policies toward Iran so inconsistently fluctuating.

Similar swinging from one position to another is evident in the case of Russia's relations with Ukraine. Depending on the political context, Ukraine may be portrayed by the Kremlin as either the culturally closest neighbor to Russia and even an indispensable part of Russian identity, or as a source of existential security threats stemming from Kiev's NATO membership plans, or from the financial damage to Russia's energy supplies to Europe caused by Ukraine. In Putin's metaphor, Ukraine is "drinking Russia's blood"[5] (a rude allusion to the alleged losses suffered by Russia in the energy transportation through Ukrainian territory), which appears to be an example of securitization of this neighboring country by Russia.

Security for Domestic Audience: a Genealogy of Russian Fears

Perlocutionary effects of Russian security discourses, i.e. those that require persuasion of target groups (Stritzel, 2011), are different for the domestic audience (where the key issue is threat construction and mobilization of public opinion) and international society (where the chief problem for Russia is gaining stronger legitimacy for its security posture). In the following sections, I will argue that, domestically, Russian security discourse is meant to mobilize those groups within society that are sensitive to the nation-centric and "Russia first" arguments, while internationally, Russia seeks to receive greater feedback and reception exactly from those Western countries that it vilifies domestically.

The dominating security discourse aimed to reach the domestic audience is an amalgam of rhetorical approaches representing a mixture of nationalist and patriotic worldviews.[6] First, its most important element is diversion of attention from numerous internal sources of insecurity to unfriendly encroachments by external forces. Domestic security discourse is very much grounded in a post-colonial type of reasoning that tends to identify Russia with semi-peripheral countries, especially when it comes to the accusations of the West stimulating the brain drain, and sponsoring domestic upheavals through supporting pro-Western groups, etc. In this type of discourse, the West is portrayed as an aggressive political subject eager to intentionally harm the Russian interests. The alleged threats from the West may be postulated as "evident and requiring no additional debate" (Yemelianov, 2005). This type of securitization is based on an anti-Western mythology that draws a deep distinction between the West and Russia, and helps demonize certain countries ("nowadays all the surface of the earth and its oceans are proclaimed the sphere of US national interests" (Panchenko, 2005)). Within this ideologically biased world outlook, all political changes in the world are perceived as programmed and presaged by the "world elite", and allegedly directed against Russia. Russia's marginalization in international relations is portrayed as a result of conscious policies of inimical subjects (Drozdov and Illarionov, 2005) that are aimed at subduing national governments to supranational control. Besides, the narrative suggests that Russia is surrounded by unthankful neighbors against whom the Kremlin must, in some instances, take tough measures (such as economic sanctions, peace enforcement operations, etc.) (Grozmani, 2005).

Second, Russia is often depicted in domestic security discourses as an exceptional country, a kind of "benevolent empire" (Sheichuk, 2011). The myth of Russian exceptionality leads to two political effects: it justifies Russia's claims for "special rights" in what it dubs its "near abroad", and attempts to lay the conceptual foundation for Russia's chronic unilateralism.

Third, Russia tends to portray regional issues as necessarily having a global significance. This vision is closely related to the spheres-of-influence type of thinking. One such example is the Russian–Georgian war of August 2008 to which Moscow ascribes much wider meaning due to the alleged ability to militarily challenge the world hegemon. Another example could be the (mis)interpretation of the France-promoted Union for Mediterranean as an indispensable element of the geopolitical encirclement of Russia by a US-led Euro–Atlantic coalition eager to reduce Russian influence in the Middle East, North Africa, and the wider Black Sea region (Pavlenko, 2009).

Fourth, selective attempts to artificially desecuritize issues pertaining to other nations are also part of the Russian security discourse. Thus, some authors claim that "nobody in the world threatens United States", a statement that evidently ignores the 9/11 security repercussions for the sake of delegitimizing US military policies in Iraq and Afghanistan (Rog, 2005).

Fifth, domestic security discourses in Russia are very much grounded in a top–down imposition of rigid ideological and populist concepts with fuzzy content ("spiritual security", "information violence", etc. (Goncharov, 2005)). In particular, information security is overwhelmingly understood to be the cleansing of the "undue" content on the Internet, subjectively defined by a blend of aesthetic criteria ("propaganda of perversions") and political considerations (promotion of non-traditional religious beliefs, or appeals to extremism which remain subject to politically motivated assessments) (Stroev, 2005). Even alternative interpretations of Russian history may be lambasted as "manifestations of cultural and spiritual aggression of the West against Russia" and even "information warfare" (Ozerov, 2005).

Under closer scrutiny, domestic security discourses appear to lack consistency and coherence. They completely ignore the fact that in many regions it is exactly the military preponderance of the United States that guarantees at least minimal stability and prevents the arms race and nuclear proliferation (Fiodorov, 2011). They contain elements of solidarity with the post-colonial resistance to Western domination, and at the same time assert Russia as a type of "new empire". They may embed both mimicry of and enmity to the West in general and the United States in particular. Needless to say that this type of security discourse is not accepted in the West where Russia is viewed rather as an "eroding empire" than as a power center of its own: "taken together, Beijing, Brussels, Ankara or Washington have provided the post-Soviet states with alternative sources of political legitimacy, loans, investment and security partnership, which they readily used to expand their foreign policy options and move a step away from Russia's orbit" (Judah, Kobzova, and Popescu, 2011).

Russia's Visions of International Security: the Challenges of Legitimation

Russian outward-oriented security discourses look profoundly different from what I have discussed earlier. The major problem that Russia faces at the international security scene is the much-needed legitimization of its security posture, which is unattainable without institutional participation in the dominating security structures. It is exactly the institutional deficit of Russian security policies that is conducive to major policy failures. Even if, in certain situations, Russia might have a point (like in the August 2008 military operation against Georgia, or in the bitter dispute with Estonia caused by the removal of the Bronze Soldier monument from downtown Tallinn), Russian arguments are overwhelmingly rejected, which dooms Russia to a politically costly role as a unilateral security actor. To put it differently, Russia's speech acts often fail to reach the goal of persuading the external audience and thus remain ineffective policy tools.

The first possible way of legitimizing Russian security policies is by referring to the centrality of the United Nations as the pivotal institution in charge for global security. Yet Russia's adherence to the United Nations is basically explained by its status as the permanent Security Council member with the veto power. The Russian position on Syria is a clear manifestation of the power logic camouflaged by the references to seemingly normative arguments (sovereignty, non-intervention, etc.). In displaying its power ambitions, Russia faces at least two substantial challenges. First, in the Syrian debate, the Kremlin *de facto* defends the premises of the traditional Westphalian (nation–state–centric) system that is no longer shared by Russia's key international partners. By doing so, Russia intentionally widens the gap that separates it from the West. Second, by applying its veto power in the UN Security Council and associating its position with the support for cruel dictatorship, Russia in fact loses other important elements of its influence in the world, mainly associated with soft power.

Apart from this, in Russian security thinking, the UN role is reduced to simply safeguarding the Westphalian structure of international relations, which leaves beyond Russia's attention (and, perhaps, due comprehension) a much wider spectrum of UN-generated norms of good governance, sustainable development, human security, and international humanitarianism. The post-Cold War UN sustains a liberal institutional order with pivotal roles for multilateralism, oversight and monitoring mechanisms, and a close nexus between legitimacy and democracy. All this justifies greater interference in domestic affairs from the part of the international society structures, and recognition of domestic democracy as the ultimate guarantor of peace. Yet these conceptual departures are alien to Russian security thinking, which sometimes leaves Russia isolated, even within the UN institutions.

The second way of legitimizing Russian security policy is through membership of regional security organizations. Two of them play the most important roles for Moscow – the Shanghai Cooperation Organization (SCO) and the Collective Security Treaty Organization (CSTO). The problem with CSTO is that Russia treats it, not as a classical security alliance, but rather as an instrument for supporting the local elites in the neighboring countries (Nikitina, 2009) and keeping them within the Russian sphere of influence. This explains Russia's reliance on bilateral rather than multilateral security policies in its relations with Belarus, Kazakhstan, Armenia, and Kyrgyzstan. In the case of SCO, security integration is complicated by the economic expansion of China, which is perceived by many international experts as a rival to Moscow rather than as its strategic partner.

> The only options left for Russia are bandwagoning and engagement with the rising China which will give Beijing much greater leverage and manoeuvrability over Moscow than ever before in history … Russia will have very few possibilities to balance or contain its political and economic dependency on China. (Nojonen, 2011, pp. 17–18)

By the same token, "the speed and vigor with which the SCO supported China's crackdown on Urumqi demonstrators in July 2009 and its recent declaration criticizing the award of the Nobel Peace Prize to Lu Xiaobo suggest that Beijing remains the primary driver of the SCO's security agenda" (Cooley, 2011). Ultimately, neither of these two organizations supported Russia in its war against Georgia in August 2008 or in recognition of the two separatist territories, Abkhazia and South Ossetia. Russia also did not have institutional support from its allies in its tug-of-war with the United States over the antimissile system in Europe. Russia's declared military buildup in response to the NATO deployment of antimissile[7] was a typical unilateral act not even rhetorically supported by those Russian allies who are geographically located in close vicinity to NATO, including Belarus.

Third, Russia tries to forge some sort of cooperation between CSTO and NATO. Sergei Lavrov has referred to putative possibilities for joint operations of these two organizations in the Euro–Atlantic and Eurasian regions. These rhetorical efforts have so far failed, which signals a lack of due legitimacy and trust for the Moscow-patronized organization on the part of the North Atlantic bloc.

Fourth, the search for legitimacy takes the form of Russia's gradual adaptation of international security vocabulary. Indeed, Russian security discourse is influenced by a number of Western security concepts, such as "hard" and "soft" security, a dichotomy that was positively accepted in the Russian academic community and unleashed intensive discussions on information, energy, environmental, and other types/forms of security. In the meantime, most Russian politicians are more skeptical about the adaptability of the Western security vocabulary in Russia. In their opinion, a wider approach to security, bereft of clear focus on the most deadly threats, is conducive to unfortunate securitization of the entire gamut of social relations, including environment, human rights, energy relations, and so forth. They believe that it is the gradual marginalization of military aspects of security in negotiations with Russia that the European Union and NATO are interested in. It is also claimed that a wider understanding of security leads to the lack of "geographic specialization" in security provision (Khot'kova *et al.*, 2010), which is a euphemism denoting division of spheres of influence. In particular, the "soft security" concept may lead to potentially divisive effects, leaving Russia as a source of security threats to the West.

What is missed in Russian debate is that the EU's and NATO's extended security agendas may widen the areas of possible cooperation with Russia to include a variety of soft security issues, such as migration, drug trafficking, border control management, etc. The same goes for the human security concept that was intentionally misinterpreted in the official discourse of the Kremlin and reduced to technical matters of survival in conditions of disasters, post-crisis management, state regulation of medical and pharmaceutical standards, etc.

Russia's Security Roles

In this section, I will dwell upon a variety of roles that Russia can play in international security politics. These roles are by no means mutually exclusive, and some of them may be performed simultaneously.

Russia as a Security Architect – Yet What Kind of Security?

The key rationale for Russia's insistence on institutionalization of a new "security architecture" in a wider Europe is a long-standing fear of being excluded from the mechanisms of decision making in the key issues of international politics (Rogov, 1999, p. 177). This role is based on Moscow's belief that all forms of integration without Russia are meant against Russia (Maximychev, 1999, p. 197). The feeling of being left outside the emerging security governance is a major source of danger for Russia, which sees itself as a major European power bereft of the appropriate place in European security. Concomitantly, Russia is interested not in launching a wide-scale Cold War-like confrontation, but in bargaining for elevating its role in a wider Europe. Against this background, the crux of Medvedev's "new security architecture" proposal lies in an attempt to join the hegemonic security community of Euro–Atlantic partnership that NATO and European Union consider, by and large, as already established and relatively efficiently functioning. The problem is that inclusion in such a community requires applicants to become "more like us" and, consequently, is premised on a sense of "we"-ness and togetherness. In such a community, difference and pluralism are externalized, and Russia is one of those outsiders that is perceived as external to Western security (Joenniemi, 2010). Some of the language games reflect this perceptional gap: while Russia prefers to speak about "*Euro–Atlantic* security" (presupposing Russia's participation), most Europeans think in terms of "*trans-Atlantic* security" (which does not envision Russia's inclusion).

However, the Russian vision of a new security architecture is grounded in a number of approaches that are either contradictory or ill-conceptualized. Some of them are in disharmony with the dominating Western conceptions. First, Russia is sympathetic with the idea of "network diplomacy", a concept that seems to be in tune with the Western political vocabulary – but this similarity is only assumed. In the Russian context, the references to "network diplomacy" connote traditional state-centric policies of multilateralism at best, while in the West this concept signi-fies a globalization-friendly type of horizontal interaction between social and profes-sional groups that constitutes an alternative to state hierarchies (Metzl, 2001).

Second, Russia is committed to the principle of equal security, which also raises a number of conceptual issues boiling down to various understandings of the idea of equality in the security domain. It can be interpreted, for example, as the right of each country to choose its own security instruments, including membership in mil-itary alliances (Yurgens, Dynkin, and Baranovskiy, 2009, p. 49). This interpretation evidently does not suit Moscow, which makes some pro-Kremlin experts claim that "autonomy of states in security sphere requires certain limitations", and that "the freedom to join alliances should not be taken as a dogma" (Entin, 2009). These remarks only reveal the real intentions behind Moscow's strategy – to constrain the freedom of choice of its neighbors and strengthen its preeminence in the "near abroad".

The Kremlin-friendly version of equal security reduces this concept to its purely legal(ist) components. But this logic seems to be of only limited utility because the references to international law often fail to work in situations of contested norms. That is why, at a certain point, the politicization of the demand for equality becomes inevitable, and this is exactly what happens when Russian authors claim that unrec-ognized territories, including Abkhazia, South Ossetia, and Transdniestria, have to be accepted as fully fledged participants of the all-European security "concert" (Sytin, 2009). Yet this apparent radicalization of the concept of equality seems to be hardly acceptable for most of Russia's Western partners.

What further complicates the practical implementation of the idea of equality is Russia's skepticism about the existence of spheres with different mechanisms of influence, commitments, and regulations within a wider Europe. Yet the secu-rity concerns of Nordic Europe are definitely very much different from – and thus unequal to – security troubles faced by the Black Sea countries. In particular, the idea of equal security may question such regional mechanisms of security provision as BLACKSEAFOR. Besides, it may require the repudiation of the spheres-of-influence type of policy that Russia pursues in its "near abroad".

Third, Russia is keen on supporting the idea of collective security, which comes in a variety of versions. In one of them, "collective security should not be substituted by bloc-based approaches" (Entin, 2011), which implies that collective security ought to unfold beyond blocs. Yet in Sergey Lavrov's version, collective security is articulated exactly as a combination of regional security "segments", or blocs: NATO plus CSTO, Asian Pacific, Persian Gulf, Middle East, the South Caucasus (Lavrov, 2012). Experts assume that even within CSTO there are three regions of "collective security": East European, Caucasian, and Central Asian. This fragmented vision certainly presupposes different security instruments and institutions for dif-ferent regions. Thus, the idea of collective security in the CSTO segment may be interpreted as "an ensemble of inter-state governmental bodies, forces and measures that provide the legally framed defense of member states' interests grounded in sovereignty and territorial integrity" (Yurgens, 2011, p. 13). Placing sovereignty as the key reference object of securitization raises substantial theoretical issues – as we well know, in many cases the strongest challenges to sovereignty might emanate from within states and result from mismanagement, corruption, lack of due transparency, etc. Presumably, in other regions such an interpretation of collective security may be questioned.

Fourth, Russia's adherence to the principle of indivisibility of security may also be a matter of debate. Thus, a former Russian Foreign Minister Igor Ivanov (2011) claims that indivisibility should not be confused with the belief in almost automatic linkages between regional conflicts and global security – such a vision is a relic of the Cold War and only leads to greater tensions between the key powers. Neither must indivisibility be equated with the search for universal institutions able to solve the entire plethora of security concerns in the world. In Ivanov's view, the most effective frame for the implementation of the idea of indivisibility is a combination of different security regimes, each one representing a flexible coalition of state and non-state actors eager to collectively solve issues of common concern (energy, environment, migration, cyber crime, etc.). In his reading, regimes are more democratic and inclusive than traditional institutions because they are not grounded in a domination of great powers, or envision the veto power (Ivanov, 2011, pp. 33–34).

Fifth, Russian diplomatic vocabulary contains multiple references to the prospects of a bloc-free structure of global security relations ("vneblokovost"). Semantically, this concept may be viewed as applicable to a limited number of countries that have chosen neutrality (Ukraine, Switzerland, Sweden, Finland), but, as seen from the Russian perspective, this principle ought to be foundational for the overall "security architecture" in Europe. What stands behind the Russian interpretation of a "bloc-free" structure of international security is the desire to delegitimize NATO as the pivotal military bloc. Yet it is evident that the declared propensity toward a "bloc-free" security is in conflict with Moscow's policy of strengthening CSTO and delineating its sphere of security responsibility.

Russia as a Unilateral Peace Enforcer

This role is an alternative to the previous one because it presupposes Russia's strengthening of its own power resources in its "near abroad", rather than co-sponsoring collective security for the entire Euro–Atlantic area. Thus, an expert in the journal published by the state-funded *Russian Institute for Strategic Studies* claims that Russia has to choose between the liberal principles of security that emphasizes collective peacekeeping and humanitarian operations grounded in a wider interpretation of security on the one hand, and a more traditional balance of forces between the key poles with well-fixed spheres of influence for each of them on the other. According to Sytin (2009), the second option seems to better fit the Russian security interests. In this interpretation, instead of participating in multilateral coalitions, Russia should opt for freedom of hands in the area of its vital interests, as well as for claiming its "right" to veto unfriendly enlargement of the rivaling military bloc and instead of looking for cooperative management of security conflicts, it should be wary about its competitors' interference in what it considers zones of its exceptional interest. This role recognizes the possible areas of privileged security responsibilities of countries like Turkey, but intends to reduce the EU's involvement in the post-Soviet countries to bilateral relations bereft of institutional background (Sytin, 2009).

This largely unilateral type of security conduct deserves critical analysis from at least two vantage points. First, Russia is destined to imitate the US policies without having comparable resources. The August 2008 Russian military action against Georgia and the Kremlin's recognition of the two breakaway territories were marked by multiple references to the Kosovo precedent. Well before 2008, Russian experts admitted that "we are doing in Abkhazia what NATO did in Kosovo, having separated it from Serbia" (Krasnosiolov, 2003, p. 123). In fact, Russia imitated the artificial grants of sovereignty and the equal rights stemming from it to territories with no resources for independent development, which "undermines the legal and political order and creates a fictional order without substantive content" (Chandler, 2008).

Second, Russia has to pay a costly political price for unilateral military action, finding itself in a diplomatic isolation on the issue of recognition of the two rebellious republics. Russia also proved unable to mastermind the political situation in its *de facto* protectorates: the President of Abkhazia was a target of numerous assassination attempts, while in South Ossetia, Moscow was incapable of guaranteeing electoral victory to its favorite for presidency, which resulted in the cancellation of the results of the presidential election in 2011. Weak political position on the ground is the price that Moscow pays for its unilateralism in the Caucasus.

Russia as a Peace Mediator

A third role for Russia to play is that of peace maker in the areas of its "near abroad". This role, which is natural due to Russia's declared "special" interests in this vast area, however, faces serious challenges. To begin with, Russia is not an "honest broker". In conflicts in Nagorno-Karabakh and Transdniestria, it takes sides, and by doing so, complicates its relations with the more important actors, Azerbaijan and Moldova. Also, Russia's interest in peace mediation and conflict resolution seems to be dubious to many in the West. Meister (2011) claims that, "Russia continues to use the conflicts in order to exert influence on the participating states and does not have a genuine interest in their resolution … Russia does not see the post-Soviet conflicts as a threat to its security, but as a means to maintain its influence".

In the meantime, then President Medvedev signed the Meseberg declaration that opened the prospects for a more intense Russian–German security dialogue on the basis of cooperation over the Transdniestria conflict. Moscow tried to exert strong pressure upon Igor Smirnov, but ultimately failed to dissuade him from running again for the presidency of this breakaway territory. Nevertheless, the Meseberg process is one of few instances of Russia's tacit acceptance of the principle of conditionality that it verbally rejects.

There are two key explanations for the lack of Russia's success in playing the role of peacemaker. One is Russia's reluctance to take political stands and thus make choices that would apparently dissatisfy one of the conflicting parties, while the other is the deficit of multilateral diplomatic efforts, which are one of the weakest links in Russian diplomacy. Of course, Western countries can't boast of their success stories in conflict resolution either, but the lack of progress is, first of all, detrimental to the Russian pretentions to hegemonize the political and security landscape of the post-Soviet region.

Russia as the Key Element of European Energy Security

Russia's role as energy security provider can be viewed in several aspects. First, it represents an extension of the idea that Russia is a corporate state, void of strong value-based identity, and interested mainly in economic and financial transactions. This role envisions a domination of energy companies' interests (especially those of "Gazprom") in Russia's relations with transit and consuming countries. The key paradox here is that this positioning, being conceived in Russia as a manifestation of its propensity toward technological approaches in its relations with its partners, was reinterpreted in the West as a political gesture entailing strong security effects, ranging from the appearance of an "energy gendarme" metaphor in the Western media to NATO's readiness to include energy disruption into the list of major security threats to the Euro–Atlantic region.

Second, the practical implementation of this role appears to be most effective within the framework of a bilateral and pragmatic co-management of energy issues between Russia and Germany, as exemplified by the Nord Stream project. Russian and German interests in energy security seem to coincide. For Russia as an exporter country, the main source of energy insecurity is dependence on transit across the territory of countries in political circles where the mood is hostile. In addition, moving to the forefront of Russian understanding of energy security is maximizing capitalization of petroleum resources, and using them for promoting Russian economic interests in the West. For Germany as a user country, raising the level of energy security is connected with partial access to Russia's energy resources through working with "Gazprom" and other large companies. As most European countries do, Germany defines energy security as providing acceptable (that is stable and reasonable) prices for oil, gas, and their future equivalents, derived from reliable and diversified sources. The two main threats from this point of view are high prices for energy and instability of supply. As the Russian–German cooperation makes clear, energy security is a means of creating regulatory regimes that would lower the risks of unexpected price changes and provide, at the same time, an appropriate level of openness in the markets.

Yet for potential transit countries, energy security is associated with the possibility of controlling the process of transit itself and receiving rent for it. In particular, in the opinion of a Lithuanian specialist, for their country "losing the position of transit state will make Lithuania more vulnerable to Russian politics" (Janeliunas and Molis, 2006). Poland, Ukraine, and the Baltic countries accuse Moscow of marginalizing their roles and of constructing politically motivated energy transportation routes, while Russia itself thinks of its energy projects as strictly technological ones, dictated primarily by economic rationale and in this sense depoliticized. In fact, the Russian message, expressed technologically yet based upon a certain political reasoning, stretches far beyond energy security matters: it reads in fact that Russia does not need "assistants"/"facilitators" in its energy dialogue with major European powers – a situation that may question the relevance of such self-ascribed roles for Russia's neighbors as "brokers", "bridges", "connectors", "communicators", etc. Moreover, Russia treats most of its neighbors as security challengers. Georgia, Poland, Ukraine – the three Baltic states – all may, in one sense or another, qualify for a role as a security threat to Russia. In their turn, each of these countries build their energy security perceptions on the unfriendly portrayal of Russia, which becomes a key factor of securitization of otherwise technical issues in the oil and gas sphere.

Arguably, this peculiar type of securitization is a product of two clashing logics: politicization and depoliticization. Each time the parties diverge in their qualification of the problem as either political or economic, the securitization perspective augments. In particular, as is the case of Russian–Latvian relations, Russia claims that it never advanced any preconditions in energy negotiations, while Latvia demands that Russia has to make a political move – namely to apologize for the 1940 occupation (Spruds, 2006, p. 18).

The key problem for Russia in this respect is that its energy security policies are in conflict with its role as the locomotive of post-Soviet integration. Instead of demonstrating its special relations with the near-abroad countries, Russia not only charges them at world prices (as each corporation would do), but also intends to bypass some of them (first of all Ukraine) as unreliable and troublesome partners.

Russia as a Bulwark Against Terrorism

Russia's security policy in the North Caucasus, due to a number of reasons (rampant terrorism in Chechnya, Ingushetia, and Kabardino-Balkaria; the uncertainty of the status of South Ossetia; and the forthcoming Sochi Olympics), has become the object of increased international attention. The developments in Russia's Caucasian regions are increasingly dictated by security considerations, which necessarily presuppose their distinctness from the rest of Russia, not only in terms of specific cultural identity, but also (geo)political orientation. The Republics of Dagestan, Ingushetia, Kabardino-Balkaria, and Karachaevo-Cherkessia were always relatively immune from the fluctuations of the federal center's policies because their traditional systems of governance, being products of the distribution of power resources among indigenous clan-like groups, were decided locally. Yet the sharpening of security concerns – partly stemming from the overall complication of the geopolitical situation in the aftermath of the war with Georgia in August 2008, and the subsequent recognition by Russia of Abkhazia and South Ossetia – only added new constrains to the policies of Moscow in these peripheral regions and exacerbated their claims for exceptional treatment by federal authorities.

Chechnya has been able to preserve its special status in Russia, not only because it was the only other region – besides Tatarstan – that signed a bilateral treaty with Moscow, but also because Putin practically left Chechnya under the full control of Ramzan Kadyrov and his military forces. As poignantly noted by some commentators, Chechnya achieved the degree of independence from Russia it had sought in the 1990s (Latynina, 2006). Keeping in mind the outrageous murders of Kadyrov's opponents that took place in Moscow, it could be suggested that his influence is not limited to the Chechen territory. Kadyrov's reach was extended officially, after the murder of Ingushetia's president in June 2009, when he was selected by the federal center as the man responsible for establishing security and order in the whole of Russia's Caucasus (Malashenko, 2009). The termination by Moscow of the "regime of counter-terrorist operation" in Chechnya in 2010, a decision strongly lobbied for by Kadyrov, may also be viewed as an example of successful regional pressure upon Moscow. In short, it is evident that as long as the Chechen president remains personally loyal to the Kremlin, he is allowed a practically free hand in ruling over Chechnya, and now even control of the situation in neighboring republics.

Yet the reverse side of the Putin–Kadyrov deal is the growing violence in Russia's southern margins where the Kremlin's policy

> is more likely to sustain rather than to quell violence. This is because centralization inevitably suppresses political competition, which leads to erosion of government legitimacy and transparency. With clan networks, nepotism, and traditions of honorable revenge especially strong in the North Caucasus, diminishing transparency has been enhancing systemic corruption of institutions responsible for security and antiterrorist defense. Through this process, Putin's centralization of government has unwittingly contributed to the most serious acts of communal violence in the region, including police shakedowns, guerilla operations, kidnapping rackets, terrorism, and rioting. (Alexseev, 2004)

As another expert suggests,

> Moscow has effectively granted sovereignty over Chechnya to its appointed leader, Ramzan Kadyrov who now has a virtual monopoly over the use of legitimate force on Chechen territory ... Yet, no one knows what Kadyrov might do for money ... Chechnya could very well become a haven for activities that Moscow regrets. At a prosaic level, this might mean drug smuggling or gunrunning. If Kadyrov's loyalties are less firm than he claims, however, it could mean cooperating with foreign interests that contribute to the further weakening of the Russian state. Moscow has risked a very unpleasant future for short-term stability. (Marten, 2008, p. 2)

Conclusion

As I have shown in this chapter, the Russian case seems to prove that security is not a static concept, but is always in the making. The variety of Russia's security roles reflects the flexibility and mobility of its security agenda and the discourses that sustain it. The key problem that looms large at this juncture is the lack of conceptual clarity, which not only sometimes makes the Russian discourses on security either disassembled or hollow, but also impedes the search for understanding between Russia and the West in the security domain.

Security itself is a very volatile and fuzzy concept, and its merging with other equally less certain concepts, such as sovereignty, identity, or equality, only complicates the comprehension of Russian discourses in the international arena. Thus, pointing to sovereignty as the major reference object of securitization is premised on a specific political logic of modernity, but becomes vulnerable in situations of dispersion of sovereignty as an effect of globalization and trans-nationalization. Politically and instrumentally, the rigidity of the security–sovereignty nexus opens possibilities for securitizing domestic protests and opposition forces, which only dissociates Russia from the Western normative order. Equally problematic is the grounding of security in the issues of identity, which is a fuzzy concept in itself and is open to endless interpretations. This makes it possible to securitize the broadest variety of issues pertaining to culture, mentality, language, religion, ethnicity, worldviews, and even the uncanny Russian spirituality. The same is true for advancing the concept of equality as the key determinant of Russia's security ideal: this conceptualization makes Russia an anti-*status quo* actor, a role that Russia is likely loathe to play, and even denies, through its sympathies, the hierarchical structure of international relations.

As a reaction to the discursive extension of the security terrain, the Kremlin – as the key securitizing actor in Russia – tends to move to an explicitly narrow vision of security in its hard (i.e. army- and physical force-based) version; yet this artificial reduction of the security agenda to matters of military balance and state financing of the defence industry is of little help for building a communicative milieu with Russia's Western partners, who are committed to a significantly wider transnational security agenda.

Arguably, neither overall securitization of the whole spectrum of social phenomena and processes nor the reductionist limitation of security to the issues of military force may constitute a fertile ground for Russia's positive and constructive interaction with its Western security counterparts. Concomitantly, Russia needs to keep searching the most effective signifiers of its security discourse that would prevent it from taking retrograde positions (such as, for example, *de facto* defending repressive autocrats in countries like Syria), and, vice versa, allow for fully fledged security cooperation with the strongest and most normatively appealing members of international society. As a minimum, a new Russian security agenda has to embrace two important issues – multilateralism (as opposed to spheres of influence and unilateral security policies) and human security (as opposed to regime security). To bring results, both ideas, which are well articulated academically, need much stronger political underpinning and institutional framing.

Notes

1. Vladimir Putin. Russia and the Changing World, available at http://premier.gov.ru/eng/events/news/18252/
2. EASI, chaired by Igor Ivanov, Wolfgang Ischinger and Sam Nunn, makes a strong case for a trilateral cooperation between NATO, European Union, and Russia in security domain, with potential participation of OCSE and international NGOs.
3. *Towards a Euro-Atlantic Security Community*. Euro-Atlantic Security Initiate Final report, February 2012, http://carnegieendowment.org/2012/02/03/toward-euro-atlantic-security-community/9d3j#
4. The mass murder of Polish officers by the Stalinist security forces.
5. "Regnum" Agency, December 20, 2011, available at http://www.regnum.ru/news/polit/1481957.html
6. I will draw most of the illustrations from "Politika" journal published by the Federation Council, the upper chamber of the Russian parliament.
7. Zayavlenie Prezidenta v sviazi s situatsiei, kotoraya slozhilas' vokrug systemy PRO stran NATO v Evrope, 23 November 2011, available at http://news.kremlin.ru/news/13637/print

References

Alexseev, Mikhail. 2004. "Security Sell-Out in the North Caucasus, 2004: How Government Centralization Backfires." *PONARS Policy Memo 344*, November.

Balzacq, Thierry. 2011. "A Theory of Securitization. Origins, Core Assumptions, and Variants." In *Securitization Theory. How Security Problems Emerge and Dissolve*, edited by Thierry Balzacq. London: Routledge.

Bogomolov, Alexander, and Oleksandr Lytvynenko. 2012. *A Ghost in the Mirror: Russian Soft Power in Ukraine*, January 2012. London: Chatham House Briefing Paper.

Chandler, David. 2008. "The Revival of Carl Schmitt in International Relations: The Last Refuge of Critical Theorists?" *Millenium: Journal of International Studies*, 37(1): 27–48.

Cooley, Alexander. 2011. "The Kyrgyz Crisis and the Political Logic of Central Asia's Weak Regional Security Organizations." *PONARS Eurasia Policy Memo*, No. 140 (May).

Drozdov, Yu. I., and S.I. Illarionov. 2005. "Kuda Rossia derzhit put'?" *Politika*, 80. Accessed December 13, 2013 from http://www.politika-magazine.ru/80.html

Entin, Mark. 2009. "Predlozhenia po rabote nad zakliucheniem dogovora o evropeiskoi bezopasnosti obrastaiut konkretikoi." *All Europe*, Spring/Summer. Accessed December 13, 2013 from http://www.alleuropa.ru/predlozheniya-po-rabote-nad-zakliucheniem-dogovora-o-evropeyskoy-bezopasnosti-obrastaiut-konkretikoy

Entin, Mark. 2011. "Chto trebuetsa dlia propyrva k real'noi mezhdunarodnoi bezopasnosti." *Vsia Evropa*, 9(58). Accessed December 13, 2013 from http://www.alleuropa.ru/chto-trebuetsya-dlya-proriva-k-utverzhdeniiu-realjnoy-mezhdunarodnoy-bezopasnosti

Fiodorov, Yurii. 2011. "Glazami liberala: na krugi svoya." *Index Bezopasnosti*, 2(97).

Goncharov, Sergey. 2005. "Rossia v epokhu terror." *Politika*, 93. Accessed December 13, 2013 from http://www.politika-magazine.ru/

Grozmani, Tatiana. 2005. "Potentsial'nie ugrozy vnutri strany." *Politika*, 92. Accessed December 13, 2013 from http://www.politika-magazine.ru//92.html

Ivanov, Igor. 2011. "Nedelimost' bezopasnosti v globalnom mire." *Index Bezopasnosti*, 17/4(99).

Janeliunas, T., and A. Molis. 2006. "The NEGP ends Lithuania's hopes of becoming a transit country." *The Baltic Mosaic. Analytical Notes*, 1(5).

Joenniemi, Pertti. 2010. "Difference within Similarity: Transatlantic Relations as a Community of 'Neighbours'." In *The Struggle for the West*, edited by Christopher S. Browning and Marko Lehti. London: Routledge.

Judah, Ben, Jana Kobzova, and Nicu Popescu. 2011. "Dealing with a Post-BRICS Russia." London: European Council on Foreign Relations.

Kaldor, Mary, and Vaquer i Fanes, Jordi. 2010. *Helsinki Plus: towards a human security architecture for Europe: the first report of the EU-Russia Human Security Study Group*. CIDOB Monographs, CIDOB Foundation, Barcelona, Spain.

Khot'kova, E.S., and G.G. Tischenko, *et al.* 2010. "O perspektivakh zakliuchenia Dogovora o Evropeiskoi bezopasnosti." *Problemy natsional'noi strategii*, 2: 7–24.

Krasnosiolov, Alexei. 2003. "Tak kto poterial Gruziyu?" *International Trends Journal of Theory of International Relations and World Politic*, 1.

Latynina, Yulia. 2006. "Khoziain Chechni: Odin den' s prem'erom." *Novaya gazeta*, September, 25. Accessed December 13, 2013 from http://2006.novayagazeta.ru/nomer/2006/73n/n73n-s11.shtml

Lavrov, Sergey. 2012. "Speech at the International Security Conference, Munich." February 4. Accessed December 13, 2013 from http://www.mid.ru/brp_4.nsf/0/45D5CC6F7F1EACF04425799A005B12EC

Malashenko, Alexei. 2009. *Ramzan Kadyrov: Rossiiskii politik kavkazskoi natsional'nosti*. Moscow: Carnegie Center.

Marten, Kimberly. 2008. *Russia, Chechnya, and the Sovereign Kadyrov*. Policy Memo No. 116. Washington, DC: PONARS Eurasia.

Maximychev, Igor. 1999. "Russia's Concept of a New European Security Architecture." In *Russia's place in Europe: a security debate*, edited by Kurt Spillmann, Andreas Wenger, Derek Müller, and Perović Jeronim, 191–202. Bern: Peter Lang.

Meister, Stefan. 2011. "A New Start for Russian – EU Security Policy?" *Genshagener Papiere*, 7.

Metzl, Jamie. 2001. "Network Diplomacy." *Georgetown Journal of International Affairs*, Winter/Spring.

Nikitina, Yulia. 2009. *ODKB i ShOS: modeli regionalizma v sfere bezopasnosti*. Moscow: MGIMO & Navona Publishers.

Nojonen, Matti. 2011. "Introduction: Adjusting to the great power transition." In *Russia – China Relations. Current State, Alternative Futures, and Implications for the West*, edited by Arkady Moshes and Matti Nojonen. Helsinki: Finnish Institute of International Affairs.

Ozerov, Viktor. 2005. "Informatsionnaya bezopasnost' Rossiiskoi Federatsii." *Politika*, 40. Accessed December 13, 2013 from http://www.politika-magazine.ru/45.html

Panchenko, Valery. 2005. "K voprosu o natsii i natsional'noi bezopasnosti." *Politika*, 86. Accessed December 13, 2013 from http://www.politika-magazine.ru/86.html

Pavlenko, Vladimir. 2009. "Kontseptsia vneshnei politiki: ispytanie krizisom." *Obozrevatel' – Observer*, 1. Accessed December 13, 2013 from http://www.rau.su/observer/N1_2009/006_024.pdf

Pouliot, Vincent. 2010. *International Security in Practice: The Politics of NATO-Russia Diplomacy*. Cambridge: Cambridge University Press.

Rog, Valentin. 2005. "O natsional'noi bezopasnosti Rossii." *Politika*, 53. Accessed December 13, 2013 from http://www.politika-magazine.ru/53.html

Rogov, Sergey. 1999. "Security Relations between Russia and the Western World." In *Russia's Place in Europe. A Security Debate*, edited by Kurt Spillmann and Andreas Wenger. Bern: Peter Land Publishers.

Rotberg, Robert. 2009. "How Corruption Compromises World Peace and Stability." In *Corruption, Global Security, and World Order*, edited by Robert Rotberg, 1–26. Cambridge, MA: World Peace Foundation and American Academy of Arts and Sciences.

Sheichuk, Ivan. 2011. "Rossia – garant mirovoi stabil'nosti." *Politika*, 90. Accessed December 13, 2013 from http://www.politika-magazine.ru/90.html

Spruds, Andris. 2006. "The NEPG and Russia's Gas Diplomacy: Latvian Perspective." *The Baltic Mosaic. Analytical Notes*, 1(5).

Stritzel, Holger. 2011. "Security, the translation." *Security Dialogue*, 41(4–5): 343–355. DOI:10.1177/0967010611418998

Stroev, Egor. 2005. "Bol'she gosudarstva, bol'she bezopasnosti." *Politika*, 40. Accessed December 13, 2013 from http://www.politika-magazine.ru/40.html

Sytin, Alexander. 2009. "Aktual'nye aspekty novoi arkhitektury bezopasnosti na postsovetskom prostranstve." *Problemy natsional'noi strategii*, 1: 48–61.

Trenin, Dmitry. 2011. "Putin the Peacemaker?" *Foreign Policy*, February 28. Accessed December 13, 2013 from http://www.foreignpolicy.com/articles/2012/02/28/putin_the_peacemaker

Trenin, Dmitri, and Alexey Malashenko. 2010. *Iran: a View from Moscow*. Washington, DC: Carnegie Endowment for International Peace.

Yemelianov, Gennadiy. 2005. "Zadachi obespechenia informatsionnoi bezopasnosti Rossii na sovremennom etape." *Politika*, 45. Accessed December 13, 2013 from http://www.politika-magazine.ru/45.html

Yurgens, Igor, ed. 2011. *ODKB: otvetstevennaya bezopasnost*. Moscow: INSOR.

Yurgens, Igor, A.A. Dynkin, and V.G. Baranovskiy, eds. 2009. *Arkhitektura Evroatlanticheskoi bezopasnosti*. Moscow: INSOR & Econ-Inform Publisher.

Chapter 24

Contextualizing Global Security: The Case of Turkey

Aslı Çalkıvik

Introduction

"Globalization imposes on us a moral responsibility; it forces on us the responsibility to see and hear other people's problems and the responsibility to solve them" (Aksam, 2012a). These observations belong to the Turkish Prime Minister Recep Tayyip Erdogan, which he articulated in a speech delivered at the 2012 UNCTAD Conference held in Qatar. It was a speech that unfolded in slightly provocative terms as Erdogan went on to suggest that "the global moral conscience that worried about dolphins, whales in extinction, rain forests" should not remain oblivious to what it has seen, heard and felt of "... the pain of children who are dying in Kabul, Gaza, Mogadishu, Bagdad, Hama and Hummus." Delivered at a time when the waves of the Arab uprising continued to pound the streets of Syria, and Turkey's insistent requests for NATO to adopt a determined stance in defense of the country's national security interests had little resonance in Brussels, this address was expressive of a broader trend in Turkey's security policies in the post-Cold War era, namely, a contested, yet, unequivocal re-orientation towards being a more vocal defender of globalized conceptions of security and a proactive actor in global security governance.

This chapter engages with the transformation in Turkey's security policies by attending to the contemporary developments and debates as it surveys Turkey's role in the formulation and implementation of the agenda of global security. While the popular uprisings in the Maghreb and the Middle East brought forth the country's role as a stabilizing factor and a model to be upheld in a region undergoing major transformations, this was only one example of the increasing number of episodes showing Turkey's emergence into the spotlight of global peace efforts and humanitarian initiatives since the 1990s. Apart from its contributions to the global security architecture through peacekeeping and humanitarian relief operations (ranging from Somalia to the former Yugoslavia, from Iraq to Afghanistan), Turkey has also been

The Handbook of Global Security Policy, First Edition. Edited by Mary Kaldor and Iavor Rangelov.
© 2014 John Wiley & Sons, Ltd. Published 2014 by John Wiley & Sons, Ltd.

increasingly at the forefront of non-military initiatives to mediate and help resolve conflicts, as exemplified by the initiatives undertaken to negotiate with Iran on its nuclear weapons program and its reconciliation efforts between Israel and Syria, Bosnia, and Serbia among others. Enhanced activism on the part of Turkey in relation to the global security agenda has not been devoid of controversies, however. Most prominent in this regard was the "Gaza Freedom Flotilla" incident when a Turkish nongovernmental organization (NGO) took part in an attempt to challenge the Israeli blockade of the Gaza Strip. The killing of Turkish civilians during the Israeli military operations carried out to prevent the ship from reaching the shore led to the deterioration of Turkey–Israeli relations as both sides condemned each other and questioned the legitimacy of their intentions. While Israel maintained that the close ties of the NGO to Hamas cast heavy doubt on its peaceful intentions, the Turkish state insisted on the idea that this was purely a civil society initiative that aimed to deliver humanitarian aid, arguing that Turkey approached the Middle East not "only through security and stability prisms, but also through [the prism] of human rights."

The first section of this chapter focuses on the impact of global security on policy formulation and implementation at the state level as it maps out the various ways in which Turkey has become a visible actor contributing to humanitarian relief efforts, peacekeeping and peacebuilding operations. Such a survey, while necessary, would itself be inadequate in terms of grappling with the multiple ways in which global security traverses local circumstances. Consequently, the second section attends to the historical background and institutional context of security policy making in Turkey. It elaborates the ways in which the policymaking context has been transforming since the 1990s and highlights the growing influence of civilian actors in a policy realm that has, until recently, been dominated by military and bureaucratic elites. One of the points that is emphasized in the discussion is the way conceptions of security has itself become a site of major contestation to the extent that globalized insecurities have provided a platform for the questioning/problematizing of the traditional state-centric security agenda, the latter being mainly articulated in terms of the principles of territorial integrity and cultural homogeneity of the nation-state. Finally, the third section turns to the points of contention and ongoing debates about Turkey's role in global security arrangements and the ongoing challenges confronting efforts to redefine the meaning of security.

Becoming a Global Security Actor

March 2012 marked the deadliest incident involving Turkish soldiers in Afghanistan when a military helicopter on a mission for the US-led NATO forces crashed to the ground, resulting in the death of 12 Turkish military personnel on board. With hardly any tribute paid to the four Afghan civilians on the ground, who were also killed during the crash, the ensuing public debate in Turkey revolved around a single question: "What are the Turkish soldiers doing in Afghanistan?" (TimeTurk, 2012). Opposition parties poured their outrage: some arguing that "Turkey [had] its own domestic problems, which need[ed] to be addressed first" while others suggested that Turkish soldiers were being used as shields by "Americans who cannot stroll safely through the streets" (Aksam, 2012b). Government representatives and the Turkish

Armed Forces were united in their defense of Turkey's participation in the peace-keeping operations. The announcement posted on the website of the Chief of General Staff highlighted the international obligations that Turkey had committed itself to since 2001 as a part of the international efforts to establish peace and stability in a key region for global security by educating Afghanistan's national defense forces, and aiding the Afghani population in matters of security, stability, and development. The Minister of Defense was unequivocal about the stance of Turkey, asserting that "national interests [could not] be defended solely within state borders" (TimeTurk, 2012). His statement was echoed by the Minister of Foreign Affairs Ahmet Davutoglu, who argued that "those who remain indifferent to the destiny of humanity by locking themselves up within their territorial borders would not be able to defend those borders either" (TimeTurk, 2012).

The public puzzlement over Turkish soldiers being on duty in a far off land for national security purposes would come as a surprise to observers of the transformations in Turkish state security policies in the post-Cold War era. As noted by a variety of scholars and policymakers, the last few decades witnessed a dramatic turn in Turkish foreign and security policy from a "minimalist, non-interventionist, *status quo* oriented" posture to an increasingly assertive, proactive one on a regional and global scale (Mufti, 2009). To fulfill its "increasing security responsibilities and security concerns in the aftermath of the Cold War", as suggested by a Turkish diplomat, the country had "significantly broadened its contributions to global security agenda, both in hard and soft terms, in a vast geography ranging from the Balkans to Afghanistan" (Ziyal, 2004). Consequently, it is argued that Turkey now stands as "an emerging hub of globalization and an internationalist humanitarian actor" (Bayer and Keyman, 2012) making crucial contributions to confronting the challenges posed by globalized insecurities.

Turkey's increasing contributions to international peacekeeping and peacebuilding operations is primary evidence lending support to the idea that Turkey is a major contributor to the implementation of the global security agenda (Oguzlu and Gungor, 2006; Bayer and Keyman, 2012). Prior to the 1990s, the only instance when Turkish troops were deployed abroad as part of an international peacekeeping operations was the Korean War between 1950 and 1953. As a strategic decision to demonstrate Turkey's commitment to the Western bloc and become a member of NATO, 15,000 military personnel were sent to Korea in a controversial move that bypassed the National Assembly (Lippe, 2000). Apart from this instance, fear of provoking the Soviet Union, the relative stability in Turkey's regional environment, and the prioritization of internal development over projecting power abroad, are given as the primary reasons for this reluctance in taking part in peacekeeping operations (Oguzlu and Gungor, 2006).

In sharp contrast to the Cold War years, Turkish security forces have started to actively participate in an increasing number of international and regional initiatives to manage globalized insecurities in the post-1990 era. Apart from serving on the UN military observer missions monitoring Iran–Iraq (1998–1991) and Iraq–Kuwait (1991–2003), Turkish armed forces have taken part in UN operations in Somalia, which was put under the command of a Turkish Lieutenant General for over a year; in the former Yugoslavia (where Turkey was responsible for monitoring the embargo on and implementing flight restrictions over Bosnia-Herzegovina); in the UN Protection

Force in Bosnia-Herzegovina; and in the UN observer missions in Georgia and Sudan (Guney, 2007; Oguzlu and Gungor, 2006). As of the December 1, 2011, Turkey was participating in nine UN peacekeeping operations around the world with a total of 505 personnel including 352 soldiers, 152 civilian police officers, and 1 expert (Republic of Turkey Ministry of Foreign Affairs, 2012a). In addition, Turkey has joined all NATO operations in the Balkans since 1995 – including Implementation Force (IFOR), Stabilization Force (SFOR), and Kosovo Force (KFOR) – and Turkish armed forces led the International Security Assistance Force (ISAF-II) in Afghanistan, taking over its command for six months in 2005, as well as contributing to NATO's Partnership for Peace Programs (Oguzlu and Gungor, 2006).

Turkey's non-military efforts in promoting global peace and stability by providing humanitarian assistance, contributing to developmental efforts, and acting as a mediator in a number of protracted conflicts are regarded as indicators of Turkey's commitment to maintaining global security (Bayer and Keyman, 2012). Viewing preventive diplomacy as "the most effective and economic method in terms of settlement of disputes" (Republic of Turkey Ministry of Foreign Affairs, 2012b), the Turkish Ministry of Foreign Affairs has been active in the internal reconciliation process in Iraq, Lebanon, and Kyrgyzstan; has contributed to trilateral cooperation processes with Serbia and Croatia in Bosnia-Herzegovina, and with Pakistan to ensure peace and security in Afghanistan; and has attempted to negotiate a nuclear swap deal with Iran (Republic of Turkey Ministry of Foreign Affairs, 2010). Furthermore, the significant increase in official development assistance and aid provided by Turkey is seen as expressive of its emergence as a donor country (United Nations Development Programme (UNDP), 2009). According to the Ministry of Foreign Affairs, the value of Turkey's in-cash and in-kind humanitarian assistance has exceeded US$250 million in 2005 and 2006 (Republic of Turkey Ministry of Foreign Affairs, 2012c). The Turkish International Cooperation and Development Agency (TIKA) has started to serve in 25 countries, undertaking over 100 projects in the areas of infrastructure, education, health, social services, agricultural production, and technological assistance (TIKA, 2010). While the Agency's operations have mostly focused on Central Asia, the Caucasus, and the Balkans, the most notable expansion of its activities has been in Africa, where TIKA allocated US$10 million in aid to 34 countries in 2010 (Fidan and Nurdun, 2008). While Turkey's recent "discovery of Africa" has mostly been economically driven (Ozkan, 2010), TIKA's projects in the region are interpreted as an indication of Turkey's "main foreign policy objectives, which see economy, security, and human betterment as intertwined aspects of regional and global stability and peace" (Bayer and Keyman, 2012, p. 77).

Because of its geographical position as a transit country between the East and the West, bordering eight countries in Asia and Europe, Turkey's role in combatting transnational organized crime – illicit trafficking of arms and drugs, human trafficking, and illegal immigration – is also noted by scholars as an important aspect of the country's responsibility in facing up to the challenges posed by globalization (Keser and Ozel, 2008). Apart from introducing new laws into the legal system, making new arrangements for police investigations and secret monitoring of suspected criminals, Turkey set up new institutions such as the National Force to Combat Human Trafficking to address such crimes, signed an agreement with the European Union on Precursors and Chemical substances, and started to enter into collaborative agreements with Europol on these issues (Toktas and Selimoglu, 2012). Lacking effective migration policies until very recently (Icduygu and Keyman, 2000), Turkey became a member of the International Organization of Migration (IOM) in 2004, and Turkish officials started to cooperate closely with the UN High Commissioner for Refugees, the IOM, as well as non-governmental organizations like the Human Resources Development Foundation to prevent human trafficking and illegal migration and provide assistance to victims of trafficking. The country has also been an active participant in the international campaign against pirates and arms smugglers in the Northern Indian Ocean (Republic of Turkey Ministry of Foreign Affairs, 2012d).

As this brief survey suggests, security policy and practice in Turkey have been transforming in the face of the multiple and complex security challenges posed by globalization. In order to elaborate how global security concerns traverse local circumstances, the next section attends to the historical background and institutional context of security policy making and elaborates the ways in which, not only Turkey's security policies, but also the very context of policymaking has been transforming in the post-Cold War era, with significant consequences on the conceptualization of national security.

Continuity and Change in Turkey's Security-Policies

Sovereign decision on who is an enemy and who is a friend is what gives the modern nation-state as a political organization its distinctive feature (Schmitt, 2007). Tightly knit with existential questions of survival, securing the sovereign state and the nation against its enemies has been an enduring aspect of modernity's politics of security. In this regard, Turkey parallels other nation-states with different political, social, and cultural structures. As the Ministry of Foreign Affairs notes, security is primarily defined as "ensuring the survival of the population; protecting territorial integrity and preserving the basic identity of a nation, as shaped by political, economic, social and cultural traits" (Republic of Turkey Ministry of Foreign Affairs, 2012e). Despite this continuity in the politics of security in Turkey, what has been changing – in tandem with the changing international context in the post-Cold War era – is the definition of what constitutes a danger and who can legitimately participate in the political process of defining the enemies.

The constitutive aspect of all nation-states noted earlier – namely, the fear that binds the nation to the state through the fear of enemies – takes the particular form of what is termed "Sevres Phobia" (or Sevres syndrome, Sevres complex) in the context of Turkey due to the historical legacy of the insecurities inherited from the Ottoman Empire. Named after the Sevres Treaty (1920), which was drawn up by the victors of World War I and foresaw the carving up of Ottoman territories into occupational zones, this phobia entails the fear that the historical experience of the former Empire can be relived anytime and that securing the Turkish Republic requires being constantly vigilant against enemies – internal as well as external – who seek to bring about the dissolution of the nation-state (Jung and Piccoli, 2001). As a consequence of this historical legacy, the concept of security has become synonymous with the term "foreign policy" since the founding of the Republic, where the military and ministry of foreign affairs have constituted the two pillars of Turkish foreign policy establishment (Candar, 2004, pp. 55–56). Perpetuating a perspective on the world that sees

Turkey as the loneliest country in the world surrounded by the largest number of internal and external enemies, this fear finds receptive ears in the public, largely as a result of the process of dissemination of militarist values in society through education, and every day reproduction of the nationalist discourse that envisions modern Turkey as a country that is "for the Turks, by the Turks" (Altinay, 2004).

While the realpolitik understanding and military definition of the concept of security has been one of the consistent features of the security culture in Turkey until recently (Karaosmanoglu, 2000; Aydin, 2003), geopolitical discourse has played a pivotal role in the reproduction of the fear of existential threats and the militarized conceptions of national security. As Turkey's geo-strategic location, with its borders in Europe, the Middle East, and the Caucasus, is recognized as a factor in allowing Turkey to play a role in world politics far beyond its size, population, and economic strength (Aydin, 1999), it is also utilized to highlight the country's unique security needs and interests due to its position amidst three different security complexes – termed as the "Turkish Bermuda triangle" (Kazan, 2005) – which require Turkey to be vigilant in its security assessments and military capabilities. The assumption of "geographical determinism", i.e. that geographic location determines state interests defined in terms of national security, works towards consolidating the already dominant role of the military in formulating and implementing state security policies by virtue of its mastery of geopolitical knowledge (Bilgin, 2007b).

One of the most significant consequences of the traditional conception of security as defending the territorial integrity and the cultural homogeneity of the nation-state has been the enduring prominence accorded to the Turkish military as the main actor that formulates and implements policies to eradicate the "dangers" to national security (Cizre, 2003; Drorian, 2005). Consolidating its political power thorough legal and constitutional provisions and becoming a collective economic actor in its own right (Akca, 2002), the Turkish Armed Forces (TAF) has exerted its influence over security policies mainly through the National Security Council (NSC), which was established in the aftermath of the 1960 military coup d'etat and incorporated a year later in the new Constitution. As the main institution responsible for the formulation of the national security policy, the NSC underwent a number of changes in terms of its composition and the power it wielded over security policymaking, most notably, in the aftermath of the 1980 military coup. Its responsibility "to prepare the guidelines for the national security policy as well as to amend and revise this policy" was later changed with the 1982 Constitution and defined as the power "to formulate views with regard to taking decisions on the identification, formulation and implementation of the national security policy and ensuring the necessary coordination" (Secretariat-General of the National Security Council, 2013). The influence of the military was further enhanced by the National Security Council Law of 1983, which stipulated that the Secretary-General of the NSC would serve the high-ranking officers in the military. This was a crucial move because the Secretary-General of the NSC was responsible for the preparation of the National Security Policy Document (NSPD) that constitutes the foundations for Turkey's security policies. The legal provisions that granted it complete autonomy in determining the military budget, production and procurement of arms and weapons, and promotions within its ranks, as well as military jurisdiction through the system of State Security Courts (which were endowed with the responsibility to oversee the trials of "crimes against the state" and other breaches of Anti-Terror Law as a part of its bestowed duty by the Constitution to protect and preserve the Turkish Republic) consolidated the central role played by the military in shaping Turkish politics in general and security policies in particular (Cizre, 2003; Drorian, 2005).

The concept of national security – whose circulation had remained limited to the military circles throughout the 1950s – was introduced into the political lexicon in Turkey and incorporated in legislation around the same time when the NSC was established in 1960. After its introduction, national security served as the primary means to legitimize the status of the military's new representative organ, the NSC (Ozcan, 2010), and eventually become "the key concept organizing thinking and action" (Bilgin, 2007a, p. 562) in matters relating to security.[1] Although prioritizing the survival of the state – its territorial integrity, its secular, culturally homogenous characters as sacrosanct – over the rights of its citizens has been an enduring aspect of security discourses and policies since the early days of the Turkish Republic, after the introduction of national security to the political lexicon in the 1960s, the concept became the principle criterion by which to determine foreign policy and set the nation-state's security agenda (Cizre, 2003; Ozcan, 2010). A deeply ambiguous term that paves the way to arbitrary practices, national security has operated as the vanishing point where domestic politics and foreign policy converge, and securing the nation-state becomes the principle means to bloc rights claims. The overlapping of domestic policing and foreign security policy through the concept of national security became especially pronounced during the 1990s as the perception of strategic threats were undergoing profound transformations within the post-Cold War context. During the 1990s, the NSPD (also known as "the Red Book") was modified twice, broadening the national security agenda where internal threats had started to take precedence over external enemies. While the 1992 NSPD identified Kurdish separatism and terrorism as the foremost security concerns, the 1997 NSPD added reactionary Islamism (irtica) to the list as a paramount threat to national security. Although less noted by security analysts, national security has also served to delimit and to police, not only separatist or religious movements, but also other forms of oppositional politics and dissent. The NSC meeting of September 28, 1995 provides an illuminating example in this regard. Convening primarily to discuss the developments in Northern Iraq, the Council incorporated the ongoing massive strikes in the public sector as a "[threat to] the security of the country" and demanded that they immediately be postponed (Urhan and Celik, 2010). By the end of the 1990s, one analyst notes, it had become difficult to find a political or societal topic that did not concern national security (Ozcan, 2000).

These transformations in state security policies – namely, the securitization of political questions and the enhancement of oppressive state practices in the name of national security – need to be contextualized within two major developments occurring a decade apart: the domestic political transformations of 1980 and the restructuring of the international system in 1990. Turkey entered 1980 with the introduction of a major plan (commonly known as the "January 24 decisions") to restructure the economy along neoliberal lines as a response to the economic crisis of 1977–1980. The provisions of the 1961 Constitution and the social reactions it provoked were a great hindrance to its implementation. The military take-over that occurred only months after (September 12, 1980) allowed for the top–down imposition of the Structural Adjustment Programs and the move towards full liberalization of the economy by eradicating any possible reactions from the Leftist movements through the imprisonment of its leaders and cadres, closing down of its parties and unions, and the banning of strikes and union activities under martial law. The severe repression during the military rule took a heavy toll on the Kurdish nationalist movement as well, with reportedly 81,000 Kurds detained between 1980 and 1982, paving the way for the "Kurdish Nationalist Resurgence" in the 1980s under the leadership of the Kurdistan Workers Party (PKK) (Romano, 2006, p. 49). Heavy prohibitions on freedom of thought and expression, political organization, and protest would be inscribed in the 1982 Constitution and the penal code. Consolidation of the national security state could go on uninterrupted after the return to civilian rule in 1983 because Turkish governments continued to act "with the mentality and approach of the *de facto* martial law" – a situation termed as civil martial law (Uskul, 1997) – and refrained from repealing constitutional and legal regulations that restricted rights and freedoms for national security purposes.[2]

Coming to terms with the post-Cold War developments in Turkey's security policies requires taking note of these domestic political developments because it was under the agency of the civilian inheritors of the post-1980 military regime that a "fundamental change" (Karaosmanoglu, 2000) in Turkey's foreign policy and security culture in the 1980s and 1990s would occur. The importance of this era is also highlighted by scholars who suggest that understanding Turkey's security policies in the 2000s would be inadequate unless "the legacy of this era [were born] in mind" (Kirisci, 2006). Turgut Ozal (author of the January 24 decisions, Prime Minister 1983–1989, and President until his death in 1993) and the ruling Motherland Party stand as the ideological precursor to the Adalet ve Kalkinma Partisi (AKP) (Justice and Development Party) with its nationalist, conservative posture and full embracement of the neoliberal project and free-market fundamentalism. It was during the 1990s that Turkey steered away from being a *status quo* oriented, cautious actor that refrained from taking risks in international politics towards playing an active role in regional and global politics by pursuing a diversified foreign policy enabled by the post-Cold War political context (Aral, 2001; Kirisci, 2006; Larrabee, 2010; Sayari, 2000). It was also around this political period that "neo-Ottomanism" – initial pronouncements that would concretize in the visions of "strategic depth" formulated by the current Minister of Foreign Affairs Ahmet Davutoglu – would emerge as one of the guiding threads shaping Turkish foreign and security policies (Yavuz, 1998).[3]

At the international level, the ending of the Cold War and the developments in its aftermath had a deep impact on Turkey given the pace and the depth of change that happened in the country's geographical proximity with the breaking-down of the Soviet Union, dismantling of the Warsaw Pact, the break-out of civil war in Yugoslavia, the changing political map of the Balkans, Iraq's invasion of Kuwait and the ensuing Gulf War, the establishment of Palestinian National Authority, and the developments in Northern Iraq. Initial disorientation and the problem of adaptation to the new security environment by the Turkish state and the security establishment has led some observers to term the 1990s as Turkey's "longest decade" (Ozcan and Kut, 2000). One of the initial concerns in diplomatic circles was the fear that Turkey would lose its strategic importance in the Western community's security arrangements. Having served as a reliable member of NATO throughout the Cold

War, the dissolution of the Soviet threat and new debates about the future of the alliance, exacerbated these worries. Joining the international coalition to oust Iraq from Kuwait during the Gulf War I (1990–1991) was therefore an important turning point in terms of proving Turkey's geo-strategic importance in the new world order (Lesser, 1999; Sayari, 2000). As Sayari (2000, p. 171) notes, despite the reluctance shown by the military elites, President Ozal, "who was convinced that Iraq's invasion of Kuwait offered an opportunity to demonstrate his country's geo-strategic importance to the West, managed to maneuver Turkey into becoming a central player in the Allied coalition." Tracing Turkey's current security policies in the Middle East to this era, Cook (2011a, p. 718) also notes that the new activism in the region during Ozal's tenure constituted an "exception" because Turkey "traditionally sought to avoid entangling Ankara in the politics, rivalries, and conflicts of the Middle East."

Yet, the new entanglement in the region introduced new concerns for the State's security agenda during the 1990s. Apart from the economically adverse effects of the Gulf War due to loss of trade and closure of the Kurkuk–Ceyhan pipeline, its aftermath witnessed the internationalization of the Kurdish question and the creation of an allied-protected autonomous region in Northern Iraq through "Operation Provide Comfort" led by the United States, Britain, and, early on, France. This development enhanced fears that a potentially independent Kurdish region would encourage an already active Kurdish separatist insurrection led by the PKK. What complicated matters more was Syria's provision of safe heaven to the PKK and its leader Ocalan as a bargaining chip in the contentious water issue with Turkey that came about with the Southeast Anatolia Project (GAP), which comprised 22 dams controlling the flow of Euphrates and Tigris (Altunisik and Martin, 2011). Improvements in bilateral relations with Syria and the ensuing close cooperation in tourism, trade, investment, and even joint military maneuvers would have to wait until Ocalan's expulsion from the country in 1999 under intense military pressure from Turkey.

Whilst "hard issues" remained on the agenda throughout this decade, "one of the most striking developments in the 1990s with respect to Turkish foreign policy was that the concept of security became much more complicated and multifaceted" (Kirisci, 2006, p. 31) and insecurities started to be reconceptualized within the context of globalization (Bilgin, 2005). Perhaps most telling in this regard is the statement made by Ismail Hakki Karadayi (then Chief of General Staff), which defined two main categories of threats in the post-Cold War context. The first category included "illegal trafficking of arms and drugs, international terrorism … the proliferation of weapons of mass destruction and environmental damage" while the second category referred to "ethnic conflicts, intolerance, radical nationalism and all kinds of separatism, and human trade in the form of migration" (Bilgin, 2005, p. 190). One of the important consequences of the broadening of the security agenda beyond "high politics" to include "low politics" was the increasing involvement of agencies, beyond the military and Ministry of Foreign Affairs, in foreign policymaking (Kirisci, 2006). This not only included other state agencies such as the police, Ministry of Interior, social security agencies, but also some NGOs started to become active in addressing these novel sources of insecurity.

In addition to the broadening of the security agenda to include "soft threats", another noteworthy development was that the Turkish armed forces, which would remain the most influential actor in shaping the security policies throughout the decade, started to undergo its own Revolution in Military Affairs in response to the changing nature of war-making in the era of globalization (Balta Paker, 2010). The concept of "total war" was abandoned in favor of "low-intensity conflict" – institutional changes were introduced to decrease reliance on manpower and troops were restructured to acquire more flexibility and speed as a response to the new geo-strategic circumstances.

The post-Cold War dynamics, according to security analysts, had "transformed Turkey from a flank country of collective security arrangements of a collective security mechanism into the epicenter of a new strategic zone" (Candar, 2004, p. 51). Despite various non-military efforts towards securing the new world order (such as the initiatives taken to build cooperative ties in the Black Sea region, attempts to strengthen economic relations with the newly independent states in the former Soviet Republic, diplomatic efforts in the Balkans and other militarized disputes such as the Armenian–Azeri conflict), the main legacy of this era with respect to Turkey's security policies is the confrontational stance taken against neighboring countries and the continuation of a militarized approach to the political questions posed by Kurdish aspirations, as reflected by the "$2^{1}/_{2}$ War Strategy" (Ozcan and Kut, 2000). Developed in the mid-1990s, the latter called for strategic planning and building military capacities to fight simultaneous wars on two fronts (against Greece and Syria) and a civil war (against Kurdish separatism). Although Turkey's security policies "seem[ed] to follow the global developments insofar as it has become increasingly preoccupied with responding to soft security concerns" during this era, "contrary to global trends, the Turkish military's search for a wider reading of the idea of security remain[ed] fixated on the conventional understanding of the problem" (Cizre, 2003, p. 4).

At the turn of the millennium, however, Turkey's security policies started to take a drastically different course as a result of the domestic political transformation and reform process (Aras and Karakayapolat 2007). One of the significant developments has been the increasing problematization of traditional conceptions of national security by political actors, most vocally in the aftermath of the European Union's granting of candidacy status to Turkey in 1999. In a "path-breaking speech" (Cizre, 2003, p. 1) delivered at his Party Convention in 2001, former Deputy Prime Minister and the leader of the Motherland Party Mesut Yilmaz identified the main obstacle for Turkey's integration with the European Union as "the national security syndrome". According to Yilmaz, not only was "national security" too broadly defined, but that there was no civilian oversight in the course of determining security priorities and strategies. The significance of this speech can not be overstated because it was the first time that a civilian political actor had openly criticized the national security discourse (Bilgin, 2007a; Cizre, 2003). Although Yilmaz's speech received mixed reactions, his vision of increased involvement and oversight of civilians over security policymaking would eventually be realized through the constitutional reforms and institutional changes introduced after 1999. Enhancing the power of civilian government vis-à-vis the military, these reforms included the changing balance of power at the NSC towards civilian members, appointment of a civilian Secretary to the NSC, removal of representatives from the Council of Higher Education and the Radio and Television High Council, and bringing the Turkish Armed Forces under the judicial control of the Court of Accounts (Aras and Karakayapolat, 2007, p. 474). Although the extent to which the military has actually lost its authority over matters of security with these reforms (Bilgin, 2005) and whether the civilian governments in power have departed from the Kemalist[4] military line in foreign policy making (Robins, 2007) are ongoing points of debate, the civilianization of the security-policy making process and the advances made towards "de-mythologization of the national security concept" (Cizre, 2003), are nevertheless significant developments that cannot be simply dismissed.

The impetus provided by the accession process to the European Union played an important role in these reform efforts. Until very recently, the conditions put forth by the European Union towards democratization – especially the calls for decentral-ization of political authority and the recognition of social, cultural, and educational rights of different ethnic communities – were received by the traditional state elite as a threat to the unitary nation-state character of the Republic, inhibiting Turkey's internalization of the EU's security identity (Oguzlu, 2003). The 1999 decision of the European Union to grant candidacy to Turkey laid the background for the AKP-led efforts towards constitutional amendments improving political and human rights and strengthening of the rule of law (Kirisci, 2006; Bilgin, 2007a). Furthermore, Turkey's position on two issues, that are regarded as high priority to its vital strategic interests – ongoing territorial disputes with Greece and the Cyprus issue (Yilmaz, 2006) – has undergone a transformation during the post-1999 era. This change became most manifest in the dramatic turn, by Turkey, on the Cyprus problem, from the traditional *status quo* oriented stance, toward a more conciliatory approach (Kirisci, 2006).[5]

There is almost a consensus among scholars and policymakers about the role played by AKP in carrying out political reforms away from a state-centric secu-rity paradigm, and contributing to the transformation of Turkey's national security agenda from a "conservative, traditional, and NATO-centric" conception towards a multi-faceted understanding that "embrace[s] aspects of economic security, human security, security of identity, other 'soft' matters" (Lesser, 2010, p. 258; see also Altunisik and Martin, 2011; Aras and Karakayapolat, 2007). Coming to power as a majority government a year after it was established by a splinter group (calling themselves "reformers") from the Islamist Virtue Party, AKP has won three gen-eral elections in a row (2002, 2007, and 2011), receiving half of the ballots cast in the latest general elections. Holding a clear majority in the parliament, the Party pushed through political and legislative reforms, restructuring the judiciary and civil–military relations. With their claim to speak for those who were marginalized and oppressed by the dominant political, cultural, and economic elite throughout the Republican era, the party has presented itself as the agent of change, not only at the domestic level, but also in terms of its foreign and security policies.

The contours of Turkey's new security policy vision and the principles inform-ing those policies are encapsulated in the "zero problems with neighbors" concept articulated by Ahmet Davutoglu, who served (2002–2009) as the chief advisor to the Prime Minister after AKP came to power and was appointed as the Minister of Foreign Affairs in 2009 (Hounshell, 2010). Depicted by some observers more as "an aspiration and strong preference rather than as an invariable guide to practice" (Falk, 2012), this policy is presented as an adaptation of the Kemalist principle of "peace at home, peace abroad" to contemporary global circumstances by viewing Turkey's neighborhood through the prism of opportunities, rather than perception of threats, and of aiming, not merely to settle problems with neighbors, but to transform Turkey's neighborhood itself (Davutoglu, 2012). According to Davutoglu, realizing these goals calls for a new policy approach that breaks with Turkey's decades of alienation from its surrounding region and makes use of its historical and geographical ties dating back to the Ottoman era as a strategic advantage ("strategic depth") in pursuing a multidimensional policy towards providing stability and security in its areas of influence (Davutoglu, 2009). The new security vision highlights the need to dispense with Sevres phobia in shaping security policies; a point most vividly captured by an anecdote delivered by Davutoglu (2011) in his "Vision 2023" speech:

> "[E]ven in the families, you cannot have zero problems. You will have problems. The most important thing [is] to change the mentality, the psyche that we are surrounded by enemies … In the Council of Europe … an Armenian parliamentarian said: "What do you think about Armenian–Turkish relations?" I said we have two categories of state. She thought that I will be saying friends and enemies. I said "friends and potential friends. No third category."

An important transformation, noted by scholars, in Turkey's security policies pursued under the AKP regime pertains to "the government-led desecuritization process in which previously securitized issues are now being gradually defined as political issues" (Oguzlu, 2007, p. 88), most significantly in the realm of ethnic and religious identity politics. Transformation of policies pursued in Iraq (reliance on a holistic approach and, rather than using the Turkoman community as a strategic card against the Kurds, attempting to build cooperative relations with the Kurdish Regional Government) and improving relations with Iran (a development that stands in sharp contrast to the dominant approach in the 1990s that viewed Iran as a major source of threat for attempting to export the Islamic Revolution to Turkey and dismantling the secular Republic) are regarded as the significant policy outcomes of this transformation (Aras and Karakayapolat, 2007).

Emphasis put on the notion of human security and the importance of international cooperation for the effective governance of globalized insecurities represents another significant aspect of the new security policy discourse and practice. Problematizing the privileging of military understanding of security, the new approach calls for "a much more comprehensive understanding of security" that would include economic, cultural, and political dimensions (Davutoglu, 2010). The methods that need to be used to achieve human security, according to Davutoglu, should combine "preventive security" with "visionary security" and, rather than merely responding to crisis, crises should be prevented before they emerge by pursuing "a policy of proactive peace diplomacy." What is interesting to note, is that in this broader understanding of security, *human* security and *national* security are not regarded as mutually exclusive. Instead, respect for the territorial integrity and sovereignty of the nation-state, it is argued, are the *sine qua non* for building trans-border relations as the conditions of possibility for achieving human security.

Paralleling the changing security discourse and practices, the last decade has also witnessed the emergence of a new group of civil society actors as dynamic agents in the implementation of this broader understanding of security, through humanitarian assistance and development initiatives. Most notable among them are the Gulen Hizmet (Service) Movement and Insan Hak ve Hurriyetleri Insani Yardim Vakfi (IHH, The Foundation for Human Rights and Freedoms and Humanitarian Relief) (Eissenstat, 2011). Regarded as "the largest and the most successful transnational Muslim outreach movement of the contemporary age" (Pandya and Gallagher, 2012, p. 1), the Hizmet movement has been active in education, operating schools attended by more than 2 million students. It has also founded institutions across the world to promote interfaith and intercultural dialogue. Through its charity organ "Kimse yok mu?" (Is there no one?), it has been providing aid and carrying out other humanitarian projects across the world in places ranging from the tsunami-hit Indonesia to Palestine, Peru, Bangladesh, Sudan, and Haiti. Attracting international attention with the Gaza Flotilla incident of 2010, IHH provides emergency relief and social aid, undertaking educational, cultural, and sanitation programs in different parts of the world (IHH, 2012). Most recently, during the Syrian Crisis when more than 35,000 Syrian took refuge within Turkey's borders, IHH, in collaboration with Qatar Charity, carried out a number of aid projects as part of the "Syria Cries for Help Campaign", providing food, medical aid packages, clothes, tents, and generators.

Lingering Questions

Turkey's new security vision and policy agenda gained renewed attention and interest during the massive popular uprisings in the Maghreb and the Middle East against neoliberal economic policies and decades-old corrupt, oppressive governments. Amidst ongoing debates over the extent to which Turkey could serve as an "attractive political and democratic model for both secularists and Islamists in the region" (Taspinar, 2011; also Dede, 2011), a more vexing question that emerged during the course of these tumultuous developments pertained to the sustainability of Turkey's regional security policy and whether the Arab Spring meant a "Turkish Fall" (Cook, 2011b). Even before the uprisings, there were already signs that the "zero problems with neighbors" policy might be "colliding with intractable realities on the ground" (Tisdall, 2010), but the crises in Syria and Libya represented a turning point for the Turkish state's new foreign policy direction because they were where "the mismatch between Turkey's regional foreign policy rhetoric and practice became much more apparent" (Dall, 2012, p. 257). Building closer economic and cultural ties and using "soft power" to encourage a gradual transformation in Syria towards a functioning liberal order had utterly failed in the face of the hard politics of geopolitical calculations. Furthermore, the dramatic reversal in the stance taken by Turkey towards these crises (in the case of Libya, the government's initial reluctance to support international efforts to pressure Gaddafi to step down and its resistance even to putting in place economic sanctions gave way to full support of a NATO-led intervention; in the case of Syria, initial diplomatic attempts to persuade the Assad regime to end the oppression and take the necessary steps towards a peaceful transition was replaced by an ardent support for international pressure on Syria and armed opposition groups) and its utter silence in the face of other oppressive Sunni regimes in the region raised questions about the double standards in Turkey's new foreign and security policy (Vahedi, 2011).

The developments in Libya and Syria are also significant in terms of ongoing debates about Turkey's international orientation. The deterioration of bilateral relations with Israel in the aftermath of the Gaza War of 2008–2009, the rapprochement with Iran, close relations with the Sudanese regime accused of genocide, and open contacts with Hamas, had led critics to declare that Turkey was shifting axis and diverging from Western policies towards the Middle East (Altunisik and Martin, 2011). Increasing self-confidence about the role Turkey could play in the region, coupled with the stalling membership process to the European Union, were regarded as contributing factors to a new self-understanding that Turkey was not entirely dependent on the West (Walker, 2007). Yet, the unfolding of the Libyan and Syrian crises also cast doubt on hasty conclusions about a possible shift of axis for Turkey. Initial hesitations aside, in both cases the AKP government closely coordinated its policies with the West. According to some analysts, the crisis in Syria, where a power struggle with Iran is at issue, is bound to bring Turkey and the United States into closer cooperation (Zaaiter, 2012). In this regard, it is worth noting Turkey's decision to host NATO's American-designed missile shield, which was hailed as "the most significant military cooperation between Washington and Ankara since 2003" when Turkey refused to allow US troops to cross Turkish territory during the invasion of Iraq (Shanker, 2011). Consequently, whether or not Turkey's "new" security policies are the regional expression of the global hegemony of the United States (Mufti, 2011; Tugal, 2007) is a question that needs to be carefully examined by avoiding dichotomous approaches that seek an either/or answer to Turkey's international orientation.

Another question pertains to the extent to which a cosmopolitan understanding of security has actually started to take root in domestic politics and political culture. Pertinent in this regard is the extent to which the demythologization of the national security concept discussed earlier has translated into actively breaking away from the national security reflex. Given that national security still bears its imprint in dealing with the Kurdish question, and the concept is frequently evoked as a stop gag during debates on constitutional reform as a way to block progressive change (Human Rights Watch, 2010),[6] a crucial question awaits answers: is the understanding of security in Turkey still confined within the national security paradigm, this time dressed up in civilian costumes?[7]

The Arab uprisings in general, and the ongoing conflict in Syria in particular, has so far had a sobering effect in terms of understanding the limits posed to Turkey playing the role of a global security actor – a vision that the Turkish state elite has been more vocally aspiring to in the recent years. According to one observer, the "events in Syria are testing Turkish foreign policy to the limits" (Hakura, 2011). The failure of Ankara's initial strategy of mediating a democratic transition in Syria was replaced with open support to the Syrian National Council and the Free Syrian Army – a move interpreted as a declaration of war by the permanent representative of Syria at the United Nations. The prospects of a military confrontation was heightened in October 2012 as Turkey attacked targets in Syria and the Turkish Parliament authorized military offensives into foreign countries in response to the errant landing of Syrian artillery shells in the Turkish border town of Akcakale, killing five people. Although NATO's approval of the deployment of Patriot missiles along the Turkey–Syria border has assuaged fears of possible unilateral action, it has been met with protests in

Turkey, where the public at large continues to oppose a military confrontation with Syria (Eurasianet, 2012). Anxious about Turkey's lining up with the Western-backed Sunni coalition in the region (Tugal, 2012), the decision has also raised tensions with neighboring Iran, whose military chief of staff has asserted that the deployment of missiles could lead to a world war. In the light of these developments, perhaps the key question to be posed is: can Turkey be considered as "yet another victim of the unforeseen consequence of the Arab Spring" (Seale, 2012)?

Notes

1. National security is a concept that is adopted not only by other nation-states, but also by supranational organization as evidenced by the European Convention on Human Rights, which states that "There shall be no interference by a public authority with the exercise of [the right to respect for his private and family life, his home and his correspondence] except such as is in accordance with the law and is necessary in a democratic society in the interests of national security, public safety or the economic well-being of the country, for the prevention of disorder or crime, for the protection of health or morals, or for the protection of the rights and freedoms of others." Accessed December 13, 2013 from http://www.echr.coe.int/Documents/Convention_ENG.pdf In the context of Turkey, what is generally recognized as problematic is not the national security concept per se, but the imbalance between the civilian and military authorities in drafting the policies towards protecting national security. See, for instance, Bilgin 2007a.
2. Recognizing that human rights had become an international issue and a major obstacle during this era, affecting negatively the relations with the European Community, two fundamental steps were taken by the Turgut Ozal government to raise Turkey's domestic and international credentials: the lifting of the ban on former politicians and the release of political prisoners in 1986–1987 and the acceptance of the right for an individual petition to join the European Human Rights Council. Both of these steps were taken because they were regarded as instrumental at a time when Turkey was applying for full membership to the European Union (Dagi, 2001). Speaking at the National Assembly, Ozal would suggest that human rights could be exploited in foreign policy and "would lead to an interventionist international system and end up with destabilization in domestic and international politics" (Dagi, 2001, p. 57). Ongoing cases of torture and hunger strikes reported by Amnesty International during this period would cast heavy doubt on the idea that the progressive steps taken towards the recognition and respect of human rights amounted to more than superficial moves.
3. Although contemporary debates privilege the Islamic orientation of the AKP as the driving factor behind neo-Ottomanism (Rubin, 2004; Schenker, 2009), it is necessary to recall that the neo-Ottoman vision was enabled by the ideological reorientation in the aftermath of the 1980 military coup "which reformulated the main principles of Kemalism, nationalism and Islam" and, as declared by the Bulent Ulusu government (1980–1983), the Turkish–Islamic synthesis became accepted as the new state ideology (Yavuz, 1998, p. 30).
4. Named after the founder of the Republic Mustafa Kemal, Kemalism denotes an ideology founded on six core principles of which secularism, republicanism, and nationalism are regarded as sacrosanct. For an authoritative discussion of Kemalism in English, see Parla and Davison, 2004.
5. For a discussion of the challenges posed to this novel approach aiming at desecuritizing the Cyprus issue, see Bilgin, 2007a.

6. The nationalist turn of the JDP's stance since 2005 is reflected not only in the stepped up military campaign against the PKK, but also through the imprisonment of oppositional voices of all stripes (ranging from students, to journalists and academics).
7. For a careful exposition of this argument, see Gambetti, 2013.

References

Akca, Ismet. 2002. "Kollektif Bir Sermayedar Olarak Turk Silahli Kuvvetleri." *Birikim*, 161/162: 80–101.

Aksam. 2012a (April 21). "Kuresel Vicdan Olen Cocuklari da gormeli." Accessed October 24, 2012 from http://www.aksam.com.tr/kuresel-vicdan-olen-cocuklari-da-gormeli–111994h.html

Aksam. 2012b (March 16). "Turk Askerinin Afganistan'da Ne isi Var?" Accessed October 24, 2012 from http://www.aksam.com.tr/turk-askerinin-afganistanda-ne-isi-var–105204h.html

Altinay, Ayse Gul. 2004. *The Myth of the Military-Nation: Militarism, Gender, and Education in Turkey*. New York, NY: Palgrave MacMillan.

Altunisik, Meliha B., and Lenore G. Martin. 2011. "Making Sense of Turkish Foreign Policy in the Middle East under AKP." *Turkish Studies*, 12(4): 569–587.

Aral, Berdal. 2001. "Dispensing with Tradition? Turkish Politics and International Society during the Ozal decade, 1983–1993." *Middle Eastern Studies*, 37(1): 72–88.

Aras, Bulent, and Rabia Karakayapolat. 2007. "Turkey and the Middle East: Frontiers of the New Geographic Imagination." *Australian Journal of international Affairs*, 61(4): 471–488.

Aydin, Mustafa. 1999. "Geographical Blessing versus Geopolitical Curse: Great Power Security Agendas for the Black Sea Region and a Turkish Alternative." *Southeast European and Black Sea Studies*, 9(3): 271–285.

Aydin, Mustafa. 2003. "Securitization of History and Geography: Understanding of Security in Turkey." *Southeast European and Black Sea Studies*, 3(2): 163–184.

Balta Paker, Evren. 2010. "Dis Tehditten Ic Tehdide: Turkiye'de Doksanlarda Ulusal Guvenligin Yeniden Insasi." In *Turkiye'de Ordu, Devlet ve Guvenlik Siyaseti*, edited by Evren Balta Paker and Ismet Akca, 407–432. Istanbul: Bilgi Universitesi Yayinlari.

Bayer, Resat and Fuat Keyman. 2012. "Turkey: An Emerging Hub of Globalization and Internationalist Humanitarian Actor?" *Globalizations*, 9(1): 73–90.

Bilgin, Pinar. 2005. "Turkey's Changing Security Discourse: The Challenge of Globalisation." *European Journal of Political Research*, 44: 175–201.

Bilgin, Pinar. 2007a. "Making Turkey's Transformation Possible: Claiming 'Security-speak' – Not Desecuritization!" *Southeast and Black Sea Studies*, 7(4): 555–571.

Bilgin, Pinar. 2007b. "'Only Strong States Can Survive in Turkey's Geography': The Uses of 'Geopolitical Truths' in Turkey." *Political Geography*, 26: 740–756.

Candar, Cengiz. 2004. "Turkish Foreign Policy and the War on Iraq." In *The Future of Turkish Foreign Policy*, edited by Lenore G. Martin and Dimitris Keridis, 47–60. Cambridge, London: MIT Press.

Cizre, Umit. 2003. "Demythologizing the National Security Concept: the Case of Turkey." *The Middle East Journal*, 213–230.

Cook, Steven A. 2011a. "The USA, Turkey, and the Middle East: Continuities, Challenges, and Opportunities." *Turkish Studies*, 12(4): 717–726.

Cook, Steven A. 2011b. "Arab Spring, Turkish Fall." *Foreign Policy*, May 5 2011. Accessed October 24, 2012 from http://www.foreignpolicy.com/articles/2011/05/05/arab_spring_turkish_fall

Dagi, Ihsan. 2001. "Human Rights and Democratization." *Southeast European and Black Sea Studies*, 1(3): 51–68.

Dall, Emel Parlar. 2012. "The Transformation of Turkey's Relations with the Middle East: Illusion or Awakening?" *Turkish Studies*, 13(2): 245–267.

Davutoglu, Ahmet. 2009. *Stratejik Derinlik: Turkiye'nin Uluslararasi Konumu*. Istanbul: Kure Yayinlari.

Davutoglu, Ahmet. 2010. Speech delivered at the 7th ISSS Regional Security Summit of the Manama Dialogue, December 3, 2010. Accessed October 24, 2012 from http://www.mfa.gov.tr/statement-by-h_e_-ahmet-davutoglu_-minister-of-foreign-affairs-of-the-republic-of-turkey-at-the-7th-iiss-regional-security-summit-of-the-manama-dialogue_-3-december-2010.en.mfa

Davutoglu, Ahmet. 2011. "Vision 2023: Turkey's Foreign Policy Objectives." Speech delivered at the Turkey Investor Conference: The Road to 2023 organized by Goldman Sachs, London. Accessed October 24, 2012 from http://www.mfa.gov.tr/speech-entitled-_vision-2023_-turkey_s-foreign-policy-objectives__-delivered-by-h_e_-ahmet-davutoglu_-minister-of-foreign-af.en.mfa

Davutoglu, Ahmet. 2012. "Interview with AUC Cairo Review." Accessed October 24, 2012 from http://www.mfa.gov.tr/interview-by-mr_-ahmet-davutoğlu-published-in-auc-cairo-review-_egypt_-on-12-march-2012.en.mfa

Dede, Alper Y. 2011. "The Arab Uprisings: Debating the 'Turkish Model'." *Insight Turkey*, 13(2): 23–32.

Drorian, Sevgi. 2005. "Turkey: Security, State and Society in Troubled Times." *European Security*, 14(2): 255–275.

Eissenstat, Howard. 2011. "A Tale of Two Flotillas." *SSRC, The Immanent Frame*. Accessed October 24, 2012 from http://blogs.ssrc.org/tif/2011/08/02/a-tale-of-two-flotillas/

Eurasianet. 2012 (October 11). "Turkey: Public Support Low for Possible Fight Against Syria." Accessed December 16, 2012 from http://www.eurasianet.org/node/66033

Falk, Richard. 2012. "Zero Problems with Neighbors Revisited." *Sunday's Zaman,* February 2012. Accessed October 24, 2012 from http://www.todayszaman.com/newsDetail_getNewsById.action?newsId=270478

Fidan, Hakan, and Rahman Nurdun. 2008. "Turkey's Role in the Global Development Assistance Community: the Case of TIKA (Turkish International Cooperation and Development Agency." *Journal of Southern Europe and the Balkans*, 10(1): 93–111.

Gambetti, Zeynep. (2013). "'I'm No Terrorist, I'm a Kurd': Societal Violence, the State and the Neoliberal Order." In *Rhetorics of Insecurity: Belonging and Violence in the Neoliberal Era*, edited by Zeynep Gambetti and Marcial Godoy-Anativia, 125–152. New York, NY: New York University Press.

Guney, Nursin Atesoglu. 2007. "The New Security Environment and Turkey's ISAF Experience." In *Contentious Issues of Security and the Future of Turkey*, edited by Narusin Atesoglu Guney, 177–190. Farnham: Ashgate.

Hakura, Fadi. 2011. "Turkey and the Middle East: Internal Confidence, External Assertiveness." *Chatham House Briefing Paper*. Accessed December 16, 2012 from http://www.chathamhouse.org/sites/default/files/public/Research/Europe/bp1111_hakura.pdf

Hounshell, Blake. 2010. "Mr. 'Zero Problems'." *Foreign Policy,* December 2010. Accessed October 24, 2012 from http://www.foreignpolicy.com/articles/2010/11/29/mr_zero_problems

Human Rights Watch. 2010. *Protesting as a Terrorist Offense. The Arbitrary Use of Terrorism Laws to Prosecute and Incarcerate Demonstrators in Turkey*. New York, NY: Human Rights Watch Publications.

Icduygu, Ahmet and Fuat Keyman. 2000. "Globalization, Security, and Migration: The Case of Turkey." *Global Governance*, 6: 383–398.

Insan Hak ve Hurriyetleri Insani Yardim Vakfi (IHH). 2012. "Activities." Accessed December 13, 2012 http://www.ihh.org.tr/en/main/activity/

Jung, Dietrich, and Wolfango Piccoli. 2001. *Turkey at the Crossroads. Ottoman Legacies and a Greater Middle East*. London: ZED books.

Karaosmanoglu, Ali. 2000. "The Evolution of the National Security Culture and the Military in Turkey." *Journal of International Affairs*, 54: 199–216.

Kazan, Isil. 2005. "Turkey: Where Geopolitics Still Matters." *Contemporary Security Policy*, 26(3): 588–604.

Keser, Nurdan, and Ali Ozel. 2008. "Geo-Political Position and Importance of Turkey in the Crime Trafficking Between the Continents Asia, Europe and Africa." *International Journal of Environmental & Science Education*, 3(2): 75–81.

Kirisci, Kemal. 2006. "Turkey's Foreign Policy in Turbulent Times." *Institute for Security Studies, Chaillot Papers No. 92*.

Larrabee, Stephen F. 2010. "Turkey's New Geopolitics." *Survival*, 52(2): 157–180.

Lesser, Ian O. 1999. "Turkey's Strategic Options." *The International Spectator: Italian Journal of International Affairs*, 34(1): 79–88.

Lesser, Ian O. 2010. "The Evolution of Turkish National Security Strategy." In *Turkey's Engagement with Modernity: Conflict and Change in the Twentieth Century*, edited by Celia Kerslake, Kerem Oktem, and Philip Robins, 258–276. New York, NY: Palgrave MacMillan.

Lippe, John M. Vander. 2000. "Forgotten Brigade of the Forgotten War: Turkey's Participation in the Korean War." *Middle Eastern Studies*, 36(1): 92–102.

Mufti, Malik. 2009. *Daring and Caution in Turkish Strategic Culture*. New York, NY: Palgrave MacMillan.

Mufti, Malik. 2011. "A Little America: The Emergence of Turkish Hegemony." *Middle East Brief*, Crown Center for Middle East Studies, 51. Accessed October 24, 2012 from http://www.brandeis.com/crown/publications/meb/MEB51.pdf

Oguzlu, Tarik. 2003. "An Analysis of Turkey's Prospective Membership in the European Union from a 'Security' Perspective." *Security Dialogue*, 34(3): 285–299.

Oguzlu, Tarik. 2007. "Soft Power in Turkish Foreign Policy." *Australian Journal of International Affairs*, 61(1): 81–97.

Oguzlu, Tarik, and Ugur Gungor. 2006. "Peace Operations and the Transformation of Turkey's Security Policy." *Contemporary Security Policy*, 27(3): 472–488.

Ozcan, Gencer. 2000. "Doksanlarda Turkiye'nin Ulusal Guvenlik ve Dis Politikasinda Askeri Yapinin Artan Etkisi." In *En Uzun Onyil: Turk Dis Politikasinda Doksanli Yillar*, edited by Gencer Ozcan and Sule Kut, 65–98. Istanbul: Buke Yayinlari.

Ozcan, Gencer. 2010. "Turkiye'de Milli Guvenlik Kavraminin Gelisimi." In *Turkiye'de Ordu, Devlet ve Guvenlik Siyaseti*, edited by Evren Balta Paker and Ismet Akca, 307–350. Istanbul: Bilgi Universitesi Yayinlari.

Ozcan, Gencer, and Sule Kut, eds. 2000. *En Uzun On Yil: Turkiye'nin Ulusal Guvenlik ve Dis Politika Gundeminde Doksanli Yillar*. Istanbul: Buke Yayinlari.

Ozkan, Mehmet. 2010. "What Drives Turkey's Involvement in Africa?" *Review of African Political Economy*, 37(126): 533–540.

Pandya, Sophia, and Nancy Gallagher. 2012. *The Gulen Hizmet Movement and its Transnational Activities: Case Studies of Altruistic Activism in Contemporary Islam*. Boca Raton, FL: BrownWalker Press.

Parla, Taha, and Andrew Davison. 2004. *Corporatist Ideology in Kemalist Turkey: Progress or Order?* Syracuse, NY: Syracuse University Press.

Republic of Turkey Ministry of Foreign Affairs. 2010. "Disisleri Bakanligi Sozcusu Burak Ozugergin'in Olagan Basin Toplantisi Metni." Accessed October 24, 2012 from http://www.mfa.gov.tr/disisleri-bakanligi-sozcusu-burak-ozugergin_in-olagan-basin-toplantisi-metni-_27-mayis-2010_.tr.mfa

Republic of Turkey Ministry of Foreign Affairs. 2012a. "The United Nations Organization and Turkey." Accessed October 24, 2012 from http://www.mfa.gov.tr/the-united-nations-organization-and-turkey.en.mfa

Republic of Turkey Ministry of Foreign Affairs. 2012b. "Resolution of Conflicts and Media-tion." Accessed October 24, 2012 from http://www.mfa.gov.tr/resolution-of-conflicts-and-mediation.en.mfa

Republic of Turkey Ministry of Foreign Affairs. 2012c. "Humanitarian Assistance by Turkey." Accessed October 24, 2012 from http://www.mfa.gov.tr/humanitarian-assistance-by-turkey.en.mfa

Republic of Turkey Ministry of Foreign Affairs. 2012d. "Piracy (Armed Robbery) off the Coast of Somalia." Accessed October 24, 2012 from http://www.mfa.gov.tr/piracy-_armed-robbery_-off-the-coast-of-somalia.en.mfa

Republic of Turkey Ministry of Foreign Affairs. 2012e. "Turkey's Perspectives and Policies on Security Issues." Accessed October 24, 2012 from http://www.mfa.gov.tr/i_-turkey_s-security-perspective_-historical-and-conceptual-background_-turkey_s-contributions.en.mfa

Robins, Philip. 2007. "Turkish Foreign Policy since 2002: Between a 'Post-Islamist' Govern-ment and a Kemalist State." *International Affairs*, 83(1): 289–304.

Romano, David. 2006. *The Kurdish Nationalist Movement: Opportunity, Mobilization and Identity*. Cambridge: Cambridge University Press.

Rubin, Michael. 2004. "Shifting Sides? The Problems of Neo-Ottomanism." *National Review Online*, August 10. Accessed October 24, 2012 from http://www.nationalreview.com/articles/211825/shifting-sides/michael-rubin

Sayari, Sabri. 2000. "Turkish Foreign Policy in the Post-cold War Era: The Challenge of Multi-Regionalism." *Journal of International Affairs*, 54(1): 169–182.

Schenker, David. 2009. "A NATO without Turkey? Ankara's Islamist Government is Turning Away from the Western Alliance." *Wall Street Journal Europe*, November 5. Accessed Octo-ber 24, 2012 from http://online.wsj.com/article/SB1000142405274870401300457451721 0622936876.html

Schmitt, Carl. 2007. *The Concept of the Political*. Chicago, IL: University of Chicago Press.

Seale, Patrick. 2012. "The Collapse of Turkey's Middle East Policy." *Middle East Online*. Accessed December 16, 2012 from http://www.middle-east-online.com/english/?id=54209

Secretariat General of the National Security Council. 2013. "About the National Security Council and the Secretariat-General of the National Security Council." Accessed Decem-ber 13, 2013 from http://www.mgk.gov.tr/en/index.php/secretariat-general/about-us

Shanker, Thom. 2011. "US Hails Deal with Turkey on Missile Shield." *New York Times*, September 15. Accessed October 24, 2012 from http://www.nytimes.com/2011/09/16/world/europe/turkey-accepts-missile-radar-for-nato-defense-against-iran.html

Taspinar, Omer. 2011. "The Arab Spring and the Duality of the Turkish Model." *Today's Zaman*, August 7. Accessed December 13, 2013 from http://www.todayszaman.com/columnists/omer-taspinar_252992-the-arab-spring-and-the-duality-of-the-turkish-model.html

TimeTurk. 2012. "Turk Askerinin Afganistan'da Ne Isi Var?" March 20. Accessed Octo-ber 24, 2012 from http://www.timeturk.com/tr/2012/03/20/turk-askerinin-afganistan-da-ne-isi-var.html

Tisdall, Simon. 2010. "Turkey's 'Zero Problems' policy is a Flop." *The Guardian*, June 21. Accessed October 24, 2012 from http://www.guardian.co.uk/commentisfree/2010/jun/21/turkey-zero-problems-policy

Toktas, Sule, and Hande Selimoglu. 2012. "Smuggling and Trafficking in Turkey: An Analy-sis of EU–Turkey Cooperation in Combating Transnational Organized Crime." *Journal of Balkan and Near Eastern Studies*, 14(1): 135–150.

Tugal, Cihan. 2007. "NATO's Islamists: Hegemony and Americanization in Turkey." *New Left Review*, 44: 5–34.

Tugal, Cihan. 2012. "Democratic Janiessaries? Turkey's Role in the Arab Spring." *New Left Review*, July/Aug: 5–24.

Turkiye Isbirligi ve Koordinasyon Ajansligi Baskanligi (TIKA). 2010. "Faaliyet Raporu." Accessed October 24, 2012 from http://store.tika.gov.tr/yayinlar/faaliyet-raporlari/faaliyet-raporu-2010.pdf

United Nations Development Program (UNDP). 2009. "Turkey as an Emerging Donor." *UNDP Monthly Newsletter,* 46. Accessed October 24, 2012 from http://www.undp.org.tr/Gozlem2.aspx?WebSayfaNo=2155

Urhan, Betul, and Seydi Celik. 2010. "Perceptions of 'National Security' in Turkey and Their Impacts on the Labor Movement and Trade Union Activities." *European Journal of Turkish Studies*, 11: 2–19.

Uskul, Zafer. 1997. *Siyaset ve Asker*. Ankara: Imge.

Vahedi, Elias. 2011. "Arab Spring and Double Standards in Turkey's Foreign Policy." *Iranian Review,* 13. Accessed October 24, 2012 from http://www.iranreview.org/content/Documents/Arab_Spring_and_Double_Standards_in_Turkey's_Foreign_Policy.htm

Walker, Joshua. 2007. "Learning Strategic Depth: Implications of Turkey's New Foreign Policy Doctrine." *Insight Turkey*, 9(3): 25–36.

Yavuz, Hakan. 1998. "Turkish Identity and Foreign Policy in Flux: The Rise of Neo-Ottomanism." *Critique*, 7(1)2: 19–41.

Yilmaz, Suhnaz. 2006. "Turkey and the European Union: A Security Perspective." In *Turkey and European Security: IAI TESEV Report*, edited by Giovanni Gasparini, 51–64. Rome: Istituto Affari Internazionali.

Zaaiter, Haifa. 2012. "Turkey: The Death of 'Zero Problems' Foreign Policy." *Al Monitor,* February 14. Accessed October 24, 2012 from http://www.al-monitor.com/pulse/politics/2012/02/for-these-reasons-turkey-renounc.html

Ziyal, Ugur. 2004. "Re-conceptualization of Soft Security and Turkey's Contribution to International Security." *Turkish Political Quarterly*, 3(2).

Chapter 25

The United States

Adam Quinn

Introduction

The United States has been the most powerful single state in the international system – measured in terms of military capacity, economic size, and political influence – since the end of the Second World War in 1945. Since the dissolution of the Soviet Union in 1991, it has been the hegemonic force within a unipolar order. This long period of superiority has brought with it many advantages of strength: a high level of security against conventional attack on its own territory, an unmatched ability to project force over distance beyond its borders, and a huge base of resources available for deployment in service of its chosen priorities. The official defense budget – a conservative figure that excludes certain defense-related expenditures elsewhere – for 2011 was recorded at US$793.3 billion, 45.7% of the world's defense spending (International Institute of Strategic Studies, 2011). At over US$15 trillion, its gross domestic product remains the largest in the world today, even after the worst recession in a generation (International Monetary Fund, 2012).

This status has also brought with it some of the burdens of great power. One is an obligation to take on an appropriately hegemonic share of the effort required to maintain its desired international order. The United States regularly finds itself obliged to play the leadership role in orchestrating a coordinated international response to security crises, from managing the global response to economic meltdown, to defusing stand-offs between dangerous antagonists such as India and Pakistan or Israel and the Palestinians, to devising strategies for dealing with disruptive regional actors, whether in Tripoli, Tehran, Caracas, or Pyongyang. A second liability, to some extent derivative of the first, is that the United States is the largest and most visible target for those whose grievances against existing political settlements, local or global, need a concrete focus for blame.

The Handbook of Global Security Policy, First Edition. Edited by Mary Kaldor and Iavor Rangelov.
© 2014 John Wiley & Sons, Ltd. Published 2014 by John Wiley & Sons, Ltd.

Over the course of coming decades, the United States must continue to wrestle with the security issues currently in its inbox while also factoring two additional trends into its calculations. First, its preeminent status in the scales of relative national power is likely to be declining. Second, threats of escalating seriousness emanate from sources beyond the command and control of states, and these cannot easily be defended against by recourse to the twentieth century security policy toolkit. The need to make policy in this context presents many questions to which American leaders and officials will need to construct at least provisional answers.

On what measures and at what speed will the United States' lead in capabilities, relative to others, erode over the coming years? Which actors will make the greatest relative gains, and what might the implications be for the global security environment and the American national interest? Which of myriad potential threats merit greatest focus on the part of the American national security apparatus? And can the United States take steps against any of the most serious challenges on its agenda (e.g. rising powers, "rogue" states, jihadist terrorism, economic instability, weapons proliferation) without producing unintended consequences that aggravate other threats, or perhaps indeed the very same threat, they were seeking to ameliorate? The answers to all these questions are subject to debate. In the worst scenarios, they provide the sort of ironic dilemmas that haunt the corridors of security policy. At the least, they require of American policymakers the kind of judgment and delicate balancing of priorities that illustrate why statesmanship is better understood as art than science.

The Context for Policy: Managing Decline or Reasserting Hegemony?

At core, the debate surrounding America's world role centers on this question: can trends that now suggest the United States' relative decline somehow be arrested, or is the task at hand that of managing transition to a "post-American" world, in which the United States is only one of several front-rank powers? This representation, however, although it does capture the spirit of the debate, it risks – to borrow Dean Acheson's phrase – stating things a little clearer than truth. Beneath the headlines, the debate between "declinism" and its critics involves a number of divergent points of view regarding reasonable timescales, the plausibility of hypothetical counterfactuals, the question of whether the underlying cause of America's shrinking capacity is domestic or external, and indeed our understanding of the nature of national power itself.

The case for relative decline is not difficult to grasp given the accepted facts of the United States' present circumstances. It has been set out in detail elsewhere by a number of scholars and analysts, including the author of this chapter (Quinn, 2011a, 2013; Layne, 2012a, 2012b, forthcoming). The precise numbers change regularly as economic data is revised and new budgets are passed and old ones renegotiated, but a central truth remains: on present trends the capacity of the United States to devote present levels of resources to national security, in the medium and long terms, is under threat. The United States has short-term budget deficits arising from the financial crisis and "Great Recession", which are projected to segue into long-term underfunded commitments to medical care and social security. Without significant increases in revenue or cuts in spending, these form a pincer movement driving the nation into structural insolvency (Congressional Budget Office, 2010).

Under any plausible future scenario, the US government must seek significant spending cuts over coming decades. Policymakers will face difficult choices between promises made to future recipients of medical care and pensions and other "non-entitlement" budgetary items. Since defense is the largest of the latter, there is a significant probability that defense spending will face a period of austerity. Before departing from the post of Secretary of Defense in 2011, Robert Gates outlined plans for a reduction of US$78 billion from the defense budget over four years. His successor Leon Panetta was then directed by President Obama to find further savings on top of this of a further US$450–500 billion over 12 years (Quinn, 2011b). The defense budget has since been made vulnerable to still further, deeper cuts as part of the US Congress's ongoing battles over government debt and spending cuts.

These reductions will be made from a relatively high base in historical terms, but nevertheless, for the first time in a generation, the pool of resources harnessed by the US government for devotion to national security will be shrinking in real terms, in contrast to rapid growth over the preceding period. This will come at a time when the defense budget is already wobbling under the pressure of ballooning costs for healthcare and veterans (Pincus, 2012; Congressional Budget Office, 2012a). It also coincides with compound year-on-year growth in the double-digit percentage points in military investment on the part of China, the most conspicuously rising power in the international system (Quinn, 2011b).

While none of these facts will be sufficient to stop the United States being the single most capable military power in the world within the next ten years, two conclusions are inescapable: the first is that in terms of conventional measures of military capability, the gap between the United States and at least one other major power will be decreasing significantly. The second is that although the United States may well be able to retain some capabilities at the highest level, and even develop new ones in areas to which it accords heightened priority (see later for reference to cyber security), it is entering an era of strategic choice, in which resources devoted to one purpose can only come at the expense of others, as the overall budgetary pie shrinks. The US government's own National Intelligence Council's projections reflect this reality of a world in which the United States will increasingly be one of several major players, less dominant than before and obliged to make hard choices between priorities at home and abroad (National Intelligence Council, 2008, 2012).

This picture of the United States as a declining power in the scales of international security has attracted various objections from scholars over recent years. Some question the plausibility of decline in any imminent sense of the word (Brooks and Wohlforth, 2008, 2009, 2012). Others highlight the challenges that still face rising powers, i.e. China, and war against simple extrapolation from present trends (Miller, 2010; Nye, 2010; Clark, 2011). Liberal thinkers highlight the importance of the structures of order built by the United States during its hegemony (Ikenberry, 2008), the residual "soft power" of its values and agenda (Nye, 2002, 2010) and the fading relevance of hard coercive capacity in a world of networks that still favors America (Slaughter, 2009). Nevertheless, these seem to be qualifications or caveats regarding the timing of relative decline in traditional terms, or advice on how it might be managed and mitigated, rather than persuasive arguments that it is not occurring (Quinn, 2011a).

It is also true that the United States is not over-extended in the classic sense of "imperial overstretch", as coined by Paul Kennedy (1989), in which a great power declines as its commitments overseas outstrip the capacity of its economic base to possibly meet them. Rather, the threat to America's status stems from a domestic politic that rejects the increases in taxation and/or reform of entitlement spending that would be needed to free up the resources required for sustaining national security policy on the present scale (Gelb, 2009; Altman and Haass, 2010). But the fact that the forces driving long-term decline in America's relative advantage in defense-spending lie largely in choices being made within its own borders does not mean that one should be signally more optimistic that they will reverse course.

Kenneth Waltz, one of the founding fathers of modern International Relations scholarship, argued that power should be defined as one's capacity to affect others with one's actions disproportionately to the extent that they could in turn affect oneself (Waltz, 2010, p. 192). Power of this sort cannot be assured of eliciting the behavior that one wants from others – that requires putting power to use behind good strategy – but it can insulate one to some degree from the consequences of error. The United States, if it plays its remaining cards wisely, may be able to secure a strong position for itself for years to come. At the same time, its margin for unforced error in the playing of those cards is shrinking.

Policy Priorities for the United States

The grand strategic challenge that the United States faces over the coming years is thus to steer a safe course for security policy in a world where its share of resources, and its strategic superiority over other powers will, in all likelihood be decreasing. Below the level of this grand strategic challenge, however, there are a number of specific issue areas that the United States is likely to prioritize contending. Broadly speaking, the American national interest can be defined as the preservation of the safety of American citizens from physical attack, and the stable continuity of the American "way of life" – social, political, and economic – against threats liable to grievously disrupt it. Threats to this come from many sources: other states, non-state actors such as terrorist groups, and complex impersonal phenomena such as economic dysfunction. Importantly, when it comes to addressing these latter two categories, the threats to American interests are not only located externally, but also within.

Economic Recovery

The fiscal constraints faced by the US government have already been outlined earlier. Two additional observations might be made, however. First, that it is the priority that stands above all others for the United States to restore its economy to a position of convincing annual growth and international competitiveness. Without this, resourcing any other policies or achieving any other objectives becomes vastly more difficult. Second, that until such time as a more sustainable and balanced economic model can be established, the growing indebtedness of the United States might justifiably be considered to pose in itself a threat to the country's well-being. In September 2011, Admiral Mike Mullen, the Chairman of the Joint Chiefs of Staff, the primary military advisor of the President of the United States, declared that he considered debt to be the greatest threat to American national security (American Forces Press Service, 2011).

Presently, the US economy remains in a fragile condition. Aside from the large federal government deficit, the financial crisis and the Great Recession have also resulted in severe downward pressure on spending at the state level where borrowing is, in most cases, difficult or prohibited, and where, in many cases, long-term solvency looks questionable (State Budget Crisis Task Force, 2012). The financial sector, while saved from total collapse during the crisis of 2008, remains a source of concern for government in terms of both its own solvency and the spillover effects of its policies on the remainder of the economy. Persistently high unemployment, which as of mid-2012 remained above 8% of those seeking work, continues to pose a threat to the skill base and the morale of the general population (Peck, 2010). Meanwhile, the longer-standing problem of America's balance of trade deficit, whereby the national economy spends money abroad in greater quantities than it earns it, continues unabated. This imbalance is particularly apparent in the US–China relationship, which will be covered later (Wolverson and Alessi, 2011).

Government debt is problematic for at least two reasons. One is that through the growing burden of interest and repayments it steadily erodes the resources available for future spending. As the total debt burden climbs, a vicious cycle between new spending, debt repayment, and fresh borrowing can take hold that threatens the nation's long-term solvency. The second is that a very large quantity of American Treasury bonds has, for some time, been purchased by other states, especially China. This does not in any simplistic sense give China a lever to exercise control over the US government; because China is investing its own wealth in US debt, any hostile act on its part, making use of its debt holdings, e.g. flooding the market with US debt to harm US credit-worthiness or shutting down its purchasing of further debt, could destroy the value of its own assets. Furthermore, because American consumption remains essential to Chinese economic growth, any act threatening the health of the US economy would amount to self-harming on the part of the Chinese leadership. Nevertheless, with these caveats in place, it must remain at least a source of concern for foresighted US strategists that the nation's autonomy may in the final analysis be circumscribed by a dependence on foreign sovereign credit to meet its day-to-day obligations. At the least, the symbiotic relationship between the American and Chinese economies makes it more difficult for America to push back against those Chinese policies that compound the trade imbalance, such as holding the value of the renminbi artificially low.

The solution to this problem, if there is one, is not simple. Persuasive economic analysis suggests that an immediate hard turn towards closing the deficit by means of tax increases and sizeable spending cuts would risk triggering a new wave of recession (Congressional Budget Office, 2012b). This would aggravate the problem it seeks to solve because recession increases the proportional burden of existing debt, further depresses revenues, and adds to entitlement spending on assistance to the unemployed or poor. The balancing act thus required of US policymakers is to simultaneously prop up the economy in the short term, even if this must come at the cost of further government borrowing, while laying out a credible plan for the reform of entitlement spending and/or the raising of new revenue in the long term, and somehow encourage private sector recovery. The debate within American politics on the way forward has been, to put it mildly, contentious (Krugman, 2012; Economist, 2012a).

Reconfiguring Counterterrorism

The threat of a terrorist attack did not materialize in 2001 as a new problem, even for mainland United States let alone for the world. But the events of September 11 of that year did unarguably elevate it to a new status in the world of security policy. The scale of those attacks, and the shock of their location and method, made an indelible impression on contemporary American leaders. Many of those at the top of the national security apparatus at the time of the attacks, who have gone on to write memoirs, have explicitly highlighted the attacks not simply as a crisis event they were required to address, but as an event that shifted their thinking about terrorism, risk, and appropriate response in profound and lasting ways (Bush, 2010; Cheney, 2011; Rumsfeld, 2011; Rice, 2011). Resources devoted to fighting terrorism have grown beyond all prior imagining since that time, as an exhaustive *Washington Post* investigation revealed to the public in 2010 (Priest and Arkin, 2010).

Responding to 9/11, the Bush administration constructed a new paradigm for confronting the threat of terrorism. The previously prevailing model treated terrorism primarily as a problem for law-enforcement, albeit a very serious one, to be prevented if possible by prior detection and arrest; otherwise to be punished retrospectively through trial and conviction. After 2001, however, terrorism was reconfigured as a fully "securitized" existential threat, to be met preemptively with the tools of warfare. This came to include, among other things: the detention and interrogation of suspected terrorists outside the civilian justice system in offshore locations and by intelligence service operatives using methods beyond those permissible in standard military interrogations; the threat to use force against any government (such as that of Afghanistan in 2001) deemed to be knowingly harboring terrorist actors; and the use of lethal force on the territory of countries with which the United States is not at war (Pakistan, Somalia, Yemen) in order to kill those designated as active members of anti-American terrorist movements. In its broadest sense, this campaign has also involved attempts at "regime change" and nation-building in Afghanistan and Iraq, one rationale offered being the goal of undermining extremism and religious militancy through the countervailing appeal of modernity, democracy, and "freedom".

The "War on Terror", as it was entitled by President Bush, has been criticized by scholars on multiple grounds, ranging from the conceptual clarity and wisdom of the terminology (Howard, 2002), to the proportionality of response relative to the actual threat faced (Mueller, 2006), to the more radical critique that the language of "terrorism" and "counterterrorism" serves chiefly as a tool to shore up the power structures of a *status quo* of questionable legitimacy (Jackson, 2005).

The Obama administration came to office having publicly criticized some of the practices that emerged under Bush. The new president made it official policy from the outset to close the detention center at Guantanamo Bay and apply the military's code of interrogation to intelligence operatives. Over time, however, the continuities between the Obama and Bush era approaches to counterterrorism have become more striking to some than the differences (Klaidman, 2012; Goldsmith, 2012).

Guantanamo Bay remains in operation, and efforts to channel detained terrorists, such as Khalid Sheikh Mohammed, into the civilian court system have hit insurmountable obstacles. President Obama's use of unmanned aerial vehicle ("drone") strikes to kill targets abroad, including some American citizens, has far exceeded that of his predecessor (Becker and Shane, 2012). Indeed, the killing of Osama Bin Laden, one of Obama's most-touted foreign policy achievements, was a successful instance of targeted killing on foreign soil, albeit one that took little justifying in the context of American domestic politics. The Obama administration has arguably framed these continuities in a more orderly and transparent framework than did its predecessor (Cole, 2012). Nevertheless, it is evidence that the US government remains engaged in a global campaign against terrorism in which it has assumed the right to detain and kill without reference to authority beyond its own institutions.

The coming years will continue to test US counterterrorism policy severely. The present administration policy appears inclined to lean away – on grounds of expense and practicality – from repeating the large-scale efforts at nation-building along the lines of that attempted in Iraq and echoed in Afghanistan, focusing instead on the intelligence-led targeting and elimination of known terrorist operatives. Though this policy appears to be meeting with success on its own terms at present, there are legitimate questions regarding its long-term sustainability and indirect consequences. Does the killing of specific militants offer a lasting solution to the threat against the United States, or will the dead simply be replaced from a pool of willing volunteers? Do strikes from the air, which inevitably produce civilian casualties as the price even of their successes, foster resentment of the United States among those populations with whom America needs to find a peaceful *modus vivendi* if it is to escape a cycle of action and reaction? Is it sustainable for the United States to continue to strike militarily within the territory of a nation, e.g. Pakistan, with which it is not officially at war when its government, officially at least, opposes such operations? And, perhaps most importantly, will the precedents the United States is setting by assuming the right to strike on foreign soil with drones prove discomfiting when other states acquire the technology to do likewise in pursuit of their own purposes?

Nation-Building, Counterinsurgency and the Military's Strategic Priorities

During the first decade of the twenty-first century – at the peak of its post-Cold War power and in response to the major security shock of the 9/11 attacks – the United States went through a period of immense strategic ambition in which it linked its security to a policy of transformational nation-building on a grand scale. This began in Afghanistan, where the overthrow of the Taliban and a desire to exclude similar forces from power in the future led the United States to install and seek to preserve a new political regime. It was pursued at first with a relatively limited direct military footprint, but escalated as the decade progressed, including NATO troop deployments, large-scale American resourcing of the Afghan government's security and training, and a "surge" in US troops after the election of Barack Obama (Woodward, 2002, 2010). Even bolder was the US invasion and occupation of Iraq in 2003, which began with a disarmament rationale to the fore, but evolved into the centerpiece of a strategy on the part of the Bush administration to remake world order in line with American preferences, with Iraq as the first advance in a project of "ending tyranny" (Bush, 2005). This broader agenda of democracy promotion under the Bush administration is discussed later. In parallel, however, these expeditions also presented concrete problems of military strategy when it came to bringing about stabilization and "nation-building".

The United States encountered huge problems – if not altogether unforeseeable ones – in attempting to bring about stability in Iraq, owing to a lethal combination of resistance and division among Iraqi actors and poor planning and execution on its own part (Ricks, 2006; Chandrasekaran, 2006). By late 2006, this had brought American policy to the brink of failure, with violence out of control on the ground and political support disappearing at home (Iraq Study Group, 2006). From this moment of crisis, with the president seeking alternatives to open failure and withdrawal, emerged a resurgence of population-centric counterinsurgency doctrine, advanced within military circles especially by retired general John M. Keane (Woodward, 2008). These were then put into place in 2007 via a troop "surge", and a change of commanding general in Iraq, with the appointment of David Petraeus, a rising star who had rewritten the Army's counterinsurgency field manual after serving in Iraq. Over the years since, the combination of high troop levels and counterinsurgency strategy has been credited with achieving something passing for success in Iraq, but also conceived by some as a transferable strategy, and indeed was applied by Petraeus himself in Afghanistan as lead commander in 2010. In the process, Petraeus, and those who shared his commitment to counterinsurgency, became prominent figures in the power-structure of the US military (Kaplan, 2013).

At the same time, however, there has been push-back against the rise of counterinsurgency as a central feature of US military doctrine and planning. On the political side, Vice President Joseph Biden prominently opposed the embrace of a counterinsurgency approach and troop surge in Afghanistan, favoring a counterterrorist approach focused more on targeted killing and less on troop-intensive counterinsurgency (Woodward, 2010). President Obama gave his assent to temporary troop number increases in Afghanistan with reluctance and, in his approach to intervention in Libya, spelled out unambiguous opposition to any repeat of an Iraq-style deployment (Obama, 2011a). Within the military itself, the wisdom and desirability of steering the US military's resources and attention towards counterinsurgency capacity has been a matter of fierce debate, with many unconvinced that the costs of such operations are worth bearing in Afghanistan specifically, or that preparing to do so represents the best focus for future-oriented preparations resources (Kaplan, 2010; Anderson, 2010).

Though President Obama's commitment of extra troops to Afghanistan in 2010 appeared to be a victory for counterinsurgency, in the longer term it appears that this victory may prove fleeting. As the US military faces up to the difficult budgetary scenario outlined earlier, and contemplates the challenges it faces in coming decades in maintaining a technical advantage over a rising China (Economist, 2012b; Engdahl, 2012), and an ability to defend its allies and the global commons, it does not seem able or inclined to invest in the sort of manpower-heavy military that would be required for making counterinsurgency scenarios a mainstay of US policy. The resulting policy seems likely to be a balancing act that tilts somewhat away from Iraq- and Afghanistan-type operations, attempting to preserve the capabilities required to scale up to wage competent counterinsurgency if required, but making it a core principle to avoid initiating such scenarios where at all possible (Gates, 2009, 2011a, 2011b).

While counterinsurgency skills and doctrine will not be discarded with the same totality as they were after Vietnam, counterinsurgency seems to all appearances to have peaked in its level of influence over US military strategy.

Rogue Actors and Weapons of Mass Destruction

As by far the strongest actor in the international system and the leading power in defining the normative shape of the international order, the United States has for two decades made reference to a perceived stand-off between the "international community", i.e. those who abide by a baseline of acquiescence with the *status quo*, and a handful of "rogue states" who refuse to do so (Lake, 1994). The most notable members of this select group of self-identified enemies of the United States today are Iran and North Korea, and before the American invasion of 2003, Saddam Hussein's Iraq was a prominent member of the category. Given the United States' massive conventional military superiority, the greatest perceived threat from these nations has long been that they might succeed in developing weapons of mass destruction, especially nuclear weapons. Whether or not one believes that the spread of such weapons increases the risk of their actual use, US policymakers legitimately fear that attaining nuclear status would embolden a rogue state in regional power politics because they would believe that any American military intervention to check for the weapons could now be deterred. Since the 9/11 attacks, this fear has been compounded by anxiety that rogue states might – whether for reasons of ideology, profit, or the plausible deniability of attack through proxies – be willing to share such technology with non-state actors. Iran, for example, has long been considered by the United States as an official state sponsor of terrorism. The government of Pakistan, while officially an ally of the United States and an aid-recipient, has a history of instability, close association between its intelligence services and Islamist militant groups, and proliferation of nuclear technology through the Khan network.

The policy response to these fears has varied significantly from case to case, with no course of action resulting in a clear template for success. In the case of Iraq in 2003, fear of weapons proliferation and state-sponsorship of terrorism was the primary *casus belli* for regime change. In the aftermath of a large-scale American military invasion and overthrow of the Hussein government, however, the United States was obliged to contend with a lengthy period of occupation and political violence. The costs associated with the invasion and occupation, both financial and in terms of political capital, have made it seem, in retrospect, a poor template for dealing with similar problems in future (Stiglitz and Bilmes 2008). In recent years, both the Bush and the Obama administrations have sought to deal with Iran and North Korea by means of coercive diplomacy. In the case of Iran, the United States has orchestrated punitive sanctions through the United Nations Security Council in order to persuade the regime to make its nuclear technology programs more transparent and deter it from using them as a platform to press on to developing weapons. In the case of North Korea, a mixture of regional six-party talks and bilateral diplomacy has been used to try and persuade Pyongyang to agree to a disarmament bargain, but with very limited success. Iran continues to express its determination to develop higher uranium enrichment capacity than the United States regards as legitimate, while North Korea has already successfully tested a nuclear weapon and missile delivery systems. In both cases, the debate within American politics runs a spectrum between those more and less willing to invoke the threat of military force to compel a change of course. The options for achieving success at acceptable cost should the logic of escalation unfold are limited, but this has not prevented a significant body of opinion within the United States from pushing for it, especially in the case of Iran, while Obama has explicitly kept the option of force on the table.

Meanwhile, in Pakistan, the United States officially maintains a friendly relationship with the government in which substantial military aid is traded for security cooperation in the fight against Islamic militant groups. In reality, however, the relationship is fraught with tensions stemming from the suspicion that the Pakistani security services play a double game at the expense of both the Americans and militant groups. The United States' deepest fear is that should the perennial instability of Pakistani politics tip over into genuine internal collapse, the country's nuclear weapons might fall into the hands of a hostile and/or extremist political movement (Goldberg and Ambinder, 2011).

Rival Great Powers and Regional Stability

It has been observed that the United States is a historical rarity, if not unique, in seeking not just hegemony in its own region but across all regions of the globe (Layne, 2006). While other large states in the world may envision themselves playing a dominant, or at least veto-wielding, role in the strategic set-up of their own environs, only the United States attempts to play the role of front-rank power across all of these theaters simultaneously. The two most obvious cases are China in Asia and Russia in Eastern Europe and Central Asia.

In East Asia, the United States maintains longstanding alliances with Japan and South Korea, and Australia to the south, as a platform for sustaining its status as an eminent projector of power in the region. As China's economic and military capacities grow, American strategists can seek to cultivate those powers that may fear Chinese domination in the absence of a continued American presence, such as Vietnam or Thailand. The greatest danger of a flashpoint lies in Taiwan, over which China maintains an internationally recognized claim of sovereignty, but whose *de facto* sovereign autonomy the United States is pledged to defend. While neither side can possibly have an interest in provoking an armed confrontation over this issue, given the economic and military fallout from such a conflict even presuming it did not escalate to a nuclear exchange, it cannot be entirely ruled out, given the unacceptability to Beijing of a Taiwanese declaration of independence and the limits to the United States ability to contain the escalation of such a scenario should it unfold. As it makes its military plans for the future, with the capabilities required for winning "Air–Sea Battle" capability a declared priority, the United States seems to have China clearly in its strategic sights (Economist, 2012b; Quinn, 2011b).

In the case of Russia, the United States does not face a rising new power as such; the Russia of 2012 is less intimidating by some distance than the Soviet Union in its heyday, and Russia has a number of demographic, economic, and military shortcomings that constrain its ability to assert itself anew as a superpower. Nevertheless, its vast residual arsenal of nuclear weapons allows it to negotiate as the United States' only peer competitor in that realm. Furthermore, through a combination of NATO expansion and other friendships, the United States has opted to take a strategic interest in the autonomy of a number of former Soviet states over which Russia considers itself entitled to exercise primary sway through the twin levers of military intimidation and control of natural resources. Over the course of the 12 years since the Vladimir Putin era of post-Soviet Russian assertiveness began, its relationship with the United States has fluctuated. As George Bush's term unfolded, an initially sympathetic alliance in the War on Terror devolved into acrimony during the post-Iraq years, reaching a nadir during Russia's military incursion into Georgia in 2008. Under President Obama, hopes of a "reset" in relations, bolstered by success in negotiating a new arms reduction agreement ("new START"), subsequently appeared to be stymied by tension over Putin's 2012 crackdown on domestic enemies, poor Russian treatment of the American ambassador, Michael McFaul, and persistent differences at the United Nations over whether to intervene in civil conflicts such as those in Libya and Syria in 2011–2012. While US–Russian relations are far from Cold War levels of discord, they have returned to a level of tension that led the Republican presidential candidate for 2012 to declare Russia a "geopolitical foe" (Oppel, 2012).

The Creeping Importance of Cyber Warfare

Although it is clear that China's ongoing military investment program is significant, and Russia's capacity to act with force in its own strategic backyard remains great, the United States' conventional military superiority should guarantee its ability to sustain a decisive strategic presence in those regions in which it operates in the short and medium term. There is one wild card in play, however, namely the incipient threat of cyber warfare as a tool of international confrontation. With both civilian and military infrastructure crucially dependent upon sophisticated electronics, satellite communications, and computer software, the ability to interfere with such systems has become an increasingly dangerous weapon. Already the potential for cyber attack to be mobilized for aggressive foreign policy purposes has been hinted at in alleged Russian cyber attacks on Estonia in 2007 (Finn, 2007) and Georgia in 2008 (Markoff, 2008), and an apparent North Korean "denial of service" attack on 40 South Korean government and private websites in 2011 (Associated Press, 2011). Meanwhile the US Office of the National Counterintelligence Executive has explicitly warned that Russia and China are guilty of large-scale hacking against the United States for economic purposes (Office of the National Counterintelligence Executive, 2011).

In its new "Strategic Concept", officially unveiled in 2010, NATO highlighted the increasing centrality of defense against cyber attack in its mission (NATO, 2010). Even as it warns of the dangers presented by this kind of warfare, the United States has itself been revealed as both developing and unleashing its own weapons of cyber warfare (Gross, 2011; Sanger, 2012). Clearly, even as the conventional military balance continues to be a core part of assessing the international security environment, it also will become more important to pay attention to the growing capacity of cyber attack to substitute for conventional warfare, to complement it, or – in ways yet to be fully realized – subvert it by enabling skilled practitioners to disable key capabilities of those states who are reliant on high technology for key functions.

Democracy Promotion versus Strategic Stability

For as long as the United States has existed, it has been obliged to navigate tensions in its foreign policy between its professed political ideals, most especially liberal values of individual rights and democracy, and its more prosaic international interests, i.e. safety from physical attack, economic gain, and access to essential resources. The often-fraught effort to find a workable balance between these priorities has produced substantial sophisticated literature (Osgood, 1953; Williams, 1972; LaFeber, 1963, 1993; Hunt, 1987; McDougall, 1997; Lieven, 2004; Dueck, 2006; Quinn, 2010). Over the last ten years, administrations of both parties have continued a longstanding practice of American leaders by glossing over the reality of such tensions rhetorically by proclaiming American values and interests to be in virtuous harmony (Bush, 2005; Rice, 2008; Obama, 2011b). In each case, the argument has been made that the most effective way of promoting the United States interests lies in supporting the spread of democracy and "freedom". Yet even as this proposition has been put forward in the highest-profile policy speeches, American policy towards specific countries has continued to struggle with inescapable tension in practice, not only between the categories of "values" and "interests" but also within them.

These tensions reveal themselves most clearly when US policymakers are tempted to take a view on the internal affairs of others, especially in the case of nations whose records on democracy and human rights are dubious but whose governments' orientation is not hostile to American interests in strategic and economic affairs. In recent years, this has been most keenly felt in the United States' relationship with the Muslim Middle East and North Africa, where longstanding nondemocratic allies, such as Egypt and Bahrain, enemies such as Iran and Syria, and states in a complex intermediate state, such as Libya, have all been roiled by internal uprisings by groups demanding more say in the governance of the state. In most of these countries, even those where protestors calling for "democracy" have been successful in toppling the existing government, the long-term outcome remains uncertain, as groups ranging from liberal democrats to Islamists to reactionary militarists contend for power in the space created by revolutionary instability.

In this context, the United States has a variety of interests, including a desire that whatever regimes result from the turmoil will cooperate with American counterterrorism efforts, maintain or adopt a conciliatory policy towards Israel, and refrain from disrupting the flow of oil from the Middle East to the West. It is far from clear that there is a correspondence between securing these objectives and the level of democracy that emerges in each case; those groups which are best able to mobilize support at the ballot box or on the streets are not always those whose politics are in closest correspondence to American preferences. The Muslim Brotherhood in Egypt, and other harder-line Islamist groups in the region, provides one ready example of organized and popular movements with some views antithetical to US objectives for the region. This uncertainty over the reconcilability of US rhetoric on democracy and the hard security interests of the United States in each case – as well as the intrinsic difficulty in any case of an outside power exercising decisive sway in such circumstances – has contributed to what has appeared to many a largely reactive and wary approach on the part of the US government (Lizza, 2011).

Over the coming years, the United States will continue to find itself challenged to balance rival narratives – one suggesting that its long-term security requires determined advocacy for the spread of the liberal model of government, the other counseling a pragmatism needed to cooperate with nondemocratic actors in order to maintain America's harder interests in economic exchange and strategic stability. In the case of inveterate enemies such as Iran, it remains the easy option to find harmony in combining the logic of advancing US security interests and the logic of regime change and democracy promotion. In the case of other undemocratic states with which the United States has essential relationships, e.g. China and Saudi Arabia, US policymakers will continue to find that the theory of democratic peace and the imperatives of day-to-day peace make awkward bedfellows. In dealing with those states where the shape of the domestic order is presently "up for grabs" amid what may be a once-in-a-generation tumult, difficult judgment will be required.

Conclusion

In formulating its security policy, the United States must negotiate a context in which its hegemonic lead in terms of the conventional resources of state power is diminishing. It may be possible for it to leverage its existing advantages into continued outsize influence through the residual effect of its institutional and soft power. Nevertheless, in as much as a shrinking lead in proportional ownership of the world's economic resources and military capabilities means something, American dominance will be lessening. In this context, US policymakers will need to contend with a range of issues that defy simple resolution. How can it renew the strength of its economic engine while also addressing the threat posed by its large deficit and imbalanced economy? Can it continue to proactively eliminate terrorist and militant non-state actors hostile to the United States without producing consequences that damage its security in other areas? Can it manage the ambitions of strong regional powers such as China and Russia, maintaining a balancing presence in these regions but without slipping over into counterproductive hostility? Can it master the techniques of cyber warfare for itself, and establish a new framework for their use before they are used by others to undermine America's conventional superiority in military affairs? And can it find a way to ensure its hard interests are defended in the world without finding itself on the wrong side of struggles for popular government, finding a workable balance between its ideological and material interests? American success in these efforts will lie in the measured application of careful judgment rather than the application of rigid paradigms, and while we may discern the parameters within the American polity, the precise direction of policy is not knowable in advance.

References

Altman, Roger C., and Richard N. Haass. 2010. "American Profligacy and American Power: the Consequences of Fiscal Irresponsibility." *Foreign Affairs*, 89(6): 25–34.

American Forces Press Service. 2011. "Debt is Biggest Threat to National Security, Chairman Says." September 22. Accessed January 6, 2013 from http://www.defense.gov/news/newsarticle.aspx?id=65432

Anderson, Col. Gary. 2010. "Counterinsurgency vs. Counterterrorism." *Small Wars Journal*. February 24. Accessed January 6, 2013 from http://smallwarsjournal.com/blog/journal/docs-temp/375-anderson.pdf

Associated Press. 2011. "South Korea government websites targeted in cyber attack." *Guardian*. March 4. Accessed January 6, 2013 from http://www.guardian.co.uk/world/2011/mar/04/south-korea-websites-cyber-attack

Becker, Jo, and Scott Shane. 2012. "Secret 'Kill List' Proves a Test of Obama's Principles and Will." *New York Times*. May 29. Accessed January 6, 2013 from http://www.nytimes.com/2012/05/29/world/obamas-leadership-in-war-on-al-qaeda.html?pagewanted=all

Brooks, Stephen G., and William C. Wohlforth. 2008. *World out of balance: international relations and the challenge of American primacy*. Princeton, NJ: Princeton University Press.

Brooks, Stephen G., and William C. Wohlforth. 2009. "Reshaping the world order: how Washington should reform international institutions." *Foreign Affairs*, 88(2): 49–63.

Brooks, Stephen G., and William C. Wohlforth. 2012. "US Primacy. The Big Picture: a One Superpower World." In *US Foreign Policy*. 2nd ed., edited by Michael Cox and Doug Stokes, 421–429. Oxford: Oxford University Press.

Bush, George W. 2005. "Second Inaugural Address." January 20. Accessed January 6, 2013 from http://georgewbush-whitehouse.archives.gov/news/releases/2005/01/20050120-1.html

Bush, George W. 2010. *Decision Points*. London: Virgin Books.

Chandrasekaran, Rajiv. 2006. *Imperial Life in the Emerald City*. New York, NY: Alfred A. Knopf.

Cheney, Dick, and Liz Cheney. 2011. *In My Time: A Personal and Political Memoir*. New York, NY: Threshold Editions.

Clark, Ian. 2011. "China and the United States: A Succession of Hegemonies?" *International Affairs*, 87(1): 13–28. DOI: 10.1111/j.1468-2346.2011.00957.x

Cole, David. 2012. "Obama and Terror: The Hovering Questions." *New York Review of Books*. July 12. Accessed January 6, 2013 from http://www.nybooks.com/articles/archives/2012/jul/12/obama-and-terror-hovering-questions/

Congressional Budget Office. 2010. "The Long-Term Budget Outlook." June 30. Accessed January 6, 2013 from http://www.cbo.gov/publication/21546

Congressional Budget Office. 2012a. "The Budget and Economic Outlook: Fiscal Years 2012 to 2022." January 31. Accessed January 6, 2013 from http://www.cbo.gov/publication/42905

Congressional Budget Office. 2012b. "Economic Effects of Reducing the Fiscal Restraint That Is Scheduled to Occur in 2013." May 22. Accessed January 6, 2013 from http://www.cbo.gov/publication/43262

Dueck, Colin. 2006. *Reluctant Crusaders: Power, Culture and Change in American Grand Strategy*. Princeton, NJ: Princeton University Press.

Economist. 2012a. "Paul Ryan Doubles Down." March 24. Accessed January 6, 2013 from http://www.economist.com/node/21551104

Economist. 2012b. "The China Syndrome." June 9. Accessed January 6, 2013 from http://www.economist.com/node/21556587

Engdahl, F. Robert. 2012. "Obama's Geopolitical China 'Pivot': The Pentagon Targets China." *Global Research*, 24 August. Accessed January 6, 2013 from http://www.globalresearch.ca/obama-s-geopolitical-china-pivot-the-pentagon-targets-china/32474

Finn, Peter. 2007. "Cyber Assaults on Estonia Typify a New Battle Tactic." *Washington Post*. May 19. Accessed January 6, 2013 from http://www.washingtonpost.com/wp-dyn/content/article/2007/05/18/AR2007051802122.html

Gates, Robert. 2009. "A Balanced Strategy: Reprogramming the Pentagon for a New Age." *Foreign Affairs*, January/February. Accessed January 6, 2013 from http://www.foreignaffairs.com/articles/63717/robert-m-gates/a-balanced-strategy

Gates, Robert. 2011a. "Statement on Department Budget and Efficiencies." January 6. Accessed January 6, 2013 from http://www.defense.gov/speeches/speech.aspx?speechid=1527

Gates, Robert. 2011b. "American Enterprise Institute (Defense Spending)." May 24. Accessed January 6, 2013 from http://www.defense.gov/speeches/speech.aspx?speechid=1570

Gelb, Lesley. 2009. "Necessity, Choice and Common Sense: A Policy for a Bewildering World." *Foreign Affairs*, May/June.

Goldberg, Jeffrey and Mark Ambinder. 2011. "The Ally from Hell." *The Atlantic*, December. Accessed January 6, 2013 from http://www.theatlantic.com/magazine/archive/2011/12/the-ally-from-hell/8730/

Gross, Michael Joseph. 2011. "A Declaration of Cyber-War." *Vanity Fair*, April. Accessed January 6, 2013 from http://www.vanityfair.com/culture/features/2011/04/stuxnet-201104

Goldsmith, Jack. 2012. *Power and Constraint: The Accountable Presidency after 9/11*. New York, NY: W.W. Norton & Co.

Howard, Michael. 2002. "What's in a name? How to fight terrorism." *Foreign Affairs*, 81(1): 8–13.

Hunt, Michael H. 1987. *Ideology and US Foreign Policy*, New Haven, CT: Yale University Press.

Ikenberry, G. John. 2008. "The Rise of China and the Future of the West: Can the Liberal System Survive?" *Foreign Affairs*, 87(1): 23–37.

International Institute of Strategic Studies. 2011. *The Military Balance*. Chart publicly available at http://www.iiss.org/publications/military-balance/the-military-balance-2012/press-statement/figure-comparative-defence-statistics/?locale=en [accessed July 16, 2012].

International Monetary Fund. 2012. "Report for Selected Countries and Subjects (United States)." Accessed January 6, 2013 from http://preview.tinyurl.com/cctmecs

Iraq Study Group. 2006. "The Iraq Study Group Report." Accessed December 13, 2013 from http://media.usip.org/reports/iraq_study_group_report.pdf

Jackson, Richard. 2005. *Writing the War on Terrorism: Language, Politics and Counter-terrorism*. Manchester: Manchester University Press.

Kaplan, Fred. 2010. "CT or COIN." *Slate*. March 24. Accessed January 6, 2013 from http://www.slate.com/articles/news_and_politics/war_stories/2009/03/ct_or_coin.html

Kaplan, Fred. 2013. *The Insurgents: David Petraeus and the plot to change the American way of war*. New York, NY: Simon & Schuster.

Kennedy, Paul. 1989. *The Rise and Fall of the Great Powers: Economic Change and Military Conflict from 1500 to 2000*. London: Fontana Press.

Klaidman, Daniel. 2012. *Kill or Capture: The War on Terror and the Soul of the Obama Presidency*. Boston, MA: Houghton Mifflin Harcourt.

Krugman, Paul. 2012. "How to End This Depression." *New York Review of Books*. May 24. Accessed January 6, 2013 from http://www.nybooks.com/articles/archives/2012/may/24/how-end-depression/?pagination=false

LaFaber, Walter. 1963. *The New Empire: An Interpretation of American Expansionism 1860–1898*. London: Cornell University Press.

LaFaber, Walter. 1993. *Inevitable Revolutions: The United States in Central America*. New York, NY: W.W. Norton & Co.

Lake, Anthony. 1994. "Confronting Backlash States." *Foreign Affairs*, 73(2): 45–55.

Layne, Christopher. 2006. *The Peace of Illusions: American Grand Strategy from 1940 to the Present*. Ithaca, NY: Cornell University Press.

Layne, Christopher. 2012a. "The End of Pax Americana: How Western Decline Became Inevitable." *The Atlantic*, April 26. Accessed January 6, 2013 from http://www.theatlantic.com/international/archive/2012/04/the-end-of-pax-americana-how-western-decline-became-inevitable/256388/

Layne, Christopher. 2012b. "US Decline." In *US Foreign Policy*. 2nd ed., edited by Michael Cox and Doug Stokes, 410–420. Oxford: Oxford University Press.

Layne, Christopher. Forthcoming. *After the Fall: International Politics, US Grand Strategy, and the End of the Pax Americana.* Ithaca, NY: Yale University Press.

Lieven, Anatol. 2004. *America Right or Wrong: an Anatomy of American Nationalism.* London: HarperCollins.

Lizza, Ryan. 2011. "The Consequentialist." *New Yorker,* May 2. Accessed January 6, 2013 from http://www.newyorker.com/reporting/2011/05/02/110502fa_fact_lizza?printable=true &currentPage=all?currentPage=all#ixzz1KXeJjYM2

Markoff, John. 2008. "Before the Gunfire, Cyberattacks." *New York Times,* August 12. Accessed January 6, 2013 from http://www.nytimes.com/2008/08/13/technology/13cyber. html

McDougall, Walter A. 1997. *Promised Land, Crusader State: The American encounter with the world since 1776.* Boston, MA: Mariner Books.

Miller, Ken. 2010. "Coping with China's financial power: Beijing's financial foreign policy." *Foreign Affairs,* July/August: 96–109.

Mueller, John. 2006. *Overblown: How Politicians and the Terrorism Industry Inflate National Security Threats, And Why We Believe Them.* New York, NY: Free Press.

National Intelligence Council. 2008. *Global Trends 2025: A Transformed World.* Accessed December 13, 2013 from http://info.publicintelligence.net/GlobalTrends2030 .pdf

National Intelligence Council. 2012. *Global Trends 2030: Alternative Worlds.* Accessed January 6, 2013 from http://www.dni.gov/files/documents/GlobalTrends_2030.pdf

North Atlantic Treaty Organisation (NATO). 2010. "Strategic Concept." Adopted in Lisbon. Accessed January 6, 2013 from http://www.nato.int/lisbon2010/strategic-concept-2010-eng.pdf

Nye, Joseph S. 2002. *The Paradox of American Power: Why the World's only Superpower Can't go it Alone.* New York, NY: Oxford University Press.

Nye, Joseph S. 2010. "The Future of American Power: Dominance and Decline in Perspective." *Foreign Affairs,* November/December: 2–22.

Obama, Barack. 2011a, "Remarks by the President in Address to the Nation on Libya." March 28. Accessed December 13, 2013 from http://www.whitehouse.gov/the-press-office/2011/03/28/remarks-president-address-nation-libya

Obama, Barack. 2011b. "Remarks by the president to parliament in London, United Kingdom." *White House,* May 2011. Accessed January 6, 2013 from http://www.whitehouse .gov/the-press-office/2011/05/25/remarks-president-parliament-london-united-kingdom

Office of the National Counterintelligence Executive. 2011. "Foreign Spies Stealing US Economic Secrets in Cyberspace." October. Accessed January 6, 2013 from http://www.ncix .gov/publications/reports/fecie_all/Foreign_Economic_Collection_2011.pdf

Oppel, Richard A. 2012. "Romney's Adversarial View of Russia Stirs Debate." *Washington Post,* May 11. Accessed January 6, 2013 from http://www.nytimes.com/2012/05/12/us/ politics/romneys-view-of-russia-sparks-debate.html?pagewanted=all

Osgood, Robert E. 1953. *Ideals and Self-Interest in American Foreign Relations.* Chicago, IL: University of Chicago Press.

Peck, Don. 2010. "How a New Jobless Era Will Transform America." *The Atlantic,* March. Accessed January 6, 2013 from http://www.theatlantic.com/magazine/ archive/2010/03/how-a-new-jobless-era-will-transform-america/7919/

Pincus, Walter. 2012. "CBO says military health-care costs could soar." *Washington Post,* July 16. Accessed January 6, 2013 from http://www.washingtonpost.com/ world/national-security/cbo-says-military-health-care-costs-could-soar/2012/07/16/gJQAF LVQpW_story.html

Priest, Dana, and William M. Arkin. 2010. "Top Secret America." *Washington Post,* July. Accessed January 6, 2013 from http://projects.washingtonpost.com/top-secret-america/

Quinn, Adam. 2010. *US Foreign Policy in Context: National Ideology from the Founders to the Bush Doctrine*. London: Routledge.

Quinn, Adam. 2011a. "The Art of Declining Politely: Obama's Prudent Presidency and the Waning of American Power." *International Affairs*, 87(4): 803–824. DOI: 10.1111/j.1468-2346.2011.01005.x

Quinn, Adam. 2011b. "Hard Power in Hard Times: Relative Military Power in an era of Budgetary Constraint." In *The United States after Unipolarity*, LSE IDEAS Report. December, Accessed January 6, 2013 from http://www2.lse.ac.uk/IDEAS/publications/reports/pdf/SR009/quinn.pdf

Quinn, Adam. 2013. "Obama and Systemic Constraint." In *Obama's Foreign Policy: ending the war on terror*, edited by Michelle Bentley and Jack Holland. London: Routledge.

Rice, Condoleezza. 2008. "Rethinking the National Interest." *Foreign Affairs*, July/Aug. Accessed January 6, 2013 from http://www.foreignaffairs.com/articles/64445/condoleezza-rice/rethinking-the-national-interest

Rice, Condoleezza. 2011. *No Higher Honor: a memoir of my years in Washington*. London: Simon & Schuster.

Ricks, Thomas E. 2006. *Fiasco: the American military adventure in Iraq*. London: Penguin.

Rumsfeld, Donald. 2011. *Known and Unknown: a memoir*. London: Sentinel.

Sanger, David. 2012. "Obama Order Sped Up Wave of Cyberattacks Against Iran." *NY Times*, June 1. Accessed January 6, 2013 from http://www.nytimes.com/2012/06/01/world/middleeast/obama-ordered-wave-of-cyberattacks-against-iran.html?_r=3&pagewanted=1&pagewanted=all

Slaughter, Anne-Marie. 2009. "America's Edge: Power in the Networked Century." *Foreign Affairs*, 88(1): 94–113.

State Budget Crisis Task Force. 2012. "Ravitch–Volcker Report." Accessed January 6, 2013 from http://www.statebudgetcrisis.org/wpcms/report-1/

Stiglitz, Joseph, and Linda Bilmes. 2008. *The Three Trillion Dollar War: The True Cost of the Iraq Conflict*. New York, NY: W.W. Norton & Co.

Waltz, Kenneth. 2010 [1979]. *Theory of International Politics*. Long Grove, IL: Waveland Press.

Woodward, Bob. 2002. *Bush at War*. London: Simon & Schuster.

Woodward, Bob. 2008. *The War Within*. London: Simon & Schuster.

Woodward, Bob. 2010. *Obama's Wars*. London: Simon & Schuster.

Williams, William Appleman. 1972. *The Tragedy of American Diplomacy*. New York, NY: Dell.

Wolverson, Roya, and Christopher Alessi. 2011. "Confronting US–China Economic Imbalances." *Council on Foreign Relations*, November 2. Accessed January 6, 2013 from http://www.cfr.org/china/confronting-us-china-economic-imbalances/p20758

Chapter 26

Civil Society in Fragile Contexts[1]

Willemijn Verkoren and Mathijs van Leeuwen

Introduction

What does civil society (CS) look like in so-called "fragile states"? What civil society actors have a potential to contribute to peace in fragile contexts, and what roles do they play, or may they play, in bringing peace closer? How can they be strengthened by international development organizations?

In (policy) literature, "civil society" actors are allocated diverse roles in democratization and peacebuilding, including advocacy, peace education, local mediation, and service delivery. Given the importance attached to CS in promoting peace and democracy, increasingly, policies to promote peace in conflict-torn societies have included "CS building" or "strengthening" as an aim. Among US-based development organizations and donors, the idea is often that citizens' associations create a space between the citizen and the state, which is used to discuss and negotiate public issues. This allows for a check on government actions, the representation of citizens' interests, and the creation of a "social contract" between both parties. More European-oriented traditions emphasize the transformative role of societal groups in striving for political reform and emancipating citizens. Based on such ideas, over the last decade, we have seen an increasing interest in "civil society building" in developing countries.

Such ideas about CS have also found strong resonance in the context of so-called "fragile states"[2] or unstable societies: those places where the state is largely absent and has lost legitimacy, where people expect little of the state or even more harm than good from it. In such contexts, CS is seen as an alternative that is less corrupt and more responsive to local needs. In order for peace to be sustainable, it is vital that it reaches down to the "grassroots". Thus, CS actors are seen to add a bottom–up dimension to processes of peacebuilding, statebuilding, and democratization.

The Handbook of Global Security Policy, First Edition. Edited by Mary Kaldor and Iavor Rangelov.
© 2014 John Wiley & Sons, Ltd. Published 2014 by John Wiley & Sons, Ltd.

However, how do such ideal images compare with practice in fragile societies? Ideal images of CS can seldom be encountered in real life. At the local level, there is large diversity of actors that may be considered "CS". These include churches, local religious or occupational associations, traditional groups (e.g. age groups), and traditional authorities (e.g. chiefs, clan leaders). Often, amid insecurity, people fall back on clan and family structures. Similarly, where the state does not function, people often rely on patronage networks or even on protection by warlords. Alternatively, they create security communities. And finally, there are the nongovernmental organizations (NGOs), which in many fragile contexts have been created in large numbers in response to the availability of donor funds. In practice, those different manifestations of CS differ highly in the extent to which they are inclusive and have local legitimacy. Local institutions may be exclusivist or sectarian. Organizations that do have strong local ties are often highly political or clan-based and may contribute to exclusion, sectarianism, and even conflict. On the other hand, more formal organizations like NGOs may lack local constituencies.

This chapter aims to shed more light on the role of different local CS actors in peacebuilding and development in fragile states, and what this implies for intervening organizations. It starts with an overview of debates on strengthening CS, and its contribution to democratization and peacebuilding in fragile states in particular. The second part of the chapter illustrates what these debates come down to in the practices of intervention. It explores the practical experiences of the staff of a Dutch peacebuilding organization with identifying local CS partners that could help bring peace closer in Ituri in the Democratic Republic of the Congo (DRC), and what issues and dilemmas come up in working with such actors in fragile contexts.

The chapter paints a picture of fluidity and high complexity that starkly contrasts with theories of CS. In particular, the analysis brings two issues to the fore. First, in fragile contexts it is difficult, if not impossible, to distinguish between state and society or between "civil" and "uncivil". Local governments and informal structures of power, such as traditional authorities, interlink. Not all of those actors conventionally referred to as CS aim to mediate between citizens and the government. Some, instead, aim to govern a particular area or deliver services or implement donor policies. And while the concept of "CS" is often associated with values such as tolerance, inclusiveness, and nonviolence, various "uncivil" local actors, which are exclusivist and/or do not reject violence by definition, may nonetheless have local legitimacy, and play important roles in service provision or even building peace.

Second, there is a tension between different types of CS legitimacy. The chapter introduces a distinction between local and international legitimacy. Local legitimacy refers to the extent to which CS actors have a local constituency and are seen as representative of local interests. International legitimacy refers to the extent to which CS comply with international norms such as tolerance, inclusiveness, nonviolence, and gender equity – things that are usually prerequisites for international donor support. The issue is that these two kinds of legitimacy rarely overlap. Groups that are most deeply rooted, completely trusted, and experienced as legitimate on the ground are often not the same as those most in step with Western norms. This yields complex dilemmas for those aiming to strengthen CS in support of peace.

Strengthening Civil Society, What Is It All About?

The term "CS" refers to the sphere of organized society that exists outside of government and the private sector (for example, Van Rooy, 1998a; Biekart, 1999). As such, CS may constitute a wide variety of actors, ranging from internationally operating development organizations to very localized initiatives and traditional forms of association. Depending on the definition,[3] CS may include media, labor unions, political parties, human rights activists, NGOs, traditional and religious institutions, and sports and welfare associations (e.g. Diamond, 1992; Barnes, 2005; Kaldor, 2003). Yet, while much debate on the definition of CS concerns what kind of actors it includes, alternatively, CS may also be seen as a "public sphere". From such a perspective, the public sphere is an area in social life where people come together to discuss societal issues of common interest. The public sphere mediates between the private sphere and the sphere of public authority. In the public sphere, public opinion is formed and translated into political action (Habermas, 1989).

In the field of development collaboration during the 1980s, CS grew to be the "imagined agent of development" (Pearce, 2005), being considered more effective than – and therefore an alternative to – governments in providing development needs (Rupesinghe, 1998; Crowther, 2001). Such high expectations of CS developed particularly in post-conflict contexts, where state institutions failed in providing security, accountability, and basic services. Here, CS would represent the forces in favor of peace in a society, and was seen as more representative and closer to the grassroots than government institutions (e.g. ECCP, 2004; Van Rooy, 1998b, p. 6). A strong CS came to be seen as a key component of democratization and peacebuilding because it would contribute to reforming state-society relations and fostering responsive and legitimate institutions that can effectively deal with conflict (see e.g. Bebbington and Riddell, 1997; Biekart, 1999; Cousens, Kumar, and Wermester, 2001, p. 12; Woodward, 2007). CS building therefore concerns efforts to support those actors in society who can bring about such reforms. Alternatively, if CS is rather seen as a "public sphere", CS building is about establishing conditions for free debate and alternative political ideas.

Increasingly over the past decade, the idea has arisen of a "global civil society", both in a descriptive and a normative sense. Taking success stories such as the global campaigns against small arms, land mines, and HIV/Aids as an example, authors like Kaldor (2003) argue that transnational networks of citizens' groups are increasingly significant in international relations, and may or should be part of the solution to the ills of globalization, such as the decreasing ability of democratically elected governments to regulate globalized issues, as well as the ways in which contemporary warfare is globalized. From such thinking, CS building is also about stimulating international or global civic action and interconnectedness.

Nowadays, in (policy) literature, "CS" actors are allocated a variety of roles in promoting democracy and peace. The World Bank, for example, lists seven functions for CS in this regard: protection, monitoring/early warning, advocacy, socialization/peace education, social cohesion, mediation, and service delivery (World Bank, 2007; see also Barnes, 2006). From such a perspective, "CS strengthening" in the first place is about supporting CS actors in fulfilling such roles; yet often ambitions are even higher and CS strengthening is seen as an objective in itself. Such approaches of "CS building" consider that a strong CS both plays vital roles in bringing about peace and is a condition for making it last.[4]

Despite a convergence in policy discourse that CS has important roles to play in development, democratization, and peacebuilding, different emphases are placed, reflecting also different analytical traditions. Building on the classic work of De Tocqueville, contemporary authors like Putnam underscore the importance of organized groups of citizens in maintaining peaceful social relations and a functioning democracy. Citizens' associations create a space between the citizen and the state – a public sphere – that is used to discuss and negotiate public issues. This allows for a check on government actions and the representation of citizens' interests. In addition, civil organizations are seen to cultivate values like tolerance and nonviolence, enhance trust and connectedness (social capital) and allow people to develop democratic debating and organizing skills (De Tocqueville, 1996 [1864]; Putnam, 1993). Such notions of CS have found resonance, particularly among donors and international agencies in the United States. A neoliberal perspective on CS developed that positions CS sharply in contrast against the state, serving as a watchdog on the state or protecting citizens from the state. More European-oriented traditions that emphasize the transformative role of societal groups goes further than providing a balance to the government, but strives to reform the government and bring about fairer social relations. Particularly in Europe, donor agencies and internationally operating NGOs acknowledge the active role citizens may have in shaping the character of their state, and in emancipating citizens (Howell and Pearce, 2001; White, 2004; Paffenholz and Spurk, 2006).

A key idea in both perspectives is that CS building would affect the so-called "social contract" between the state and its citizens. The notion of a social contract captures the idea that state authority is based on the consent of its citizens, which forfeit some of their freedoms in exchange for the benefits of social order through the rule of law. Particularly important in a context of conflict and state failure is the notion of a monopoly on violence, which, in the process of state formation, people handed to the government in exchange for protection and law enforcement. Another aspect of the social contract may be that citizens pay tax in exchange for social services, and also for being represented in government (Rousseau, 2009[1762]; Tilly, 1975). Legitimacy of a government is therefore based upon the extent to which it can live up to its side of the social contract. Where it does not offer its citizens protection from harm, people no longer see a reason for the state to maintain its monopoly on violence. They may start to organize their own forms of governance or even their own militia. A government further loses legitimacy if it fails to provide for the development needs of its citizens. This, put very simply, is the essence of ideas about "state failure". If war represented a failure of the social contract between a state and its citizens, CS became increasingly seen as the intermediate sphere where this social contract can be renegotiated (White, 2004; Kaldor, 2003, p. 79).

This interest in "CS building" in developing countries has resulted in much discussion about the questions of how to effectively strengthen CS, and what kind of actors, initiatives, and processes to focus on. Important debates have developed about the extent to which CS can actually fulfill the democratizing and peacebuilding roles attributed to it. It has been argued, for instance, that the focus on CS is at the expense of other actors that might play important roles in those processes, such as local state actors (Hewitt de Alcantara, 1998; Crowther, 2001; Hohe, 2005). A lot of critique has focused on the tendency of development actors to narrow CS down to professional NGOs; their preference for working with local NGOs comes at the expense of other forms of local organization (Biekart, 1999; Douma and Hilhorst, 2004; Pouligny, 2005; van Leeuwen and Verkoren, 2012). More broadly, a recurring question is whether CS is necessarily representative of the grassroots or speaking on behalf of a constituency at all (Chandler, 1999; World Bank, 2009, p. ii). A key critique concerns the extent to which CS building is a donor-driven rather than an endogenous process, in which donors set the agendas of their local partners (see various contributions to Bebbington, Hickey, and Mitlin, 2008; Fisher and Zimina, 2008). Such questions have also found resonance in debates on so-called "fragile states".

Hybrid Providers of Development in "Fragile States"[5]

The discussions we have described so far tend to take an interventionist perspective, focusing on the question of whether and how CS can be supported, developed, or built, but few analyses take the local situation as the starting point, or question the applicability of CS theory to non-Western settings in general, or fragile states in particular. Underlying aspirations for CS building, however, are often behind models of Western states and state formation. In such abstract models, core tasks of the state are the protection of the security of citizens and the regulation of relations between citizens, supported by taxation of citizens (e.g. Tilly, 1975). Such models present the state as an effective bureaucracy that provides services for the well-being of its citizens. Such states are critically followed, scrutinized, and checked on by an independent CS, which is clearly separated from the state and which has its own roles. This ideal picture does not always correspond with reality, even in "developed" countries.[6] But in fragile contexts, it scarcely applies at all.

The concept of the "fragile state" has become a guide in much of the contemporary policy literature. A typology of states developed by the Department for International Development (DFID) conveniently summarizes much of the literature on fragile states. DFID defines fragile states as states in which the government is either unwilling or incapable to deliver basic services. Such a definition assumes four types of environments: (1) situations of strong state capacity, a reasonable commitment of the state to promoting human welfare, and assuring that all social groups benefit from development (example: Costa Rica); (2) situations where the government is committed to development and inclusiveness, yet government capacity is an obstacle to implementing policy (example: East Timor?); (3) situations where the state is strong (has authority, economic, and implementation capacity) but unresponsive (example: Bahrain); and (4) situations where both state capacity and political will are lacking (example: DRC) (Moreno-Torres and Anderson, 2004). The label "fragile state" therefore applies to situations (2) and (4), i.e. situations where the state may or may not be willing to provide basic services, but where it is certainly lacking in capacity to do so. Often, these situations are characterized by violence and instability.

If, in many developing countries, the state already has a limited presence at the local level, in fragile settings, the involvement of state actors in conflict has delegitimized the state in the eyes of many citizens, or the state has simply collapsed or faded away. In such situations, actors, other than those of the state, play core roles in providing basic needs and represent a form of public authority. Alternative institutions develop that take care of core government tasks, such as the provision of human security, local justice, and taxation (Menkhaus, 2007; Raeymaekers, Menkhaus, and Vlassenroot, 2008; Hohe, 2005; Sikor and Lund, 2009). These may include arrangements set up by people themselves, arrangements supported directly or indirectly by the warring parties, by outside aid agencies, by remnants of state organizations, or frequently by a mixture of these. Such unwieldy configurations are found in conflict contexts in Africa (Lund, 2006; Vlassenroot and Raeymaekers, 2008), Latin America (Arias and Goldstein, 2010), South Asia (Vandekerckhove, 2009) and Central Asia (Goodhand, 2004). Such arrangements may include local institutions, (inter)national NGOs, representatives of the business community, and even armed groups. As of yet, little is known about how public authority and responsibility are shared and/or negotiated in such complex, fluid, and conflictive contexts. What we can say, however, is that the theoretical distinction between state and CS becomes artificial in such circumstances.

For instance, traditional structures and authorities often provide security and take care of conflict resolution. Yet, in fragile states, notions of citizenship are often rather limited. People do not expect a lot from the state, but neither do they see a reason to fulfill obligations towards the state. There is no "social contract" in the sense in which it is understood in the West. Social relationships are considered as more important than the obligations as a citizen (Boege, Brown, Clements, and Nolan, 2009, p. 6 ff.). In many such arrangements, patronage, personalized leadership, and clientelism (Joseph, 1999) play a role. To local citizens, such practices are not corrupt or illegitimate by definition: they represent a logic of their own, or even a different kind of social contract, in which those with power offer favors to their followers in exchange for loyalty (Chabal and Daloz, 1999; van Leeuwen and Verkoren, 2012). Such local forms of public authority are often deeply rooted and, in conflict situations, they are what people fall back on.

Even if the state is barely present, local institutions seldom operate completely disconnected from the state. Statebuilding efforts by the colonial and post-colonial authorities have often resulted in "hybrid political orders", in which customary forms of order and governance do not exist in isolation from the state, but permeate and interact with each other (Boege, Brown, Clements, and Nolan, 2009; Roberts, 2009). For instance, analysts of African political systems have, for a long time, analyzed how patrimonial relationships linger under a thin layer of formal bureaucracy in many countries. Many local institutions find themselves in the "twilight zone" between state and non-state (e.g. Menkhaus, 2007; Vlassenroot and Raeymaekers, 2008). And even those institutions that consider themselves explicitly non-state often legitimize themselves in ways similar to those of the state, or in fact promote the notion of statehood (Lund, 2006).

In cases as diverse as eastern DRC, Liberia, and southern Sudan, for many people with political aspirations, civil society has at times functioned as an alternative to inaccessible government structures. As soon as opportunities arise, representatives of civil society enter state governance structures (van Leeuwen, 2009). Rather than operating as a check on the state or holding state institutions accountable, there may be considerable competition for authority and legitimacy between representatives from local CS institutions and the state (e.g. Hohe, 2005). Sikor and Lund (2009), for instance, argue how local level resource conflicts may provide both CS and state institutions with ample opportunities for strengthening their own authority. Violent conflict and state collapse may create opportunities for local CS actors to take over from the state.

Agents of Peace and Democratization?

The question is to what extent such diverse local manifestations of CS may contribute to peace and democratization. In literature on reconciliation and transitional justice, a lot of attention is given to the role that local conflict-resolving mechanisms or traditional justice systems might have in contributing to peace. Such institutions are believed to be rooted in the local culture and history, to have intimate knowledge of local realities, and to be more trusted or effective than state institutions in arriving at locally accepted solutions (see e.g. Prendergast, 1997; Wardak, 2004; Dexter and Ntahombaye, 2005; Edossa et al., 2007). However, other analysts doubt whether such institutions can still fulfill their traditional roles, having been eroded by conflict or perceived as elitist (e.g. Reijntjens and Vandeginste, 2001; Deslaurier, 2003). Traditional institutions may also be insufficiently geared to deal with new challenges that arise. For instance, in post-genocide Rwanda, the question is whether the roles of such traditional institutions can be stretched to comprise dealing with violence on a massive scale (Molenaar, 2005).

The extent to which such local forms of CS have the power to represent a check on national state power, renegotiate local authority, or contribute to local peacebuilding varies enormously. History and culture influence how citizenship is defined and what forms social mobilization takes (Leach and Scoones, 2007). Some localities have a long tradition of civil organization and activism, while in other areas hardly any forms of civil organization are present.

The political context also shapes the roles that CS can play. In settings where the state lacks political will or institutional capacity for delivering core development needs, as in South Sudan and Somaliland, CS and other local actors tend to take over state functions, sometimes quite successfully. A challenge for outside supporters in such settings is how not to obstruct the development of the state's capacity. At the same time, in such settings CS might still have a role to play in advocacy for good governance, which is not easy, especially when populations see service delivery as the first priority (Dowst, 2009). On the other hand, in states that have strong capacity, but lack political will or that are even repressive, CS may have a key role in advocacy rather than in service provision. Here, civil society plays delicate roles in negotiating space vis-à-vis the government, and urging for alternative ways of policy making (see also DFID, 2005). However, precisely in such settings, space for making contentious claims may be reduced (Tilly, 2003). Further, the character of the political context may change over time, with important implications for the most appropriate roles for civil society (see Tarrow, 1998).

Legitimacy and "Civilness"

An important issue is the legitimacy of CS actors, both local (are they locally seen as representative, do they have a constituency) and international (do they comply with international norms such as tolerance, inclusiveness, nonviolence, and gender equity) (Tiemessen, 2004; Fierens, 2005). These two kinds of legitimacy may not always be in correspondence with one another. The organizations that are most deeply rooted, completely trusted, and experienced as legitimate on the ground, need not be the same as those most in step with Western norms.

In fragile contexts, some of the organizations providing social services may be closely related to military actors. Hamas, Hezbollah, and the Sadrists in Iraq are well-known examples of this. They provide security and services, but they also have exclusivist tendencies and employ violent means. Another example comes from southern Sudan. During the war, the humanitarian organization Sudan Relief and Rehabilitation Association (SRRA) was one of the few actors providing the population with social or conflict resolving services, yet this organization was closely affiliated with the resistance movement Sudan People's Liberation Movement and Sudan People's Liberation Army (SPLM/SPLA).

Even if they are not associated with armed actors, CS actors may have substantially different visions, partisan biases, and political connections (Cardoso, 2003). As Crowther (2001) indicates, "civil organisations are often set up precisely to cope with and strengthen an interested party's hand in conflict". In the Philippines, for example, several civil society organizations (CSOs) that implemented development activities or provided services had their roots in the underground revolutionary movement (Hilhorst, 2003). Many of the CSOs in pre-genocide Rwanda that received the wholehearted support of international agencies were part of a clientelist system linking them to an exclusionist government (Uvin, 1998; for more instances, see various contributions to Paffenholz, 2010).

Another issue is that many CSOs may primarily be serving the interests of their staff, rather than the wider societal aims. Often founded to get access to available donor money, such organizations provide employment and income under difficult economic circumstances. Their main aim may be to survive as an organization. Adopting "donor jargon" and becoming versed in fundraising will then take the foreground; however, stated aims may not reflect the priorities of the local people that the organization claims to represent.

A major problem in assessing the "true nature" and ambitions of CSOs is that they constitute multiple realities that may coexist. A CS representative may be sincerely concerned about the suffering of indigenous people, while also being concerned about personal – financial, emotional, political – interests. An organization's partisan interests, or past affiliation with guerrillas does not necessarily prevent it from making a real contribution to peace (Hilhorst and van Leeuwen, 2005).

Global Connections and Difficulties of Outside Support

Recent thinking on "global civil society" suggests that global civic action and inter-connectedness may play important roles in dealing with contemporary globalized conflicts. The question therefore arises, to what extent civil society in fragile contexts is indeed becoming part of the global civil network or sphere? Many of the groups we have described in this chapter are very much local; however, sometimes they are connected to actors in other places – members of the diaspora, civil society networks (often created by partner/donor NGOs from Western countries) and, particularly, international NGOs who act as partners/donors. Global NGO networks are on the rise – in the field of peacebuilding the Global Partnership for the Prevention of Armed Conflict (GPPAC) is an interesting case. Even if clearly established from the outside-in, or top-down, the network has managed to connect a large number of peace groups around the world, including some very local ones, in order to have their voices heard in global policy forums (Verkoren, 2008).

The question is how far can such examples of "globalized" civil society retain legitimacy and representativeness. For instance, with regard to the diaspora, in a country like Cambodia we see that diaspora returnees dominate the NGO sector. These people speak the language and understand the way of thinking of foreign donors and are therefore best able to access international funding channels. There are, however, few linkages between these returnee NGOs and more localized civil society groups, which often lack global connections (Hughes, 2009; Pouligny, 2005). The question is to what extent, after years in exile and different exposure, the diaspora still shares the same interpretations of and attitudes towards the conflicts as those that stayed behind (Demmers, 2002).

Such issues become all the more prominent when partnership is established between highly different entities, such as international NGOs and local civil society actors. Here, a number of tensions emerge between (Western) theory and (non-Western) reality, and the ensuing complexity yields a number of difficult dilemmas. In a "hybrid political order", where societal actors may carry out state (and security) functions and may be both "civil" and "uncivil" at the same time, how does one select local partners? And what is the best way to support them? Who are considered suitable partners in pursuit of peace, and what roles these partners should play depends strongly on the context and, in particular, on the capacity, legitimacyy, and roles of state and societal actors. Simply aiming to strengthen CS in order to function as an intermediary between the state and citizens may make sense within the traditional theory of CS, but may not apply when CS actors are not intermediaries in the first place but are alternative service providers, or intermingled with state institutions, or highly antagonistic towards the state. In view of the complexity of the context, choosing the right strategy, and the right CS partners, is not easy.

This complexity also applies to CS actors themselves. Given the circumstances, the perfect peace-promoting CS actor does not usually exist. As we have seen earlier, there is often a tension between local and international legitimacy. Would-be supporters of CS usually aim to select local partners that have both a high mobilizing capacity and the same values as the supporting organization. If it is not possible to find CSOs that meet both these requirements, then compromises will have to be sought. In this regard, supporting organizations tend to opt for international legitimacy. Much has been written about donors' preference for local NGOs over other CS groups. Either new local NGOs are created or local CS groups are assisted to become professional NGOs. These local partners speak the language of international human rights and associated norms, but they often lack local support, and as a result, their capacity to achieve societal transformation is limited (see various contributions to Bebbington, Hickey, and Mitli, 2008; Fisher and Zimina, 2008). The dilemma of international versus local legitimacy remains unsolved.

When we look at what intervening actors currently do, we see an emphasis on strengthening *organizations* rather than approaching CS as a public *sphere*. If CS is treated as a public sphere, then the dominant activity might not be organization building (or "NGO-ization") but increasing the space for public debate and civic action. Rather than just strengthening the services-providing capacities of CSOs, there is need for explicit support for the political and reformist roles of CS. Indeed, from a public sphere perspective, the focus may not be on CSOs at all, but on the government and the extent to which it enables citizen-state interaction. To renegotiate social contracts and reform relationships of governance, CS needs access to public information, opportunities to voice opinions and grievances, opportunities for association, and space and mechanisms for dialogue with the government (World Bank, 2009). Such enabling factors are strongly related to the nature of the state; thus, building CS as a space for negotiating state-society relations cannot be done without reforming the state.

More basically, statebuilding may be a requirement for CS building because CS cannot function as a space for state-citizen interaction unless functioning (local) state institutions are present and represent a minimum of economic and political power (Crowther, 2001; Hohe, 2005). In this connection, a difficult question is the extent to which local (CS/state) institutions should be formalized. As traditional institutions are often in competition with the state for authority and legitimacy (e.g. Hohe, 2005), efforts to strengthen local institutions may easily feed into local struggles for power. For instance, the acknowledgement of local institutions by the state may contribute to their authority and legitimacy, but their affiliation to the state could erode their local standing as well (see e.g. van Leeuwen, 2010).

Case Study – Strengthening "Agents of Change" in Ituri[7]

To illustrate the issues and dilemmas discussed in this chapter, we now describe the experiences of the Dutch peace organizations IKV Pax Christi (IPC) in Ituri in DRC. IPC's policy conforms to much policy thinking about "fragile states", which emphasizes institutional weakness and the need to (re)build strong and legitimate state institutions and (re)create a "social contract". At the same time, the partnership policy of IPC recognizes the complexity of fragile contexts, and the range of actors that could potentially be partners is deliberately left wide. IPC aims to team up with so-called "agents of change", which are defined as "individuals and informal groups that have a strong mobilizing capacity in their society". However, another important criterion in the selection of counterparts is "shared values". This may be seen to reflect norms of both local and international legitimacy.

Civil Society in Ituri

The Ituri district in the north-east of DRC has experienced serious violence between 1999 and 2003. During this time, longstanding grievances about land issues between Lendu and Hema have played an important role (see e.g. Pottier, 2008, Vlassenroot and Huggins, 2005). Conflict increasingly affected the whole population due to the presence of various armed groups participating in the Second Congo War, which began in 1998.

CS in Ituri is relatively weak. War has had a devastating effect on CS: leaders fled or were killed; churches and NGOs were cut off from the hinterland and henceforth lacked any public basis outside the district capital, Bunia; NGOs became proxies of particular (ethnic) communities; and all organizations closed down their regular activities.

Important non-state actors in Ituri are traditional authorities, NGOs, the Catholic Church and other churches, security arrangements organized by the community themselves, local militia, and traders. When exploring the roles of these actors in the unstable Ituri society, it is often difficult to distinguish unambiguously between state and society. Many of these actors have taken over governmental roles, and to an extent, we may consider them as representing public authority. Moreover, they are often not completely disconnected from the state.

In a similar vein, a distinction "civil" or "non-civil" also appears useless. All main non-state actors play mixed roles – sometimes "drivers of peace", sometimes "drivers of conflict". For example, many NGOs in Ituri are mono-ethnic in nature or perceived as such (Frerks and Douma, 2007), and are formed by elites from single ethnic communities. They serve mainly the (humanitarian or development) interests of their own ethnic communities, and may represent partisan opinions and possibly contribute to resentment of others. They are neither representative nor legitimate in the eyes of all groups. A case in point is the Catholic Church, which is perceived as biased towards the Hema and therefore has no legitimacy among a significant part of the population of some regions. Various NGOs, as well as the Catholic Church, are involved in land conflicts. NGOs also tend to be elite-based and are often perceived as far removed from the "grassroots". Nonetheless, they are important actors because they are representative of the important political forces in the region. In addition, they employ many of the more talented and educated people. According to observers, if ever something of a Congolese state has to emerge, it may have to originate from the NGO sector.

This mixed picture also applies to other CS groups. In many places, customary chiefs play important roles in conflict resolution (Mongo, Nkoy Elela, and Puijenbroek, 2009), and have certain local legitimacy; however, chiefs are not by definition in pursuit of peace. In Aru, for instance, customary chiefs have been heavily implicated in deals through which communal land was taken over by outsiders (Frerks and Douma, 2007). In addition, different types of "vigilante" groups have developed at community level. Such groups may have positive effects when they alert the population to take refuge in case of insecurity or play a role in reporting misconduct by policemen and soldiers to the local authorities. At the same time, they risk developing into a force of their own with their own interests, outside the political framework, and with limited accountability (Risch and Hoebeke, 2010).

In some instances, even militia might promote peace and development. There are accounts of militia extorting the population, who already contribute to the maintenance of roads, to pay at roadblocks. Vlassenroot and Raeymaekers (2008) describe how businessmen's needs for predictability and security have resulted in strategic alliances with rebel leadership to protect their trade. In Beni-Lubero, such arrangements even incidentally turned the local business elite to act as some sort of local governors. A case in point is the militia belonging to the N'giti clan, one of the most deprived communities in Ituri. This militia has been instrumentalized in illegal gold trafficking, even by traders from the adversary community, and partly they degenerated to banditism, sometimes even looting their own community. At the same time, this militia is enjoying popular support because they are the only ones assuring that the interests of this marginalized group remain on the political agenda. Further, sustainable peace seems unachievable without an arrangement for the N'giti community to access their fishing grounds and for their political emancipation.

Identifying Peace-Minded Partners

IKV-Pax Christi has been present in Ituri since 2002. Its intervention strategy was based on the assumption that predatory segments of the state had an interest in maintaining the situation as it was. This was to be countered first by strengthening community committees and organizing dialogue between all local government actors (chiefs, formal government, local army commanders, and police commanders). Thereafter, dialogue would be organized between communities and higher-level government.

The single-ethnic basis of most societal organizations in Ituri led IPC to conclude that it should not work with one particular organization, but with a network of organizations from different backgrounds. In other words, the antagonisms of local society and conflict had to be incorporated within the partner network – and the leading criterion was to be as inclusive as possible and to make sure that the main actors in society would be present in the network.

Yet, in practice, it turned out to be difficult to identify a series of partners that fitted this intervention strategy and those criteria. Although the idea was to include a diversity of local non-state actors, in practice there were few other options than a program with more conventional CS organizations, like NGOs, associations, and churches. Customary authority was very fragmented, local government had not resumed yet and the main commercial actors were also outside Ituri – above all, no other organizations existed that worked specifically on the theme of peace and security at the early stages.

The selection of partners and arriving at a right mix of people was therefore a process of trial and error. In the end, the network of partners that developed largely originated from an initial conference, held in 2003 and organized by a local organization. With hindsight it can be concluded that this network is largely the result of the efforts of one particular local organization. Some argue that this organization is basically an elite affair. At the same time, so were most local organizations in Ituri. The elites that are part of the network are well connected, and in the eyes of IPC staff, that also has its merits. Over the course of time, other members have been added to the initiative of IPC in agreement with the network. When looking for partners who could join the network, however, one difficulty was the lack of reliable information about potential partners.

In this process, IPC struggled to reconcile principles of international and local legitimacy. While the leading criterion for the network as a whole was inclusiveness, it was realized that to contribute to peace, partners needed to have strong local legitimacy, and capacity to generate inclusive dialogue. Few potential partners lived up to all these criteria at the same time. NGOs run by Congolese from outside Ituri had the technical capacity to act as bridge builders but lacked local legitimacy. The church had strong legitimacy, yet only among one particular group. Many CSOs were rather involved in the conflict. At the start of the program, only one significant local organization had activities outside Bunia town, and so managed to bring the militia to participate in the meetings. In the end, partners had to be sought outside the territories affected by the Ituri conflict.

As much as on the formal criteria or conflict analysis, the establishment of partnerships depended on chance and the gut feeling of the program staff, personal connections, and networking. Perhaps it was even the case that rather than a strategy leading to certain criteria for partner selection on which partners were then identified, in practice, partnerships were established with interesting organizations, after which this selection was then legitimized with reference to the desired general objectives.

Finally, in practice, those who were seen as "agents of change" turned out to depend a lot on what peace is being aimed at and on one's analysis of the conflict. Communities were increasingly concerned about assuring community security. This required the involvement of "agents of change", like the community members themselves, but also like the army and police. Further, with the return of internally displaced people, land conflicts between returnees and the on-staying population were on the increase. Such intra-community conflicts required other CS actors than the previous inter-community land conflict. In the past, there was no central leadership and intercommunity conflict had to be addressed by the communities themselves. As chiefs, formal administration and churches began to re-establish themselves, and once they had regained legitimacy they became important again. It was also expected that in the future, commercial actors might become an interesting party to work with because the root cause of the Ituri conflict lies, amongst other things, in equal access to economic opportunities.

Connecting back to the earlier discussion of international involvement with local civic actors, the question arises how the presence and activities of IPC shaped the local public sphere. It is difficult to satisfactorily answer this question. IPC created a platform in which local organizations could enter into dialogue with one another. There were no cross-ethnic civil society actors, and IPC created one. This is a potentially significant, but not necessarily permanent contribution to civil society in Ituri. It may be that this construction requires ongoing investment by outsiders. Also, the extent to which IPC's engagement has changed local civil society dynamics and initiatives is not yet clear. It is also a broader theoretical question; for example, in the literature on hybrid political orders, the way in which hybrid orders can be fed and supported is identified as an important question for further research. This is, indeed, a central question that external interveners will need to actively engage with.

Conclusion

In this chapter, we have highlighted the complexity and fluidity of CS in fragile contexts. Where theories of CS ascribe clear and positive roles to CSOs in promoting peace and democracy, in practice, we see that things are not as clear-cut in fragile settings. Based on the Western experience of state formation, protection of human security, and regulation of relations between citizens are conceptualized in political theory as core tasks of the state. In some non-Western contexts, however, the state has never fully developed these capacities, whilst in others they have come under severe pressure from the combined forces of fragmentation and globalization that characterize new wars and complex emergencies.

Where the state lacks institutional capacity for delivering core functions, and/or the state is mistrusted, the tendency is for a wide diversity of local actors to step in to provide security and other basic needs and to further the interests of the group. Such local actors include not only "non-state" and "civil" actors conventionally identified with CS, e.g. NGOs and churches, but may also comprise traditional authorities, clan and family associations, local security communities, entrepreneurs, and even armed actors. This raises questions about the meaning of the concept "CS", which is often associated with actors that embody values such as tolerance and nonviolence. However, "uncivil" local actors, which do not reject violence by definition, may be relevant players in bringing about peace in fragile contexts. Local actors in fragile contexts often play mixed roles, playing peacebuilding roles on the one hand but simultaneously being associated with armed actors, or being highly partisan and political. Local legitimacy (representativeness and a strong support base) and international legitimacy (living up to norms of inclusiveness and nonviolence) rarely overlap.

This reality challenges two core components of civil society theory: the distinction between state and society (with CS either being on the society side or being an intermediary sphere between the two), and the "civilness" of CS actors. Those active in CS strengthening in fragile states have not yet found answers to this discrepancy between theory and reality. Although they usually recognize the problem, they struggle to find the right intervention strategy. Through trial-and-error and by relying on their gut feeling, interveners find solutions that meet the fluidity and complexity of fragile contexts. In Ituri, creating a network out of a variety of single-ethnic organizations has become a core role of IPC. Since there were no cross-ethnic organizations to partner with, and inclusivity was one of IPC's guiding principles, creating this network seemed the only way to have a suitable local partner that was inclusive and representative.

The struggle to find appropriate ways of understanding, and supporting CS in pursuit of peace would be helped by more fundamental reflection. This reflection would entail recognition of the Western bias of CS theory and a more careful contextualization and problematization of the role of the state and CS in fragile settings.

In their strategies for CS strengthening, intervening actors tend to focus exclusively on CSOs, and even on NGOs. In doing so, they lose an important part of the picture. Alternatively conceiving of CS as a "public sphere" would make for a reorientation away from organizations and toward the political conditions that create space for public debate and civic action. This would better recognize the fact that CS is never neutral, as many CS policies appear to assume, but is itself very political. Indeed, often CS groups consider taking a stance in the conflict as the best way to achieve peace. Or they may see the conflict itself as a necessary process to redress injustice.

A public sphere approach to CS would aim at fostering avenues for nonviolent ways of conflict management and societal transformation through public debate and civic action. Still, the concept of a public sphere connecting citizens to the state would look very different in situations where state and society are not separate and where the primary connection between citizens and power holders is through patronage networks and clan ties.

Awareness of such complexities does not make intervention in fragile contexts easier. Indeed, this chapter has painted a picture of high complexity and difficult choices. It is not easy to do the right thing in fragile contexts and any decision has a trade-off. Explicit reflection on these choices and dilemmas will be helpful to all involved. If anything can be concluded from this chapter, it is that there is a world to be gained in adapting CS policies to the realities of fragile contexts.

Notes

1. This chapter builds on a study about civil society strengthening in fragile states that was carried out within the Dutch peace organization IKV Pax Christi by the current authors together with Mient-Jan Faber, Marlies Glasius, Gijsbert van Iterson Scholten, Joost van Puijenbroek, and Ben Schennink. We are indebted to all of them for the ideas and findings that found their way into this chapter. The arguments and possible mistakes in this chapter are the responsibility of the current authors.
2. The term "fragile states", while widely used in policy circles, is not unproblematic. It is more a label used by donors than an analytically useful category. One issue is that the concept focuses on state institutions and the national level, and implies that strengthening the state is the solution to the ills of those societies concerned.
3. The coverage of the concept is subject to discussion, for instance whether or not to include organizations from the business sphere, associations that do not have a representative function towards government, or even northern NGOs that depend heavily on state financing.
4. For a more complete overview of the roles of civil society in democratization and peacebuilding, see e.g. Paffenholz & Spurk (2006).
5. The authors wish to thank Marlies Glasius for her inputs to an earlier version of this section.
6. For example, there are questions as to the independence of NGOs that are financially dependent on the state.
7. We would like to thank Joost van Puijenbroek for his inputs in this case study.

References

Arias, E.D., and D.M. Goldstein, eds. 2010. *Violent Democracies in Latin America*. Durham, NC: Duke University Press.

Barnes, C. 2005. "Weaving the Web: Civil Society Roles in Working with Conflict and Building Peace" In *People Building Peace II: Successful Stories of Civil Society*, edited by P. Van Tongeren, M. Brenk, M. Hellema, and J. Verhoeven, 7–24. Boulder, CO: Lynne Rienner.

Barnes, C. 2006. *Agents for Change: Civil Society Roles in Preventing War & Building Peace*. The Hague: European Centre for Conflict Prevention.

Bebbington, A.J., and R. Riddell. 1997. "Heavy Hands, Hidden Hands, Holding Hands? Donors, Intermediary NGOs and Civil Society Organisations." In *NGOs, States and Donors: Too Close for Comfort*, edited by D. Hulme and M. Edwards, 107–127. New York, NY: St Martin's Press.

Bebbington, A., S. Hickey, and D. Mitlin, eds. 2008. *Can NGOs Make a Difference? The Challenge of Development Alternatives*. London: ZedBooks.

Biekart, K. 1999. *The Politics of Civil Society Building: European Private Aid Agencies and Democratic Transitions in Central America*. Utrecht: Arkel.

Boege, V., A. Brown, K. Clements, and A. Nolan. 2009. "On Hybrid Political Orders and Emerging States: What is Failing – States in the Global South or Research and Politics in the West?" In *Building Peace in the Absence of States: Challenging the Discourse on State Failure*, edited by M. Fischer and B. Schmelzle, 15–35. Berlin: Berghof Research Centre for Constructive Conflict Management.

Cardoso, F.H. 2003. *High Level Panel on UN-CS; CS and Global Governance*. Contextual paper prepared by the Panel's Chairman. New York, NY: United Nations.

Chabal, P., and J.-P. Daloz. 1999. *Africa Works: Disorder as Political Instrument*. Bloomington, IN: International African Institute, James Currey, Indiana University Press.

Chandler, D. 1999. *Bosnia: Faking Democracy after Dayton*. London: Pluto Press.

Cousens, E., C. Kumar, and K. Wermester. 2001. *Peacebuilding as Politics: Cultivating Peace in Fragile Societies*. Boulder, CO: Lynne Rienner.

Crowther, S. 2001. "The Role of NGOs, Local and International, in Post-war Peacebuilding." *CTTS Newsletter*, 15.

Demmers, J. 2002. "Diaspora and conflict: locality, long-distance nationalism, and delocalisation of conflict dynamics." *The Public*, 9(1): 85–96.

Deslaurier, C. 2003. "Le 'Bushingantahe'; Peut-il Réconcilier le Burundi? Politique Africaine." *Justice et Réconciliation; Ambiguïtés et Impensés*, 92: 76–96.

De Tocqueville, A. 1996 [1864]. *Democracy in America*. Ware: Wordsworth Editions Ltd.

Dexter, T., and P. Ntahombaye. 2005. *The Role of Informal Justice Systems in Fostering the Rule of Law in Post-Conflict Situations; The Case of Burundi*. Geneva: Centre for Humanitarian Dialogue.

DFID. 2005. *Why We Need to Work More Effectively in Fragile States*. London: Department for International Development.

Diamond, L. 1992. "Economic Development and Democracy Reconsidered." In *Re-examining Democracy. Essays in Honor of Seymour Martin Lipset*, edited by G. Marks and L. Diamond, 93–139. London: Sage Publications.

Douma, N., and D. Hilhorst. 2004. *'Beyond Conflict'; Peacebuilding in Policies and Practice of Cordaid and its Partners in the Great Lakes Region (The Experience of DR Congo, Rwanda and Burundi)*. Wageningen: Disaster Studies.

Dowst, M. 2009. *Working with Civil Society in Fragile States*. Policy Briefing Paper No. 23. Oxford: INTRAC.

ECCP. 2004. *European Conference on the Role of Civil Society in the Prevention of Armed Conflict*. Report of a conference held at Dublin Castle, Dublin, 31 March – 2 April, 2004. Utrecht: European Centre for Conflict Prevention.

Edossa, D.C., S.B. Awulachew, R.E. Namara, et al., 2007. "Indigenous Systems of Conflict Resolution in Oromia, Ethiopia." In *Community-based Water Law and Water Resource Management Reform in Developing Countries*, edited by B. Van Koppen, M. Giordano, and J. Butterworth, 146–157. Wallingford, WA: CABI.

Fierens, J. 2005. "Gacaca Courts: Between Fantasy and Reality." *Journal of International Criminal Justice*, 3(4): 896–919.

Fisher, S. and L. Zimina. 2008. "Just Wasting our Time? Provocative Thoughts for Peacebuilders." Accessed from www.berghof-handbook.net

Frerks, G., and P. Douma. 2007. *Local peace initiatives in Ituri, DRC, 2003–2007*. Pax Christi Best Practice Study, No. 3. Utrecht: Pax Christi.

Goodhand, J. 2004. "From war economy to peace economy? Reconstruction and statebuilding in Afghanistan." *International Affairs*, 58(1): 155–174.

Habermas, J. 1989. *The Structural Transformation of the Public Sphere: An Inquiry into a Category of Bourgeois Society*. Cambridge, MA: MIT Press.

Hewitt de Alcantara, C. 1998. "Uses and Abuses of the Concept of Governance." *International Social Science Journal*, 50(155): 105–113.

Hilhorst, D. 2003. *The Real World of NGOs; Discourses, Diversity and Development*. London: Zed Books.

Hilhorst, D., and M. van Leeuwen. 2005. "Global Peace Builders and Local Conflict: The Feminization of Peace in Southern Sudan." In *The Gender Queston in Globalization; Changing Perspectives and Practices*, edited by T. Davids and F. Van Driel, 93–108. Aldershot: Ashgate.

Hohe, T. 2005. "Developing Local Governance." In *Postconflict Development: Meeting New Challenges*, edited by G. Junne and W. Verkoren. Boulder, CO: Lynne Rienner.

Howell, J. and J. Pearce. 2001. "Civil Society, Democracy, and the State: the Americanization of the Debate." In *Civil Society and Development: A Critical Exploration*, edited by J. Howell and J. Pearce, 39–62. Boulder, CO: Lynne Rienner Publishers.

Hughes, C. 2009. *Dependent Communities: Aid and Politics in Cambodia and East Timor*. Ithaca, NY: Cornell University Press.

Joseph, Richard. 1999. "State, Conflict, and Democracy in Africa." In *State, Conflict, and Democracy in Africa*, edited by Richard Joseph, 3–14. Boulder, CO: Lynne Rienner Publishers.

Kaldor, M. 2003. "The Idea of Global Civil Society." *International Affairs*, 79(3): 583–93.

Leach, M. and I. Scoones. 2007. *Mobilising Citizens; Social Movements and the Politics of Knowledge*. IDS Working Paper, 276.

Lund, C. 2006. "Twilight Institutions; Public Authority and Local Politics in Africa." *Development and Change*, 37(4): 685–705.

Menkhaus, K. 2007. "Governance without Government in Somalia; Spoilers, State Building, and the Politics of Coping." *International Security*, 31(3): 74–106.

Molenaar, A. 2005. *Gacaca: Grassroots Justice after Genocide; The Key to Reconciliation in Rwanda?* Leiden: African Studies Centre.

Mongo, E., A.D. Nkoy Elela, and J. Van Puijenbroek. 2009. *Conflits fanciers en Ituri, Poids du passé et défis pour l'avenir de la paix*. RHA/IKV Pax Christi, Bunia.

Moreno-Torres, M., and M. Anderson. 2004. *Fragile States: Defining Difficult Environments for Poverty Reduction*. Department for International Development.

Paffenholz, T., ed. 2010. *Civil Society and Peacebuilding: A Critical Assessment*. Boulder, CO: Lynne Rienner.

Paffenholz, T., and C. Spurk. 2006. *Civil Society, Civic Engagement, and Peacebuilding*. Social Development Papers: Conflict Prevention & Reconstruction Paper 36. Washington, DC: World Bank.

Pearce, J. 2005. "The International Community and Peacebuilding." *Development*, 48(3): 41–49.

Pottier, J. 2008. "Displacement and ethnic reintegration in Ituri, DR Congo: challenges ahead." *Journal of Modern African Studies*, 46(3): 427–450.

Pouligny, B. 2005. "Civil Society and Post-Conflict Peace-building: Ambiguities of International Programmes Aimed at Building 'New' Societies." *Security Dialogue*, 36(4): 495–510.

Prendergast, J. 1997. *Crisis Response; Humanitarian Band-Aids in Sudan and Somalia*. Chicago, IL: Pluto Press.

Putnam, R. 1993. *Making Democracy Work: Civic Traditions in Modern Italy*. Princeton, NJ: Princeton University Press.

Raeymaekers, T., K. Menkhaus, and K. Vlassenroot. 2008. "State and non-state regulation in African protracted crises: governance without government?" *Africa Focus*, 21(2): 7–21.

Reijntjens, F. and S. Vandeginste. 2001. "Traditional Approaches to Negotiation and Mediation: Examples from Africa; Burundi, Rwanda and Congo." In *Peacebuilding: A Field Guide*, edited by L. Reychler and T. Paffenholz, 128–138. Boulder, CO: Lynne Rienner Publishers.

Risch, L., and H. Hoebeke. 2010. "Local Initiatives of Community-based Security in DR Congo." In *Multi-stakeholder Security Partnerships in Post-conflict Reconstruction*, 178–217. Hamburg: Institute for Peace Research and Security Policy.

Roberts, D. 2009. "The Superficiality of Statebuilding in Cambodia: Patronage and Clientelism as Enduring Forms of Politics." In *The Dilemmas of Statebuilding: Confronting the contradictions of postwar peace operations*, edited by R. Paris and T. Sisk, 149–170. London: Routledge.

Rousseau, J.J. 2009 [1762]. "The Social Contract or Principles of Political Right." Accessed December 15, 2012 from http://www.constitution.org/jjr/socon.htm

Rupesinghe, K. 1998. *Civil Wars, Civil Peace; An Introduction to Conflict Resolution*. London: Pluto Press.

Sikor, T., and C. Lund. 2009. "Access and Property; A Question of Power and Authority." *Development and Change*, 40(1): 1–22.

Tarrow, S. 1998. *Power in Movement: Social Movements and Contentious Politics*. Cambridge: Cambridge University Press.

Tiemessen, A.E. 2004. "After Arusha: Gacaca Justice in Post-genocide Rwanda." *African Studies Quarterly*, 8(1): 57–76.

Tilly, C. 1975. *The Formation of National States in Western Europe*. Princeton, NJ: Princeton University Press.

Tilly, C. 2003. *The Politics of Collective Violence*. Cambridge: Cambridge University Press.

Uvin, Peter. 1998. *Aiding Violence: The Development Enterprise in Rwanda*. West Hartford, CT: Kumarian Press.

van Leeuwen, M. 2009. *Partners in Peace; Discourses and Practices of Civil-society Peacebuilding*. Aldershot: Ashgate.

van Leeuwen, M. 2010. "Crisis or Continuity? Framing Land Disputes and Local Conflict Resolution in Burundi." *Land Use Policy*, 27: 753–762.

van Leeuwen, M. and W. Verkoren. 2012. "The complexity of civil society building: Key challenges for enhancing post-conflict civil society approaches." *Journal of Peacebuilding and Development*, 7(1): 81–94.

Vandekerckhove, N. 2009. "'We are sons of the soil'; The Endless Battle over Indigenous Homelands in Assam, India." *Critical Asian Studies*, 41(4): 523–548.

van Rooy, A. 1998a. "The Art of Strengthening Civil Society." In *Civil Society and the Aid Industry; The Politics and Promise*, edited by A. Van Rooy, 197–220. London: Earthscan Publications Ltd.

van Rooy, A. 1998b. "Civil Society as Idea; An Analytical Hatstand?" In *Civil Society and the Aid Industry; The Politics and Promise*, edited by A. Van Rooy, 6–30. London: Earthscan Publications Ltd.

Verkoren, W. 2008. *The Owl and the Dove: Knowledge Strategies to Improve the Peacebuilding Practice of Local NGOs*. Amsterdam: Amsterdam University Press.

Vlassenroot, K. and C. Huggins. 2005. "Land, Migration and Conflict in Eastern DRC." In *From the Ground Up; Land Rights, Conflict and Peace in Sub-Saharan Africa*, edited by C. Huggins and J. Clover, 115–194. Pretoria: Institute for Security Studies.

Vlassenroot, K. and T. Raeymaekers. 2008. "New Political Order in the DR Congo? The transformation of regulation." *Afrika Focus*, 21(2): 39–52.

Wardak, A. 2004. "Building a Post-war Justice System in Afghanistan." *Crime, Law, and Social Change*, 41(4): 319–341.

White, G. 2004. "Civil Society, Democratization and Development: Clearing the Analytical Ground." In *Civil Society in Democratization*, edited by P. Burnell and P. Calvert, 6–21. London: Frank Cass.

Woodward, S. 2007. "Do the 'Root causes' of Civil War Matter? On Using Knowledge to Improve Peacebuilding Interventions." *Journal of Intervention and Statebuilding*, 1(2): 143–170.

World Bank. 2007. *Civil Society and Peacebuilding; Potential, Limitations and Critical Factors*. Washington, DC: Social Development Department, World Bank.

World Bank. 2009. *Cambodia: Linking Citizens and the State*. Washington, DC: World Bank.

Chapter 27

Protest and Politics: How Peace Movements Shape History

David Cortright

Movements against war and nuclear weapons have generated some of the largest social mobilizations in modern history, yet their impacts on policy change are seldom acknowledged. Social movement scholars tend to focus more on mobilization tactics and framing strategies than on the evaluation of political effectiveness. Political scientists rarely acknowledge the role of peace movements in helping to shape security policy. National leaders deny that their decisions are influenced by public pressure and often dismiss the impact of peace activism. Myopia exists even within the peace movement. Because activists rarely see their specific demands met by government officials, they sometimes fail to recognize the policy changes their actions make possible.

In this paper, I examine the largest peace movements of recent decades – the Vietnam antiwar movement, the disarmament campaigns of the 1980s, and the worldwide mobilization against war in Iraq – and trace the ways in which these movements were able to exert impact on US and international policy. Resistance to the Vietnam War limited US war-making options and ultimately forced the withdrawal of American troops. The disarmament campaigns of the 1980s resulted in a partial nuclear freeze and a ban on intermediate nuclear forces and contributed to the ending of the Cold War. Opposition to the war in Iraq produced the largest single-day social mobilization in history but could not prevent the US-led invasion, although antiwar activists in the United States played a key role in electing a president who carried out his campaign pledge to end the war.

I was an active participant in all of these movements and am hardly a disinterested observer; yet I try to bring political realism and scholarly rigor to this analysis. While I acknowledge the transnational dimensions of these movements, my primary focus is on actions and impacts in the United States. I combine my insider perspective with the study of important published literature by leading scholars, participants and analysts, drawing from the works and insights of Charles Chatfield, Charles DeBenedetti,

The Handbook of Global Security Policy, First Edition. Edited by Mary Kaldor and Iavor Rangelov.
© 2014 John Wiley & Sons, Ltd. Published 2014 by John Wiley & Sons, Ltd.

Daniel Ellsberg, Barbara Epstein, Mary Kaldor, Thomas Rochon, Melvin Small, Rebecca Solnit, Pam Solo, Jonathan Schell, Tom Wells, Lawrence Wittner, and others.

These peace movements employed both unconventional means of social contention and conventional tools of political participation. Because of this, they do not fit easily into the categories of social analysis. The movements achieved change in gradual, partial, and indirect ways. Their specific demands – end the war now, abolish nuclear weapons, stop the invasion – were not fully accepted by government leaders, yet pressures on behalf of those goals achieved important results – blocking escalation, generating support for arms reduction, and creating political pressure for the withdrawal of troops. In the pages that follow, I develop these themes and give examples of specific ways in which peace activism helped to achieve significant change in government policy.

A Global Context

The Vietnam, disarmament, and Iraq movements I examine take place in an era of growing civil society mobilization on issues related to war and peace. Citizens have spoken out against war and nuclear weapons all over the world in recent decades. Among the many examples that could be cited are the massive protests and movements against nuclear weapons in Japan over the decades, opposition in France to the war in Algeria, the massive "peace now" movement that emerged in Israel in 1982 against the war in Lebanon, protests against nuclear weapons testing in Kazakhstan in the 1980s, opposition in Russia to the costly and disproportionate use of force during the first Chechen War, worldwide protests against French nuclear weapons testing in the Pacific, movements in the former Yugoslavia to prevent war and ethnic intolerance in the region, protests in Calcutta and other cities against India's decision to test nuclear weapons, the *"no mas"* protests against terrorism and kidnappings in Columbia, and citizen demands for peace and an end to violence during the wars in Liberia and Sierra Leone. In these and many other movements, citizens have sought to promote pluralism, peace, and human rights and have worked to create social space for advocates of nonviolence and cooperation.

These global movements for peace and disarmament have contributed to emerging social norms against war and nuclear weapons and help to explain the global trend toward fewer inter-state wars. A few years after the end of the Cold War, Randall Forsberg, founder of the nuclear freeze movement in the United States, called attention to the declining incidence of great-power war. In a little-noticed but important essay published in 1997, Forsberg evoked the possibility of a future in which war would no longer be socially sanctioned and would increasingly diminish in scope and frequency (Forsberg, 1997). In 2006, retired British General Rupert Smith declared that the old paradigm of industrial inter-state war "no longer exists" (Smith, 2006). That same year Finnish scholar Raimo Väyrynen edited an important volume on *The Waning of Major War* (Väyrynen, 2006). More recently, Steven Pinker, Joshua Goldstein, and Andrew Mack have published books and reports confirming Forsberg's observation of a global trend toward less armed conflict. In *The Better Angels of Our Nature*, Pinker presents evidence of a long-term trend in human affairs toward a reduction in armed violence, which he describes as perhaps "the most important thing that has ever happened in human history." (Pinker, 2012).

Most of the studies that examine the decline of inter-state war attribute the trend to structural factors – economic development, the spread of democracy, the empowerment of women, global interdependence, the rise of multilateralism, and the increasing lethality of military technologies. Few consider the role of social agency or the impact of evolving cultural values in contributing to the declining legitimacy of war. Social norms do not emerge automatically. They are socially constructed and often arise out of social movements and political contention.

A case can be made that movements for peace and human rights in recent decades have strengthened social norms for peace and the prevention of war and have contributed to the lessening of armed conflict. The sharp global reaction to the wars in Vietnam and Iraq makes it more difficult for the United States and any other state to consider similar invasions or inter-state war in the future. Worldwide protests against nuclear weapons have helped to establish what political scientists refer to as the "nuclear taboo" (see Tannenwald, 2007). The influence of peace and disarmament movements is perhaps most apparent in the ending of the Cold War. As Mary Kaldor and her colleagues have noted, the Cold War ended not with war but with nonviolent revolutions in Eastern Europe. This was a victory for civil society and created a "profound rupture in international relations". It led directly to greater international cooperation for peacemaking and has reinforced social disdain for militarization and threats of violence as means of resolving political differences (Kaldor, Kostovicova, and Said, 2006).

Opposing War in Indochina

The movement against US military aggression in Indochina was the largest, most sustained and intensive antiwar campaign in American history. For a decade, as the US war escalated, reached its furious peak, and then gradually diminished, millions of citizens in the United States and around the world campaigned continuously to bring the unpopular war to an end. Antiwar protests occurred on every continent, fueling political radicalization and the development of a counterculture that shaped global values and consciousness.

The antiwar movement in the United States was huge but was plagued by divisiveness. Three distinct tendencies emerged – a "new left" rooted in student radicalism and pacifist organizations such as the War Resisters League, an "old left" tendency dominated by Trotskyist groups such as the Social Workers Party, and a liberal wing involving moderate groups such as Americans for Democratic Action (ADA). Many activists felt a profound sense of frustration and anguish over their seeming inability to stop the killing, despite the mass scale of the movement and the countless number of protests, but over time the cumulative impact of the movement played a significant role in constraining, de-escalating, and ultimately ending the war (Wells, 1994).

The first significant demonstration against the war, organized by new left Students for a Democratic Society, brought 25,000 people to Washington in April 1965. Over the next decade hundreds of thousands of activists remained continuously opposed to the war, organizing educational events, mass marches, sit-ins, direct action (often against the military draft), and civil disobedience (more than 12,000 people were arrested on May Day 1971 for attempting to shut down Washington). As the war dragged on, some activists resorted to disruptive action and property damage and a handful engaged in terror attacks. Old left groups focused on organizing large, legal demonstrations and took advantage of the rising mass movement to gain influence and attempt to recruit new members. Liberal antiwar activists sought to lobby members of Congress and used the electoral system to build an antiwar political constituency.

Historians differ on which elements of the movement had the greatest impact. Charles DeBenedetti favored the liberal wing of the movement and argued that radical tendencies turned off potential supporters and hurt the antiwar cause (Chatfield, 2004). Tom Wells (1994) emphasized the radical elements of the movement as the most important source of antiwar action, but he acknowledged the diversity of the movement and argued that each dimension had an impact in building pressure to end the war.

In this analysis, I focus on four episodes and dimensions of the antiwar movement that show clear impacts: the reaction to the Tet Offensive and the "Dump Johnson" campaign of 1968, the popularity of the Vietnam moratorium of 1969, the campaign to stop war funding in the final years of the conflict, and the spread of antiwar resistance within the ranks of the military. I also emphasize the strategic impact of the movement's general role in undermining domestic political support for the war. My purpose is to illustrate the multiple ways in which antiwar resistance played a role in helping to end the war.

Challenging the War-Making President

As President Lyndon Johnson continually escalated the war in 1966 and 1967, many liberals within the Democratic Party became increasingly concerned and began to speak out. ADA leader Allard Lowenstein organized a campaign to unseat the war-making president. Lowenstein convinced Minnesota Senator Eugene McCarthy to challenge Johnson in the 1968 Democratic Party primaries and organized thousands of volunteers to back his candidacy. McCarthy was a dull and uninspiring speaker and many doubted his electability, but large numbers of young people trekked to snowy New Hampshire, site of the first primary, to support the McCarthy campaign. When the ballots were tallied in March, McCarthy polled a remarkable 42 per cent of the vote, compared to 49.5 per cent for the president who was a write-in candidate (DeBenedetti, 1980, pp. 211–212). McCarthy lost the vote count but won what DeBenedetti termed "an astonishing psychological victory" that stunned Johnson and the political establishment in Washington (DeBenedetti, 1980, pp. 181–182).

Opposition to the war increased greatly in February 1968 following the Tet Offensive by Vietnamese liberation forces. The shocking images of bloody attacks across South Vietnam contrasted sharply with the rosy picture of supposed US military success painted for the media just a few weeks before by Commanding General William Westmoreland, who was brought back to Washington by the Johnson administration to claim military gains in Vietnam in his infamous "light at the end of the tunnel" testimony. As historian Melvin Small (1988, pp. 121–122) noted, the public relations campaign using Westmoreland was a direct response to the October 1967 March on the Pentagon, the largest antiwar action to date, which had substantial media and political impact. The administration launched its media campaign in response to the October march. A military officer later testified, "as the antiwar movement grew there was growing need to demonstrate success" (quoted in Small, 1988, p. 109). The March on the Pentagon and the administration's false claims in response thus set the stage for a rapid erosion of public confidence in the president's conduct of the war.

The strong public reaction to the Tet Offensive and McCarthy's political success marked a turning point in the conduct of the war. Lyndon Johnson's "wise men" (a group of eminent former statesmen to whom he turned for advice) called for de-escalation. Senator Robert Kennedy entered the primaries as a more effective and electable antiwar candidate to challenge the president. Then came the shocker: Johnson's surprise announcement in late March that he would not run for reelection and would begin negotiations on ending the war. The president also announced a bombing halt and rejected the Pentagon's request for 206,000 more troops. This ended the process of troop escalation and opened the door to an eventual peace agreement. It would take several more agonizing years for the United States to withdraw its troops, but this was the beginning of the end – brought about by peace movement pressures and the administration's unexpected responses to them.

Blocking Escalation

Another significant challenge to presidential war-making occurred in the fall of 1969 through the Vietnam moratorium movement. The antiwar cause ebbed early in 1969 after the election of Richard Nixon. To help rejuvenate the movement former McCarthy campaign activists conceived of a different kind of peace action that would bring antiwar activism into the political mainstream. They called for people to take action in their communities and workplaces, to pause and interrupt business as usual to help end the war. The moratorium idea caught on like wildfire and gained the endorsement of a wide range of organizations, trade unions, and many prominent intellectuals, artists, and former officials. The moratorium actions that began on October 15 that year were hugely successful, engaging millions of Americans in local activities that ranged from a gathering of 100,000 people on the Boston Common, to prayer vigils in hundreds of small towns, to the wearing of peace signs and armbands by troops in Vietnam. The moratorium events were, in DeBenedetti's words, "the largest mass volunteer actions in American history" (DeBenedetti, 1980, p. 184). They had a significant impact on Nixon's conduct of the war. That impact was unknown at the time but turned out to be decisive in preventing a planned escalation of military violence.

Nixon had campaigned for office on a pledge to end the war, but his supposed peace plan was a threat of massive bombing if North Vietnam did not sue for peace on US terms. He explained his plan to senior aide H.R. Haldeman as the "madman theory": a threat of major military escalation by an unpredictable president obsessed about communism (Haldeman, 1978, p. 98). In 1969, Nixon instructed Henry Kissinger to deliver just such a warning to the Vietnamese and their Soviet supporters, giving Hanoi until November to accept his terms or face the consequences. The administration began preparations for Operation Duck Hook, which was to be a huge, rapid expansion of military pressure, including mining the harbors of Haiphong and bombing in the northern part of Vietnam along the Chinese border. The administration also placed nuclear forces on alert and ordered

B-52 bombers with nuclear weapons to fly north over Alaska to circle outside Soviet airspace in what was called Operation Giant Lance (Sagan, 2006). The Vietnamese and the Soviets were not swayed by these military threats, and they called the president's bluff. Nixon knew at this point that his plan would fail, for he could not afford the political risks of carrying out his threatened escalation in the face of deepening skepticism about the war and a rising tide of antiwar activism.

The president claimed to be unimpressed by the ubiquitous moratorium events and the giant November 15 rally in Washington that followed. In truth, the White House was extremely concerned and feared that the prospect of further demonstrations and public resistance would make it impossible to carry out the planned military escalation (for an account of these events, see Ellsberg, 1981). Nixon later admitted that antiwar protests undermined his ultimatum to Hanoi: "these highly publicized efforts aimed at forcing me to end the war were seriously undermining my behind-the-scenes attempts to do just that." He noted the "irony" that "protest[s] for peace … destroyed whatever small possibility may still have existed of ending the war in 1969." This was an admission that antiwar resistance prevented a major military escalation and constrained US military options. As Nixon wrote, "although I continued to ignore the raging antiwar controversy, I had to face the fact that it had probably destroyed the credibility of my ultimatum to Hanoi" (Nixon, 1978, pp. 401, 403).

Seeds of Watergate

Nixon did not abandon his attempts to escalate military pressure, and in late April 1970 he sent US troops into Cambodia. In communities all over the country, tens of thousands of people poured into the streets in angry protest. On May 4 at Kent State University Ohio, National Guard troops fired into a crowd of antiwar protestors and killed four students, sparking a further convulsion of protest. Sit-ins and student strikes shut down hundreds of colleges and universities. Dozens of military training programs on campuses were attacked and burned. National Guard units were mobilized in 16 states. More than a hundred thousand people gathered within days in Washington and an even greater number demonstrated in San Francisco. Nixon withdrew US troops from Cambodia after just 60 days, prompted in part by Senate passage of the Cooper-Church amendment cutting funds for military operations in Cambodia after June. The president claimed a great military success, but the invasion caused only temporary disruption to North Vietnamese operations, while sparking a new upsurge of antiwar action.

The massive protests that followed the Cambodian invasion and the Kent State killings turned Washington into a "besieged city" said Henry Kissinger. Haldeman remembers sleeping in the White House bomb shelter for several days. According to Haldeman, Nixon was under "unbearable pressures which caused him to order wiretaps and activate the plumbers (a secret break in and dirty tricks squad) in response to antiwar moves" (quoted in Small, 1988, pp. 203, 209). The Watergate crisis thus originated in part from Nixon's obsession with and attempts to silence antiwar opposition.

Several of the White House's dirty tricks operations were directed at antiwar critics, including the break-in at the office of Daniel Ellsberg's psychiatrist, and the infiltration and filing of conspiracy charges against Vietnam Veterans Against the War (VVAW) – which Attorney General John Mitchell considered the most dangerous group in the country (Stacewicz, 1997, p. 336). As presidential paranoia increased, White House agents conducted their ill-fated break-in at the Watergate complex, apparently hoping to find evidence of foreign or radical connections to the Democratic Party. The bungled burglary and subsequent White House cover-up and obstruction of justice undermined the President's credibility and political standing. This emboldened antiwar critics in Congress to challenge the president's attempts to keep the war going.

Defunding the War

Even after the last US ground troops left Vietnam in early 1973, the Nixon administration tried to stave off defeat of US client regimes through massive bombing raids in Vietnam, Laos, and Cambodia. Its policy of Vietnamization provided weapons and money for the Saigon government to continue the fighting. Peace activists responded by creating the Coalition to Stop Funding the War and used conventional political methods to lobby members of Congress to restrict US involvement and cut funding. Activists employed legislative lobbying methods, although with an emphasis on grass roots education and mobilization to put pressure on members of Congress.

These lobbying efforts began to bear fruit in June 1973 when Congress passed legislation that terminated all US military activity "in or over or off the shores" of Indochina (Belasco, Cunningham, Fischer, and Niksch, 2007). The restriction went into effect on August 15, 1973. This was the definitive end of US military involvement in Vietnam, brought about by a congressionally imposed restriction. Antiwar activists actively supported this legislation and worked in concert with a growing number of members of Congress to end all forms of further American military involvement in Indochina.

The next priority for the movement was to halt the flow of funds to the Saigon regime, which launched major military attacks against communist-controlled territory in South Vietnam. The Nixon administration requested US$1.6 billion in military aid for fiscal year 1973, but Congress cut that amount to US$1.1 billion. In March of 1974, the administration requested US$474 million in supplemental funding, but Congress rejected the request – a decision described by the *Washington Post* as a "stunning defeat" for the White House (Wells, 1994, p. 574). In August, Congress reduced the overall level of military aid for Saigon to US$700 million, less than half the US$1.6 billion requested by the administration. This was right before Nixon's resignation. All of these congressional votes occurred in the shadow of the deepening Watergate crisis and growing public revulsion at the president's actions. Antiwar voices in Congress became increasingly assertive in calling for an end to any further US military involvement. Their numbers grew substantially in the landslide Democratic Party victory in the congressional mid-term elections of November 1974 that followed Nixon's resignation.

The final blow against the war came in early 1975. As communist-led troops closed in on Saigon and Phnom Penh, President Gerald Ford attempted to continue Nixon's war policy by requesting US$300 million in supplemental aid for Saigon and $200 million for the beleaguered military regime in Cambodia. Three thousand activists gathered in Washington in January for an antiwar assembly and lobbying effort against further aid. Graham Martin, the US ambassador in Saigon, cabled Washington to urge support for the funding, but his urgent plea fell on deaf ears. In March, Congress rejected the president's requests, thereby sealing the fate of both the South Vietnamese and Cambodian governments, which fell a few weeks later.

Graham attributed Congress's decisions during this period to what he called "one of the best propaganda and pressure organizations the world has ever seen." It was a backhanded but respectful acknowledgement of the power of the antiwar lobby. "I have watched these operations over the world for a long period of time," he later testified before Congress: "these individuals deserve enormous credit for a very effective performance." It was "the constancy of the drumming in day after day" and "the building of the pressure from the constituencies" that produced an "enormously effective" and "beautifully orchestrated campaign" to end US involvement in the war (Wells, 1994, pp. 576–577).

Resistance in the Ranks

Antiwar activism directly affected US military capabilities through widespread opposition to the military draft and resistance within the military itself. Millions of young men avoided the draft in those years by claiming phantom disabilities, flocking to exempt occupations and schools, or marrying early and having children. Hundreds of thousands of draft-age youth actively resisted military service as part of a vast movement that began to cripple the conscription system and led to the government's decision to introduce an all-volunteer force. More than 500,000 young men were classified as draft offenders during the Vietnam era (Baskir and Strauss, 1978; Whiteclay Chambers II, 1999).

Many of those who entered the military also opposed the war. I was one of them and participated actively in the GI peace movement. Antiwar groups emerged within the enlisted ranks and among junior officers throughout the military, emerging first in the Army and Marine Corps and spreading to the Navy and Air Force as the air war intensified. During the years 1968–1972, more than 300 "underground papers" were published by service members on nearly every major US military base and on many ships. More direct forms of disobedience and resistance also multiplied. Desertion rates soared to record levels, and racial rebellions wracked major military bases and ships. Most horrifying was the rise of deadly assaults against officers and sergeants ("fragging"). This was grim evidence of an army literally at war with itself.

Dramatic proof of the collapse of the Army in Vietnam exists in the prevalence of combat refusal. A few instances of open defiance by troops were reported at the time, including two incidents during the Cambodia invasion when small groups of soldiers refused to advance with their units into the country. Two other combat refusals were reported in March 1971 when groups of US troops refused orders to support a South Vietnamese incursion into Laos (see Cortright, 1975). Subsequent research revealed that combat avoidance was widespread, and that hundreds of incidents of combat refusal may have occurred in the latter years of the war (Stanton, 1985, p. 349). When commanders sent their units into the field, they could not be certain that the troops would follow orders. In the face of such pervasive resistance and noncooperation in the ranks, US combat effectiveness in Vietnam slipped away. Dissent and disobedience in the military played a decisive role in limiting the US ability to continue the war.

The Invisible Participant

Historians writing about the Vietnam era rarely mention the full extent of the collapse of the US military, or acknowledge the important ways in which the antiwar movement constrained US war-making options. US political leaders faced determined opposition that forced them to search for ways to bring the war to an end. The movement had a major strategic impact in undermining domestic political support for US policy. The state of public opinion was a key variable in the strategic calculations of both the Johnson and Nixon administrations. National leaders made decisions about the conduct of the war based on their assessment of political impacts at home and the effects on antiwar dissent. Small (1988, 336–337) described this as "irrefutable evidence" of the movement's impact on policymaking.

In his book about the war, former CIA Director William Colby acknowledged the role of public pressure in forcing the government to pursue a negotiated solution. He described the antiwar movement as an "invisible participant" in the peace talks, a force standing behind reluctant US officials pushing them toward the bargaining table while limiting available military options (Colby, 1989, pp. 336–337). For the peace movement, it was an extraordinary accomplishment, however long and difficult, which helped to change the course of history.

Campaigning for Disarmament

Opposition to nuclear weapons has been a central focus of peace activism throughout the atomic age. Over the decades, three major waves of citizen activism and antinuclear protest have swept through Western society and much of the world. The first came in the wake of the Hiroshima and Nagasaki bombings. Led by the atomic scientists who created the bomb, it sought to place nuclear energy under international control. The second wave came in the late 1950s and early 1960s and was focused on ending atmospheric nuclear testing. The third and largest wave, the focus of this discussion, produced the popular Nuclear Weapons Freeze Campaign in the United States and massive movements for disarmament in Western Europe.

The disarmament movements of the late 1970s and 1980s were a response to an increasingly dangerous nuclear buildup by the Soviet Union and the United States. The immediate catalyst was the deployment by the Soviet Union of new intermediate range nuclear missiles (the SS-20) in Eastern Europe in the late 1970s and the corresponding deployment in the early 1980s by the United States and NATO countries of Cruise and Pershing II missiles. These highly accurate first strike weapons created widespread nuclear anxiety in Europe and North America. Opinion polls found a huge jump in the percentage of people fearing nuclear war in Europe and the United States (*Washington Post*, 1981; Rochon, 1988, pp. 46–47).

Freezing the Arms Race

In the United States, the Nuclear Weapons Freeze Campaign emerged in response to a proposal by researcher Randall Forsberg. Her idea of a bilateral nuclear freeze was simple and direct and spoke powerfully to the public desire for an end to the nuclear danger: the United States and the Soviet Union should halt all testing, production, and deployment of nuclear weapons. The idea swept across American society like a proverbial prairie fire, with hundreds of nuclear freeze groups forming in communities all over the country. Opinion polls at the time consistently showed 70–80% approval for the nuclear freeze proposition (Cortright, 1993, p. 80). Organizations such as SANE (the Committee for a Sane Nuclear Policy), which was formed during the second wave of disarmament activism in the late 1950s, expanded rapidly during the nuclear freeze campaign, gaining tens of thousands of new members.

The nuclear freeze campaign was enormously successful in attracting public support. In 1982, local freeze groups placed referenda in support of the nuclear freeze proposal on the ballot in nine states and dozens of cities. One quarter of the American electorate – 18 million people – voted on nonbinding nuclear freeze resolutions that year. In some states, placing the freeze referendum on the ballot required a major mobilizing effort. In California, for example, local organizers collected more than 700,000 valid signatures in just a few months, twice the number needed to qualify for the ballot. Voters overwhelmingly approved the freeze resolution. It was endorsed in every city where it was on the ballot and in all but one state. Overall, the freeze won 10.6 million votes, 60% of those cast. This decisive electoral affirmation had significant political impact, as Congressman Ed Markey (D-MA) observed:

> It was the closest our country has ever come to a national plebiscite on nuclear arms control. Within a very brief time the freeze had taken education at the grassroots and translated it into political muscle at the ballot box, delivering to the White House a resounding vote of no confidence in its nuclear buildup. (Cortright, 1993, p. 80)

Nuclear freeze groups also mobilized people in the streets. On June 12, 1982, a million people marched in New York and gathered in Central Park for the "rally to freeze and reverse the arms race". It was the largest disarmament demonstration ever held in the United States. A week before, 90,000 people participated in a "Peace Sunday" event at the Rose Bowl in California. The Central Park and Rose Bowl rallies were cultural and social expressions as much as they were forms of political protest, with rock stars, artists, and celebrities performing at the events and lending their support to the freeze movement.

Riding the crest of popular support and cultural appeal, the freeze movement helped to shape the political climate in the United States. The Reagan administration entered office on a hardline Cold War platform of nuclear buildup, but the rise of the freeze movement and the growing demand for reducing nuclear dangers forced the White House to adapt. The administration began to soften its rhetoric and agreed in late 1981 to begin negotiations with the Soviet Union on eliminating medium range missiles in Europe – despite initial assertions that negotiations would begin only after the nuclear buildup was completed. On Capitol Hill, members of Congress faced demands from constituents to support the nuclear freeze and arms control. These increasing political pressures led to limits on the MX missile and other specific weapons systems and created a political climate conducive to arms reduction.

Disarmament groups in the United States succeeded in forcing Congress to cut off funding for nuclear testing. The concept of a mutual nuclear test ban was part of the original freeze proposition. Its importance increased significantly when Soviet leader

Mikhail Gorbachev announced a unilateral moratorium on Soviet nuclear testing in August 1985 on the 40th anniversary of the Hiroshima bombing. In the three months following Gorbachev's announcement, SANE and the Nuclear Freeze campaign gathered more than a million signatures on a petition urging the United States and the Soviet Union to join together in a mutual halt to nuclear testing. The petitions were delivered by a peace movement delegation in which I participated at the first Reagan–Gorbachev summit in Geneva that November.

Disarmament groups also mounted a successful, multi-year congressional lobbying campaign for a test ban. Beginning in 1986 and for several years afterwards disarmament groups succeeded in winning passage of measures to cut funding for US nuclear testing. An amendment approved by the House of Representatives in 1986 cut funds for testing all but the smallest nuclear weapons. Similar measures passed in the House in 1987 and 1988, although in each case the Senate refused to go along and the legislation died. The campaign continued into the early 1990s, led by newly elected Congressman Mike Kopetski (D-OR), with support from Oregon Peaceworks and disarmament groups across the country. Kopetski's amendment calling for a moratorium on nuclear testing gained majority support in the House of Representatives. In 1992, for the first time, the Senate also passed the legislation, approving a moratorium on nuclear testing in August by a vote of 68 to 26. President George H.W. Bush opposed the measure and considered the testing moratorium language "highly objectionable", but he reluctantly signed the legislation in October 1992. This was a significant achievement – an end to US nuclear testing, brought about by the pressure of the disarmament movement and its arm control allies in Congress. As historian Lawrence Wittner (2003, p. 441) wrote, "years of efforts by the anti-nuclear movement came to fruition, and US nuclear testing came to a halt, unilaterally."

Saying No to New Missiles

The widespread public opposition to NATO and Soviet intermediate range missiles in Europe generated a massive wave of protests in October 1981. More than half a million people took to the streets in several cities in Italy, an estimated 250,000 people gathered in Bonn, 100,000 in Brussels, 250,000 in London, and tens of thousands in Paris and other cities (New York Times, 1981a, 1981b, 1981c). In November, nearly half a million people jammed the streets of Amsterdam (New York Times, 1981d). A huge banner in the streets of Paris captured the movement's message: "Neither Pershings nor SS-20s." In Milan, a banner read "No to the Pentagon! No to the Kremlin!"

One of the most significant antinuclear protests occurred at Greenham Common, a British military base slated to receive Pershing and Cruise missiles. In September 1981, members of Women for Life on Earth marched to the base and stayed, maintaining a continuous presence for several years. In December 1982, nearly 30,000 women descended upon Greenham Common for a major protest. Their actions attracted significant media attention and prompted the creation of similar peace camps at more than a dozen sites in the United Kingdom and Europe, and also one at Rome Air Base near Seneca, New York, site of the founding congress of the women's suffrage movement more than 100 years earlier (Cook and Kirk, 1983).

The Reagan administration responded to antinuclear sentiment in the fall of 1981 by proposing the "zero option" plan, which called for the elimination of all intermediate-range nuclear weapons in Europe. Reagan supported the zero option, contrary to the advice of senior military officials, because it appealed to his desire to see nuclear weapons eliminated (Lettow, 2005, p. 60). Some of his White House aides saw value in the proposal as a way of co-opting peace movement demands. An administration official told disarmament leader and peace scholar Mary Kaldor, "We got the idea from your banners ... the ones that say 'No Cruise, No Pershing, No SS-20s.'" (Kaldor, 1987). The White House fully expected that Brezhnev-era Soviet leaders would reject the proposal, which they did. Even Mikhail Gorbachev was initially skeptical and tried to link Soviet acceptance of the plan to limits on the US Strategic Defense Initiative (SDI), which Reagan flatly refused.

The culmination of the European disarmament movement came in October 1983, when nearly three million people poured into the streets of cities all across Western Europe. In London, more than 300,000 people assembled for what the *New York Times* called the "largest political protest of its kind in British history" (*New York Times*, 1983). Similar mobilizations of hundreds of thousands occurred in Rome, Vienna, Brussels, Paris, Dublin, Copenhagen, and other cities. The biggest protests occurred in West Germany, where on a single day, 400,000 marched in Bonn, 400,000 in Hamburg, and 250,000 in Stuttgart. More than 200,000 people participated in a human chain that stretched continuously for 64 miles (Rochon, 1988, p. 6). The October 1983 demonstrations were the largest mobilizations for peace in history up to that time (the worldwide mobilizations against war in Iraq in February 2003 were even larger).

Despite this massive outpouring of antinuclear protest, NATO governments disregarded public opinion and proceeded with the deployment of Pershing and Cruise nuclear missiles. On the surface, it appeared that the peace movement had lost the battle against the new weapons, and that all the massive mobilization effort had been for naught.

In 1987, Gorbachev unexpectedly dropped the demand for SDI linkage and accepted the zero option without conditions. This was a dramatic breakthrough that ironically placed NATO leaders in a difficult position. Although many NATO officials were skeptical, and Henry Kissinger and other conservative leaders expressed misgivings, they had no choice but to accept Gorbachev's approval of their proposal. This led to the Intermediate-Range Nuclear Forces (INF) Treaty eliminating all intermediate range missiles. In the end, the peace position prevailed. Peace advocates crafted the message ("No to Soviet and NATO missiles") and created the anti-nuclear political climate that helped to produce the 1987 treaty banning intermediate missiles. The peace movement had prevailed in the larger political struggle against new nuclear weapons in Europe.

Who Won the Cold War?

In the West, Ronald Reagan and Margaret Thatcher are lauded as heroes who won the Cold War. Thatcher famously claimed that Reagan "won the Cold War without firing a shot" (quoted in D'Souza 1997). According to this perspective, it was Reagan's military buildup, especially his cherished SDI, that broke the back of Soviet power and forced the Kremlin to sue for peace. This conventional interpretation of the ending of the Cold War is a serious distortion of history. The Soviet Union was indeed overburdened by excessive military spending, but the crisis that brought the system down resulted most fundamentally from the inherent dysfunction and corruption of its centralized planned economy. Reagan deserves credit for accepting the compromises Gorbachev was willing to offer, but he was slow to recognize the significance of Gorbachev's reforms and some of his actions impeded the process of change.

The ending of the Cold War was due principally to the actions of Gorbachev and to the pressures applied by popular movements for disarmament in the West and for freedom in the East. Gorbachev's *perestroika* reforms and "new thinking" in international affairs broke decisively with the logic of the Cold War. Gorbachev's demilitarization initiatives were encouraged by and were a response to the global disarmament movements that created a political climate conducive to arms reduction. The Berlin Wall came down because of popular resistance in East Germany, Poland, Czechoslovakia, and other states in the disintegrating Soviet empire. When Gorbachev announced that the Red Army would no longer intervene to prop up these regimes, millions of people in the East took to the streets in the historic "Velvet Revolution" that brought an end to the Soviet system.

In his memoirs, George Kennan described the triumphalist interpretation of the ending of the Cold War as "silly and childish". Military pressures from the West during the Cold War were usually counterproductive and often reinforced Soviet repression and militarism, he wrote. "The general effect of Cold War extremism was to delay rather than hasten the great change that overtook the Soviet Union at the end of 1980s" (Kennan, 1992, 1996, p. 185). Soviet leaders who worked with Gorbachev and participated in changing Kremlin policy also described the triumphalist interpretation as "absolute nonsense", to use the words of Georgi Arbatov (1992). Alexander Yakovlev, the principal architect of *perestroika*, said that US hard-line policies "played no role. None. I can tell you with full responsibility. Gorbachev and I were ready for changes in our policies regardless of whether the American president was Reagan, or … someone more liberal" (quoted in Wittner, 2003, p. 487). The pressures that brought change in the East came mainly from within, not without.

Missing from the conventional description of the ending of the Cold War is any recognition of the role of the peace movement. Some political leaders went out of their way to deny the role of social agency and denigrate disarmament activism. President George H.W. Bush said in the 1992 election debates that "if we had listened to the freeze crowd, we never would have ended the Cold War." In fact the nuclear freeze campaign and European disarmament movement played a significant role in helping to make that possible. By challenging Reagan's hardline policies and creating a political climate for peace and arms reduction, they made it possible for the two sides to compromise. Gorbachev's most significant concession, the one that provided the breakthrough for nuclear reduction and the improvement in East–West relations, was the decision to separate the question of intermediate-range missiles from the issue of SDI. This was made possible in part by the strong public desire for disarmament that was made visible in the actions of peace movements. Gorbachev declared at a meeting of Soviet officials in 1987, "untying the package on the medium-range missiles ... will be our response to the state of public opinion in the world" (Wittner, 2003, p. 397).

The disarmament movement in the United States contributed to ending the nuclear standoff by building political support for arms reduction. Through pressure applied on members of Congress, the movement helped to create a significant arms control lobby on Capitol Hill, which compelled the Reagan administration to adopt a more flexible negotiating posture toward the Soviet Union. The decision to begin arms control negotiations, the shaping of the zero option, and other bargaining positions at the Geneva talks, the stalemating of the MX missile program, the rejection of the Crisis Relocation Plan civil defense program – all of these developments were the result of peace movement activism and occurred before Gorbachev came to power (Wittner, 2003, pp. 403, 446). Peace movement pressures during the decade also placed significant constraints on the SDI program and, as noted, were successful in stopping nuclear testing.

In Europe, the disarmament movement had an explicitly anti-Cold War message. Groups such as European Nuclear Disarmament rejected the entire system of East–West militarized confrontation and insisted on linking peace and human rights. They engaged in dialogue with civil society networks and peace and human rights advocates in Eastern Europe, establishing links with members of some of the groups that emerged after the Helsinki Final Declaration in 1975 and that later went on to play a major role in bringing down communist regimes in 1989. This grass roots dialogue between West and East was described by Dutch disarmament leader Mient Jan Faber as "détente from below" (Kaldor, 1999, p. 481). As Mary Kaldor and her colleagues write,

> A significant contribution to the ending of the Cold War was the dialogue between peace and human rights groups across the Cold War divide, which produced an emerging consensus that freedom is more likely to be achieved within a framework of international peace and vice versa – international peace is more likely to be achieved in democracies. (Kaldor, Kostovicova, and Said, 2006, p. 97)

This breakdown in the previous separation between peace and human rights contributed in important ways to the 1989 revolutions and the end of the Cold War (Kaldor, 1999, p. 477).

What is Success?

In October 1987, I was invited by the Green Party in Germany to participate in a meeting to evaluate the recently signed INF Treaty. The German Greens had battled these NATO and Warsaw Pact missiles for a decade, helping to organize the mass demonstrations of 1981 and 1983. At the 1987 meeting, the Greens were surprisingly diffident and even glum about the historic treaty banning the weapons they had opposed. Because the movement had not succeeded in preventing NATO deployment in November 1983, activists had come to look upon the struggle as a failure. I argued that they should take pride in the signing of the Treaty and claim it as their own. We may have lost the battle against initial deployment, I said, but we won the larger war to get rid of the missiles.

Change often occurs in unanticipated and unplanned ways. Movements may win when they seem to be losing. The freeze movement never succeeded in convincing the US government to support the bilateral freeze resolution, but it had a significant impact in changing the political climate in Washington to allow for negotiations with the Soviets and generated pressure for arms reduction. This is not what activists wanted or intended, but it was a positive result. SANE and other groups mounted a major campaign to stop the MX missile, managing to defeat the mobile basing system and cut the number of deployed missiles by three quarters, but they were not able to stop the missile program entirely. During the course of the campaign, disarmament groups exerted pressure on members of Congress, who deflected that pressure onto the Reagan administration to adopt a more accommodating stance in negotiations with the Soviets. This is not what opponents of the MX missile intended, but it was a beneficial side effect. When movements apply pressure, they can never be sure how political establishments will respond, but if they persist and generate mass political support, they can bring about significant and unexpected policy change.

Resisting the Iraq War

On February 15, 2003, an estimated 10 million people demonstrated against the Iraq war in hundreds of cities across the globe, the largest single day of antiwar protest ever recorded. More than a million people demonstrated that day in London, Rome, and Barcelona, and hundreds of thousands poured into the streets in dozens of other cities on every continent. In New York, an estimated 400,000 gathered in subfreezing temperatures, and tens of thousands demonstrated in San Francisco. In Cairo, tens of thousands protested in Tahrir Square in an officially permitted rally that was a precursor for the mass protests that brought down the Mubarak dictatorship eight years later.[1] A month later on the eve of the invasion, another massive wave of global protest occurred, this time at the local level, as millions of people gathered in 6000 candlelight vigils in more than one hundred countries in a last minute plea against war.

The Iraq campaign was more international in character than any previous antiwar movement. Protests were coordinated throughout the world and activists understood themselves to be part of a truly global struggle. In dozens of countries, national coalitions were created, encompassing a wide range of movements and organizations. The various coalitions set up websites that were linked to each other, and many adopted the same slogan and graphic design – a missile crossed out with the words "stop the war". People across the globe spoke out as never before in a unified voice against invading Iraq.

The *New York Times* dubbed this mass movement a global "superpower", an unprecedented transnational mobilization that exerted significant influence on numerous governments (Tyler, 2003). Opposition to the war helped German Chancellor Gerhard Schröder win re-election in September 2002. In Turkey, public pressure persuaded Parliament to deny the Bush administration's request to use the country's military bases for the invasion, turning aside an estimated US$20 billion in financial inducements. At the United Nations, the Security Council refused to support the Bush administration's proposed resolution authorizing the use of military force – the first time in history, according to Immanuel Wallerstein, that "Washington, on an issue that mattered to it, could not get a majority on the Security Council" (Wallerstein, 2003). In the March 2004 national elections in Spain, the socialist opposition unseated the pro-war conservative government and promptly implemented its pledge to withdraw Spanish troops from Iraq.

A Diverse Movement

In the United States, the antiwar movement reached levels of mobilization in the course of a few months that during the Vietnam era took years to develop. Almost every major religious body in the country spoke out against the war, as did many trade unions, women's organizations, Hollywood artists, musicians, and others. The Iraq movement contained different factions, but political sectarianism was less intense than during the Vietnam antiwar movement. On the left was ANSWER (Act Now to Stop War and End Racism), a racially diverse anti-imperialist coalition founded by the Trotskyist Workers World Party. Also on the left, but more focused on Iraq, was United for Peace and Justice (UFPJ), a broadly based nonsectarian coalition of national and grass roots pacifist and social justice organizations. ANSWER and UFPJ focused on organizing demonstrations and rallies nationally and at the local level. The third coalition, Win Without War, adopted a more centrist approach and focused on media communications, online organizing, and congressional lobbying.

The Iraq antiwar movement was able to communicate effectively to the media – aided by advertising and media campaigns from the public relations firm, Fenton Communications, and from progressive business executives and Hollywood artists. The mainstream media generally portrayed opposition to the war in Iraq as "diverse, legitimate and representative", which Rebecca Solnit (2003) described as a "watershed victory" for the cause of peace activism. The Iraq movement was not hindered by the negative stereotypes that limited the appeal of the Vietnam antiwar movement.

An important innovation of the Iraq antiwar movement, one that is now common for all forms of social mobilization, was the extensive use of the Internet for communicating and organizing mass action. The Iraq campaign was an early manifestation of the power of online activism to mobilize massive levels of social participation on short notice with limited resources. The leading force in this development was MoveOn.org, a major player in the Win Without War coalition. In addition to helping build support for the February 15 rallies, MoveOn led the "virtual march on Washington" on February 26, during which hundreds of thousands of constituents contacted their congressional representatives, clogging phone lines, fax machines, and email inboxes across Capitol Hill. MoveOn also helped organize a petition to the UN Security Council signed by a million people that was delivered to UN representatives a few days before the invasion. During the course of these mobilizing efforts, the MoveOn list tripled in size from 700,000 to more than 2 million. It continued to grow after the invasion, reaching 5 million names on the eve of the Obama electoral campaign.

Ultimately, of course, the movement could not stop the Bush administration's preplanned invasion. As Jonathan Schell (2003) wrote poignantly at the time, "candles in windows did not stop cruise missiles". Given the obdurate determination of Bush and his advisers to invade Iraq regardless of law, logic, or the facts, the movement probably had no chance of preventing the war. Nor did activists have much time to organize, less than six months from the founding of UFPJ and Win Without War, until the bombs started falling. Antiwar action continued after the invasion, with hundreds of local protests urging an end to the occupation on the first and second-year anniversaries of the invasion and on other occasions, but protest action gradually diminished. By 2006, the movement in the streets was barely visible.

The Turn Toward Conventional Politics

Opposition to the war did not end, however. It changed form and employed more conventional means of political action. As during the Vietnam antiwar movement, many activists began to utilize the political process. This was especially true of MoveOn, which was closely aligned with the Democratic Party. The emerging political strategy consisted of two components, legislative and electoral. On Capitol Hill, activists urged members of Congress to support legislation urging the withdrawal of US troops and cutting funds for continued military occupation. In the Republican-dominated 108th and 109th Congresses (2003–2006), neither approach garnered much support. This prompted many to shift toward electoral politics, with the goal of electing an antiwar Congress and hopefully an antiwar President.

The 2006 congressional elections were a turning point. Antiwar activists were heavily involved in many local races and played a role in the election of dozens of new antiwar members of Congress. Democrats regained control of the House of Representatives and gained a slight edge in the Senate, a result widely seen as swayed by antiwar sentiment (Heaney and Rojas, 2011; Grunwald, 2006). As writer Mike Davis (2007) observed, pundits and exit-poll surveys agreed that "Iraq was the Archimedean lever" that shifted independent voters massively toward the Democrats. In Virginia, antiwar activists helped Jim Webb win a razor-thin victory for the Senate, and in Connecticut they propelled Ned Lamont's upset victory over pro-war Senator Joe Lieberman in the Democratic primary, although Lamont lost to Lieberman in the general election. The results of the elections sent a clear message that antiwar activists were a force to be reckoned with in the Democratic Party – a message that was not lost on the junior Senator from Illinois.

The improbable candidacy of Barack Obama was built on his opposition to the war in Iraq and his pledge to bring the troops home. As a political unknown, Obama was a long-shot for the Democratic Party nomination. He faced a formidable rival in Hillary Clinton, who had substantial financial backing and the support of many Democratic Party leaders. The principal distinction of Obama's candidacy was his forthright stance against the Iraq War. Clinton by contrast waffled on ending the war and was burdened by her Senate vote in 2002 to authorize the use of military force. Obama had spoken against the invasion at an October 2002 antiwar rally in Chicago, and he remained unequivocally opposed to continuing the war. His unwavering commitment to ending the war won him the endorsement of MoveOn's support base and generated a huge wave of volunteer and financial support from the antiwar movement.

Activists supported Obama as the candidate who would bring the troops home from Iraq, but most had no illusions that he was antiwar in a broader sense. In his Chicago speech in 2002 he declared, "I don't oppose all wars. What I am opposed to is a dumb war." During his 2008 campaign he reiterated his commitment to withdraw from Iraq, but he was equally clear in pledging to increase US military involvement in Afghanistan. He vowed to expand military operations in Afghanistan and to use force wherever he deemed necessary to counter terrorist threats. As President he followed through on those pledges, much to the chagrin of many antiwar activists who supported him.

Helping to Elect a President

Obama's 2008 electoral strategy played to the strengths of the antiwar constituency. His campaign created an extensive field presence in dozens of states, built on the foundations of already existing activist networks – principally the antiwar movement, but also labor, women's, environmentalist, African American, Latino, and other established organizing networks. Obama's victories were concentrated in caucus states, where success is determined by the strength of local activism rather than big name endorsements and large television advertising budgets. In the state of Washington, Obama won two-thirds of the caucus delegates but only 51 per cent of the popular vote and came away with two-thirds of the state's delegates. In Texas, Clinton won the popular vote, but Obama won more of the caucus delegates and ended up with the majority of the state's delegates. Nationwide, Clinton won the popular vote, but Obama held a two-to-one margin in the 13 caucus contests, enough to win the nomination. Obama's victory was the result of his superior ability to mobilize tens of thousands of strongly committed loyalists from the antiwar movement.[2]

That activist support base also propelled Obama to victory in the general election. The Obama campaign pioneered the use of social media to harness volunteer and donor support. The campaign had 13 million people on its various email and Facebook lists. Many of those names were drawn from the MoveOn list and other pre-existing activist networks. With 8 million visitors a month, the Obama web site was used to create 35,000 volunteer groups and organize 200,000 offline events. The campaign had 3 million online donors, who gave a total of 6.5 million contributions at an average gift size of $80. Obama raised twice as much money as McCain, a record $750 million, two-thirds of it from grass roots contributions (Walker, 2008; Vargas, 2008; OpenSecrets.org, 2008; Lutz, 2009).

Scholars often consider participation in institutional politics and mobilization for street protest as distinct subjects, but in the case of the Iraq antiwar movement the connection between the two was direct and strategic. Organizers made a conscious decision to shift their activism from street protest to voter canvassing. A similar pattern occurred during the Vietnam antiwar movement, although with less impact. The "Dump Johnson" movement on behalf of Eugene McCarthy in 1968 was surprisingly strong and showed the power of the antiwar constituency. It contributed to Johnson's decision to withdraw from the race.

The election of Obama was more decisive and led directly to the end of the war. Soon after taking office, Obama established a schedule for the withdrawal of troops. In December 2011, he announced that the last troops had left the country. The Pentagon and most military analysts had expected that at least some troops would remain. Writer Tom Ricks (2009) predicted that the United States would keep 25,000 to 50,000 troops in Iraq indefinitely. The Iraqi government would not stand for it, however, and insisted on sticking to the December 2011 target date for the departure of US troops stipulated in the security agreement signed with the Bush administration in 2008. As the deadline approached in 2011, Generals David Petraeus and Raymond Odierno called for keeping a residual force in place, but Obama stood firm. His decision was made easier by the fact that he was following the timeline originally established by Bush. He and his advisers also recognized that attempting to renege on the agreement might have triggered a political crisis in Iraq and that any troops remaining beyond the deadline likely would face renewed insurgent violence. Nonetheless Obama deserved credit for staying with the scheduled plan for withdrawal and fulfilling his pledge to end the war.

Some antiwar activists marked the occasion of the last troops leaving Iraq by expressing gratitude for the President's action. Many also noted the role of the peace movement in opposing the war and helping to get Obama elected. On the day the final departure was announced, I received a phone call from the White House Office of Public Engagement. "We just want to call to say thank you," the director of the office said, "to you and other activists in the antiwar movement. What the president accomplished today would not have been possible without the work you and many others did over the past few years." I was humbled and overjoyed to receive the call and grateful that what he said was true.

Some activists were dissatisfied and skeptical when the Iraq war ended. It had taken too long to bring the troops home, they said. Thousands of US contractors remained behind to try to exert continuing American influence. Many were disappointed by Obama's military escalation in Afghanistan and were outraged by his administration's extensive drone warfare program. These were valid concerns, yet on the issue that mattered most, ending the occupation of Iraq, they were vindicated. Many considered this a victory for the antiwar movement.

Understanding Change

The withdrawal from Iraq, like the US defeat in Vietnam and the ending of the Cold War, did not meet the hopes or expectations of most peace activists. Many did not see their hand in these events or recognize the role of the antiwar movement in bringing about political change. At the end of the Vietnam and Iraq Wars, the dominant mood was not satisfaction with success but profound sorrow and regret at the senseless loss of life and the staggering waste of resources. The nuclear reductions at the end of the Cold War also brought confusion, as the millions of activists who campaigned for disarmament were ignored, while those who had long opposed disarmament claimed credit for its success.

Political change is often ambiguous and rarely happens quickly enough for activists or in the manner they intend. This is especially true for peace movements, which contend against deeply entrenched structures of militarism. Changes on matters of war and peace in the United States tend to come incrementally rather than rapidly. For idealists, these realities may be difficult to accept. Those who campaign for an end to war and nuclear weapons are rarely satisfied with gradual military withdrawals or partial limits on specific weapons.

Social analysts also have difficulty understanding the dynamics of social change. They tend to view social movements as noninstitutionalized forms of contention embodied in demonstrations and disruption. Lobbying and electoral work are often examined separately without reference to social mobilization. Social movements are in the streets, not the suites. When demonstrations and protests are no longer visible, the movement is assumed to be inactive. Peace activism is not so sharply bifurcated, however. Many activists participate in both street action and conventional politics and move seamlessly back and forth between the two.

The success of the former may create conditions for the latter. When protests in the street generate social pressure, they create opportunities for conventional political action. Activists initially turn toward protest when conventional legislative or electoral approaches are unresponsive or unavailable. As movements grow and exert effective street pressure, new opportunities may emerge for conventional lobbying and electoral campaigns. In the Vietnam era, Congress refused to challenge presidential conduct of the war until the final years when, encouraged by an effective antiwar lobby, legislators prohibited further US involvement and cut military funding. During the freeze movement, activists used an electoral form – nonbinding local referenda – to mobilize mass support. They channeled this pressure into effective lobbying to constrain the weapons buildup and stop nuclear testing. Opponents of the Iraq War brought their mobilizing assets into the political arena and helped elect a president who pledged to withdraw US troops.

Ultimately, it is persistent mobilization that makes these conventional political efforts successful. Through continuous educational campaigns, demonstrations, rallies, vigils, civil disobedience, and various forms of disruptive action, movements establish themselves as a political force. At times, the scale of social mobilization and protest is sufficient to constrain government action, as when Nixon abandoned his threat of escalation in November 1969 or the Reagan administration adopted a more flexible approach in negotiating with the Soviet Union. At other times, activism is channeled into conventional political forms. Movements influence political decision-making in complex and subtle ways. Often denied by government leaders and sometimes overlooked even by activists who work for change, the impacts of peace movements are nonetheless real and have helped to change the course of history.

Notes

1. Estimates of the numbers of demonstrators and antiwar events are drawn from the website of United for Peace and Justice. United for Peace and Justice, "The World Says No to War," February 15, 2003. Available online at *United for Peace and Justice* http://www .unitedforpeace.org/feb15.html (accessed November 24, 2003). In San Francisco, police and organizers estimated the crowd at 200,000, but a careful analysis by the *San Francisco Chronicle*, employing an innovative aerial observation method, put the crowd at approximately 65,000. See "Counting Crowds: Using Aerial Photography to Estimate the Size of Sunday's Peace March in S.F.," *San Francisco Chronicle*, February 21, 2003. Available online at *SFGate* http://sfgate.com/cgi-bin/article.cgi?f=/c/a/2003/02/21/MN20213.DTL (accessed February 14, 2007). For newspaper accounts of the protests, see Angelique Chrisafis *et al.*, "Threat of War: Millions Worldwide Rally for Peace," *Guardian* (London), February 17, 2003, p. 6; Glenn Frankel, "Millions Worldwide Protest Iraq War," *Washington Post*, February 16, 2003, A1; Alan Cowell, "1.5 Million Demonstrators in Cities Across Europe Oppose a War Against Iraq," *New York Times*, February 16, 2003, A20.

2. See "2008 Democratic Primary Election Results" http://uselectionatlas.org/RESULTS/nati onal.php?f=0&year=2008&elect=1; see also "Caucuses vs. Primaries: A Report" http:// www.talkleft.com/story/2008/5/27/92144/7994 (accessed December 12, 2013).

References

Arbatov, Georgi. 1992. *The System: An Insider's Life in Soviet Politics*. New York, NY: Random House.

Baskir Lawrence M., and William A. Strauss. 1978. *Chance and Circumstance: The Draft, the War and the Vietnam Generation*. New York, NY: Alfred Knopf.

Belasco, Amy, L.J. Cunningham, H. Fischer, and L.A. Niksch. 2007. *Congressional Restrictions on US Military Operations in Vietnam, Cambodia, Laos, Somalia, and Kosovo: Funding and Non-funding Approaches*. Congressional Research Service, January 16, p. CRS-6.

Chatfield, Charles. 2004. "At the Hands of Historians: The Antiwar Movement of the Vietnam Era." *Peace and Change*, 29(3/4): 483–526. DOI: 10.1111/j.0149-0508.2004.00300.x

Colby, William. 1989. *Lost Victory: A Firsthand Account of America's Sixteen-Year Involvement in Vietnam*. Chicago, IL: Contemporary Books, 1989.

Cook, Alice, and Gwyn Kirk. 1983. *Greenham Common Everywhere: Dreams, Ideas and Actions from the Women's Peace Movement*. Cambridge, MA: South End Press.

Cortright, David. 1975. *Soldiers in Revolt: GI Resistance during the Vietnam War*. Chicago, IL: Haymarket Books.

Cortright, David. 1993. *Peace Works: The Citizen's Role in Ending the Cold War*. Boulder, CO: Westview Press.

Davis, Mike. 2007. "The Democrats After November." *New Left Review*, January– February. Accessed December 12, 2013 from http://newleftreview.org/II/43/mike-davis-the-democrats-after-november

DeBenedetti, Charles. 1980. *The Peace Reform in American History*. Bloomington, IN: Indiana University Press.

D'Souza, Dinesh. 1997. "How Reagan Won the Cold War." *National Review*, 49(22).

Ellsberg, Daniel. 1981. "Introduction: Call to Mutiny." In *Protest and Survive*, edited by E.P. Thompson and Dan Smith, pp. xv–xvi. New York, NY: Monthly Review Press.

Forsberg, Randall. 1997. "Toward the End of War." *Boston Review*, October/November.

Grunwald, Michael. 2006. "Opposition to War Buoys Democrats." *The Washington Post*, November 8.

Haldeman, H.R. 1978. *The Ends of Power*. New York: Times Books.

Heaney Michael T., and Fabio Rojas. 2011. "The Partisan Dynamics of Contention: Demobilization of the Antiwar Movement in the United States, 2007–2009." *Mobilization: An International Journal*, 16(1): 45–64.

Kaldor, Mary. 1987. "'We Got the Idea from Your Banners'." *New Statesman*, 113 (No. 2920), March 13.

Kaldor, Mary. 1999. "Ideas of 1989: The Origins of the Concept of Global Civil Society." *Transnational Law and Contemporary Problems*, 9(2): 475–488.

Kaldor, Mary, Denisa Kostovicova, and Yahia Said. 2006. "War and Peace: The Role of Civil Society." In *Global Civil Society 2006/7*, edited by Helmut K. Anheier, Mary Kaldor and Marlies Glasius, pp. 97–98. London: Sage Publications.

Kennan, George. 1992. "The G.O.P. Won the Cold War? Ridiculous." *New York Times*, October 28.

Kennan, George. 1996. *At a Century's Ending: Reflections, 1982–1995*. New York, NY: W.W. Norton & Co.

Lettow, Paul. 2005. *Ronald Reagan and His Quest to Abolish Nuclear Weapons*. New York, NY: Random House.

Lutz, Monte. 2009. "The Social Pulpit: Barack Obama's Social Media Toolkit." Washington, DC: Edelman.com.

Nixon, Richard. 1978. *RN: The Memoirs of Richard Nixon*. New York, NY: Grosset & Dunlap.

New York Times. 1981a. "250,000 at Bonn Rally Assail US Arms Policy," *New York Times*, October 11, 1981, A 1, 9.

New York Times. 1981b. "50,000 March in Paris to Protest Weapons Build Up," *New York Times*, October 26, 1981, A 11.

New York Times. 1981c. "In Italy, the Bomb's a Political Issue for the First Time," *New York Times*, November 14, 1981, A 2.

New York Times. 1981d. "350,000 in Amsterdam Protest A-Arms," *New York Times*, November 22, 1981, A 16.

New York Times. 1983. "Vast Crowds Hold Rallies in Europe Against U.S. Arms," *New York Times*, October 23, 1983, A 16.

OpenSecrets.org. 2008. "Banking on Becoming President." Accessed December 12, 2013 from http://opensecrets.org/pres08/index.php

Pinker, Steven. 2012. *The Better Angels of Our Nature: A History of Violence and Humanity*. London: Penguin.

Ricks, Tom. 2009. *The Gamble: General David Petraeus and the American Military Adventure in Iraq, 2006–2008*. New York, NY: Penguin Press.

Rochon, Thomas R. 1988. *Mobilizing for Peace: The Antinuclear Movements in Western Europe*. Princeton, NJ: Princeton University Press.

Sagan, Scott. 2006. "The Vietnam War and Richard Nixon's Secret Nuclear Alert." Podcast, Torn Curtain: The Secret History of the Cold War, Episode 3, Radio National, ABC News, 28 May 2006. Accessed December 12, 2013 from http://www.abc.net.au/radionational/programs/hindsight/past-programs/index=2006?page=4

Schell, Jonathan. 2003. "The Other Superpower." *The Nation*, March 27.

Small, Melvin. 1988. *Johnson, Nixon, and the Doves*. New Brunswick, NJ: Rutgers University Press.

Smith, Rupert. 2006. *The Utility of Force: The Art of War in the Modern World*. London: Penguin.

Solnit, Rebecca. 2003. "Acts of Hope: Challenging Empire on the World Stage." *Orion*, May 20.

Stacewicz, Richard. 1997. *Winter Soldiers: An Oral History of the Vietnam Veterans Against the War*. New York, NY: Twayne Publishers.

Stanton, Shelby L. 1985. *The Rise and Fall of an American Army: US Ground Forces in Vietnam, 1965–1973*. Novato, CA: Presidio Press.

Tannenwald, Nina. 2007. *The Nuclear Taboo: The United States and the Non-use of Nuclear Weapons Since 1945*. Cambridge: Cambridge University Press.

Tyler, Patrick E. 2003. "Threats and Responses: News Analysis; A New Power in the Streets." *New York Times*, February 17.

Vargas, Jose Antonio. 2008. "Obama Raised Half a Billion Online." *The Washington Post*, November 20.

Väyrynen, Raimo. 2006. *The Waning of Major War: Theories and Debates*. London: Routledge.

Walker, Martin, 2008. "The Year of the Insurgents: The 2008 US Presidential Campaign." *International Affairs*, 84: 1095–1107.

Wallerstein, Immanuel. 2003. "US Weakness and the Struggle for Hegemony." *Monthly Review*, 55(3): 23–29.

Washington Post. 1981. "Poll Finds 7 out of 10 Imagining Outbreak of Soviet Nuclear War." September 27.

Wells, Tom. 1994. *The War Within: America's Battle over Vietnam*. Berkeley, CA: University of California Press.

Whiteclay Chambers II, John. 1999. "Draft Resistance and Evasion," In *The Oxford Companion to American Military History*, edited by John Whiteclay Chambers II. New York, NY: Oxford University Press.

Wittner, Lawrence S. 2003. *Toward Nuclear Abolition: A History of the World Nuclear Disarmament Movement, 1971 to the Present*. Stanford, CA: Stanford University Press.

Chapter 28

Corporate Actors

Shantanu Chakrabarti

Introduction

One issue on which social scientists across the spectrum mostly agree is that, while human organizations and systems are becoming more complex in nature, institutional structures, such as government, are failing to cope with these complexities (Foster, 1994, pp. 4–5). This has accelerated a trend towards denationalization and privatization, leading to the private actors becoming involved in diverse fields like legitimatization of standards; provision of social welfare; enforcement of contracts; and even provision of security (Biersteker and Hall, 2002, p. 203). Ensuring security, in particular, considered for long as one of the principal tasks of the post-Westphalian state, has also been affected by the myriad challenges affecting the state in recent times. The New Security Dilemma (NSD), it has been argued, significantly reduces the effectiveness of traditional state-based and state-systemic approaches to international politics as a range of transnational and subnational actors and structures are forging alliances beyond state determined boundaries (Cerny, 2000, p. 645). This, however, does not mean, as several analysts have suggested, the complete loss of state monopoly, or even loss of its status as the leading security actor resulting from globalization-induced pressure to outsource essential elements of governance, including security provision. In reality, a more appropriate explanation would suggest creation of new, "global security assemblages; settings where a range of different global and local, public and private security agents and normativities interact, cooperate and compete to produce new institutions, practices, and forms of security governance" (Abrahamsen and Williams, 2009, p. 3). This process, however, has led to a shift from the state and territorial-based system of governance to a more polyarchical, nonterritorial, and network-centric governance pattern bringing together governments, nongovernment organizations (NGOs), military establishments, and private companies as part of an emerging system of global liberal governance

The Handbook of Global Security Policy, First Edition. Edited by Mary Kaldor and Iavor Rangelov.
© 2014 John Wiley & Sons, Ltd. Published 2014 by John Wiley & Sons, Ltd.

(Duffield, 2005, p. 2). Such networks have been defined by Duffield as "strategic complexes" where security and development gets merged due to more interactive and integrative policymaking.

Within most fragile and conflict-prone states, a significant portion of the state-controlled security mechanism has already been privatized, with varied non-state security delivery and maintenance agencies being incorporated, sometimes surreptitiously, within the state's security and justice delivery system. Private security has also become a prominent feature of internal security governance in developed countries. It may now be easier to conceive provisioning of security taking place along a continuum, with most of the service delivery occurring somewhere in the middle of the spectrum, between the opposing poles of "state" and "non-state" provision (Scheye, 2009, p. 12). The process of security privatization is not restricted to conflict zones or fragile states only, but has become a part of the normal process of governance in developed parts of the world, giving it a truly global character. While security privatization is a complex process that involves a slew of actors dependent upon local specificities and historical roots, the most striking feature of the post-Cold War phase has been the rise of the Private Security Industry (PSI) with greater involvement of corporate actors.

Outlining the Rise of the PSI

While having a historical precedence, the PSI has been witnessing a phenomenal growth in recent decades. The Small Arms Survey Yearbook 2011, for instance, estimates that the formal private security sector employs between 19.5 and 25.5 million people worldwide. Greater involvement of private players in the realm of security provision has given rise to the concept of "security economy". Security economy incorporates a cluster of economic activities dealing with security threats. At its broadest level, it could include all matters related to defense and counterintelligence, the public police force, private policing, armed guards, and security technology provision (Stevens, 2004, p. 8). The global security economy is also expanding, with even highly conservative estimates putting the PSI's global turnover between US$100 billion and US$120 billion. States are also turning into consumers of private security services themselves in their quest for greater cost-efficiency, relying on private firms for threat analysis and policy implementation (Krahmann, 2008, p. 396). The private sector is also doing most (in the range of 90% plus) of the research and development in the field of new security technologies and countermeasures (Arquilla, 2003, p. 218).

To an extent, this dependence is an outcome of the changing nature of conflict itself. As Singer (2001–2002, p. 195) argues:

> At high-intensity levels of conflict, the military operations of great powers have become more technologic and thus more reliant on civilian specialists to run their increasingly sophisticated military systems. At low-intensity levels, the primary tools of warfare have not only diversified but, as stated earlier, have become more available to a broader array of actors. Increasingly, the motivations behind many conflicts in the developing world are either criminalized or driven by the profit motive in some way. Both directly and indirectly, these parallel changes have heightened demand for services provided by the privatized military industry.

Particularly significant is the rising incidence of irregular or asymmetric warfare, often characterized as the Fourth Generation Warfare (4GW) (for details, see Hammes, 2006), which the conventional forces are not well suited to tackle and which require long-term engagement at local conflict zones, thereby increasing the demand for private contractors.

This trend towards privatized security has also led to a process of "commodification" of security. According to Loader (1997, pp. 377–378), for instance:

> The provision of security is becoming … ever more fragmented and commodified. The protection of person and property is less and less the exclusive province of the public police, but is now increasingly being delivered by a plethora of public, commercial, and voluntary agencies. … We are at the very least witnessing the emergence of an uneven patchwork of security provision, increasingly determined by people's willingness and ability to pay.

The global PSI also indicates its dynamism by evolving in a fast manner through shifting patterns and trends. In contrast to the boom years of the 1990s, there are hardly any firms today that strictly fall into the category of military provider firms, ready and able to engage in offensive combat operations, reflecting their failure to convince the world about their legitimacy (Spear, 2011, p. 3). In contrast, the military consulting firms and the military support firms have fared better. But given the rising levels of multitasking and assemblage, any definitive classification of the corporate actors in the security field has become difficult, if not impossible. Some analysts in recent years have also advocated greater use of private naval security companies to deal with the threat of coastline piracy, terror activities, and clandestine trade (see for instance, Berube, 2007).

It should also be noted that security privatization also involves "quasi-corporate" organizations like vigilante groups, militias, non-state armed groups, crime syndicates, mafia, or even terrorist networks in the maintenance of security and justice, often with tacit or overt support from states or other transnational entities. Such groups, however, fall outside the scope of this chapter, which deals with private security providers that are legal entities and have corporate character.

Security Privatization: Historical Roots

The growth of the PSI in recent times, though startling, is not unprecedented. It has been argued, for instance, that the role played by the irregular or alternative forces in the historical process of wars and state building is yet to be adequately analyzed (see for instance, Davis, 2003, p. 5). Privatization of security, although it takes place in a qualitatively new context, should be understood, in part, as the re-emergence and re-legitimization of non-state and commercial forms of violence and protection (Berndtsson, 2009, p. 135). Though commentators like Machiavelli (1469–1527) criticized their use, deployment of militias and mercenaries continued to be a common practice throughout the human history of conflict. Following the Thirty Years War (1618–1648) and the Treaty of Westphalia (1648), as tentative steps toward formation of the modern nation-state were being undertaken, efforts were made to substitute the mercenary groups with modern standing armies. The practice of employing mercenaries was, however, continued because it was considered to be cheaper and convenient. In the eighteenth century, for instance, it was quite common for the major European countries to employ large private forces during warfare. The practice was prevalent outside Europe also – mercenaries were, for instance, employed by both sides during the American War of Independence. Use of mercenaries and private contractors was quite common during the American Civil War (1861–1865) and the Spanish–American War (1898). Nor was this a particularly Western phenomenon. Mercenaries were regularly employed in the non-Western armies maintained by indigenous rulers. In India, for instance, there existed a huge military market consisting of armed men who were not formally attached to the armies but could be recruited during specific campaigns (for details, see Kolff, 1990). During the second half of the nineteenth century, the Chinese emperors also maintained mercenary groups that were often manned by foreigners like the Filipino Foreign Rifle Corps raised by the American adventurer Frederick Townsend Ward; the French-controlled Ever Triumphant Army; and the Ever Victorious Army under the British General, Gordon (Barkawi, 2006, pp. 45–46).

Gradually, however, monopoly over any legitimate form of violence was increasingly considered to be a vital function of the state. This, however, did not put an end to the trend of outsourcing certain noncore military functions to civilians in many armies. Civilian contractors became a part of the wars fought during the twentieth century, including the two World Wars. Nor was this phenomenon restricted to the Western armies or the US army, in particular. During the course of the Second World War, the Imperial Japanese Army, for instance, employed groups of civilian contractors known as the *Gonzoku* for construction works and guarding of Allied prisoners of war (CBC News, 2007). In the US army, by the time of the Vietnam War, outsourcing had risen to such a level that the *Business Week* described the war in Vietnam as a "contractor war" (McBride, 2003, p. 5).

Internally, the rising importance of the private security companies (PSCs) in providing various security-related services also has a historical precedence. Functions such as crime control and guarding activities by the professional security services belonging to the state was, in fact, quite a late development, with the first modern police force emerging only in the nineteenth century. As a result, private security agencies played an important role in ensuring internal security. In the United States, for instance, the Pinkerton Company, founded in 1850 as a detective agency, also provided armed guards and strikebreakers to industrial firms.

The Post-Cold War Spurt

Changing nature of conflicts and the rise of new security threats have acted as essential catalysts to large scale proliferation. Martin van Creveld (1991, p. 207), for instance, had predicted that:

> The spread of sporadic small-scale war will cause regular armed forces themselves to change form, shrink in size, and wither away. As they do, much of the day-to-day burden of defending society against the threat of low-intensity conflict will be transferred to the booming security business; and indeed the time may come when the organisations that comprise that business will, like the condottieri of old, take over the state.

According to Singer (2003, p. 61), "warfare is undergoing several key transformations – diversification, technologization, civilianization, and criminalization-each of which creates opportunities for private firms to play increasing roles." What has been, however, a more significant development since the 1990s has been the proliferation of Private Military and Security Companies (PMSCs) assisting the state in its various security-related initiatives in both domestic and external spheres. In developed Western societies, the increased capacity of the global media to inflame and influence popular concerns regarding "casualty sensitivity" or the "body bag syndrome" has caused concern among the policymakers, making the deployment of regular forces in conflict zones politically difficult. According to Edward Luttwak, most post-Cold War conflicts are "discretionary" by nature, incapable of posing any serious existential threat to the state and, thus, given the evolving moral and social norms in the "post-industrial" societies, makes the issue of military casualty a highly sensitive affair (for details, see Luttwak, 1995, 1996) In this connection, extensive use of the PSCs in security operations and training of personnel in conflict zones, apart from outsourcing of logistical and other noncore army functions, have contributed to their rise. Involvement of PSCs like the Executive Outcomes (EO) and Sandline International in conflict-ridden countries like Angola, Sierra Leone, and Papua New Guinea during the 1990s provided an indication of their potentiality. The US government, for instance, gave a contract to DynCorp International helping the Sudanese Peoples' Liberation Movement involved in the civil war in Sudan. During the Bosnia war, another US-based PSC, Military Professional Resources Inc. (MPRI, now L3 MPRI) provided supplies and training to the Croatian army in spite of an existing UN embargo.

PSCs are now operating in virtually every country of the world. Within Asia, although there is a historical precedence of external PSCs involvement in various conflict zones, the post-Cold War period has witnessed expansion of the PSI involving proliferation of corporate PSCs, domestic and international, as well as more amorphous pro-government vigilante groups (for details, see Chakrabarti, 2009, pp. 49–58). Particularly significant is the rapid growth of the domestic PSI in the Asian countries in recent years. In China, for instance, it was the need for elaborate security arrangements for the Beijing Olympics (2008) that had given a real boost to the industry. At present, China's private security industry is booming, with nearly 2767 registered companies in the sector, generating about US$1.2 billion a year and employing more than 2 million security workers (Bardsley, 2011). Shandong Huawei Security Group is reported to be a top-ranking Chinese PSC, which now appears to be set for overseas operations (Erickson and Collins, 2012).

Another major Asian country to experience a sharp growth in PSI has been India. Many Indian ex-servicemen, for instance, are reported to be serving in the PSCs operating in Iraq. Though the Indian personnel are mostly not engaged as armed contractors, many of them are deployed for guarding key installations like oil wells, refineries, and government offices (Dogra, 2004). Indian contractors as well as South Asian contractors also generally seem to enjoy greater public confidence in conflict zones. In Afghanistan, for instance, local people seem to be more favorably inclined towards the non-Western PSCs and Asian contractors, for instance, the Gurkhas. During a field survey conducted by the Swiss Peace Foundation in 2008, among the focus group discussants, the Gurkha private security contractors were particularly mentioned for having the most courteous and professional behavior (Joras and Schuster, 2008, p. 22).

Within India, there is also greater internal demand for private security. According to India's Central Association of Private Security Industry (CAPSI), India's private security industry had grown to, "approximately 5.5 million security guards employed by about 15,000 security companies and as an industry, is now the country's largest corporate taxpayer" (Bennett, 2009). Such trends towards security privatization had initially been criticized by most analysts as crass commercialism unleashed by globalization. According to Bharadwaj (2003, p. 327), for instance:

> The ideology of globalisation has similar aversion to the concept of national security as it has to the national-welfare economy. The globalists would like to see both dismantled and substitute them with a private military and security network, in the larger interest of global capitalism.

Over time, however, there is a greater acceptability for the PSI with even the Indian government taking certain steps interpreted as favorable to the PSI. In order to regulate the activities of private security agencies, the Indian government introduced the The Private Security Agencies (Regulation) Act 2005, which came into effect from March 2006. Under this Act, a Controlling Authority is to be appointed by every state government for granting licenses to agencies for carrying on the business of security agencies and other related matters. The Central Government has also framed the Private Security Agencies Central Model Rules 2006, which have been sent to all the state governments for their guidance, enabling them to frame their own rules in conformity with the Central Model Rules (Ministry of Home Affairs (MHA), India, 2011, pp. 217–218). The new regulation also stipulates the introduction of a detailed training syllabus for security personnel, including a minimum period of 100 hours of classroom teaching and 60 hours of field training for new recruits and a condensed course of 40 hours of classroom instructions and 16 hours of field training for ex-servicemen and former police personnel (The Gazette of India Extraordinary, 2006, p. 26).

The Indian government now also deploys PSC personnel for guarding and detection services at government installations after approval from the Indian Home Ministry (in charge of internal security), supplementing the role of Central Industrial Security Force (CISF), who is entrusted with the task of providing security cover for all the important installations in the country (Guha and Narayan, 2011). Faced with a manpower crunch of nearly 30% in the Railways Protection Force (RPF), the government-controlled Indian Railways is also depending upon private security agencies to guard its installations and properties. One senior spokesman of the Railways (Jha, 2011) defended the decision by claiming:

> There is no policy of engaging private security guards for security duties. However, private guards are being allowed on experimental basis in non-core areas. This is being done under the supervision of RPF staff, after proper verification and due recommendation and diligence by a committee of senior officers.

A proposal to allow private security agencies registered under the Private Security Agencies (Regulation) Act 2005 to possess arms is also under consideration. Decision to grant arms licenses to such PSCs, fulfilling certain criteria, would enable them to carry a certain number of weapons of prescribed description (Ministry of Home Affairs (MHA) India, 2010, p. 12). According to an Indian government official, "this would enable the security agencies to buy better weapons and focus on the quality of trained guards they recruit" (Tikku, 2011). With rising incidents of attacks on cargo ships by Somali pirates, many countries, including India have allowed their merchant ships to hire armed private security contractors on board (Kurup, 2012). The Indian government is also set to limit foreign direct investment (FDI) in private security services at 49%. This development is expected to help domestic security firms to consolidate their position in the fast-growing sector and force foreign players to restructure their holdings and offload the surplus FDI in favor of domestic players (Guha and Kumar, 2010).

Such trends towards security privatization, however, raise concerns. Lack of proper monitoring has led to the proliferation of unorganized players, which now accounts for nearly 80% of India's PSI that has around 15,000 agencies today (Krishnan, 2011). Essentially, these are illegal operators because they operate without licenses and hardly implement the required training schedule or basic norms as stipulated in the government regulation. Non-state agencies like the vigilante groups also continue to play a major role in the largely unorganized realm of privatized security in developing countries, including India.

The merging of development and security has also made the humanitarian agencies and the NGOs engaged in conflict zones more vulnerable. For these organizations, turning to PSCs for protection often provides a better alternative. According to one estimate, in recent years more than 40 NGOs have signed contracts with private military firms (Singer, 2006, p. 69). The United Nations Report of 2007, criticizing the PMSCs, had noted that some of these companies have stimulated and fuelled the demand in "third world countries for former military personnel and ex-policemen to be recruited as security personnel, who in fact, are private militarily armed soldiers" (United Nations, 2007, p. 20). As a sign of changing priorities and greater acceptability, it has been reported that the United Nations has increased its own use of PSCs – with close to 60% or 12,000 facilities worldwide using such services, although it is yet to finalize a comprehensive policy concerning the vetting and monitoring of these companies and their personnel (United Nations, 2010).

Categorization of PMSCs

In the post-Cold War period, the process of delivering security involves many actors whose inputs were previously negligible or nonexistent (Webber *et al.*, 2004, p. 16). PSCs as security providers are essentially commercial enterprises, hierarchically organized into registered businesses that trade and compete openly and are vertically integrated into the wider global marketplace (Singer, 2003, p. 45). It is generally recognized that the new PMSCs, particularly those which operate in global battle zones are different from traditional mercenaries, and are legitimate national corporations following proper legal codes existent in their respective locations or where these are registered (Smith, 2003, p. 112). The "old" mercenaries were usually regarded as colorful adventurers or, at best, groups of former soldiers sometimes managing to form *ad hoc* organizations. The PMSCs, on the other hand, have a distinct business identity often with subsidiary branches or tie-ups with other business entities, with a permanent core staff and on-going marketing, and their operations emphasize private enterprise, efficiency, and expertise (Adams, 2003, pp. 55–56). According to Tim Spicer, a veteran operator of the former PSC, the Sandline International, and the chief of the Aegis Defence Services (cited in, Pelton, 2007, p. 274):

> "Mercenary" and "private military company" are not the same. There are very distinct differences. Essentially a mercenary is there as an individual. The private military company has led to people using the pejorative distinction. Most private security companies will not consider mercenary work. My view has always been that there is plenty of legitimate work to be done.

The categorization of the PSCs is, however, a difficult task given the range of multitasking and overlapping in the services provided. Peter Singer (2003, pp. 88–101), classifies them into three basic groups: (1) the Military Provider Firms commonly called PMCs and sometimes PSCs, which offer direct tactical military assistance including participation in combat roles; (2) the Military Consulting Firms, which draw on retired and noncommissioned officers to provide military advice and training, but do not take part in operations themselves; and (3) the Military Support Firms, which generally provide logistics, intelligence, and miscellaneous maintenance services. According to Singer, the distinction between "offensive" and "defensive" functions is essentially subjective and is not analytically useful. Moreover, such classifications often degenerate into a division of the PSI in which security/defensive firms are "good", and military/offensive firms are "bad", which does not represent a true picture of the industry (Singer, 2006, p. 68). According to another analyst, the PSCs could be grouped into categories like: (1) Private Combat Companies (PCCs) (still analytical and not real); (2) PMCs, Proxy Military Companies, PSCs, Commercial Security Companies; and (3) Freelance Operators (Kinsey, 2006, pp. 13–21). Doug Brooks, the president of the International Peace Operations Association (IPOA, now International Stability Operations Association, ISOA), an umbrella association of the US-based PSCs, divided the existing PSI into three categories – support companies, PSCs, and PMCs – predicting more opportunities for the PMCs to flourish in the near future, particularly through their involvement in training of security forces in the developing world (PBS, 2005).

Such classifications, though somewhat confusing, in effect, reveal the increasing capacity and greater involvement of the PSCs in performing diverse security related tasks.

Major Activities and involvement

Military Service Industry

There has been a strong expansion in the military services industry in the post-Cold War period. This has involved both the growth of new specialist military services companies and the increasing diversification of established arms-producing companies into military services (Perlo-Freeman and Skons, 2008, p. 2). Such services range from maintenance of advanced weapons systems and communication networks to logistical services and various support functions. The privatization process is not restricted to Western armies. It has been recently reported, for instance, that within the Chinese Peoples' Liberation Army (PLA), the General Logistics Department (GLD) has begun implementing privatization measures to reduce the size of the standing army. As a part of the process, functions like managing barracks and building maintenance have been shifted from PLA units to civilian companies, thereby linking civilian and military logistics (Payne, 2008).

Vital Inputs to Military and Counterinsurgency Operations

The PSI is very much a part of the new security-related operations, as PSCs appear well-placed to act as force multipliers, bolstering internal security without necessarily incurring a concomitant rise in security-related expenditure (Jones, 2006, p. 356). As an indication of their greater acceptability to policymakers, the US Army Manual on Counter-Insurgency, for instance, while highlighting the need for expanding the counterinsurgency agenda, advocated recruitment from diverse backgrounds including private security contractors along with other groups like diplomats, police, politicians, humanitarian aid workers, and local leaders (US Army Field Manual, 2006, 2.1). The deployment of PMSCs, in fact, can be achieved more quickly than the regular army. It has been argued, for instance, that the average deployment time for most regular militaries is around two to four months, while for the UN forces it is six to eight months. PMSC personnel, in contrast, can be deployed for similar missions within two to six weeks (Brooks and Chorev, 2008, p. 120).

Adding private actors into the mix is, however, another complicating variable for military leaders and policymakers to consider and manage in conflict zones (Spearin, 2003, p. 42). The most serious problems arise from the fact that armed contractors are being injected into an international security arena that lacks recent experience in regulating them (Hammes, 2010, p. 14). According to one US Department of Defense report, contracting local nationals could be an important element in counterinsurgency strategy because employing local nationals injects money into the local economy and provides job training, which may help in winning "hearts and minds" of local nationals (Schwartz and Swain, 2011, p. 7). In Afghanistan and Iraq, however, the percentage of local contractors has steadily declined from a high of 86% in September 2008 to a low of 51% in March 2011 (Schwartz and Swain, 2011, p. 11).

Many PMSC personnel (particularly foreigners) have also been accused of unwarranted aggression and a "trigger-happy" attitude, leading to harassment and killing of innocent civilians and torturing of prisoners. In Iraq, for instance, the Fallujah shooting of 2004, leading to the death of at least 20 Iraqi civilians and the subsequent lynching of four American private security personnel from the PSC Blackwater, followed by the Nisour Square (Baghdad) firing by Blackwater personnel again in September 2007 leading to 17 civilian casualties, made Blackwater the center of media attention and giving negative publicity to the entire PSI.

Blackwater's (subsequently renamed as Xe and at present, Academi) rise as one of the leading PSCs within a short span of time is representative of the rapid proliferation of the global PSI itself. Beginning as a multimillion-dollar business designing and manufacturing targets and shooting ranges, under the leadership of ex-marine and businessman Eric Prince, Blackwater soon became a massive organization engaged in providing a range of security-related services, including training of personnel belonging to various departments and agencies of the US government, and won major contracts in Iraq and Afghanistan (for details on Blackwater's rise see, Scahill, 2007). Prince's resignation as CEO of Blackwater in March 2010 did not reduce the dependence of the US government on the company. It has been recently reported that the Pentagon, in its plan to outsource its anti-drug operations in South America to PSCs, also plans to involve a subsidiary of Academi (Marquez, 2012). Academi also currently operates a forward operating base in Afghanistan called "Camp Integrity". The facility, located near the Kabul International Airport, has been home to Blackwater/Academi's Afghanistan operations since 2009. The base features a, "24/7 operations center, fueling stations, vehicle maintenance facility, lodging, office and conference space and a fortified armory" (Ackerman, 2012).

Essential Element of Security Sector Reform Process

Internal Security   The growing participation of the corporate sector in internal security governance does not occur in a vacuum, but is intrinsically associated with the evolving nature of the state and changes in procedures of governance. Security management and governance are increasingly becoming complex and the corporate security actors, as vital components of the Security Sector Reform (SSR) projects, are specializing in providing security services that were previously monopolized by the government. Apart from the PMSCs, the corporate sector also includes other bodies that provide a variety of security services like investigation, crime prevention, order maintenance, systems planning, technical consulting, and security design, etc. (Steden and Sarre, 2007, p. 223). PSCs are also increasingly being deployed as part of disaster management programs. After Hurricane Katrina, for instance, Blackwater personnel were used to maintain order in some of the affected areas in New Orleans in 2005.

There is, however, significant criticism as to their efficiency. Problems related to poor performance of the PSCs are nothing new. The RAND Report of 1975, for instance, highlighted several problems associated with the use of private security employees in domestic contexts (for details, see Wildhorn, 1975).

Private Prisons   Although running juvenile offender centers or illegal immigrant detention centers had not been uncommon, the private sector began to get involved in prison running around 1980s. In Texas, the Corrections Corporation of America (CCA) and the Wackenhut Corrections Corporation (WCC) won contracts and began to operate four privately run prisons in 1989, beginning the trend (Harding, 2001, p. 267). With 2.3 million prisoners, the United States employs nearly 800,000 workers in various prisons nationwide, which are still considered to be inadequate thereby fuelling demand for private prisons. Private companies hold about 130,000 people, or 8% of American inmates (Msnbc, 2011). CCA is the largest private prison provider with 69,000 beds (inmates) managed in 63 state and federal facilities, or more than 50% of all private prisons. Private prisons have their own accrediting agency, the American Correctional Association (ACA), which sets standards for penal facilities and provides monitoring services (Verkuil, 2007, p. 39).

Becoming a global phenomenon, private prisons in England and Wales now account for 11% of the prison population, while Australia has 17% of its prisoners held in private prisons (Verkaik, 2009). In Asia, the first privately operated prison (run by a Protestant group) was set up in South Korea in 2010.

The regulatory system and accountability mechanisms that govern the operations of the private prisons, however, leave scope for improvement. Governments, when privatizing activities, are often tempted to reduce regulatory resources at the same time. With private prisons, above all, this could prove to be problematic (Harding, 2001, pp. 340–341).

Protecting the Neoliberal Agenda

It has been argued that the growth of the corporate security industry helps in protecting the neoliberal agenda being pursued through the process of globalization. This widens the economic gap, which perpetuates and enhances conflicts at intra-societal level as well as making conflict the major characteristic in state-society interface. This, in turn, generates and perpetuates more demand for security, particularly among affluent groups, fueling demand for gated communities. As Weiss argues (2007, pp. 12–13):

> In their geopolitical conflict over precious resources, advanced capitalist states draw on private contractors as an option that is more flexible, politically palatable … less expensive in the long run. Low-level warfare involving private military forces will be used to contain resistance movements, while private guards will be called in for labor struggles over job security, unionization, and compensation, as well as to police against organized crime and other predators attracted to the sudden displays of wealth. The future of the security industry is bright, but the prospect of harmonious social relations is not certain.

Whether employed by the government agencies or privately employed in developing countries, PMSCs often aim to secure specific resource rich geographic areas in order to facilitate resource extraction. In many cases, the usage of services offered by PSCs have gone hand-in-hand with such developments, with PSCs being engaged, for instance, to guard mining installations (Muthien and Taylor, 2002, p. 187). What unites private armies and transnational corporations in the exploration business is their profit motive. This process, arguably, is exacerbated by globalization and the dominance of neoliberalism (Muthien and Taylor, 2002, p. 189).

Problems Related to Monitoring and Regulation

One major international concern regarding the proliferating PSCs has been the relative absence of legal provisions in dealing with them. Most existing international regulations are geared around the concept of "mercenary" rather than modern corporate PSCs. Existing international laws and treaties to control mercenary activities include The Hague Conventions (1907); the Geneva Conventions (1949); the UN Charter and related Resolutions; Article 47 of Protocol 1, additional to the

Geneva Convention of 1949 (1977); declarations and conventions of the Organi-zation of African Unity (OAU); and the UN International Convention against the Recruitment, Use, Financing, and Training of Mercenaries adopted in 1989. But none of these international conventions, or more specific country-wise legislative attempts as attempted from time to time in South Africa, United Kingdom and the United States, have really been able to specifically address the issue of PSCs in a satisfactory manner.

The Abu Ghraib prisoner torture issue perhaps exemplifies the problem of reg-ulating PSCs. The US detention facility at Abu Ghraib entered the news following the release of shocking pictures of prisoner abuse. Apart from the military personnel, employees from PSCs (CACI International and Titan Corporation) were also accused of involvement in prisoner abuse on a massive scale in 2003. Since then, eleven sol-diers have been convicted, but so far no CACI or Titan personnel have been charged (Human Rights First, 2008, p. 2). When a group of former detainees tried to bring a case against the private contractors in 2011, the US Supreme Court declined to take up the lawsuit, ruling that "During wartime, where a private service contrac-tor is integrated into combatant activities over which the military retains command authority, a tort claim [for damages] arising out of the contractor's engagement in such activities shall be preempted" (Richey, 2011).

While monitoring remains a problem, improper recruitment procedure is often leading to selection of poorly qualified personnel. Regulation of the PSI, in fact, has proven to be a difficult task even before the post-Cold War boom. One analyst, writ-ing in the 1980s, had predicted that as the "social, demographic, and legislative fac-tors were making the selection process increasingly difficult, the quality of service provided by the industry was likely to decline in the near future" (Lipman, 1988). The problems within the PSI, as highlighted in a RAND Corporation report in 1975, included abuse of authority such as unnecessary use of force; problems of dishon-est or poor business practices; and negligence of duties (Wildhorn, 1975). The report continued to state that the "licensing and regulation of private security businesses and employees, is at best, minimal and inconsistent, and, at worst, completely absent" (Wildhorn, 1975, pp. 2–3). The same issues continue to hamper proper functioning of the PSI, even in recent years.

Another noticeable trend, particularly within the Western PMSCs operating glob-ally, has been to hire personnel from developing and underdeveloped parts of the world at comparatively cheaper rates. It has also been alleged that these recruits are often inadequately trained, given insufficient protective clothing or weapons, and provided with poor health and insurance coverage (Caparini, 2008, p. 173). Even in countries where national regulatory frameworks are relatively developed, as in the United States, South Africa or the United Kingdom, states confront challenges in monitoring, oversight, and accountability for the PSI's off-shore activities (Cockayne et al., 2009, pp. 6–7).

There have been attempts to develop an array of internal management systems, ethics programs, and controls on the use of force, both individually and in coop-eration with PMSC associations (for example, through the British Association of Private Security Companies (BAPSC), ISOA, and the Private Security Company Association of Iraq (PSCAI) (Cockayne et al., 2009, p. 7). Steered self-regulation, constituting a middle-way between self-regulation and state regulation, through public authorities assisting private parties in developing self-regulatory goals has also been attempted. An example is the "Voluntary Principles on Security and Human Rights" of December 20, 2000 from the extractive sector, which was initiated by the UK and US governments in conjunction with human rights organizations, labor unions, and the concerned PSCs. The code sets obligations and standards that extractive industry companies should respect while employing PSCs and standards that PSCs are expected to observe in their activities (Thurer and MacLaren, 2007, pp. 355–356). The "Montreux Document on Pertinent International Legal Obligations and Good Practices for States related to Operations of Private Military and Security Companies during Armed Conflict" finalized in 2008, although not legally binding, also helps in generating greater awareness about the need for a universally accepted standard for PMSCs.

Quest for Legitimacy

Notwithstanding existing criticism, it has been argued that there is little empirical evidence to suggest that non-state actors are more prone to committing human rights violations than state institutions, and the existing evidence suggests that non-state/local justice and security networks are open to improvement and learning (Scheye, 2009, p. iv). One PSC, GardaWorld, the Global Risk Group of Garda World Security Corporation (TSX:GW), for instance, was awarded the Foundation for Relief and Reconciliation in the Middle East 2007 Prize for Peace in the Middle East, the first time that the prize has been presented since the formation of the Foundation in 2005.[1] Interestingly, the PMSCs themselves are also making serious efforts to highlight their nonpartisan attitude and responsible behavior through intense lobbying and propaganda. The ISOA mission statement, for instance, highlights its role in promoting high operational and ethical standards of firms active in the peace and stability operations industry and to engage in a constructive dialogue and advocacy with policymakers about the growing and positive contribution of these firms to the enhancement of international peace, development, and human security.[2]

The ISOA also produces the *Journal of International Peace Operations*, touted as the world's only publication devoted to the study of the private sector's role in peace and stability operations. In one of its issue, the president of the ISOA Doug Brooks (2012) comments:

> Not surprisingly, too many commentators are referring to an "army" of contractors – terminology which may make their articles a more compelling read, but also provides an unfortunate mischaracterization of the civilian reality ... Contractors are conducting logistics, facilities management, medical evacuation and many different kinds of training. Yes, many are providing site security and body guard services as well, defensive, protective roles as is common domestically in the West. While this unique operation with international policy implications should indeed be covered by the media, the sensationalization is unhelpful to the public.

Though it is true that only a small fraction of the PSC personnel actually work as armed security guards (Perito, 2009, p. 5), what causes concern is a recent survey that has estimated that the PSCs hold between 1.7 and 3.7 million firearms worldwide. If undeclared and illegally held weapons were to be included, the global PSC stockpile would be even higher (Small Arms Survey, 2011, p. 101). Greater and easier availability of small arms increases the lethality and the potentiality of the armed PSC personnel in conflict zones. Little wonder that many analysts continue to regard the PMSCs as mutated forms of erstwhile mercenary groups. According to Guy Arnold (1999, p. 47), for instance:

> The emergence into the public eye of mercenary organizations or companies ... suggests both a new public acceptance of the role that mercenaries are expected to play and an increasingly brash certainty on the part of the mercenary community that its services are needed and that its members will continue to be lucratively employed round the world. Indeed, as the twentieth century drew to an end and the governments of more and more states appeared less and less able to maintain law and order so the openings for mercenaries and organized mercenary interventions multiplied.

Conclusion

The evolving concept of "New public management" (NPM) of security focuses more on the growing public–private interface in this sector (for details, see Ortiz, 2010, pp. 35–41). The PSI, in this connection, is still involved in a search for standardization, which is essential for long-term institutionalization and legitimization, even if it is not essential for their *ad hoc* existence and acceptance. Their use, however, may reduce the state's capacity to control them in the long run. As Deborah Avant argues (2005, p. 26):

> The privatization of finance gives private entities budgetary control over the use of forces. The privatization of delivery devolves control over the institutional setup of forces to private entities. The privatization of both moves the state out of a direct consequential role altogether.

The reputation of the PSI is, however, conditional on, among other things, there being transparency in the relevant market (which in the case of the PMSCs cannot be relied upon) and there being an expectation from customers of certain service standards (as noted, states and international organizations may not always demand law-abiding conduct from PMCs) (Thurer and MacLaren, 2007, p. 355). To many other analysts, however, the trend towards privatized security represents the "new face" of neocolonialism, operating under the guise of neoliberal market policies through "corporate mercenarism", providing viable foreign policy proxies for Western governments in the pursuit of their national interests (Francis, 1999, p. 319). However, given the rising strategic relevance of the PSI, its use, however, cannot be completely avoided. This trend, when coupled with the fact of diminishing state authority creates the danger of undermining the state's legitimacy and relevance for the citizens, leading to destabilization (Ungar, 2008, p. 34). Within the context of diminishing state control over security provision, corporate security could act as a proverbial double-edged sword ending up perpetuating, and generating, more security threats rather than solving them.

Notes

1. Source: http://www.marketwire.com/press-release/GardaWorld-Awarded-First-Peace-Prize-from-Foundation-Relief-Reconciliation-Middle-East-651642.htm (accessed January 7, 2012).
2. Source: Website of the International Stability Operations Association (ISOA) http://www.stability-operations.org (accessed January 24, 2012).

References

Abrahamsen, Rita, and Michael C. Williams. 2009. "Security beyond the State: Global Security Assemblages in International Politics." *International Political Sociology*, 3(1): 1–17. DOI: 10.1111/j.1749-5687.2008.00060.x

Ackerman, Spencer. 2012. "Blackwater's Afghan HQ Is Really Called 'Camp Integrity'." *Wired*, March 26. Accessed April 6, 2012 from http://www.wired.com/dangerroom/2012/03/academi-camp-integrity/

Adams, Thomas K. 2003. "Private Military Companies: Mercenaries for the 21st Century." In *Non-State Threats and Future Wars*, edited by Robert J. Bunker, 54–67. London: Frank Cass.

Arquilla, John. 2003. "Thinking about new security paradigms." *Contemporary Security Policy*, 24(1): 209–225. DOI: 10.1080/13523260312331271879

Arnold, Guy. 1999. *Mercenaries: The Scourge of the Third World*. London: Macmillan.

Avant, Deborah D. 2005. *The Market for Force: The Consequences of Privatizing Security*. Cambridge: Cambridge University Press.

Bardsley, Daniel. 2011. "China's new wealthy on guard." *The National*, January 17. Accessed April 6, 2012 from http://www.thenational.ae/thenationalconversation/industry-insights/economics/chinas-new-wealthy-on-guard

Barkawi, Tarak. 2006. *Globalization and War*. London: Rowman & Littlefield.

Bennett, Jody Ray. 2009. "India's Private Security Metamorphosis." *ISN Security Watch*, November 27. Accessed December 15, 2013 http://www.isn.ethz.ch/Digital-Library/Articles/Detail//?lng=en&id=109996

Berndtsson, Joakim. 2009. *The Privatisation of Security and State Control of Force: Changes, Challenges and the Case of Iraq*. Doctoral Dissertation in Peace and Development Research. Gothenburg: School of Global Studies, University of Gothenburg.

Berube, Claude. 2007. "Blackwaters for the Blue Waters: The Promise of Private Naval Companies." *Orbis*, 51(4): 601–615. DOI: 10.1016/j.orbis.2007.08.005

Bharadwaj, Atul. 2003. "Understanding the Globalisation Mind Game." *Strategic Analysis*, 27(3): 309–331. DOI: 10.1080/09700160308450093.

Biersteker, Thomas J., and Rodney Bruce Hall. 2002 (Online 2009). "Private authority as global governance." In *The Emergence of Private Authority in Global Governance*, edited by Rodney Bruce Hall and Thomas J. Biersteker, 203–222. Cambridge: Cambridge University Press. DOI: 10.1017/CBO9780511491238.011

Brooks, Doug. 2012. "The Realty of Withdrawal." *Journal of International Peace Operations*, 74.

Brooks, Doug, and Matan Chorev. 2008. "Ruthless Humanitarianism: Why Marginalizing Private Peacekeeping kills people." In *Private Military and Security Companies: Ethics, Policies and Civil–Military Relations*, edited by Andrew Alexandra, Deane-Peter Baker, and Marina Caparini, 116–130. New York, NY: Routledge.

Caparini, Marina. 2008. "Regulating Private Military and Security Companies: The US Approach." In *Private Military and Security Companies: Ethics, Policies and Civil–Military*

Relations, edited by Andrew Alexandra, Deane-Peter Baker, and Marina Caparini, 171–188. New York, NY: Routledge.

CBC News (Robin Rowland). 2007. "Private Military Contractors Subject to Rule of Law: Second World War Gonzoku Provide Precedent." *CBS News*, 15 October. Accessed December 15, 2013 from http://www.clrd.ca/articles/article-4.html

Cerny, Philip G. 2000. "The New Security Dilemma: Divisibility, Defection and Disorder in the Global Era." *Review of International Studies*, 26(4): 623–646.

Chakrabarti, Shantanu. 2009. *Privatisation of Security in the Post-Cold War Period: An Overview of its Nature and Implications*. New Delhi: Institute for Defence Studies and Analyses (IDSA).

Creveld, Martin van. 1991. *On Future War*. London: Brassey's UK.

Cockayne, James, Emily Speers Mears, Iveta Cherneva, Alison Gurin, *et al.* 2009. *Beyond Market Forces Regulating the Global Security Industry*. New York, NY: International Peace Institute.

Davis, Diane E. 2003. "Contemporary Challenges and Historical Reflections on the Study of Militaries, States, and Politics." In *Irregular Armed Forces and Their Role in Politics and State Formation*, edited by Diane D. Davis and Anthony W. Pereira, 3–34. Cambridge: Cambridge University Press. DOI: 10.1017/CBO9780511510038.002.

Dogra, Chander Suta. 2004. "Our Hitmen in Iraq." *Outlook India*, May 3. New Delhi. Accessed April 6, 2012 from http://www.outlookindia.com/article.aspx?223783

Duffield, Mark. 2005. *Global Governance and the New Wars: The Merging of Development and Security*. London: Zed Books.

Erickson, Andrew and Gabe Collins. 2012. "Enter China's Security Firms." *The Diplomat*, February 21. Accessed December 15, 2013 from http://thediplomat.com/2012/02/enter-chinas-security-firms/

Foster, Gregory D. February 1994. *In Search of a Post-Cold War Security Structure*. McNair Paper No. 27. Washington, DC: Institute for National Strategic Studies, National Defense University.

Francis, David J. 1999. "Mercenary Intervention in Sierra Leone: Providing National Security or International Exploitation?" *Third World Quarterly*, 20(2): 319–338.

Guha, Rajat, and Nirbhay Kumar. 2010. "Security services players to face 49% FDI ceiling." *The Financial Express*, July 21. Accessed April 6, 2012 from http://www.financialexpress.com/news/security-services-players-to-face-49-fdi-ceiling/649521/

Guha, Rajat, and Subhash Narayan. 2011. "Pvt security cos can now guard PSU installations." *The Financial Express*, October 14. Accessed April 6, 2012 from http://www.financialexpress.com/news/Pvt-security-cos-can-now-guard-PSU-installations/859874/

Hammes, T.X. 2006. *The Sling and the Stone: On War in the 21st Century*. Minneapolis, MN: Zenith Press.

Hammes, T.X. 2010. "Private Contractors in Conflict Zones: The Good, the Bad, and the Strategic Impact." *Strategic Forum*, 260. INSS, National Defense University. Accessed December 15, 2013 from http://www.researchgate.net/publication/235022609_Private_Contractors_in_Conflict_Zones_The_Good_the_Bad_and_the_Strategic_Impact

Harding, Richard. 2001. "Private Prisons." In *Crime and Justice: A Review of Research*, Vol. 28, edited by M. Tonry, 265–346. Chicago, IL: University of Chicago.

Human Rights First. 2008. *Private Security Contractors at War: Ending the Culture of Impunity*. Report. Washington, DC: Human Rights First.

Jha, Srinand. 2011. "Manpower crunch forcing Rlys to hire pvt security." *Hindustan Times*, August 8. Accessed December 15, 2013 from http://www.hindustantimes.com/india-news/newdelhi/manpower-crunch-forcing-rlys-to-hire-pvt-security/article1-730584.aspx

Jones, Clive. 2006. "Private Military Companies as Epistemic Communities." *Civil Wars*, 8(3): 355–372. DOI: 10.1080/13698240601060660

Joras, Ulriche, and Adrian Schuster (eds.). April 2008. "Private Security Companies and Local Populations: An Exploratory Study of Afghanistan and Angola." *Working Paper No. 1/2008*. Swiss Peace Foundation.

Kinsey, Christopher. 2006. *Corporate Soldiers and International Security: The Rise of Private Military Companies*. New York, NY: Routledge.

Kolff, D.H.A. 1990. *Naukar, Rajput and Sepoy: The Ethno History of the Military Labour Market in Hindustan 1450–1850*. Cambridge: Cambridge University Press.

Krahmann, Elke. 2008. "Security: Collective Good or Commodity?" *European Journal of International Relations*, 14(3): 379–404. DOI: 10.1177/1354066108092304

Krishnan, Karthik. 2011. "India's private security industry is being hamstrung by illegal operators, who dominate the sector." *Outlook India*, May 28. Accessed December 15, 2013 from http://business.outlookindia.com/article_v3.aspx?artid=271960

Kurup, N.K. 2012. "Ships with armed guards: Govt may fix responsibility on flag-state." *The Hindu, New Delhi*, February 19. Accessed April 6, 2012 from http://www.thehindubusinessline.com/industry-and-economy/logistics/article2910600.ece?css=print

Lipman, Ira A. 1988. "Personnel Selection in the Private Security Industry: More Than a Résumé." *Annals of the American Academy of Political and Social Science, The Private Security Industry: Issues and Trends*, 498(1): 83–90. DOI: 10.1177/0002716288498001009

Loader, Ian. 1997. "Thinking Normatively about Private Security." *Journal of Law and Society*, 24(3): 377–394. DOI: 10.1111/j.1467-6478.1997.tb00003.x

Luttwak, Edward. 1995. "Toward Post-Heroic Warfare." *Foreign Affairs*, 74(3): 109–122.

Luttwak, Edward. 1996. "A Post-Heroic Military Policy." *Foreign Affairs*, 75(4): 33–44.

Marquez, William. 2012. "Privatiza Estados Unidos la guerra contra las drogas?" *BBC Mundo*, January 16. Accessed April 6, 2012 from http://www.bbc.co.uk/mundo/noticias/2012/01/111208_eeuu_pentagono_guerra_drogas_mercenarios_wbm.shtml

McBride, Michael T. April 2003. *The Proliferation of Contractors on the Battlefield: A Changing Dynamic that Necessitates a Strategic Review*. Strategy Research Project. US Army War College, Carlisle Barracks, PA.

Ministry of Home Affairs (MHA), India. 2010. "Arms and Ammunition Policy for Individuals." Accessed December 15, 2013 from http://www.mha.nic.in/hindi/sites/upload_files/mhahindi/files/pdf/AaAPolicyInd-080410.pdf

Ministry of Home Affairs (MHA), India. 2011. *Annual Report, 2010–2011*. New Delhi: Government of India.

Msnbc.com (Scott Cohn). 2011. "Private prison industry grows despite critics." Accessed January 24, 2012 from http://www.msnbc.msn.com/id/44936562/ns/business-cnbc_tv/t/private-prison-industry-grows-despite-critics/#.Tx5XjXLTnKQ

Muthien, Bernedette, and Ian Taylor. 2002. "The return of the dogs of war? The privatization of security in Africa." In *The Emergence of Private Authority in Global Governance*, edited by Rodney Bruce Hall and Thomas J. Biersteker, 183–200. Cambridge: Cambridge University Press. DOI: http://dx.doi.org/10.1017/CBO9780511491238.010

Ortiz, Carlos. 2010. "The new public management of security: the contracting and managerial state and the private military industry." *Public Money & Management*, 30(1):35–41. DOI: 10.1080/09540960903492356

Payne, David A. 2008. "Chinese Logistics Modernization." *Army Logistician*, 40(4). Accessed October 24, 2011 from http://www.almc.army.mil/alog/issues/JulAug08/chinese_log_mod.html

PBS. 2005. "Interview – Doug Brooks." *PBS*, June 21. Accessed July 12, 2007 from http://www.pbs.org/wgbh/pages/frontline/shows/warriors/interviews/brooks.html

Pelton, Robert Young. 2007. *Licensed to Kill: Hired Guns in the War on Terror*. New York, NY: Crown Pub.

Perito, Robert. January 2009. "The Private Sector in Security Sector Reform: Essential But Not Yet Optimized." *USIPEACE Briefing*, United States Institute of Peace (USIP).

Perlo-Freeman, Sam, and Elisabeth Skons. September 2008. "The Private Mili tary Services Industry." *Sipri Insights on Peace and Security*, No. 2008/1. SIPRI.

Richey, Warren. 2011. "Supreme Court declines to take up Abu Ghraib detainee lawsuit." *Christian Science Monitor*, June 27. Accessed April 6, 2012 from http://www.csmoni tor.com/USA/Justice/2011/0627/Supreme-Court-declines-to-take-up-Abu-Ghraib-detainee-lawsuit

Scahill, Jeremy. 2007. *Blackwater: The Rise of the World's Most Powerful Mercenary Army*. New York, NY: Nation Books.

Scheye, Eric. 2009. *Pragmatic Realism in Justice and Security Development: Supporting Improvement in the Performance of Non-State/Local Justice and Security Networks*. Netherlands: Netherlands Institute of International Relations, Conflict Research Unit.

Schwartz, Moshe, and Joyprada Swain. 2011. "Department of Defense Contractors in Afghanistan and Iraq: Background and Analysis. CRS Report for Congress." *Congressional Research Service*. Accessed December 15, 2013 from http://www.fas.org/sgp/crs/natsec/R40764.pdf

Singer, Peter W. 2006. "Humanitarian Principles, Private Military Agents: Some Implications of the Privatised Military Industry for the Humanitarian Community." In *Resetting the Rules of Engagement: Trends and Issues in Military-Humanitarian Relations. Humanitarian Policy Group Report 22*, edited by Victoria Wheeler and Adele Harmer, 67–79. London: Overseas Development Institute.

Singer, Peter W. 2003. *Corporate Warriors: the Rise of the Privatized Military Industry*. New York, NY: Cornell University Press.

Singer, Peter W. 2001–2002. "The Rise of the Privatized Military Industry and Its Ramifications for International Security." *International Security*, 26(3): 186–220. DOI: 10.1162/016228801753399763

Small Arms Survey. 2011. "A Booming Business: Private Security and Small Arms." In *Small Arms Survey 2011: States of Security*, 101–103. Cambridge: Cambridge University Press. Accessed January 12, 2012 from http://www.smallarmssurvey.org/fileadmin/docs/A-Yearbook/2011/en/Small-Arms-Survey-2011-Chapter-04-EN.pdf

Smith, Eugene B. 2003. "The New Condottieri and US Policy: The Privatization of Conflict and Its Implications." *Parameters: US Army War College Quarterly*, XXXII(4)4: 104–119.

Spear, Joanna. 2011. "The Maturing Market for Private Security." *Privatizing the Battlefield: Contractors, Law and War, (World Politics Review Feature Report)*, (14): 1–7.

Spearin, Christopher. 2003. "American Hegemony Incorporated: The Importance and Implications of Military Contractors in Iraq." *Contemporary Security Policy*, 24(3): 26–47. DOI: 10.1080/1352326032000247136

Steden, Ronald van and Rick Sarre. 2007. "The Growth of Private Security: Trends in the European Union." *Security Journal*, 20: 222–235. DOI: 10.1057/palgrave.sj.8350052

Stevens, Barrie. 2004. "Chapter One: The Emerging Security Economy: An Introduction." In *The Security Economy*, 7–16. Paris: Organisation for Economic Cooperation and Development (OECD).

The Gazette of India Extraordinary. 2006. Part II Section 3, Subsection (ii), No.416, Ministry of Home Affairs(MHA) Notification. April 26, 2006/*Vaisakha* 6, 1928, New Delhi, MHA.

Thurer, Daniel, and Malcolm MacLaren. 2007. "Military Outsourcing as a Case Study in the Accountability and Responsibility of Power." In *The Law of International Relations – Liber Amicorum Hanspeter Neuhold*, edited by A. Reinisch & U. Kriebaum, 347–369. Netherlands: Eleven International.

Tikku, Aloke. 2011. "Pvt Security firms to shop for arms?" *Hindustan Times, New Delhi*, August 8. Accessed April 6, 2012 from http://www.hindustantimes.com/News-Feed/newdelhi/Pvt-security-firms-to-shop-for-arms/Article1-730597.aspx

Ungar, Mark. 2007. "The Privatization of Citizen Security in Latin America: From Elite Guards to Neighborhood Vigilantes." *Social Justice*, 34(3/4): 20–37.

United Nations. August 2007. *United Nations Working Group Report*, A/62/301, *Use of Mercenaries as a Means of Violating Human Rights and Impending the Exercise of the Right of Peoples to Self-Determination.* United Nations.

United Nations. November 2010. *Intergovernmental Working Group Established by Human Rights Council to Elaborate Convention on Regulating Private Security Companies.* Sixty-fifth General Assembly, Third Committee. General Assembly. GA/SHC/3991. Accessed April 6, 2012 from http://www.un.org/News/Press/docs/2010/gashc3991.doc.htm

US Army Field Manual 2–24. December 2006. *Counterinsurgency.* US Army.

Verkaik, Robert. 2009. "Private prisons 'performing worse than state-run jails'." *The Independent*, June 29. Accessed January 24, 2012 from http://www.independent.co.uk/news/uk/home-news/private-prisons-performing-worse-than-staterun-jails-1722936.html

Verkuil, Paul R. 2007. *Why Privatization of Government Functions Threatens Democracy and What can we do about it.* Cambridge: Cambridge University Press.

Webber, Mark, Stuart Croft, Jolyon Howorth, Terry Terriff, and Elke Krahmann. 2004. "The Governance of European Security." *Review of International Studies*, 30(1): 3–26. DOI: 10.1017/S0260210504005807

Weiss, Robert P. 2007. "From Cowboy Detectives to Soldiers of Fortune: Private Security Contracting and Its Contradictions on the New Frontiers of Capitalist Expansion." *Social Justice*, 34(3/4): 1–19.

Wildhorn, Sorrel. 1975. "Issues in Private Security." *The Rand Paper Series*, RAND Corporation. Accessed December 12, 2011 from http://www.rand.org/content/dam/rand/pubs/papers/2008/P5422.pdf

Index

Note: Italic page numbers indicate figures; bold page numbers indicate tables. A page number followed by the letter *n* and a number indicate a note.

9/11 terrorist attacks (2001) 41, 42, 71, 94
  border security following 45–6
  EU response to 364
  and "global terrorism" after 131–3
  rise in terrorism following 128
  and US invasion and occupation of Iraq 452–3
  see also War on Terror

Abraham, Itty 111, 112
accountability
  and peace, tensions between 302–3
  and state-building 273–4
Accra Agenda for Action (AAA) 289, 290–1
Acton, James M. 117
Adalet ve Kalkinma Partisi (AKP), Turkey 315, 433, 436, 437, 439
Afghanistan 95
  drugs trade 165–6
  India's relations with 393–5
  Taliban 94–5, 165–6, 266, 395, 452
  terrorist incidents *128*
African Union (AU) 90, 220, 251, 252, 257–8, 311–12
Agenda for Peace, An (Ghali) 306
Ahmadinejad, Mahmoud, Iranian president 157–8

Ahtisaari, Martti 317
air quality index (AQI), China 374
airport security screening 72–3
al-Qaeda 131–3, 307
Alt, Suvi 96
Amoore, Louise 45–6, 71, 72–3
Angrist, Joshua D. 184–5, 186
Annan, Kofi 154, 303, 316, 317, 395
ANSWER (Act Now to Stop War and End Racism) 497
antiterrorism 137–42
antiwar movements 482–3
  Cambodia invasion 487–8
  Coalition to Stop Funding the War 488–9
  military opposition 489
  moratorium movement 486–7
  opposition of Indochina war 484–6
  public pressure, role of 490
  resistance to Iraq war 496–500
Appadurai, Arjun 17
Arab League 224, 317, 329, 379
Arab Spring/uprisings 289
  stance taken by Turkey 439–40
Arbatov, Georgi 494
Argentina, criminal trials 343
arms race, freezing 490–2
Aron, Raymond 26, 364

The Handbook of Global Security Policy, First Edition. Edited by Mary Kaldor and Iavor Rangelov.
© 2014 John Wiley & Sons, Ltd. Published 2014 by John Wiley & Sons, Ltd.

ASEAN 376, 397
Ashton, Catherine 367, 380–1
Asia
  growth of private security 509–11
  rise of 390
  see also China; India
Assad regime, Syria 315, 438
Atrocities Prevention Board, US 146, 156, 158
Australia 114
Automated Targeting System (ATS) 72–3

Baker, James, US Secretary of State 358, 361
Bakker, Karen 196
Balkan wars
  EU's powerlessness during 363–4
  failure to protect civilians 255
  gender-based violence 53, 54, 56–7
Ball, Nicole 6
Barakat, Sultan 296
Barcelona Report (2004) 365
  human security principles 92–4
"bare life" 97, 99
Barnett, Michael 154
Bauman, Zygmunt 16
Bazzi, Samuel 184, 185
Beardsworth, Richard 24
Beck, Ulrich 1, 70, 81–2
  global risk 77–9
  risk society and reflexive modernity 79–81
Bellamy, Alex 239
Bergoffen, Debra 55
Berlin Wall, fall of 304–5, 393, 494
Besley, Timothy 183
Better Angels of Our Nature, The (Pinker) 483
Bharatiya Janata Party (BJP), India 400, 403
Bigirumwami, Joseph 58–9
bin Laden, Osama 132, 133, 452
Biological Weapons Convention (BWC) 120
biometric border 44–6
biopower 99–100
bioterrorism 19
biothreats 19–20
Blackwater PSC 513–14
Blattman, Christopher 184, 185
Bloxham, Donald 149
"body bag syndrome" 509
Bojicic-Dzelilovic, Vesna 6

Booth, Ken 3–4, 39–40, 322
border conflicts, China 372–3
border security 44–6
Borowiak, Craig Thomas 273
Bosnia-Herzegovina 273, 313, 428–9
Bosnia war
  debate about mass rapes 56
  EU's failure to resolve 360–1
  international criminal court, ICTY 340, 342, 344, 346
  intervention debate 89
Bottom Billion (Collier) 176
bottom-up approach, human security 93
Boutros Ghali, Boutros 301–2, 306, 311–12, 317
Brahimi Report on UN Peace Operations 251
Brauman, Rony 235, 240
Braut-Hegghammer, Malfrid 118
Brazil 112, 227, 255–6, 328, 403
Bright, Charles 16
Broeckling, Ulrich 76
Bruckner, Markus 181, 184
Brunnschweiler, Christa 180–1
Bulte, Eric H. 180–1
Burford, Lyndon 106, 120
Burundi–Netherlands Security Sector Development (SSD) program 292–3, 295
Bush, George W. 98, 152–3, 324, 456, 494
  post-9/11 "War on Terror" 41, 42–3, 71, 98
Buzan, Barry 20–1, 193, 359

Calhoun, Craig 233, 242
Çalkıvik, Aslı 7
Cambodia, genocide 145
Campbell, David 42, 43, 44
capital-intensive resources, link to violence 184–5
capitalist system, protests against 38–9, 40
Caracas Declaration 379
care work, undervaluing of 60–1
Carhuancho water conflict 191
Carius, A. 194
cartels 163–4, 166, 167, 168, 170
Carter, Jimmy 315
Caselli, Francesco 183, 185
Castels, Robert 73
"casualty sensitivity" 509
Catholic Church, Ituri 473

Central African Republic 90
Central America, TCOs 166–8
Chakrabarti, Shantanu 8
Chandler, David 85, 94, 271, 274
Chard, Margaret 296
Charny, Israel 158
Chechnya 421–2
chemical weapons 95
Chemical Weapons Convention (CWC) 120
Chen, Qi 380
Chen, Shui-bian, Taiwan President 373
Chesterman, Simon 274
China 371
    capabilities 375–6
    defense budget 375
    definition of security 372
    economic development 375
    military capabilities 375–6, **389**
    military spending **390**
    relations with India 398–9
    role in global security 376–82
    security threats facing 372–5
    socio-economic indicators **398**
Ciccone, Antonio 181, 184
civil society activism 332–3
civil society (CS) 463–5
    contributing to peace and
        democratization 469–70
    in fragile states 467–9
    IKV-Pax Christi in Ituri, DRC 472–4
    legitimacy of CS actors 470
    outside support vs local CS actors 471–2
    strengthening 465–7
civil society organizations (CSOs) 470
civilian command, human security
    operations 94
civilian protection 211–13
    during armed conflict 214–17
    and international humanitarian law
        227–8
    military strategies 224–7
    R2P (Responsibility to Protect) concept
        222–4
    UN peacekeeping operations 217–22
    UNSC resolutions 89–90
Clark, General Wesley 362–3
climate change 19
    and international law 330–1
    and US unilaterallism 332
    and water scarcity 195
"climate chaos" 19

Clinton, Bill 154
Clinton, Hilary 91, 381, 395, 498
Cluster Munitions Convention (CMC) 120
Cockayne, James 169–70
Cockburn, Cynthia 53
codependency and water security 198–9
Cohn, Carol 35–6
Colby, William, CIA director 490
Cold War
    aftermath of and security reform 284
    Berlin Wall, fall of 304–5, 393, 494
    nuclear proliferation 109
    post-Cold war actors 308–17
    post-Cold war issues 302–8
    post-Cold war trends 317–18
    winning of 493–6
"collective conflict management" (CCM)
    318
collective security, Russia 417–18
Collective Security Treaty Organization
    (CSTO) 411, 415, 417
Collier, Paul 178–9, 181
Colombia
    cartels 164
    coca-growing, link to violence 184–5,
        186
    drug-related violence 161–2, 186
Commission on Global Governance 15
Commission on Human Security 59, 88
Common Foreign and Security Policy
    (CFSP) 357–8, 359–60, 365, 366
Communism, post-Second World War 150
Conference on Disarmament (CD) 120–1
Conflict Humanitarian and Security
    Department (CHASE) 286
conflict persistence/recurrence 270, 317,
    344
consent issues, peacekeeping presence
    253–4
Convention on the Prevention and
    Punishment of the Crime of Genocide
    (Genocide Convention) 145, 146–7,
    150, 151, 154, 156, 222–3
conventional wars 18
Cook, Catherine 193
Cook, Steven A. 424
corporate actors *see* private security
    industry
corrections corporations, US 514
Cortright, David 8
"cosmopolitanism" 23, 24, 80–1

Cotet, Anca M. 181, 185
counterinsurgency 91, 95
    civilian protection, NATO 220
    failures 133
    private security companies 513–14
    security assistance for 288
    United States 453–4
counterterrorism 288
    measures 96, 138–42, 451–8
Cox, Robert 39
Craig, Susan L. 372
Cramer, A. 194
crime, transnational 160–71
crimes against humanity 55, 145, 146, 147,
    155
"criminal enclaves" 164–5, 168, 169–70
criminal insurgency 167–8
Critical Security Studies 32, 41
    feminism and the critique of violence
        33–8
    the Occupy Movement 40–1
    poststructural approaches 41–6
    security as emancipation 38–40
    and social critique 32–3
Critical Theory 38–40
Crocker, Chester 317–18
cross-country studies, criticisms of 181
Crowther, S. 470
Cruise missiles 34, 490, 492, 493
CS see civil society
cyber warfare 456
Cyprus issue 315, 327, 436

Dal Bó, Ernesto 182, 184
Dal Bó, Pedro 182, 184
Dallaire, General Romeo 154
Darfur, Western Sudan
    Chinese donation to UN Trust Fund 379
    climate conflict 196
    genocide 153, 155–6
Davis, Diane E., "fragmented sovereignty"
    170
Davis, Mike 498
Davutoglu, Ahmet 428, 433, 436–7
de Andrés, Amado Philip 168–9
de Cuellar, Perez 307–8
De Gaulle, Charles 357
de Goede, Marieke 71, 72–3
de Larrinaga, Miguel 98
de Soto, Alvaro 6
De Soysa, Indra 178

De Tocqueville, A. 46
de Wilde, Jaap 193
DeBenedetti, Charles 485, 486
DeChaine, Robert 240
decolonization 304, 327
defense budgets
    China 375
    United states 448
DelZotto, Augusta 54, 56–7
Democratic Republic of Congo (DRC) 90,
    252, 365–6
    IKV Pax Christi (IPC) in Ituri 472–5
democratization
    civil society's role in 463, 464, 465, 466,
        469–70
    conflict and violence associated with
        153–4
    democracy promotion vs. strategic
        stability 457–8
    "third wave" of, justice dilemma in
        343–5
Deng, Francis 238
Department of International Development
    (DFID) 285, 286, 467
Department of Peacekeeping Operations
    (DPKO) 218, 219, 222
depolitization of security policy-making
    72–3
desecuritization 411, 437
Development Assistance Committee (DAC),
    security sector reform 282–3, 285,
    286, 287
diamond production 177, 178
"dilemma of rising powers" theory, China
    377–8
diplomacy and mediation 300–2
    post-Cold war actors 308–17
    post-Cold war issues 302–8
    post-Cold war trends 317–18
disarmament see nuclear disarmament
disarmament, demobilization, and
    reintegration (DDR), Sierra Leone 60
Doucet, Mark 98
drug cartels/trafficking 162, 164, 166
drug violence 161–2
drug wars 169–70
Dube, Oeindrilla 184, 185
Duchêne, François 361–2
Duffield, Mark 3, 99, 100, 241, 506
Dunant, Henry 234
Dunlap, Charles 216

Dutch peace organization, IKV Pax Christi 472–5
Dwan, Renata 6

Economic Cooperation Framework Agreement (ECFA) 373
economic system, protests against 38–9, 40
Edkins, Jenny 242
Egypt, Nile River conflict 190–1, 198, 199–200
elections, violence associated with 153–4
emancipation, critical theory 38–40
emancipatory threats 14, 15, 20–2
eminent individuals as peacemakers 316–17
enemies, fear of 430–1
"enemy", killing of the 214–15
energy security, Russia 420–1
Enloe, Cynthia 53
environmental degradation 19
environmental determinism 195–6
environmental problems, China 374
envoys, UN 309–11
Erdogan, Recep Tayyip, Turkish PM 426
Ericson, Richard V. 75
ethical traditions, civilian harm 214–15
ethnic cleansing 55, 147, 149, 154
   during Yugoslav wars 151, 152
   in Kosovo 323, 363
European Convention on Human Rights 440n1
European Defence Community (EDC) 355–6
European External Action Service (EEAS) 367
European integration 357–8
European Political Co-operation (EPC) 356, 357
European Security and Defence Policy (ESDP) 90, 360, 363, 364, 366
European Security Strategy (ESS) 361, 363, 365, 371
European Union (EU) 355–6
   debate on China's role 381–2
   energy security, Russia's role 420–1
   integrated security 357–61
   norms and values 361–5
   peacekeeping role 312
   relations with China 380–1
   relations with Russia 410–11, 416
   security capabilities 365–7
Euro–Atlantic Security Initiative (EASI) 410

Evangelista, Matthew 115–16, 119
Evans, Gareth 87, 114
Evert, Steven 363
"everyday" peace approaches 275–6, 277
exception, sovereignty constructed through 98
existential threats 14, 15–16, 17–20, 98

Faber, Mient-Jan 495
Falk, Richard 6, 12
Fassin, Didier 242
Fearon, James 177, 178–9
Featherstone, Mike 16
Felbab-Brown, Vanda 165, 169
feminism
   and the critique of violence 33–8
   gender and security research 51–63
   human security 96–7
   poststructural 44
Finnemore, Martha 118
Fissile Material Cutoff Treaty (FMCT) 107, 120–1
Foot, Philippa 11–12
Forest, James J.F. 169
Forsberg, Randall 483
Forsyth, T. 194–5
Foucault, Michel 45, 99
Fouchet Plan 356, 357
"fragile states" 467–9
France 357, 360, 362
Frankel, Benjamin 109
Frankfurt School, social critique 39
Fritz, Verena 267
funding
   for nuclear testing 491–2
   of Vietnam war, efforts to stop 488–90

g7+ governments 289–90
Galtung, Johan 12
Gandhi, Indira 391
Gandhi, Mahatma 391, 393
gangs 162–4
GardaWorld 517
Garfinkel, Michelle 182, 185
Garland, David 68
Gates, Robert (former US Defense Secretary) 91, 381, 448
"Gaza Freedom Flotilla" incident 427, 438
gender and security 51–2
   human security discourse 57–61
   sexual and gender-based violence 53–7

gender and security (*Continued*)
  state-centric security 52–3
  and the "War on Terror" 61–2
Geneva Conventions 215, 232, 327, 334, 515–16
genocide 145–6
  conceptual and legal issues 146–8
  factors associated with 152–4
  global (post-Cold War) era 149–52
  historical perspective 148–9
  limitations of global genocide policy 156–8
  policies and politics of genocide prevention 154–6
Genocide Convention (1948) 145, 146–7, 150, 154, 156, 222–3
Genocide Prevention Task Force (GPTF) 156
geographical determinism 431
George, Jim 32
Georgia 410, 411, 413, 414, 415, 419, 420–1
Gerlach, Christian 149
Germany
  disarmament movement 493
  energy security 420
  Green Party 495
  nuclear decision making 109
Geyer, Michael 16
Ghadaffi, Colonel Muammar 156–7, 303
Ghani, Ashraf 271
GHG emissions 330–1
Giddens, Anthony 16, 69
Gilmore, Elizabeth 177, 178
Gleditch, Nils Petter 177, 178
global citizenship 23, 24–5
"global civil society" 21, 24, 25, 437, 465, 471
global consciousness 23–4
global emancipatory threats 14, 15, 20–2
global existential threats 14, 15–16, 17–20
global identity formation 25–6
global institutional reform 26–8
"global jihad" terrorism 132, 133, 141
"global", meaning of term 12–13
global movements for peace and disarmament 483–4
Global Partnership for the Prevention of Armed Conflict (GPPAC) 471
"global risk" concept, Beck 77–9, 80, 81–2

global security 1–3
  definition of term 14
  threats to 13–15
Global Terrorism Index (GTI) 127, 128, 129
global zero, nuclear disarmament 114, 115–16
Gorbachev, Mikhail 492, 493, 494, 495
government debt, United States 450
government quality mechanism, natural resources 182, 185–6, 187
Gramsci, Antonio 18, 24, 25
Grant, Charles, Powerless Europe 363
"Great Reckoning" 16–17, 22
Green Party, Germany 495
Greenham Common Peace Camp 34–35, 47n3, 492
Grombach Wagner, Johanna 239–40
Guantanamo Bay detention center 451–2
Gulen Hizmet (Service) Movement, Turkey 438
Gulf War 434

Habermas, Jürgen 22
Haggerty, Kevin D. 75
Hague Conventions 215, 515–16
Haldeman, H.R. 487
Hammarskjöld, Dag 300–1
Hammond, Laura 241
Hansen, Lene 55–6
Harrington de Santana, Anne 118
Hassan, Margaret, murder of 241
hegemonic masculinity 2, 37, 53–4, 61, 63n
Hegre, Havard 179
Helsinki Agreement (1975) 87, 495
Hitchens, Christopher 94–5
Hoeffler, Anke 178–9, 181
Holocaust 146, 148, 149, 157
  Ahmadinejad's denial 157–8
Holslag, Jonathan 381–2
Holzgrefe, J.L. 236, 237
homeland security 71, 72–3, 74–5
Hopgood, Stephen 239
Houdret, A. 194
Huang, Yuxing 380
Hubic, Meliha 53
Hughes, Caroline 274
Hughes, Llewelyn 116
human development, India 401–3
Human Development Report (1994), UNDP 20, 86–7, 175, 358–9

human rights 21, 87, 92, 97
  modern human rights movement 212–13
  and protection of civilians 217–18
  Turkey's moves 427, 436, 438, 440n 2
human rights violations *see* genocide;
  transitional justice
Human Rights Watch 95
human security 20, 85–6
  Barcelona version of 91–4
  context 88–91
  critiques of 96–100
  gendered discourse 57–61
  impact of war on terror 94–6
  India 401–3
  origins of concept 86–8
  reconstruction of 100
  reports 87–8
Human Security Study Group 91–2
humanitarian assistance 232–3
  classical 234–6
  and insecurity of humanitarians 240–1
  as a mechanism of governance 241–3
  and Responsibility to Protect (R2P)
    238–9
  types of humanitarian space 239–40
  without consent, military intervention
    236–8
Humanitarian Dialogue (HD) 315–16
humanitarian intervention
  contradictions in 157
  criteria justifying 95
  dilemmas of 156–7
  Holzgrefe's definition 236, 237
  military interventions as 223, 233, 236–8
  political suspicions of 226
  Rieff's disillusionment with 96, 237–8
humanitarian projects, Turkey 438
humanitarian space 95–6, 239
  humanitarians in peril 240–1
  humanitarians in power 241–3
  types of 239–40
Humphreys, Mcartan 177
Hussein, Saddam 94–5, 157, 454
hybrid (liberal) peace approach 275, 276–7
Hyde-Price, A. 362
hydrological cycle 191, 195
Hymans, Jaccques 109, 110–11, 119

Ica Valley, water security issues 191, 196,
  198
ideational causes for nuclear
  nonproliferation 110–11

identities, created through "risk"-based
  measures 73
ideologies 16–17
  "global jihad" 132, 133, 141
  militarized masculinity 36–7
  of terrorism 130–1, 135–6
  undermining terrorists' 141–2
Ignatieff, Michael 94–5
IHH movement, Turkey 438
IKV Pax Christi (IPC), Ituri 472, 474–5
illicit pharma/drugs market 161–2
Independent International Commission on
  Kosovo (IICK) 238
India 388–90
  in Afghanistan 393–5
  emerging global profile 403–4
  foreign policy, early foundations of 391–2
  human security at home 401–3
  maritime reorientations 395–7
  military capabilities **389**
  multidimensional poverty index **402**
  "Non-alignment 2.0", foreign and
    strategic policy 392–3
  nuclearization and non-proliferation
    treaty 399–401
  private security companies 510–11
  relations with China 398–9
  relations with United States 397–8
  socio-economic indicators **398**
  wars, conflicts, and terrorist attacks **394**
Indian Ocean Region (IOR) 395–7
individual engagement, "global citizens"
  24–5
Indochinese region, opposition of war in
  484–90
"industrial, techno-economic decisions and
  considerations of utility" (Beck),
  potential consequences of 78–9, 80
insecurity 1–2
intelligence cooperation 140
inter-state wars, decline in 483–4
interdependency, and water security
  198–200
Intermediate Range Nuclear Forces (INF)
  treaty 113, 493, 495
internal security, PSCs 514
"internalization" of global security issues
  74–5
internally displaced persons (IDPs) 153,
  166, 220, 238, 269, 475
International Commission on Intervention
  and State Sovereignty (ICISS) 87, 98

International Committee of the Red Cross (ICRC) 212, 234, 239–40
International Criminal Court (ICC) 33–4, 90, 146, 155, 158, 223
  accountability and peace 302–3
  non-ratification of, India 403
International Criminal Tribunal for the former Yugoslavia (ICTY) 57, 155, 156, 340, 344, 346
international criminal tribunals 146, 154–5, 342, 346
International Crisis Group (ICG) 162
International Dialogue on Peacebuilding 289–90
international humanitarian law (IHL) 212, 214, 227–8
  implementation of, factors impeding 215–16
  and the Red Cross movement 234–5
international law 320–3
  and climate change 330–1
  "deterrance" and retention of nuclear weapons 325–6, 330
  and global security 325
  governance of use of force 324–5
  recourse to threats and uses of force 326–9
  relating to civilian harm 215
  relevance of 323–4
International Network on Conflict and Fragility (INCAF) 291, 296
international peacekeeping 247–8
  China 376
  current implementation challenges 253–8
  multidimensional and multi-actor 249–51
  new and old models 251–3
  rethinking 258–62
  traditional 248–9
  UN civilian protection 217–22
international relations (IR) theory/theorists 12, 25, 26, 52
  Chinese perspectives/debates 377–80
interrogation of terrorist suspects 325, 451
Iran 157–8
  enemy of US 454
  nonproliferation 107
  nuclear programs 326, 454–5
  Russia, ally or threat to 412
  Turkey's relations with 437

Iraq
  antiwar movement 496–500
  civil war following US invasion 152–3
  and humanitarian assistance 95–6
  invasion of Kuwait 42
  terrorist incidents 128
  US invasion and occupation of 452–3
Israel
  nuclear weapons 326
  occupation of Palestinian territories 327
  Turkey relations 315
  US relations 157–8, 313
Ituri, DRC, Dutch peace organization IKV Pax Christi 473–5
Ivanov, Igor, Russian Foreign Minister 418

Jackson, Robert R. 271
Janus, Thorsten 182–3
Japan 109, 112, 116, 150, 373, 399
"jihadi" terrorist cells 133
Jintao, Hu, Chinese President 372, 375–6
Johnson, C.L. 198
Johnson, President Lyndon 485–6, 499
Jones, Adam 54, 56–7
Just War Ethic/tradition 213, 215
justice see transitional justice
"justice dilemma" 342–5

Kadyrov, Ramzan 421–2
Kagan, Robert 362–3
Kaldor, Mary 4, 21, 70, 117, 183, 272, 465, 484, 493, 495
Kant, Immanuel 15, 362
Kargil conflict, India–Pakistan 115
Karl, Terry Lynn 183
Keen, David 235
Kelleher, Catherine 116
Kennan, George 494
Kennedy, Paul, "imperial overstretch" 449
Khilnani, Sunil 392–3
Ki-Moon, Ban 87–8, 303
Kimberley Process Certification Scheme (KPCS) 186–7
Kissinger, Henry 114, 320, 486, 487, 493
Kosovo war 317
  agreement with Serbia 367–8
  ethnic cleansing 323, 363
  EU's failure in resolving 360–1
  NATO intervention 151, 238, 242, 251
  US vs. European war tactics 362–3
Kostovicova, Denisa 6

Kouchner, Bernard 236–7, 241–2
Krasmann, Susanne 73
Kremlin 412, 417, 423
Kugler, Adrian D. 184–5, 186
Kurdistan Workers Party (PKK) 433, 434
Kutchesfahani, Sara 119
Kuwait, Iraqi invasion of 42, 434

labor-intensive resources, link to violence
    184, 187
Laitin, David 177, 178–9
land mines 120, 121, 332
Lantis, Jeffrey 111
Latin America
    Caracas Declaration 379
    Mexican cartels 166–8
    nuclear acquisition 112
    transitional justice processes 341
Lavoy, Peter, nuclear "mythmakers" 119
Lavrov, Sergey 415, 417
Law of the Seas Treaty (1982) 330
Law of Armed Conflict (LOAC) see
    international humanitarian law (IHL)
Lee, Teng-hui, Taiwan former President 373
"Left Wing Extremist" (LWE)-affected
    regions, India 403
legitimacy of civil society organizations 470
legitimacy of state-building 271–2
legitimate political authority, human
    security 92–3
Lemarchand, Rene 153
Lemkin, Raphael 145, 147–8, 154
Levite, Ariel 111
Li, Anshan 380
liberal peace 3, 266, 267–8
    alternatives to 275–7
    critiques of 269–70
Liberia 250, 273, 288–9, 483
Libyan crisis (2011)
    and civilian protection 224–5, 226, 227,
        228
    and genocide prevention 156–7
    India's concerns 403–4
    limited military intervention 212, 224,
        259
    referral to ICC 90, 303
Lieberthal, Kenneth 381
Linklater, Andrew 12
Lisbon Treaty (2007) 365, 367
"locked-door" policy, schools 46
Lockhart, Clare 271

logic of "risk" 69, 69–70
    in security policymaking 70–7
Loughnan, Arlie 77
Lubanga, Thomas 33, 38
Luhmann, Niklas 69–70, 73
Lujala, Paivi 177, 178
Lund, C. 469
Luttwak, Edward 509
Lyon, David 73

Ma, Ying-jeou, ROC President 373–4
Maastricht Treaty 357–8, 359–60, 361, 365
Mackenzie, Donald 117
"madman theory" 486
"madness of sanity" 22–7
mafias 161
Magsig, B.-O. 194
major powers, mediation role 313
Makarychev, Andrey 7
Malet, David 111
Mali 259
Mandela, Nelson 304, 314
Mann, Michael 149, 152, 154
Manners, Ian 364
Marhia, Natasha 4
maritime expansion, India 395–7
Martin, Graham, Saigon US ambassador
    489
Martin, Mary 7
Marx, Karl 16, 26, 38–9, 118
masculinity
    hegemonic 37, 63n 2
    militarized 36–7
    sexual violence against men 53–4
mass murder 42, 95, 148, 235
Mathews, Jessica Tuchman 32
Mbeki, Thabo 314
McCarthy, Senator Eugene 485, 486, 499
McFaul, Michael, US ambassador to Russia
    456
McGuinty, "locked-door" policy 46
McLuhan, Marshall 15
Mearsheimer, John 31, 39, 47
Médecins Sans Frontières (MSF) 235, 236,
    240
mediation see diplomacy and mediation
Meister, Stefan 419
MEND (Movement for the Emancipation
    of Niger Delta) 169
Mennell, Stephen 15
Menocal, Alina R. 267

mercenaries 507–8, 511–12, 518
Mexico, TCOs 166–8
middle powers, as mediators 313–15
migration policy, Turkey 430
"militarized masculinity" 36–7
military humanitarian intervention 236–8
military interrogations 451
military interventions to protect civilians
    224–7
military modernization, China 375–6
military services industry 512–13
military spending 2, 185, **390**
Milosevic, Slobodan 317, 362–3
Mine Ban Treaty (MBT) 120
missiles
    deployment of, Turkey–Syria border
        439–40
    protests against new 34–5, 492–3
    testing of, India 401
    see also nuclear disarmament
Mitchell, Audra 275–6
modernization and terrorism 134
mono-ethnic states, creation of 149–50
moratorium on nuclear testing 492
Morgenthau, Hans 52
Morris, Jill 58–9
MoveOn.org 497
Mozambique 315
multilateral interventionism 89–90
multilateralism, human security 93
Mutimer, David 4
MX missiles 34, 491, 495, 496

Napolitano, Janet, Secretary, US Homeland
    Security 71, 74
"Narco-Jihad" 165, 166
narcotics trade 161–2, 165–6
nation-building 267
    Afghanistan and Iraq 451, 452–3
    economic assistance directed at 89
    (post-)liberal and critical framings
        267–70
National Intelligence Council 448
National Security Council (NSC), Turkey
    431–2, 435–6
National Security Policy Document
    (NSPD), Turkey 431–2
National Security Strategy, Russia 410
National Security Strategy, UK 70
National Security strategy, US 363

natural resources and civil war 175–6
    cross-country studies 176–81
    empirical evidence 184–6
    policy implications 186–7
    theoretical models and mechanisms
        181–4
    see also water security
Nazi concentration camps, Red Cross relief
    235
"Nazi genocide" 148, 149
Nehru, Jawaharlal 391, 393
Neocleous, Mark 46–7
Netanyahu, Benjamin, Israeli PM 158
New Agenda Coalition (NAC),
    disarmament 114
"new security architecture", Russia
    416–18
Nile Basin Initiative (NBI) 190–1, 198,
    199–200
Nile River conflict 190–1, 198, 199–200
Nixon, Richard 486–8
non-alignment debate, China 378–9
non-alignment, India 391–3
non-interference debate, China 379–80
non-intervention 328–9, 379
nongovernmental organizations (NGOs)
    civil society actors 464, 471–3, 475
    peacemaking role 315–16
    use of private military security firms
        511
nonproliferation see nuclear
    nonproliferation
non-traditional security threats, China
    374–5
North Korea, nuclear weapons threat 116,
    326, 454–5, 456
Norway 314, 411
Nuclear Deal (2008), Indo–US 398,
    399–401
nuclear deterrence 35, 109, 115–16, 325,
    326
    questioning of 117–18
nuclear disarmament 105
    achievability of 116–17
    desirability of 115–16
    history of negotiations for 112–15
    norm entrepreneurs 118
    NPT compared to other treaties 119–21
    vs. nonproliferation 105–7
nuclear freeze campaign 490–2

nuclear hedging 111–12
Nuclear Non-Proliferation Treaty (NPT)
    106, 108, 110, 111, 112, 113–14
    comparison with other disarmament
        treaties 119–21
    and India, nuclear testing 399–401
nuclear nonproliferation
    causes of 108–11
    history of 107–8
    nuclear programs 326, 454–5
    restraint, hedging or ambiguity
        111–12
    vs. disarmament 105–7, 119–20
nuclear politics
    norm entrepreneurs 118–19
    questioning deterrence 117–18
    rogue states 454–5
nuclear proliferation 17–18, 105–6
    global zero causing 115–16
    norm entrepreneurs promoting 118
    scholarly work on 118–19
Nuclear Proliferation Prevention Act
    (1994), US 399–400
nuclear restraint, causes of 108–11
nuclear "wargasm", Kahn 13
nuclear-weapon-free zones (NWFZ) treaties
    112–13
nuclear weapons 17–18
    acquisition by rogue states 454–5
    and international law 325–6
    retention of 321–2
    testing of, India 400–1
    see also nuclear disarmament; nuclear
        nonproliferation
Nuclear Weapons Convention (NWC)
    114–15
Nussbaum, Martha 58

Obama, Barak
    antiwar movement aiding election of
        498–500
    call for disarmament 114, 115
    counterinsurgency approach 453–4
    counterterrorism policy 451–2
    dealings with rogue states 454–5
    and genocide prevention 156
    and international law 320, 321
    Israeli–Palestinian conflict 313
    policy towards Asia–Pacific 381
objectivity and risk 72–3

Occupy Movement 38, 40–1
"Occupy Wall Street" protest 38
Office for the Coordination of
    Humanitarian Affairs (OCHA) 232,
    236, 240
Office of the National Counterintelligence
    Executive, US 456
Ogata, Sadako 88
Operation Allied Force 216, 224, 225–6
Operation Artemis, DRC 220, 365
Operation Atalanta 396
Operation Deliberate Force 313
Operation Desert Storm 214
Operation Duck Hook 486–7
Operation Giant Lance 487
Operation Provide Comfort 434
Operation Turquoise 224
Operation Unified Protector (OUP) 224–5
opium trade, AfPak region 165–6
opportunity costs of conflict mechanism
    183, 184–5, 186, 187
oppositional nationalists 110–11
Orford, Anne 98
Organization of African Unity (OAU) 89,
    90, 304, 311–12, 516
Organization for Security and Cooperation
    in Europe (OSCE) 312
organized crime see transnational criminal
    organizations
ownership
    and aid effectiveness 289–92
    issues in state-building 274–5
Ozal, Turgut, Turkey PM 433, 434

Pakistan 115, 128–9, 133, 326, 395
    drugs trade 165–6
    instability of 454
    military spending 390
    nuclear capability 400
    relations with the US 455
    socio-economic indicators 398
    terrorist incidents (2001–11) 128
    wars with India 391, 394
Panchasheela 391, 392, 393
partnerships, peacekeeping 257–8
Passonen, Karl-Erik 118
past grievances, dealing with 303–4
"patting the missile" metaphor 35–6
Paul, T.V. 108
Pauli, Markus 7

peace movements 482–3
  defunding the Vietnam war 488–9
  disarmament movement 490–6
  global context 483–4
  Iraq antiwar movement 496–500
  opposing Indochina war 484–6
  political and social mobilization 500–1
  protests following Cambodian invasion 487–8
  resistance within the military 489
  Vietnam moratorium movement 486–7
Peace Support Operations, NATO 220
peacekeeping see international peacekeeping
Peoples, Columba 40
People's Liberation Army (PLA), China 372, 373, 375, 376, 513
Pérez de Cuéllar, Javier, UN Secretary-General 307–8
Perkovich, George 117
Pershing missiles 34, 490, 492, 493
Persson, Torsten 183
Petersburg Declaration 359, 360
Peterson, V. Spike 52–3
Piche, Genevieve 45
Pinker, Steven 483
piracy, Somalia 165
PKK (Kurdistan Workers Party) 433, 434
PLA (People's Liberation Army), China 372, 373, 375, 376, 513
POC (Protection of Civilians) 212, 217–22, 226–7
political acts, decoupling from grounds of actuality 72
political change, understanding 500
pollution, China 374
"post conflict" 269
post-liberal peace 267–9, 275–7
  critiques of 269–70
post-Marxist Critical Theory 38–40, 46
post-structural approaches 41–6
post-war reconstruction see reconstruction interventions
poverty 398
  India 401, **402**, 403
  link to terrorism 134
  "Voices of the Poor" study, World Bank 284
Power, Samantha 154, 156
Price, Richard 121
prisoner abuse 513, 516

prisons, private sector 514–15
Private Military and Security Companies (PMSCs) 509
  categorization of 511–12
private security agencies regulations, India 510–11
private security industry (PSI) 505–6
  categorization of PMSCs 511–12
  historical roots 507–8
  major activities and involvement 512–15
  monitoring and regulation issues 515–17
  post-Cold War increase 508–11
  protecting the neoliberal agenda 515
  quest for legitimacy 517–18
  rise of 506–7
Protection of Civilians (POC), UN peacekeeping 212, 217–22, 226–7, 254–5
proximity paradoxes 15–16
Pupavac, Vanessa 274
Putin, Vladimir 408, 412, 421, 422, 456
Putnam, R. 466

Qatar 314
Qin, Yaqing 377
quality of government mechanism, natural resources 182, 185–6, 187
"quasi-corporate" organizations 507
Quinn, Adam 7
quotidian "everyday" peace approach 275–6, 277

R2P see Responsibility to Protect
Radice, Henry 5–6
Raeymaekers, T. 474
Railways Protection Force (RPF), private security, India 510
Rampton, David 6
Rangelov, Iavor 6–7
rape in wartime 55–6
Rasmussen, Mikkel Vedby 75
Razack, Sherene 36
Reagan, Ronald 113, 493–4
RECOM Coalition, war crimes 348–9
reconstruction interventions 266, 267
  accountability, lack of 272–3
  criticism of 269
  legitimacy issues 271–2
  and ownership 274–5
  sovereignty issues 270–1

Red Cross movement 234–5
Rees, Martin 19–20
reflexive Modernity, Beck 79–81
reform
   global in stitutional 26–7
   see also security sector reform
refugee camps 235
regime change 224, 225, 226
   intervention in cases of 380
   interventions to achieve 327–8
regional organizations, mediation efforts
   311–13
regionalization of Al-Qaeda 132–3
regulations, private security companies
   515–17
Reith, Gerda 69
Responsibility to Protect (R2P/RTP) 5–6,
   98, 212
   concept of 222–4
   formulation of 87–8, 323
   and genocide prevention 146, 155
   and humanitarian assistance 238–9
   military interventions to protect civilians
   224–7
   seen as a Trojan Horse 240
responsibilization of society 74–5
returns to conflict mechanism 182, 183,
   185
Ricks, Tom 499–500
Rieff, David 96, 237–8
Rigterink, Anouk 5, 184, 185
risk 68–70
   "global risk" 77–9, 81–2
   "risk contract" 80
   "risk society" 79–82
   and security policies 70–7
rival great powers and regional stability
   455–6
Roberts, Sir Ivor 300
Robinson, Fiona 60–1, 96–7
Robinson, James A. 180
rogue states and weapons of mass
   destruction 454–5
Rome Declaration 358
Rome Statute, ICC 90, 302–3, 403
Rosberg, Carl G. 271
Ross, Michael 177–8
Rousseau, Jean-Jacques 27
RTP see Responsibility to Protect
Rublee, Maria Rost 4–5, 110, 118, 119
rule of law reforms 259–60

Russia 408–9
   Europe's energy security provider 420–1
   genealogy of russian fears 412–16
   methodological issues, securitization
     concept 409–12
   new security architecture 416–18
   peace mediator role 419
   security policy in the North Caucasus
     421–2
   unilateral peace enforcer 418–19
Ruzicka, Jan 119
Rwandan genocide 146, 148, 152, 153,
   154, 342
   international criminal tribunal 155

Sagan, Scott 110, 115
Sahnoun, Mahmoud 87
Said, Yahia 183
Saigon 488–9
Salter, Mark 45
Sambanis, Nicholas 179
Sayari, Sabri 434
Schabas, William A. 147
Schell, Jonathan 497–8
Scheuerman, William 26–7
Schmidt-Semisch, Henning 73
Schmitt, Carl 98, 99, 242
school shootings, USA 46
Schöttli, Jivanta 7
Seckinelgin, Hakann 58–9
"second order legality" 325–6
Secretary-General of the UN see UN
   Secretary-General
securitization 2, 7
   of development 393
   expansion of 75–6
   and human security 58–9
   meaning of 97–9
   Russian security-making 409–23
   of sexual and gender-based violence 54–7
security 11–12
   Chinese definition 372
   meanings of 97–9
   rethinking of 90–1
security dilemma vs. dilemma of rising
   powers, China 377–8
security policies and the logic of risk 70–1
   dynamic of the decoupling political acts
     from grounds actuality 72
   dynamic of an expanding process
     securitization 75–6

security policies and the logic of risk
(*Continued*)
  dynamic of an internalization global
    security issues and the process
    responsibilization 74–5
  dynamic of a depolitization security
    policymaking 72–3
Security Sector Development (SSD)
    program, Burundi–Netherlands 292–3
security sector reform (SSR) 282–3
  donor approaches, effectiveness of
    294–5
  evolution of concept 283–7
  importance of process 295–6
  internal security 514
  international political and security
    climate 288–9
  ownership issues 289–92
  politics of 292–4
  prison security 514–15
Selchow, Sabine 4, 77
self-determination principle 327, 334n 17
Sen, Amartya 88
Serbia 334n 17, 304, 367–8
"Sevres Phobia" 430
Sewell, Sarah 5
sexual violence 37–8, 52, 53
  securitization of 54–7
  Sierra Leone, DDR process 59–60
  and state-centric security 52–4
Shanghai Cooperation Organization (SCO)
    415
Shaw, Martin 5
Shepherd, Laura J. 54, 57, 62
Sierra Leone 59–60, 89, 94, 250, 303
Sikkink, Kathryn 118
Sikor, T. 469
Singer, Peter W. 24–5, 506, 509, 512
Singh, Manmohan, India PM 403
Sivakumaran, Sandesh 54
Skaperdas, Stergios 182, 185
Small, Melvin 485–6, 490
Snyder, Jack 344
social change 41, 500–1
social contract 276–7, 463, 466, 468
social critique 31–2
  feminism and critique of violence 33–8
  poststructural approaches 41–6
  security as emancipation 38–41
  and security studies 32–3

social movements 41, 482
  use of Internet 497
societal security 20–1
Solana, Javier 91, 312, 367, 410
Solingen, Etel 109–10
Solnit, Rebecca 497
Somalia
  African Union Mission (AMISOM) 214,
    220
  peacekeeping operations 250, 252,
    257–8, 259
  piracy 165, 376, 511
  "Somalia Affair" 36–7
South Africa 116, 295, 314, 315, 339
South Sudan 155–6, 199, 294, 304, 470
sovereignty 98–9
  fragmentation of 170
  humanitarian assistance violating 236
  and post-war reconstruction 270–1
  and responsibility to protect 223, 238,
    240
  and state-building 272
Soviet Union
  and the disarmament movement 491–3
  and ending of the Cold War 493–5
  nuclear nonproliferation 107, 109, 113
Spicer, Tim 512
Spinardi, Graham 117
Squassoni, Sharon 113
Srebrenica massacre 90, 151, 154, 235
SSR *see* security sector reform
standards for PSCs 517
state-building 265–6
  alternative peace frameworks 275–7
  definition 266–7
  dilemmas and contradictions 270–5
  (post-)liberal and critical framings
    267–70
state-centric security 52–3
state-centrism, UN 321
state reconfiguration, gangs and cartels 170
Stepanova, Ekaterina 5
Strategic Defense Initiative (SDI), US 493–4
strategic military interventions to protect
    civilians 224–7
Straus, Scott 148
Stumbaum, May-Britt 7
sub-Saharan Africa
  organized criminal networks 169
  state fragmentation 304

Suhrke, Astri 274
Sullivan, John 5
Sun, Xuefeng 7
surveillance 44, 46, 82
    screening at airports 72–3
sustainability of peace after intrastate
    conflict 305–6
Switzerland, neutrality of 313–14
Sylvester, Christine 34, 44
Syria
    Anann as joint envoy for 316–17
    nonintervention consensus 85
    and protection of civilians 85–6, 255
    proxy war 328–9
    Qatar's stance 314
    restricting access of UN peacekeepers 253
    role of civil society 323
    Turkey's involvement 315, 438–40
Syropoulos, Constantinos 182, 185
Sytin, Alexander 418

Taiwan sovereignty issues 373–4, 455
Taliban 94–5, 165–6, 266, 395, 452
Tang, Shiping 378
Taylor, Charles 250, 303
Taylor, R. 195
Teitel, Ruti 6–7, 338
territorial disputes 326–7, 372–4
terrorism 126
    in aftermath of 9/11 attacks 131–3
    antiterrorism 137–42
    causes and explanations of 133–7
    progress in defining 126–7
    rise of in early 21st century 127–30
    transnationalization of 130–1
Tesei, Andrea 185
Tet Offensive, Vietnam war 485, 486
Thatcher, Margaret 34, 493–4
"third wave" of democratization 341, 343
Tickner, J. Ann 52–3
torture 35, 57, 62, 513, 516
    US authorization of post 9/11 325
Torvik, Ragnar 180
trade bans 186–7
traditional security threats, China 372–4
trafficking
    by criminal networks 162, 163, 170–1
    Turkey's role in fighting 429–30
    West Africa 168, 169–70
transboundary water dynamics 199–200

transitional justice 338–40
    challenges for policy and scholarship
        345–9
    evolution of 340–2
    justice dilemma and its critics 342–5
transnational criminal organizations
    (TCOs) 160–1, 162, 163–4
    Afghanistan/Pakistan (AfPak) 165–6
    Mexico and Central America 166–8
    and state reconfiguration 170
    West Africa 168–70
transnational organized crime (TOC)
    160–1, 165, 170, 171
    illicit networks of crime and disorder
        170–1
    statemaking potential of 170
    Turkey's role in combatting 429–30
transnationalization of terrorism 130–1
transparency initiatives 187
tribunals 90, 146, 154–5, 328, 342, 346
True, Jacqui 52–3
Tsai, Ing-wen, Taiwan DPP 373
Tsui, Kevin K. 181, 183–4, 185
Turkey 426–7
    becoming a global security actor 427–30
    intervention in Cyprus 327
    involvement in Libya and Syria crises
        438–40
    mediation role 314–15
    security policies, continuity and change in
        430–8
"Turkish Bermuda triangle" 431
types/categories of people, created through
    "risk"-based measures 73

Ukraine 106, 410, 412, 420–1
UN Charter 87, 262n2, 321
    Article 99 319n4
    non-intervention 328
    self-determination 304, 327
    use of force 223, 324, 326
    regional arrangements (chapter VIII) 258,
        310, 311
UN Development Programme (UNDP) 20,
    285, 306
    Human Development Report (1994) 20,
        86–7, 175, 358–9
UN peacekeeping missions 247–53
    implementation challenges 253–8
    re-evaluation of 258–62

UN Secretary-General 309–11
  Annan, Kofi 154, 303, 316, 317, 395
  Boutros Ghali, Boutros 301–2, 306,
    311–12, 317
  Hammarskjöld, Dag 300–1
  Ki-Moon, Ban 87–8, 303
  nuclear disarmament negotiations
    120–1
  Pérez de Cuéllar, Javier 307–8
UN Security Council Resolutions (UNSCRs)
  civilian protection 89–90, 218, 224
  and former Yugoslavia 346
  Israel's withdrawal from occupied
    territory 327
  women, peace and security 37–8, 54–5
UN Trust Fund for Human Security 87
uncertainty, risk discourse 69, 72, 75, 77–8,
  80
"unconventional" terrorism 136–7
underdevelopment see poverty
unilateralism, Russia 418–19
United for Peace and Justice (UFPJ),
    anti-Iraq war movement 497
United States 446–7
  alliances in East Asia 455
  and China, "strategic distrust" 381
  counterinsurgency 453–4
  counterterrorism policy 451–2
  declining power 447–9
  democracy promotion vs. strategic
    stability 457–8
  economic recovery 449–51
  genocide-prevention politics 156
  military capabilities 389
  military spending 390
  nation-building 452–3
  relations with India 397–8
  relations with Russia 455–6
  rogue states, dealing with 454–5
  socio-economic indicators 398
  threat of cyber warfare 456
Universal Declaration of Human Rights
    (UDHR) 145, 321
"universal" vs. "global" 13
UNSCRs see UN Security Council
    Resolutions
Uppsala Conflict Data Program (UCDP)
    129, 394
US VISIT programme 45
USA PATRIOT Act (2001) 98

van Creveld, Martin 508
van Leeuwen, Mathijs 7–8
Vargas, Juan 184, 185
Vaughan-Williams, Nick 40
Vaux, Tony 234
Vayrynen, Faimo, The Waning of Major
    War 483
Verdier, Thierry 180
Verkoren, Willemijn 7–8
Vietnam antiwar movement 484–90
"Vietnam Syndrome" 329
vigilante groups 473, 509, 511
Vinjamuri, Leslie 344
violent non-state actors (VNSAs) 162, 170,
    171
"virtual water" 191, 193–4, 195, 198
Vlassenroot, K. 474

Waever, Ole 193, 359
Walker, RBJ. 43
Wallerstein, Immanuel 496–7
Waltz, Kenneth 47, 115, 116, 449
Wang, Jisi 378–9, 381
War on Terror 4, 6, 18, 41, 42–3, 44
  criticism of 451–2
  gender narratives 61–2
  impact on human security 85, 94–6
  impact on SSR agenda 288
  and treatment of "terrorists" 307, 311
  and US's biometric borders 44–6
war crimes in former Yugoslavia, RECOM
    Coalition 348–9
war crimes courts 55, 303
  see also International Criminal Court
    (ICC)
Wartner, J. 198
water resources security 193–4
water security 190–2
  literature review 192–4
  narrow and determinist views 195–6
  orthodox thinking 194–5
  see also web of water security
Watergate 487–8
weapons of mass destruction (WMD) 94–5,
    136–7
  and rogue actors 454–5
web of water security 196–8
  analytical and policy implications 200–1
  interdependency and sustainability
    198–200

Weiss, Robert 515
Weiss, Thomas 240, 241
Wells, Tom 485
Welsh School 40, 41
West Africa, TCOs 168–70
Western European Union (WEU) 358, 359,
    365–6
Wheeler, Nicholas 119
Whitworth, Sandra 36–7
Williams, Michael J. 71
Williams, Phil 160, 169–70
Wilson, Ward 117–18
Win Without War coalition 497
Wittner, Lawrence 118
Wolfers, Arnold 13–14
World Bank 176, 344
    civil society functions 465–6
    Nile project 190–1, 199, 200
    security reform 286, 294
    Voices of the Poor study 284
world order 331–3
"world" vs. "global" 13
Writing Security (Campbell) 42, 43,
    44
Wunderlich, Carmen 118
Wyn Jones, Richard 41

Xuefeng, Sun 7

Yahuda, Michael 380
Yakovlev, Alexander 494
Yan, Xuetong 372, 377, 378, 379
Yang, Jiechi 380
Yang, Zewei 379
Yilmaz, Mezut, Motherland Party, Turkey
    435
Young, Iris Marion 62
Yuan, Peng 379
Yugoslavia (former) 249, 250, 304
    EU–UN collaboration 312–13
    genocide in 151–2
    international criminal tribunal (ICTY)
        57, 154–5, 156, 346
    war crimes, RECOM 348–9
Yuxing, Huang 380

Zaire *see* Democratic Republic of Congo
Zarkov, Dubravka 54
Zeitoun, Mark 5
zero option 493, 495
Zhang, Wenmu 378
Zhu, Feng 378–9
Zuccotti Park protests 38